THE GREAT TERROR

The Great Terror

STALIN'S PURGE OF THE THIRTIES

Revised Edition

Robert Conquest

Collier Books

NEW YORK, NEW YORK

For Caroleen

The Macmillan Company
866 Third Avenue, New York, N.Y. 10022
Collier-Macmillan Canada Ltd., Toronto, Ontario

The Great Terror is also published in a hardcover
edition by The Macmillan Company.

Library of Congress Catalog Card Number: 72-90541

FIRST COLLIER BOOKS EDITION 1973

Printed in the United States of America

CONTENTS

PREFACE TO THE PRESENT EDITION

THE present world cannot be understood if we do not understand the Soviet Union. The Soviet Union as it is today cannot be truly understood without a clear understanding of the way in which its present system came into being; knowledge of the events recorded in this book remains essential—indeed is more essential than ever—to any real grasp of its nature and development.

The second edition (published by Penguin Books in 1971) incorporated a fair amount of new material, the nature and origins of which are described in the Preface to that edition, printed below. Since then, some further information has become available, which is provided here in the form of an Addendum.

As with the second edition, most of it is from *samizdat* sources. Much comes from a work by Roy Medvedev, which only reached the West in 1971—his monumental *Let History Judge*. Peter Yakir, too, has given us new information in his *A Childhood in Prison*. Nadezhda Mandelstam, widow of the poet, has also succeeded in sending out of Russia her memoirs, published here as *Hope Against Hope*. And there is certain other *samizdat* information.

Once more, it is the case that the new material usually shows things to be rather worse than I had originally suggested. For example, in the first edition, I spoke of I. V. Kossior as dying a natural death, one of the few recorded of Central Committee members at the time; in the second edition, the fact that it was a suicide had become known. The similar "natural death" of Corps Commander Goryachev is still so recorded in the second edition; for this edition we now learn (from Peter Yakir) that this too was a suicide.

From official sources, a few further details have also accumulated. For example, in the large-scale political and military massacre at the end of July 1938, which had not been

recorded anywhere before *The Great Terror* first came out,
the names of more victims continue to emerge. The first edition named ten victims among senior army and navy officers.
We now know of fourteen. For the second edition we were
able to add, for instance, Army Commander Alksnis, Commander-in-Chief of the Soviet Air Force. For this edition,
we now have Army Commissar Yan Berzin, formerly, under
the pseudonym 'Grishin,' effective Commander-in-Chief of
the Spanish Republican Army. We may expect more of this
sort of information as time passes.

The way in which such apparently petty detail, almost all
that is nowadays released by the authorities, may yet cast an
important light on the period emerges in the extraordinary
death dates given by an obscure official source (*Ukrainian
Soviet Encyclopedic Dictionary*) for Yenukidze and Karakhan. Their trial, in December 1937, was the only major one
to be publicized, but not held in public. The death dates now
given indicate that those concerned had been shot months
previously (see Addendum, note to p. 371). This importantly
affects our view of events.

More generally, the information newly available once again
substantially confirms the story told in the first edition in
every way. I am especially glad, and touched, to be able to
add that the book, which was well reviewed in the Soviet
underground press, has now itself been translated and is circulating in two-chapter sections in *samizdat* in Moscow. Soviet
readers have good cause to study the forbidden period of their
own history. So, for the reasons I adduce at the beginning of
this preface, do we.

R. C.

PREFACE TO THE PENGUIN EDITION

THE flow of information from Soviet official sources about the events of the thirties virtually ceased in 1965–6. Enough material had emerged, if only in partial and episodic form, to make it possible at last to give a full and coherent account in which recent Soviet, and earlier unofficial, information complemented and confirmed each other. It then looked as if we could expect practically no additional knowledge until such a time as the Soviet political scene changed radically.

However, a certain amount of important new information has after all emerged from various sources. In particular, the past few years have seen a marked increase in one type of document – the so-called *samizdat*, 'self-publication', material circulating in typescript in the Soviet Union and often reaching the West. Thus, though the story as a whole is not substantially affected, for this new edition I have been able to use a number of new facts, and give detailed confirmation of others which had previously been probable rather than certain – in particular from the essays, open letters and so forth of Peter Yakir (son of the executed Army Commander); Leonid Petrovsky (son of the executed Peter Petrovsky and grandson of the Politburo member); Roy Medvedev, the historian; his brother Zhores Medvedev the scientist; and Academician Andrei Sakharov, the atomic physicist. Similarly a certain amount of new material about methods of preparing a show trial was made public after the Prague Spring by Czechoslovaks concerned with the Slansky case . In addition correspondents (to whom I am most grateful) have drawn my attention to two or three points I had simply missed.

It is a melancholy fact that in almost every case the new information shows things to have been rather worse than I had originally suggested. For example, I wrote that unlike his four brothers I. V. Kossior died in good odour, as a member of the Central Committee, on 3 July 1937 – one of the few natural deaths of the period. It now appears (from Peter Yakir's account) that his death was actually a suicide, in circumstances similar to Ordzhonikidze's. Again, where I was able to deduce that the lists for execution personally signed by Stalin must have contained a minimum of seven to eight thousand names, we now have from Roy Medvedev a substantive figure – about 40,000. Where I had estimated the number of party members arrested as 'not far short of a million', we are now told by Academician Sakharov that it was 'over 1,200,000'. And so on.

That these men of the younger generation are still deeply concerned with the events of the terror is both natural and significant. The subject is now once again virtually taboo in official circles. But the failure of the political leadership to face the facts about a period crucial to the whole development of the country and to its present structure is an unending strain on all Russians with an intellectual conscience.

There is now no official story, true or false, about the purge as a whole. In fact, one might say, the terror has yet to be abreacted. Researchers in the U.S.S.R. are not in a position to discover or publish the full truth. Until they can, this account must continue to do duty.

R. C.

PREFACE

STALIN'S Purge is, in a sense, the event among all those of the past generation which affects the world most directly today. The wounds left by Nazism, and by the Second World War, are deep and painful. But they are part of the past in a way which is not nearly so true of Stalinism. While the Hitler regime is over twenty years dead, that created by Stalin, and those founded on his model, survive. They have passed through important changes, but it remains true that their political principles derive from the new state he built on the ruins left in 1938. The whole world, indeed, still lives under Stalin's shadow.

The Great Purge by which he established himself as unchallenged dictator is distinctive in three main respects: above all, its immense scale, in which millions perished and every member of the population was held under immediate threat; secondly, its methods, and in particular the extraordinary device of the confession trial, with the ruler's leading critics publicly denouncing themselves for treason; and thirdly, its secrecy – apart from the public trials and a few announcements of other executions, nothing was officially said of the whole vast operation. For the barest facts of Stalin's terror were long concealed or misunderstood: and it was for decades a main source of doubts and falsehoods which ate deep into the consciousness and conscience of the West.

It has been my purpose in this book to give a coherent and connected account of these events. It is only now that it has become possible to do so.

For twenty years the Russians had a clear and consistent story for the purges. A vast conspiracy, led by disgraced members of the Party leadership itself, had penetrated every part of Soviet life. Its objects, pursued in conjunction with the intelligence services of Germany, Poland, Britain and Japan, were the assassination of the Soviet leadership, the defeat of the U.S.S.R. in war, the dismemberment of the country, the restoration of capitalism and sabotage of every phase of the national life from the mines to the ministries. This conspiracy had been discovered, its leaders had in turn confessed, and they had been fairly tried and justly punished, to the complete satisfaction of the whole Soviet people. In addition to these few death sentences, a number (though not a large number) of delinquent citizens had been sent to perform 'corrective labour', by which society was rapidly redeeming them. The alternative view – held by many outside Russia, and, as we now know, by more inside – was that the whole alleged plot was a vast cycle of frame-ups by Stalin and his entourage, that terror had raged with unprecedented fury throughout the country, that mass executions had been supplemented by a vast system of slave-labour camps in the Arctic and desert areas of the country. This relied largely on 'defector' information and on deduction.

In the last decade, the old Soviet version was abandoned, and all the essentials of the former 'anti-Soviet slanders' were admitted. During the Khrushchev period, though more particularly in 1961–4, a large amount of relevant information was put out in the Soviet Union. There was, indeed, no full and coherent account of the Purge as a whole; but in memoirs, articles and even novels a mass of particulars emerged, often both striking and revealing. It was confirmed that there had been a 'period of mass repression', in which many innocent lives had been lost. It was made clear that at least some of the confessions in the public trials were false, and this, if only by implication, destroyed the credibility of all. The large-scale existence, and the horrible conditions, of the labour-camp system were confirmed. On almost every major point covered in this book, it will be found that the evidence comes both from those who have defected or escaped from the U.S.S.R., and from material published lately in the U.S.S.R. itself.

The Purge raises, at every step, the most profound moral issues. On most of these the facts speak for themselves, by any normal standards; and I hope I have been able to avoid too much tedious moralizing. But there are cases in which judgement became perhaps a trifle confused by the claims of the regime that the ends it supposedly held in view permitted it to transcend 'bourgeois morality'. Every sacrifice of humanist principles was made in the name of the true interests of humanism. And the sacrifices were very complete, reminding one of Sir Boyle Roche's alleged remark in the eighteenth-century Irish Parliament:

In the great cause of civil liberty, Mr Speaker, I should be prepared to sacrifice not only a part of our glorious constitution but, if necessary, the whole of it – in order to preserve the remainder.

Every nation has its own cant. In the 'humanism' so much insisted on as an accompaniment of Stalin's rule, one might see something specifically Russian. Tolstoy, in his story *Hadji Murad*, describes Nicholas I ordering the punishment of a Polish student who had attacked and slightly wounded his professor:

He took the report and in his large handwriting wrote on its margin with three orthographical mistakes:
'Diserves deth, but, thank God, we have no cpitle punishment, and it is not for me to introduce it. Make him run the gaunlet of a thousand men twelve times. – Nicholas.'
He signed, adding his unnaturally huge flourish. Nicholas knew that twelve thousand strokes with the regulation rods were not only certain death with torture, but were a superfluous cruelty, for five thousand strokes were sufficient to kill the strongest man. But it pleased him to be ruthlessly cruel and it also pleased him to think that we have abolished capital punishment in Russia.

There is another implied attitude of some oddity, met with occasionally not only in the Communist apparatuses themselves, but even in old admirers of the Stalin system in the West. A lot of killing seems to convince people of the seriousness, and thus the justifiability, of a cause. Similarly, Arthur Koestler in *Darkness at Noon* has the N.K.V.D. interrogator Gletkin say that it is the Stalinist willingness to face the 'necessary' filth and horror of historical progress that gives a superiority over sentimental humanism. I have myself heard an almost identical justification from a serving N.K.V.D. officer.

Marx and Engels were, in fact, opposed to terror, and from their point of view it was one of the blemishes on Jacobin rule. In one of several similar passages, Engels remarks:

Terror consists mostly of useless cruelties perpetrated by frightened people in order to reassure themselves. I am convinced that the blame for the Reign of Terror in 1793 lies almost exclusively with the over-nervous bourgeois, demeaning himself as a patriot, the small petty bourgeois beside themselves with fright [*Hosenscheissenden*] and the mob of riff-raff who know how to profit from the terror.*

The Terror of the French Revolution is not comparable with the Stalinist Terror. It resembles rather – and even then on a much smaller scale – the Terror of the first phases of the Russian Revolution. The Jacobins and the Communists of the early years had much in common. The lower-level delegates and operatives of terror were often coarse and violent brutes. But at the top there were fanatical idealists, men, with all their ruthlessness, not without gleams of certain perverse nobility of character. Saint-Just – even the repulsive Robespierre – show something of the narrow, honest violence of Lenin.

This is not to exculpate political fanaticism, which has so many horrible acts to its discredit in our century. But Stalin's Terror was something else again. Its methods were those of vulgar crime. Its procedure was 'the reign of the lie', the imposition on the people not of mistaken ideas, but of allegations about the opposition known to be false even to the imposer.

And the frightful slaughter of the thirties was not, like the terrors of Lenin and Robespierre, launched in time of crisis, of revolution and war. It was not even done – like Stalin's own liquidation of the *kulaks* – for misconceived but at any rate debatable economic ends. On the contrary, it was launched in the coldest of cold blood, when Russia had at last reached a comparatively calm and even moderately prosperous condition.

But the most important consideration remains the mere extent of the Terror. In the First World War the killing was on a scale wholly disproportionate to any military or political objective attainable by either side – to the degree, indeed, that our whole civilization was badly shaken, and almost ruined. This has long been widely understood. The Great Purge in Russia (and the previous killings of the collectivization period) are a similar case, but one which has perhaps not yet been grasped so clearly. Even leaving aside the question of whether the ends involved were good ones, the casualties were too great for any attainable political or social objective.

* Engels, letter to Marx, 4 September 1870.

The sacrifice could only have been justified (if at all) by it having led to, or at least contributed to, the establishment of a social order unarguably superior to any alternative; just as the sacrifices of the First World War might have been found tolerable in retrospect if it had indeed been a 'war to end war'. It would now perhaps be accepted almost everywhere that the U.S.S.R. is not, and shows no particular promise of becoming, the unquestionably superior community for which such sacrifices might arguably have been called for.

The present writer cannot conceal that he has views on these ethical and political matters; but it seems to him that the open admission of them tends to force the historian into the practical limits of objectivity as regards evidence, and that it is an error to suppose the contrary. He hopes, in any case, that the prejudices he feels are those of most civilized men. But though there is general agreement about the nature, and about the indefensibility, of the Great Purge, the approach to it of the present Soviet rulers, and even of their predecessor, is different from our own. I would agree with the Soviet General Gorbatov that 'It will be a long time before the significance of this period in the history of our country has been fully assessed'.* I hope, nevertheless, that even readers whose attitudes to these events may be different from, or contrary to, my own may meanwhile find this account of the facts useful.

I wish to thank Professor Tibor Szamuely for much and invaluable discussion and criticism; Mr Seweryn Bialer and Mr Stephen Cohen, who have helped me in many ways; Professor Herbert Dinerstein, Professor Gleb Struve, Professor Alexander Dallin, Mr Leo Labedz, Mr John Erickson and Mrs Jane Shapiro for valuable comment or information. My gratitude is also due to my editor, Mr Peter Ritner, who constructively cut much material of interest to myself, but doubtfully relevant to my theme; to Mrs Joan Sutton; to Mrs Joan Baylis; and, above all and as ever, to my wife.

R. C.

* General A. V. Gorbatov, *Years off My Life*, English ed., London, 1964, p. 126.

BOOK ONE

The Purge Begins

A harvest of sorrow came over the land of Russia.
The Armament of Igor

THE ROOTS OF TERROR

> The remedy invented by Lenin and Trotsky, the general
> suppression of democracy, is worse than the evil it was
> supposed to cure. ROSA LUXEMBURG

LENIN'S PARTY

THE Purge was not a sudden and total surprise. It had its roots
in the Soviet past. It would doubtless be false to argue that it
followed inevitably from the nature of Soviet society and of the
Communist Party. It was itself a means of enforcing violent
change upon that society and that party. But all the same, it
could not have been launched except against the extraordinarily
idiosyncratic background of Bolshevik rule; and its special
characteristics, some of them hardly credible to foreign minds,
derive from a specific tradition. The dominating ideas of the
Stalin period, the evolution of the oppositionists, the very confessions in the great show trials, can hardly be followed without
considering not so much the whole Soviet past as the development of the Party, the consolidation of the dictatorship, the
movements of faction, the rise of individuals and the emergence
of extreme economic policies.

After his first stroke on 26 May 1922 Lenin, cut off to a certain
degree from the immediacies of political life, contemplated the
unexpected defects which had arisen in the revolution he had
made.

He had already remarked, to the delegates to the Party's Xth
Congress in March 1921: 'We have failed to convince the broad
masses.' He had felt obliged to excuse the low quality of many
Party members: 'No profound and popular movement in all
history has taken place without its share of filth, without adventurers and rogues, without boastful and noisy elements. . . . A
ruling party inevitably attracts careerists.'[1] He had noted that
the Soviet State had 'many bureaucratic deformities', speaking
of 'that same Russian apparatus . . . borrowed from Tsardom

and only just covered with a Soviet veneer'. And just before his stroke he had remarked 'the prevalence of personal spite and malice' in the committees charged with purging the Party.[2]

Soon after his recovery from this first stroke he was remarking, 'We are living in a sea of illegality',[3] and observing, 'The Communist kernel lacks general culture'; the culture of the middle classes in Russia was 'inconsiderable, wretched, but in any case greater than that of our responsible Communists'.[4] In the autumn he was criticizing carelessness and parasitism, and invented special phrases for the boasts and lies of the Communists: 'Com-boasts and Com-lies.'

In his absence his subordinates were acting more unacceptably than ever. His criticisms had hitherto been occasional reservations uttered in the intervals of a busy political and governmental activity. Now they became his main preoccupation. He found that Stalin, to whom as General Secretary he had entrusted the Party machine in 1921, was hounding the Party in Georgia. Stalin's emissary, Ordzhonikidze, had even struck the Georgian Communist leader Kabanidze. Lenin favoured a policy of conciliation in Georgia, where the population was solidly anti-Bolshevik, and had only just lost its independence to a Red Army assault. He took strong issue with Stalin.

It was at this time that he wrote his 'Testament' (see Appendix B). In it he made it clear that in his view Stalin was, after Trotsky, 'the most able' leader of the Central Committee; and he criticized him, not as he did Trotsky (for 'too far-reaching self-confidence and a disposition to be too much attracted by the purely administrative side of affairs'), but only for having 'concentrated an enormous power in his hands' which he was uncertain if Stalin would always know how to use with 'sufficient caution'. A few days later, after Stalin had used obscene language and threats to Lenin's wife, Krupskaya, in connexion with Lenin's intervention in the Georgian affair, Lenin added a post-script to the Testament recommending Stalin's removal from the General Secretaryship on the grounds of his rudeness and capriciousness – as being incompatible, however, only with that particular office. On the whole, the reservations made about Trotsky must seem more serious when it comes to politics proper, and his 'ability' to be that of an administrative executant rather more than a potential leader in his own right.

The Testament was concerned to avoid a split between Trotsky and Stalin. The solution proposed – an increase in the size of the Central Committee – was futile. In his last articles Lenin went on to attack 'bureaucratic misrule and wilfulness', spoke of the condition of the State machine as 'repugnant', and concluded gloomily, 'We lack sufficient civilization to enable us to pass straight on to Socialism although we have the political requisites'.

'The political requisites . . .' – but these were precisely the activity of the Party and governmental leadership which he was condemning in practice. Over the past years he had personally launched the system of rule by a centralized Party against – if necessary – all other social forces. He had created the Bolsheviks, the new type of party, centralized and disciplined, in the first place. He had preserved its identity in 1917, when before his arrival from exile the Bolshevik leaders had aligned themselves on a course of conciliation with the rest of the Revolution. There seems little doubt that without him the Social Democrats would have reunited, and would have taken the normal position of such a movement in the State. Instead, he had kept the Bolsheviks intact, and then sought and won sole power – again against much resistance from his own followers.

It is clear from the reports of the meeting of the Central Committee nine days before the October Revolution in 1917 that the idea of the rising was 'not popular', that 'the masses received our call with bewilderment'. Even the reports from most of the garrisons were tepid. The seizure of power was, in fact, an almost purely military operation, carried out by a small number of Red Guards, only partly from the factories, and a rather larger group of Bolshevized soldiery. The working masses were neutral.

Then, and in the Civil War which followed, by daring and discipline a few thousand comrades* imposed themselves on Russia, against the various representatives of all political and social trends, and with the certain prospect of joint annihilation if they failed. The 'Old Bolsheviks' among them had the prestige

*The effective central core of the Party at the time of the October Revolution is estimated at 5,000–10,000, a third of them intellectuals.[5]

of the underground years, and the evident far-sightedness which had led them to form such a party gave them a special cachet: the *myth* of the Party, and the source of its leading cadres right up to the mid thirties, was the underground struggle. But the vital force which forged in those concerned an overruling Party solidarity was the Civil War, the fight for power. It transformed the new mass Party into a hardened and experienced machine in which loyalty to the organization came before any other consideration.

When the Civil War ended, the Mensheviks and Social Revolutionaries quickly began to gain ground. The rank and file of the trade unions turned away from the Bolsheviks. And as the failure of the first attempt to impose strict State control of the economy became obvious, Lenin began to realize that to continue on those lines would lead to ruin. He determined on the economic retreat which was to be the New Economic Policy. But with this admission that the Bolsheviks had been wrong, the way was open for the moderate parties, to whom the workers were already turning, to claim political power.

At the Xth Party Conference, in May 1921, Radek, with rather more frankness than Lenin, dotted the i's by explaining that if the Mensheviks were left at liberty, now that the Communists had adopted their policy, they would demand political power; while to concede freedom to the Social Revolutionaries when the 'enormous mass' of the peasants was opposed to the Communists would be suicide.[6] They had now either to be fully legalized or completely suppressed. The latter course was naturally chosen. The Menshevik Party, which had operated under enormous disadvantages but had not been completely illegalized, was finally crushed. The Social Revolutionaries followed, receiving the death blow at a trial of their leaders in 1922.

Within the Communist Party itself centres of discontent, to some degree linked with the workers' feelings, had built up: the Democratic Centralists, led by Sapronov, and the Workers' Opposition, led by Shlyapnikov. The former stood for at least freedom of discussion within the Party, and both opposed the increasing bureaucratization – though as so often with Com-

munist oppositions Lenin was able to ask Shlyapnikov and his
supporters why they had not been such keen opponents of Party
bureaucracy when they themselves held Cabinet posts.

At the Xth Party Congress in 1921 Lenin suddenly introduced
two resolutions forbidding the formation of such groups or
'factions' within the Party. From then on the Secret Police took
on the suppression of the even more radical opposition groups
which refused to disband. But its chief, Dzerzhinsky, found that
even many loyal Party members regarded them as comrades and
refused to testify against them. He went to the Politburo to
obtain an official decision that it was the duty of every Party
member to denounce other Party members who were engaged in
agitation against the leadership. Trotsky pointed out that of
course it was an 'elementary' obligation for members to denounce
hostile elements in Party branches.

The illegal 'Workers' Truth' group started issuing, at the end
of 1922, proclamations attacking the 'new bourgeoisie', speaking
of 'the gulf between the Party and the workers', of 'implacable
exploitation'. The class, they added, which was supposed to be
exercising its dictatorship was 'in fact deprived of the most
elementary political rights'.[7] And in fact the Party, which had
crushed opposition parties and had openly denied the rights of
the non-proletarian majority in the name of the proletarian class
struggle, was now on the brink of a breach of its last meaningful
link to a loyalty outside itself.

When the Constituent Assembly, with its large anti-Bolshevik
majority, was dispersed by force in January 1918 almost as soon
as it met, Lenin had openly proclaimed that the 'workers' would
not submit to a 'peasant' majority.

But as early as 1919 he found it necessary to remark: 'We
recognize neither freedom, nor equality, *nor labour democracy*
[my italics] if they are opposed to the interests of the emancipa-
tion of labour from the oppression of capital.'[8] In general the
working class itself began to be regarded as unreliable. Lenin
insisted that 'revolutionary violence' was also essential 'against
the faltering and unrestrained elements of the toiling masses

themselves'.[9] The Right-wing Communist Ryazanov chided him. If the proletariat was weighed down with unreliable elements, he asked, 'on whom will we lean?'[10]

The answer was to be – on the Party alone. Early in 1921 it had become obvious that the workers opposed the Party. Karl Radek, addressing the War College cadets, put the case clearly:

> The Party is the politically conscious vanguard of the working class. We are now at a point where the workers, at the end of their endurance, refuse any longer to follow a vanguard which leads them to battle and sacrifice. . . . Ought we to yield to the clamours of workingmen who have reached the limit of their patience but who do not understand their true interests as we do? Their state of mind is at present frankly reactionary. But the Party has decided that we must *not* yield, that we must impose our will to victory on our exhausted and dispirited followers.[11]

The crisis came in February 1921 when a wave of strikes and demonstrations swept Petrograd, and culminated in the revolt in March of the Kronstadt naval base.

Kronstadt saw the Party aligned finally against the people. Even the Democratic Centralists and the Workers' Opposition threw themselves into the battle against the sailors and workers. When it came to the point Party loyalty revealed itself as the overriding motive.

War was openly waged on the *idea* of libertarian radical socialism, on proletarian democracy. On the other side there remained only the idea of the Party. The Party, cut off from its social justification, now rested on dogma alone. It had become, in the most classical way, an example of a sect, a fanaticism. It assumed that popular, or proletarian, support could be dispensed with and that mere integrity of motive would be adequate, would justify everything in the long run.

Thus the Party's mystique developed as the Party became conscious of its isolation. At first, it had 'represented' the Russian proletariat. Even when that proletariat showed signs of flagging, the Party still 'represented' it as an outpost of a world proletariat with whose organizations it would shortly merge when the World or the European Revolution was completed. Only when the revolutions in the West failed to mature was the Party left quite evidently representing no one, or not many, in the actual world. It now felt that it represented, not so much the Russian proletariat as it existed, but the future and real interests of that proletariat. Its justification came no longer from the politics of actuality, but from the politics of prophecy. From within itself, from the ideas in the minds of its leading members, stemmed the sources of its loyalty and solidarity.

Moreover, Lenin had established within the Party all the seeds of a centralized bureaucratic attitude. The Secretariat, long before Stalin took it over, was transferring Party officials for political reasons. Sapronov had noted that local Party committees were being transformed into appointed bodies, and he put the question firmly to Lenin: 'Who will appoint the Central Committee? Perhaps things will not reach that stage, but if they did, the Revolution will have been gambled away.'[12]

In destroying the 'democratic' tendency within the Communist Party, Lenin in effect threw the game to the manipulators of the Party machine. Henceforward, the apparatus was first to be the most powerful and later the only force within the Party. The answer to the question 'Who will rule Russia?' became simply 'Who will win a faction fight confined to a narrow section of the leadership?' Candidates for power had already shown their hands. As Lenin lay in the twilight of the long decline from his last stroke, they were already at grips in the first round of the struggle which was to culminate in the Great Purge.

STALIN CRUSHES THE LEFT

When one of the factions is extinguished, the remainder subdivideth.   FRANCIS BACON

It was in the Politburo that the decisive confrontations took place. Over the following years Trotsky, Zinoviev, Kamenev, Bukharin, Rykov and Tomsky were to meet deaths at the hands of the only survivor, Stalin. At the time such a denouement seemed unlikely.

Trotksy was the first, and on the face of it the most dangerous, of Stalin's opponents. On him Stalin was to concentrate, over the years, the whole power of his immense capacity for political malice. The personal roots of the Great Purge extend back to the earliest period of Soviet rule, when the most bitter of the various bitter rivalries which possessed Stalin was centred on the man who seemed, at least to the superficial observer, the main claimant to the Lenin succession, but who, for that reason, roused the united hostility of the remainder of the top leadership.

Trotsky's revolutionary record, from the time he had returned from abroad to become President of the St Petersburg Soviet during the 1905 Revolution, was outstanding. His fame was European. In the Party, however, he was not as strong as his repute suggested. Right up to 1917 he had stayed clear of Lenin's tightly organized Bolshevik group and operated, with a few sympathizers, as an independent revolutionary, though in some ways closer to the Mensheviks. His own group had merged with the Bolsheviks in June 1917 and he had played a decisive role in the seizure of power in November of that year. But he was regarded as an outsider by most of the Old Bolsheviks. And at the same time he was lacking in the experience of intrigue which they had picked up in the long and obscure inner-Party struggles in which he had tried to operate as a conciliator. They also thought of him as arrogant. The respect he won by his gifts and intellect was wrung from them reluctantly. Though he had a number of devoted adherents, on the whole he repelled as much as he attracted. With Lenin's partial support, he was undoubtedly the second man in the Party and State. But Lenin had opposed his later political line. With Lenin dead, he became vulnerable. But, in spite of the weakness of his position, it had its strength. He had powerful backing, not only from many able Bolsheviks, but also from the students and younger Communists. The 'Left' associated with Trotsky had opposed Lenin on the great issues of the early twenties. By the New Economic Policy, Lenin had saved the country from collapse, and at the same time kept the Party's grip on power, but at the expense of large concessions to 'capitalism': the rich peasant proprietor and the profiteering 'NEP-man' flourished. All this was repulsive, even sinful, to the purists. While Lenin now foresaw a very long process of inducing the independent peasantry to accept some form of collectivization, the Left longed for their early and urgent suppression. They were often not particularly devoted to Trotsky in person, but rather held to the views – dogmatic or principled, depending on how one looks at it – which Trotsky had come to personify in the early twenties, as Bukharin had in 1918. When Stalin himself went 'Left' in 1928, most of them ceased to support Trotsky in his opposition.

This group included Pyatakov, one of the six men named by Lenin in his Testament; Lenin saw him, with Bukharin, as the ablest of the younger men. Pyatakov, a tall dignified man with a long, straight beard and a high domed forehead, had started his political career as an anarchist, becoming a Bolshevik about 1910. During the Civil War, his brother had been shot by the Whites in the Ukraine, and he had only just escaped the same fate himself. His modesty and lack of personal ambition were admired as much as his ability.

Other leading 'Trotskyites' were Krestinsky, member of the first Politburo, and original senior Secretary of the Central Committee till the Left were removed from administrative power by Lenin; Rakovsky, the handsome Bulgarian veteran who had virtually founded the Balkan revolutionary movement; Preobrazhensky, the great theorist of the creation of industry on the basis of squeezing the funds out of the peasantry, who has been described as the true leader of the Left in 1923-4;[13] Radek, ugly and intelligent, who had come to the Bolsheviks from Rosa Luxemburg's Polish Social Democratic Party, and had also worked in the German Socialist Left. He had operated with great daring and skill in the revolutionary Berlin of 1919, where he had been imprisoned. But his element was very much that of underground intrigue and the political gamble, and as an able journalist, sharp and satirical. His image in the Party was that of an erratic, unreliable, cynical talker rather than a serious politician; during his last years, he became thoroughly corrupted.

Trotsky was, however, quite isolated in the Politburo itself. His greatest strength was his control of the War Commissariat. An old Trotskyite later took the view that Trotsky could have won in 1923 if he had held his base in the Army and personally appealed to the Party workers in the great towns. Trotsky did not do so (this observer felt) because his victory would then have meant a sure split in the Central Committee, and he hoped to secure it by negotiation.[14]

But this was the wrong arena. Trotsky's weaknesses as a politician were demonstrated:

... the great intellectual, the great administrator, the great orator lacked one quality essential – at any rate in the conditions of the Russian Revolution – to the great political leader. Trotsky could fire masses of men to acclaim and follow him. But he had no talent for leadership among equals. He could not establish his authority among colleagues by the modest arts of persuasion or by sympathetic attention to the views of men of lesser intellectual calibre than himself. He did not suffer fools, and he was accused of being unable to brook rivals.[15]

His hold on Party workers was dependent on great gestures and great speeches. A listener remarks:

But as soon as he [Trotsky] had finished he left the hall. There was no personal contact in the corridors. This aloofness, I believe, may partly explain Trotsky's inability as well as his unwillingness to build a large personal following among the rank and file of the Party. Against the intrigues of Party leaders, which were soon to multiply, Trotsky fought only with the weapons he knew how to use: his pen and his oratory. And even these weapons he took up only when it was too late.[16]

Above all, Trotsky's self-dramatization, his conviction that he would triumph by mere personal superiority, without having to condescend to unspectacular political actions, was fatal. A devastating comment from an experienced revolutionary sums it up: 'Trotsky, an excellent speaker, brilliant stylist and skilled polemicist, a man cultured and of excellent intelligence, was deficient in only one quality: a sense of reality.'[17]

Stalin left the fiercest attacks on Trotsky to his allies. He insistently preached moderation. When Zinoviev and Kamenev urged the expulsion of Trotsky from the Party, he opposed it. He said that no one could possibly 'conceive of the work of the Political Bureau ... without the most active participation of Comrade Trotsky'.[18] But his actions were far more effective than his allies' words. His Secretariat organized the dispersal of Trotsky's leading supporters. Rakovsky was sent to the Soviet

Legation in London, Krestinsky on a diplomatic mission to Germany, others to similar exile. By these and similar means Trotsky was isolated and outmanoeuvred with little trouble. His views, which had already been in conflict with those of Lenin, were officially condemned and by 1925 it was possible to remove him from the War Commissariat.

Stalin now turned on his erstwhile allies Zinoviev and Kamenev. Only to a lesser degree than Trotsky himself they were to be pivotal to the Great Purge.

It is hard to find anyone who writes of Zinoviev in other than a hostile fashion. He seems to have impressed oppositionists and Stalinists, Communists and non-Communists, as a vain, incompetent, insolent and cowardly nonentity. Except for Stalin himself, he is the only Bolshevik leader who cannot be called an intellectual. But, at the same time, he had no political sense either. He had no understanding of economic problems. He was a very effective orator, but his speeches lacked substance, and were only temporarily effective in rousing mass audiences. And yet this was the man who was for a time the leading figure in the Soviet State just before and after Lenin's death. He owed his position simply to the fact that he had been one of the most useful amanuenses and hangers-on of Lenin (often a poor judge of men) during the period from 1909 to 1917 – in fact his closest collaborator and pupil. Just before, and for some time after, the October Revolution, he often opposed what he thought to be the risks in Lenin's policies, on occasion resigning his posts. But he always came back with apologies. And from 1918 on he had again followed Lenin loyally.

Lenin is said to have complained, 'He copies my faults';[19] nevertheless he had forgiven him his weakness in 1917, and relied on him heavily in important posts. He had also said that Zinoviev was bold when danger was past.[20] 'Panic personified' was Sverdlov's comment.[21] Yet Zinoviev had worked in the underground until joining Lenin abroad in 1908, and his conduct in opposition to Stalin, including long spells in jail, though neither firm nor reasonable, was not pure cowardice. With all his faults he did at least make a serious bid for power, which is more than can be said for either Trotsky or Bukharin. He built up his

Leningrad fief and he and Kamenev exerted all their capacities
to defeat Stalin. But perhaps the best thing to be said in his favour
is that Kamenev, a more reputable figure, worked loyally with
him for many years, and in fact right up to the time of their
execution.

Like Stalin, Kamenev had lived in Tbilisi as a boy, and had
gone from the Tbilisi Gymnasium to be a law student in Moscow.
He was again in Tbilisi, representing the Party, in the early years
of the century, when Stalin was barely known. He had been in the
Butyrka jail when a student. After his underground work, he had
stayed abroad between 1908 and 1914 as Lenin's nearest collaborator after Zinoviev. He did not follow Lenin quite so closely
as Zinoviev did, but worked for compromise with the Mensheviks
and later, in Russia, dissociated himself from Lenin's defeatism
in the First World War. After the February Revolution in 1917,
he came back from exile in Siberia with Stalin and they launched
a programme of support for the Provisional Government. When
Lenin returned and insisted on a more revolutionary attitude,
Kamenev alone continued to resist this view. In October 1917 he
had joined Zinoviev in opposing the seizure of power, attracting
Lenin's violent, though temporary, rage. From 1918 on he had
stuck to the Party line. He was not ambitious, and always inclined
to moderation. In any case, he had neither the will-power nor
the judgement to compete adequately in the new phase.

Zinoviev and Kamenev had no truly outstanding adherents,
but their following nevertheless included men like Lashevich
(Vice-Commissar for War, and later to die before the Purges),
G. E. Evdokimov (Secretary of the Central Committee) and a
number of other powerful figures. Moreover, Zinoviev still
controlled the Leningrad Party, and it voted solidly against
Stalin's majority. There was thus the curious sight of the organizations of the Party 'representing' the workers of Leningrad and
of Moscow respectively passing *unanimously* resolutions condemning each other. 'What,' Trotsky asked ironically, 'was the
social explanation?'[22]

Once again, Stalin was able to appear the moderate. He represented Zinoviev and Kamenev as wanting to destroy the
majority. In passages which were to require much amendment

in later editions of his *Works*, he asked: 'You demand Bukharin's blood? We won't give you his blood.' And again:

The Party was to be led without Rykov, without Kalinin, without Tomsky, without Molotov, without Bukharin . . . The Party cannot be led without the aid of those comrades I have just named.[23]

Defeated, Zinoviev and Kamenev, who had been particularly strong against Trotsky, now turned to him for support, forming 'the United Opposition'. This involved their accepting the Left-wing line on economic policy, and it automatically ranged against them the followers of Lenin's line, in particular Bukharin and his supporters. By 1926, as Souvarine remarks,[24] Trotsky had 'more or less already handed Stalin the dictatorship by his lack of foresight, his tactic of patient waiting broken by sudden and inconsequent reactions, and his mistaken calculations', but his final mistake was the forming of this bloc with Zinoviev and Kamenev, 'men devoid of character or credit who had nothing concrete to offer to offset the disrepute they brought with them'. Trotsky did not understand what the Party now was, nor the nature of the problem he faced.

In April 1926 Evdokimov, the only Zinovievite on the Secretariat, was removed. In July, Zinoviev was expelled from the Politburo, being replaced by the Stalinist Rudzutak, and in October Trotsky and Kamenev were expelled in turn. In October the opposition submitted. Zinoviev, Kamenev, Trotsky, Pyatakov, Sokolnikov and Evdokimov denounced their own offences,[25] a most striking precedent for the long series of self-denunciations by the oppositionists.

In 1927 the Trotsky–Zinoviev bloc made one last effort. Defeated and isolated in the ruling councils of the Party, they thought to appeal to the 'Party masses' and the workers. (This was a measure of their lack of contact with reality – the masses were now wholly alienated.) In the autumn came the setting-up of an illegal Trotskyite printing-press, and illegal demonstrations in Moscow and Leningrad. Mrachkovsky, Preobrazhensky and Serebryakov accepted responsibility for the printing-shop. They were all immediately expelled from the Party, and Mrachkovsky was arrested. Stalin gave the whole thing a most sinister air by

representing the G.P.U. *provocateur* who had exposed the opposition printing in an entirely false role as 'a former Wrangel
officer'. Opposition demonstrations on 7 November were a fiasco.
The only result was that on 14 November Trotsky and Zinoviev
were expelled from the Party, and Kamenev, Rakovsky, Smilga
and Evdokimov from the Central Committee. Their followers
everywhere were also ejected. Zinoviev and his followers recanted.
Trotsky's, for the moment, stood firm. The effective number of
Trotskyites and Zinovievites is easy to deduce: 2,500 oppositionists recanted after the 1927 Congress, and 1,500 were expelled.
The leading Trotskyites were sent into exile. In January 1928,
Trotsky was deported to Alma-Ata. Rakovsky, Pyatakov,
Preobrazhensky and others of the Left followed him to other
places in the Siberian and Asian periphery.

On 16 December 1928 Trotsky refused to abjure political
activity. In spite of efforts by Bukharin, together with Tomsky
and Rykov, with the support, apparently, of the moderate Stalinist Kuibyshev, the Politburo agreed to his expulsion from the
U.S.S.R. He was arrested on 22 January 1929 and expelled
to Turkey.

STALIN'S MEN

As his rivals fell one by one, Stalin was promoting a following
with different qualities. Not one of them had any status as a
theoretician, though most were capable of putting a line to a
Party Congress in the conventional Marxist phrasing, which to
some degree disguised this disability. Few of them had great
seniority in the Party. But they were all Old Bolsheviks, and their
characteristics were doggedness, and a willingness to work at
the dull detail of administration.

They included men of ability, if not of brilliance. It was natural
that Molotov, Russia's best bureaucrat, should gravitate to
Stalin's side. He had been one of the first leadership in Petrograd
when the underground Bolsheviks emerged in 1917, and before
that he had edited *Pravda*. He had become a candidate member
of the Politburo in 1921. In 1922 he was joined in that capacity
by the administrative tough V. V. Kuibyshev. But it was not until

January 1926 that a further intake of Stalin's men took place: Voroshilov, his creature since the Civil War, became a full member; Yan Rudzutak, a Latvian who typified the *durs* of the old underground, and G. I. Petrovsky, formerly member of the Duma and latterly an executive of Stalinist policy, came in as candidates.

Later in 1926 Rudzutak was promoted to the full membership lost by Zinoviev, and the candidates were reinforced by five more Stalinists, including the Georgian 'Sergo' Ordzhonikidze, who had been a member of the Central Committee even before the war; Sergei Kirov, appointed to head the Leningrad Party on the rout of the Zinovievites; Lazar Kaganovich; and Anastas Mikoyan.

Ordzhonikidze, whom Lenin had proposed to expel from the Party for two years for his brutality to the Georgian Communists in 1922, was a *feldsher*, or medical orderly. Uneducated, except in Party matters, he gave foreigners the impression of being genial but sly. He seems to have intrigued with Zinoviev in 1925 and with Bukharin in 1928 and then let each of them down.[26]

On the other hand, his vacillations appear to have been due to weakness rather than ill-will. He was temperamental rather than cold and calculating. He was apparently willing to accept Zinoviev and Kamenev back into the Party in 1927 on better terms than Stalin granted, describing them as men 'who have brought a good deal of benefit to our Party',[27] and he expressly dissociated himself from some of the more extreme charges against Trotsky.[28] He was reasonably popular in the Party, and in the years to come was to be to some extent a moderating influence.

Kirov had joined the Party at the age of eighteen in Tomsk in 1904. Arrested or deported four times under Tsarism, the February 1917 Revolution had found him leader of the Bolshevik organization at Vladikavkaz in the Caucasus – a typical minor but highly testing post for the underground militant. He, too, was lacking in some of the worst Stalinist characteristics. He, too, was fairly popular in the Party. He was a Russian, as Stalin was not. He was also, alone among the Stalinists, a very effe***
orator. Though he unflinchingly enforced Stalin's collec***

and industrialization policies, he does not seem to have had that streak of malice which characterized Stalin and his closest associates. Though ruthless, he was neither vicious nor servile. A foreign Communist who had dealings with him says that his Leningrad office had no air of revolutionary enthusiasm, and he himself 'by his remarks and methods, reminded me of the cultured high officials of the Austrian administration I had known at Brünn'.[29]

Such men as Kirov and Ordzhonikidze, Rudzutak and Kuibyshev, whose fates were to be important cruxes in the Great Purge, were supporters and allies of Stalin rather than real devotees. They did not see the logical tendencies of Stalin's political attitude, nor penetrate the obscure potentialities of his personality. The same seems to apply to such men as Vlas Chubar, who joined the Politburo as a candidate member in November 1926, and S. V. Kossior, who came in the following year – both of them Bolsheviks since 1907, and of worker origin.

There was a story in the early thirties of Stalin telling Yagoda that he preferred people to support him from fear rather than from conviction, because convictions could change.[30] When it came to the point, he could not rely on these men to support him through everything. He was to deal with them just as ruthlessly as with the oppositionists, reminding one of Cosimo de Medici's remark that 'We are nowhere commanded to forgive our friends'.

The truest Stalinist of these promotions of the twenties was Lazar Kaganovich. He was brought in by Stalin in 1922 as leader of the then 'Organization and Instruction' Section of the Central Committee under the Secretariat. He was raised to the Central Committee and to the Secretariat at the XIIIth Congress in 1924. Thenceforward he undertook Stalin's most important assignments – as First Secretary in the Ukraine from 1925 to 1928, being withdrawn as part of the concessions Stalin then felt worth making (see p. 345); from 1930 to 1935 he was First Secretary in the Moscow Party organization, and in 1933 ran in addition the key Agricultural Department of the Central Committee.

Kaganovich, though to some degree shallow in his appreciation of problems, was a brilliant administrator. A clear mind and a powerful will went with a total lack of the restraints of humanity. If we have used the word ruthless as generally descriptive of Kirov, for Kaganovich it must be taken quite literally – there was no ruth, no pity, at all in his make-up.

In the Purge, he took the extreme line that the Party's interest justified everything. Fixing him 'with his steely blue eyes', he told an industrial official that as the Party was cleansing itself there were bound to be occasional mistakes: 'When the forest is cut down the chips fly.' He added that a Bolshevik must be ready to sacrifice himself for the Party: 'Yes, ready to sacrifice not only his life but his self-respect and sensitivity.'[31] His public speeches, too, arc full of appeals for ruthlessness and self-sacrifice. When he himself was removed, in rather easier circumstances, in 1957, he telephoned the victor begging not to be shot. It is not difficult to conclude that we have here a bully and a coward.

We may also note here the rise of future Politburo members. Andrei Zhdanov, First Secretary of the important Nizhni–Novgorod (later Gorki) province, was typical of the younger Stalinist generation. A strong, if not profound, intelligence went in him with an ideological fanaticism much more dominant than in most of his generation. To him is due one of the few benefits of the Stalin epoch as compared with the twenties – the re-establishment of an educational system which, though narrow and sycophantic, at least restored in the non-political subjects the rigour and effectiveness of Russian education, which had deteriorated in the experimental interlude. Georgi Malenkov, an equally ruthless and equally intelligent young man, worked in the Party apparatus. His mind ran less in the channels of ideological conviction and political fanaticism than in the skills and details of political manoeuvre, the apparatus and its personalities. Lavrenti Beria, a former O.G.P.U. operative, was appointed by Stalin in 1931 to head the Party organization in Transcaucasia, against the objections of local leaders. In Moscow a slightly older man, Nikita Khrushchev, was being groomed in the local Party machine. These four were to combine some political capacity with satisfactory ruthlessness and to rise high in the State. Their roles in the Purge were particularly murderous.

One view commonly held at the time was that the essential

struggle of the early thirties was waged between the Stalinist 'moderates' and men of the Kaganovich type, for 'priority of influence over Stalin'. In fact, Stalin himself was occasionally giving in with apparent good grace to hostile majorities while leaving Kaganovich and company the task of overtly putting the extreme case. As a result, the moderates seem to have thought that Stalin might have been induced to accept compromise, and make shift with less than autocratic power. This mistake weakened them, as it had weakened all the previous oppositions to Stalin.

There seems, indeed, no doubt that Kaganovich and others identified with terrorism did their best to dissuade Stalin from any policy of relaxation. For the Party would have forgiven Stalin, but a change in line would certainly have led to the fall of this cabal. That Stalin needed their encouragement is a more dubious proposition: his suspicions and ambitions were so strong as not to be notably affected by the efforts of these advisers. Khrushchev probably has the hierarchy of influence right when he comments: 'Arbitrary behaviour by one person encouraged and permitted arbitrariness in others.'[32]

Apart from the true politicians operating the overt machinery of Party and State, Stalin began from the twenties to build up a personal group of agents, chosen for their lack of scruple and totally dependent on and devoted to himself. There is a Russian proverb, 'Out of filth you can make a prince', which, Trotsky says, Stalin was fond of quoting.[33] These men were truly disgusting characters by any standards, a cadre which had abandoned all normal political or even Communist standards, which may be regarded as in effect a personal group of hatchet-men, ready for any violence or falsification at the orders of their leader. At the same time, the political mechanism – containing comparatively reputable figures – continued to exist and was held to the front, just as Al Capone's rule over Cicero was fronted for by civic officials, and employed the usual quota of economic and administrative cadres.

The 'bloodthirsty dwarf' Yezhov – he was only about five feet high – joined the Party in March 1917. Stalin found him in provincial posts and brought him into the Secretariat. He became a member of the Central Committee in 1927. An old Communist remarks, 'In the whole of my long life I have never seen a more repellent personality than Yezhov's.'[34] He was reminded of one of those slum children whose favourite occupation was to tie paraffin-soaked paper to a cat's tail and set fire to it – and this was long before Yezhov had shown his full potentialities.

The intelligence of Yezhov himself has universally been described as low. But that is not to say that he, and the others, did not have adequate organizational and 'political' capacities. Such have been found also in leading gangsters: these latter have, indeed, also been known to nourish a sense of allegiance to the mystique of an organization in much the same way as Yezhov and his colleagues. For such men the Party was indeed *cosa nostra* – 'our thing'.

Another such character, even closer to Stalin, was his secretary Poskrebyshev – tall, slightly hump-backed, heavily pock-marked. He was accustomed to speak quietly, but in the coarsest possible language, and gave a general impression of being almost totally uneducated. As head of the 'Special Sector' of the Central Committee for many years, he was Stalin's closest confidant up till 1952.

Similar men, who were to play important roles in the Terror, were Mekhlis and Shchadenko, who destroyed the Army, Shkiryatov, Yezhov's chief Purge assistant, and a dozen others of lesser note.

A last figure, more important than most, was Andrei Vyshinsky. Educated, intelligent, cowardly and servile, he had been a Menshevik up to 1921 and had joined the Bolshevik Party only after it established itself as victor. He was thus vulnerable to pressures and threats, and soon sought the protection of the faction best able to provide it. He made a quasi-academic career for himself in the Faculty of Law at Moscow University, and rapidly became its Rector on the intervention of the Party apparatus. Later he was a high official in the Commissariat for Education and deeply involved in the purge of the academic world.

Vyshinsky was originally only on the fringe of the Purges, like a gangland lawyer. He was despised, and often openly snubbed, by the police and Party operatives. He was to survive them, after a career of unrelieved falsification and slander. He struck the present writer, who spoke with him in the last years of his life when he was Foreign Minister, as both physically and spiritually a creature who gave life to the worn image of a 'rat in human form'.

Machiavelli mentions several instances of actual criminals rising to control the State – Agathocles of Syracuse, for example. Georgian Communists used to refer to Stalin as a *kinto* – the old Tiflis equivalent of the Neapolitan *lazzaroni*. This tendency in his character is most clearly seen in his selection of followers. In the 1937 Trial Vyshinsky was to say of the oppositionists, 'This gang of murderers, incendiaries and bandits can only be compared with the medieval *camorra* which united the Italian nobility, vagabonds and brigands.'[35] There is a sense in which this analysis is not inappropriate to the victors.

DEFEAT OF THE RIGHT

Zinoviev and Trotsky were no sooner defeated than Stalin turned against his 'Right'-wing allies. Far the most influential was Nikolai Bukharin. He had been described by Lenin as 'the favourite of the Party'. But Lenin had earlier referred to him as '(1) credulous towards gossip and (2) devilishly *unstable* in politics'.[36] He was much the most intellectual of the Bolsheviks, and had an intense interest in theory (being, in Lenin's peculiar formation, 'a most valuable and most eminent Party theoretician' who nevertheless did not properly understand Marxism). In 1917 Lenin thought of Sverdlov and Bukharin as the natural successors if he and Trotsky were killed.[37]

But in the following year Bukharin had led the 'Left Communists' in opposition to the Brest–Litovsk Treaty, in a struggle that at one time reached the point of tentative plans for Lenin's overthrow. He had worked with the 'Left' tendency until 1921, when he had suddenly become the strongest supporter of the N.E.P., a line he was to maintain until his fall.

Deutscher describes Bukharin as combining 'angularity of intellect' with 'artistic sensitivity and impulsiveness, a delicacy of character, and a gay, at times almost schoolboyish, sense of humour '.[38] He was also possessed from time to time by a soggy, tearful romanticism – even about the Secret Police (see p. 724). Trotsky speaks of 'his behaving in his customary manner, half hysterically, half childishly'.[39]

His main associate was Alexei Rykov, Lenin's successor as Premier, who had worked in the underground top leadership since it first stabilized, but who had consistently tended to compromise with the Mensheviks. With Bukharin and Rykov stood the striking figure of Tomsky, leader of the trade unions, the only worker in the Politburo. He had led one of the earliest of all Soviets, that in Reval, in the 1905 revolution, and had been one of the three representatives of underground organizations at the conference of Bolshevik leaders in Paris in 1909.

Bukharin's Right won men like Uglanov, successor to Kamenev as leader of the Moscow Party; and around Bukharin in particular there grew up a group of younger men, mainly intellectuals, who were perhaps the best minds in the Party in the early thirties.

There was a real problem. Though the countryside was now comparatively flourishing, it was not providing an adequate marketable surplus for the towns. Bread rationing was introduced in some provincial towns in 1928 and in Moscow and Leningrad at the beginning of 1929.

During the attack on the Left, Stalin strongly censured the idea of 'fantastic plans for industry without reckoning up our reserves' and rebuked 'people who look on the mass of labouring peasants as ... an object to be exploited for the benefit of industry'.[40] But he now began to take a different line, adopting the Left-wing policy in its most rigorous form.

On 11 July 1928 Bukharin had a secret meeting with Kamenev, organized by Sokolnikov. Kamenev made a résumé of the conversation, which finally leaked and was published abroad. Bukharin had finally seen, as he said, that the political divergences between his own Right-wing faction and the Left-wing faction of Zinoviev and Kamenev were as nothing compared with the total divergence of principle which separated them all from Stalin. It was not a question of ideas, since Stalin did not have any. 'He changes his theories according to the need he has of getting rid of somebody at such-and-such a moment.' Stalin had concluded that the advance to socialism would meet more and more popular resistance. Bukharin commented, 'That will mean a police State, but nothing will stop Stalin.' On the peasant issue Bukharin added in true Party style, 'The *kulaks* can be hunted down at will, but we must conciliate the middle peasants.'

Bukharin's appeal to the disgraced Kamenev was the poorest possible tactics. Not only was Kamenev no use, and the news of the approach to him highly damaging to Bukharin, but the real forces of the Left were beginning to be reconciled to the Party line, now that it had evidently swung their way: Pyatakov capitulated as early as February 1928. By mid 1929 Krestinsky, Radek and most of the other 'Trotskyites' had petitioned for readmission to the Party. Of the leaders Rakovsky alone held out (until 1934). An observer remarks that Communists who had become involved in the opposition and needed to redeem their past faults were 'particularly ruthless'.[41]

Towards the end of 1928 Bukharin, Rykov and Tomsky put in their resignations, in anger at Stalin's steady undermining of their positions. It was too soon for Stalin and he immediately made his usual verbal concessions, passed a Politburo resolution compromising with the Right, and thus obtained 'unanimity'. Thereafter, the attack on the Rightist deviation went on as before but without any naming of the leaders.

In January 1929 Bukharin submitted a declaration to the Politburo. This has never been published, although its sense can be partially reconstructed from various allusions. It protested against plans to squeeze the peasantry, and strongly criticized the absence of intra-Party democracy. It included the remarks: 'We are against one-man decisions of questions of Party leadership. We are against control by a collective being replaced by control by a person, even though an authoritative one.' This, it was charged, was ' direct slander of the Party, direct slander of Comrade Stalin, against whom they try to advance accusations of attempting the single-handed direction of our Party'.[42]

Stalin's success in organizational detail now bore fruit. The Rightists were supported in the Central Committee by a mere handful of members.[43] That body, meeting in April 1929, condemned the Right wing's views, removed Bukharin from his editorship of *Pravda* and chairmanship of the Comintern, and dismissed Tomsky from the trade union leadership. As Kaganovich was to say of the trade unions: 'The greater part of the leadership . . . has been replaced. It could be said that this was a violation of proletarian democracy, but, Comrades, it has long been known that for us Bolsheviks democracy is no fetish . . .'[44]

In April, too, the principles of crash industrialization and of collectivization were adopted at the XVIth Party Conference. After their views had been condemned, the Rightists submitted. On 26 November 1929 they published a very general recantation of their views on 'a series of political and tactical questions'.

As the Right made its submission, Stalin ordered a swing to the left on the collectivization issue far greater even than that to which they had objected. The decision of the XVIth Party Conference that in 1933 the 'public sector' of agriculture was to comprise 26 million hectares, or $17\frac{1}{2}$ per cent of all ploughland, and account for $15\frac{1}{2}$ per cent of gross grain production, was suddenly given a radical amendment:

Molotov, with the agreement and approval of Stalin, criticized the very idea of carrying out collectivization over a five-year period. 'For the basic agricultural districts and regions, with all their different rates of collectivization, we must now think not in terms of a five-year plan, but in terms of the coming year . . .' Molotov ascribed all talk of the difficulties of collectivization to Right-opportunists . . .[45]

Stalin's political problem was not yet solved. Though he had beaten the Right, there was no true guarantee against a revival of their fortunes. But with the launching of the Party into the bitter adventure of sudden collectivization, the effect on any wavering section might be calculated to be a swing to more solidarity. The effect on the Leftist element, already opposed to Bukharin's views, would be further to disarm their complaints against Stalin's policies, and to make them start thinking of the old Party loyalty in the presence of the enemy. As for the just-defeated Rightists, how could they rock the boat during the crisis?

Whenever the Party had been unpopular, this sort of solidarity had been demonstrated. At Kronstadt, all the oppositionists – even the Workers' Opposition – had rallied to the leadership for the critical period.

The last pretence that persuasion, or even economic pressure, was to be the method of enforcing the Party will on the peasantry had disappeared. Pure force, a frontal assault, was the chosen method. Without any serious preparation or planning on the economic side, the Party was launched into a civil war in the rural areas. It was the first great crisis of the Stalin regime, and it marks the beginning of a whole new era of terror.

As a political move against the Right, Stalin's plunge to extreme militancy in the countryside had its tactical merits. Seen as a serious policy move, it shows all the signs of economic ignorance, a belief that administrative methods can cope with anything, and an almost frivolous failure to make any real preparations.

It is worth remarking that Stalin had no economic experience and little economic knowledge. The Bolsheviks had started with the almost total destruction of the skilled entrepreneur class in industry. Now came, in the villages, the elimination precisely of the most productive and efficient of the peasantry. A myth-dominated economy led also to the virtual annihilation of the skilled economists in the Party. Stalin so pilloried the economists and planners in 1929 for their ideas about achieving a balanced economy that 'he choked off any desire on the part of either scientific or practical workers to take the matter up'.[46]

The economists mainly took the view that large-scale public investment based on internal resources could be coupled with anti-inflationary policies. Public investment would increase the private wealth in agriculture, but this would not endanger the regime because the public sector would be advanced more rapidly still. The Bukharinites argued in addition that collectivization could not be made attractive, or even practical, in the countryside until more advanced agricultural methods were ripe and ready. The Stalinist scheme – which amounted to seizing the peasant's surplus in order to pay for tractors which would only begin to arrive some time later – in fact resulted in there being no incentive whatever to the peasantry. The collective farms were set up on a starvation basis by force alone. In their anger against the collectivization the peasantry destroyed a vast amount of Russia's agricultural wealth. And the tractors were never delivered in tolerable numbers. Moreover, owing to the same lack of preparation, the provisions for their maintenance were quite unsatisfactory and a large proportion were wasted.

Meanwhile, the new policy went forward. On 5 January 1930 the Central Committee issued a decision, switching from the original plan of collectivizing 20 per cent of the sown area during the Five-Year Plan to the *complete* collectivization of the more important regions by the autumn of 1930 or at the very latest the autumn of 1931, and in other areas the autumn of 1931 or at the very latest the autumn of 1932.[47] In one way or another, everything got out of hand, and in a few weeks the Party had been carried to the brink of disaster. Between January and March 1930 the number of peasant holdings brought into the collective farms increased from 4 million to 14 million. Over half the total peasant households had been collectivized in five months. And in the countryside the peasants fought back with 'the sawed-off shotgun, the axe, the dagger, the knife'.[48] At the same time they destroyed their livestock rather than let it fall into the hands of the State.

Kalinin, Ordzhonikidze and other members of the Politburo visited the provinces and seem to have reported realistically about the disaster. There are also a number of stories in 1930 of Voroshilov's objection to crash collectivization.[49] Stalin is said not to have bothered to obtain Politburo permission for his key article 'Dizziness with Success', in *Pravda* of 2 March 1930.[50] The article put most of the blame on excesses committed by local Party workers, and this, it is said, came as a shock to local enthusiasts. It was followed on 14 March by a condemnation of 'distortions' of the Party line in the application of compulsion to the peasantry – which, the statement said, was a Leftist deviation which could only help to strength Right-wing elements in the Party. Bauman, who had replaced Uglanov as First Secretary in Moscow and candidate member of the Politburo, was now made a scapegoat on charges of Left deviation, removed from his post and sent to a lesser position in Central Asia.[51]

Defeat had been accepted. The peasants left the *kolkhozes*. Stalin's policy lay in ruins.

In any other political system this would have been the moment for the opposition to stand forward. They had been proved right. And support for the Rightist leadership sprang up spontaneously in Party branches all over the country. Among the people as a whole, they were of course stronger still. But to this vast potential support Bukharin, Tomsky and Rykov gave no lead. On the contrary, they went out of their way to say that to come out against 'the Party', especially with the support of peasants, was unthinkable. So Stalin's policy defeat was accompanied by a political victory. Tomsky was removed from the Politburo in July 1930, and Rykov in December. Henceforth it was purely Stalinist.

The Rightist leaders privately regarded Stalin's leadership as catastrophic, and hoped for his fall, but advised their closest adherents to wait in patience for a change in the Party mood. Bukharin favoured working up a general support of the idea of a change without any direct organized struggle for the time being. He is described as having counselled the younger oppositionists to rely on the masses, who must sooner or later realize the fatal consequences of the Stalin line.[52] Patience would be necessary. So he accepted defeat in the vague hope of some improvement later on.

The Trotskyists voiced a similar hope for a change. Ivan Smirnov, a 'capitulator', now considered: 'In view of the incapacity of the present leadership to get out of the economic and political deadlock, the conviction about the need to change the leadership of the Party is growing.'[53]

Stalin, though retreating, had not given up his plans for collectivization. He now proposed to bring it into being over a longer period – by means just as inhuman but not so ill-prepared. Everywhere in the countryside the Party, faced with a hostile peasantry, regrouped and prepared further desperate action.

By a far better prepared combination of ruthlessness and

economic measures, the almost complete collectivization of the bulk of the country was again attained by the end of 1932. Resistance was now met by a simple method. If the peasant had produced only enough for his own subsistence, leaving none for the State, local enforcement officials reversed that procedure. The last sacks of grain were taken from the barns for export while famine raged. Butter was sent abroad while the Ukrainian infants were dying for lack of milk.*

The famine can be blamed quite flatly on Stalin. The crop in 1932 was about 12 per cent below average. This was far from being famine level. But procurements of food from the peasantry were up by 44 per cent. The result was, and could not have been other than, large-scale starvation. It is perhaps the only case in history of a purely man-made famine.

It is also the only major famine whose very existence was ignored or denied by the governmental authorities, and even to a large degree successfully concealed from world opinion. The process by which this happened is a very unfortunate one, involving political reactions which are still with us to this day. It was not, of course, possible to make the concealment absolute. It was widely known in Moscow, and the low-level Government official occasionally spoke of it to a foreigner. Some foreigners – including Malcolm Muggeridge and Tom Jones, Lloyd George's secretary – even penetrated the famine area and saw for themselves. But the information was naturally taken up and given widest publicity in the West by those most hostile to the Soviet Union in principle. By a common – though thoughtless and unfortunate – reaction, Left-wing and even moderate circles were able to persuade themselves that the story was untrue or (a much easier view) greatly exaggerated. The Soviet Government had not admitted it. Occasionally, specially shepherded travellers (for example, Sir John Maynard) had been taken to prepared spots in the area and had generalized from that.

The Soviet authorities, as far as can be seen, let through only

* Grain export during the early thirties was higher than at any time since the Revolution, running at around 5 million tons a year in 1930–31 and 1¾ million tons even during the famine period 1932–33. In 1929–30 it had been less than 200,000 tons.

one accidental admission – an accusation that members of the People's Commissariat of Agriculture then on trial for sabotage had used their positions 'to create a famine in the country'.[54] The Ukrainian President Petrovsky told a Western correspondent that millions were dying.[55] Thirty years later, there was a brief lifting of the curtain in the Soviet press – as in the serial *People Are not Angels* by Ivan Stadnyuk, who sums up: 'The men died first, then the children, and finally the women.'[56]

As is always the case when the authorities will not provide information nor permit research into the relevant archives, it is not easy to estimate the casualties. A careful examination of all the estimates, and all the accounts, seems to show that over 5 million deaths from hunger and from the diseases of hunger is the best estimate.[57] Only one famine listed in the *Encyclopaedia Britannica* (that of China in 1877–8) is cited as more destructive.*

Starvation was compounded by terror. Arbitrary rule by Party gangs flourished. But in any case, normal process of law was Draconian: for example, a law of August 1932 imposed a sentence of ten years' imprisonment for any theft of grain, however small. Already, deportation quotas were laid down for different areas.[62] Mass execution also played its part. Stalin later told Churchill that 10 million *kulaks* had to be dealt with,† and that 'the great bulk' were 'wiped out', others being transferred

*Of the 5–6 million who perished, more than 3 million were in the Ukraine; Kazakhstan, the North Caucasus and the Middle Volga also suffered particularly heavily.[58] Even on official figures, the Ukraine's population had sunk from 31 million to 28 million between 1926 and 1939. The O.G.P.U. figures sent to Stalin gave deaths from starvation alone as 3·3–3·5 million.[59] Even higher estimates are said to have been given by Skrypnik and Balitsky to an American Communist.[60] Some notion of losses among newborn children can be estimated from the fact that in 1941 there were a million fewer 7-year-old children than 11-year-olds in the schools. The point is greatly strengthened by a comparison between the 1941 figures for Kazakhstan, which was much affected by the 1933 famine, and for Moldavia, most of which, at the time of the famine, had not formed part of the U.S.S.R. at all. In Kazakhstan, the 7-year-old group was less than two fifths the size of the 11-year-old, while in Moldavia the 7-year-old group was two thirds as large again as the 11-year-old.[61]

† A recent Soviet account estimates that in a typical village sixteen households (of five to eight persons each) were 'repressed' as *kulaks*, only five of them being economically *kulak* even by the official definition.[63]

to Siberia.[64] Over 3 million seem to have ended up in the newly expanding labour-camp system (see p. 454).

Collectivization destroyed about 25 per cent of the productive capacity of Soviet agriculture.[65] The Five-Year Plan had postulated a grain output for its last year of over 100 million tons. It did not reach 70 million, and the original target was not achieved before the outbreak of war. From 1933 on, Soviet statistics of grain output are falsified by a matter of up to 30 per cent, owing to the introduction of the method of counting the grain thought to be present on the stalk, rather than that actually harvested – as revealed in 1953. The power available on the farms was actually less in 1938 than it had been in 1929. Although many tractors ·appeared, they were not in anything like adequate numbers to make up for the death or slaughter of half of Russia's horses during the first Five-Year Plan.[66]

There seems little doubt that the main issue was simply crushing the peasantry at any cost. One high official told a Ukrainian who later defected that the 1933 harvest 'was a test of our strength and their endurance. It took a famine to show them who is master here. It has cost millions of lives, but the collective farm system is here to stay. We have won the war.'[67] In fact, we find that mass terror was now already in existence in the countryside, and thousands of police and Party officials had received the most ruthless operational experience.

On the other front, that of crash industrialization, a similar atmosphere of discipline prevailed. The great steelworks went up among ramshackle barracks packed with ill-fed workers. But in this field there was economic achievement. It was not that presaged by the plans, or claimed by the propaganda authorities. The idea of smoothly planned progress was quite inapplicable.

Even in theory the idea of plan fulfilment gave way to a race for the maximum. 'Over-fulfilment' was the target, and awards went to the director who produced 120 per cent of his quota. But if he did so, how did he get the raw materials? They must, of course, have been obtained at the expense of some other industry. The method, in fact, is not strictly speaking that of a planned economy: it is rather that of a competitive expansion without regard to allocation of resources, or the necessity of the goods produced. This system gave rise to enormous dislocations. It resulted in a great increase in productivity, particularly in certain industries, but with a wastage probably at least as bad as those of uncontrolled capitalism during its own period of '*Sturm und Drang*'.

For example, an attempt to increase copper production from 40,000 tons to 150,000 tons in a single year, which was not simply very difficult but totally impossible, was resisted by the leaders of the metallurgical industry, Serebrovsky and Shakh-Muradov. The latter attempted to have the target brought down to 100,000 tons, and was dismissed. The former, his chief, then publicly accepted the official target, knowing that it could not be reached, as a matter of Party discipline. Immense effort was put in, but production never went above 50,000 tons, and 'It took a long time to stabilize even that, during the Five-Year Plan'.[68]

Even admitting the basic validity of the crash programmes, the Party had not by 1930 had time to prepare adequate technical and managerial staffs or to educate the workers and peasants. Hence, everything had to be handled on the basis of myth and coercion rather than rationality and cooperation. The new proletariat was 'alienated' even more thoroughly than the old. In October 1930 the first decree was issued forbidding the free movement of labour, followed two months later by one that forbade factories to employ people who had left their previous place of work without permission. At the same time unemployment relief was abolished on the grounds that 'there was no more unemployment'. In January 1931 came the first law introducing prison sentences for violation of labour discipline – confined for the time being to railwaymen. February brought the compulsory Labour Books for all industrial and transport workers. In March punitive measures against negligence were announced, followed by a decree holding workers responsible for damage done to instruments or materials. Preferential rations for 'shock brigades' were introduced, and in 1932 the then very short food supplies were put under the direct control of the factory managers through the introduction of a kind of truck-system for allocation by results. July 1932 saw the abrogation of Article 37 of the 1922 Labour Code, under which the transfer of a worker from one enterprise to another could be effected only with his consent. On 7 August 1932 the death penalty was introduced for theft of State or collective property – a law which was immediately applied on a large scale. From November 1932 a single day's unauthorized absence from work became punishable by instant dismissal. Finally, on 27 December 1932, came the re-introduction of the internal passport, denounced by Lenin as one of the worst stigmata of Tsarist backwardness and despotism.

The trade union system became simply an appendage of the State. Tomsky's view that 'it is impossible simultaneously to manage production on a commercial basis and to express and defend the workers' economic interests', and that 'first wages must be raised, and only then can we expect a rise in productivity' were publicly rejected at the IXth Trade Union Congress in April 1932, and his successor Shvernik put forward instead, as 'the trade unions' most important task', the mass introduction of 'piecework on the basis of ... norms' – that is, the rigid payment-by-result which was to be the instrument of sweating the worker over the following decades.

However, the workers did not, on the whole, die. Industrial advances were made. The system of coercion, which became institutionalized at a less desperate level, worked in the sense that industry was created. It is probable that other methods could have produced at least equal advance at far less human cost. But there were tangible results and the Party could feel that the policy had proved successful.

Stalin's other evident political objective had also been attained. In the struggle with the people there was no room for neutrality. Loyalty could be called for from the Party membership on a war basis. He could demand absolute solidarity and use all rigour in stamping out weakness. The atmosphere of civil war resembled that of the foreign wars which autocrats have launched, throughout history, to enable them to silence the voices of criticism, to eliminate waverers. It was, once again, a question of 'My party right or wrong'. The oppositionists made no move. The Menshevik Abramovitch is not being unfair when he says 'The famine evoked no reaction on the part of Trotsky, who found time and space to write of the "dreadful persecution" of his own partisans in Russia and to denounce Stalin for the latter's falsification of Trotsky's biography. The "proletarian humanist" Bukharin and the tempestuous Rykov likewise remained silent.[69]

Bukharin was, however, beginning to understand that 'rapid socialization', involving as it was bound to so much ruthlessness, dehumanized the ruling party. During the Revolution, he said privately, he had seen

things that I would not want even my enemies to see. Yet 1919 cannot even be compared with what happened between 1930 and 1932. In 1919 we were fighting for our lives. We executed people, but we also risked our lives in the process. In the later period, however, we were conducting a mass annihilation of completely defenceless men, together with their wives and children.[70]

But he was even more concerned with the effect on the Party. Many Communists had been severely shaken. Some had committed suicide, others had gone mad. In his view, the worst result of the terror and famine in the country was not so much the sufferings of the peasantry, horrible though these were. It was the 'deep changes in the psychological outlook of those Communists who participated in this campaign, and instead of going mad, became professional bureaucrats for whom terror was henceforth a normal method of administration, and obedience to any order from above a high virtue'. He spoke of a 'real dehumanization of the people working in the Soviet apparatus'.[71]

He and his friends nevertheless remained silent, awaiting a moment when Stalin, at last realized to be an unsuitable leader of State and Party, would somehow be removed from power. They had misunderstood the nature of this last problem.

CHAPTER ONE

STALIN PREPARES

Resolv'd to ruin or to rule the state. DRYDEN

IT was while he was securing his victory in the countryside that Stalin made the first moves towards the new style of terror which was to typify the period of the Great Purge.

While the opposition leaders thrashed about ineffectively in the quicksands of their own preconceptions, lesser figures in the Party were bolder and less confused. Three movements against Stalin came in the period 1930–33. The first, in 1930, was led by men hitherto his followers – Syrtsov, whom he had just raised to be candidate member of the Politburo (in Bauman's place) and Chairman of the R.S.F.S.R. Council of People's Commissars, and Lominadze, also a member of the Central Committee. They had obtained some sort of support from various local Party Secretaries (among them the Komsomol leader Shatskin and Kartvelishvili, First Secretary of the Transcaucasian Party) for an attempt to limit Stalin's powers.[1] They both objected to authoritarian rule in the Party and State, and to the dangerous economic policies. They seem to have circulated a memoir criticizing the regime for economic adventurism, stifling the initiative of the workers, and bullying treatment of the people by the Party. Lominadze had referred to the 'lordly feudal attitude to the needs of the peasants'.[2] Syrtsov had described the new industrial giants, like the Stalingrad Tractor Plant, as so much eyewash.[3]

Stalin learned of the plans of this group before they could complete their preparations, and they were expelled in December 1930. Lominadze committed suicide in 1935; all the others concerned were to perish in the Purges.*

And now we come to a case crucial to the Terror – that of Ryutin. Throughout the ensuing years, this was named as the

---

*Syrtsov and Lominadze are named as conspirators in the Zinoviev and Bukharin Trials.[4]

original conspiracy; all the main oppositionists in turn were accused of participating in the Ryutin 'plot'.

A group of lesser Rightists, headed by Ryutin and Slepkov, had ignored the policy of inaction recommended by Bukharin and produced at the end of the summer of 1932 the celebrated 'Ryutin Platform'. This document of 200 pages they circulated widely in the leading circles of the Party.

The 'Platform' is known in its essentials from various sources.[5] A key phrase from it is 'The Right wing has proved correct in the economic field, and Trotsky in his criticism of the regime in the Party'.[6] It censured Bukharin, Rykov and Tomsky for their capitulation. It proposed an economic retreat, the reduction of investment in industry, and the liberation of the peasants by freedom to quit the *kolkhozes*. As a first step in the restoration of democracy in the Party it urged the immediate readmission of all those expelled, including Trotksy.

However, it was mainly notable not so much for its frank statement of a Rightist programme as for its severe condemnation of Stalin personally. Fifty of its pages were devoted to this theme, and called forcefully for his removal from the leadership. It described Stalin as 'the evil genius of the Russian Revolution, who, motivated by a personal desire for power and revenge, brought the Revolution to the verge of ruin'.[7] For Ryutin saw, far more clearly than his seniors in the opposition, that there was no possibility of controlling Stalin. It was a question either of submission or of revolt.

Stalin interpreted the 'Platform' as a call for his assassination. In the Bukharin–Rykov Trial in 1938, it was to be spoken of at length as 'registering the transition to the tactics of overthrowing the Soviet power by force; the essential points of the Ryutin platform were a palace coup, terrorism . . .'[8] This was, of course, untrue. But we may take it that such a remark, put into the mouth of the accused by the authorities, shows Stalin's attitude to the Ryutin case – that he regarded it as the occasion for starting to accuse the opposition of capital crimes.

Stalin seems to have hoped that the O.G.P.U. might shoot Ryutin without involving the political authorities. But they referred the question first to the Party's Central Control Commission. This was supposed to be a body, outside the normal Party hierarchy, in which disciplinary matters could be decided independently. Its chief was normally a man of Politburo standing, who gave up membership of the Politburo for the time being. Since Lenin's death the post had been held by a series of Stalinists – Kuibyshev, Ordzhonikidze, Andreyev, and now Rudzutak. Rudzutak felt that the Ryutin affair was a political issue going far beyond the simple question of discipline, and referred it on to the Politburo. There Kirov is said to have spoken 'with particular force against recourse to the death penalty. Moreover, he succeeded in winning over the Politburo to this view.'[9] Another account says that, in addition to Kirov, Ordzhonikidze, Kuibyshev, Kossior, Kalinin and Rudzutak spoke against Stalin, who was only supported by Kaganovich. Even Molotov and Andreyev seem to have wavered.[10]

Such a division of views is suggested (in connexion with a much lesser figure who happens, however, to have been rehabilitated) by a recent Soviet article. It represents Stalin attempting at this time to purge the Armenian Communist Nazaretyan, but being unable to do so because Ordzhonikidze defended him and Stalin knew that 'Kirov and Kuibyshev would also speak out in the Politburo on the same lines'.[11] This is a definite assertion of the existence of what amounts to a moderate bloc and one, presumably, able to obtain a Politburo majority. For the first time, in fact, Stalin was faced with powerful opposition from his own allies.

Ryutin's would have been the first such execution within the ranks of the old Party.* It was particularly unacceptable, in any case, to start applying such measures in what on the face of it was no more than a straight political dispute (even though the O.G.P.U. is said to have already concocted a story about a plot at the Military Academy to go with the Platform).[12] The old Party loyalty, whatever its bad side, had involved not merely the submission of intra-Party oppositions of the will of the majority: it had also defended at least the skins of the oppressed Party

---

* Blyumkin (the ex-Social Revolutionary who had shot the German Ambassador in 1918) had been executed as a secret envoy of Trotsky in 1929, but that was a rather different matter.

minorities. Lenin could work amicably with Zinoviev and Kamenev although he had for a time denounced them as traitors when
they attacked the plan for the armed uprising in October 1917.
Bukharin could later admit his talk in 1918 of arresting Lenin
and changing the Government, without thereby forfeiting Party
esteem. Now, it emerged that Stalin's new Stalinist Politburo
would not automatically accept his decisions when they contradicted such deep-set Party traditions.

It is certain that the defeat rankled. In each of the Great Trials
of 1936, 1937 and 1938, the accused confessed to complicity in
the Ryutin plot, which marked, they said, the first coming
together of all the oppositions on a terrorist basis. It was precisely
four years after the exposure of Ryutin that Stalin significantly
remarked that 'the O.G.P.U. is four years behind' in unmasking
Trotskyites. The four years from September 1932 to September
1936 were, in fact, for him a period in which he set himself the
task of breaking resistance to the physical destruction of his
Party enemies.

The first lesson he seems to have drawn was that he could not
easily obtain his followers' consent to executions of Party members for purely political offences. The attempt to read an assassination programme into the Ryutin Platform was too unreal. A
genuine assassination might prove a better theme.

At the same time, he saw among his own adherents men whose
resistance could not easily be broken, and for whose removal it
was difficult to find any political excuse. Over the next two years,
he was to put these two thoughts together and find a logical
solution – the assassination of Kirov.

A plenum of the Central Committee was held from 28 September to 2 October 1932 on the case. The Ryutin group were
expelled from the Party 'as degenerates who have become
enemies of Communism and the Soviet regime, as traitors to the
Party and to the working class, who, under the flag of a spurious
"Marxism–Leninism", have attempted to create a bourgeois-
kulak organization for the restoration of capitalism and particularly kulakdom in the U.S.S.R.'[13]

Many of the old oppositionists had, while failing to support
Ryutin, seen copies of the Platform and failed to report it to the

authorities. Now a new repression was launched against this indiscipline. Zinoviev and Kamenev were expelled from the Party again on these grounds, and deported to the Urals. Ivan Smirnov, who, on his readmission to the Party, had become head of the Gorki Automobile Works, was rearrested on 1 January 1933 and sentenced to ten years' jail, going to the 'isolator' at Suzdal. Smilga received five years, and with Mrachkovsky was sent to Verkhne-Uralsk.

A resolution on a more general purging of the Party was passed by a plenum of the Central Committee on 12 January 1933. More than 800,000 members were expelled during the year, and another 340,000 in 1934.

The method of the Party purge was in itself an encouragement to informers, lickspittles and conscienceless careerists. The local Purge commissions, in the presence of the entire local membership, would examine each member about every detail of his political and personal past. Intervention from the audience was welcomed. In theory, all this was a sign of Party democracy and comradely frankness. In practice, it attracted – and of course increasingly so as conditions got worse – first the inflation of true though pettifogging points from the past, such as distant relationship or acquaintance with former White Army officers, and finally simple invention or misrepresentation.

At the January 1933 plenum, too, the last of the new cycle of plots was exposed. The distinguished Old Bolshevik A. P. Smirnov, Party member since 1896 and formerly member of the Central Committee's 'Orgburo', was charged with two other Old Bolsheviks, Eismont and Tolmachev (members since 1907 and 1904 respectively), with forming an anti-Party group.

A. P. Smirnov's group is said to have had wide contact with Old Bolshevik workers, mainly in the trade unions, in Moscow, Leningrad and other cities. Realizing that no legal methods could break Stalin's grip, they had to a large degree gone underground, with a view to organizing for a struggle. Their programme seems to have covered the revision of the unbalanced industrial schemes, the dissolution of most of the *kolkhozes*, the subjection of the O.G.P.U. to Party control, the independence of the trade unions. Above all, they had discussed the removal of

Stalin. When taxed at the plenum Eismont said, 'Yes, there were such conversations among us. A. P. Smirnov started them.' None of the three had had any connexion with the Trotskyite or Rightist oppositions. The exposure of this plot was described in the Khrushchev era as 'the beginning of reprisals against the old Leninist cadres'.[14]

In his speech on the matter Stalin significantly remarked, 'Of course, only enemies could say that to remove Stalin would not affect matters.'[15]

Again, an attempt to have the oppositionists shot seems to have been made and blocked. It appears that Kirov, Ordzhonikidze and Kuibyshev again played the main role in opposing the death penalty. Kalinin and Kossior supported them; Andreyev, Voroshilov and, to some degree, Molotov took a vacillating position and once again only Kaganovich supported Stalin to the end.[16]

The top Rightists had refused to have anything to do with Smirnov's plans. And even in the published Resolution on this group it is only alleged that Rykov, Tomsky and V. V. Shmidt had 'stood aside from the struggle with anti-Party elements and even maintained relations with Smirnov and Eismont, thus in fact encouraging them in their anti-Party activities'.

At the plenum, Bukharin, not implicated even to this extent, made a speech typical of the extravagant and insincere tone which was now conventional in ex-oppositionist statements, demanding 'the severe punishment of A. P. Smirnov's grouping'; and he spoke of his own earlier 'Right-opportunist, absolutely wrong general political line', of his 'guilt before the Party, its leadership, before the Central Committee of the Party, before the working class and the country', mentioning Tomsky and Rykov as his 'former companions in the leadership of the Right opposition'.[17]

Eismont and Tolmachev were expelled from the Party, and A. P. Smirnov from the Central Committee.* Over the winter Eismont, Tolmachev, Ryutin, Uglanov and others were given jail sentences.[19]

* Smirnov was expelled from the Party in December 1934, after the Kirov murder, for 'double-dealing and continuing his struggle against the Party'.[18]

The views of A. P. Smirnov and his followers mark an important crux. For we find veteran senior officials who had never been associated with any opposition speaking not merely of a policy change, but specifically of Stalin's removal. This lends considerable plausibility to the rather vague assertions that similar discussions took place a year later at the time of the XVIIth Congress.[20]

Neither the Ryutin nor the A. P. Smirnov groups had any serious chance of success. The significance of the cases was, rather, in the opposition offered to Stalin by his own supporters in the Politburo on the issue of executing the conspirators.

The revulsion of Kirov, Ordzhonikidze and the others against the proposal was quite genuine. The extraordinary strength of the idea of Party solidarity is nowhere better shown.

It is here that the true *dvoeverye* – 'double belief' – of the Party 'moderates' lay. It explains, as nothing else can, the horrified resistance of many who had cheerfully massacred the Whites, and at least uncomplainingly starved and slaughtered the peasantry, to the execution of prominent Party members, to 'shedding the blood of Bolsheviks'. It reflects a double standard of morality comparable to the attitude of sensitive and intelligent men in the ancient world to slaves, or of the French nobility of the eighteenth century to the lesser classes. Non-Party people were hardly more taken into account, even by the better Old Bolsheviks, than slaves were by Plato. They were, in effect, nonmen. One is reminded of a famous scene in *Salammbô* when Hamilcar discovers, but is not quite able to grasp, that a slave is capable of sorrow at the proposed death of his son. For it is not, indeed, wholly impossible to maintain humanist virtues within a limited circle and at the same time to treat outsiders with indifference or brutality.

A view of the Purges which requires us to sympathize with the loyal Party victim, while withholding our sympathy from such men as those who suffered in the Shakhty Case (see Appendix F), is unlikely to be accepted very widely. It is, indeed, defensible, but only from a narrow and rigorist Party viewpoint. It may perhaps be argued, from the opposite viewpoint, that those at least of the Party victims who had themselves committed or

connived at similar repressions against non-Party figures are
entitled not to a greater, but to a considerably smaller, meed of
sympathy for their own later sufferings.

All the apparatus of oppression under which they themselves
were to suffer was already in existence. They had raised no
objection to its employment so long as the animus of the State
was directed against men and women they too believed to be
enemies of the Party. If Bukharin in the Politburo had spoken
up against the Shakhty Trial, if Trotsky in exile had denounced
the Menshevik Trial – if they had even objected not to the injustice as such but merely to the blemish on the reputation of the
Party and State – the oppositionists would have been on solider
ground.

We are perhaps in danger of romanticizing the better actions
of some of these men. When Isaac Deutscher – or even Arthur
Koestler – puts the fate of the oppositionists in a tragic light, we
should nevertheless recall that they themselves in their time had
thought nothing – as Bukharin himself said at his trial[21] – of
killing political opponents on a large scale and for no other
reason but to establish the power of their own Party against
popular resistance. They had, moreover, at least not effectively
protested against the trials in which non-Party people were
convicted on patently falsified evidence. Few of them had stood
for anything resembling democracy even within the Party (and
it is notable that those few, men like Sapronov, never came to
public trial).

All the same, even avoiding the romanticizing of revolution (a
habit to which the British, who do not have to go through
revolutions themselves, are perhaps particularly prone), we need
not fall into denying any virtue to men some of whose actions
may appear to us to be dubious. For this would be to lay down
criteria as narrow in their way as those of the Stalinists themselves. Dr Goebbels was one of the most unpleasant characters
in Europe; yet it does not seem amiss to grant him a certain
admiration for his courage and clear-headedness in the last days
of the Third Reich, particularly in comparison with the cowardly
and stupid intrigues of most of his colleagues.

In fact, courage and clear-headedness are admirable in themselves. And if they do not rank high among the moral virtues, we can see in some of the Soviet oppositionists something rather better. It is true that those who did not confess, and were shot secretly, demonstrated not merely a higher courage, but a better sense of values. In them, however touched by the demands of Party and revolutionary loyalty, loyalty to the truth and the idea of a more humane regime prevailed. But even among those who confessed, we can often see the struggle between Party habits and the old impulses to justice which had originally, in many cases at least, been one of the motives for joining the Party.

If the oppositionists were not spotless, it is at least true of their conduct during the Civil War that to have acted

> right or wrong
> Within that furious age

was different from planning the cold-blooded Terror shortly to be launched. Even the attempt by those who had just decimated the Ukraine to save Ryutin, absurd though it may appear to logical Stalinist and logical humanist alike, perhaps indicates not merely a wish to preserve privilege, but also a residuum of humane feeling.

There is, after all, a moral difference between some restraint and none. Though indulgence in terrorist action against any section of the population may corrupt the entire personality, as it clearly had done in the cases of Yezhov and others, nevertheless the contrary is also true – that the preservation of more or less humanist attitudes, even if only in a limited field, may, when the particular motives for terror against others have lapsed, spread out again and rehumanize the rest.

Over the next few years, Stalin was to burn out the last roots of humanism. There was no longer to be a section of the community reserved from the operation of arbitrary rule. And, in itself, this was not unwelcome to the non-Party members. We often find in the prison and concentration-camp literature accounts of ordinary victims being cheered up at the sight of some notorious persecutor from the N.K.V.D. or the Party machine appearing in the same cell or barrack.

For the general objection to the Terror is not that it was to strike at the Party members as well as at the population, but that the sufferings of the population itself under it increased immeasurably. The true crux of the Ryutin dispute resides less in preserving the privileged sanctuary of Party membership, than in the fact that it was the issue on which Stalin was to fight the battle with his own colleagues to decide if Russia was or was not to submit unreservedly to his single will. In an oligarchical system there is at lowest always the possibility of some members of the ruling elite taking moderate views, or at least acting as a brake on their more repressive fellows. In an autocracy, the question depends entirely upon the will of one man. There have been comparatively mild autocrats. But Stalin was not one of them.

In this period when Stalin was the effective binding power of the State, the pressures he met penetrated his personal life as well. On 5 November 1932 his wife Nadezhda Alliluyeva committed suicide. But neither personal loss nor public crisis broke his will. And this was widely understood as the decisive factor in the terrible struggle just concluded. He had met wavering and refused it countenance. We are told that 'in 1932 Stalin was adamant against the proposal to surrender the positions already gained'.[22] An official of the period comments, 'Loyalty to Stalin at the time of which I am writing [1932] was based principally on the conviction that there was no one to take his place, that any change of leadership would be extremely dangerous, and that the country must continue in its present course, since to stop now or attempt a retreat would mean the loss of everything.'[23] Even a Trotskyite could comment: 'If it were not for that so-and-so . . . everything would have fallen into pieces by now. It is he who keeps everything together . . .'[24]

By the beginning of 1933, many circles in the Party previously unconvinced about the possibility of success began to alter their attitude and to accept that Stalin had in fact won through. As Kamenev was made to remark at his trial in 1936: 'Our banking on the insuperability of the difficulties which the country was experiencing, on the state of crisis of its economy, on the collapse of the economic policy of the Party leadership had obviously failed by the second half of 1932.'[25] The 'victory' did not amount to the creation of an efficient industry and agriculture. But the

Party, which had staked its existence on winning the battle against the peasantry, had succeeded in crushing them, and a collective farm system was now firmly established.

By early summer a certain relaxation took place in all fields. In May 1933 a decrease of peasant deportations to a figure of 12,000 households a year was ordered by a secret circular signed by Stalin and Molotov.[26] In the same month Zinoviev and Kamenev were brought back from Siberia to make another confession of error. *Pravda* published a piece by Kamenev, condemning his own mistakes and calling on the oppositionists to cease any resistance.[27]

The former theological students among them – and there were always a surprising number of these in the Party, from Stalin and Mikoyan down to men like Chernov – might have remembered the scenes which took place after the Council of Nicaea, when one of the more extreme Arians remarked to a colleague who had surrendered, 'Thou hast subscribed to escape banishment, but within the year thou shalt be as I am.' But it is also true that even the opposition was often won over by the victory of Stalin's line, and the successes gained, at whatever cost, in industry.

Moreover, the rise of Nazism in Germany was a strong shock. Stalin had played on a quite implausible war scare in the late twenties, trapping Trotsky in particular into implying that even in war he would oppose the leadership – a sure formula for accusations of 'traitor'. But no serious figure had been shaken by the manoeuvre. Now Rakovsky and Sosnovsky, the last leading oppositionists in exile, finally made their peace with the regime, giving the war danger as their main motive. Rakovsky, who earlier seems to have been badly hurt in an attempt to escape, had pointed out that even Lenin had expressed qualms about the power of the Party, and that since his death it had become ten times more powerful. Getting to the heart of the dispute, he had said, 'We have always based ourselves on the revolutionary initiative of the masses and not on the apparatus.' He had added that no more faith could be placed in 'enlightened bureaucracy' than in 'the enlightened despotism of the seventeenth century'.[28] But now he was persuaded. He was welcomed back by Kaganovich in person.[29] It was plain that an air of general reconciliation was prevalent.

Radek had long since become a shameless adulator of Stalin, detested by the less venal oppositionists. He pleased Stalin greatly by an article purporting to be a lecture delivered in 1967 at the School of Interplanetary Communications, on the fiftieth anniversary of the October Revolution. At this date (which is now behind us), the World Revolution had evidently triumphed and looked back on Stalin as its most brilliant architect. Radek was put up early in 1934 to distinguish between the old oppositionists who merely lacked 'proper understanding and will' and the 'alien' Trotsky – a striking token of peace with the Zinovievs and Bukharins.[30] (Trotsky himself had been meanwhile writing that the slogan 'Down with Stalin' was wrong[31] and that 'at the present moment, the overthrow of the bureaucracy would surely serve counter-revolutionary forces'.[32])

If Stalin's special talents had been vital during the crisis, he now no longer seemed quite so essential to the Party's survival. But if it had been impossible to remove Stalin at a time when the Party and the regime were engaged in a desperate struggle, it now became difficult for a different reason: he was the victor, the man who had won against all the odds. His prestige was higher than ever.

It began to be hoped, not so much that Stalin would be removed, as that he would take a more moderate line, lead a movement of reconciliation, adjust to the Party's desire to enjoy the fruits of victory in comparative peace. He might be expected to retain the leadership but to let many of his powers devolve. 'In seasons of great peril, 'Tis good that one bear sway'; but when the danger is past, more constitutional ways return.

Stalin, Khrushchev later told the world, had not been to a farm since 1928: for him, the collectivization operation was a desk-bound one. Those who had to carry it out in the field had a more shaking time. With all the ruthlessness with which men like Kossior put through the Stalin policies, there seems no doubt that their nerves were strained and they felt something of the battle exhaustion which affected the entire organization in the field.

Now the worst tensions had somewhat slackened. The Party

machine everywhere was firmly in the hands of operators who had shown their devotion to Stalin's policies. If Stalin wanted only this – political victory and the enforcement of his plans – he had won. It was now only necessary to consolidate – to consolidate, and perhaps to relax, to re-establish the Party's links with the people, and to reconcile the embittered elements in the Party itself.

Such were the ideas which seem to have entered the minds of many of the new Stalinist leadership. But they did not enter Stalin's. His aim remained, as is now clear, unchallenged power. So far, he had brutalized the Party, but he had not enslaved it. The men he had brought to the top were already adequately crude and ruthless, but they were not all vicious and servile. And even the hard-won brutality might peter out if reconciliation were practised, if terror became thought of as not an institutionalized necessity, but only a temporary recourse.

For the moment, however, the new 'unity' of the Party was celebrated. In January 1934 its XVIIth Congress, the 'Congress of Victors', assembled. The 1,966 delegates (of whom 1,108 were to be shot over the next few years)[33] listened to the unanimously enthusiastic speakers.

Stalin himself set the theme:

Whereas at the XVth Congress it was still necessary to prove the correctness of the Party line and to fight certain anti-Leninist groupings, and at the XVIth Congress, to finish off the last supporters of these groupings, at the present Congress there is nothing to prove and, it seems, nobody to beat.[34]

Former oppositionists were allowed to speak: Zinoviev, Kamenev, Bukharin, Rykov, Tomsky, Preobrazhensky, Pyatakov, Radek and Lominadze. It is usually said that they were received respectfully, and it is true that on the whole there was much less bitterness expressed against them than at the previous Congress.* The line they took was one of complete Stalinist

---

*Pyatakov's speech was welcomed by 'prolonged applause'. Zinoviev and Bukharin were not interrupted and gained 'applause'. Radek and Kamenev were interrupted, but applauded. Rykov and Tomsky were interrupted and not applauded. But even these last were comparatively well received.

orthodoxy, replete with compliments to the General Secretary, and abuse of his enemies.

Kamenev said that the first wave of anti-Party opposition had been Trotskyism, the second the Right wing, and went on:

The third was not even a wave, but a wavelet; this was the ideology of the most rabid *kulak* scum, the ideology of the Ryutinites. . . . It would have been absurd to fight them by theoretical means, by ideological exposure. Other, more tangible weapons were needed, and these were brought to bear against the members of this group and their accomplices and protectors alike.[35]

We have spoken of the miscalculation, as it turned out, in the oppositionist line of abject repentance, now repeated. Their basic error was that they did not understand Stalin. If he had been less determined and unprincipled, they might have succeeded. Doubtless Zinoviev had little chance of returning to power. But the Rightists, at least, were not in a bad tactical position. During the extreme crisis of 1930 they had not rocked the boat, and, as a result, the crisis had been overcome by methods which represented at least to some slight degree a concession to their views. Their admission of their faults to the Congress was received in much better part than had been the case on previous similar occasions. At the same time, there was everywhere hope that the worst strain was over, that the terrible efforts and sufferings of the first Five-Year Plan and of the collectivization drive could now be forgotten. The second Five-Year Plan pointed to a rather more moderate approach to the economy.

All these circumstances were favourable for the Right. They were most unfavourable to Stalin. The mood, in fact, was one of intra-party reconciliation, and of an attempt to rebuild the bridges between the Party and the people. And such a formulation seems to have been the conscious line of thought of Kirov and others.[36]

Between sessions, some delegates seem to have discussed in this context the whole question of Stalin's leadership. A recent *Pravda* account remarks that Stalin was already 'deviating further and further from Leninist norms', becoming 'more and more isolated' and 'abusing his position'; the 'abnormal situation' in connexion with this 'alarmed many Communists'; some delegates to the Congress got the idea that the time had come to transfer Stalin from the post of General Secretary to other work. This could not but have reached Stalin; 'he knew that the old Leninist cadres of the Party would be a decisive hindrance to the further strengthening of his position and the concentration in his own hands of even greater power'.[37] The *Pravda* article immediately goes on, without logical connexion, but with obvious implications, to speak of 'that splendid Leninist S. M. Kirov', whom it describes as 'the favourite of the Party' and whose speech to the Congress is reported as arousing great enthusiasm. This story of a plan – or at any rate of conversations – on the desirability of transferring Stalin is repeated in a recent life of Kirov.[38]*

Thus 'the old Leninist cadres', including that 'marvellous Leninist' Kirov, were planning to limit Stalin's power; their intention was to relax the dictatorship and effect a reconciliation with the opposition; and Stalin, having found out their plans, saw them as a 'decisive hindrance' to his own desire to extend his power. Politically, in 1934, it looked as though Stalin was not indeed beaten, but on the point of being blocked in his drive for unlimited authority. And this may have been a sound view, within the limits of politics proper.

It had taken years of manoeuvre to defeat the old oppositionists. The new men who had blocked Stalin were neither so vulnerable nor so naïve. Yet to allow the situation to stabilize while the oppositionists were still alive, and while men like Kirov were gaining popularity in the Party, must have seemed a dangerous policy to Stalin. Sooner or later he might have to face the emergence of a more moderate alternative leadership.

But what action was open to him? These trends could only be contained by force. Stalin had manned the machinery of terror

---

* A more official, and perhaps more authentic, comment[39] has been that such accounts lack documentation. This is doubtless inevitable, as they are clearly based on personal reports. (The author of the *Pravda* article had a number of relatives who had held high Party positions.) However, the story, even if exaggerated, accords with rumours of the period, and harmonizes with the events which followed.

with his own men. But it was necessary that the highest Party organs should approve his using it, and they had refused. To create a situation in which they could be panicked or bullied into consent – such was Stalin's problem.

For the moment nothing was done on either side. A Central Committee was elected, consisting almost solely of Stalinist veterans of the intra-Party struggle, but including Pyatakov among its full members and Sokolnikov, Bukharin, Rykov and Tomsky among its candidates. Of the 139 members and candidate members now elected, '98 persons, i.e. 70 per cent' (or more: see p. 632), were to be 'arrested and shot (mostly in 1937-8)'.[40]

The leading organs elected by the new Committee reflected a stalemate. The Politburo was no more satisfactory to Stalin than the one which had blocked him over the Ryutin issue in 1932. And, in particular, this time Kirov was elected not only to the Politburo, but to the Secretariat as well, where he joined Stalin, Kaganovich and Stalin's equally sinister protégé Zhdanov.

The Central Control Commission which had failed Stalin in 1932 was reduced in status and lost its remnant of independence from the political leadership; Kaganovich became its head. But Rudzutak was brought back to the Politburo, though with reduced seniority. He had been a full Politburo member before taking up the C.C.C. post. Now he was the junior candidate member. This was the only change in the Politburo apart from the addition to candidate membership of Pavel Postyshev, 'tall and thin as a lath, with a grating bass voice. No fool . . . but careless of others' feelings',[41] Stalin's latest and toughest emissary in the Ukrainian campaign (see p. 347).

The leading Party organs elected by the Congress were not to be the only bodies to play important roles in the forthcoming period. While the overt political struggle of the past decade had been going on, more sinister developments were taking place in what might be called the technical side of despotic rule. The Secret Police, founded in 1917, had become a large and highly organized body, and had gained great experience in arbitrary arrest, repression and violence. None of the oppositionists had objected to it: Bukharin in particular had been effusively enthusiastic about its role (see Appendix E for a brief account of its history).

In July 1934 the O.G.P.U. was abolished, or rather subsumed into a new All-Union N.K.V.D. The thin-faced terror veteran Genrikh Yagoda was placed at the head of the new organization. His First Deputy was an old adherent and friend of Stalin, Ya. D. Agranov, who had been in charge of the brutal 'investigation' of the Kronstadt rebels.[42]

The new body was to be efficiently deployed over the following years. Its increasingly privileged and powerful officers were to make its emblem – a serpent being struck down by a sword – prevail everywhere against the hammer and sickle of the Party membership. From Politburo members down, no one was to be exempt from their attentions. They themselves were to remain under the careful control of the supreme political authority, Stalin.

In addition to police organization proper, a number of key measures date from this period. After the announcement in January 1933 of the forthcoming purge of the Party, a central Purge Commission was formed (on 29 April) which included Yezhov and M. F. Shkiryatov.

It is at this time too that what was to be, in many respects, the most important body of all came to the surface – the 'Special Sector' of the Central Committee,[43] headed by Poskrebyshev. It was in effect Stalin's private secretariat, the immediate organ for carrying out his will. It has been compared with Nicholas I's 'Personal Chancellery of His Imperial Majesty'. All sensitive issues were effectively handled through this channel – for example, the assassination of Trotsky.[44]

In connexion with this personal secretariat a special State Security Committee appears to have been organized: the main figures are believed to have been Poskrebyshev, Shkiryatov, Agranov and Yezhov, at that time head of the Records and Assignment Depart of the Central Committee.[45] Shkiryatov's key role is implied in an official description of his being 'representative of the Central Control Commission to the Politburo and the Orgburo'.[46]

On 20 June 1933 a Prosecutor-Generalship of the U.S.S.R. was established. Andrei Vyshinsky, thought at first ranking only as First Deputy Prosecutor-General, was the most important figure. Links with the O.G.P.U., the 'legality and regularity' of whose acts the Prosecutors were supposed to check, were provided for.

Another major element in the Stalinist State had already emerged: the show trial. In 1922, a trial expressly designed by Lenin to crush the Social Revolutionary Party had been presided over, ironically enough, by Pyatakov. Though there was an important element of falsification, in that many of the supposed prisoners were *agents provocateurs*, the genuine Social Revolutionaries were given reasonable freedom of defence. And death sentences (much to Lenin's anger) were abandoned under heavy pressure from the Socialist parties of Western Europe. In 1928 came the first trial in a newer mode – that of the Shakhty engineers, presided over by Vyshinsky. This was the first testing-ground of the more recent technique of founding a case upon false confessions extracted by terror. Over the following years came three similar great set-pieces – the so-called 'Industrial Party' of 1930, the Mensheviks in 1931, and the Metro-Vic engineers in 1933. The oppositionists, including Trotsky in exile, made no public objection to these horrible farces (see Appendix F for an account of these early trials).

Thus a positive machinery of despotism had been created outside of and independent of the official political organs. Everywhere, in fact, the potential mechanisms for further terror were in existence, and manned for Stalin not by allies who might balk, but by accomplices who could be relied on against enemies, or friends, inside or outside the Party.

Meanwhile, the official leadership retained its power. The Stalinist writer Alexander Fadeyev commented on the Politburo: 'They are bound together by the manly, principled, iron, gay friendship of the *bogatyrs*.'[47] Half were to meet death or disgrace in the next four years. Kirov was the first to go.

There is little in his past record to suggest that he could have been a major leader. Even if Stalin had dropped dead, the Politburo contained men at least equally forceful, and more experienced, who would not willingly have submitted to Kirov.

Pyatakov's opinion was that if Stalin went, Kaganovich would be able to take over. Even granted the defeat of the entire Stalinist wing, we have no ground for any certainty that Kirov could have coped with his seniors among the 'moderates'. But meanwhile, he seems to have presented the most awkward immediate problem from Stalin's point of view.

Kirov was the best orator the Party had produced since Trotsky. And the concern he had shown, now that the Stalinist victory was complete, for the welfare of the Leningrad workers was beginning to gain him a certain amount of personal popularity. In the Party itself, this popularity was genuine and unqualified. But the most significant thing was the fact that Kirov controlled a definite source of power – the Leningrad organization. When the Leningrad delegates demonstratively led the applause for Kirov at the XVIIth Congress, it may have reminded Stalin of the similar support given by an earlier Leningrad Party generation to Zinoviev.

Throughout Stalin's career this powerful fief was viewed as a seedbed of rebellion – from his removal of Zinoviev in 1926 to his slaughter of the third generation of Leningrad Communists in 1950. And it is true that in the great northern metropolis, no longer – since 1918 – capital of Russia, a certain alienation from the great mass of the hinterland was still present. Russia's 'window on Europe' had always been a sort of advanced outpost. Its citizens thought of themselves as far ahead, even dangerously far, of the rest of the country in civilization and the arts of the West. In this youngest of the great cities of Europe – founded, indeed, after New York, Baltimore, Boston and Philadelphia – Kirov was truly showing signs of a certain independence.

It was not easily possible for Stalin to attack Kirov for deviationism. He had never belonged to the oppositions and had fought them firmly. But he had been generous to them in defeat. The N.K.V.D. had already turned up the fact that a number of minor oppositionists or former oppositionists were working quite freely in Leningrad. Officials taxed with permitting this were able to say that Kirov had personally ordered it. In particular, encouraging the cultural life of the city, he had allowed many of them to take posts in publishing and other similar activities. He had also worked in Leningrad in reasonable concord with Party veterans who were not strictly speaking oppositionists, but whose views tended well to the right of the Party line. If he and his Politburo colleagues with similar views had come to power, their standing was scarcely great enough to enable them to rule the Party without appealing to the old oppositionists and effecting a reconciliation with at least the Right wing. One could perhaps envisage a situation in which Kirov, Ordzhonikidze and Kuibyshev sat in the Politburo with Bukharin and Pyatakov, and even Kamenev, on a moderate programme.

Meanwhile Kirov had used his position in Leningrad in other ways unwelcome to Moscow. On one account, he was in dispute with the Stalinist members of the Politburo on various issues, and in particular on the matter of the food supply to the Leningrad workers. He had blamed Mikoyan for disorganization in this field, and had requisitioned, without Moscow's permission, part of the food reserves of the Leningrad Military District. To this Voroshilov objected, speaking of it as an attempt to seek cheap popularity. Kirov retorted hotly that if the Leningrad worker was to produce he must be fed. When Mikoyan said that Leningrad workers were better fed than the average, Kirov replied that the value of the increased output more than counterbalanced this. Stalin then intervened in Mikoyan's favour, upon which Kirov became heated.[48]

Kirov's election to the Secretariat seems to have been made with a view to his transfer to Moscow, where he would be under Stalin's eye. In August Stalin asked Kirov down to Sochi, where he was holidaying with Zhdanov. Here they discussed the proposed transfer, and Stalin eventually had to settle for Kirov's agreement to come to Moscow 'at the end of the second Five-Year Plan' – that is, in 1938. But Stalin clearly believed that the political issues before him must be settled one way or another in the immediate future.*

* The proposal to transfer Kirov was known in the Party, but the precise issue has been obscured in certain reports. In particular, the 'Letter of an Old Bolshevik' presents it as a question of Stalin disliking the prospect of an almost immediate move of Kirov to Moscow already decided upon. A recent Soviet book,[49] with which the best defector source[50] substantially agrees, makes it clear that the circumstances were as given above.

It must have been about this time that Stalin took the most extraordinary decision of his career. This was, that the best way of assuring his political supremacy and dealing with his old comrade, Secretary of the Central Committee, Member of the Politburo, First Secretary of the Leningrad Party Organization, was murder.

CHAPTER TWO

THE KIROV MURDER

That many men were undone by not going deep enough in roguery; as in gaming any man may be a loser who doth not play the whole game. HENRY FIELDING, *Jonathan Wild's 'Principles of Greatness'*

ON 1 December 1934, at about four o'clock in the afternoon, the young assassin Leonid Nikolayev entered the Smolny, headquarters of the Communist Party in Leningrad. The few hours of the city's thin winter daylight were over, and it was quite dark. The lights of the former aristocratic girls' school, from which Lenin had organized the 'ten days that shook the world', shone out over its colonnade and gardens, and eastward up the icy Neva. The outer guard examined Nikolayev's pass, which was in order, and let him in without trouble. In the interior, the guard posts were unmanned, and Nikolayev wandered down the ornate passages until he found the third-floor corridor on to which Sergei Kirov's office opened. He waited patiently outside.

Kirov was preparing a report on the November plenum of the Central Committee from which he had just returned. He was shortly supposed to deliver it to the *aktiv* of the Leningrad Party now assembling in a conference room farther along on the same floor. At 4.30[1] he left his office and turned towards the office of the Leningrad Second Secretary, his trusted aide, Mikhail Chudov.[2] He had gone only a few steps[3] when Nikolayev moved from a corner,[4] shot him in the back with a Nagan revolver, and then collapsed beside him.

At the sound of the shot Party officials came running along the corridor. They were astonished at the complete absence of guards. Even Kirov's chief bodyguard, Borisov, who according to standing instructions should have been with him, was nowhere to be seen.

This killing has every right to be called the crime of the century. Over the next four years hundreds of Russians, including the most prominent political leaders of the Revolution, were shot for direct responsibility for the assassination, and – literally – millions of others went to their deaths for complicity in one or another part of the vast conspiracy which allegedly lay behind it. Kirov's death, in fact, was the keystone of the entire edifice of terror and suffering by which Stalin secured his grip on the Soviet peoples.

Fairly sound accounts of the murder have been available in the West for many years. Until recently, however, they lacked confirmation – indeed they were hotly rejected – by Soviet sources. No full story of the Kirov murder has yet appeared in Russia: but strong hints have been given, details have been confirmed or amended, and statements have appeared which are incompatible with any version but the one long since published in the West by certain of Stalin's enemies, and often previously rejected even here as coming from biased sources and, in any case, being beyond reasonable belief.

The truth is, indeed, beyond reasonable belief.

The first official Soviet line, accepted by many in the West, was that Nikolayev was a Zinovievite indirectly inspired by Zinoviev and Kamenev. Then, in 1936, the fallen leaders were accused of being directly involved, of having ordered the killing. Finally, in 1938, the Soviet view took the form it was to keep until 1956: Zinoviev and Kamenev, together with Trotsky, had ordered the assassination. It had been facilitated by Yagoda, head of the N.K.V.D., who, as a Rightist under Yenukidze's instructions, had ordered Zaporozhets – the second-in-command of the Leningrad N.K.V.D. – to remove all obstacles to the assassin.

This change of line, which contained some elements of truth, was evidently designed to mask or neutralize the real version, which began to circulate in the N.K.V.D. within weeks of the crime – that Nikolayev was an individual assassin, and Stalin had arranged his opportunity. This has never been said quite flatly in the Soviet Union, (though the young Soviet 'unofficial' historian Leonid Petrovsky has put Kirov's name, in the most natural fashion, in a list of Stalin's victims).[5] There is no doubt that it is the correct explanation: we can now reconstruct the details.

The problem Stalin faced in 1934 admitted of no political solution entirely satisfactory to him. But he saw one way out. It was extremely unorthodox. It shows more clearly than anything else the completeness of his lack of moral or other inhibitions. To kill Kirov would remove the immediate obstacle, and at the same time create an atmosphere of violence in which the enemies on to whom he shifted the blame for the murder could be wiped out without the sort of arguments he had encountered over Ryutin.

Stalin seems to have been impressed by the 30 June 1934 Purge in Nazi Germany. But he did not himself proceed in the same way. The one principle firmly established in the Nazi Party, that the will of the leader is the highest law, had no equivalent in the Communist Party. Even when, later on, Stalin was in practice able to destroy his critics at least as freely as Hitler, it was always done either in the form of some sort of trial accompanied by some sort of justification, or was carried out in complete secrecy. The only case in which Stalin struck with a simulacrum of the urgency of Hitler's June Purge was when he destroyed the generals in June 1937. It is true that Hitler really had some fear of Roehm and the S.A. as a rival power centre, against whom no other method could be risked, and something of the same sort of argument seemed at least plausible as regards the Soviet High Command. (Stalin could have learned another point from Hitler's June Purge, though there is no reason to suppose him incapable of discovering the same tactics for himself. When destroying one group of enemies, it is helpful to throw in, and accuse of the same plot, a variety of other hostile figures in no way connected with them.)*

During the Zinoviev Trial, the planning of the Kirov murder was said to have taken place in the summer of 1934.[6] Of course, the form in which this was put was untrue, but the date was no doubt thought plausible because it was around this time that

---

*There are earlier assassinations in Russia's own history which may also have inspired Stalin; for example, the killing of the Prime Minister, Stolypin, in 1911 by an assassin who seems to have been a double agent and who was certainly widely thought to have acted with the approval and connivance of the Tsarist Secret Police, which objected to Stolypin's policies.

Stalin himself, as we have suggested, had actually started to organize the murder. It was in August that he had spoken with Kirov about his future, and in the interim Kirov was in Central Asia, only returning to Leningrad on 1 October.[7] By that time the plot was already in preparation.

According to one account, Stalin's original plan involved replacing Philip Medved, the head of the Leningrad N.K.V.D., by his own crony E. G. Evdokimov, the old Secret Policeman of Shakhty fame, who was on cool terms with the rest of the N.K.V.D. officers. However, this transfer was blocked by Kirov,[8] who protested against such moves being made without the permission of the Leningrad Provincial Committee, and it had to be countermanded.

Stalin could only approach Yagoda. But, even as second choice, it is an extraordinary idea that the head of the N.K.V.D. could be approached with an order to procure the death of a Politburo member. The natural explanation would be that Stalin had some special hold over him. This would be quite in accord with Stalin's style. There are a number of cases in which Stalin seems to have secured support by blackmail of this type (for example, Voroshilov, whose conduct in 1928 convinced Bukharin that this was true in his case). The rumour in Russia was that Stalin had discovered some discreditable incident in Yagoda's pre-Revolutionary career, involving acting in some way for the Tsarist police. In the N.K.V.D., it was said that in 1930 Yagoda's then deputy Trilisser made an investigation of Yagoda's past and found that he had almost entirely falsified his pre-Revolutionary record. When Trilisser reported this to Stalin, Stalin merely censured and dismissed Trilisser. But Stalin was in fact glad to have the information, and to keep on as effective head of the police a man he had something against.[9]

Yagoda selected a suitable N.K.V.D. man in Leningrad. This was Medved's assistant, Zaporozhets. Zaporozhets would naturally not accept such an assignment just at Yagoda's orders, so he had to receive instructions from Stalin. For the junior man in particular (in Yagoda's case, ambition must have played a more important role) the idea of Party discipline must already have been corrupted into something unrecognizable.

When Yagoda himself came to trial with the 'Bloc of Rights and Trotskyites' in 1938, he testified that he had been instructed by Yenukidze 'to assist in the murder of Kirov'. Although he objected, he said, 'Yenukidze insisted.' If anyone in Soviet political life was totally unqualified to insist on anything, it was Yenukidze, a far less powerful figure than Yagoda himself. If we were to substitute for him the name of a man who *was* in a position to insist, we should not have to look far.

Yagoda went on: 'Owing to this, I was compelled to instruct Zaporozhets, who occupied the post of Assistant Chief of the Regional Administration of the People's Commissariat of Internal Affairs, not to place any obstacles in the way of the terrorist act against Kirov.'[10]

During Yagoda's cross-examination things did not go smoothly. Without giving anything away, he yet managed to imply that there was something fishy about the whole business. Asked what methods he used in the other alleged murders, he answered, 'In any case not such as . . . described here', and when questioned as to whether he would confirm his own testimony at the preliminary investigation, said, 'It is exaggerated, but that does not matter.' When it came to the Kirov murder itself, the following exchange was particularly odd:

Yagoda: I gave instructions . . .
Vyshinsky: To whom?
Yagoda: To Zaporozhets in Leningrad. That is not quite how it was.
Vyshinsky: We shall speak about that later. What I want now is to elucidate the part played by Rykov and Bukharin in this villainous act.
Yagoda: I gave instructions to Zaporozhets. When Nikolayev was detained . . .
Vyshinsky: The first time?
Yagoda: Yes. Zaporozhets came to Moscow and reported to me that a man had been detained . . .
Vyshinsky: In whose briefcase . . .
Yagoda: There was a revolver and a diary. And he released him.
Vyshinsky: And you approved of this?
Yagoda: I just took note of the fact.
Vyshinsky: And then you gave instructions not to place obstacles in the way of the murder of Sergei Mironovich Kirov?
Yagoda: Yes, I did . . . It was not like that.

Vyshinsky: In a somewhat different form?
Yagoda: It was not like that, but it is not important.[11]

In Leningrad Zaporozhets looked around for a method and found on the files a report on a disillusioned and embittered young Communist – Nikolayev. Nikolayev had told a friend that he intended to assassinate some Party figure as a protest. The friend had reported him. Through the friend, Zaporozhets got into contact with Nikolayev and saw that he was provided with a pistol. In addition, Zaporozhets got the friend to persuade Nikolayev to select Kirov as his victim.[12]

Zaporozhets' next task was to steer his gunman to the heavily guarded Kirov. As so often in real life, his plans did not run smoothly. The revolver had been got to Nikolayev.* He was worked up to assassination pitch. But his attempts to get into the Smolny did not at first succeed. He was arrested (it is now said) twice in that neighbourhood. The first time, 'a month and a half before the killing',[14] that is, within a couple of weeks of Kirov's return from Kazakhstan, he was 'not even searched'. The second time, only a few days before his successful attempt, he got as far as the outer guard in the Smolny. There the guard found on him 'a revolver and a chart of the route Kirov usually took' (according to Yagoda at the 1938 Trial) or 'a notebook and a revolver' (according to the evidence of Yagoda's secretary Bulanov on the same occasion); in any case, 'arms were found on him. But upon Zaporozhets' instructions he was released on both occasions' (as Khrushchev was to put it in his speech to the XXIInd Party Congress in 1961).

It says a good deal for Nikolayev's nerve that he brought himself to make his last, and successful, attempt.

Apart from instructions to the outer guard to let Nikolayev through unsearched, Zaporozhets's arrangements included the 'temporary' abandonment of the internal guard posts on each floor. He also managed to detain the bodyguard Borisov. And

---

* According to one account it was stolen from Zaporozhets's neighbour, the former member of the Central Committee Avdeyev, a supporter of Zinoviev's – but if so, this point does not seem to have been investigated, unless it was worked into Avdeyev's disgrace soon afterwards in connexion with the errors of the Society of Old Bolsheviks.[13]

finally, after all the earlier muddles, Stalin's plan succeeded, and his colleague lay dead in the Smolny corridors. But there was still much to do.

When the news reached Moscow it was announced to the accompaniment of a strong expression of grief and comradeship for the dead man by Stalin and the Politburo. Stalin, with Voroshilov, Molotov and Zhdanov,[15] left for Leningrad the same evening to 'conduct the inquiry'. Yagoda, Agranov and Mironov, Head of the N.K.V.D. Economic Department, accompanied them.

Stalin and his entourage took over an entire floor of the Smolny. But before the investigation, there were political moves to be made.

An official speaker remarked at the XXIInd Party Congress in 1961:

On the day of the murder (which at that time had not yet been investigated, of course), upon Stalin's instructions from Leningrad, a law was adopted on an accelerated, simplified and conclusive examination of political cases. This was immediately followed by a wave of arrests and political trials. It is as if they had been waiting for this pretext in order, by deceiving the Party, to launch anti-Leninist, anti-Party methods of struggle to maintain a leading position in the Party and State.*[16]

(It is difficult to see how Stalin could have given instructions from Leningrad on the day of the murder. He travelled by train, and Leningrad and Moscow are 400 miles apart by rail. He could scarcely have arrived earlier than 'the crack of dawn on 2 December' – a time given by the most recent Soviet source.[18] The Decree is indeed dated 1 December. Stalin doubtless put it in hand before he left and telephoned after arriving in Leningrad to have it signed by the State authorities and issued.)

The Decree, decided on without consultation in the Politburo,[19] was to be a Charter of Terror over the following years. It ran:

*The last sentence puts Stalin's attitude accurately and succinctly. Western historians who accepted that the assassination was a surprise to Stalin reversed the order of things when they said, for example, 'Stalin . . . drew the conclusion that the time for quasi-liberal concessions was over'.[17] For the 'conclusion' preceded and caused the assassination, not the reverse.

1. Investigative agencies are directed to speed up the cases of those accused of the preparation or execution of acts of terror.
2. Judicial organs are directed not to hold up the execution of death sentences pertaining to crimes of this category in order to consider the possibility of pardon, because the Presidium of the Central Executive Committee of the U.S.S.R. does not consider as possible the receiving of petitions of this sort.
3. The organs of the Commissariat of Internal Affairs are directed to execute the death sentence against criminals of the above-mentioned category immediately after the passage of sentences.

This was published the following day, and the Politburo, presented with a *fait accompli*, approved it 'casually' the day after that.*[20]

Stalin then turned to the inquiry, which was, we are now told, conducted in 'the conditions established at that time by the cult of Stalin's personality'.[22] He at once discovered various snags. First, Borisov, whose devotion to Kirov was well known, had become suspicious.[23] This was dealt with at once. On 2 December 'Zaporozhets so arranged it that an accident occurred to the automobile which took Borisov to the Smolny. Borisov was killed in the accident, and in this way they got rid of a dangerous witness' (Bulanov's evidence in the 1938 Trial). This was, much later, interestingly expanded by Khrushchev:

When the chief of Kirov's bodyguard was being taken for questioning – and he was to be questioned by Stalin, Molotov and Voroshilov – the car, as its driver said afterwards, was involved in an accident deliberately arranged by those who were taking the man to the interrogation. They said that he died as a result of the accident, even though he was actually killed by those who accompanied him.

In this way, the man who guarded Kirov was killed. Later, those who killed him were shot. This was no accident but a carefully planned crime. Who could have done this? A thorough investigation is now

*This was the first exercise in Stalin's new technique, by which the state of emergency was used to justify personal, and technically unconstitutional, action. In the circumstances any attempt at disapproval would have been extremely difficult. And thus even what poor guarantees Soviet law gave to 'enemies of the State' were destroyed. On 10 December new Articles 466–70 of the Code of Criminal Procedure of the R.S.F.S.R. were enacted to bring it into line. We are told that the extra-judicial bodies set up at this period were instituted on the basis of a draft by Kaganovich.[21]

being made into the circumstances of this complicated affair. It transpires that the driver of the car in which the chief of Kirov's bodyguard was being taken for questioning is alive. He has said that an N.K.V.D. operative sat with him in the cab during the drive. They went in a lorry. It is, of course, very strange why a lorry was used to take the man for questioning, as if no other vehicle could be found for the purpose. Evidently, everything had been planned in advance and in detail. Two other N.K.V.D. operatives were in the back of the lorry together with Kirov's chief bodyguard.

The driver continued his story. When they were driving through one street, the man sitting next to him suddenly took the steering wheel from his hands and steered the car directly at a house. The driver regained control of the wheel and steered the car, and it only hit the wall of the house sideways. He was told later that Kirov's chief bodyguard lost his life in this accident. Why did he die when no other person in the car suffered? Why were both officials of the People's Commissariat for Internal Affairs, escorting Kirov's chief bodyguard, later shot? This means that someone wanted to have them liquidated and to remove all traces.[24]

Why did Stalin dispose of Borisov in such a roundabout way? It seems that in view of Borisov's known loyalty to Kirov, to have him shot or 'disappear' as an accomplice of Nikolayev's would have aroused instant incredulity in the Leningrad Party organization. It was not until 1938, when such considerations no longer applied, that Borisov was alleged to have been an accomplice.[25]

And here we may note that the Khrushchevite version of the Kirov affair, with all its air of throwing fresh light, did not produce any *facts* incompatible with Stalin's own final version. As we see, on the murder of Borisov, Bulanov had already testified to the essentials at the 1938 Trial. Almost every detail of Yagoda's and Zaporozhets's involvement was given at that trial. Why, then, we may ask, did Khrushchev produce the same material – with insubstantial additional detail – as though it amounted to a great revelation? The answer clearly is that he meant to *imply* something further. And this method of dealing with the case – of implication – is the one that was pursued in Russia from 1956 to 1964.

In his Secret Speech of February 1956 Khrushchev said:

It must be asserted that to this day the circumstances surrounding Kirov's murder hide many things which are inexplicable and mysterious and demand the most careful examination.

This was said in the context of an attack on Stalin. But nothing was made explicit. At the XXIInd Party Congress in October 1961 Khrushchev said, this time in public:

Great efforts are still needed to find out who was really to blame for his death. The more deeply we study the materials connected with Kirov's death, the more questions arise . . . A thorough inquiry is now being made into the circumstances of this complicated case.

The same cautious line was taken by other speakers. But the 'inquiry' was slow to produce results. And in a *Pravda* article of 7 February 1964 the hint was conveyed by remarking that Kirov represented an obstacle to Stalin's ambitions and going on immediately to add:

Less than a year had passed after the XVIIth Congress when a criminal hand cut short the life of Kirov. . . . This was a premeditated and carefully prepared crime the circumstances of which, as N. S. Khrushchev declared at the XXIInd Congress, have not yet been fully cleared up.

Short of actually saying that Stalin was responsible, an announcement which still seemed to stick in the Soviet throat, it would hardly be possible to make the point more clearly. If we still have 'to find out who was really to blame', then obviously the case against the previously blamed – Zinoviev and Kamanev, and later the Rightists – is no longer sustained. Only one major suspect remains. Stalin's daughter, writing in 1963, rightly speaks of 'transparent hints' then being given in Russia that her father was responsible. And there is no doubt that they were so intended and so taken.[26]*

With Borisov liquidated, Stalin was left with the major problem – Nikolayev.

Leonid Nikolayev had, indeed, been a dupe of Stalin, Yagoda

---

*Stalin's similar complicity in the murder of the Yiddish actor–producer Solomon Mikhoels in Minsk in 1948 now seems well established. Described at the time as an accident, it was admitted in the Khrushchev era to have been the work of the M.G-B.[27]

and Zaporozhets. But he had also acted on his own beliefs. He has, naturally, been treated in a hostile fashion by every generation of Soviet and of oppositionist commentators, including the present one. And his act, far from bringing any benefit to Russia, was made the excuse for worse tyranny than ever. For these and other reasons, it is not easy to get a clear idea of the thirty-year-old tyrannicide.

Like many revolutionaries, he seems to have been something of a misfit. He had fought in the Civil War as a teenager, and afterwards had been unable to make a successful career amid an increasingly bureaucratic society. He was a typical member of a young and energetic, but wild and unamenable, generation which had been broken by the new regime in the Party. Unlike the others he had taken action.

A Party member since 1920, he had not been known as an oppositionist. Practically the whole vote of the Leningrad Party had gone to Zinoviev in 1925, and doubtless Nikolayev's too, but he had not been penalized and so cannot have been active, or obnoxious to the victors.

Nikolayev had been out of work since March 1934, when he seems to have attacked a decision demoting him which he believed to be a piece of bureaucratic intrigue.[28] He had been expelled from the Party for this breach of discipline,[29] but his membership had been restored two months before the crime on his making a declaration of repentance.[30]

In the meantime he had brooded considerably on the degeneration of the Party. He saw himself as an avenger in the old Russian style. He is said to have answered, when Stalin pointed out to him that he was now as good as dead, 'What does it matter? Many are going under now. But for the days to come my name will be coupled with those of Zheliabov and Balmashev'[31] – the great terrorists of the People's Will and the Social Revolutionaries respectively.

For Stalin was personally conducting the interrogations. Accounts of his approach to Nikolayev agree that he spoke in an extremely mild way:[32] 'Why did you kill such a nice man?'

Nikolayev answered firmly, 'I did not fire at him. I fired at the Party.'[33]

For, as Zaporozhets had already found out in a hurried inter-rogation before Stalin's arrival, this was 'not a weak neurasthenic shaken by his horrible crime and arrest, but a composed and fearless fanatic'.[34] Moreover, he now understood how Zaporoz-hets had used him. He refused point-blank to implicate Zinoviev. Even if he could be tortured into temporary submission, it was out of the question to produce him in open court.

Ordering Agranov to follow up the 'Zinovievite' line as best he could, Stalin returned to Moscow, and for the moment satisfied himself with other measures to intensify the atmosphere of terror.

Back in the capital, Kirov's body lay in state. The highest in the land mounted guard over it in the Hall of Columns. When Stalin saw the corpse, the Soviet press noted, he appeared so overcome by emotion that he went forward and kissed it on the cheek. It would be interesting to speculate on his feelings at that moment.

It is a trifle ironic that Zinoviev too had just expressed his sorrow over Kirov's death, in an obituary rejected by *Pravda*, and that at the 1936 Trial Vyshinsky was to speak of it in these terms:

The miscreant, the murderer, mourns over his victim! Has anything like it ever occurred before? What can one say, what words can one use fully to describe the utter baseness and loathsomeness of this: Sacrilege! Perfidy! Duplicity! Cunning![35]

On 4 December it was announced that Medved had been dis-missed (and replaced by Agranov), and that he and seven of his subordinates would be brought before a court for their failure to protect Kirov; Zaporozhets' name was not among them. A long list of those arrested in connexion with the case in Moscow and Leningrad, all 'White Guards', was given at the same time. Within a few days, 'trials' of these, under the new decree, were announced. In Leningrad the Stalinist judge I. O. Matulevich chaired a circuit court of the Military Collegium which, on 5 December, sentenced thirty-seven named 'White Guards' to death for 'preparation and organization of terrorist acts against officials of the Soviet regime', and in Moscow a similar session under the even more notorious V. V. Ulrikh did the same for thirty-three others.[36]

On 13 December Ulrikh went down to Kiev to preside over the sentencing to death of twenty-eight Ukrainians. They too were charged with 'organizing acts of terror against officials of the Soviet Government', and it was also said that most of them had been 'apprehended with revolvers and hand-grenades'.[37] In this Ukrainian case we chance to know more about those concerned than we do about the victims of Leningrad and Moscow. Though the accused in all three cases were charged with having, in their majority, crossed the frontier from abroad for their terrorist purposes, we find that these Ukrainians were almost all fairly well-known writers and cultural and social workers. Apart from one minor diplomat, and a poet who had visited Germany, they had been living in the Ukraine for years.[38] There was later a brief attack on one of them, the deaf poet Vlyzko.[39]

These official executions were supplemented by scores of others performed with less formality. This was welcomed by the Leningrad N.K.V.D. on technical grounds, since prison space was now at a premium. A description of the executions there has prisoners queueing up by the elevator and being taken down, one by one, to the cellar and shot at intervals of two to two and a half minutes, throughout the night. In the morning, 200 corpses lay in the cellars.[40] But the crowding in the cells was relieved only temporarily. Throughout the country a great wave of arrests swept in thousands of those listed in the N.K.V.D. records as in one way or another politically suspect. The period of comparative relaxation was now abruptly at an end.

The last great assassination and attempted assassination had been in August 1918, when Social Revolutionaries killed Uritsky and wounded Lenin. Following that, Sverdlov had issued an hysterical call for 'merciless mass terror', adding that there was no doubt that the assassins would turn out to be 'hirelings of the English and French'. In the event, hundreds of prisoners were shot as reprisals. Few Bolsheviks (apart from the brave Olminsky) made any protest. Now that a similar case had arisen, how could they object to the slaughter of a few score 'White Guards' from Leningrad and Moscow?

There was one typical distinction between the two terrors. Stalin implied that the victims of his terror decree were actually associated with the crime, while in Lenin's time those shot had quite frankly been no more than class hostages.

Amid this orgy of shootings, the Soviet press was launched into one of those campaigns replete with calls for vigilance and ruthlessness towards the hidden enemy, which were to appear at intervals throughout Stalin's life. An atmosphere was created, in fact, in which no voice of even comparative reason or moderation could raise itself. The mutual denunciation sessions in which Communists fought for their Party membership, and indeed for their lives, by panicky and sycophantic accusations against their own accusers, had died down to some considerable extent since 1933; they now revived. The 'moderate' line towards the rank-and-file opposition was reversed. Thousands who had been re-admitted to the Party were expelled.

In December 1934 a secret letter from the Central Committee, entitled 'Lessons of the Events Connected with the Evil Murder of Comrade Kirov', was sent to all Party Committees. It amounted to a call to them to hunt down, expel and arrest all former op-positionists who remained in the Party. Towards the end of the month it was discussed in all Party organizations and was followed by a storm of indiscriminate denunciations. At this early phase in the Purge, however, some discrimination was still shown in the action taken on these. Friendship with an exposed 'Trotskyite' usually received a severe reprimand rather than expulsion: 'only a few years later,' Professor Fainsod comments, 'such mild punishment would come to be regarded not merely as extreme liberalism, but as clear indication of the complicity of the judges in counter-revolutionary activity.'[41] Throughout the month the press attacked Trotskyites discovered in various parts of the Union, censured Party organizations for 'rotten liberalism', and called for vigilance. Mass deportations to Siberia and the Arctic took place. Within a few months 30,000–40,000 Leningraders had already been taken.[42]

Everyone who was remotely connected with the case was seized. One woman had worked as a librarian at the 'Young Communist Club' in Leningrad which had been disbanded in the mid twenties but with which Nikolayev had in some way been associated. Not only was she arrested, but also her sister with whom she lived, her sister's husband, the secretary of her Party cell, and all those who had recommended her for jobs.[43]

A typical case from the times, of which dozens might be related, has lately been treated in the Soviet press.[44] The writer Alexander G. Lebedenko was arrested in Leningrad in January 1935 and exiled. One and a half years later – that is, in mid 1937 – he was sentenced without trial or investigation, by decision of an N.K.V.D. Troika, to twenty years' isolation, and was released after the XXth Congress in 1956.

Meanwhile, Agranov had been working on the Zinoviev connexion. He established a connexion between Nikolayev and the men who had been leading figures in the Leningrad Komsomol during Zinoviev's ascendancy in the city. The most prominent was I. I. Kotolynov, former member of the Central Committee of the Komsomol. It had been Kotolynov who had boldly protested at the Stalinist bully-boys who were then taking over the youth organization, saying of them: 'They have the mentality – if he is not a Stalinist, put on the screws, let him have it, chase him so hard that he won't open his mouth again.'[45] He had, in fact, been a real oppositionist – and one against whom a real grudge persisted. Right through the Purge, this was to be a bad combination.

Agranov found that Kotolynov and some others of this group had met for discussion in 1934, because the local Party Institute was talking of producing a history of the Leningrad Komsomol. These meetings were quite open, and under Party control, and Nikolayev had also attended them. Agranov built this up into a 'conspiracy'. Nine other men who had been present, including another former member of the Komsomol Central Committee, Rumyantsev, were arrested. They were under arrest, or some of them were, by 6 December.[46] 'Severe' interrogation methods were employed.

Even so, most of the young oppositionists refused to capitulate. This method of dealing with Party members was new, and they could not have had the feeling of hopelessness which later set in in similar circumstances. On the contrary, the whole thing must have seemed a dangerous and horrible lunacy of the interrogators, which might be overruled at any moment. By 12–13 December,[47] Agranov nevertheless had one or two confessions ready. These connected the former oppositionist Komsomols of Leningrad with Kamenev and Zinoviev, who had met their former supporters once or twice in an innocent way.[48] Agranov's report to Stalin represented this as Kamenev and Zinoviev going back on their various promises to 'disarm' politically, and in effect as a sort of conspiracy.

When this report came before the Politburo, in 'an atmosphere of extreme tension',[49] the majority still supported the liberalization envisaged by Kirov. Stalin accepted this warmly, but added that it should be amended at one point: since the opposition had failed to disarm, the Party should in self-defence undertake a check-up of all former Trotskyites and Zinovievites. This was agreed to with some hesitation, and as to the assassination itself, it was to be left to the investigating authorities.[50]

Before the middle of the month, G. E. Evdokimov, former Secretary of the Central Committee of the Party, and Bakayev, who had been Zinoviev's head of the Leningrad N.K.V.D., were arrested. Zinoviev then drafted a letter to Yagoda saying he was disturbed by these arrests and asking to be summoned so that he could establish that he had no connexion with the murder. Kamenev dissuaded him from sending it.[51]

On 16 December, Pauker, Head of the Operations Department of the N.K.V.D., and Bulanov, Yagoda's personal assistant, arrested Kamenev, and at the same time Molchanov, Head of the Secret Political Department, and Volovich, Deputy Head of the Operations Department,* pulled in Zinoviev.[52] It says something for the respect which leading Old Bolshevik oppositionists even now commanded in the Party that the routine 'search' was dispensed with.[53]

For the first four or five days after the murder the press had been full of the demands of workers' meetings for revenge; accounts of Kirov's life; descriptions of his lying in state and his funeral; listings of executed 'White Guard' terrorists; and so on.

* All four N.K.V.D. officers were later themselves to be denounced and shot as conspirators – Pauker and Volovich as German spies in addition.

Then came, for a week or ten days, a curious pause. But now, on 17 December, the Moscow Committee of the Party passed a resolution to the effect that 'loathsome, hateful agents of the class enemy, foul dregs of the former Zinoviev anti-Party group, have torn Comrade Kirov from our midst', the first public reference to the alleged political feelings behind the murder.[54] The Leningrad Committee, which had just 'elected' Andrei Zhdanov as Kirov's replacement (on 16 December), passed a resolution in almost identical terms.

As yet, no N.K.V.D. announcement had *directly* blamed the assassination on anyone but Nikolayev. The 'White Guards' had been vaguely charged with 'terrorism'. On 21 December, it was at last officially stated that Kirov had been murdered by a 'Leningrad Centre', headed by Kotolynov, and consisting of him, Nikolayev and six others – all of them categorized as former members of the Zinoviev opposition who had 'at various times been expelled from the Party', though mostly restored to membership after statements of solidarity with the Party line.[55]

On the following day a list was given for the first time of the arrested Zinovievite leaders, with a decision on the conduct of their cases.

There were distinguished names among them: Zinoviev and Kamenev, formerly members of the Politburo; Evdokimov, formerly member of the Secretariat; other former members and candidate members of the Central Committee – Zalutsky, who had formed with Molotov and Shlyapnikov the first Bolshevik Committee in Petrograd after the February Revolution; Kuklin; Safarov.[56] For the moment a partial accusation went forward. On seven of those arrested, including Zinoviev, Kamenev, Zalutsky and Safarov, it was announced that the N.K.V.D., 'lacking sufficient data for bringing them before a court', would take them before a Special Board, with a view to sending them into administrative exile. With the others, headed by Bakayev, 'further investigation' would take place. It was a typical Stalin move – suitable for gradually getting his colleagues and the Party used to the idea of Zinoviev's guilt, and at the same time complicated and confusing enough to mask or blur his real intent.

Of the fifteen now mentioned, ten were to appear in the first Zinoviev–Kamenev Trial the following month, together with nine not previously named. The five who were not to appear again included two of those now under too grave suspicion to be simply exiled; of the other three Safarov was to appear as a witness in January 1935, and to be denounced at the Great Trial of 1936. But his fate was unknown until recent Soviet publications[57] referred to him curtly as having been expelled from the Party in 1934, convicted, and having died in 1942. Zalutsky, of whom nothing whatever was said in the interim, is reported as expelled in 1934, convicted, and died in 1937.[58] They seem to have been among the ninety-seven oppositionists secretly sentenced early in 1935* to five years in labour camps[60] – then the Special Board maximum – but this does not preclude later and severer penalties.†

On 27 December the formal accusation against the Nikolayev group was published. Now fourteen in number, they had allegedly been working since August, keeping a watch on Kirov's flat and office, and deducing his usual movements. 'Witnesses' were mentioned – Nikolayev's wife and brother and others. The conspirators were accused of having planned to kill Stalin, Molotov and Kaganovich in addition to Kirov. And Nikolayev was also said to have been passing anti-Soviet material to an unspecified foreign consul, who later turned out to be the Latvian

---

* At the same time, leaders of other former oppositions were sent to the Verkhne-Uralsk 'isolator' – Shlyapnikov and Medvedev from the former Workers' Opposition, Sapronov of the Democratic Centralists, the Trotskyite Smilga and others.[59]

† Anticipating further, we may note that of the nineteen accused in the January 1935 Trial, only *four* came to public trial in 1936. Of the others, eight were then mentioned in incriminating evidence, and two of these were named as allotted to future trial (of which no report was ever to be published). The remaining seven were simply not heard of again. For whatever reason, this means that one in three were dropped between December 1934 and January 1935; and more than one in three between January 1935 and August 1936. The point is worth making as it probably implies either failure to produce reliable confession (or, alternatively, death under interrogation) in a high proportion of cases, and so gives a broader perspective on the whole business of the confession trials.

Bissenek, though the N.K.V.D. are said to have originally favoured his Finnish colleague.[61]* The already executed 'White Guards' were vaguely worked in through connexions Nikolayev was said to have formed with 'Denikinists'.

'Documentary evidence' was mentioned, including a diary of Nikolayev's and statements he had prepared. Apparently these showed clearly that he had no accomplices. It could not be totally suppressed at this stage, as too many uninitiated investigators and others seem to have seen it. So the official account, mentioning the document, says that it was a forgery designed to give the impression that there was no conspiracy, but only a protest against the 'unjust treatment of individuals',[63] or, as a later and fuller version has it:

> The accused Nikolayev prepared several documents (a diary, declarations addressed to various institutions, etc.) in which he tried to represent his crime as a personal manifestation of despair and discontent arising from the aggravation of his material situation and as a protest against the unjust attitude of certain members of the Government towards a living person.[64]

Three volumes of testimony are cited, each of them at least 200 pages long, including various confessions.[65] From all this it might have been expected that the prosecution could have held an open trial. It did not do so. On 28–9 December a court presided over by the ubiquitous Ulrikh sat behind closed doors.

For the more important of Nikolayev's alleged accomplices seem still to have refused to confess in spite of severe interrogation.[66] There were rumours, to put it no higher, that fellow-prisoners had seen Kotolynov at the time of his interrogation, badly scarred and beaten.[67] But he and the other Zinovievite ex-Komsomols are said to have resisted to the end. The published announcement of their 'trial' reported the conspirators as saying that their motive for killing Kirov was to replace the leadership with Zinoviev and Kamenev.[68] Nikolayev and all the others were sentenced to death and executed on 29 December.

At least they presumably were. But it is entirely possible that

* And a prisoner mentions a Finn in his camp who had been arrested in Leningrad as a bearer of secret instructions from Finland to the assassin.[62]

many of them were dead already. Nikolayev, in particular, is said to have been executed soon after Stalin saw him. And, on the other hand, there is a reference by Vyshinsky in the Zinoviev Trial of 1936 to Levin – one of Nikolayev's 'fellow-plotters' – having been shot 'in 1935';[69] if this is not a slip, it may perhaps mean that he was held past his official execution date with a view to providing evidence against later accused.*

The result so far was not entirely satisfactory to Stalin. The Party would still scarcely have accepted a direct incrimination of Zinoviev and Kamenev simply on trust, without the assassin being produced to testify to it in public. Moreover, after the first shock of Kirov's death had died down, a strong element in the Politburo and elsewhere continued to put Kirov's own line of reconciliation and relaxation.

Negotiations were afoot with the imprisoned opposition leaders to get them to assume the entire guilt for reasons of Party discipline, but these were unproductive. On the other hand, they began to feel that it was in their own interests to do all they could to discourage terrorism, which could only lead to worse repressions against themselves and their followers. So they finally agreed to accept 'moral responsibility' for the murder – in that the assassin could conceivably have been encouraged to his act by their political attitudes.

On 15–16 January Zinoviev, Kamenev, Evdokimov, Bakayev, Kuklin and fourteen others were brought to trial in Leningrad as the 'Moscow Centre'. Ulrikh again presided, and Vyshinsky prosecuted. The line taken was that, knowing the terrorist inclination of Kotolynov's 'Leningrad Centre', those now accused had given it political encouragement.

The new trial was not, however, reported fully. Only a three-quarter-page summary appeared in the press, with a few quotations from the evidence of Zinoviev and others admitting their partial guilt. The group was said to have been 'exposed' by Bakayev and by Safarov, who was not on trial.[71] Bakayev, who had been under interrogation for over a month, seems to have made the fullest confession.

* Kotolynov too is reported, rather inconclusively, in Leningrad's Nizhegorodsky Prison in February 1935.[70]

Zinoviev was reported as saying in court:

The former activity of the former oppositon could not, by the force of objective circumstances, but stimulate the degeneration of those criminals.[72]

He took full responsibility for those he had misled, and summed up by remarking that 'the task that I see confronting me on this subject is to repent fully, frankly and sincerely, before the court of the working class, for what I understand to be a mistake and a crime, and to say it in such a way that it should all end, once and for all, for this group'.[73]

But though this general acceptance of the moral responsibility of the opposition was made, charges of more sinister involvement were rejected. Evdokimov stoutly denied all connexion with the murder.[74] Kamenev expressed his lack of trust in the 'witness' Safarov; he also stated flatly that he did not know of the existence of the 'Moscow Centre', of which it now turned out he was an active member, though in so far as it existed he took responsibility for it.[75] Zinoviev, too, said that many of those in the dock were unknown to him,[76] and added that he had learned of Kotolynov's role only from the indictment in the 'Leningrad Centre' Case.[77] In spite of the partial surrender of the oppositionists, it is clear that their stand was not fully satisfactory to Stalin and that a public trial would not have been a success.

On 16 January 1935 Zinoviev was sentenced to ten years' imprisonment, Evdokimov to eight, Bakayev to eight, and Kamenev to five. The other sentences ranged from ten years to five. The length of the sentences was in any case to prove unimportant, as there is no known instance of any of these figures, major or minor, ever being released.

Two days after the trial (18 January 1935) a further secret circular on vigilance was issued by the Central Committee – an official call to all branches to start rooting out 'enemies', which significantly condemned lack of vigilance as 'a re-echoing of the Right deviation'.[78] A fresh wave of arrests, running into tens of thousands, now struck all the former opposition and other suspects at local levels.

There was still one batch of prisoners from the Kirov Case left to be dealt with – the Leningrad N.K.V.D. leadership whose forthcoming trial had been announced on 4 December. On 23 January these finally came before a court under, as ever, Ulrikh. Instead of the nine originally charged, there were now twelve – and Zaporozhets was among them. Medved and Zaporozhets were charged with failure to observe the basic requirements of State security, in that 'having received information about the preparations for the attempt on S. M. Kirov ... they failed to take the necessary measures to prevent the assassination ... although they had every possible means of arresting it'.[79]

The sentences were extremely light. One official, Baltsevich, got ten years for – in addition to the main charge – unspecified wrongful acts during the investigation. Medved got three years, and the others either two or three. The sentences were specifically to be served in a *kontslager* (concentration camp), a word soon to fall into disuse.

These sentences struck observant N.K.V.D. officers as totally out of proportion to the charges. Stalin's natural reaction to a criminal failure to guard against a genuine assassination attempt – of the sort which might strike him next – would have been the exemplary execution of all the N.K.V.D. defaulters: in fact they could scarcely have avoided a charge of complicity in the actual crime. But the whole thing became even odder and more sinister when it was discovered that Medved and Zaporozhets were being treated as though the sentences were little more than a tedious formality.

As was later admitted at the 1938 Trial, Yagoda displayed 'exceptional and unusual solicitude' towards them. He had 'entrusted the care of the family of Zaporozhets and Medved' to his personal secretary, Bulanov; he had 'sent them for detention to the camp in an unusual way – not in the car for prisoners, but in a special through car. Before sending them, he had Zaporozhets and Medved brought to see him.'[80]

This is, of course, impossible to conceive as a personal initiative of Yagoda's. A higher protection was being provided. Moreover, N.K.V.D. officers learned that Pauker and Shanin (Head of the N.K.V.D. Transport Department) were sending records and radio sets to Zaporozhets in exile – contrary to the strict Stalinist rule of instantly breaking even with one's best friend, once arrested.[81]

After the various odd circumstances of the whole Kirov Case, it was this above all which convinced many officials that Stalin had approved, if not arranged, the Kirov killing. The true story gradually filtered through the N.K.V.D. apparatus. Even then it was recounted with great reserve. Both Orlov and Krivitsky were told, as the former puts it, 'The whole affair is so dangerous that it is healthier not to know too much about it.'[82]

A prisoner from the White Sea Canal camps reports that Medved appeared at the headquarters of the camp complex, arriving by train in a special compartment and being put up by the head of the project, Rappaport, in his own house, where he gave a party for him. Medved was wearing an N.K.V.D. uniform without the insignia of his rank. He then went on, in the same style, to Solovetsk.[83]

Zaporozhets went to the Lenzoloto gold-mining camps in the Far East,[84] and is soon reported as head of the road-building administration in the Kolyma Camp complex – with another Leningrad N.K.V.Der, Fomin, under him.[85] Medved, who was meanwhile able to make a visit to Moscow,[86] seems to have joined them there later.[87]

As to the final fate of these N.K.V.D. exiles, Khrushchev was to remark twenty years later:

> After the murder of Kirov, top functionaries of the Leningrad N.K.V.D. were given very light sentences, but in 1937 they were shot. We can assume that they were shot in order to cover the traces of the organizers of Kirov's killing.[88]

Khrushchev's point is fairly taken; but it is too crudely put. No doubt, in a general way, Stalin favoured silencing those who knew his secrets. In fact, during the Zinoviev–Kamenev Trial of 1936, the accused are represented as planning, 'after their seizure of power, to put Bakayev in charge of the N.K.V.D. with a view to "covering up traces" by killing all officials who might have knowledge of the plot, and also so that the conspiratorial group could destroy its own activists, its own terrorist gunmen'. As the conspiracy was simply an invention of Stalin's, with evidence faked to suit, this shows that he thought it natural to shoot N.K.V.D. men and others who knew too much.

But, on the other hand, Stalin could scarcely liquidate everyone who knew of, or suspected, his crimes. It was not practical politics to execute Yagoda's subordinates until – or nearly until – he was ready to destroy Yagoda himself. And even when echelon after echelon of the Secret Police operatives had been killed, there had been time for all sorts of leaks. If it comes to that, several men who were in possession of some of Stalin's worst secrets – like Shkiryatov, Poskrebyshev, Vyshinsky, Beria and Mekhlis – survived until 1953–5, while Kaganovich is still alive.

It is true that in 1937 a great purge swept the N.K.V.D. in Kolyma. Its chief, Berzin, and most of the leading engineers were shot, and with them went Medved and all the other ex-Leningrad N.K.V.D. officers – with the extraordinary exception of Zaporozhets.[89] For though Stalin may have found it convenient to silence awkward witnesses by killing them, this was by no means the natural and necessary move Khrushchev implies. For what could they say or do? If it had been learned that they had dropped the slightest hint of their inside information, they would soon have been denounced. Perhaps the innocent Medved might have lapsed. But Zaporozhets, who *knew*, had every motive for silence.

Moreover, even if they had actually escaped to the West, and published their experiences in the press of Britain or France or the U.S.A., it would have mattered little. Indeed, the truth did come out through N.K.V.D. defectors, yet failed to convince many.

In any case, Zaporozhets became expendable soon afterwards. Once it was decided to expose Yagoda's part in the Kirov murder, and to tell the whole story of the N.K.V.D. involvement, it was time to sacrifice all concerned. At the 1938 Trial Zaporozhets's role was plainly described; and it was announced that he had not appeared in court because he was being made the 'subject of separate proceedings'. This seems to confirm that he was then still alive but that, if such was the case, he would not long remain so.

With the January 1935 trial of the Leningrad N.K.V.D. chiefs, the Kirov Case was wound up – for the time being. The old Zinoviev oppositionists were all in prison. Leningrad had been taken from independent hands and put under Stalin's devoted satrap, Zhdanov. A terror expressed mainly in mass deportations, but partly in mass executions, had struck the city and – to a lesser extent – the country as a whole.

Nevertheless, Stalin had not been able to crush his opponents entirely or to overcome the resistance of his less enthusiastic allies. The *coup de grâce* had not been given. And meanwhile hostility to his actions was once again arising in the lower levels of the Party.

In the Komsomol, for example, there was surprisingly frank resistance to Stalinism as late as 1935. The Secret Archive [90] from Smolensk province reveals the extent of this feeling. In a Komsomol discussion on the Kirov assassination one member is quoted as saying, 'When Kirov was killed they allowed free trade in bread; when Stalin is killed, all the *kolkhozes* will be divided up.' A Komsomol school director, serving as a propagandist, declared: 'Lenin wrote in his will that Stalin could not serve as leader of the Party.' Another teacher accused Stalin of having transformed the Party into a gendarmerie over the people. A nine-year-old Pioneer was reported to have shouted 'Down with Soviet Power! When I grow up, I am going to kill Stalin.' An eleven-year-old schoolboy was overheard saying 'Under Lenin we lived well, but under Stalin we live badly.' And a sixteen-year-old student was said to have declared 'They killed Kirov; now let them kill Stalin.' There were even occasional expressions of sympathy for the opposition. A worker Komsomol was quoted as saying 'They have slandered Zinoviev enough; he did a great deal for the Revolution.' A Komsomol propagandist in answer to a question denied that Zinoviev had any hand in the Kirov affair and described him as an 'honoured leader and cultivated man'. An instructor of a district Komsomol committee 'came out in open support of the views of Zinoviev'.

In fact, there was much to do before a situation satisfactory to Stalin could be established.

CHAPTER THREE

ARCHITECT OF TERROR

A Prince must possess the nature of both beast and man.
MACHIAVELLI

THE events of December 1934 and January 1935, so horrible, but above all so extraordinary, lead to the question of the mind behind them. The nature of the whole Purge depends in the last analysis on the personal and political drives of Stalin.

If we have put off any consideration of this personality until after we have seen him in characteristic action, it is because we can recount what he did (and, later, describe the results of the State he brought into being) more easily than we can describe him as an individual. He was not one of those figures whose real intentions were ever openly declared, or whose real motives can readily be deduced. If, on the one hand, Stalin's personal drives were the motive force of the Purge, it is also true that his ability to conceal his real nature was the rock on which all resistance to the Purge foundered. His opponents could not believe that he would either wish to, or be able to, do what he did.

Stalin was now fifty-five. Until the age of thirty-seven he had been a not particularly prominent member of a small revolutionary party whose prospects of coming to power in his lifetime even Lenin had doubted as late as 1916.

When the Revolution came, Stalin appeared to be outshone by many glittering contemporaries. The time since had been spent in ceaseless political manoeuvre. As a result he had defeated in turn every rival, and had now been for five years the undisputed head of State and Party; he had lately had his methods put to the severest test in the collectivization campaign and, against all prediction, had won through. This had not proved enough for him. Contrary to all that Marx had thought, we shall find in the Soviet Union of the Stalin epoch a situation in which the economic and social forces were not creating the method of rule. On the contrary, the central factor was ideas in the mind of the ruler impelling him to action very often against the natural trend of such forces. An idealist conception of history was for once correct. For Stalin created a machine capable of taking on the social forces and defeating them, and infused it with his will. Society was reconstructed according to his formulae. It failed to reconstruct him.

As the physicist Alexander Weissberg, himself a victim of the Great Purges, points out, a Marxist view of history – and, one might say, any sociological interpretation of politics – has its validity restricted 'to systems which allow of the application of the statistical conception',[1] just as with the other true sciences. When a society is so organized that the will of one man, or a small group, is the most powerful of the political and social forces, such explanations must give way, at least to a very considerable degree, to a more psychological style.

And so we are driven to an examination of the individual Joseph Stalin. But, as Arthur Koestler remarks,

What went on in No. 1's brain? . . . What went on in the inflated grey whorls? One knew everything about the far-away spiral nebulae, but about them nothing. That was probably the reason that history was more of an oracle than a science. Perhaps later, much later, it would be taught by means of tables of statistics, supplemented by such anatomical sections. The teacher would draw on the blackboard an algebraic formula representing the conditions of life of the masses of a particular nation at a particular period: 'Here, citizens, you see the objective factors which conditioned this historical process.' And, pointing with his ruler to a grey foggy landscape between the second and third lobe of No. 1's brain: 'Now here you see the subjective reflection of these factors. It was this which in the second quarter of the twentieth century led to the triumph of the totalitarian principle in the East of Europe.' Until this stage was reached, politics would remain bloody dilettantism, mere superstition and black magic . . .[2]

Stalin's head 'had a solid peasant look about it',[3] but his face was pock-marked and his teeth uneven. His eyes were dark brown with a tinge of hazel. He had a stiff left arm and shoulder, the result of an accident when he was about ten. His torso was short and narrow and his arms were too long.* Like many ambition-driven

* By the time of the Second World War, when many Western observers first saw him, he had changed. He had developed quite a large paunch; his

men he was very short, only about five feet two inches. He raised himself an inch or so by specially built shoes, and at the May Day and 7 November parades stood on a wooden slab which gave him another inch or two. Bukharin said:

It even makes him miserable that he cannot convince everyone, including himself, that he is a taller man than anybody else. That is his misfortune; it may be his most human trait and perhaps his only human trait; his reaction to his 'misfortune' is not human – it is almost devilish; he cannot help taking revenge for it on others, but especially those who are in some way better or more gifted than he is . . .[4]

Such psychological science as we have would turn also to Stalin's childhood. W. H. Auden wrote of the origins of another dictatorship:

> Accurate scholarship can
> Unearth the whole offence . . .

and not only in the history of a country, but in the early life of a dictator:

> Find what occurred at Linz . . .

But it seems doubtful if it will ever be possible really to trace what occurred at Gori, where Stalin was born and grew up, in anything like the detail implied. In any case, the necessary type of research, the free questioning of relatives and contemporaries and others in the area, has not been possible: even if it were soon to become so, it is by now presumably too late. Not that any definitive and generally accepted psychological study of the formation even of Hitler has emerged either; *a fortiori*, on the little and dubious evidence before us in Stalin's case, it would seem best not to venture even the sketchiest reconstruction.

There are, anyhow, probably few historians today who would care to deduce the essentials of a personality from a few second-hand reports about a long-past childhood. With Stalin, moreover, the bare facts are in dispute. His father was, according to some

---

hair had become very thin; and his face was now white with ruddy cheeks. This coloration was common in high Soviet circles, where it was known as 'Kremlin complexion' and attributed to working through the night in its offices.

accounts, a worthless drunkard; according to others this was not so. The biographers are faced with pursuing the matter, but in the circumstances we may be excused. This is a pity, in a way, for if it were possible to describe with rigour a set of childhood conditions likely to produce a Stalin, world-wide legislation everywhere to prevent their recurrence would be a laudable enterprise.

Legends clung even about his birth. Georgians, anxious for the reputation of their country, represented him as really of Tatar or Ossetian origin.[5] In the period of his greatness there was a story that he was the illegitimate son of a Georgian prince and a servant girl.[6] In fact, one of the few things about his earlier career on which there is no doubt is that he was the son of a peasant cobbler (who treated him either well or badly – for as early as this discord descends on the accounts). His father died when he was eleven, leaving a hard-working and strong-minded mother to bring up the boy. When nearly fifteen Stalin left the Gori elementary school for the Theological Seminary at Tiflis, being expelled, or removed for health reasons, when he was about twenty.

This was in 1899. He had already joined the Party circles in which he was to pass the remainder of his life, and by 1901 had given up all other activity to become a professional revolutionary.

His early life in the Social Democratic organizations in the Caucasus is still a very obscure subject. The Trotskyite line, that he was unimportant and inactive, is clearly exaggerated. The hagiological stories which appeared in the thirties and forties representing Stalin as a 'Lenin of the Caucasus' are even more baseless. But he seems, at least, to have been elected a member of the Executive of the All-Caucasus Federation of the Social Democratic Party in 1903. The whole early history of the Bolsheviks in Transcaucasia has been thoroughly obfuscated by a series of historians. The main point is that Bolshevism never struck root in Georgia, and most of those who later became Bolsheviks were little more than occasionally mutinous hangers-on of the large and efficient Menshevik organization.[7]

When, after the failure of the 1905 Revolution, Lenin started to rely on bank robbery as a source of funds for the Party, Stalin was prominent in organizing raids on banks in the Caucasus, though he never directly took part in them. At this time, these 'expropriations' were being widely condemned in the European and the Russian Social Democratic movement, and Trotsky, among others, was pointing to the demoralization involved. Even Lenin saw this to some degree, and attempted to bring the 'fighting squads' under strict control and to eliminate the semi-bandit elements which had got into them. But Stalin seems to have had no qualms of any sort. However, after his rise to power, nothing was ever said about this activity.

Whatever Lenin's tactical qualms, this ruthlessness appealed to him, and in 1912 Stalin was co-opted on to the Central Committee of the Party. Thenceforward, in Siberian exile or at the centre of power, he remained a high though unobtrusive figure in the Bolshevik leadership. In Lenin's last days, his estimate of the 'wonderful Georgian' changed. He said of him, 'This cook's dishes will be too peppery.' Trotsky tells us, plausibly enough, that Lenin admired Stalin for 'his firmness and his direct mind', but finally saw through 'his ignorance ... his very narrow political horizon, and his exceptional moral coarseness and unscrupulousness'.[8] But it was only in a last personal quarrel, and only on grounds of personal unpleasantness – not of political unreliability – that he urged Stalin's removal, not from positions of power, but from the particular post of General Secretary, where 'rudeness' was inappropriate.

At about the same time, Stalin is reported as saying to Kamenev and Dzerzhinsky:

To choose one's victims, to prepare one's plans minutely, to slake an implacable vengeance, and then to go to bed ... there is nothing sweeter in the world.[9]

This often quoted story is entirely in accord with Stalin's practice, but it is perhaps a little unlikely that he would have spoken in quite these terms in front of possible, and not yet forewarned, rivals. His opponents, on the whole, only realized his implacability too late. But it is unnecessary today to labour the point of Stalin's unscrupulousness, nor yet the extreme vindictiveness of his nature.

The Stalin method of argument, which is still prevalent in the

Soviet Union, can be traced as early as his first articles in 1905. Its particular marks are expressions like 'as is well known' (*kak izvestno*), used in lieu of proof to give weight to some highly controversial assertion; and 'it is not accidental' (*ne sluchayno*), used to assert a connexion between two events when no evidence, and no likelihood, of such a connexion exists. Readers will find many examples of these and similar expressions in current Soviet speeches.

Such phrases are extraordinarily illustrative and significant. A statement like 'As is well known, Trotskyites are Nazi agents' is difficult to object to in an authoritarian State; while the idea that nothing is accidental, a strictly paranoid formulation, makes it possible to construe every fault and weakness as part of a conscious plot.

This attitude accords with Stalin's notoriously suspicious nature. Khrushchev tells us:

> . . . Stalin was a very distrustful man, sickly suspicious; we knew this from our work with him. He could look at a man and say: 'Why are your eyes so shifty today?' or 'Why are you turning so much today and avoiding looking me directly in the eyes?' The sickly suspicion created in him a general distrust even toward eminent Party workers whom he had known for years. Everywhere and in everything he saw 'enemies', 'double-dealers' and 'spies'.[10]

A result of this attitude was that he almost never let down his guard. In politics, particularly in those of the sharpest style, this was to prove an excellent tactical principle.

We cannot know how far Stalin really cherished the principles he professed. Khrushchev, in his Secret Speech of February 1956, concludes a series of appalling revelations of terror by remarking of them that

> Stalin was convinced that it was necessary for the defence of the interests of the working class against the plotting of the enemies and against the attack of the imperialist camp. He saw this from the position of the working class, the interests of the working people, the interests of the victory of Socialism and Communism. We cannot say that these were the deeds of a giddy despot. He considered that this should be done in the interests of the Party, of the working masses, in the name of defence of the revolution's gains. In this lies the whole tragedy.

Most people would not perhaps regard it as the *whole* tragedy. But, more to our point, there is no way of telling what Stalin's true motivation was. The fact that to all appearances he took the view attributed to him by Khrushchev does not prove that he held it sincerely. Whether he consciously thought of the state of things he created and found good as the Socialism taught in his youth, or whether he saw it as an autocracy suitable to his own aims and to Russian reality, we cannot say.

A Soviet Air Force expert who had attended a number of meetings with the top Soviet leadership in connexion with plans for an inter-continental rocket mentions Stalin saying that the project would make it 'easier for us to talk to the great shop-keeper Harry Truman and keep him pinned down where we want him', but then turning to him with 'a curious remark' – 'You see, we live in an insane epoch.'[11]

None of the other Soviet leaders has ever been reported as expressing in private anything but a straightforward and cynic-ally-put desire to crush the West. This philosophical comment certainly goes deeper. Whether it represents Stalin's real thinking and self-justification, or is a sign of that same sensitivity to the attitude of others often reported of him, cannot be guessed.

When Litvinov was discarded in 1947, he used to meet regu-larly with his old friend Surits, another of the rare survivors of the old Soviet diplomatic service. They frequently discussed Stalin. They both agreed that he was a great man in many ways. But he was unpredictable. And he was stubborn, refusing to consider facts which did not correspond to his wishes. He imag-ined, they thought, that he was serving the people. But he did not know the people and he did not wish to know them, preferring the abstract idea, 'the People', made up to his own liking.[12]

For what it is worth, the evidence seems to be that Stalin really believed that the abolition of incomes from capital was the sole necessary principle of social morality, excusing any other action whatever. Djilas's summary is perhaps correct:

All in all, Stalin was a monster who, while adhering to abstract, absolute and fundamentally utopian ideas, in practice had no criterion but success – and this meant violence, and physical and spiritual exter-mination.[13]

Except for the priceless, though limited, light thrown on it by his daughter's book, the more personal side of his character must remain to a large degree enigmatic.

But it seems that the human moments, few as they were, arose in connexion with his wives. When the first, Ekaterina Svanidze, died, a friend who went to the cemetery with him says that he remarked, '. . . this creature softened my stony heart. She is dead and with her died my last warm feelings for all human beings.'[14]

His second wife, Nadezhda Alliluyeva, held to the old revolutionary ideas. She is said to have become horrified with what she had learned of the sufferings of the collectivization campaign. She seems to have obtained most of her information from students at a course she had been allowed to take, and these were arrested as soon as Stalin found out.

Her suicide on 9 November 1932 took place as the result of the last of a series of violent quarrels with her husband, whom she accused of 'butchering the people'. All early accounts agree that Stalin lost his temper with her and cursed her in front of his friends (though this is somewhat toned down in the version later given to his daughter).[15] For if Nadezhda, following Ekaterina, touched him in a comparatively soft spot, it was not as soft as all that, and remarkable only in comparison with his usual conduct. She left him a letter which 'wasn't purely personal: it was partly political as well'.[16] We are told that this made him think – and, of course, rightly – that he had enemies everywhere, and that it much exacerbated his suspiciousness. Stalin seems to have been deeply affected by Nadezhda's death. He felt it for the rest of his life, blaming it on 'enemies' (and on Michael Arlen, whose book *The Green Hat* she had been reading at the time).[17]

Nadezhda's brother, the Old Bolshevik Paul Alliluyev, was Political Commissar of the Armoured Forces. He was put under special surveillance. Later he told an old acquaintance that he had been kept away from Stalin since his sister's death and had had his Kremlin pass taken from him. It was clear to him that Yagoda and Pauker had suggested that he might be personally dangerous to Stalin in revenging his sister. He was removed from this post in 1937 and given a minor job in the Soviet Trade

Delegation in Paris.[18] He seems to have died naturally,* though his wife was later given ten years for poisoning him.[19]

An interesting family sidelight arises too in Stalin's attitude to his younger son Vasili. With his elder son Yakov, by his first wife, he was always on poor terms, occasionally subjecting him to minor persecutions. The feeling was mutual. With Vasili, Nadezhda Alliluyeva's son, his attitude was quite different. The young man is described with contempt and detestation by all who came in contact with him. He was a stupid bully, a semi-literate drunkard, 'a beastly pampered schoolboy let out into the world for the first time'.[20] In spite of a very poor record at the Kachinsky Flying School, where he received special tuition, he was passed into the Soviet Air Force without a single bad mark, and by the time he was twenty-nine was already a Lieutenant-General. In his intemperate outbursts, he invariably traded on his father's name.[21]

But Stalin finally removed him from his command for drunken incompetence. And it does not seem that he ever intervened directly to advance his career. It was rather that his subordinates did not dare to do other than recommend the young man enthusiastically in spite of his lack of qualifications. All the same, there seems to be a faint echo here of Napoleonic vulgarities. H. G. Wells writes of Napoleon's relation to the French Revolution:

And now we come to one of the most illuminating figures in modern history, the figure of an adventurer and a wrecker, whose story seems to display with an extraordinary vividness the universal subtle conflict of egoism, vanity and personality with the weaker, wider claims of the common good. Against this background of confusion and stress ... this stormy and tremendous dawn, appears this dark little archaic personage hard, compact, capable, unscrupulous, imitative and neatly vulgar.[22]

Many people have felt something of the same about the squat, vulgar figure of Stalin against the tremendous dawn of the

*There is no evidence (though it has been strongly suggested) that his death in 1937 was unnatural; even the fact that Stalin did not sign his obituary in spite of their very old Party acquaintance proves nothing.

Russian Revolution. But, in the first place, Wells is more than a little unfair to Napoleon. His political, as well as military, talents were considerable. Doubtless the Emperor vulgarized the Revolution; but it had already vulgarized itself.

No doubt all revolutions are doomed to vulgarization. On the other hand the idealization of the first glories of the new regime often contains a large element of vulgar sentimentalism, and the change to vulgar cynicism may constitute only a comparative deflation. Napoleon and Stalin, however that may be, both established their rule largely, though not entirely, by to some degree replacing the motivation of general ideas by that of careerism and personal loyalty.

Napoleon was of course a vain man. Stalin's vanity has also been much remarked on. But it did not, at least until his last years, run to palatial ostentation. Until the Second World War, he dressed with traditional Bolshevik modesty in a plain brown military coat and dark trousers stuffed into leather boots. He lived unpretentiously in a small house in the Kremlin, formerly part of the Tsar's servants' quarters. Ownership and money as such played no part in his life. In the thirties, his official salary was about 1,000 roubles a month – in purchasing power, perhaps $40. One of his secretaries accepted and dealt with this small sum, paying the superintendent of the Kremlin a modest rent for his apartment, and dealing with his Party dues, his payment for his holiday, and so on. He owned nothing but had immediate right to everything, like the Dalai Lama or the Mikado in the old days. His country villa at Borovikha and his seaside Government Summer House No. 7 at Sochi were 'State property'.[23]

With all this personal simplicity, his reputation for envious emulation arose early among his colleagues. When the Order of the Red Banner began to be awarded in the Civil War, and had been given to Trotsky, Kamenev proposed that Stalin should receive it too. Kalinin, the new Head of State, asked in surprise 'For what?' Bukharin intervened: 'Can't you understand? This is Lenin's idea. Stalin cannot live unless he has what someone else has. He will never forgive it.'[24]

In the final stages of the 'cult of personality', he was built up with the most astonishing adulation as a genius not only in politics, but also strategy, the sciences, style, philosophy and almost every field. His picture looked down from every hoarding, his bust was carried by Soviet alpinists to the top of every Soviet peak, he was elevated to be, with Marx, Engels and Lenin, the fourth of the great political geniuses of the epoch. The histories were, of course, rewritten to make his role in the Revolution a decisive one. Khrushchev describes him inserting in a draft of his own *Short Biography* the following passage:

Although he performed his task as leader of the Party and the people with consummate skill and enjoyed the unreserved support of the entire Soviet people, Stalin never allowed his work to be marred by the slightest hint of vanity, conceit or self-adulation.

Khrushchev goes on to say:

In the draft text of his book appeared the following sentence: 'Stalin is the Lenin of today.' This sentence appeared to Stalin to be too weak, so, in his own handwriting, he changed it to read: 'Stalin is the worthy continuer of Lenin's work, or, as it is said in our Party, Stalin is the Lenin of today.' You see how well it is said, not by the nation but by Stalin himself.

... I will cite one more insertion made by Stalin concerning the theme of the Stalinist military genius. 'The advanced Soviet science of war received further development', he writes, 'at Comrade Stalin's hands. Comrade Stalin elaborated the theory of the permanently operating factors that decide the issue of wars, of active defence and the laws of counter-offensive and offensive, of the cooperation of all services and arms in modern warfare, of the role of big tank masses and air forces in modern war, and of the artillery as the most formidable of the armed services. At the various stages of the war Stalin's genius found the correct solutions that took account of all the circumstances of the situation.'

And further, writes Stalin: 'Stalin's military mastership was displayed both in defence and offence. Comrade Stalin's genius enabled him to divine the enemy's plans and defeat them. The battles in which Comrade Stalin directed the Soviet armies are brilliant examples of operational military skill.'[25]

On the other hand, it can be argued that precisely because his claim to leadership was shakily based, it had to be exaggerated and made unchallengeable. Lenin, whose dominance in the Party was genuine and accepted, had had no need of such methods.

For Stalin they were, in part at least, the necessary cement of autocracy. One shrewd Soviet diplomat in the thirties writes, 'Anyone who imagines that Stalin believes this praise, or laps it up in a mood of egotistical willingness to be deceived, is sadly mistaken. Stalin is not deluded by it. He regards it as useful to his power. He also enjoys humiliating these intellectuals . . .'[26]

To discuss Stalin's character and beliefs is not to estimate his abilities. There have been two main views of these. On the first, he was an infallible genius, a 'Coryphaeus of science', an inspired leader of the human race, and so forth. On the second, he was a mediocrity. The first view, taken (during Stalin's lifetime) by Professor Bernal, Khrushchev and others, has been submitted to enough destructive criticism, and we need hardly deal with it. The view that he was a nonentity who reached the top by luck and low cunning still has influence. It is true that most of those who hold it would concede that he was also a monster. But they would grant him few other active qualities.

The Menshevik historian Sukhanov, soon to be his victim, described him in 1917 as making no more impression than a grey blur. Trotsky called him 'the most outstanding mediocrity in our Party'.[27] And Khrushchev later said, in his Secret Speech of 1956: 'I shall probably not be sinning against the truth when I say that ninety-nine per cent of the persons present here heard and knew very little about Stalin before 1924.' He had, in fact, made little impression on the talkative politicians of the Party at that time. Thus there was some basis for the judgement of Trotsky and his successors. But on the whole it was a shallow one, as later events bore out. The qualities Stalin lacked and Trotsky possessed were not the essentials for political greatness. And Lenin alone among the Bolshevik leaders had recognized Stalin's ability.

It is early yet to look at his career objectively, with his technique of despotism simply 'considered as a fine art'. Nevertheless, we can avoid dismissing with the negative estimate of his unsuccessful rivals and their intellectual heirs the brilliant politician who was able to produce such vast and horrible effects.

He had a good average grasp of Marxism, and though his adaptations of that flexible doctrine to suit his purposes were not so elaborate or so elastic as the similar interpretations of his rivals and predecessors, they were adequate to his purpose. His lack of the true theoretician's mind was noted by many, and he seems to have resented it.

Bukharin told Kamenev in July 1928 that Stalin was 'eaten up with the vain desire to become a well-known theoretician. He feels that it is the only thing he lacks.' The old Marxist scholar Ryazanov once interrupted Stalin when he was theorizing: 'Stop it, Koba, don't make a fool of yourself. Everybody knows that theory is not exactly your field.' Nevertheless, as Isaac Deutscher rightly comments,[28] his great theoretical departure – 'socialism in one country' – however crude and even un-Marxist a notion, was a powerful and appealing idea.

Deutscher says that 'the interest of practitioners of Stalin's type in matters of philosophy and theory was strictly limited. . . . The semi-intelligentsia from whom socialism recruited some of its middle cadres enjoyed Marxism as a mental labour-saving device.' But this view exaggerates Stalin's philosophical clumsiness. Or rather, perhaps, it overrates the more philosophical Bolsheviks, such as Lenin, with whom Deutscher goes on to compare him. Lenin's only adventure into philosophy proper – *Materialism and Empirio-Criticism* – is his least impressive work. On the other hand, Stalin's brief summary of Marxism, which appears in Chapter 4 of the 'Short Course' *History of the All-Union Communist Party*, is, in an unpretentious way, as clear and able an account as there is. Georg Lukács, the leading Communist theoretician, who has shown some revulsion from Stalinism, recently commented, 'Since we have to do with a popular work written for the masses, no one could find fault with Stalin for reducing the quite subtle and complex arguments of the classics on this theme to a few definitions enumerated in schematic textbook form.'[29]

With the exception of Zinoviev, Stalin was the only non-'intellectual' in Lenin's leadership. But his knowledge of more truly relevant matters was not small. Djilas tells us that 'Stalin had considerable knowledge of political history only, especially Russian, and he had an uncommonly good memory. Stalin really did not need any more than this for his role.'[30]

In 1863 Bismarck reminded the Prussian Chamber that 'politics is not an exact science'. It would have been a truism to every previous generation, and he was perhaps provoked into giving the idea such definite expression by the rise of the new rationalism in historical science, of the claims to rigour of the social and political professors. Among the Russian Communists of the post-Revolutionary period this tendency had reached its fullest development. They were political scientists, they were using the methods of *the* political science devised by Marx, the Darwin of society. Everything was discussed in theoretical terms.

Unfortunately, the theories were not correct, and the claim to scientific rigour was, to say the least, premature. Even if their formulations had been closer to the definitiveness claimed for them, it is still perhaps doubtful if such leaders would have prevailed in actual politics: professors of ballistics do not necessarily make good baseball players. As it was, the more intuitive Stalin, less able to analyse and plan his moves in theoretical terms, had a fuller operational grasp of reality.

As his daughter remarks, in spirit Stalin was completely Russianized. He had not learnt Russian until he was eight or nine, and always spoke it with an accent. But he spoke it well, and his conversation was often rich and vivid in a coarse way. Though not well educated, he was widely read in the Russian classics – in particular, the satirists Shchedrin and Gogol. He had also read when young a number of foreign authors in Russian translation – in particular Victor Hugo, and popular works on Darwinism and social and economic matters. Gendarmerie reports on the Tiflis Theological Seminary in the last part of the nineteenth century mention the reading by students of 'seditious' literature of this sort, and Stalin's name appears in the seminary bad-conduct book a number of times for the discovery of such works from the local 'Cheap Library', showing that he was engaged in absorbing this sort of self-education.[31]

His style of writing was unsubtle and here again his opponents sneered at him. Djilas associates it, and its crudeness, with the backward nature of revolutionary Russia. 'It contains simplicities from the writings of the church fathers, not so much the result of his religious youth, as the result of the fact that this was the way of expression under primitive conditions.' Djilas adds elsewhere that 'His style was colourless and monotonous, but its over-simplified logic and dogmatism were convincing to the con-formists and to common people.'[32] But there is more to it than that. Clear and plain arguments are appealing not only to 'common' minds. A Soviet official writes, 'It was precisely his lack of brilliance, his plainness, which inclined us to believe what he said.'[33]

He is often described as having a curious effect of sullenness, but he could be charming enough, and had 'a rough humour, self-assured but not entirely without subtlety and depth'.[34] In this he contrasts with the humourlessness of Lenin, and of Trotsky too.

It seems doubtful that he would have had the same sort of success in a more experienced political community, but in the political circumstances in which Stalin found himself he proved a master. Tactically he far outshone his rivals. Bukharin com-mented of him that he was a master of 'dosing' – of giving the right dose at the right time. It is a measure of Bukharin's own comparative ineptitude that he seems to have thought of this as an insult. In fact it is a sound compliment to one of Stalin's greatest strengths.

He won his position by devious manoeuvre. It is notable that from 1924 to 1934 there are none of the abrupt *coups* which mark the post-Stalin period. Stalin would attack and discredit a man, then appear to reach a compromise, leaving his opponent weakened but not destroyed. Bit by bit their positions were undermined and they were removed one by one from the leader-ship.

Lenin saw this side to Stalin's political methods. When he was working to defeat Stalin on the Georgian issue in the last days of his active life, he told his secretary not to show Kamenev the notes he had prepared for Trotsky, or they would leak to Stalin, in which case 'Stalin would make a rotten compromise in order then to deceive'.[35] And this indeed Stalin did in the months following Lenin's death, exhibiting, as Gibbon says of Alaric, 'an artful moderation, which contributed to the success of his designs'.

It was because Stalin never committed himself irretrievably until he was certain of success that his opponents were so often put into a dilemma. They were never sure how far he was intending to go. And they could – and did – frequently delude themselves into thinking that he had submitted to the will of the Politburo majority, and would henceforth be possible to work with. Even when he was pressing forward hard to the terrorist solution of the question of the oppositionists, they were able to feel that this was partly due to the influence of Kaganovich and others, whom Stalin might well be induced to abandon if suitable arguments were produced. It is notable that few of the alternative solutions seriously put forward from 1930 onwards envisaged the total removal of Stalin from positions of power which alone could have saved the situation.

Thus, in a manner almost unprecedented in history, he continued his '*coup d'état* by inches', culminating in a vast slaughter, while *still* giving an air of moderation. Through his silences and unprovocative talk, he not merely deceived many foreigners, but even in Russia itself, at the height of the Purge, he was to some degree able to avoid popular blame.

A friend who had contact in the higher circles in both Stalin's Russia and Rákosi's Hungary remarks that Rákosi was indeed much the more educated and in a sense more intelligent man. But he laid himself open in the most unnecessary way. The most important example was that during the period of the Rajk Trial in 1949 he made a speech saying that he had spent sleepless nights until he himself had unravelled all the threads of the conspiracy. When Rajk was rehabilitated, this was a deadly weapon against Rákosi. But quite apart from that, it meant that even at the time he personally was blamed by the people and the Party for all malpractices in connexion with his purge.[36] Stalin, who never said a word more than was necessary, would not have dreamed of making so crude a revelation. It was his triumph that the Great Purge was very largely blamed on Yezhov, the head of the N.K.V.D. 'Not only I but very many others thought the evil came from the small man they called "the Stalinist Commissar". The people christened those years the 'Yezhovshchina' [the Yezhov times]', remarks Ilya Ehrenburg. Ehrenburg also tells[37] of meeting Pasternak in the Lavrushensky Lane on a snowy night. Pasternak raised his hands to the dark sky and exclaimed 'If only someone would tell Stalin about it!' Meyerhold, too, remarked, 'they conceal it from Stalin'.[38]

In fact, the opposite was true. The cartoonist Boris Efimov describes his brother Mikhail Koltsov telling him of a conversation with Mekhlis, who explained how the arrests were taking place. Mekhlis showed him, in confidence, 'a few words in red pencil addressed to Yezhov and Mekhlis, laconically ordering the arrest of certain officials'. These were, Koltsov noted, 'people still at liberty and at work, who had in fact already been condemned and . . . annihilated by one stroke of this red pencil. Yezhov was left with merely the technical details – working up the cases and producing the orders for arrest'.[39]

Stalin's achievement is in general so extraordinary that we can hardly dismiss him as simply a colourless, mediocre type with a certain talent for terror and intrigue. He was, indeed, in some ways a very reserved man. Even in his younger days it is said that if beaten in an argument he would show no emotion, but just smile sarcastically. His former secretary penetratingly remarks 'He possessed in a high degree the gift for silence, and in this respect he was unique in a country where everybody talks far too much.'[40] His ambitions, and even his talents, were not clear to most of his rivals and colleagues.

Because he did not elucidate and elaborate his views and plans, it was thought that he did not have any – a typical mistake of the garrulous intellectual. 'His expression', an observer remarks, 'tells nothing of what he feels.'[41] A Soviet writer speaks of 'the expression which he had carefully devised for himself over the years as a fixture and which Comrade Stalin, as he had long since been in the habit of calling himself in his thoughts and sometimes aloud, in the third person, had to assume in the presence of these people'.[42] He would listen quietly at meetings of the Politburo, or to distinguished visitors, puffing at his Dunhill pipe, doodling aimlessly – his secretaries Poskrebyshev and Dvinsky write that his pads were sometimes covered with the phrase 'Lenin–teacher–friend', but the last foreigner to visit him, in February 1953, noted that he was doodling wolves.

All early accounts agree that one of Stalin's characteristics was 'laziness' or 'indolence' – which Bukharin impressed on Trotsky as Stalin's 'most striking quality'.[43] Trotsky remarked that Stalin 'never did any serious work' but was always 'busy with his intrigues'. Another way of putting this is that Stalin paid the necessary attention to the detail of political manoeuvre. In his own words, 'Never refuse to do the little things, for from the little things are built the big.'[44] One may also be reminded of a remark by a former German Commander-in-Chief, Colonel-General Baron Kurt von Hammerstein-Equord, about his officers: 'I divide my officers into four classes. . . . The man who is clever and industrious is suited to high staff appointments; use can be made of the man who is stupid and lazy; the man who is clever and lazy is fitted for the highest command, he has the nerve to deal with all situations; but the man who is stupid and industrious is a danger and must be dismissed immediately.' In the political struggle Stalin's great characteristic is precisely 'nerve'. He had complete determination and considerable patience, together with an extraordinary ability to apply and to relax pressure at the right moment, which carried him through a series of critical situations, until his final victory.

At the centre of Stalin's superiority over his competitors was certainly his intense will, just as Napoleon ranked what he called 'moral fortitude' higher in a general than genius or experience. When Milovan Djilas said to Stalin during the Yugoslav–Soviet discussions in Moscow during the war that the Serbian politician Gavrilović was 'a shrewd man', Stalin commented, as though to himself: 'Yes, there are politicians who think shrewdness is the main thing in politics . . .'[45] His was a will-power taken to a logical extreme. There is something non-human about his almost total lack of normal restraints upon it.

He is said to have been a constant reader of Machiavelli, as indeed is reasonable enough. In Chapter XV of *The Prince*, he would find the simple advice that rulers should in no case practise villainies which might lose them the State, but must nevertheless, if it comes to the worst, 'not flinch from being blamed for vices which are necessary for safeguarding the State', making whatever effort is feasible to 'escape the evil reputation' involved. Or, again, in Chapter XVIII, Machiavelli recommends the appearance of mercy, faithfulness, and so forth, while noting that the Prince 'and especially a new Prince, must often act in a fashion contrary to those virtues'.

When the great film director Eisenstein produced his film on Ivan the Terrible, Stalin objected to his attitude. He had been inclined to treat Ivan, in the way most people have, as a ruthless and paranoid terrorist. Stalin told Eisenstein and the actor N. K. Cherkasov that, on the contrary, Ivan had been a great and wise ruler who had protected the country from the infiltration of foreign influence and had tried to bring about the unification of Russia; 'J. V. Stalin also remarked on the progressive role played by the Oprichnina [Ivan's Secret Police]'; Stalin's criticism of Ivan was limited to his having 'failed to liquidate the five remaining great feudal families'. On that point Stalin added humorously 'There God stood in Ivan's way' – since Ivan after liquidating one family would repent for a year 'when he should have been acting with increasing decisiveness'.*

Stalin also understood how to destroy his enemies' political reputations. He could have learned in certain respects from another totalitarian leader whom he to some extent admired. Hitler gives a recipe for the whole tenor of the Purges:

> The art of leadership, as displayed by really great popular leaders in all ages, consists in consolidating the attention of the people against a single adversary and taking care that nothing will split up that attention into sections. . . . The leader of genius must have the ability to make different opponents appear as if they belonged to the one category; for weak and wavering natures among a leader's following may easily begin to be dubious about the justice of their own cause if they have to face different enemies. . . . Where there are various enemies . . . it will be necessary to block them all together as forming one solid front, so that the mass of followers in a popular movement may see only one common enemy against whom they have to fight. Such uniformity intensifies their belief in their own cause and strengthens their feeling of hostility towards the opponent.[46]

---

* Cherkasov gives an account of this conversation in his *An Actor's Notes*, Moscow, 1953, pp. 380–82. This book was passed for publication while Stalin was still alive, and (we are told in the Soviet historical journal *Voprosy Istorii*, no. 8, 1956) he raised no objection.

But Stalin was deeper and more complex than Hitler. His view of humanity was cynical, and if he too turned to anti-Semitism it was as a matter of policy rather than dogma. We can see traces of this later anti-Semitism, or rather anti-Semitic demagogy, as early as 1907, when he was remarking, in the small underground paper he then controlled at Baku, 'Somebody among the Bolsheviks remarks jokingly that since the Mensheviks were the faction of the Jews and the Bolsheviks that of the native Russians, it would be a good thing to have a pogrom in the Party.'[47]

The Yiddish writers shot in August 1952 were accused of the *political* offence of wishing to set up a secessionist State in the Crimea – a charge faintly linked with reality through the fact that a proposal had indeed arisen in the Jewish Anti-Fascist Committee, after the war, to resettle Jews in the then desolate peninsula. In the Doctors' Plot of 1952–3 a majority of those accused were Jews, but some were not. The Jewish element was publicly emphasized, but it was under the guise of a link with 'Zionism': just as in the campaign leading up to it, Jewish literary men were called 'cosmopolitans' ('cosmopolitans . . . that long-nosed lot', a bureaucrat comments in one of Avram Tertz's stories). When critics in the West pointed out the undoubted anti-Semitic element in the alleged 'Plot', there were still people to come forward and say that, no, Gentiles were being accused too, and that Zionism was, after all, more or less implicitly anti-Soviet. For, as we shall see, Stalin's policies in strictly political matters were never elaborated clearly in such a fashion that they could be refuted. There was never any complete certainty in an individual case about what his disposition would be.

This enigmatic attitude misled even experienced and clever people. Lion Feuchtwanger (Ehrenburg remarks), a passionate defender of the Jews, could never believe that Stalin persecuted Jews – just as Romain Rolland, devoted to freedom in the arts, was easily deceived by him on the absence of freedom in Soviet literature.[48]

The 'anti-Semitism', thus disguised, was in accord with Stalin's general exploitation of prejudices, and of the gullibility and pliability of men in general. In a broader sense, this was doubtless at the root of Stalin's acceptance of the theories of the physiologist Pavlov (who loathed the Soviet regime). Moreover, he interpreted Pavlov in the crudest way as applying to human beings, sponsoring an attack on the view that Pavlov had dealt with the elementary nervous process of animals only and that in the case of man it was necessary to take into account the phenomenon of 'resistance to the formation of conditioned reflexes'.[49]

But the dull, cool, calculating effect given cumulatively through Stalin's long career, the air of a great glacier moving slowly and by the easiest path to overwhelm some Alpine valley, is only part of the picture. At various times – and especially in his early career – the calm of his general manner was broken, and expression given to the driving emotions that possessed him.

In Lenin's time, if offended, he would sulk and stay away from meetings for days.[50] Lenin noted of Stalin that he often acted out of anger or spite and that 'spite in general plays the very worst role in politics'. He also noted Stalin's hastiness, and his tendency to solve everything by administrative impulse. At the time of Lenin's death, he had nearly ruined himself by this 'capriciousness' and needed all his skill to retrieve the situation.

Nor, later, was his terrorism wholly rational. He 'practised brutal violence, not only toward everything that opposed him but also toward that which seemed, to his capricious and despotic character, contrary to his concepts'.[51] As George Kennan has remarked, to Stalin's 'darkly mistrustful mind no political issue was ever without its personal implications'.[52] His daughter takes it as central to his character that 'once he had cast someone he had known a long time out of his heart, once he had mentally relegated that someone to the ranks of his enemies, it was impossible even to talk to him about that person any more'.[53] There can be no doubt that Stalin pursued his grudges implacably, even after many years. But, of course, this cannot be more than a partial motive for the killings he ordered. For these involved friends as well as enemies, and men he hardly knew as much as personal rivals. Men who had injured him did not survive the Terror. And nor, of course, did men whom he had himself injured, like Bauman.

Nevertheless, when Khrushchev represents Stalin as a capricious tyrant, this is not necessarily incompatible with a basic rationale. It is true that anyone Stalin had a personal grudge against was almost automatically included on the death-list; but even a long life of quarrelsome intrigue could not provide anything like the required number of victims from that source alone. To obtain the terror effect, after all those who really stood in his way or annoyed him had been dealt with, the quota could just as efficiently be made up by caprice as by any other method.

Stalin's Terror, in fact, begins to show a more rational pattern, if it is considered as a statistical matter, a mass phenomenon, rather than in terms of individuals. The absence of strict categories of victims, such as a Trotsky might have listed, maintained the circumspect deviousness of the Purge and avoided presenting any clear-cut target to critics. The effect of terror is produced, he may have argued, when a given proportion of a group has been seized and shot. The remainder will be cowed into uncomplaining obedience. And it does not much matter, from this point of view, which of them have been selected as victims, particularly if all or almost all are innocent.

Ilya Ehrenburg, as late as 1964, still asks himself why some were shot and some spared. Why Litvinov was never in serious trouble (though kept away from active work for years), while all the diplomats associated with him were eliminated; why Pasternak, independent and unyielding, survived while Koltsov, anxious to do everything required of him, was liquidated; why the biologist Vavilov perished, and the even more independent-minded Kapitsa remained in favour.[54]

Whatever the 'statistical' rationale, the way Stalin's caprice operated is a useful sidelight on his character. A British writer of great political experience noted in the forties, 'It seemed almost . . . as if Stalin simultaneously demanded and hated the sycophancy of absolute obedience.'[55] This is confirmed and elaborated in a more recent Soviet account by the novelist Konstantin Simonov, who had much direct contact with the high Soviet leadership. In his *Soldiers Are Made, Not Born*, Stalin receives a letter from a general during the war asking for the release of a colleague, whose Civil War services he recounts:

Serpilin's recalling of past efforts had failed to touch Stalin. It was the directness of the letter that had interested him. In his ruthless character side by side with a despotic demand for total subservience, which was the rule with him, there lay the need to come across exceptions – which was the obverse side of the same rule. At times he evinced something akin to flashes of interest in people who were capable of taking risks, of expressing opinions which ran counter to his own opinions, whether genuine or assumed. Knowing himself, he knew the degree of this risk and was all the more capable of setting store by it. Sometimes, that is! Because it was far more frequently the other way around and this was where the risk lay.

Stalin gives Serpilin an interview, which goes fairly well:

Still, on his way out, Serpilin considered that his fate had already been finally settled during his conversation with Stalin. But in actual fact it had been settled not while they had been talking but a moment ago when Stalin had silently looked at his back as he left. That was the way he often finally decided people's fate, looking at them not in the eyes but from behind as they left.[56]

With certain categories Stalin seems to have had different standards. His former Georgian rivals and friends were mostly shot, like their Russian counterparts. But whereas Stalin showed nothing but contempt for most of his victims, the execution of his Georgian Old Bolshevik brother-in-law Alyosha Svanidze in 1942, on charges of being a Nazi agent, brought out a different attitude:

Before the execution, Svanidze was told that Stalin had said that if he asked for forgiveness he would be pardoned. When Stalin's words were repeated to Svanidze, he asked: 'What am I supposed to ask forgiveness for? I have committed no crime.' He was shot. After Svanidze's death, Stalin said: 'See how proud he is: he died without asking forgiveness.'[57]

An even more extraordinary example is that of another Georgian, S. I. Kavtaradze. He had been Chairman of the Council of People's Commissars in Georgia from 1921 to 1922, and had fallen with the rest of the Georgian leadership during Stalin's clash with them before and after Lenin's death. He was expelled from the Party as a Trotskyite in 1927, and was among those not readmitted during the following years. He was of course arrested and sentenced during the Purges. He is reported in Maryinsk and Kolyma labour camps in 1936, thoroughly disillusioned.[58] In 1940 he was still in camp. One day the commandant called him and he was sent off to Moscow. Much to his surprise, instead of being shot, he was taken directly in his prison clothes to see Stalin, who greeted him affably, asking him where he had been all these years. He was at once rehabilitated, and sent to the Commissariat of Foreign Affairs, where he shortly became Assistant People's Commissar. After the war he was Ambassador in Romania for a time. In his biography, as given in various Soviet reference books, a bare mention is made of the thirteen-year gap in his Party membership between December 1927 and December 1940![59] Kavtaradze had been a Menshevik, and Stalin was on the whole comparatively lenient with ex-Mensheviks who had not become involved in the later Party struggles. Nevertheless, this is a clear and conscious example of his indulging a caprice.

Of his leading opponents in post-revolutionary Georgia, while he had Mdivani shot, he made a remarkable exception to the Purge in sparing Philip Makharadze. Makharadze, though publicly censured for various errors in the particularly sensitive field of Georgian Party history,[60] remained Chairman of the Presidium of the Georgian Supreme Soviet until he died, in good odour, in 1943. His survival is very peculiar – unless indeed, we regard the reprieve as amounting to no more than four years' imminent expectation of arrest, and see in it a particularly subtle piece of vengeance.

What may be a curious remnant of Caucasian chivalry can be seen in one of Stalin's more general omissions from the Purge lists. He had no objection to killing or imprisoning women – in fact 'wife' is mentioned as a normal category for execution (see p. 355). But within the inner Party itself there is a curious survival of Old Bolshevik women. Krupskaya, Lenin's widow, is in a sense a special case, though she had been strong in the opposition to Stalin in the twenties and had given him personal offence. But it would not by any means be beyond Stalin's powers or beyond the usual scope of his malice to prove that Lenin's wife had betrayed her husband.

But there are many other cases of Old Bolshevik women surviving. Elena Stasova lasted right through the Stalin epoch. L. A. Fotieva, Lenin's secretary, who must also have known a

good deal about what was one of Stalin's most sensitive points –
the quarrel with Lenin in his last days – was also spared. So was
K. I. Nikolayeva, the only woman full member of the 1934 Central
Committee apart from Krupskaya, who was one of the few
who was carried over into the Committee elected in 1939, and
she was an ex-Zinovievite at that. Another case was R. S.
Zemlyachka, member of the 1904 Central Committee. A brutal
terrorist, she had been Béla Kun's chief colleague in the great
slaughter in the Crimea in 1920, to which Lenin himself had
objected. She survived, while Kun went to the execution cellars.
Alexandra Kollontai, the star of the Workers' Opposition, had
been married to Dybenko and had lived with Shlyapnikov. On
top of all this, after her acceptance of the Stalin line she remained
as Ambassador (in Sweden) – a profession which was anyhow
almost invariably fatal. Yet she survived the Stalin epoch unscathed, *en poste*.

Psychologists might make something about this trait of Stalin's.
In any case, it is a comparatively human characteristic and one
perhaps harking back to Caucasia as much as the blood-feud
does. Another 'category' to be spared has no such obvious
source: the former Bolshevik members of the Duma (including
Grigori Petrovsky, was under the direst threat in 1939) all
survived.

But when all is said, we are still peering into the glooms of an
extreme reticence. A shrewd Soviet official was impressed by
Stalin's patience and also by his capriciousness, and comments,
'That rare combination is the principal key to his character.'[61]
Doubtless this is a sound view, yet it only takes us into the out-
skirts of a full understanding.

Even as to his political aims, he never spoke his mind. That he
knew in general what he was doing cannot be doubted. It is
much more difficult, as we have seen, to tell how far he had made
his aims explicit even in his own mind, and how far ahead he
looked during a given crisis. What he had, politically speaking,
was less definite than a planned control of developments. It was
rather the feel of events, the flow. In this he was unsurpassed
among his contemporaries.

We do not need to posit a conscious long-term plan to say that in a general way the drive for power was Stalin's strongest and most obvious motivation. There have been men, like Cromwell, whose paths to supreme power were truly accidental, who neither planned, nor particularly wished for, the result. This is quite certainly not true of Stalin.

Bukharin said plainly, 'At any given moment he will change his theories in order to get rid of someone.'[62] But politically speaking, this shows a basic consistency. The one fundamental drive that can be found throughout is the strengthening of his own position. To this, for practical purposes, all else was subordinate. It led him to absolute power. As Machiavelli points out, though the actual seizure of power is difficult in despotic States, once seized it is comparatively easy to hold. And Stalin seized it and held it.

Over the next four years he carried out a revolution which completely transformed the Party and the whole of society. Far more than the Bolshevik Revolution itself, this period marks the major gulf between modern Russia and the past. It was also the deepest trauma of all those which had shaken the population in the turbulent decades since 1905. It is true that only against the peculiar background of the Soviet past, and the extraordinary traditions of the All-Union Communist Party, could so radical a turn be put through. The totalitarian machinery, already in existence, was the fulcrum without which the world could not be moved. But the revolution of the Purges still remains, however we judge it, above all Stalin's personal achievement. If his character is to some degree impenetrable to direct investigation, we shall see it adequately displayed in his actions over the following years, and in the State he thus created and found good.

CHAPTER FOUR

OLD BOLSHEVIKS CONFESS

'In what did his fascism show itself?'
'His fascism showed itself when he said that in a situation
like the present we must resort to the use of every possible
means.'
Exchange between VYSHINSKY *and* ZINOVIEV *at the
August 1936 Trial*

THE six months following the Medved–Zaporozhets Trial is one
of the most obscure periods of the Purge. It starts with the death,
in circumstances which are still unknown, of another member of
the Politburo, and ends with another trial, of which even the
charges have never been made public, of Kamenev and others.
But the pattern is clear, and much of the detail can now be constructed.

After the first wave of terror following the Kirov murder, the
moderate faction in the Politburo continued to urge the policy of
relaxation. It could, after all, equally well be argued that the
assassination was the sign of tensions which might best be dealt
with by a more popular policy, as the opposite, that it indicated the
need for further terror.

In the Politburo, Valerian Kuibyshev, head of the State
Planning Commission (Gosplan), is believed to have been particularly active along Kirov's line, and is said to have opposed
the January Zinoviev–Kamenev Trial.[1] Outside, the influence of
Maxim Gorki, and of Lenin's widow Nadezhda Krupskaya, was
of importance. The Society of Old Bolsheviks, which had long
acted as a sort of Party conscience, strongly opposed the idea of
death sentences for the opposition. Among Stalin's immediate
entourage Abel Yenukidze, who was Secretary of the Central
Executive Committee and (among other duties) responsible for
the administration of the Kremlin, urged the same view.

Yenukidze was the first target of Stalin's counter-measures. As
if to emphasize the connexion, he was required on 16 January
1935, the very day Zinoviev and his adherents were sentenced, to

perform a significant though minor act of self-denunciation – on the always thorny theme of the origins of Georgian Bolshevism. In a half-page of *Pravda*,[2] he wrote of his errors in articles in the encyclopaedias and elsewhere, where he had attributed too big a role to himself. This marked the beginning of his rapid decline.

The next great blow to moderation was the death of Kuibyshev on 26 January. Most of his subordinates in Gosplan, including his deputy, Professor Osadchy, had been purged for opposing ill-prepared crash programmes in the first years of the decade. Although Kuibyshev's death was at first described as being from natural causes, it was later to be alleged that he was murdered by wilful medical mistreatment on the orders of Yagoda. It is still difficult to be certain about the Kuibyshev case. Common sense gets us nowhere. There are, in fact, two different 'commonsensical' ways of looking at it. The first would say that what appears to be a natural death should be taken as such if there is no absolutely firm evidence to the contrary. After all, Kuibyshev had to be ill in the first place if he was being treated medically; people do die naturally, and we should not strain to fit every death into a preconceived pattern. The other view is that Kuibyshev had, as is now officially said (see p. 53), been one of three Politburo members who had blocked Stalin, and that of this group one had been shot just before Kuibyshev's death and the other was to perish later of a faked heart attack; that 'medical murder' in the conditions of the time is not in the least implausible; and that moreover Stalin was making moves against other advocates of moderation such as Gorki and Yenukidze at precisely this time. Against a member of the Politburo, at once more dangerous and less vulnerable, what sanction was left him except the one that had succeeded with Kirov?*

Kuibyshev was photographed at a meeting of the Council of People's Commissars on 22 January.[3] On the 26th, his death was

---

*The reader may feel this to be taking suspicion too far. But a certain amount of suspicion seems reasonable when we consider that *all* the other nine Politburo members (and ten ex-Politburo members) to die in the years 1934–40 were victims of the Purge; that *all* those of his own supporters who opposed him on the Purge perished; and, perhaps most important, that the others of his own Politburo supporters who died before 1938 were disposed of by him, but in ways not easily attributable to his own actions.

announced – of heart disease. The signatories to the medical bulletin included Kaminsky, Khodorovsky and Levin, all of whom were to sign the certificate of Ordzhonikidze's equally sudden death from the same cause, which is known to be a fake.

Kuibyshev seems to have had a bad heart, and to have been under treatment at least since August 1934. An attack of tonsillitis and an operation weakened him still further. But he was not at this stage particularly ill, and was still at work within an hour or two of his death.[4]

The account of his death given at the Bukharin Trial was that he had some sort of *angina pectoris* attack while at his office at the Council of People's Commissars, was allowed to go home unaccompanied, and climbed to his flat on the third floor. There chanced to be a maid at home who telephoned his secretary and the doctor on duty, but by the time they arrived Kuibyshev was dead.[5]

It was alleged that it was the purposely incorrect treatment which had been given him which caused his death, and that the doctors should anyhow have insisted on his being in bed.[6] The doctors (and Kuibyshev's secretary Maximov) were later accused of working under Yagoda's orders. There is nothing impossible about this: after all a leading N.K.V.D. officer had just aided in the Kirov murder, and Levin at least was an N.K.V.D. doctor. But it seems equally likely that if Kuibyshev did not die naturally he was killed in some other way than that stated – perhaps by another member of the Council of People's Commissars dropping in from a nearby office with a glass of non-medicine. If so, it is possible that the true facts were known only to a few now dead, and that they are no longer available even to investigators in Russia.

Among those actively opposed to the persecution of oppositionists throughout this period, another of the most forceful was Maxim Gorki. Moreover, his great ambition was to assist in a reconciliation between the Party and the intelligentsia – to lead the Soviet regime, of which he had originally disapproved, into the socialist humanism he believed it capable of. It was for this that he had compromised himself by returning from Italy in 1928, and defending the regime against its external critics.

Gorki is said to have personally worked to reconcile Stalin with Kamenev and to have apparently succeeded in doing this early in 1934,[7] even securing a friendly personal meeting. Kamenev was given a job in the Akademia publishing house.

Gorki is said to have at first been greatly enraged against the supposedly anti-Party assassins of Kirov, but soon to have reverted, as far as general policy went, to his 'liberal' position. Stalin's resentment at his stand was expressed by the appearance, for the first time, of articles highly critical of him.* However, Gorki continued in his efforts to reconcile Stalin with the oppositionists. So did Krupskaya, who had been Kamenev's and Zinoviev's main ally in 1924.

Krupskaya, up to a point, represented a moral threat to Stalin's plans. But unlike Gorki, she was a Party member and subject to that same Party discipline which had led her to acquiesce in the suppression of her husband's Testament. Her sympathies with the Zinovievite opposition over the years had been common knowledge in the Party. By now she had as a result lost most of the prestige she had once enjoyed on the higher levels, even though her name was still useful with the Party masses. The exact methods by which Stalin silenced her are unknown. He is said to have once remarked that if she did not stop criticizing him, the Party would proclaim that not she, but the Old Bolshevik Elena Stasova, was Lenin's widow: 'Yes,' he added sternly, 'the Party can do anything!'[8]

In any case, there was little she could do. It was not difficult to keep foreigners away from her, to surround her with N.K.V.D. men, and at the same time to call on her to obey the Party's orders – a situation quite different from that of Gorki. It is said that she was in fear for her life in her last few years. But, by his standards, Stalin treated her comparatively well, neither framing her nor (as far as is known) poisoning her.

On 1 February, a plenum of the Central Committee elected Mikoyan and Chubar to the posts on the Politburo left vacant by the deaths of Kirov and Kuibyshev, and promoted Zhdanov and Eikhe to candidate membership. To the extent that Mikoyan, at least, was to support the extreme Stalinist line throughout the Purge period (as, of course, was Zhdanov among the candidate

* For example, one by the writer Panferov in *Pravda* of 28 January 1935.

members), this was a gain for Stalin. But he was not yet ready wholly to overwhelm the 'moderates' in the leading policy bodies.

In the key organizational posts in the Party and Purge machinery it was another matter. Nikolai Yezhov, a tested and ruthless operator, became a member of the Secretariat, and on 23 February was appointed in addition to the key post of Head of the Party Control Commission.[9] Another prominent young Stalinist, Kaganovich's protégé Nikita Khrushchev, was made First Secretary of the Moscow Party organization a few days later.[10] Andrei Vyshinsky had been made Prosecutor-General by June. And by 8 July 1935 Georgi Malenkov was Yezhov's chief deputy as Assistant Director of the Cadres Department of the Central Committee.[11]

Thus by mid 1935 Stalin had men of his personal selection, who were to prove themselves complete devotees of the Purge, in control of Leningrad and Moscow, and in the Transcaucasus where Beria ruled; in the Control Commission and the key departments of the Party Secretariat; and in the Prosecutor-Generalship; and if the leadership of the N.K.V.D. was later to prove unsatisfactory to him, it was at least totally under his control.

In the formal organs of Party power, the Central Committee and the Politburo, he had not yet achieved the same total grip. Many of the provincial committees were still headed by men who dragged their feet. And the Ukraine was under the control of the same style of leadership which it had been necessary to remove in Leningrad by an assassin's bullet. But a firm basis for attack on these old cadres had been established.

The same piecemeal progress was being made, during this outwardly quiet period, in thought control and in the Party purge. A circular of 7 March 1935 ordered the removal from libraries of all the works of Trotsky, Zinoviev and Kamenev. Another, dated 21 June, extended the list to include Preobrazhensky and others.[12]

A secret letter dated 19 May 1935 from the Central Committee called for the special investigation of 'enemies of the Party and the working class' who had remained within the Party. On 27

June a special (and evidently typical) Central Committee resolution on the Western province censured the local officials in charge of the Party purge for insufficient vigilance.

A secret circular of 13 May 1935 had called for another 'verification'. As a result, in the Smolensk *rayon*, 455 out of 4,100 members examined were expelled – after 700 oral and 200 written denunciations.[13] One member was denounced for having admitted that he had in his possession 'a platform of the Trotskyites'. A professor had given a favourable character reference to a Trotskyite and now 'never expressed his attitude toward the Trotskyite counter-revolution'. A group of worker members of the Party wrote denouncing their local leadership for refusing to listen to denunciations. Typical of remarks at Party meetings were such attacks as 'There is information that Smolov is married to the daughter of the merchant Kovalev, and that the Party organizer of the second group of the Institute is the son of a person who was given a strict reprimand.'[14] By 1 August, as a report signed by Yezhov and Malenkov noted, 23 per cent of the Party cards in this representative area had been withdrawn or held pending investigation.[15]

Even more striking were some of the changes in Soviet law. A decree of 30 March made the illegal carrying of a knife punishable by five years' imprisonment. A decree of 9 June, later incorporated into the Criminal Code (Article 58 [i.*a*, i.*b*, i.*c*]), was a much more startling departure, exemplifying in full the style of the Stalin epoch. It provided the death penalty for flight abroad by both civil and military; in the case of the military, members of the family aware of the intended offences were subject to up to ten years' imprisonment; while – the real novelty – those who knew nothing whatever about it – 'the remaining adult members of the traitor's family, and those living with him or dependent on him at the time' – were made liable to five years' exile.

A Soviet law book, justifying this, speaks approvingly of

the application of special measures in respect of the adult members of the family of a serviceman-traitor in the event of the latter's flight or escape across the frontier in those cases where the adult member of the family in no way contributed to the act of treachery that was being prepared or executed and did not even know of it. . . . The political significance of it consists in the strengthening of the overall preventive action of the criminal law for the purpose of averting so heinous a felony as the action of a serviceman in crossing or flying across the frontier, as the result of which the guilty party cannot himself be subjected to punishment.[16]

In fact, we have a crude and frank institution of the hostage system – a sign of the way Stalin was thinking in other cases as well.*

More extraordinary still, and just as relevant to Stalin's general plans, was the decree of 7 April 1935 extending all penalties, including death, down to twelve-year-old children.[18]

This decree was noted in the West, where it made very bad anti-Soviet propaganda. Many people wondered why Stalin had made such a law public. Even if he meant to shoot children, this could be done without publicity. Indeed, an N.K.V.D. veteran tells how the *bezprizorniye* – homeless orphans of the wars and famines – had been reduced by indiscriminate shooting two or three years earlier.[19]

Stalin's motives, as it turned out, were centred elsewhere. He could now threaten oppositionists quite 'legally' with the death of their children as accomplices if they did not carry out his wishes. The mere fact of his accepting the disadvantages of publicizing the law gave it a sinister seriousness.

Why the age-limit of twelve was chosen is uncertain. Presumably there were oppositionists whose children were just within that limit. On the other hand, it might be suggested that Stalin had a rough precedent to which the opposition had made no objection. The youngest member of the Tsar's family, executed in the cellar at Ekaterinburg on 16 July 1918, was the Tsarevich Alexis, aged thirteen.

As to the precise timing, while it is true that Stalin often showed great foresight in these manoeuvres, it seems that we must associate this decree with another case that was just coming up.

Almost nothing has been published on the matter. But in effect it was an attempt to link the opposition with a plot against the life of Stalin. There seems to have been a grain of truth behind

*This was extended during the War to provide for 'the punishment of relatives of those who had been taken prisoner'.[17]

the story. There are several accounts of an alleged attempt on Stalin's life in the library of the Central Executive Committee by a young woman.[20] In the spring of 1935 about forty people were arrested.[21] They included Kremlin guards and N.K.V.D. men who seem to have been the alleged links in an assassination plot.[22] The covert struggle over this case dominated the ensuing period.

For once again Stalin determined to involve the opposition. Kamenev had a brother, the painter Rosenfeld, who was married to a doctor who worked in the Kremlin. Through this tenuous link he was now implicated. Yezhov, as Chairman of the Control Commission, demanded the death penalty. Opposition remained strong. Gorki was particularly outspoken.

Another leading advocate of moderation had already been silenced. Yenukidze's job as Secretary of the Central Executive Committee included general supervision of the Kremlin. It was easy to accuse him of negligence – or even complicity – in any plot formed in the old palace. Moreover, he had long been giving a certain amount of protection to minor non-political survivors from the pre-Revolutionary classes – with, of course, Stalin's concurrence. This too was now turned against him. He seems to have been removed from his posts as early as March, with the promise of an important position in the Caucasus, which never materialized.

Another prominent Kremlin figure and confidant of Yenukidze went with him. The Latvian Peterson, who had commanded Trotsky's train[23] – the celebrated mobile G.H.Q. of the Civil War – was Commandant of the Kremlin. He was not at once arrested, but was transferred to a post in the Kiev Military District, which he held until 1937, when he was liquidated.[24] He was later (in 1938) to be named as one of the military conspirators who were thinking in terms of a Kremlin *coup*, having allegedly been selected for the purpose by Yenukidze.[25]

Yenukidze was not the only Party veteran who had experienced qualms at the fierceness of the assault on the opposition. The Society of Old Bolsheviks, and the equally distinguished Society of Former Political Prisoners, had been collecting signatures in influential circles for a petition to the Politburo against the death penalty for the opposition.[26] This was now treated as factional activity. On 25 May a brief decree by the Central Committee abolished the Society of Old Bolsheviks, and appointed, to deal with its dissolution, a commission headed by Shkiryatov and consisting mainly of Stalin's young adherents, including Malenkov.[27]

The Society had had its own publishing house which printed the memoirs of its members and certain theoretical works. It was almost impossible that these, particularly the memoirs, should not have been offensive to the new regime. In fact Stalin was, as usual, combining a political move with the settlement of a personal grudge. Starting at the end of July, *Pravda* itself prominently serialized an example of what was now to be the only right sort of record of the Party's past, a 'History' of pre-Revolutionary Bolshevism in the Caucasus by Beria, which is simply Stalinist hagiography. The facts had previously been distorted, with hostile intent, it was said, by Yenukidze and Orakhelashvili. They had not given due prominence to Stalin – though in their time their works had appeared to strain facts in his favour rather than not: standards of adulation were changing.

Yenukidze's fall has lately been attributed entirely to Stalin's desire to inflate his own role in the history of the Caucasian Bolsheviks, and the responsibility is put on 'the notorious falsifier of Party history, the *provocateur* and adventurist, Beria'.[28] Beria's role, and the whole question of these memoirs, can only have been secondary; and this sort of interpretation anyhow takes too superficial a view of Stalin's motives. But still, this concern with suppressing and transforming the past certainly played its part. In fact, Old Bolshevik memoirs now ceased to be published. Kossior, who had evidently thought of writing some, was told by Petrovsky that Stalin was opposed to this.[29]

Early in June Yenukidze was politically outlawed. He was denounced, in one of the main items of the agenda at a Central Committee meeting held on 5–7 June, for 'political and personal dissoluteness'.[30] Yezhov reported on his errors, and the former Secretary of the Central Executive Committee was expelled from the Central Committee and from the Party.* Over the following weeks, the papers printed violent attacks on him by Stalin's

*He was replaced by Akulov, who had been serving as Prosecutor-General. It was now that Vyshinsky received that post.

young Party Secretaries in Leningrad and Moscow, Zhdanov
and Khrushchev. He was accused of taking 'enemies' under his
wing – 'former princes, ministers, courtiers, Trotskyites, etc. . . .
a counter-revolutionary nest',[31] and in general of 'rotten liberalism'.

These 'former princes' and so on seem to have been represented
by an aged quasi-aristocratic woman who tended the Kremlin
antiques,[32] and who was now inflated into an agent of the class
enemy. In one account, the girl alleged to have plotted against
Stalin's life was a countess.[33] In any case, the link with the case
boiling up in the Kremlin is undoubted. Yenukidze was not put
on trial at this time, being presumably charged with negligence
only. But he seems to have been under arrest not later than early
1937.[34]

The next blow was at the Society of Former Political Prisoners,
which was dissolved on 25 June, in the same way as the Society of
Old Bolsheviks had been. A commission headed by Yezhov was
appointed to deal with its effects. A number of its members who
had been especially closely involved in the campaign for clemency
were already, or were shortly to be, under arrest. The veteran
Lobov, particularly active in putting the case against intra-Party
terror, is said to have died of a heart attack while under interrogation.[35]

If the old revolutionaries had been offering a certain resistance,
the main revulsion from Stalin and his new line was to be found
in the very youngest generation of Communists. As we have seen,
openly seditious remarks were noted in their ranks by the
N.K.V.D. More threatening still, the Kirov murder inspired
various groups to talk of, and even to plan, in an amateurish
fashion which was no match for the police of the new regime,
the killing of Stalin. Either way, such circles were now invariably
arrested and shot. But the Komsomol as a whole also needed
thorough purging. Its reorganization with a view to eliminating
'enemies of the Party' was announced at the end of June.[36]

In general, Stalin's moves over the past six months had
strengthened his position in obvious ways. Even so, they had not
broken down the resistance to a death sentence on Kamenev. It
was clear that this could only be done by a massive purge of the

Stalinist moderates. And for this, the ground had not yet been adequately prepared. For the moment Stalin abandoned the project.

And so, on 27 July, Kamenev was sentenced at a secret trial to ten years' imprisonment under Article 58 (viii) of the Criminal Code, dealing with terrorist actions against Soviet officials.[37] His brother Rosenfeld appeared as a witness against him.[38] It is not known if any other oppositionists were accused. Nor do we know if the others accused of the alleged Kremlin plot came to trial at the same time as their alleged senior accomplice, or whether they had been dealt with already. Of the forty-odd sentences, only two death penalties are reported.

The heavy pressure exerted by Stalin over the summer had to some degree advanced his plans for a purge. The dissolution of the society uniting the Old Bolsheviks, the campaign against the 'rotten liberalism' of Yenukidze, the fresh sentence on Kamenev, had taken things a step further. Nevertheless, the going had been hard, and it had been impossible to produce a public trial or even a death sentence for Kamenev. Further and more thorough preparation was evidently necessary. The next months were spent in consolidating the gains achieved and laying the groundwork for an N.K.V.D. set-piece to crush the opposition.

THE N.K.V.D. PREPARES A TRIAL

From the point of view of the purges, the period from July 1935 to August 1936 was to all outward appearances something of an idyllic interlude. In the sense that nations without any history are the happiest, it seemed a greatly improved time. There were no deaths of Politburo members, no trials of important opposition-ists, no removals of leading political figures. The harvest, too, was reasonably good.

A plenum of the Central Committee held in December 1935 passed a long resolution on checking Party documents, which was later to be the organizational basis of the Purge at the grass roots. But in itself it appeared harmless. Moreover, it was an-nounced at the same time that the purge of the Party ordered in 1933 was now complete.

The Draft of a new Constitution had been occupying the minds of Bukharin and Radek, as the active members of a Commission set up for the purpose in February 1935.[39] It was ready in June 1936, and Bukharin, in particular, thought of it as a document which would make it impossible for the people any longer to be 'pushed aside'.[40]

It was indeed a model document, giving, for example, guarantees of freedom from arbitrary arrest (Article 127), inviolability of the home and secrecy of correspondence (Article 128), and indeed freedom of speech, of the press, of meetings and of demonstrations (Article 125). That Bukharin, who was mainly responsible for it, thought that it might be implemented shows that even he now imagined that a genuine relaxation was taking place.

Bukharin's view of the Communists at this time was 'They are all good people, ready for any sacrifice. If they are acting badly now, it is not because they are bad, but because the situation is bad. They must be persuaded that the country is not against them, but only that a change of policy is necessary.' He had come around to the view that Bolshevism needed humanizing, and had looked to the intellectuals – in particular, Ivan Pavlov and Gorki – to help him. Pavlov, the great physiologist, was strongly opposed to the Communists. When Bukharin's name was put up for election to the Academy of Sciences in the mid-twenties, Pavlov spoke against him as 'a person who is up to his knees in blood'. Eventually, however, the two men had become friendly. Bukharin is even quoted as wanting the intelligentsia to put up candidates under the New Constitution as a sort of 'second party',[41] not to oppose the regime, but to give constructive criticism – a vague utopianism, indeed.

In reality, Stalin had simply changed his tactics. Under the calm façade there was furious activity. He had ready all the ingredients which he was to bring together into the set-pieces of the Great Purge. First, he had developed direct control of the Secret Police, and set up other mechanisms of power responsible to himself alone, and capable, given careful tactics, of overcoming the official hierarchy of Party and State. Second, the tradition of faked trials for political purposes had been established, and not objected to in the Party, whose tradition of maintaining flat untruths for political purposes was in any case of still longer standing. Third, the former oppositionists had, under the particular pressures available in Communist life, already been induced to make admissions of error which they did not sincerely believe to be correct, in what they took to be the Party's interest. Fourth, his operatives were accustomed to the use of torture, blackmail and falsification – if as yet mainly on non-Party figures.

If his technical arrangements were complete, the same was evidently not so of his political preparations. It was still quite possible that he might have met with formidable opposition if he had set about the problem in the same way again. He chose a different method. The case was to be prepared in secret – not too difficult a matter, as the doomed Zinovievites and Trotskyites were already under arrest. It would take its course during the summer vacation, and in the absence of Stalin in particular. The death sentences would not be mentioned until they were pronounced; and even then every indication would be given that they would be commuted. But they would, on the contrary, be carried out without discussion.

At the very moment in the summer of 1935 when Stalin was retreating on the question of a death sentence for Kamenev, he was taking the first steps to gain the same result by his alternative method. A group of Komsomol students in the town of Gorki, said to have planned an attempt on Stalin, was one of many arrested at this time. They had not actually done anything beyond discussion, but already even this made the death penalty a foregone conclusion. The trial routine was about to be gone through, in the late summer, when the case was held for 'further investigation', under instructions from the Secretariat.[42]

The N.K.V.D. had selected this particular group because it had a ready-made way of linking them with Trotsky, and hence of building a vast political conspiracy around them. The link was through one of their own men, Valentin Olberg.

Olberg was a former agent of the Foreign Department of the N.K.V.D., and had worked in Berlin as a secret informer among the Trotskyites. In 1930 he had attempted to get a post as Trotsky's secretary, one of the first of the many N.K.V.D. attempts to penetrate Trotsky's ménage (which ended in success in 1940). Since 1935, Olberg had been working for the N.K.V.D. Secret Political Department, exposing Trotskyite tendencies in the important Gorki Pedagogical Institute, where the students in question worked. His nomination had been opposed by the local Party officials, in particular Yelin, head of the Provincial Committee's Propaganda and Education Section, since Olberg lacked qualifications and was a foreigner. Yelin, moreover, rightly complained that his documents seemed forged, and appealed to the Central Committee; but Yezhov then personally imposed Olberg.

By the beginning of 1936, the N.K.V.D. had made a good beginning in extending the scope of this Komsomol conspiracy. A number of professors at the Institute were arrested. And Olberg, with his foreign contacts, was ordered as a matter of Party and police discipline to confess to being a link between them and Trotsky. He was told that this was simply an N.K.V.D. assignment, and that whatever the verdict of the court he would be freed and given a post in the Far East. He signed whatever was required of him.[43] This was, in brief, that he had been sent by Trotsky to arrange the assassination of Stalin, recruiting professors and students to make the attempt when they went to Moscow for the 1936 May Day Parade.

The processing of the Olberg case was not straightforward, and took time. Yelin, who knew too much, was executed without trial,[44] though he was to be mentioned several times during the public hearings. Olberg's brother, P. Olberg, was implicated and his evidence was quoted in court, though he was not produced. Other accused included the Head of the Pedagogical Institute, Fedotov. He confessed, but perhaps did not seem reliable enough to present in public, for he was not brought to trial. Nelidov, a teacher of chemistry who was required as the hypothetical maker of bombs, was not a Communist and, in spite of violent pressure by one of the most vicious of the interrogators, the younger Kedrov, was not broken.

But by late February 1936 Olberg's story had been worked up into a usable version,[45] and the N.K.V.D. definitely selected it as the basis of the whole oppositionist 'plot'. However, Olberg's connexions were simply with Trotsky. It became necessary to provide the 'Trotskyite–Zinovievite Centre' with some Zinovievite links.

The head of the Secret Political Department, G. A. Molchanov, now held a conference of about forty N.K.V.D. executive officers. He told them that a vast conspiracy had been uncovered and that they would all be released from their ordinary duties and set to investigating it. The Politburo regarded the evidence as absolutely trustworthy, and the task was therefore simply to discover the details. The question of any accused being not guilty did not arise.[46]

The officers at once realized that the whole business was a frame-up, since they themselves were the men who had for years been in charge of supervision of the oppositionists, and they had detected no such activity. Moreover, if such a plot had come into being without their discovering it, they would clearly have been reprimanded at the very least. How little Stalin himself must have believed in the existence of any real plots was shown by the mere fact of his withdrawing so many of the most experienced officers from all the active departments of the Secret Police into what he knew to be an investigative farce.

In the N.K.V.D. as it was now, Stalin had a powerful and experienced instrument. At its head stood Yagoda. His deputy in security matters was Stalin's crony Agranov: the latter had finished his special operations at Leningrad and handed over that city to the dreadful Zakovsky, who is said to have boasted that if he had Karl Marx to interrogate he would soon make him confess that he was an agent of Bismarck.

The Secret Police machine proper was concentrated in the N.K.V.D.'s Chief Administration of State Security. This consisted of a highly organized array of departments, skilled in the ways of their trade, and practised in all modes of investigation, interrogation and falsification. Its leading officers had almost all been with it for a decade, and had coped with the great cases of the late twenties and early thirties. (The N.K.V.D. controlled, in addition to this Secret Police machine, the 'militia' [ordinary police], the frontier guards, its own internal troop formations, the fire service, and the labour camps, whose main administration, GULAG, under Matvei Berman, was already receiving a vast number of assorted purgees.)

Yagoda and Agranov themselves, and Yezhov representing the Central Committee, played a prominent part in the organization of the trial, and Stalin personally conducted the key conferences. Under them, the Secret Political Department was technically responsible for the whole operation, though it now had at its disposition the services of a number of officers from the other departments of State Security, including their chiefs.

The *Secret Political Department*, which had been the kernel of the Cheka from the beginning,[47] was still the key centre of Secret Police operations. That is, it had the overall responsibility of supervising all the country's organizations, and carrying on the political struggle against all hostile political elements. It was headed by G. A. Molchanov, an unscrupulous careerist, and his deputy G. Lyushkov.

The *Economic Department* had security responsibility for all industry and agriculture (except for transport, dealt with by the Transport Department). In Soviet conditions, this gave it a role as weighty, in a general way, as that of the Secret Political Department, and it had the main responsibility for trials such as the Shakhty which, though in a general sense political, were centred on economic crimes. Its head, L. G. Mironov, was a man with an extraordinary memory, which was to be of great use in composing and mastering the details of the first two trials. At the same time as he ran his vast department, he acted as assistant to Yagoda in the whole of the State Security side of the N.K.V.D. He is described as a conscientious Party man who was depressed by the prosecution of the Old Bolsheviks.[48] Previous cases that he had organized, and which do not seem to have depressed him similarly, included the 'Industrial Party' and the Metro-Vic Trials – cases, with all their political importance, definable as 'economic'. The Zinoviev Trial had no economic component. Nevertheless, Mironov was given an important role.

The *Operative Department* was responsible for guarding leading personnel and installations and investigating terrorist acts against them. Its main concern at this time was the protection of Stalin.

Its head K. V. Pauker or his Deputy Volovich were almost continually with him except when he was actually in his heavily guarded offices, and Chertok, their chief subordinate, also spent much time organizing his local defence.

Pauker was a sort of evil buffoon. He had been a barber and valet to opera stars in Budapest, and had himself a turn for comic acting. Taken prisoner by the Russians in 1916, he had become one of the group of Communists which emerged from that milieu. An ignorant and uneducated man without any political convictions, he was recruited to the Cheka, like so many other foreigners in those days, to work on searches and arrests. He rose by becoming a personal attendant again, this time to Menzhinsky, who came to rely on him and finally appointed him head of the Kremlin bodyguard and chief of the Operative Department. He was on close terms with Stalin, who even allowed him to shave him.⁴⁹

The *Special Department* in general ran the administration and registration of all the Secret Police networks and centralized the information about the various grades of 'anti-Soviet elements'. Its head was M. I. Gay.

The *Foreign Department* dealt with espionage and terror abroad. Its head, A. A. Slutsky, was a sly intriguer, who played an important role in the major interrogations. His deputies were Boris Berman and Shpigelglas.

The *Transport Department*, under A. M. Shanin, was the only one not deeply involved, having its hands full with Kaganovich's endless purges on the railways.

There was a good deal of flexibility in these arrangements. Postings between departments were fairly frequent. And reorganization involving the transfer of lesser matters between the departments was also quite common.

Such was the order of battle of the shock troops of repression Stalin was now launching on the helpless prisoners in the Lubyanka.

They were assisted by another organization – the Prosecutor's Office. This had not been centralized on an All-Union basis until 1933, when it became one of the most centralized bodies in the U.S.S.R., having all its legal agencies completely and uniformly subordinate to the Prosecutor-General in Moscow, who was now Vyshinsky. He announced his operative principle – that any discrepancies between the commands of the law and those of the Revolution 'must be solved only by the subordination of the formal commands of law to those of Party policy'.[50] His chief assistant was G. Roginsky, a fanatic who was to defend mass liquidation even after he himself had been purged and sent to a penal camp.

A former oppositionist, Isak Reingold, Chairman of the Cotton Syndicate, was now pulled in. He was a friend of Sokolnikov's and was connected with Kamenev. A strong man, still only thirty-eight, he proved hard to break. He was interrogated for three weeks, often for periods of forty-eight hours at a time without sleep or food, by one of the worst N.K.V.D. men, Chertok. The order to arrest his family was given in his presence. Finally, he was handed a death sentence and told it would be carried out automatically if he did not testify at once. He still refused to do so, but said that he would sign anything if so instructed by the Party. Yagoda refused to accept these terms and the interrogation dragged on. Finally Yezhov intervened and personally ordered Reingold in the name of the Central Committee to provide the evidence required. By early summer, satisfactory accusations against the Zinoviev group were being obtained from him.

The N.K.V.D. also arrested Richard Pickel, a writer and a playwright who had served in the Civil War. At the time of his arrest he was working at the Kamerny Theatre in Moscow and took no interest in politics. But he had at one time been head of Zinoviev's secretariat.

Pickel was a personal friend of a number of N.K.V.D. officers. He resisted for some time, but was promised his life by his friends. Yagoda himself confirmed this to him. Pickel agreed to give evidence against Zinoviev and himself only. As to all the others, he made a rule that he would only incriminate them if they had already been incriminated by others, or had given testimony against themselves.[51]

The confessions, apart from Olberg's, had been obtained with some difficulty. Stalin is said to have brought about 300 former oppositionists from prisons and isolators[52] for the N.K.V.D. to test for suitability as accused. By May, about fifteen suitable confessions had been obtained, and more were coming in.

It was not necessary that all these should be used in detail (in fact, the trial was to be limited to eight political figures plus eight minor 'accomplices', mainly *provocateurs*). The immediate purpose was to present the N.K.V.D.'s accumulation of confessions to the main accused, as yet untouched, with a view to putting the basic pressure on them.

In mid May Stalin held a conference with a number of the leading N.K.V.D. officials, and ordered the N.K.V.D. to produce further links with Trotsky. Molchanov, much to the anger of the Foreign Department, nominated two more N.K.V.D. agents, who had been working as its representatives in the German Communist Party and in the Comintern, Fritz David and Berman-Yurin.[53] They were arrested about the end of May[54] and had no choice but to accept their instructions. They too claimed that they had each visited Trotsky and received orders from him to kill Stalin.

Two more figures, Moissei Lurye, a scientist, and Nathan Lurye, a surgeon, whose conduct in court led even Western journalists to suspect them of being *agents provocateurs*, are also reported by fellow prisoners, in on different charges, as scarcely bothering to conceal this.[55] They were supposed to be Trotskyite terrorists. With their evidence, a mass of material was now accumulating against the oppositionists.

'THE TROTSKYITE-ZINOVIEVITE CENTRE'

By early June 1936 everything was in order, and the scenario fully prepared, but for the lack of confessions from the principal accused.

The selection of leading victims had presented certain difficulties. The Zinovievite side of the matter was clear enough. Zinoviev, Kamenev and Evdokimov were the acknowledged leaders of the faction, and with Bakayev, as their senior link to the Kirov murder, they made an entirely satisfactory group. Moreover, they had all gone through a long routine of confession, and negotiation for confession, over the past years and were already half lost. But to extend the plot to Trotsky's followers, as Stalin wished, was not so simple.

Trotsky himself was not available, and most of his former supporters, having abjured his views, were now working in responsible positions. None of them had been seriously criticized for years. Trotskyism had of course been under violent attack, and various minor Trotskyites had been arrested and exiled since the Kirov murder. But the long personal campaign which had been grinding at Zinoviev and his followers for eighteen months had no equivalent victims from Trotsky's side.

As was later pointed out, the 'Centre' contained 'not . . . a single one of the old political leaders' from the Trotskyite side.[56] The three leading Trotskyites finally selected were not politically on a level with their Zinovievite counterparts. I. N. Smirnov, Mrachkovsky and Ter-Vaganian were all, however, men of repute in the Party. (Trotsky's Army Inspector-General, the heroic giant Muralov, had been arrested on 17 April, and it was doubtless intended to use him too; but he held out until December and this had to be postponed.)

Smirnov alone had been a member of the Central Committee, but he at least was a most distinguished Old Bolshevik. He was one of the earliest and most respected of all the Communists. A factory worker, he had been an active revolutionary from the age of seventeen, and had often been arrested.[57] He had spent many years in Tsarist prisons and in Arctic exile. He had fought in the 1905 Revolution, and in the Civil War led the Fifth Red Army to its victory over Kolchak. Known as 'the Lenin of Siberia', he had ruled there for some years after the Revolution.

Smirnov had been proposed as the leading Secretary of the Party in 1922, just before the job went to Stalin.[58] After being exiled with the other Trotskyites in 1927 he had recanted but, during the Ryutin period, had spoken approvingly of the proposals to remove Stalin and had been in jail ever since. Stalin thus had a particular grudge against him.

Perhaps it was this that led Stalin to insist on his inclusion in the 'Centre' in spite of the physical impossibility of his having participated in anything of the kind. For, as even Agranov is said to have tentatively objected, there would be some difficulty in making the charge plausible, since Smirnov had been held in jail throughout the period of the alleged plot. Stalin 'gave Agranov a sullen look and said, "Don't be afraid, that's all."'[59]

Mrachkovsky had also fought in Siberia. He had run Trotsky's underground printing-press in 1927, and had been the first oppositionist to be arrested. He was regarded as simply a 'fighter'. Ter-Vaganian, an intellectual Armenian described as both honest and unambitious, had fought with great distinction in the Revolution and Civil War, and afterwards had reverted to ideology and journalism. He too had been in exile in Siberia since 1933.

A fourth Trotskyite was thrown in for good measure – Dreitzer, the former head of Trotsky's bodyguard and prominent in the 1927 demonstrations. He was not accused of being a member of the Centre, but rather as the head organizer of assassin groups.

The first examinations of the leading accused were a total failure. Smirnov, on 20 May, simply replied 'I deny that; again I deny; I deny.'[60] Mrachkovsky's key interrogation is said to have lasted ninety hours, without result, though Stalin rang up at intervals to inquire how things were going.[61] He was at this point taken before Molotov, who made him some sort of offer; but Mrachkovsky simply spat at him.[62]

Zinoviev too made 'obdurate denials'.[63] Bakayev made 'persistent denials'.[64] In general, all the genuine oppositionists refused to confess and pointed out that they had been in prison or exile in the remotest parts of the country during most of the period, and under close N.K.V.D. supervision during the rest of it. Molchanov then gave the interrogators to understand that earlier orders about not using unlawful means of interrogation were not to be taken too seriously.[65] Evdokimov, who is reported to have behaved very stoutly and to have denounced the regime as hypocrites and assassins, is said to have been treated with particular brutality.[66]

The interrogation of Zinoviev and Kamenev was put in charge of the most senior officials, Agranov, Molchanov and Mironov. Zinoviev was ill at the time with a liver ailment, and the routine interrogation was postponed.[67] He had once again written to the

Politburo vaguely accepting 'responsibility' for the assassination of Kirov. This was returned with an insistence on 'greater sincerity'.[68]

With Kamenev, the attempt was made to secure a confession by ordinary interrogative methods. Mironov conducted it. But Kamenev resisted him in spite of all his efforts, exposing Reingold at a 'confrontation' and in general standing firm.

Mironov reported to Stalin that Kamenev was refusing to confess, and later gave an account of the conversation to a close acquaintance:

'You think that Kamenev may not confess?' asked Stalin, his eyes slyly screwed up.

'I don't know,' Mironov answered. 'He doesn't yield to persuasion.'

'You don't know?' inquired Stalin with marked surprise, staring at Mironov. 'Do you know how much our state weighs, with all the factories, machines, the army, with all the armaments and the navy?'

Mironov and all those present looked at Stalin with surprise.

'Think it over and tell me,' demanded Stalin. Mironov smiled, believing that Stalin was getting ready to crack a joke. But Stalin did not intend to jest. He looked at Mironov quite in earnest. 'I am asking you, how much does all that weigh?' insisted he.

Mironov was confused. He waited, still hoping Stalin would turn everything into a joke, but Stalin kept staring at him and waited for an answer. Mironov shrugged his shoulders and, like a schoolboy undergoing an examination, said in an irresolute voice, 'Nobody can know that, Yosif Vissarionovich. It is in the realm of astronomical figures.'

'Well, and can one man withstand the pressure of that astronomical weight?' asked Stalin sternly.

'No,' answered Mironov.

'Now then, don't tell me any more that Kamenev, or this or that prisoner, is able to withstand that pressure. Don't come to report to me,' said Stalin to Mironov, 'until you have in this briefcase the confession of Kamenev!'[69]

The transfer of Kamenev's case to the third-rate bully Chertok also produced no results, though the usual pressures of sleeplessness, semi-starvation and general bullying must have begun to wear him down.[70]

THE DEATH OF GORKI

Stalin planned to carry through the execution of the opposition-ists regardless of possible revulsion in the Party. For, as ever, he was prepared to deal with this by his usual combination of hard-ness and manoeuvre. The only figure who could not be handled in this fashion and who, if alive, would be difficult to silence, was Maxim Gorki, who 'remained until his death the only person whom Stalin was compelled to take into consideration, to some extent at least'.[71] It is possible that had he lived the August Trial might have had a different denouement. He became ill on 31 May,[72] and died on 18 June.

When Gorki had opposed the October Revolution in 1917, Stalin had attacked him in a tone more venomous than any other Bolshevik's. He had even said (quite falsely), in an assault upon an article of Gorki's entitled 'I Cannot Keep Silent', that Gorki and his type had 'kept silent' when landlords and capitalists were attacking the peasantry and the proletariat, that they reproached only the Revolution and not the counter-revolution. Gorki's work had of course been one long blast at the ruling classes, and he had been associated with the Social Democrats from the start. Stalin went on to write that the Revolution was quite prepared to throw away 'great names', including Gorki's, if necessary.

Gorki's own views were by no means lacking in pugnacity. He several times remarked that if 'the enemy' did not surrender 'he must be destroyed'. Nevertheless, he had protected both Pilnyak and Zamyatin during the outcry against those writers in 1930 – and this alone must have been very galling to Stalin, particularly in the case of Pilnyak (see p. 440). And since then, more signifi-cantly still to our point, he had intervened strongly in favour of the policy of reconciliation and been an outspoken opponent of the earlier attempts to destroy Kamenev and Zinoviev.

His mere existence was a factor strengthening the morale of Kamenev and others in their ordeal. His voice, they could be sure, would be raised against the new persecution of them, as soon as this became publicly known. To some degree knowledge of this must have fortified their resistance. By the same token his death at this particular time must have been a moral blow, and have made Stalin's task easier.

As with Kuibyshev, we have a case of a death at a time very convenient to Stalin. Most deaths at times convenient to Stalin were so for the obvious reason.

The doctors attending Gorki were later to be accused of murdering him on Yagoda's orders. When we come to the Bukharin Trial of 1938, at which this charge was made, we shall consider the evidence (see pp. 540–61). Meanwhile, we may note that the current trial was held as soon after the necessary confessions as was feasible; and, moreover, seems to be dated to suit the absence on holiday of some of the Politburo. If Gorki had hung on even a few months, he would certainly have represented an impediment to Stalin's plans. The indefinite postponement of the trial would have been at the least awkward, and time would have been given for the mustering of opposition in the Central Committee. To have proceeded with the trial and *not* executed the oppositionists would have been contrary to Stalin's whole plan. But to have carried this out regardless would, with Gorki alive, have had disadvantages. A powerful voice would have supported and heartened the already restless elements in the leadership; and while it might have been possible, it would not have been easy, to silence the writer.

All such considerations are merely logical, and prove nothing. But Stalin was, in his way, a logical man. He was not averse to having people murdered, and his respect for literature was not such as to prevent his disposing of many other Russian writers of repute. And the evidence we have, as we shall see, points strongly to unnatural death.

ZINOVIEV SURRENDERS

It now seemed suitable for Stalin to make a direct political approach to Zinoviev and Kamenev. Yezhov gave them what were represented as the Politburo's instructions, to 'disarm in a manner that will preclude any hope on your part of raising your head against the Party ever again'. The alternative was a trial by military court behind closed doors and the execution of the entire opposition, including the thousands in the camps.

Zinoviev refused and a similar attempt on Kamenev was also unsuccessful, though Yezhov this time directly threatened that Kamenev's son would be shot if he did not give in.

A tighter interrogative routine was then inflicted on them. Yagoda had the heating put on in the cells, though the weather was now hot. Zinoviev's physical condition was very bad, and Kamenev was beginning to weaken under the threats to his son, whose arrest was finally ordered in his presence. In July, Zinoviev, after an all-night interrogation, asked to speak to Kamenev, and when they had discussed the matter they agreed to go on trial on condition that Stalin would confirm his promises to them, of executing neither themselves nor their followers, in the presence of the whole Politburo.

This was accepted. However, when they were taken to the alleged Politburo meeting only Stalin, Voroshilov and Yezhov were present. Stalin explained that they formed a 'commission' of the Politburo authorized to hear the case.[73]

This appeal to the Politburo, and Stalin's partial evasion of it, presents some interesting points. Both appeal and evasion suggest that there were still some men in the Politburo who might have been relied on to try to have its guarantees respected. In fact it is curious that as late as the execution of Rudzutak in 1938, some attempt at a similar appeal is suggested when we are told that 'he was not even called before the Central Committee Political Bureau because Stalin did not want to talk to him'.[74]

Though shaken by the absence of the other Politburo members, the prisoners, after some argument, finally accepted Stalin's terms, which guaranteed their lives, the lives of their supporters and the liberty of their families. (A member of Zinoviev's family told Krivitsky[75] that one reason for capitulation was 'to save his family', and in Kamenev's case the same is obviously true – and can be seen in his final plea.)

With the surrender of Zinoviev and Kamenev, the game was in Stalin's hands. The trial was on. The lesser political figures were expendable at a pinch, and in any case no stronger argument could be put to them than the willingness of their seniors to go along with the trial and accept Stalin's promises.

Pending the pulling together of these last loose threads, the political preparation for the case could now go forward. On 14 January 1936 there had been a ruling from the Central Committee that all members should turn in their Party documents for new ones, with a view to screening unworthy members. Now, on 29 July 1936, a top-secret letter of the Central Committee pointed out that several of those now under arrest had, in spite of all previous measures, managed to keep their Party cards, though 'all boundaries have been obliterated' between 'spies, *provocateurs*, White Guards, *kulaks*' and 'the Trotskyites and Zinovievites'. It called for a renewal of 'revolutionary vigilance', and asserted firmly the main duty of the Party membership in the forthcoming period: 'The inalienable quality of every Bolshevik under present conditions should be the ability to recognize an enemy of the Party, no matter how well he may be masked.' [76]

On receiving the circular, local officials began a further round of feverish delation. The First Secretary of Kozelsk *rayon*, for example, wrote to the Provincial Committee denouncing not only local inhabitants, but also people he had met in previous posts and now thought suspicious, commenting in each case, 'It is possible that up to this time he has not been unmasked.' [77]

This was, in fact, the political preparation of the Party branches throughout the country for the campaign about to be launched, in connexion with the Zinoviev Trial, against all the enemies of the General Secretary. As one result, even longer lists of anti-Soviet elements than those already in existence were compiled everywhere, and the mass Purge began to get under way.

On 20 July a U.S.S.R. People's Commissariat of Justice was set up, a minor but useful organizational change.

Meanwhile, the lesser oppositionists doomed by the Zinoviev-Kamenev capitulation were being broken down. Kamenev's own confession was under way on 13 July. Mrachkovsky was confessing by 20 July, and on 21 July he had a 'confrontation' with Smirnov. There are two slightly different accounts of this. [78] One of them, evidently based on the official record, has these old friends quarrelling because of what Smirnov regarded as Mrachkovsky's weakness in surrendering. The other shows them as still on good terms at the end. In any case, Mrachkovsky made some such remark as 'Why, Ivan Nikitich, you want to get out of a sordid bloody business with a clean shirt?' And Smirnov's firm comment was 'invention and slander!' [79]

Further pressure was brought upon Smirnov by the arrest of his former wife Safonova, who was now implicated. She signed evidence against herself and him under the promise that this was the only way to save their lives. She was then, in August, brought to a 'confrontation' with him in Gay's office, where she broke down and pleaded with him to go to trial. Since Kamenev and Zinoviev had already confessed, it would be best for him to stick with them and go to public trial, in which case there would be no question of shooting them. [80]

Smirnov seems also to have been 'confronted' with Zinoviev, who said he was confessing and argued in favour of Smirnov doing so too. Zinoviev said that he really believed that his admissions would open the way to his returning to the Party, and that Stalin – whom he referred to by his old Party nickname of Koba – was at present the focus of the Party's will, and would come to a compromise with the opposition, since in practice he could not do without the 'Lenin guard' in the long run. Smirnov replied that on the contrary it was obvious that the Politburo wanted the physical annihilation of the opposition, otherwise there was no point in the case. [81]

The interrogator told Smirnov that it was useless for him to resist, as there were plenty of witnesses against him. And, moreover, it was not only Smirnov but his family too that would suffer – as the assassin Nikolayev's had suffered. Smirnov knew nothing of the arrest of his family and took this simply to be a disgusting threat by the interrogator. But shortly afterwards, on his way to an interrogation, he saw his daughter at the other end of the corridor, held by two guards. It is not known what happened to her. Her mother was sent to a women's camp at Kotlas where she heard from her relations that the daughter was still in prison. The mother was shot in the camp in March or April 1938, during a mass execution of 1,300 undesirables. [82]

Under all these pressures Smirnov finally gave way, but he

would only consent to make a partial confession. This would not have been accepted from anyone else, but time was getting short and Stalin wanted Smirnov in the trial at all costs. Smirnov also managed to have Safonova removed from the list of defendants, and she only appeared as a 'witness' – not that this was any guarantee of survival. All this rankled with Stalin, and Yagoda and Mironov were later charged with having shielded Smirnov.[83]

By 5 August,* Smirnov was well into his confession. On 10 August Evdokimov had begun his. On the 11th the official orders for holding the trial were given by the Central Executive Committee, and the indictment was drawn up on 14 August. On the same day Ter-Vaganian, who had vaguely admitted the existence of the Centre on 16 July, was making a full confession.

The last confessions were eased, and the earlier ones fortified, by the publication on 11 August of a decree which (going back, to some extent, on that of 1 December 1934) re-established public hearings and the use of lawyers, and allowed appeals from the accused for three days after the sentence. The timing of this decree is decisive. While clearly intended to strengthen the accused's hope that a reprieve would be granted, it was also designed, of course, to put the same idea about among the apprehensive Party membership. These included some of the interrogators themselves. It seems that reassurances that no death sentences would be carried out were believed by, for example, Boris Berman, and that this led him to quite sincere advice to Ter-Vaganian that the best course open to him was to surrender.[84] And, with the publication of the indictment on 15 August, it was at last necessary to take such measures as would best put the case over to the Party as a whole. The preparatory work had been done in great secrecy. There was no preliminary discussion in the Politburo. 'The trial came as a complete surprise not only for the rank and file of Party workers but also to members of the Central Committee and some members of the Politburo.'[85]

To objectors in the current leadership, Stalin now had a simple answer: the matter was in the hands of the Prosecutor and the

*These dates are those given sporadically in the indictment and in the evidence of the trial.

court. It was they who were so keen on legality, after all. They must let justice take its course. And the 11 August decree was a considerable reassurance.

Opposition to the trial would in any case have been very difficult to organize once confessions had been obtained. But Stalin played safe by springing it on the country and the Party, and on the Politburo itself, when he himself was on holiday, and many of the rest of the leadership were also scattered around the country. Molotov and Kalinin, for example, are said to have gone on holiday in ignorance of the forthcoming massacre.[86]

Whether this is true of Molotov in quite this form seems dubious. It is true that his row with Mrachkovsky does not in itself indicate complicity in the plan to kill the defendants. However that may be, there now came a startling proof that Stalin was discontented with him.

For when the indictment came out, a sensation was caused in Moscow by the omission from the list of those the conspirators were planning to kill of one important Soviet leader – Molotov. Stalin, Ordzhonikidze, Voroshilov, Kaganovich, Kossior, Postyshev and Zhdanov were named (the last three specifically as the targets of local terrorist branches in the Ukraine and Leningrad), but not the Soviet Premier. Right through the trial, the confessions gave the same listing, and it was repeated in Vyshinsky's final speech for the prosecution. In Soviet conditions this was taken to mean, and without any doubt at all really meant, that Molotov was in disfavour. An N.K.V.D. defector account[87] says that Stalin crossed Molotov's name out of the early evidence (where it had naturally been included) with his own hand, and that Yagoda then instructed the interrogators not to bring it in again. This story must be substantially true. Without a personal decision of Stalin's, Molotov could not have been omitted.

There seem grounds for supposing that Molotov had in some way dragged his feet about the plan to destroy the Old Bolsheviks. And the episode lends at least some credence to the reports that in the discussions about the Ryutin Case in 1932 he had not whole-heartedly supported Stalin in calling for extreme measures. (It may be noted, too, that in all the unofficial stories of the period, while Voroshilov is found more than once as a trusty accomplice of Stalin's in interviews with the accused, Molotov scarcely appears at all.)

Thus, from around May 1936 until the end of the trial in August, Molotov faced elimination. He went on his holidays under careful N.K.V.D. supervision.[88]

Some weeks after the Zinoviev Trial he seems to have returned to favour. His name *was* included as a target of the conspirators in the 1937–8 Trials – even though this raised the anomaly that the later batches of conspirators had allegedly plotted with Zinoviev and Kamenev for this purpose, but Zinoviev and Kamenev had inexplicably omitted to confess it.

Stalin's pressure had brought Molotov to heel. Henceforth, there were no reports of anything but complicity on his part in the Great Purge. Why Stalin saved him cannot be more than guessed at. He was, of course (or was to be after Ordzhonikidze's removal), the only Old Bolshevik of any repute at all among Stalin's ruling group.

Meanwhile, it was impossible for Molotov, or anyone else, to interfere with the trial, though they could hope that it would end merely with prison sentences.

THE TRIAL BEGINS

At ten minutes after midday on 19 August the trial opened before a session of the Military Collegium of the Supreme Court in the little 'October Hall' of the Trade Union House – chosen in preference to the huge 'Hall of Columns' which had been the scene of earlier show trials. A large, high, bright room, decorated rather floridly in the Russian nineteenth-century style with white Corinthian columns and light blue walls, it had formerly been one of the ballrooms of what was then the Nobles' Club. In this small hall there was room for no more than 150-odd Soviet citizens and thirty-odd foreign journalists and diplomats. The foreign audience was crucial to the show. Unanimously hostile criticism might have prevented further performances. Too many of these privileged witnesses allowed themselves to be taken in by an improbable plot and incredible details. The Soviet spectators

were all selected by the N.K.V.D. and were, in fact, mainly
N.K.V.D. clerks and officials. The crowd is reported to have
been under instructions to raise a commotion at a given signal,
which might be necessary if any untoward outbreak from one of
the prisoners took place.[89] High officials of the Central Committee and the Government were not able to get in. Nor were relatives of the accused.[90]

The court commandant, in uniform tunic and breeches, and
wearing the magenta hatband and collar tabs of the N.K.V.D.,
called the court to order. Everyone stood, and the judges took
their seats. Presiding was Ulrikh, a fat man, with dewlaps like a
bloodhound and little pig eyes. His shaven head rose to a point.
His neck bulged over the collar of his uniform. His voice was soft
and oily. He had much experience in political cases.

On his right was another veteran of these trials, Matulevich,
who had presided over the mass slaughter of the Leningrad
'White Guards' in December 1934. On his left was a figure of
great interest to Westerners, the unimpressive, thin-faced
Divisional Military Jurist I. I. Nikitchenko. Ten years later he
was to appear on the Supreme Allied Tribunal at Nuremberg,
with the most distinguished judges of Britain, America and
France, to preside over the trial of Goering and others.* He
represented a judicial tradition so different from that of the rest of
the Tribunal that his mere presence may be thought to have made
a mockery of those proceedings.

One important respect in which Soviet justice differed from
that practised by his future colleagues in Nuremberg was that
sentences had been prepared beforehand by non-judicial authorities. 'The vicious practice was condoned of having the N.K.V.D.
prepare lists of persons whose cases were under jurisdiction of
the Military Collegium and whose sentences were prepared in
advance. Yezhov would send these lists to Stalin personally for
his approval of the proposed punishment. . . . He approved these
lists.'[92] It was even the case that 'Kaganovich, before court
sittings on various cases had come to an end, would personally

---

*He is also mentioned by General Gorbatov as presiding in 1939 over
the four- or five-minute farce which sentenced him to fifteen years' imprisonment.[91] He died in good odour in 1967.

edit the draft sentences and arbitrarily insert charges that suited him, such as allegations that acts of terrorism had been planned against his person'[93], while Molotov is described as personally changing a sentence on a 'wife of an enemy of the people' from imprisonment to death when the list went through his hands.[94] In the case now before Nikitchenko and his colleagues, there is no reason to doubt that the sentences were part of the original script, and had been imposed by the General Secretary himself.*

Three large and healthy N.K.V.D. soldiers, with rifles and fixed bayonets, escorted the prisoners to the dock, behind a low wooden bar along the right-hand wall of the courtroom, and took up positions guarding them. The accused had gained a little weight and caught up on their sleep in the few days just past. But they still looked pale and worn.

Just before the trial, Yagoda and Yezhov had had a conference with Zinoviev, Kamenev, Evdokimov, Bakayev, Mrachkovsky and Ter-Vaganian. Yezhov repeated Stalin's assurance that their lives would be spared, and also warned them that a single attempt at 'treachery' would be regarded as implicating the whole group.[96]

Now they sat, ill at ease among the *agents provocateurs* scattered among them and separating them. The practice of trying a group of important political prisoners with various second-rate crooks (or alleged crooks), as though they formed one group, is an old technique. At the trial of Danton and the Moderates on 13–14 Germinal, he and his four closest followers were mingled in with men accused as thieves and common spies, and each was carefully linked with the others by joint accusations. The Soviet press was doing just such a job. An angry and violent campaign filled the papers, where, meanwhile, other and contrary themes were appearing – in particular, almost daily photographs of a series of airmen, like those of the astronauts a generation later. These were men like Chkalov, who with his crew flew a new Soviet plane on a round tour of the country to the Far East and back, and Kokkinaki who produced a series of altitude records.

* Just as the Czechoslovak investigation of the Slansky Trial made in 1968 established that 'the individual sentences had been settled beforehand by the Political Secretariat'.[95]

They were photographed with Stalin and others, being received in the Politburo, being awarded Orders, and simply on their own. Through them, an air of youth and progress, of the triumph of the young Stalinist generation, was projected at the same time as the forces of darkness represented by the Old Bolsheviks were being dissipated.

At the side of the room, opposite the doomed representatives of anti-Stalinism, Vyshinsky sat at a small table, with his trim grey moustache and hair, neatly dressed in stiff white collar and well-cut dark suit.

Ulrikh went through the formalities of identification and asked if there were objections to the court and if the accused wanted defending lawyers. The answer to both questions was a unanimous negative. The secretary of the court then read the indictment. This based itself on the trial of January 1935, at which, it said, Zinoviev and his colleagues had concealed their direct responsibility for the Kirov murder. The since-revealed circumstances showed that they and the Trotskyites, who had practised terrorism earlier still, had formed a united bloc at the end of 1932. The bloc had been joined also by the Lominadze group. They had received instructions, through special agents, from Trotsky. In fulfilling these, they had organized terrorist groups which had 'prepared a number of practical measures' for the assassination of Stalin, Voroshilov, Kaganovich, Kirov, Ordzhonikidze, Zhdanov, Kossior, Postyshev and others:[97] one of these terrorist groups had actually murdered Kirov. They had no programme other than murder.

Trotsky had sent written instructions to Dreitzer, who had passed them to Mrachkovsky, to assassinate Stalin and Voroshilov. The five junior accused, together with Holtzman, had been personally sent by Trotsky or his son Sedov to assist in these acts. Olberg, in addition, had had contacts with the Gestapo. All the accused had fully admitted their guilt, with the exception of I. N. Smirnov, whose full guilt was, however, proved by the confessions of the other accused. He had made only a partial confession – of belonging to 'the united centre' and being personally connected with Trotsky up to the time of his arrest in 1933; and of having received, in 1932, instructions from Trotsky to organize terror. He had denied, however, taking part in terroristic activities.

The indictment concluded by mentioning various names of men who were to be tried separately: 'The cases of Gertik, Grinberg, Y. Gaven, Karev, Kuzmichev, Konstant, Matorin, Paul Olberg, Radin, Safonova, Faivilovich, D. Shmidt and Esterman, in view of the fact that investigation is still proceeding, have been set aside for separate trial.' [98] Matorin, who had been Zinoviev's private secretary, was elsewhere said to be still under investigation with a view to later trial 'in connexion with another case'. [99] None of these men was ever to come to public trial, and in most cases we know nothing whatever of their fate.

After the reading of the indictment, the accused pleaded guilty on all counts, with the exception of Smirnov and Holtzman. Smirnov admitted belonging to the Centre, and to having received terrorist instructions from Trotsky, but denied participation in preparing or executing terrorist acts. Holtzman, too, though admitting having brought terrorist instructions from Trotsky, denied himself participating in terrorism. After a fifteen-minute recess, *Mrachkovsky* was called upon to testify.

Under Vyshinsky's questioning, he recounted the formation of the Centre and the planning of terrorism under instructions from Trotsky and his son Sedov, partly passed through Smirnov and partly by a letter from Trotsky in invisible ink sent him through Dreitzer. Under Smirnov there had been formed a Trotskyite group consisting of himself (Mrachkovsky), Ter-Vaganian, and Smirnov's former wife Safonova. Dreitzer joined them and they had a number of lesser agents. [100]

When Mrachkovsky implicated Smirnov in direct terrorist activity, Smirnov several times denied the evidence, and there were warm wrangles between him and Vyshinsky. Zinoviev, called on to confirm the story, added that the murder of Kirov had been a joint enterprise involving both Zinovievites and Trotskyites, including Smirnov. Kamenev also confirmed this. The joint terror network was thus sketched out right at the start of the trial. For good measure Mrachkovsky also implicated Lominadze (who had committed suicide the previous year), [101] and a Red Army group of assassins headed by Divisional Commander Dmitri Shmidt. This latter charge was to be of far-reaching significance.

Mrachkovsky was followed by *Evdokimov*, who said he had deceived the court in January 1935. He then explained how he, Bakayev, Zinoviev and Kamenev had organized the Kirov assassination. The plan had been to get Stalin at the same time: '. . . Bakayev warned Nikolayev and his accomplices that they must wait for Zinoviev's signal,' said Evdokimov, 'that they must fire simultaneously with the shots to be fired in Moscow and Kiev.'[102] (Mrachkovsky had been quoted in the indictment as having said at the preliminary examination that 'Stalin was to be killed first', but in any case Kirov was not supposed to precede the General Secretary to the grave.) Evdokimov for the first time involved the Old Bolshevik Grigori Sokolnikov, former candidate member of the Politburo and still a candidate member of the Central Committee.

In the course of Evdokimov's evidence Smirnov, once more implicated, again denied the testimony.

At the evening session *Dreitzer* recounted his connexions with Sedov and his organization of two other terrorist groups for killing Stalin and Voroshilov respectively. As to Smirnov, 'Trotsky's deputy in the U.S.S.R.', Dreitzer remarked harshly, 'There could be no acting on one's own, no orchestra without a conductor among us. I am surprised at the assertions of Smirnov, who, according to his words, both knew and did not know, spoke and did not speak, acted and did not act. This is not true!'[103] Smirnov again denied the evidence, and said he had not discussed terrorism with Dreitzer. Zinoviev was again called to confirm Smirnov's role, and did so at length.

Reingold, who followed, extended the conspiracy further, speaking of negotiations with Rykov, Bukharin and Tomsky, and mentioning yet two more terrorist groups, headed by the 'Rightists' Slepkov and Eismont. He went on to tell of a plan of Zinoviev and Kamenev to put Bakayev in charge of the N.K.V.D. on their coming to power so that he could kill all police officials who 'might be in possession of the threads of the controversy', and also 'all the direct perpetrators of the terroristic acts' – an interesting sign, as we have noted, of the way Stalin's mind was working.

Bakayev, who followed, confessed to organizing the Kirov murder, and planning that of Stalin:

Vyshinsky: Did you take a number of practical measures to carry out these instructions, namely, to organize several attempts on the life of Comrade Stalin, which failed through no fault of yours?
Bakayev: That is so.[104]

But he introduced a note of reservation, of a type to be found in later cases, when he said that the other plots now attributed to the accused he had learned of for the first time when he read the indictment.[105] He also had some lesser reservations, saying, for example, that he did not go to Leningrad to meet Vladimir Levin (one of the Nikolayev 'group') for terrorist reasons.[106] These minor denials could count for nothing against the major admissions. Nevertheless, they can still perhaps be treated as slight and pathetic signals that the evidence was not to be relied on.

Pickel came next. He had agreed, he said, to take part in an attempt on Stalin's life. He mentioned a tragedy of 1933, when Zinoviev's secretary, Bogdan, had committed suicide as a protest against the Party purge then going on. A new interpretation was now imposed on this, through Pickel's mouth. Bogdan had indeed 'left a note making it appear that he was a victim of the Party cleansing', but in fact he had been ordered by Bakayev either to attempt Stalin's life or to commit suicide. Even this extravagant tale roused no incredulity from some of those present in the press box.

Pickel had been away in Spitzbergen: as a member of the Union of Soviet Writers he had been on assignment to do some work on the Soviet mining concession there. This was represented as an attempt to keep clear in order to avoid discovery.[107] Thus, when a man was away, this proved that he was a terrorist trying to escape discovery, and when (as Pickel did) he came back, he was a terrorist resuming work – in this case further attempts on the lives of Kaganovich, Voroshilov and others.

Next morning, 20 August, *Kamenev* gave his evidence. He spoke at first with a certain dignity, but as the cross-questioning went on, this began to collapse. He made an almost complete confession, repudiating only the idea that the plotters had intended to cover the traces of their crimes by physically exterminating N.K.V.D. men and others who might know about them. About Smirnov's denials, he said, 'It is ridiculous wriggling, which only creates a comical impression.'[108]

In Reingold's evidence, Sokolnikov had been named as a full member of the 'Centre'.[109] However, Kamenev now put it slightly differently:

Kamenev: . . . Among the leaders of the conspiracy another person may be named who in point of fact was one of the leaders, but who, in view of the special plans we made in regard to him, was not drawn into the practical work. I refer to Sokolnikov.
Vyshinsky: Who was a member of the Centre, but whose part was kept a strict secret?
Kamenev: Yes. Knowing that we might be discovered, we designated a small group to continue our terroristic activities For this purpose we designated Sokolnikov. It seemed to us that on the side of the Trotskyites this role could be successfully performed by Serebryakov and Radek.

He also extended the conspiracy to include the former Workers' Opposition group of Shlyapnikov.

On the involvement of the Rightists he said:

In 1932, 1933 and 1934 I personally maintained relations with Tomsky and Bukharin and sounded their political sentiments. They sympathized with us. When I asked Tomsky about Rykov's frame of mind, he replied: 'Rykov thinks the same as I do.' In reply to my question as to what Bukharin thought he said: 'Bukharin thinks the same as I do, but is pursuing somewhat different tactics: he does not agree with the line of the Party, but is pursuing tactics of persistently enrooting himself in the Party and winning the personal confidence of the leadership.'[110]

This was not a complete incrimination, in theory at least, but it could hardly be regarded as meaning anything other than an intention by Stalin to bring Bukharin and his associates into dock.

A 'witness', Professor Yakovlev, was next produced, to corroborate the testimony. Kamenev, he said, had put him in charge of a terrorist group at the Academy of Sciences.[111]

Zinoviev was now called on for his evidence-in-chief. He appeared cowed. The formerly eloquent orator was hardly able to speak. He looked puffy and grey, and gasped asthmatically. His confession was complete, involving him not only in the Zinovievite terrorist groups, but also with M. Lurye, allegedly sent by Trotsky. He invoked Tomsky's name unamibiguously, and also named Smilga, the veteran member of Lenin's Central Committee who had led the Baltic Fleet in the seizure of power. He asserted that he was in constant communication with Smirnov,[112] adding:

. . . In this situation I had meetings with Smirnov who has accused me here of frequently telling untruths. Yes, I often told untruths. I started doing that from the moment I began fighting the Bolshevik Party. In so far as Smirnov took the road of fighting the Party, he too is telling untruths. But it seems, the difference between him and myself is that I have decided firmly and irrevocably to tell at this last moment the truth, whereas he, it seems, has adopted a different decision.[113]

Next came – as witness only – Smirnov's former wife Safonova. She said that Smirnov had transmitted Trotsky's instructions on terrorism and strongly supported them. Smirnov firmly denied both assertions, but others of the accused backed her up. Vyshinsky then questioned Smirnov:

Vyshinsky: What were your relations with Safonova?
Smirnov: Good.
Vyshinsky: And more?
Smirnov: We were intimately related.
Vyshinsky: You were husband and wife?
Smirnov: Yes.
Vyshinsky: No personal grudges between you?
Smirnov: No.[114]

At the afternoon session *Smirnov* was the first to be questioned. He continued with his partial confession. He had passed on Trotsky's and Sedov's ideas about terrorism; but he had not shared them, and he had done nothing else:

I admit that I belonged to the underground Trotskyite organization, joined the *bloc*, joined the centre of this *bloc*, met Sedov in Berlin in

ɔpinion on to
...instructions on terrorism
...ugh not in agreement with them, I communicated
...ovievites through Ter-Vaganian.[115]

y (ironically): When did you leave the Centre?
mirnov: I did not intend to resign; there was nothing to resign from.
Vyshinsky: Did the Centre exist?
Smirnov: What sort of Centre . . . ?
Vyshinsky: Mrachkovsky, did the Centre exist?
Mrachkovsky: Yes.
Vyshinsky: Zinoviev, did the Centre exist?
Zinoviev: Yes.
Vyshinsky: Evdokimov, did the Centre exist?
Evdokimov: Yes.
Vyshinsky: Bakayev, did the Centre exist?
Bakayev: Yes.
Vyshinsky: How, then, Smirnov, can you take the liberty to maintain that no centre existed?[116]

Smirnov again said that no meetings of such a centre had taken place, and again three of the other members of it were made to bear him down. After the evidence of the others that it was he who was head of the Trotskyite side of the conspiracy, he turned to them sardonically and said, 'You want a leader? Well, take me!'[117]

Even Vyshinsky commented that this was said 'in rather a jocular way'.[118]

Smirnov's partial confession was a rather difficult position to maintain, but on the whole he succeeded in confusing the issue. When the contradictions in his stance became awkward, he simply did not answer the questions.

Olberg, next, told of his long membership of the German Trotskyite organization, through which he had met Sedov and by means of a forged Honduran passport had got to Russia. He gave no explanation of how, with a tourist visa on a Central American passport, he had got a job at the Gorki Pedagogical Institute; but there he had organized the terrorist act to be committed in Moscow on May Day 1936. Olberg's plan to assassinate Stalin failed because he had been arrested. Olberg was one of those of whom it was noted even at the time that his evidence was given in

an almost jau~~n~~
the same mistake. Several ~~observers~~
were *agents provocateurs.*

Following Olberg, *Berman-Yurin* gave evidence th~~at~~
had personally sent him to shoot Stalin at a Comintern pl~~en~~
He gave a very detailed account of meetings with Trotsky and his
entourage in Copenhagen in November 1932. This evidence had
been constructed by the N.K.V.D. as follows. Jack Soble, the
Soviet spy whose career only ended with his arrest in 1957 in New
York, had infiltrated Trotsky's circle in 1931. He met him for the
last time in Copenhagen in December 1932 when Trotsky had
been admitted there on a short lecture tour. Soble then lost
Trotsky's confidence. But his account of Trotsky's moves in
Copenhagen, as transmitted to the N.K.V.D., was edited to form
the basis of Berman-Yurin's evidence.[119]

Berman-Yurin concluded by saying that he was unable to get a
ticket for the XIIIth plenum at the Comintern, and so could not
shoot Stalin after all.

Ever since the publication of the indictment the Soviet press
had been violently demanding the death penalty. Resolutions
from all over the country came in and were printed. Workers of
the Kiev Red Flag Factory and the Stalingrad Dzerzhinsky
Tractor Works, Kazakh *kolkhozes* and Leningrad Party organizations, calling for the shooting of the accused, day by day made
an overwhelming build-up. Now, on the morning of 21 August,
Pravda carried something new. There were still dozens of mass
resolutions, and the usual hack verses by the poetaster Demyan
Bedny, with the title 'No Mercy'. But, in addition, there were
manifestos from Rakovsky, Rykov and Pyatakov, which showed
another aspect of Party discipline. They too all demanded the
death penalty. Rakovsky's was headed 'No Pity'. Rykov insisted
that no mercy be shown to Zinoviev. The tone of all may be
judged from Pyatakov's contribution, which said:

One cannot find the words fully to express one's indignation and
disgust. These people have lost the last semblance of humanity. They
must be destroyed like carrion which is polluting the pure, bracing air
of the land of Soviets; dangerous carrion which may cause the death of
our leaders, and has already caused the death of one of the best people

in our land – that wonderful comrade and leader S. M. Kirov. . . . Many of us, including myself, by our heedlessness, our complacency and lack of vigilance towards those around us, unconsciously helped these bandits to commit their black deeds.

. . . It is a good thing that the People's Commissariat of Internal Affairs had exposed this gang.

. . . It is a good thing that it can be exterminated.

. . . Honour and glory to the workers of the People's Commissariat of Internal Affairs.[120]

Under these mounting pressures the accused continued with their evidence. For 21 August, the last day of testimony, only one leading figure – Ter-Vaganian – remained. Otherwise there were three more 'assassins' and Trotsky's alleged emissary Holtzman.

Holtzman, a genuine ex-Trotskyite of junior rank, was a personal friend of Smirnov's. His evidence turned out to be highly unsatisfactory to the prosecution, on two grounds.

Firstly, no doubt under the influence of Smirnov's example, he had already reverted from the complete confession the indictment had attributed to him to a refusal to admit that he was implicated in terrorism. He now said flatly that though he had passed it on, he (like Smirnov) 'did not share' Trotsky's point of view about the necessity of terror. Vyshinsky was only able to get him to admit that he had remained a member of the Trotskyite organization, and to allege that this amounted to the same thing.

The second point was different. Holtzman confessed that he had met Sedov in Copenhagen, In that city he had arranged to 'put up at the Hotel Bristol' and to meet him there. 'I went to the hotel straight from the station and in the lounge met Sedov.'

When Holtzman's testimony was published, Trotsky declared it false, and immediately published a demand that the court ask Holtzman on what sort of passport and in what name he had entered Denmark – a point which could be checked with the Danish immigration authorities. This was a matter that had not been prepared, and naturally the court paid no attention to it. But soon after the trial ended, the organ of the Danish Social Democratic Party pointed out that Copenhagen's Hotel Bristol had been demolished in 1917.[121] Soviet propaganda had some difficulty with this point and belatedly settled for a story that

Holtzman had met Sedov at a Café Bristol which was near a hotel of a different name at which he was staying, a version inconsistent with the original testimony. There was, in addition, convincing evidence that Sedov had been taking examinations at the Technische Hochschule in Berlin at the time when (in 1932) he was supposed to have been in Copenhagen.[122]

The 'Hotel Bristol' error is said to have arisen as follows. Yezhov decided that the alleged meeting should take place in a hotel, and asked Molchanov to provide a name. Molchanov referred to the travel section of the Foreign Department of the N.K.V.D. To cover the inquiry, he asked the names of several hotels in Oslo as well as Copenhagen, ostensibly needed for a group of prominent Soviet visitors. Molchanov's secretary jotted down the lists telephoned to him, and in typing them out accidently put the Oslo hotels under the heading 'Copenhagen'.[123]

The two Luryes followed Holtzman. Their relationship is uncertain – they were not brothers. They had worked together. *Nathan Lurye*, the surgeon, confessed to having been sent by the Trotskyites abroad to make an attempt on Voroshilov's life. He had worked on assassinating Voroshilov from September 1932 to the spring of 1933, with two accomplices, and 'frequently went to Frunze Street and to the adjacent street armed with revolvers'.[124]

President of the Court: So that you would have committed the terroristic act had a favourable moment offered itself? Why did you not succeed in doing so?
N. Lurye: We saw Voroshilov's car going down Frunze Street. It was travelling too fast. It was hopeless firing at the fast-running car. We decided that it was useless.[125]

N. Lurye was then sent to Chelyabinsk, where he tried to meet Kaganovich and Ordzhonikidze when they visited the city. The plan, a simple one, was as follows. In Ordzhonikidze's case Moissei Lurye instructed Nathan Lurye 'to take the opportunity of a possible visit to the Chelyabinsk Tractor Works by Comrade Ordzhonikidze to commit a terrorist act against him'. N. Lurye 'tried to meet' both leaders, but 'he failed to carry out his intention'.

This unpromising assassin was then transferred to Leningrad where he was put in touch with 'Zeidel's terrorist group' (one of the miscellaneous assassin groups named throughout the trial: Zeidel was an historian). Here N. Lurye's instructions were to assassinate Zhdanov. He planned to do this at the 1 May demonstration. Ulrikh established in detail the type of revolver (a medium-sized Browning), but as Lurye made no use of it, this point lost some of its significance:

President of the Court: Why did you fail to carry out the attempt on the life of Zhdanov?
N. Lurye: We marched by too far away.[126]

He had now been involved in 'assassination attempts' on four leading figures, and no overt action of any sort had been taken – comparing most unfavourably with the efficiency of the killers of Kirov.

Mossei Lurye's evidence was of the same type. He also had instructions from Trotsky, through the German Communist oppositionist leaders Ruth Fischer and Maslow, and had met Zinoviev too. He had prepared his namesake for his various attempts.

Ter-Vaganian appeared next. He implicated a new group, the Georgian deviationists who had been terrorists, 'as is well known', since 1928. This implied Mdivani and his followers, but the only person Ter-Vaganian named was Okudzhava. He had also conducted the negotiations with his close friend Lominadze and with the Trotskyite historians Zeidel and Friedland.

Ter-Vaganian also implicated Smirnov, who again put his denials in the record, though eventually conceding that one disputed meeting 'may have taken place'.

The last accused, *Fritz David*, gave evidence of having been sent by Trotsky and Sedov and attempting to carry out 'two concrete plans to assassinate Stalin', both of which failed, one because Stalin did not attend the meeting of the Comintern Executive Committee chosen as the occasion for action, and the other because, at the Comintern Congress, David had been unable to get near enough. Sedov had (not surprisingly) been furious when he learned of these hitches. Not a single one of all the terrorists sent into Russia at such trouble and expense had even slightly inconvenienced, let alone killed, any of the Stalin leadership. In spite of this, Vyshinsky remarked that 'the Trotskyites operated with greater determination and energy than the Zinovievites'![127]

Dreitzer was recalled at the end of the evening session on 21 August to implicate Corps Commander Vitovt Putna (see Chapter Seven), who had 'ostensibly left the Trotskyites' but had actually carried instructions from Trotsky to Dreitzer for transmission to Smirnov. Smirnov here again intervened to deny that Putna was a Trotskyite, but Pickel, Reingold and Bakayev confirmed it.

At the end of the day's session Vyshinsky issued the following statement:

> At preceding sessions some of the accused (Kamenev, Zinoviev and Reingold) in their testimony referred to Tomsky, Bukharin, Rykov, Uglanov, Radek, Pyatakov,* Serebryakov and Sokolnikov as being to a greater or lesser degree involved in the criminal counter-revolutionary activities for which the accused in the present case are being tried. I consider it necessary to inform the court that yesterday I gave orders to institute an investigation of these statements of the accused in regard to Tomsky, Rykov, Bukharin, Uglanov, Radek and Pyatakov, and that in accordance with the results of this investigation the office of the State Attorney will institute legal proceedings in this matter. In regard to Serebryakov and Sokolnikov, the investigating authorities are already in possession of material convicting these persons of counter-revolutionary crimes, and, in view of this, criminal proceedings are being instituted against Sokolnikov and Serebryakov.[128]

On 22 August this announcement was printed, together with a prompt demand by a workers' meeting at the Dynamo Factory that these charges should be 'pitilessly investigated'.

Immediately on reading Vyshinsky's announcement Tomsky committed suicide in his *dacha* at Bolshevo. The Central Committee, of which he was a candidate member, next day denounced this, attributing it (truly enough) to his having been incriminated.

The morning of 22 August was devoted to Vyshinsky's speech for the prosecution. First he laid the theoretical basis of the trials, of the whole Purge:

* For some reason, the evidence implicating Pyatakov is not given in the printed version of the court proceedings – which is, however, much compressed.

Three years ago Comrade Stalin not only foretold the inevitable resistance of elements hostile to the cause of socialism, but also foretold the possibility of the revival of Trotskyite counter-revolutionary groups. This trial has fully and distinctly proved the great wisdom of this forecast.[129]

After an attack on Trotsky, he took the court at length through the history of Zinoviev's and Kamenev's various recantations and promises. He then gave great prominence to the Kirov murder:

These mad dogs of capitalism tried to tear limb from limb the best of the best of our Soviet land. They killed one of the men of the revolution who was most dear to us, that admirable and wonderful man, bright and joyous as the smile on his lips was always bright and joyous, as our new life is bright and joyous. They killed our Kirov; they wounded us close to our very heart. They thought they could sow confusion and consternation in our ranks.[130]

Vyshinsky took some time to deal with Smirnov's 'wrigglings' (and, in passing, condemned Holtzman for having 'adopted the same position as Smirnov'); Smirnov had 'stubbornly denied that he took any part in the terroristic activities of the Trotskyite–Zinovievite centre'.[131] His guilt was, however, established by the other confessions. One awkward point was dealt with thus:

I know that in his defence Smirnov will argue that he had left the centre. Smirnov will say: 'I did not do anything, I was in prison.' A naïve assertion! Smirnov was in prison from 1 January 1933, but we know that while in prison Smirnov organized contacts with his Trotskyites, for a code was discovered by means of which Smirnov, while in prison, communicated with his companions outside. This proves that communication existed and Smirnov cannot deny this.[132]

In fact, no evidence of any sort on this point had been, or ever was to be, produced.

Vyshinsky, in passing, dealt with an unfortunate idea which had evidently gained popularity,

The comparison with the period of Narodnaya Volya ['People's Will'] terrorism is shameless. Filled with respect for the memory of those who in the times of the Narodnaya Volya sincerely and honestly, although employing, it is true, their own special, but always irreproachable, methods, fought against the tsarist autocracy for liberty – I emphatically reject this sacrilegious parallel.[133]

He concluded with the appeal, 'I demand that these dogs gone mad should be shot – every one of them!'

The evening session of 22 August and the two sessions of 23 August saw the last pleas of the accused.

They spoke in the same order as they had given their evidence. Mrachkovsky started by telling of his background, a worker, son and grandson of workers, a revolutionary, son and grandson of revolutionaries, who had suffered his first arrest when thirteen years old.

'And here,' he went on in a bitter and ironical tone, 'I stand before you as a counter-revolutionary!' The judges and Prosecutor looked apprehensive, but all was well. For a moment Mrachkovsky was overcome. He stuck his hand on the bar of the dock and regained his self-control,[134] going on to explain that he had only mentioned his past so that everyone should 'remember that not only a general, not only a prince or nobleman can become a counter-revolutionary; workers or those who spring from the working class, like myself, can also become counter-revolutionaries'.[135] He ended by saying that he was a traitor who should be shot.

Most of the other pleas were simple self-condemnations; the accused described themselves as 'dregs' undeserving of mercy. But an occasional wrong note was struck, as when Evdokimov said – surely not without meaning – 'Who will believe a single word of ours?'[136]

When Kamenev had finished his plea, and had already sat down, he rose again and said that he would like to say something to his two children, whom he had no other means of addressing. One was an Air Force pilot, the other a young boy. Kamenev said that he wanted to tell them 'No matter what my sentence will be, I in advance consider it just. Don't look back. Go forward. Together with the Soviet people, follow Stalin.' He then sat down again and rested his face in his hands. Others present were shaken, and even the judges are said to have lost their stony expressions for an instant.[137]

Zinoviev made a satisfactory definition of the whole inadmissibility of opposition to Stalin: 'My defective Bolshevism became transformed into anti-Bolshevism, and through Trotskyism I arrived at Fascism. Trotskyism is a variety of Fascism, and Zinovievism is a variety of Trotskyism . . .'[138] But he ended that worse than any punishment was the idea that 'my name will be associated with the names of those who stood beside me. On my right hand Olberg, on my left – Nathan Lurye . . .'[139] And this remark is, in an important sense, incompatible with the idea of the trial: for on the face of the evidence how was Zinoviev better than the two he names?

Smirnov again denied any direct implication in any terrorist activity. However, he denounced Trotsky, though in comparatively mild terms, as an enemy 'on the other side of the barricade'.

When Fritz David had finished, the court withdrew to consider the verdict. Yagoda had it ready for them in the Council Chamber. But a decent interval was allowed to pass, and at 2.30 the following morning the court reassembled and found all concerned guilty on all counts. They were all sentenced to death.

As Ulrikh finished reading the verdict, one of the Luryes shrieked hysterically, 'Long live the cause of Marx, Engels, Lenin and Stalin!' Then the prisoners were taken out, to the police wagons that were to return them to the Lubyanka.

TO THE EXECUTION CELLARS

As soon as the trial was over, the defect in the bargain Zinoviev and Kamenev had struck with Stalin became apparent. Having carried out their side of it, they no longer disposed of any sanction to make him do the same with his.

Under the new law, seventy-two hours' grace was allowed for the accused to put in their petitions for pardon. Some of these may have been put in and rejected, though Smirnov, at least, seems not to have made an appeal. In any case, the announcement of their execution was made only twenty-four hours after the verdict.

Various accounts of the actual execution have filtered out. They are of course based on N.K.V.D. gossip, the only possible source in the circumstances.

Zinoviev was unwell and feverish. He was told he was to be transferred to another cell. But when he saw the guards he at once understood. All accounts agree that he collapsed, yelling in a high-pitched voice a desperate appeal to Stalin to keep his word. He gave the impression of hysteria, but this is probably not fair, as his voice was always very piercing when he was excited, and he was perhaps trying to make a last speech. He was, in addition, still suffering from heart and liver trouble, so that some sort of collapse is understandable. It is said that the N.K.V.D. lieutenant in charge, fearing the effect of this scene if prolonged along the corridor and down into the cellar, hustled him into a nearby cell and shot him there and then, later receiving an award for his presence of mind.[140]

When Kamenev was called from his cell to execution, he made no complaint and appeared stunned. He was executed by an hysterical N.K.V.D. lieutenant who kicked his body as it fell and shot him again. Smirnov was calm and courageous. He is reported as saying 'We deserve this for our unworthy attitude at the trial.'[141]

There is a story,[142] originating from an N.K.V.D. man under arrest, that Zinoviev and Kamenev were not executed until five days after the announcement of their deaths. The motive was to show them, alive and well, to those prospective defendants of the next trial who were already under arrest, with the implication that sentences were merely for the public. Condemned men were, the new accused were told, to be given research work in an 'isolator'. This is one of many similar stories which circulated in the prisons. There is nothing inherently impossible about it and there is at least some official evidence, however dubious, that announced sentences were not always carried out on the date stated (see p. 371). It is true, too, that Stalin's promises to spare the lives of the defendants would not be believed so easily after they had once been broken, so the motive for such action is plain. But in the absence of stronger evidence than this, the story can hardly be accepted, though we may note that it is curious that no death date is given for Ter-Vaganian, contrary to the almost invariable practice, in the note on him in the latest edition of *Lenin's Collected Works*.[143]

We can trace the fate of few of the relatives of the accused, apart from Smirnov's. Evdokimov's son was shot. Kamenev's children were sent to labour camps.[144] Olberg's wife, Betty, was sent to labour camp. In prison, very ill and thin, she had made an attempt to commit suicide by throwing herself over some banisters. She was sent back to Germany with the Communists handed over to the Gestapo by Stalin in 1940.[145]

The executions took place when many Party leaders were on holiday. Stalin himself had left for the Caucasus, and only a quorum of the formal State body, the Central Executive Committee, was available to hear appeals which their general instructions were to reject unless ordered to the contrary by the Politburo. Yezhov had remained in Moscow to see that nothing could interfere with the processes Stalin had set in motion.[146] Nothing did.

THE CREDIBILITY OF THE TRIAL

The trial had on the whole been a success for Stalin. The Communists and the Russian people could make no overt objection to his version. And the outside world whose representatives he had allowed in to authenticate it, as it were, was at least inclined not to reject it outright, from the start, as a fabrication. There was very considerable uneasiness about the confessions. But even if they had been obtained by unwarrantable methods, that did not in itself prove that they were untrue. In fact, the one phenomenon which was difficult to reconcile with the complete innocence of the accused was precisely their confessions. Thus to a considerable degree the confession method justified itself politically.

The case itself must come as something of an anti-climax to us today, who know the falsehood of the charges and something of the ways in which the whole thing was prepared. At the time, to the world, and to the Party itself, it appeared differently – as a terrible public event. The allegations were examined in detail. They were found convincing by various British lawyers, Western journalists and so forth, and were thought incredible by others. As so often, this appears to be a case in which alleged facts were accepted or rejected in accordance with preconceived opinion. Most people either felt that it was incredible that old revolutionaries should commit such actions, or that it was incredible that a

Socialist State should make false accusations. But neither position is really tenable. It was by no means absolutely inconceivable that the opposition might have planned the assassination of the political leadership. There are various reasons for thinking it is out of character and contrary to their previous views, but that is a much weaker argument.

Some Western commentators, applying 'common-sense' criteria to the situation, argued that the oppositionists should logically have seen that the removal of Stalin was the only way of securing their own lives and a tolerable future, from their point of view, for the Party and the State. So it was, yet history gives many examples of inadequate common sense.

But in any case, it seems perfectly clear that the opposition, up to the actual execution of the Zinoviev–Kamenev group, never expected that Stalin would really kill off the old leadership. The whole of their manoeuvres up to that point had been designed to keep themselves alive and, if possible, in the Party, until such time as Stalin's failures and excesses would swing Party feeling back in their favour and give them another chance. After the first executions, no oppositionists of any standing were in a position to attempt assassination whether they thought it suitable or not. The only people with any chance of getting rid of the General Secretary were those close to him.*

It seems certain that Stalin himself was really afraid of assassination. He must have known that the leading oppositionists could scarcely organize such plots, so closely did he have them watched. But at a lower level in the Party there were thousands and thousands of potential enemies. Individual assassination was

---

* We do not, indeed, know of the precise circumstances in which he finally died, in March 1953. But his death certainly took place at a moment when he was preparing further slaughter in the leadership, and it may be that this time they had more sense than to await their fate like sheep. At least (so Enver Hoxha has asserted), the Soviet leaders 'are the plotters who had the impudence to tell us openly – as did Mikoyan – that they had hatched a plot to kill Stalin'.[147] Thus it is certainly true that desperate and ruthless men, who might have been expected to learn from the events of the thirties, *may* well have planned, and perhaps even carried out, the most logical killing of all. (On the other hand, the fact that Vasily Stalin went round saying that 'father was killed by his rivals' can carry little weight.)[148]

indeed contrary to established Marxist principles. In fact Zinoviev had been supposed to be banking on this idea. Reingold
remarked: 'Zinoviev told me . . . "When under examination the
main thing is persistently to deny any connexion with the organization. If accused of terroristic activities, you must emphatically
deny it and argue that terror is incompatible with the views of
Bolsheviks–Marxists."'[149] Nikolayev, the assassin of Kirov, had
been a dupe: but, himself a Communist, he had shot down a
Party leader with a quite clear idea of what he was doing. That
others should refrain on Marxist principle from individual
terror was not a certain hope. Desperation had already, for
example, driven the Bulgarian Communist Party to the bomb
outrage in Sofia Cathedral in 1925.*

Again, the selective assassination of N.K.V.D. defectors and of
other political enemies in the West was soon to become routine.
And Stalin himself – an Old Communist too! – had organized
the killing of Kirov. In the circumstances, we may agree with the
idea that after all assassination by Zinoviev and Kamenev *was*
possible, that Reingold *could* have been telling the truth when he
deposed:

In 1932, Zinoviev, at Kamenev's apartment, in the presence of a
number of members of the united Trotskyite-Zinovievite Centre argued
in favour of resorting to terror as follows: although terror is incompatible with Marxism, at the present moment these considerations must
be abandoned . . .[152]

Moreover, some of the ideas placed in the mouths of Zinoviev
and Kamenev were plausible. It was quite reasonable to suppose
that if Stalin had been assassinated, as a result of the leadership
struggle that would ensue, 'negotiations would be opened with
us'. As Kamenev said, 'Even with Stalin we, by our policy of

---

* At the time, it is true, the Communists denied responsibility and claimed
that they had been framed by their enemies. Georgi Dimitrov, at the Reichstag Trial, said: 'This incident was not organized by the Bulgarian Communist Party . . . that act of provocation, the blowing up of Sofia Cathedral,
was actually organized by the Bulgarian police.'[150] However, in a speech in
1948, he admitted and criticized 'the desperate actions of the leaders of
the Party's military organization culminating in the attempt at Sofia
Cathedral'.[151]

double-dealing, had obtained, after all, forgiveness of our mistakes by the Party and had been taken back into its ranks.'[153] And it was also plausible that they had anticipated the rehabilitation of Trotsky as a later result.

But to support either view of the case, there was very little genuine reference to the facts. Yet at this level, the only one worth a sensible examination, the outward semblance of an established plot could easily be shown to rest on absurdities and contradictions. For its composition, as in later cases, bears many marks of crudity. It seems that these are not attributable to Molchanov and Yagoda, but to Stalin himself, who personally insisted, for example, on the inclusion of Smirnov.

In spite of the inconsistencies and incredibilities, *Pravda*, on 4 September 1937, was nevertheless able to give prominence to a statement by 'the English jurist Pritt' from the London *News Chronicle* on the complete propriety and authenticity of the trial. And this was one case among many.

But Zinoviev and Kamenev had been in exile or prison for most of the period of the active plot. Mrachkovsky had been in exile in Kazakhstan. Smirnov had been in a prison cell since 1 January 1933. Vyshinsky had spoken of ways in which 'even those not at liberty' had been able to take part in the plot. But no evidence had been produced of their methods of liaison. It might have been thought that even observers like Pritt would have found it odd that a conspiracy directed from outside the country should, when one of its members was actually in prison in a distant area, have continued to pass instructions through him, rather than use alternative channels – of which the evidence implied, they had a profusion.

A further striking point is the proportion between the number of assassinations planned and those carried out. Two separate plans to kill Stalin at the meeting of the Communist International had been made, another to shoot Voroshilov, a third to assassinate Kaganovich and Ordzhonikidze, and many others simply decided on in principle.

No reference was made during the trial to some of the previous trials in connexion with the Kirov assassination. The action of

1931, listened to his opinion on terrorism and passed this opinion on to Moscow. I admit that I received Trotsky's instructions on terrorism from Gaven and, although not in agreement with them, I communicated them to the Zinovievites through Ter-Vaganian.[115]

Vyshinsky (ironically): When did you leave the Centre?

Smirnov: I did not intend to resign; there was nothing to resign from.

Vyshinsky: Did the Centre exist?

Smirnov: What sort of Centre . . . ?

Vyshinsky: Mrachkovsky, did the Centre exist?

Mrachkovsky: Yes.

Vyshinsky: Zinoviev, did the Centre exist?

Zinoviev: Yes.

Vyshinsky: Evdokimov, did the Centre exist?

Evdokimov: Yes.

Vyshinsky: Bakayev, did the Centre exist?

Bakayev: Yes.

Vyshinsky: How, then, Smirnov, can you take the liberty to maintain that no centre existed?[116]

Smirnov again said that no meetings of such a centre had taken place, and again three of the other members of it were made to bear him down. After the evidence of the others that it was he who was head of the Trotskyite side of the conspiracy, he turned to them sardonically and said, 'You want a leader? Well, take me!'[117]

Even Vyshinsky commented that this was said 'in rather a jocular way'.[118]

Smirnov's partial confession was a rather difficult position to maintain, but on the whole he succeeded in confusing the issue. When the contradictions in his stance became awkward, he simply did not answer the questions.

Olberg, next, told of his long membership of the German Trotskyite organization, through which he had met Sedov and by means of a forged Honduran passport had got to Russia. He gave no explanation of how, with a tourist visa on a Central American passport, he had got a job at the Gorki Pedagogical Institute; but there he had organized the terrorist act to be committed in Moscow on May Day 1936. Olberg's plan to assassinate Stalin failed because he had been arrested. Olberg was one of those of whom it was noted even at the time that his evidence was given in

an almost jaunty fashion: Fritz David and the two Luryes made
the same mistake. Several observers at once concluded that these
were *agents provocateurs*.

Following Olberg, *Berman-Yurin* gave evidence that Trotsky
had personally sent him to shoot Stalin at a Comintern plenum.
He gave a very detailed account of meetings with Trotsky and his
entourage in Copenhagen in November 1932. This evidence had
been constructed by the N.K.V.D. as follows. Jack Soble, the
Soviet spy whose career only ended with his arrest in 1957 in New
York, had infiltrated Trotsky's circle in 1931. He met him for the
last time in Copenhagen in December 1932 when Trotsky had
been admitted there on a short lecture tour. Soble then lost
Trotsky's confidence. But his account of Trotsky's moves in
Copenhagen, as transmitted to the N.K.V.D., was edited to form
the basis of Berman-Yurin's evidence.[119]

Berman-Yurin concluded by saying that he was unable to get a
ticket for the XIIIth plenum at the Comintern, and so could not
shoot Stalin after all.

Ever since the publication of the indictment the Soviet press
had been violently demanding the death penalty. Resolutions
from all over the country came in and were printed. Workers of
the Kiev Red Flag Factory and the Stalingrad Dzerzhinsky
Tractor Works, Kazakh *kolkhozes* and Leningrad Party organizations, calling for the shooting of the accused, day by day made
an overwhelming build-up. Now, on the morning of 21 August,
Pravda carried something new. There were still dozens of mass
resolutions, and the usual hack verses by the poetaster Demyan
Bedny, with the title 'No Mercy'. But, in addition, there were
manifestos from Rakovsky, Rykov and Pyatakov, which showed
another aspect of Party discipline. They too all demanded the
death penalty. Rakovsky's was headed 'No Pity'. Rykov insisted
that no mercy be shown to Zinoviev. The tone of all may be
judged from Pyatakov's contribution, which said:

One cannot find the words fully to express one's indignation and
disgust. These people have lost the last semblance of humanity. They
must be destroyed like carrion which is polluting the pure, bracing air
of the land of Soviets; dangerous carrion which may cause the death of
our leaders, and has already caused the death of one of the best people

N.K.V.D. officers in Leningrad was not referred to. The allegation about the Latvian Consul was not mentioned.

No documentary evidence (except Olberg's Honduran passport) was produced. The failure of the prosecution to produce documents should have struck observers as particularly odd. For in the arrest of underground Bolsheviks, the Tsarist police repeatedly discovered documents – without which, indeed, it is difficult to see how an underground could operate. When the February 1917 Revolution opened up the police archives, hundreds of secret Party documents were found in them, including letters written by Lenin himself. And the underground Bolsheviks of that time were at least as skilled in conspiracy as the men Stalin now arrested: indeed (as Orlov points out) 'They were the *same* men.'

Again, prominent conspirators and witnesses were simply missing. Sokolnikov was clearly a relevant and important witness. But he was not called. Nor were Bukharin, or Tomsky, or Rykov – or any of the newly implicated. Among the Zinovievites who were not called but who had appeared at previous trials were Gertik, one of the main links with the 'Leningrad Centre' which had allegedly assassinated Kirov,[154] and Karev, who was supposed to have been personally instructed by Zinoviev, and by Bakayev, to prepare the Kirov murder with others of the Leningrad assassination group,[155] with whom Faivilovich was also a contact man.[156] Kuklin was actually named as a full member of the 'Centre'.[157]

But meanwhile, questions of evidence, of logic, were not decisive. The prestige of the 'Socialist State' was high. There was little choice between accepting the trial at its face value and branding Stalin as a vulgar murderer, and his regime as a tyranny founded on falsehood. The truth could be deduced, but it could not be proved. Few cared to hear it, given the more evident menace of Fascism.

In Russia itself things were different. Few, perhaps, credited the confessions. But fewer still could even hint their doubts.

*

A week after the execution of Zinoviev and his fellow defendants, Stalin ordered Yagoda to select and shoot 5,000 of the oppositionists then in camps.[158] At this time the last privileges were withdrawn from political prisoners in camps. In March 1937 some rights were temporarily restored. But a few months later another mass execution was ordered. Most of the remaining Trotskyites at Vorkuta were brought to Moscow and shot. They included Trotsky's son Sergei Sedov. In March 1938 the Armenian Sokrates Gevorkian and twenty other former Leftists were executed near their camp. From then until the end of 1938, groups of forty or so were executed there once or twice a week. Children under twelve alone were spared.[159]

There are reports of a last hunger strike by the oppositionists before they were separated, resulting in many deaths and, eventually, the disappearance of all concerned.[160]

CHAPTER FIVE

THE PROBLEM OF CONFESSION

He lies like an eyewitness. Russian saying

WHEN, at 1.45 p.m. on 19 August 1936, Mrachkovsky started to confess in public to a series of appalling crimes, it marked the beginning of a series of events which shook and astonished the entire world.

Mrachkovsky was a former worker and an Old Bolshevik, a member of the Party since 1905. He had actually been born in prison where, in 1888, his mother was serving a sentence for revolutionary activity. His father, a worker like himself, was a revolutionary too, and became a Bolshevik when that party was organized. Even his grandfather, also a worker, had belonged to one of the first Marxist groupings, the Southern Russian Workers' Union.

Mrachkovsky himself had come to prominence by leading a rising in the Urals. He had fought in Siberia in the Civil War, and been wounded several times. He had later been one of the boldest of Trotsky's followers, and had been the first to be arrested when, in 1927, he organized the Trotskyites' short-lived underground printing-press.

He was, in fact, a real epitome of revolutionary boldness, born and bred to resistance. He now stood up and complaisantly confessed to active membership of a plot to murder the Soviet leadership. Over the next few days half a dozen other Old Bolsheviks followed suit, including leaders known the world over. Lastly, they made final pleas, condemning themselves for 'contemptible treachery' (Kamenev), speaking of themselves as 'the dregs of the land' (Pickel), 'not only murderers but fascist murderers' (Holtzman). Several expressly said that their crimes were too foul to let them ask for clemency: Mrachkovsky described himself as 'a traitor who should be shot'.

Twice in the next two years the same scene was to be repeated, always to the bafflement of commentators, friendly or hostile.

The impression of unanimous surrender was not, indeed, entirely a correct one. Two of the 1936 accused (Smirnov and Holtzman) hedged considerably in their admissions: but this was hardly noticed among the self-abasement of so many others, including the two major figures, Zinoviev and Kamenev.

And similarly, the minor hitches and qualifications of later trials passed barely noticed. Krestinsky withdrew his confession on the first day of the 1938 Trial, and only reaffirmed it after a night in the hands of the investigators. Bukharin refused to confess to some of the major charges – such as that of having planned to kill Lenin. Radek, admitting that he was a treacherous liar, took occasion to point out that the case rested entirely on his evidence.

But such points were on the whole lost in the picture as it appeared in gross: everyone had confessed, the Old Bolsheviks had publicly avowed disgraceful plans and actions. The whole business almost passed belief. Were the confessions true? How had they been obtained? What did it all signify? We are told that the confessions were as little believed in Russia as abroad, 'or even less', but that the average Soviet citizen who had not been in jail found them as puzzling as foreigners did.[1]

It was curiously argued, not only by Vyshinsky, but also in the West, that the accused confessed owing to the weight of evidence against them, that they had 'no choice'. Apart from the fact that there was no evidence against them *except* their confessions and those of others, this does not accord with common experience. People, especially on capital charges, plead not guilty even if there is a great deal of evidence against them. In the past, Communists had frequently denied facts. But in any case, it was not only confession which was so strange, it was repentance – the acceptance of the prosecution's view that the acts confessed to were appalling crimes. If Zinoviev and Kamenev had really concluded that the way out of Russia's difficulties was the assassination of Stalin, this would be to say that experienced politicians had made a definite political decision suited, as they thought, to the circumstances. It would not be a decision they felt guilty about. Their natural line of reasoning – as with the terrorists of the People's

Will – would have been, if the facts were admitted, to defend their plans and actions. The complete acceptance of the opinion of their accusers was the real and crowning implausibility of the whole affair.

THE PARTY MIND

The problem of these confessions is really a double one. We have to consider the technical means, the physical and psychological pressures by which false public confessions could be secured. And this is a question that applies to non-Party as well as to Party victims.

But in the surrender and self-abasement of old revolutionaries, a further element enters. Their surrender was not a single and exceptional act in their careers, but rather the culmination of a whole series of submissions to the Party made in terms they knew to be 'objectively' false. And this attitude is a key to Stalin's victory going far beyond the trials themselves, largely accounting as it does for the extraordinary and disastrous failure of the successive Party elements who objected to his rule to take any effective action to block him.

In Soviet circumstances, where all factions had long been united in imposing the principle of the one-party State and the practice of crushing all alternative and independent political enterprise by police methods, the responsibility for saving the country and the people from Stalin rested squarely on his opponents within the Party.

They had abdicated that responsibility. The Party mystique led them to submission to the Party leadership, however packed the Congresses and committees which produced it. They could see no political possibilities outside the Party. Even when they had been expelled, they thought of nothing but a return at any price.

The oppositionists – with the exception of Trotsky himself – had made a basic tactical error. Their constant avowals of political sin, their admissions that Stalin was after all right, were based on the idea that it was correct to 'crawl in the dust', suffer any humiliation, to remain in or return to the Party. In this way, they thought, when Stalin's policies came to grief, they themselves would be there, available as the alternative leadership which the Party must then seek.

In the first place, the policy was too abjectly cunning. The constant avowals and humiliations ate into the morale of rank-and-file oppositionists, and wore away their reputations, perhaps irretrievably. But the basic miscalculation was on an even more crucial point. The members of an alternative Government have at least got to be alive. It is certainly true that some of the oppositionists – Kamenev, for instance – did not underestimate Stalin's desire to crush them at all costs. But they did not believe that it would be politically possible for him to face the Party with the execution of its veteran leaders. They underestimated not his ruthlessness, but his determination, cunning, and unscrupulousness. When he had finished, there was no such thing as a living ex-member of the Politburo, with the single exception of Grigori Petrovsky, working on sufferance as a museum administrator.

Their view of history made it hard for them to conceive that the proletarian Party could simply be converted by intrigue or any other method into an apparatus of personal dictatorship. No one had previously created a State, on a solid and stable basis, entirely hostile to the natural movements of the economy and to the aspirations of the people. It did not occur to them that it could be done, still less that an Old Bolshevik would seek to do it. And if they did not understand the unappeasable drive to power in Stalin's mentality, nor the fact that with the simplicity of genius he was prepared to undertake actions contrary to the 'laws of history', and to do what had never been done before, they also did not understand his methods. That a modern, a Marxist, State could be subverted by intrigue and manoeuvres in the political organs, this they had at least begun to grasp. It did not occur to them that their opponent could use the methods of a common criminal, could procure assassination, and frame up others for his own crime. A rank-and-file oppositionist commented (of Rykov): 'To spend twenty years with Stalin in an illegal Party, to be with him during the decisive days of the Revolution, to sit at the same table in the Politburo for ten years after the Revolution and still fail to know Stalin is really the end.'[2]

There were two great preconditions for the Purge. First, the personal drives and abilities of its prime mover, Stalin; and second, the context, the political context, in which he operated. We have traced the changes which had come over the Party after the Civil War and the trauma of Kronstadt. Since then, the final silencing of the debate and the extravagantly bitter test of the 'Second Civil War', against the peasantry, had put it on the anvil. Under these new strokes, an ever greater premium was put upon ruthlessness and will, but at the same time the idea of the Party itself as an object of devotion and of its membership as an elite brotherhood had strengthened yet further.

For his opponents as well as his supporters, Stalin's leadership was thus the authentic – or at least the only – representative of the 'Party'. While Lenin had always been prepared to split a party if he had felt the majority to be wrong, the oppositionists were now hamstrung by an abstract loyalty. Just as most of the German generals were later to be reduced to impotence by their oath of loyalty to a man who would not himself have thought twice about breaking his word, so the Rightists were brought to ruin by a similar intellectual and moral muddle.

In 1935, Bukharin, who had just been denouncing Stalin's 'insane ambition', was asked why, in that case, the oppositionists had surrendered to him, and replied 'with considerable emotion':

You don't understand, it is not like that at all. It is not *him* we trust but the man in whom the Party has reposed its confidence. It just so happened that he has become a sort of symbol of the Party . . .[3]

Bukharin's faith in the Party, as the incarnation of history, was seen again in 1936, a year before his own arrest, when he remarked to the Menshevik Nicolaevsky:

It is difficult for us to live. And you, for example, could not accustom yourself to it. Even for some of us, with our experience during these decades, it is often impossible. But one is saved by a faith that development is always going forward. It is like a stream that is running to the shore. If one leans out of the stream, one is ejected completely. (Here Bukharin made a scissor-like gesture with his two fingers.) The stream goes through the most difficult places. But it still goes forward in the direction in which it must. And the people grow, become stronger in it, and they build a new society.[4]

This view is admittedly an act of faith, of pure theoretical anticipation. Stalin held in effect that his personal rule was essential on precisely the same grounds. The moral distinction between the two attitudes is not a very clear one. The whole general ethic had been expressed most clearly by Trotsky in 1924:

> None of us desires or is able to dispute the will of the Party. Clearly, the Party is always right. .... We can only be right with and by the Party, for history has provided no other way of being in the right. The English have a saying, 'My country, right or wrong'; whether it is in the right or in the wrong, it is my country. We have much better historical justification in saying, whether it is right or wrong in certain individual cases, it is my party. .... And if the Party adopts a decision which one or other of us thinks unjust, he will say, just or unjust, it is my party, and I shall support the consequences of the decision to the end.[5]

And this, as we shall see, is absolutely cardinal in explaining, not so much Stalin's rise to power, as the almost total failure to oppose him *after* his aims and methods had declared themselves.

A very revealing account of the attitude of an old oppositionist to the already Stalinized Party – more revealing than official statements, since it was made in the heat of the moment in private – had been given in a series of remarks made by Pyatakov in 1928 to a former Menshevik friend, N. V. Volsky. Pyatakov had just 'capitulated'[6] and, meeting the Menshevik in Paris, provoked him by a suggestion that he lacked courage. Volsky replied warmly that Pyatakov's capitulation a couple of months after his expulsion from the Party in 1927, and repudiation of the views that he had held right up till then, showed a real lack of moral courage.

Pyatakov, in an excited and emotional manner, replied with a long harangue. Lenin, he said, had become a tired and sick man towards the end of his life:

> The real Lenin was the man who had had the courage to make a proletarian revolution first, and then to set about creating the objective conditions theoretically necessary as a preliminary to such a revolution. What was the October Revolution, what indeed is the Communist Party, but a miracle? No Menshevik could ever understand what it meant to be a member of such a Party.[7]

Pyatakov's 'miracle' was a reasonable description from the Marxist point of view of what the Party, as he thought, was attempting to do. For it was contrary to the natural 'Laws of Society' as propounded by Marx: instead of socialism arising as the result of the conquest of political power by a Party representing a large proletarian majority in a country already thoroughly industrialized, the Communist Party in the Soviet Union was (in theory) attempting to create by mere will-power and organization the industry and the proletariat which should in principle have preceded it. Instead of economics determining politics, politics was determining economics.

'According to Lenin', Pyatakov added, 'the Communist Party is based on the principle of coercion which doesn't recognize any limitations or inhibitions. And the central idea of this principle of boundless coercion is not coercion by itself but the absence of any limitation whatsoever – moral, political and even physical, as far as that goes. Such a Party is capable of achieving miracles and doing things which no other collective of men could achieve. . . . A real Communist . . . that is, a man who was raised in the Party and had absorbed its spirit deeply enough becomes himself in a way a miracle man.'[8]

From this attitude significant conclusions followed:

'For such a Party a true Bolshevik will readily cast out from his mind ideas in which he has believed for years. A true Bolshevik has submerged his personality in the collectivity, "the Party", to such an extent that he can make the necessary effort to break away from his own opinions and convictions, and can honestly agree with the Party – that is the test of a true Bolshevik.'

There could be no life for him (Pyatakov continued) outside the ranks of the Party, and he would be ready to believe that black was white, and white was black, if the Party required it. In order to become one with this great Party he would fuse himself with it, abandon his own personality, so that there was no particle left inside him which was not at one with the Party, did not belong to it.[9]

This idea of all morality and all truth being comprehended in the Party is extraordinarily illuminating when we come to consider the humiliations Pyatakov and others were to accept in the Party's name. For this evaporation of objective standards, though it did not affect all members of the old Party, was widespread. Many had by the end of the twenties become quite disillusioned with the idea that the workers, let alone the peasants, could play any part in a country like Russia. By 1930 a foreign Communist noted among his students in Leningrad that they thought it entirely natural for the masses to be mere instruments under both Fascism and Communism – the moral distinction being simply one of the respective leaders' intentions.[10] One Trotskyite remarked that there was much to be said for Stalin: 'No doubt Trotsky would have done it with more go and with less brutality, and we, who are more cultured than Stalin's men, would have been at the top. But one should be able to rise above these ambitions . . .'[11]

Even those who did not go to Pyatakov's self-immolating lengths no longer felt capable of the intellectual and moral effort of making a break and starting afresh:

They were all tired men. The higher you got in the hierarchy, the more tired they were. I have nowhere seen such exhausted men as among the higher strata of Soviet politicians, among the Old Bolshevik guard. It was not only the effect of overwork, nervous strain and apprehension. It was the past that was telling on them, the years of conspiracy, prison and exile; the years of the famine and the Civil War; and sticking to the rules of a game that demanded that at every moment a man's whole life should be at stake. They were indeed 'dead men on furlough', as Lenin had called them. Nothing could frighten them any more, nothing surprise them. They had given all they had. History had squeezed them out to the last drop, had burnt them out to the last spiritual calorie; yet they were still glowing in cold devotion, like phosphorescent corpses.[12]

Even the brave Budu Mdivani is quoted as saying, 'I belong to the opposition, that is clear. But if there is going to be a final break . . . I prefer to return to the Party I helped create. I no longer have the strength to begin creating a new party.'[13] As a psychological hurdle, the fresh start was too high. They fell back into submission, surrender.

This loyalty to 'the Party' has an element of unreality about it. The original Party of 1917 had been decimated by the expulsion of thousands of oppositionists. By the end of 1930, only Stalin, of the original leadership, remained in the Politburo. His nominees, from the ranks of the new men, controlled the elements of power. The Party itself, diluted by the great influxes of the twenties, had changed in the style of its membership and now contained a rank and file who had regularly, so far at least, acted as reliable voting fodder for the secretaries imposed by Stalin's Secretariat.

On the face of it, the opposition could well have argued that Stalin's control of, and claim to represent, the Party was based on no higher sanction than success in packing the Party Congresses: that in fact he had no real claim to be regarded as the genuine succession. But the oppositionists had themselves used similar methods in their day, and had never criticized them until a more skilled operator turned the weapon against themselves.

In 1923 Stalin was already able to attack such arguments from his opponents by pointing out that appeals for democracy came oddly from people like Byeloborodov and Rosengolts, who had ruled Rostov and the Donets Basin respectively in the most authoritarian fashion.[14] Even more to the point, in 1924 Shlyapni-kov ironically remarked that Trotsky and his followers had all supported the action taken against the Workers' Opposition at the Xth Party Congress in 1921, so that their claims to stand for Party democracy were hypocritical.[15] Kamenev denounced Party de-mocracy in this struggle with Trotsky in revealing terms:

> For if they say today, let us have democracy in the Party, tomorrow they will say, let us have democracy in the trade unions; the day after tomorrow, workers who do not belong to the Party may well say: give us democracy too . . . and surely then the myriads of peasants could not be prevented from asking for democracy.[16]

A year later he was asserting: 'We object to the Secretariat, uniting policy and organization in itself, being placed above the political organism.' It was too late. And the Stalinists were able to comment tellingly, as when Mikoyan said 'While Zinoviev is in the majority he is for iron discipline. . . . When he is in the minority . . . he is against it.'[17]

When Stalin proceeded to the further step of arresting those responsible for the Trotskyite underground printing-press, headed by Mrachkovsky, in 1927, he was again able to refute opposition objections, remarking:

> They say that such things are unknown of the Party. This is not true. What about the Myasnikov group? And the Workers' Truth group? Does not everyone know that Comrades Trotsky, Zinoviev and Kame-nev themselves supported the arrest of the members of these groups?[18]

Mere truth is a common casualty in all types of political system, but in non-totalitarian parties this never becomes an overt
and overriding principle, remaining sporadic and occasional, and
discrediting its authors when exposed. Among the Communists
it was consciously and systematically accepted.

It was ironically enough Trotsky who had publicly denied the
existence of Lenin's Testament. When Stalin attacked Kamenev
in 1926 for having sent a telegram of congratulations to the Grand
Duke Michael at the time of the February 1917 Revolution,
Kamenev pointed out that Lenin had personally signed a denial
of this. Stalin retorted quite matter-of-factly that Lenin had, in
the interests of the Party, knowingly stated a falsehood.[19] At the
XIVth Congress in 1925, Krupskaya appealed, as a member of
the defeated faction, to objective truth. Bukharin retorted:
'N. N. Krupskaya says truth is that which corresponds to reality,
each can read and listen, and answer for himself. But what about
the Party? Disappeared, as in the magic picture!'[20]

Also going back to the earliest days of the Party was the tradition that the best method of winning political argument was to
smear the opponent by every conceivable means. Lenin once said
to Angelica Balabanoff: 'Everything that is done in the proletarian cause is honest.' The great Italian Socialist leader Serrati,
though sympathetic to the Communists, had tried to prevent their
splitting his movement to suit their strategies, and had been
attacked in terms to which Mme Balabanoff, at that time Secretary
of the Comintern, had objected. After Serrati's death it was Zinoviev who explained the Leninist tactics to her: 'We have fought
and slandered him because of his great merits. It would not have
been possible to alienate the masses [from him] without resorting
to these means.'[21] It was natural, then, that the oppositionists
should be required to cast filth on their own motives and ideas.

At the XVth Party Congress in December 1927, Kamenev
argued that the denunciation of their own views then required of
the opposition would be meaningless. He explained the dilemma.
They now had no choice but either to constitute a second party,
which would be ruinous for the Revolution and 'lead to political
degeneration', or they must make 'a complete and thorough
surrender to the Party'. He and Zinoviev had decided on the

latter, taking the view that 'nothing could be done outside of and despite the Party'. They would obey, but he pleaded that they should not be obliged to denounce views that they had obviously held just a few weeks earlier. No one, he said, had previously made such a demand. (Though, in fact, Zinoviev had made exactly the same demand of Trotsky in 1924!)

Stalin did not accept Zinoviev's and Kamenev's recantation. They were trapped. They could hardly go back on what they had already said. Finally, they accepted the terms of the victor, denouncing their own views on 18 December as 'wrong and anti-Leninist'. Bukharin told them they were lucky to have made their minds up in time as this was 'the last moment available to them'.

Again denounced, expelled from the Party and sent into exile in 1932, Zinoviev and Kamenev were readmitted in 1933 on similar but yet more abject self-abasement. Zinoviev wrote to the Central Committee: 'I ask you to believe that I am speaking the truth and nothing but the truth. I ask you to restore me to the ranks of the Party and to give me an opportunity of working for the common cause. I give my word as a revolutionary that I will be the most devoted member of the Party, and will do all I possibly can at least to some extent to atone for my guilt before the Party and its Central Committee.'[22] And soon afterwards he was allowed to publish an article in *Pravda* condemning the opposition and praising Stalin's victories.[23]

In crawling as he did,* Zinoviev was acting logically from the point of view of Party ethics. He believed that any humiliation could be undergone for the purpose of remaining in the Party, where he might, in the future, play a useful role. But such logic was in any case to prove inapplicable. And meanwhile, the long process of deception and apology was corrupting the oppositionists. As a close observer commented:

* We should note, incidentally, that some of the earlier crop of capitulations by 'Trotskyites' had been much less abject than those of Zinoviev. Muralov had never made any declaration against the opposition. Ivan Smirnov's 'capitulation' had been in rather non-committal terms, and when he met Sedov in Berlin they had been friendly. Trotsky recognized that Serebryakov's capitulation, too, was 'more dignified than some'.

It must be admitted, that from the point of view of political morals, the conduct of the majority of the oppositionists was by no means of high quality. To be sure, the conditions prevailing in the Party are intolerable. To be loyal, to do every single thing that is demanded of us is almost impossible: to do so would mean to become an informer, to run to the Central Control Commission with reports on every utterance of opposition picked up more or less accidentally, and on every oppositionist document one comes across. A party which expects such things from its members cannot be expected to be regarded as a free association of persons of like views, united for a common purpose. We are all obliged to lie: it is impossible to manage otherwise. Nevertheless, there are limits which should not be exceeded even in lying. Unfortunately, the oppositionists, and particularly their leaders, often went beyond these limits.

. . . To plead for pardon has become a common phenomenon, on the supposition that the party in power being 'my party', the rules which applied in the Tsarist days are no longer valid. One hears this argument everywhere. At the same time, it is considered quite proper to consistently deceive 'my party', since the party does not fight its intellectual opponents by trying to convince them, but by the use of force. This has given rise to a special type of morality, which allows one to accept any conditions, to sign any undertakings, with the premeditated intention not to observe them.[24]

This attitude had a very demoralizing effect. The border between treachery and compromise became very vague. At the same time, Stalinists could point out that it was impossible to believe the opposition precisely because of their idea that telling lies was permissible.

Zinoviev and Kamenev had been expelled for the third time in 1934, on suspicion of politically inspiring Nikolayev in the murder of Kirov. And in January 1935, as we have seen, they had once again declared their political guilt, this time accepting it in a form which was already a partial plea of guilty before the criminal law.

Their successive surrenders had never been voluntary, in the sense that they would have preferred to avoid them. But they had accepted them, under pressure, as unavoidable moves in the political and moral conditions of the one-party system to which

they adhered. They had abandoned in turn each of their objections
– to falsification, to undemocratic procedures, to insincere re-
tractions, to arrest. They had chosen to do so in order to remain
in the Party, or to gain readmission when they had been expelled.
The Rightist Slepkov is reported by a Soviet writer as being
brought back from a political isolator and supplying the names of
over a hundred and fifty accomplices, on the grounds, 'We must
disarm! We must go on our knees to the Party.'[25]

In the case of the prominent Communists accused at the great
show trials of 1936, 1937 and 1938, there is no doubt that the
rational, or rationalized, component in their motives included
this idea of service to the Party. This theme has been most strikingly and persuasively developed in Arthur Koestler's *Darkness
at Noon*, and is often taken as *the* explanation of the public
confessions – though Koestler himself makes no such claim, and
on the contrary remarks:

Some were silenced by physical fear, like Hare-lip; some hoped to
save their heads; others at least to save their wives or sons from the
clutches of the Gletkins. The best of them kept silent in order to do a
last service to the Party, by letting themselves be sacrificed as scapegoats – and, besides, even the best had each an Arlova on his conscience.[26]

Koestler's last point – that the oppositionists felt they had lost
the right to judge Stalin – is confirmed in various reports. A non-
Communist prisoner notes how 'nearly every supporter of the
regime, before falling a victim to it, has in his time been involved
by it in actions which have conflicted with his political conscience'.[27] And he agrees with Koestler on the main issue:

It is true that the interrogation methods, particularly when applied
for months or years, are capable of breaking the strongest will. But the
decisive factor is something else. It is that the majority of convinced
Communists must at all costs preserve their faith in the Soviet Union.
To renounce it would be beyond their powers. For great moral strength
is required in certain circumstances to renounce one's long-standing,
deep-rooted convictions, even when these turn out to be untenable.[28]

Koestler's account is in fact extremely well founded on the
facts. For instance, when he describes an attempt to break

Rubashov's* morale by dragging a badly tortured prisoner past his cell to execution, he can base this firmly on the evidence.[30] Briefly summarized, Rubashov's surrender is based on a feeling that his own past actions have deprived him of the right to judge Stalin's, coupled with a feeling of loyalty to the Party and its conception of history; and it is largely a conscious process – the pressure of the interrogation, toothache, etc., merely intensifying his reflections leading up to the decision. In fact, he is shown in court as resisting the temptation not to confess. The key thought in his confession is formulated thus:

'I know', Rubashov went on, 'that my aberration, if carried into effect, would have been a mortal danger to the Revolution. Every opposition at the critical turning-points of history, carries in itself the germ of a split in the Party, and hence the germ of civil war. Humanitarian weakness and liberal democracy, when the masses are not mature, is suicide for the Revolution. And yet my oppositional attitude was based on a craving for just these methods – in appearance so desirable, actually so deadly. On a demand for a liberal reform of the dictatorship, for a broader democracy, for the abolition of the Terror, and a loosening of the rigid organization of the Party. I admit that these demands, in the present situation, are objectively harmful and therefore counter-revolutionary in character . . .'[31]

We have here, though in more extreme form, that extravagant identification with the Party which is to be found in Bukharin's private utterances before his arrest, and in Pyatakov's 1928 outburst. Bukharin was to say publicly in his last plea:

For three months I refused to say anything. Then I began to testify. Why? Because while in prison I made a revaluation of my entire past. For when you ask yourself: 'If you must die, what are you dying for?' – an absolutely black vacuity suddenly rises before you with startling vividness. There was nothing to die for, if one wanted to die unrepented. . . . And when you ask yourself, 'Very well, suppose you do not die; suppose by some miracle you remain alive, again what for?' Isolated from everybody, an enemy of the people, an inhuman position, completely isolated from everything that constitutes the essence of life.[32]

* His 'Rubashov' is modelled on Bukharin in his thinking and Trotsky and Radek in his personality and physical appearance.[29]

Koestler does not, as we have noted, put forward his account as a general theory of the motivation of confessions. He is simply giving an account of one presumable mechanism: and it is clear from much that has been written since that what he describes, or something like it, was genuinely involved in certain cases.

These considerations did not apply to all Party members. Ryutin and his associates were clearly prepared to remove Stalin. And similarly with the confessions. Ivan Smirnov was only induced to make his partial and derisory confession on the grounds that without it he would be shot in secret and his name dragged in the mud by those who had already decided to confess, and by the promise to spare his former wife and his family,[33] while his presence would to some extent check the smears of the Prosecutor. Even so, he is said to have gone to his death remarking that he and the other defendants had behaved despicably.[34]

And what greater contrast could there be between Pyatakov's words and those reported of Ter-Vaganian:

But in order to sign the testimony which is demanded of me, I must be sure first that it is really needed in the interests of the Party and the Revolution . . .

. . . You suggest that I do not think and rely blindly on the Central Committee, because the Central Committee sees everything more clearly than I. But the trouble is that by my very nature I am unable to stop thinking. And when I do think, I come to the inescapable conclusion that the assertions that the oldest Bolsheviks have turned into a gang of murderers will bring incalculable harm not only to our country and the Party, but to the cause of Socialism all over the world . . .

. . . If now the new programme of the Central Committee deems it necessary to discredit Bolshevism and its founders, then I don't agree with that programme and I no longer consider myself bound by Party discipline. And besides, I am already expelled from the Party, and for that reason alone I am not obliged to submit to Party discipline.[35]

When he was finally persuaded that there was no point in resisting, while Zinoviev and Kamenev, greatly senior figures, were going anyhow to smear the Party, and he was advised by the interrogator Boris Berman, with whom he had become friendly, that he might just as well save his own life this way, he gave in.

Berman remarked that in this way he hoped, after years had passed, to see Ter-Vaganian rehabilitated and given an important post. Ter-Vaganian is said to have replied:

I have not the slightest desire to be in a high post. If my party, for which I lived, and for which I was ready to die any minute, forced me to sign *this*, then I don't want to be in the Party. Today I envy the most ignorant non-Party man.[36]

And yet Ter-Vaganian was one of those who gave in. We can be sure that similar views, even more strongly held, determined the attitudes of men who could not be broken. Kuklin is reported in prison as saying that 'all was lost' as far as the Party and the Revolution were concerned, and a new start would be necessary.[37]

The argument that Party-style thinking, the idea of Party discipline, are *the* main explanation for the public confessions has one obvious objection. This logic, if it existed, was as formally true at the moment of arrest as it was later. Yet in almost every case the accused resisted for a longer or shorter period. Why was the idea of Party discipline convincing to Muralov in December 1936, when for eight months previously he had found it unconvincing? Why did Bukharin resist for three months?

Bukharin, indeed, gave an answer at his trial: cut off and exposed, removed from the Party, with nothing to live for, he started a re-examination of his thoughts, a re-evaluation which led him to surrender. If it comes to that, Boguslavsky went through the whole process in eight days, during which 'owing to my arrest, I recovered my balance and I was able to bring my still largely, if not utterly, criminal ideas in order'[38] – which, though expressed suitably to the trial, amounts to the same thing.

Thus it is not the case that good Communists automatically obeyed when told 'The Party needs your evidence': they did so after a varying length of imprisonment and interrogation. And indeed, in many cases it was impossible to persuade them at all. Even Bukharin himself (who is supposed to be the main follower of this line) did not after all produce a confession wholly in accord with the prosecution's wishes, but chose to speak in such a way that anyone of any sense could see that the charges were false.

And we have already noted that when Kaganovich, one of the

keenest supporters of the Purge, himself fell from power, he omitted to suggest that the Party's image would be best served by bringing him to trial and blackening him as a spy, terrorist and saboteur and shooting him amid public execration. On the contrary, he rang up Khrushchev and begged him 'not to allow them to deal with me as they dealt with people under Stalin'[39] – a grave dereliction from the point of view of service to the Party. Clearly, without denying that in many cases the idea of being useful to the Party was a component of the intellectual and psychological conditions of surrender, we can at least say that it took effect in combination with a good many other pressures.

It is obvious enough that the oppositionists did not expect just fair treatment and political persuasion. Tomsky's suicide the day he heard of the charges against him is enough to show that, and his was not the only one. The political argument about service to the Party can, in fact, be seen as a component in some cases (but not all) of a larger system of physical, intellectual and moral pressures. In a case like Kamenev's, where the argument about the Party's interests was combined with exhausting interrogation, heat, lack of food, threats to his family, and promises of his life, we can hardly expect to decide which played the most important part.

For, having gone into the habits of mind of the oppositionists who confessed, there are two major qualifications to add. First, as we have seen, not all the Communists held the ideas of party unity and of self-abasement in the way that Zinoviev and Kamenev, Bukharin and Pyatakov did; and from them it was often impossible to obtain public confessions. And, on the other hand, public confessions were produced from non-Communists: the doctors in the 1938 Trial, most of the Polish underground leaders in 1945, the Bulgarian Protestant pastors in 1949. The motivations just described were of primary importance in the whole great cycle of Party submission to Stalin, but in the trials themselves they were neither necessary nor sufficient causes of the particular surrender involved in public confession. In a number of the most important cases they predisposed the leading accused to giving in to the pressures put on them, and they provided the rationale of the confessions made. But it was by the merely technical action of the N.K.V.D. interrogation system that these and other predisposing factors were brought to the full fruition of the scenes in the October Hall.

TORTURE

When it came to explaining *how* the confessions had been obtained, the first thought of hostile critics was torture. Indeed, Khrushchev was to remark in 1956: 'How is it possible that a person confesses to crimes which he has not committed? Only in one way – because of application of physical methods of pressuring him, tortures, bringing him to a state of unconsciousness, depriving him of his judgement, taking away his human dignity. In this manner were "confessions" acquired.'[40]

Physical torture was, of course, practised by the N.K.V.D., and had been since the early days of the regime. In the early thirties there are many reports of police brutality: in Rostov, prisoners were hit in the stomach with a sandbag: this was sometimes fatal. A doctor would certify that a prisoner who had died of it had suffered from a malign tumour.[41] Another interrogation method was the *stoika*. It consisted of standing a prisoner against a wall on tiptoe and making him hold that position for several hours. A day or two of this was said to be enough to break almost anyone.[42]

Other 'improvised' torture methods included the 'swallow', which consisted of tying the hands and feet behind the back and hoisting the victim into the air.[43] One prisoner describes having her fingers slammed in a door.[44] Beating up was usual. Interrogators sometimes had to hand over to special heavily-built thugs known to the prisoners as 'boxers' who would carry this out.[45] Nor was this done only with peasants and socially hostile elements: a colonel, later restored to the Party, reports being badly beaten up by the N.K.V.D. in 1935.[46] There are many reports of women being beaten.[47] In general, the provincial interrogators were the more brutal. A Red Army Choir accordionist had both legs broken at Khabarovsk;[48] toenails were torn out at Baku, genitals beaten at Ashkhabad.[49]

All this was, in a sense, 'unofficial'. In most prisons physical torture remained so. Needles, pincers and so on are sporadically reported, and more specialized implements seem to have been in use at the Lefortovo.[50] But on the whole some appearance of spontaneity was maintained. Feet and fingers were stamped on. Broken-off chair legs were the usual weapon for beatings, which were sometimes distinguished from 'torture'. But as one very experienced prisoner says, this distinction was rather absurd, when a man came back after such a beating with broken ribs, urinating blood for a week, or with a permanently injured spine and unable to walk.[51]

In any case, in his Secret Speech, Khrushchev refers directly to the 'long tortures' inflicted on Kossior and Chubar. And he also gives a long account of a particular case – oddly choosing that of Kedrov. He quotes a letter of his which in most circumstances would have been unreservedly moving:

> I am calling to you for help from a gloomy cell of the Lefortovo Prison. Let my cry of horror reach your ears. . . . Please, help remove the nightmare of interrogations . . . I am firmly certain that, given a quiet objective examination, without foul rantings, without any anger and without the fearful tortures, it would be easy to prove the baselessness of the charges . . .

Kedrov himself had behaved with the most notorious cruelty as representative of the Cheka in the Archangel area during the Civil War, and his son (who shared his fate) had been one of the N.K.V.D.'s most brutal interrogators in extracting false confessions in the Zinoviev and Pyatakov cases, a fact he can scarcely have been unaware of. Whatever sympathy we may feel for him, it is bound to be greater for the many more innocent and harmless people who were enduring the same torments, whose voices (since they are not old Communists) have yet to be reproduced in the Soviet Union.

Physical torture, though not uncommon, had been contrary to regulations until 1937. Then it suddenly became the usual method of interrogation, at least in the bulk of cases at the lower level. It seems to have been late in 1936 that the first official, though secret, instructions on the use of torture were put out in Byelorussia.[52] Early in the following year an authorization from the

'Central Committee' – that is, Stalin – was given to the N.K.V.D. It was only on 20 January 1939 that a circular coded telegram formally confirmed the system to the secretaries of Provincial Committees and Republican Central Committees of the Party, and to the heads of N.K.V.D. organizations:

The Party Central Committee explains that application of methods of physical pressure in N.K.V.D. practice is permissible from 1937 on, in accordance with permission of the Party Central Committee. . . . It is known that all bourgeois intelligence services use methods of physical influence against the representatives of the socialist proletariat and that they use them in their most scandalous forms. The question arises as to why the socialist intelligence service should be more humanitarian against the mad agents of the bourgeoisie, against the deadly enemies of the working class and of the collective farm workers. The Party Central Committee considers that physical pressure should still be used obligatorily, as an exception applicable to known and obstinate enemies of the people, as a method both justifiable and appropriate.[53]

A Soviet general describes his fate under this system:

I accidentally found out that my fiend of an interrogator's name was Stolbunsky. I don't know where he is now. If he is still alive I hope he will read these lines and feel my contempt for him, not only now but when I was in his hands. But I think he knew this well enough. Apart from him, two brawny torturers took part in the interrogation. Even now my ears ring with the sound of Stolbunsky's evil voice hissing 'You'll sign, you'll sign!' as I was carried out, weak and covered in blood. I withstood the torture during the second bout of interrogation, but when the third started, how I longed to be able to die![54]

He adds that all his cell-mates had (in 1938) confessed to imaginary crimes: 'Some had done this after physical coercion and others after having been terrified by accounts of the tortures used.' In most of them the threat of further torture was enough to prevent retraction.*

Yet, in spite of Khrushchev's remarks, torture is not an ade-

---

*Various forms of humiliation were often especially effective on men weakened by torture. An Army officer who withstood beating finally broke when the interrogator pushed his head into a spittoon brim-full of spittle. Another gave way when an interrogator urinated on his head – an interrogation practice which according to reports became traditional.[55]

quate explanation of all the confessions of the oppositionists. We should record its extent, and its overwhelmingly powerful effects throughout the period. But critics were right in saying that torture alone could probably not have produced the public self-humiliation of a whole series of Stalin's enemies, when returned to health and given a platform.

We shall see, in fact, that some accused withdrew in closed court confessions obtained by torture. Others 'insisted even in the preliminary investigation or in court that their statements charging violations of socialist legality be entered in the examination record'.[56]

THE 'CONVEYOR'

The basic N.K.V.D. method for obtaining confessions and breaking the accused man was the 'conveyor' – continual interrogation by relays of police for hours and days on end. As with many phenomena of the Stalin period, it had the advantage that it could not easily be condemned by any simple principle. Clearly, it amounted to unfair pressure after a certain time, and as actual physical torture later still: but when? No absolutely precise answer could be given.

But, at any rate, after even twelve hours, it is extremely uncomfortable. After a day, it becomes very hard. And after two or three days, the victim is actually being physically poisoned by fatigue. It was 'as painful as any torture'.[57] In fact, we are told though some prisoners had been known to resist torture, it was almost unheard-of for the conveyor not to succeed if kept up long enough. One week is reported as enough to break almost anybody.[58] A recent description by a Soviet woman writer who experienced it speaks of seven days without sleep or food, the seventh standing up – ending in physical collapse. This was followed by a five-day interrogation of a milder type, in which she was allowed three hours' rest in her cell, though sleep was still forbidden.[59]

Krestinsky managed to make it clear, in his evidence at his trial, that his first interrogation had lasted a week,[60] though the point does not seem to have been taken by observers. In the case of Marshal Blyukher, 'the health of this virile man was broken by continuous interrogation'.[61] He died less than three weeks after his arrest, and the interrogation presumably lasted a shorter time still.

There is nothing new about this method. It was used on witches in Scotland. The philosopher Campanella, who withstood all other tortures during his interrogation in the sixteenth century, succumbed to lack of sleep. Hallucinations occur. Flies buzz about. Smoke seems to rise before the prisoner's eyes, and so on.

Beck and Godin report a case in which interrogation lasted without any break for eleven days, during the last four of which the prisoner had to stand. Towards the end of even lesser periods prisoners collapsed about every twenty minutes and had to be brought round with cold water or slaps.*[62] Sitting on a stool for fourteen hours is, according to one victim, more painful than standing against a wall, where you can at least shift your weight from one foot to the other. The groins swell and violent pains set in.

In Weissberg's account of his interrogation,[64] he mentions that on one occasion he was interrogated for eighteen hours, then left locked in the washroom where the floor was under water. He was, however, able to lie down on a footrack. After fourteen hours he was called out for a brief interrogation and sent back to find that the rack had been removed, so that he had to stand in an inch or so of water for forty hours, until the next interrogation. Later, he was beaten up, under the new practice, but was then returned to the conveyor. A 'technical improvement' had been made in that the seat had been taken out of the chair and it was extremely painful, even briefly.[65]

There are very few accounts of successful resistance to the conveyor. One is of a fifty-five-year-old anarchist, Eisenberg, who on being called a counter-revolutionary refused to answer any more questions. Beating up had no effect on him, and he survived a

* There is a report from the Butyrka of the interrogation of a doctor who was kept standing without sleep, with little interruption, for a week. The process was then broken off. It was said that there was then a regulation limiting such practices to precisely a week.[63]

conveyor lasting for thirty-one days – an extraordinary record. Examination by a doctor showed that though physically very sound there was something abnormal about his imperviousness to pain. He is supposed to have been sent to a lunatic asylum.[66]

Weissberg himself held out for seven days, helped by a brief interruption, but finally confessed. After a day's rest he withdrew the confession. Interrogation started again. This time he gave way on the fourth day, having already told the examiners that every confession he made he would withdraw when he recovered. The third conveyor session ended on the fifth day without his signing a fresh confession, though by now the interrogators had two 'documents'.

And here we have the defect of the 'conveyor'. Though it was almost always successful, and usually in two to three days, it had no essential advantage over torture proper (with which it was often combined), since the confessions it produced could be withdrawn.

THE LONG INTERROGATION

The interrogation system which broke down many prisoners to the extent of maintaining their confessions at public trial was conceived on rather different lines. It aimed at a more gradual, but more complete, destruction of the will to resist. With intellectuals and politicians the process often lasted a long time – some (with interruptions) up to two and a half years. The average is thought to have been about four or five months.[67]

Throughout the period the prisoner was kept with inadequate sleep, in cells either too hot or (most usually) too cold, on insufficient though attractively prepared food. The Spanish Communist general, El Campesino, speaks of $3\frac{1}{2}$ ounces of black bread and some soup 'served beautifully and tastily' twice a day,[68] with results such as scurvy, which must be taken as planned. Physical exhaustion produces increased liability to psychological disorders – a well-established phenomenon noted in the last war in, for example, boats' crews who had drifted for a long time: even persons whose stability was such that they were not likely to break down under the most difficult situation, frequently then succumbed.

Interrogation usually took place at night and with the accused just roused – often only fifteen minutes after going to sleep. The glaring lights at the interrogation had a disorientating effect. There was a continual emphasis on the absolute powerlessness of the victim. The interrogators – or so it usually seemed – could go on indefinitely. Thus the struggle seemed a losing one. The continual repetition of a series of questions is also invariably reported to disorientate both semantically and as regards the recollection, or interpretation, of facts. And there was a total lack of privacy.

A Pole, Z. Stypulkowski, who experienced the whole process in 1945 describes it:

... Cold, hunger, the bright light and especially sleeplessness. The cold is not terrific. But when the victim is weakened by hunger and by sleeplessness, then the six or seven degrees above freezing point makes him tremble all the time. During the night I had only one blanket.

... After two or three weeks, I was in a semi-conscious state. After fifty or sixty interrogations with cold and hunger and almost no sleep, a man becomes like an automaton – his eyes are bright, his legs swollen, his hands trembling. In this state he is often convinced he is guilty.[69]

He estimated that most of his fellow-accused had reached this condition between the fortieth and seventieth interrogations. International considerations made it necessary to bring the Polish underground leaders to trial before Stypulkowski (alone among the accused) was ready to confess. We have more lately had the evidence, for the first time,* of men who made a full confession – Artur London[70] and, more revealingly, Evzen Loebl, sentenced to life imprisonment in the Czechoslovak Slansky Trial in 1952.

Loebl mentions other prisoners being beaten, having their genitals crushed, being put in ice-cold water, having their heads wrapped in wet cloth which, when it dried, shrank, and caused 'unbearable pain'. But (unlike London), he was not tortured himself and confirms that torture was inadequate for the preparation of the victim of a set-piece trial, when 'the whole of the person

* If we except a short piece by Pal Justus, one of the Rajk Trial accused, which appeared in Budapest in 1956.

had to be "broken"'. He describes having to be on his feet eighteen hours a day, of which sixteen were devoted to interrogation. During the six-hour sleep period the warder pounded on the door every ten minutes, upon which he had to jump to attention and report: 'detainee No. 1473 reports: strength one detainee, everything in order'. He was, that is, 'awakened thirty or forty times a night'. If the banging did not wake him a kick from the warder would. After two or three weeks his feet were swollen and every inch of his body ached at the slightest touch; even washing became a torture. He says that the worst pain came in his legs when he lay down. He was taken six or seven times to what he was led to believe would be his execution: he did not mind it at the time, but the reaction afterwards affected him badly. Like others in various Eastern European trials, he is convinced that he was given drugs. But if so this was a late refinement and does not appear in reports of pre-war interrogations in Russia. (Loebl notes, incidentally, that the doctor's brutality was even greater than that of the interrogators.) He finally reached the stage where it did not occur to him to repudiate his confession. Having confessed, he was allowed books, adequate food and rest, but he had (as he puts it) been deprived of his ego: 'I was quite a normal person – only I was no longer a person.'[71]

There is no doubt that not only non-political defendants but even strong political opponents can be broken by the 'Yezhov method'. In this connexion the statements of the Bulgarian Protestant pastors in the February 1949 Trial are the most relevant, since no one could possibly argue that loyalty to party or creed induced them. In their confessions they all remarked that they now saw Communist rule of their country 'in a new light'. In their final pleas Pastor Naumov thanked the police for their 'kindness and consideration' and said: 'I have sinned against my people and against the whole world. This is my resurrection'; Pastor Diapkov was in tears as he admitted his guilt and said 'Do not make of me a useless martyr by giving me the death sentence. Help me to become a useful citizen and a hero of the Fatherland Front'; Pastor Bezlov, who had earlier stated that he had read 12,000 pages of Marxist literature while in prison and that this had entirely changed his outlook, declared: 'I have now an intellectual appreciation of what the new life means and I want to play my part in it.'*

In his speech to the United Nations General Assembly on 26 October 1953, Dr Mayo drew attention to the parallel between the similar treatment of the American prisoners in Korea to obtain confessions of 'germ warfare' and the work of Pavlov in establishing conditioned reflexes in dogs. Soviet psychologists and physiologists have always treated Pavlov as the basis of their work, and his method of associating stimuli to provide an automatic response accords with the reduction of prisoners to the point at which they associate survival with the single response of accepting what their captors tell them. In a human being this involves considerable degradation. An animal's response – at least to situations which it recognizes (the only ones it can cope with) – is in principle unconditional and without discrimination. Man's higher status consists precisely in his ability to distinguish and discriminate. To put it another way, among men it is only the psychotic who give an unconditional reaction to a stimulus.

But a man, even in this state, is not an animal. He needs at least the appearance of rational motives. In the case of Communists this was ready to hand in their Party principles. There were other pressures.

HOSTAGES

There is no doubt that threats to the family – the use, that is, of hostages for good behaviour – was one of the most powerful of all Stalin's safeguards. It seems a general rule that with confessions by prominent figures, members of the family were in the power of the N.K.V.D. Bukharin, Rykov and Krestinsky all had children of whom they were very fond, whereas at least some of those tried in private, such as Karakhan, did not. Several of the accused in

---

*The factual side of the confessions, as so often, contained impossibilities – as when the Head of the Congregationalist Church mentioned meetings with a British vice-consul over a long period when the man concerned had not been in the country.

their final pleas referred to their children – for example, Kamenev and Rosengolts.

Engineers under arrest as early as 1930 had been threatened with reprisals against their wives and children.[72] And the decree of 7 April 1935 which extended full adult penalties down to children of twelve was a terrible threat to those oppositionists with children. If Stalin could openly and publicly declare such an atrocity, they could be sure that he would not hesitate to apply the death penalty secretly to their own children in cases where he thought it would bring him advantage. According to Orlov,[73] it became regular practice, on Yezhov's orders, for interrogators to have a copy of the decree on their desks. We are also told that fear of reprisals was made more dramatic and emotionally effective by the display on the interrogator's desk of private belongings of members of the family.[74] Even if accepted and allowed for on the conscious level, this must have been a continual argument in the unconscious in favour of surrender.

The use of relatives as hostages, and their imprisonment or execution in other cases, was a new development in Russian history. In Tsarist times revolutionaries never had this problem. Here again, Stalin recognized no limits.

On the other side of the coin it was suggested, even at the time, that there was something about the confessions which was specifically Russian. The Dostoievsky-style habit of self-abasement was much spoken of. Bukharin denied that the *âme slave* had any bearing on the confessions. He was himself a more intellectual and in a sense more Westernized character than many of the leaders. But in any case these adumbrations of national psychology are very vague and in themselves unconvincing. It is not surprising that at the time people faced with the extraordinary phenomenon of the confessions should have sought out extraordinary explanations.

Nevertheless, like any other, the Russian culture has its own characteristics, affecting the attitudes of all those brought up in it. We can hardly quite exclude *some* effect of a tradition of self-immolation (even though the Russian tradition also contains famous examples of most outright defiance of authority, as with Archpriest Avvakum who spat in the face of the Tsar). Four out of five of the arrested Politburo members who did not come to public trial – Rudzutak, Eikhe, Kossior and Chubar – were non-Russians. The Georgians without exception were tried *in camera*. It was the Georgian, Alyosha Svanidze, who is mentioned as refusing a pardon offered on condition that he asked forgiveness.[75]

Another powerful motive was that of self-preservation. This is a paradox which confused observers in the West, and still confuses some. By the full and sometimes abject confession of capital crimes, it appeared that the defendants were actively seeking the death sentence which, they themselves sometimes said, they fully deserved. The reality was different. The absolutely certain way for a defendant to get himself shot was to refuse to plead guilty. He would then not go before an open court at all, but either perish under the rigours of the preliminary investigation, or be shot, like Rudzutak, after a twenty-minute closed trial. The logic of Stalin's courts was different from what is customary elsewhere. The only chance of avoiding death was to admit everything, and to place the worst possible construction on all one's activities. It is true that even this seldom saved a man's life. But it did sometimes, for a while – as in the cases of Radek, Sokolnikov and Rakovsky. At the August 1936 Trial, moreover, the defendants had actually been promised their lives and had reasonable expectation that the promise would be fulfilled. The same promise was evidently made to Pyatakov and others in the second trial. It must have lost a good deal of its efficacy; yet, even then, it represented the only possible hope. Besides, on the face of it, the Pyatakov situation was different. While Zinoviev and Kamenev had continued in effect to oppose the Stalin leadership, and had long since been excluded from decent Party society, Pyatakov had been of the greatest service to the dictator and had been admitted by him to his latest Central Committee. He was, in addition, under the apparently powerful protection of Ordzhonikidze. And a little hope goes a long way.

As to Communist motives proper, the Party and the old opposition had already been smeared beyond relief. Even for a man like Sokolnikov, it may have appeared that no action he could take could affect the issue one way or the other, and that the only consideration left was to attempt to save his family. So much more admirable, then, is the sense of truth and personal courage shown by men like Uglanov and Preobrazhensky who even under the pressure of such arguments seem to have 'died in silence'.

For, when everything is said of the pressures for confession, it is remarkable how many did not give way or – if they did – were not trusted to maintain their confessions in court. Non-confessors were a special breed. Koestler analyses his friend Dr Weissberg:

> What enabled him to hold out where others broke down was a specific mixture of just those character traits which survival in such a situation requires. A great physical and mental resilience – that jack-in-the-box quality which allows quick recuperation and apparently endless comebacks, both physical and mental. An extraordinary presence of mind. . . . A certain thick-skinnedness and good-natured insensitivity, coupled with an almost entirely extroverted disposition – notice the absence in Dr Weissberg's book of any contemplative passage, of any trace of religious or mystic experience which is otherwise almost inevitably present in solitary confinement. An irresponsible optimism and smug complacency in hair-raising situations; that 'it can't happen to me' attitude, which is the most reliable source of courage; and an inexhaustible sense of humour. Finally, that relentless manner of persisting in an argument and continuing it for hours, days or weeks, which I mentioned before. It drove his inquisitors nuts, as it sometimes had his friends.[76]

Similar attitudes can be seen in other known non-confessors.* We can trace the tough temperaments elsewhere. In Pervouralsk, in 1938, the chief construction engineer at the Novo-Trubni Plant, who had been in prison for thirteen months, 'little more than a skeleton in rags', and with patches of blood and bruises all over him, was interrogated by the local N.K.V.D. chief, Parshin. He was accused of putting wooden roofs over furnaces, which might well have caught fire. He continued to explain that though the roofs should have been made of iron, a Government order signed by Ordzhonikidze had ordered wood because of the iron shortage. To several similar questions he answered in the same way.[77] Similar accounts are given all through the literature, though they

*e.g. the Pole Stypulkowski and the Spaniard El Campesino.

are always treated as most exceptional: the critic Ivanov-Razumnik says that in his years in jail in Moscow and Leningrad only twelve of the thousand-odd prisoners he shared cells with had failed to confess.[78]

It is significant that many oppositionists who had repudiated the Bukharin view of Party discipline in the early thirties did not come to trial. Stalin must have wanted Ryutin in dock, but he did not get him. The same applies to Uglanov, Syrtsov, A.P. Smirnov and the others who tried to organize resistance while the Right leaders were counselling patience. The absence in their make-ups of the Party fetishism noted in Bukharin, Zinoviev and most of the other public confessors must be a factor. We know very little of the conduct under arrest of such oppositionist Communists. But it is fairly clear that neither the pressures nor the arguments were enough to break many, or more precisely (for many certainly confessed under interrogation) to keep them broken.*

According to most reports there were several hundred candidates for public trial, but only about seventy actually came into court. Of those named for complicity in the Zinoviev Trial, sixteen appeared at the time, three committed suicide, and seven were tried later. Forty-three others were never brought to trial and so never made public confessions. They included men as prominent as Uglanov, who had, after all, been Candidate Member of the Politburo and Secretary of the Central Committee, and first-line Old Bolsheviks like Shlyapnikov and Smilga.

In the Zinoviev Trial material quoted from the preliminary investigation is given as coming from a different volume of evidence from each accused. These dossiers are numbered intermittently from 1 to 38, but only sixteen accused appeared. The presumption is that twenty-two were dealt with secretly (though some – e.g. Gaven and Slepkov – were perhaps held in reserve).

In the Pyatakov Trial, where dossiers ran from 1 to 36, there are nineteen missing. The leading figures have the low numbers:

---

* Just as (it was officially revealed in 1968) a number of prominent accused were not brought to trial with Slansky in Prague because they 'would not behave in court': of fifty or sixty leading functionaries available, only fourteen were used.[79]

Pyatakov I, Radek V, Sokolnikov VIII, Drobnis XIII. Serebryakov and Muralov do not happen to be quoted; but even inserting their names, there are clearly missing volumes, and the presumption is that these existed, and covered figures at this political level not brought to trial.

Certain Soviet books about the period of the Revolution have briefly referred in their biographical notes to a number of members of the opposition. This information (which became available in the Khrushchev interlude) remains sketchy,* but it will be appropriate here to note that some are specifically said to have been 'convicted', which implies secret and hitherto undisclosed trials. These include Uglanov, implicated in all three public trials, expelled from the Party in 1936, convicted, and died 1940; Smilga, convicted, and died 1938; Sosnovsky, Sapronov, Shatskin and Preobrazhensky, convicted, and died 1937; V. M. Smirnov, expelled and convicted 1936, died 1937; Safarov (who is reported in Vorkuta in 1940),[80] convicted, died 1942. If these major ex-oppositionists could be openly branded, and yet not brought to public trial, the normal implication is that they could not be trusted in court.†

THE IDEA OF CONFESSION

The question naturally arises, not only why the accused made the confessions, but also why the prosecution wanted them. In the public trials, indeed, as Radek pointed out in the dock, there was no other evidence. A case in which there was not only no evidence against the accused, but they also denied the charges, would clearly be rather a weak one by any standards.

In fact, confession is the logical thing to go for when the accused

---

*In the notes to the new editions of the Stenographic Reports of early Party Congresses and Conferences, and the new edition of Lenin's *Collected Works*, and in various other books such as *History of the Civil War* (Moscow, 1960), *The Party in the Period of Civil War and Foreign Military Intervention* (Moscow, 1962), *Thus Was Lenin* (Moscow, 1964), etc.

† Death dates of other prominent figures not specifically referred to as convicted are Medvedev (Shlyapnikov's chief aide in the Workers' Opposition), 1937; Ryazanov, 1938; Syrtsov, 1938; Vasily Shmidt, expelled as a Rightist, 1937, died 1940; A. P. Smirnov, 1938.

are not guilty and there is no genuine evidence. For, in these circumstances, it is difficult to make people appear guilty unless they themselves admit it. And it is easier to stage-manage a trial of this sort if one can be sure that no awkward defendant is going to speak up at unpredictable intervals.

In general, moreover, in the public trials of Zinoviev and the others, the confession method can be easily accounted for. Stalin wanted, not merely to kill his old opponents, but to destroy them morally and politically. It would have been difficult simply to announce the secret execution of Zinoviev. It would have been equally difficult to try him publicly, without any evidence, on charges which he could vigorously and effectively deny.

Even if confessions seem highly implausible, they may have some effect, even on sceptics, on the principle that there is no smoke without fire and that mud sticks. Even if the confession is disbelieved, a defendant who humbly confesses and admits that his opponents were right is to some extent discredited politically – certainly more than if, publicly, he had put up a stout fight. Even if the confession is disbelieved, it is a striking demonstration of the power of the State over its opponents. It is more in accordance with totalitarian ideologies that a defendant should confess, even under duress: it is better discipline and a good example to all ranks. (Those who would not confess properly in court were sometimes provided with posthumous confessions, to keep up the standards, as with the Bulgarian Kostov in 1949.)

These are rational considerations. But it is also clear that the principle of confession in all cases, even from ordinary victims tried in secret, was insisted on. In fact, the major effort of the whole vast police organization throughout the country went into obtaining such confessions. When we read, in cases of no particular importance, and ones never to be made public, of the use of the 'conveyor' system tying down team after team of police investigators for days on end, the impression one gets is not simply of vicious cruelty, but of insane preoccupation with a pointless formality. The accused could perfectly well, it seems, have been shot or sentenced without this frightful rigmarole.

But the extraordinary, contorted legalism of the whole operation remained to the end. It would have been possible simply to have deported thousands or millions of people on suspicion. Yet perhaps 100,000 examiners and other officials spent months interrogating and guarding prisoners who did not, during that time, even provide the State with any labour.[81] One explanation advanced in the prisons was that, apart from a hypocritical wish to preserve the façade, the absence of confessions would have made it much more difficult to find fresh inculpations.

It is also clear that the confession system, involving one single type of evidence, was easier to stereotype down the whole line of investigators than more substantial methods of faking. When evidence of actual objects was involved, there was often trouble. In the Ukraine a group of Social Revolutionaries confessed to having a secret arms cache, at the instance of an inexperienced interrogator. The first 'conspirator' confessed to having put it in charge of another man. The second man, under torture, said that he had passed them on to another member. They went through eleven hands until, after a discussion in his cell, the last consignee was urged to think of someone who had died whom he knew well. He could only remember his former geography master, a completely non-political character who had just died, but maintained that the examiner would never believe him to have been a conspirator. He was finally persuaded that all the examiner wanted was to get rid of the arms somehow, so he made the confession as suggested and the examiner was so delighted that he gave him a good meal and some tobacco.[82]

We may also feel that with the establishment of the confession principle in the public trials, its abandonment with lesser accused might have been taken in N.K.V.D. usage as an implied criticism of the trials. The principle had become established that a confession was the best result obtainable. Those who could obtain them were to be considered successful operatives; and a poor N.K.V.D. operative had a short life-expectancy.

Beyond all this, one forms the impression of a determination to break the idea of the truth, to impose on everyone the acceptance of official falsehood. In fact, over and above the rational motives for the extraction of confession, one seems to sense an almost metaphysical preference for it. As early as 1918 Dzerzhinsky had remarked, of enemies of the Soviet Government, 'When con-

fronted with evidence, criminals in almost every case confess; and
what argument can have greater weight than a criminal's own
confession?'[83]

Vyshinsky was the great theorist of confession. He regarded a
confession, however obtained, as 'in itself grounds for a conviction', and recommended prosecutors and investigators to make a
practice of getting the defendant's testimony in his own handwriting as looking more voluntary. He added 'I personally prefer
a half confession in the defendant's own handwriting to a full
confession in the investigator's writing', thereby, as a recent
Soviet legal commentator remarks, 'creating the appearance of
the "voluntary nature" of this testimony'.*[84] This remark is
interesting, as showing some awareness on the part of Stalin's
entourage of the basic incredibility likely to attach to confessions.
But as to their general desirability, we can note that Vyshinsky
was not a man likely to intrude his own prejudices in a matter in
which Stalin was deeply concerned. We can take it that basically
the idea must have been Stalin's own. It involved endless thousands of men in days and months of mental and physical torment.

* One prisoner reports that after several days of bullying and beating to
make him sign a confession which he had not read, with the interrogator
showing especial rage at his obstinacy, he found himself unable to speak or
use his hand, whereupon the interrogator put a pen in his fingers and signed
it thus.[85]

BOOK TWO

The Yezhov Years

And the truth cannot be hid;
Somebody chose their pain,
What needn't have happened did.

W. H. AUDEN

CHAPTER SIX

LAST STAND

Singleness of purpose became with him duplicity of action.
KARL MARX *on Ivan III*

AUTUMN MANOEUVRES

THE Zinoviev Trial, and particularly the executions, severely shook the 'officer corps' of the Party – 'those elements who, until recently, had considered themselves the sole possessors of the right to occupy themselves with politics'.¹ Everything had been arranged without consulting them. Nothing could now be done about the dead. A dangerous precedent had been successfully established.

Preparations for the next round were already at hand. N. I. Muralov, former Inspector-General of the Red Army, had been arrested on 17 April 1936. He had previously been working in Western Siberia. On 5 and 6 August² two more ex-Trotskyites from the same area – Y. N. Drobnis and M. S. Boguslavsky – were pulled in. These were distinguished old revolutionaries of the second rank.

Drobnis, a worker, a shoemaker, an active revolutionary at the age of fifteen, who had served six years in a Tsarist prison, had survived three death sentences. From one of these, when captured and wounded by the Whites during the Civil War, he had escaped by a rare chance. He had later been a Secretary of the Ukrainian Central Committee. The giant Muralov came from a poor toiling family, and had joined workers' circles in 1899 and the Party in 1905.³ He had had an extraordinary Civil War record. Boguslavsky, too, was a veteran of both the underground and the Civil War.

Early August may also have been the date of the arrests of the much more important figures of Sokolnikov and Serebryakov, who were under interrogation soon after. Sokolnikov was already confessing, though 'vaguely', in August.⁴ And as Vyshinsky had said in his statement of 21 August, Bukharin, Rykov, Pyatakov,

Radek and Uglanov were to be the subject of further investigation, with Tomsky, who had, however, escaped by suicide.

On 27 August, two days after the executions, most of the members of the Politburo* were in Moscow, including the Kiev-based Kossior and Postyshev. On the last day of the month Molotov returned from leave.[6] Apart from Mikoyan, the only full member not there was Stalin himself, who was still holidaying at Sochi, where he was to remain for several weeks. Yezhov, however, was in Moscow, and doubtless in touch with his superior.

Over the next week or so, the Party leadership discussed the cases of the newly incriminated, and the revulsion felt among them showed itself in strong opposition to further persecution. To question the guilt of Zinoviev and Kamenev, or the conduct of the case, was now impossible, for they were proven traitors. But with Bukharin and Rykov it was different. Moreover, they were popular in the country and in the Party in a way that Zinoviev and Co. had never been. And the suicide of Tomsky had evidently been a severe shock.

On 10 September, in a small paragraph at the top of page 2, *Pravda* announced that the investigation into the charges against Rykov and Bukharin was being dropped, for lack of evidence. This reversal is said to have been made 'under pressure of some members of the Politburo'.[7]

Politically, the exculpation is understandable. From a judicial point of view, it is fantastic. The accused in the Zinoviev Case had been sentenced to execution on their own evidence against themselves. But their evidence against Rykov and Bukharin was of exactly the same status, neither more nor less credible. It might be thought that this alone would have shown Western observers the meaninglessness of the whole trial. (Moreover, though the case against the two Rightists was suspended, it was not found necessary to make amends to their colleague Tomsky. Article 107 of the Criminal Code of the R.S.F.S.R. lays down penalties for provoking suicide by moral or physical persecution. It was not applied.)

It is improbable that a majority against the Purge now existed

* Kossior, Voroshilov, Kalinin, Chubar, Kaganovich, Ordzhonikidze, Andreyev and Postyshev.[5]

in the Politburo. Voroshilov, Kaganovich, and probably Andreyev, were by now committed to it. Molotov, too, must already have learned his lesson. At least, he was back in good odour by 21 September,[8] when an alleged attempt on his life was being put into the scenario for the next trial. And this return to favour can hardly be accounted for except on the view that he had aligned himself whole-heartedly with Stalin's plans in the September discussions.

Nevertheless, the opposition was powerful, and Stalin gave in to it as far as the two Rightists were concerned. He had, it should be noted, never committed himself finally to their arrest. He may well have intended no more at this stage than a preliminary sounding, a putting of the Bukharin problem on the agenda, as it were, in his usual devious style. In that case, it was not a question of decisive votes in the supreme body. And in his absence, his own prestige was not directly involved.

Moreover, if he commanded adequate support in the Politburo, events were to show that this was not the case in the Central Committee.

We do not know if the Central Committee met at this time. A former Party official has given a circumstantial account of such a meeting, lasting four days, in early September 1936. It was on the fourth day that the Bukharin issue came up. Yezhov proposed a motion for the trial of Bukharin and the others which, he said, had already been adopted in its essentials by the Politburo. Bukharin defended himself.[9]

Doubt has always been thrown on this account[10] because there is no official reference to a plenum having taken place at this time,* and it has been suggested that Avtorkhanov is confusing the resistance in the Politburo with what took place in February 1937.† On the other hand, there is an official reference to 'one of the autumn plenums of the Central Committee of the Party',[11]

---

*It is perhaps worth noting that four announced plenums took place in 1935 and three in 1937, while in 1936 only *one* was mentioned, on 1–4 June.

†And it should be noted that Avtorkhanov omits Ordzhonikidze's name from the list of objectors, which *may* indicate confusion with a plenum in November, when Ordzhonikidze was ill, or with the February–March plenum, 1937.

which from the context must be after March 1936 and before February 1937. The reference to 'plenums' in the plural seems to imply another, which (as we shall see) must have been in November.

There is a further argument. Though Bukharin and Rykov were now acquitted, Pyatakov and Sokolnikov (with Radek, Serebryakov and Uglanov) were not. Khrushchev remarks that the Central Committee members 'arrested in 1937–8 were expelled from the Party illegally through gross violation of the Party statutes, since the question of their expulsion was never studied at a Central Committee plenary session'.[12] By implication, the arrests of Pyatakov and Sokolnikov, the only Central Committee member and candidate member known to have been arrested in 1936, *were* legalized, even if *ex post facto*. It does seem that in the conditions prevailing in the autumn of 1936 it might not have been feasible for Stalin to expel members without a plenum – indeed, he did not think fit to do so even for Bukharin and Rykov, candidate members, as late as February of the following year. It was quite a different matter, as yet, from proceeding against men like Kamenev and Zinoviev, already in jail, already expelled from the Party.

In whichever body the discussion and compromise took place, Stalin had made certain gains. The materials were in his hand for prolonging the Purge. He now had, after all, a reasonable quota for the next trial: Serebryakov and Sokolnikov, and now Radek, arrested on 22 September, and Pyatakov, who was presumably taken about the same date, by which time Sokolnikov at least was already confessing. But the failure over Bukharin and Rykov, even if Stalin had not been certain of success at the first attempt, evidently rankled. It was plain that he was going to have to deal with resistance in the Politburo and Central Committee and that a powerful effort, a new campaign, would be needed. In the Black Sea sunshine, he considered the next move. The Soviet press concerned itself with other matters: democracy, the triumph of Soviet aviation, the successful harvest, and massive support for the struggle of the Spanish Republic.

Like a general who transfers the weight of his offensive from a line where the going is heavy to an easier approach, Stalin shifted his attack to Yagoda. The temporary rehabilitation of Bukharin and Rykov was made without their having been called in for interrogation. But still, it seems undeniable that the political decision to rehabilitate them must have been accompanied, at least formally, by a report from the N.K.V.D. casting doubt on the evidence. If so, it is not clear how this was done: whether Yagoda, by arrangement with the moderates of the Politburo, gave the two men a clean bill of health which was then used for the political decision, or whether the political decision was taken first and Yagoda then complied with the formalities.

Yagoda's position at that time remains something of a mystery. It is clear that he was concerned in the preparations for the 1936 Trial from the start – though perhaps excluded from the key discussions and conversations preceding the case. He is indeed said to have 'urged that the case be discussed in the Politburo'.[13] At the same time, it seems that he was himself deceived by Stalin's assurance that Zinoviev and Kamenev would not be executed.[14] He was later to be accused of shielding I. N. Smirnov – though there was an obvious motive here, in that this was advanced as an explanation for Smirnov's unsatisfactory behaviour in the dock.[15] Nevertheless, it does seem that Yagoda may have made some attempt to temper the wind to the oppositionists.[16] He was to be similarly accused of ordering that Uglanov's testimony be kept 'within certain limits'.[17] And there are other reports of underground obstruction within the N.K.V.D. which took the form of framing questions in such a way as to protect those interrogated.[18] The most likely occasion for the development of more definite resistance on his part would be *following* the executions. This could only have manifested itself in the discussions about the fates of Bukharin and Rykov.

We can be sure that Yezhov (who was to replace Yagoda) offered stronger resistance to clearing the Rightists. He seems to have acquiesced very reluctantly in the decision. He regarded the rehabilitation of Bukharin and Rykov as temporary, 'vowing that he would yet make good the "mistake" ',[19] and he and Agranov almost immediately started accusing Yagoda of laxness.

It had never been Stalin's way to proceed directly against firm opposition. Time and time again, during the struggles of the twenties, he had accepted rebuffs, pretended to give ground – and carried on with manoeuvres designed to undermine the opposition. For the moment, Bukharin and Rykov were safe. The former continued to hold his position as editor of *Izvestia*, and both remained candidate members of the Central Committee. It was clear that many leaders hoped that the momentum of the Purge would peter out with the forthcoming Pyatakov Case. But if Stalin could not obtain the votes he needed in the highest Party bodies, he had other methods of gaining his ends. He proceeded to the *coup* which was to bring the Terror to its most frightful climax – the appointment of Yezhov as People's Commissar for Internal Affairs.

On 25 September Stalin and Zhdanov sent a telegram from Sochi to Kaganovich, Molotov 'and other members of the Political Bureau' as follows:

> We deem it absolutely necessary and urgent that Comrade Yezhov be nominated to the post of People's Commissar for Internal Affairs. Yagoda had definitely proved himself to be incapable of unmasking the Trotskyite-Zinovievite bloc. The O.G.P.U. is four years behind in this matter. This is noted by all Party workers and by the majority of the representatives of the N.K.V.D.[20]

The 'four years' is significant and sinister. It was four years almost to the day since the September sessions of 1932 which had blocked the attempt to execute Ryutin.

No one, of course, thought for a moment that Yagoda's removal indicated mere 'incapability'. It was at once noted in the Party that 'It was not a question of dissatisfaction with his insufficiently active work . . . this indicated political distrust of him.'[21]

The transfer of Yezhov to duties that he was already much concerned with in any case could hardly have been the occasion for members of the Politburo opposing the General Secretary, even if Ordzhonikidze, Chubar or Kossior might have wished this. Though the tone and the intention of the new appointment would be obvious, as a practical measure it would be hard to argue against.

The following day Molotov carried out instructions. The shift was used to rid the Soviet Government of Rykov. Next day, the papers announced Rykov's 'release', without the conventional comment that he was going to 'other work'; the appointment of Yagoda to Rykov's post of People's Commissar of Communications; and Yezhov's appointment to be head of the N.K.V.D.

On 29 September 1936 and 21 October 1936, two circulars were issued from the Central Committee. They called in effect for the end of unfair expulsions from the Party and a stepping-up of fair ones. They were followed by press censures of a number of local leaders for failure in one or other of these respects.

Yagoda handed over his office on 30 September 1936. On the same day the announcement of M. Berman as Deputy Head of the N.K.V.D. was made, while Yagoda's Second Deputy, Prokofiev, was transferred with him to be his First Deputy Commissar. On 17 October a more sinister figure still, the puffy-faced Frinovsky, was also appointed a Deputy Head of the N.K.V.D. Neither Berman nor Frinovsky had been serving in the old Secret Police apparatus proper. The former had headed the Labour Camp Administration, GULAG, while the latter had commanded the Frontier Guards. Otherwise the old N.K.V.D. chiefs were not yet disturbed. Even Yagoda's personal assistant remained in the N.K.V.D. for some time. Molchanov and the other departmental chiefs kept their posts, though Yezhov brought in his own men from the Central Committee apparatus to help them in their work, and to learn how to supplant them.

The whole force was again launched on the preparations for a trial.

The original script for this described Pyatakov and his fellow-accused simply as a 'Reserve Centre' which had plotted but not acted. By this means the case was represented as less serious than that of August, and one not implying the death penalty. It was no doubt partly by this means that Stalin had gained the leadership's consent to go forward with the Pyatakov Case – which, it might be hoped, would be no more than a tidying-up of loose ends in a fairly restrained fashion.

But after the N.K.V.D. had proceeded on these lines for a few weeks, the line suddenly changed. Molchanov, in Yezhov's presence, instructed a meeting of interrogators that 'a new line of investigation' was to be pursued. The accused were to be required to confess that they had plotted to seize power and had worked with the Nazis for this purpose.[22]

Stalin had not, since his recantation in the twenties, had anything to complain about from Radek. He had betrayed the opposition on every possible occasion, and had flattered Stalin lavishly. He was one man who had truly burned his bridges to the opposition; and at the same time he was nowhere regarded as a serious politician and there was no question of his ever competing for even the lowest rung of power. What Stalin's motive was in bringing Radek in particular into the plot at all is obscure. It may simply be that until he could secure the arrest of the Rightists, he was rather low on big names for another trial. And Radek was at least a very well-known man.

Sokolnikov seems to have had an interview with Stalin and to have been promised his life. It is not clear why Sokolnikov believed this promise. It was, in all probability, made before the execution of Zinoviev and his followers. But Sokolnikov seems to have been convinced of its efficacy even after the executions. But in any case, he had little choice. He had a young wife, and a son by a previous marriage who was in his twenties.[23]

Sokolnikov was brought to a 'confrontation' with Radek immediately after the latter's arrest.[24] This did not lead to anything at once. Radek was worked on on the 'conveyor' system by Kedrov and other interrogators.[25] At first he resisted stubbornly.

The sacrifice of Pyatakov is perhaps the clearest sign of Stalin's motives. He had been, it was true, an oppositionist, and an important one. But he had abandoned opposition in 1928, and worked with complete loyalty ever since. He was regarded by the Trotskyites as a deserter. Trotsky's son Sedov, chancing to meet him on the Unter der Linden, had publicly insulted him.[26] He had not liked, but he had honestly accepted, Stalin's leadership. There was, in his case, no real question – as might have been thought of Zinoviev and Kamenev, and of Bukharin – of any desire to present an alternative leadership.

And his services to Stalin's Government were extremely valuable. His energy and intelligence, probably unrivalled in the whole leadership, had been channelled into carrying out Stalin's industrialization plans.

What was there to be said against him?

He had loyally accepted the Stalin leadership, but he would have accepted an alternative leadership if Stalin could have been overthrown: he supported him with reservations. He had been a major critic of Stalin's in the twenties. He had made it clear that he regarded his rise to power as unfortunate. Above all, he was, even now, whatever his own desires, leadership timber. Lenin had named him among the six most important figures in the Party (of them all, Stalin was to allow none but himself to survive). He had even been thought of as an alternative Prime Minister to Lenin in the 'Left Communist' plans of 1918.

Ordzhonikidze, as People's Commissar for Heavy Industry, depended entirely on the genius of Pyatakov, and was generous enough to admit this. Pyatakov's was the brain and the driving force behind the Plan, creating a major industrial base against all the handicaps that resulted from Stalin's system – the wastages due to the purges of experts, the establishment of impossible prestige targets, and the suspicions and inefficiencies of administrators.

On 28 October 1936, Ordzhonikidze's fiftieth birthday was celebrated with lavish adulation in the press and at meetings. *Pravda* and *Izvestia* published hearty congratulations from organs of government and groups of comrades in every conceivable field. The leaders of heavy industry were prominent among them. One name was missing: that of Pyatakov, already under arrest.

There is a report that after Pyatakov's arrest, but before its announcement, the director of a scientific institute who knew of it made a public attack upon him in Ordzhonikidze's presence. Ordzhonikidze interrupted him with the remark 'It is very easy to attack a man who is not there to defend himself. Wait till Yuri Leonidovich returns.'[27]

Ordzhonikidze fought hard for Pyatakov. He came round and paid him a friendly visit in jail, promising to do all he could to help him.[28]

Stalin's main hostages against Pyatakov were his wife and child, at that time about ten years old. He was practically separated from the wife, but they were on good terms. She broke down quickly, and agreed to testify against him to save the child. Another hostage was his closest friend and secretary Moskalev, who had his own wife and young daughter to think of, but agreed to testify only after insisting on seeing Agranov and telling him he was doing so solely as a matter of Party discipline.[29]

SABOTEURS IN SIBERIA

One theme already well established in Soviet mythology, that of sabotage, had not been raised in the Zinoviev Trial. It would have been difficult, in fact, to charge men who were all either in prison or cut off from major work with such acts: anybody can commit assassination, but sabotage is carried out by industrialists and engineers or, anyhow, people with access to the relevant machines. The group now coming to trial had almost all held, till shortly before their arrests, posts as People's Commissars, Assistant People's Commissars, leaders of industrial complexes, engineers, and so forth. And to show that no breach in tradition was intended they were specifically linked with the saboteurs of the earlier period.

The concept of sabotage as a political weapon is in general an absurd one. The very word, with its implications of peasants throwing clogs into machinery, is a fair description of what is almost invariably an individual and illiterate protest. The only real exception is to be found in large underground movements in occupied countries in time of war, operating with the sympathy of most of the population. In those circumstances, on the one hand, it becomes possible on a fairly wide scale; and on the other, it becomes, or at least appears, a genuine contribution to the defeat of the enemy. In peace-time, a small conspiracy could scarcely hope to achieve any political result whatever by such means. In any case, plotters working to remove the political leadership by terror would hardly dissipate their forces, or run the extra risk of discovery, for local and indecisive actions of this type. Nor had any previous conspiracy of the sort ever done so. The illogic of the accusations was not the sort of consideration to stop Stalin, and over the following years sabotage became the theme of a mass purge at all levels.

The official definition of sabotage was now extended and the penalties for it were made more severe. 'On 29 November 1936, Vyshinsky ordered that within a month all criminal cases of major conflagrations, accidents and output of poor-quality products be reviewed and studied with the aim of exposing a counter-revolutionary and saboteur background in them and making the guilty parties more heavily liable.'[30]

In the new industrial region of the Upper Ob basin – the 'Kuzbas' – almost 2,000 miles east of Moscow, a number of reconstructed Trotskyites held posts suitable to their condition. The great plants had gone up, amid a squalor for the workers – mainly deportees – which the old industrial revolutions in the capitalist West had hardly matched. At the same time unrelenting pressure for results at all costs had led to the virtual abandonment of the usual sort of safety precautions. Frightful accidents were common.

On 23 September 1936 there was an explosion in the Tsentral-naya Mine at Kemerovo. Its director, Noskov, and several of his subordinates were at once arrested. His superior, Norkin, Head of the Kemerovo Combined Works Construction since 1932, was arrested on 30 September.[31] For the N.K.V.D. this was a most useful line of responsibility, as Norkin was an immediate link with Drobnis, and through him to Muralov. A whole 'Trotskyite nest' in West Siberia, operating moreover under the direct orders of the Deputy People's Commissar for Heavy Industry, Pyatakov, was thus laid open to easy attack. To make it yet easier, the N.K.V.D. ordered their representative in the Kemerovo industrial area, Shestov, to accept the role of *agent provocateur*.[32]

It was thus possible to establish the idea of widespread sabotage before Pyatakov and the others came to trial. On 19–22 November a great trial took place in Novosibirsk, before a court of the Military Collegium under Ulrikh, in which the accidents in the mines and factories of that city and Kemerovo were charged against Noskov and eight other defendants, including a German engineer, Stickling. In addition, the charge was now put forward that an attempt had been made to assassinate Molotov. The defendants were linked, through Drobnis and Shestov (who appeared as 'witnesses'), with Muralov and Pyatakov.

At this trial there were confessions, and even documents, about an anti-Soviet printing establishment. It seems that this actually existed. The cellar where it had stood still showed signs of its presence three years later. But the whole thing had been an N.K.V.D. operation. The job had been done at night by prisoners under guard awaiting execution. As to the thousands of leaflets supposed to have been distributed, it was clear that this had not happened, since anyone caught with such a leaflet would have been arrested, and no one in Kemerovo knew of any such arrests. One local commented 'Maybe the conspirators printed them up just to provide themselves with bedtime stories.'[33]

One of the accused, the German engineer Stickling, was not given a death sentence. Later, in the Gestapo prison in Lublin, he said that his confession was false, and implied that it had been obtained because the N.K.V.D. were able to blackmail him about his private life.[34]

A Soviet industrialist who was sent to Kemerovo in 1939, and actually took over the very office from which Norkin had allegedly organized his crimes, has produced an account of the background of the trial. As a prominent local figure pointed out, though the saboteurs were now dead, the accidents still went on. In any case, if engineers had really wished to make trouble, it was clear that they could have blown the whole place to pieces. Moreover, in the files there were many reports from the executed men sent by them to the Commissariat of Heavy Industry coal administration warning about the conditions which were bound to lead to accidents.[35]

But the Tsentralnaya Mine disaster was not the only one which a determined investigation could turn up in the Kuzbas. On 29 October a Commission of Experts was sent to Kemerovo to investigate two explosions and other accidents which had taken place in the plants of the Kemerovo Combined Works Construction Trust in February, March and April 1936. A similar body started work on a series of pit-fires in the nearby Prokopyevsk coal-mines – sixty of these had occurred up to the end of 1935.[36] The experts produced findings of sabotage. The material now available was sufficient by any standards to damn the West Siberian defendants.

Though this West Siberian group was to provide no less than seven out of the seventeen accused in the forthcoming trial, two other sabotage groups were also being prepared. One was headed by Rataichak, Chief of the Central Administration of the Chemical Industry in Pyatakov's Commissariat: on 22 October 1936 the Head of the Gorlovka Nitrogen Fertilizer Works, Pushin, was arrested in connexion with an explosion there on 11 November 1935. He confessed at once and implicated his chief.[37] This group of saboteurs was completed by an N.K.V.D. *agent provocateur*, Hrasche,[38] who worked in the Foreign Division of Rataichak's Administration, and so formed a useful link with Japanese espionage and other sinister foreign forces.

More important was the third and last of the saboteur groups – that devoted to wrecking the railways. Its three leaders were Yakov Livshits, an Old Bolshevik and reformed Trotskyite, who was now Kaganovich's Assistant People's Commissar of Communications, and the lesser figures of Knyazev, Assistant Chief of the Central Traffic Department in the Commissariat, who had formerly been Head of the South Urals Railway, and Turok, Assistant Head of the Traffic Department of the Perm Railway.

Knyazev was giving evidence in mid-December, later than the other main figures, and it seems that the railway theme was the last to be brought in. It implicated in particular Serebryakov, who had run the Commissariat in the twenties, and it linked up with Boguslavsky, who was responsible for railway-wrecking in the West Siberian set-up.

The charge of sabotage was a serious one. But, ironically enough, it could have been represented to the Central Committee as a sign of possible clemency. Professor Ramzin, the main 'saboteur' in the 'Industrial Party' Case, had not only been amnestied a couple of years after sentence and repentance, but had been restored to office and to favour, and even awarded an Order.*

---

*In the January 1937 Trial itself there was to be a curious reflection of this attitude: an engineer formerly sentenced in connexion with the Shakhty Trial, Boyarshchinov, was referred to as having become an honest Soviet engineer, killed by the conspirators because he was exposing their wrongful methods of work.

Stalin is reported back in Moscow, from his holiday, at a reception for a Mongolian delegation on 4 November. With him were several members of the Politburo, including Mikoyan – and, of course, Yezhov. At the 7 November Parade all the Politburo members based in Moscow were on the stand.

The slogans for this nineteenth anniversary of the Revolution included a violent attack on the Trotskyite–Zinovievite spies. But there was no reference to the Right deviation, which presumably shows that the issue was still in abeyance.

And now Stalin, perhaps looking ahead from the purge of the ex-oppositionists to the completer sweep he was to make of the Party, made his first move against one of his own followers. In the discussions on the fate of the Rightists one of the strongest voices for moderation had been that of Pavel Postyshev, Second Secretary of the Ukraine and candidate member of the Politburo.

Postyshev had served in Kiev from 1923, becoming a secretary of the Kiev Committee in 1924, and from 1926 to 1930 had been a member of the Ukrainian Politburo, before going to Moscow to be a Secretary of the Central Committee. He had been intruded on the Ukrainian apparatus in January 1933 to toughen it in its difficult struggle with the peasantry and Ukrainian national feeling. Though Kossior and his group were not displaced, as much power and prestige attached to Postyshev as to his theoretical superior. In addition to his Ukrainian Second Secretaryship, he held the First Secretaryship of the Kiev Provincial Committee of the Party.

During the whole period it became customary to give Postyshev what, on the face of it, looked like an anomalous seniority. When greetings were sent to the Soviet Government, or the Central Committee of the All-Union Communist Party, or to the Ukrainian Government, in each case only the single leading figure was named as the recipient. But when it came to the Ukrainian Central Committee, both Kossior and Postyshev were conventionally named.*

* For example, in *Pravda* of 6 January 1937, a Ukrainian public report is made to all four bodies: to the Central Committee in Moscow it simply goes to Stalin, to the Central Committee in Kiev to both Kossior and Postyshev. All this was later to be censured as a personality cult, reflecting years of

A younger and better-looking man than most of the others, with a clipped moustache and high hair swept back over his oval head, Postyshev was in fact an irreproachable Stalinist, but an honest one, and a comparatively popular one. His reputation for fair-mindedness (within the limits of the system) was good. It is said that he had been among the opponents of the proposal to shoot Ryutin, and had redeemed himself in Kiev. Opposition from such a source could, as with Kirov's, have been a real threat.

In accordance with his line of hostility to the Purge, Postyshev had been interpreting the Central Committee circulars on expelling Party members in the wrong fashion. He was expelling *provocateurs* and slanderers and retaining their victims. One of these delators was a woman called Nikolayenko,* who had been particularly troublesome for a year.[41] Postyshev had expelled her from the Kiev Party organization.

Clearly, this expulsion was an action totally contrary to the whole spirit of the Purge and particularly to the Central Committee decisions of 29 September and 21 October 1936, which may indeed have already been aimed at Postyshev. Everywhere, as the 'Yezhovshchina' got going, it was precisely through the denunciation by such types that the police got their grip on the leaders of the Party organizations. It was later to be alleged that in Kiev, more than anywhere else in the Ukraine, Trotskyites had been able to gain important posts.[42] Postyshev's attitude is thus plainly established as being against this system, even before the showdown. In November Stalin, seeking a pretext, took over the Nikolayenko case.[43] The Central Committee apparatus in Moscow, that is to say, examined her appeal against expulsion in a favourable fashion.

These weeks must have been the time of the second of the 'plenums of the Central Committee', if indeed it occurred at all.†

---

complacency on the part of Postyshev and his entourage, who as a result had 'let in enemies'.[39]

* Recently described in a Soviet work as 'one of the worst slanderers'.[40]

† If this is the period Avtorkhanov is referring to in his account (see p. 215), the objection of Ordzhonikidze's omission may not arise, as he had a heart attack early in November.[44] One of the 'plenums' mentioned by Ivanov in his evidence at the Bukharin Trial is to be dated presumptively in December or in November 1936.[45]

The Politburo, including the members from the provinces, were all present in Moscow on 23 November 1936, together with most of the other prominent people in the country, in connexion with the New Constitution.

It has been argued that a plenum should have been called at this time for formal reasons. After the last one, in June 1936, there had been 'popular discussion' of the draft of the New Constitution. Various amendments had been put forward, and a number of these were accepted in a final draft put up to the Congress of Soviets when it met in November. Who (this argument goes) would have agreed the final draft except the Central Committee in session? This is not entirely convincing.

The New Constitution finally passed into law amidst a fanfare of speeches, ovations, and a press campaign which culminated in a speech by Stalin on 27 November. He went at great length into the questions which had arisen about how best to guarantee democracy, freedom of the subject, and all the other attributes of a State fully attuned to the people's will.*

Plenum or no, the Politburo was certainly in session. Stalin was at a certain disadvantage in that most of the accused had not yet confessed. On the other hand, the fact that many who had held out were starting to confess by the first week in December may show that a reluctant compromise was now reached among the leadership about the trial. At any rate Ordzhonikidze seems to have obtained from Stalin a promise to save all Pyatakov's hostages and to spare his life. He then visited Pyatakov in jail and persuaded him that nothing more could be done, and that he should now go forward with the trial.[46] Pyatakov gave in. By 4 December he was confessing. On the same day Radek, too, gave his first evidence. He had in the end decided to surrender if Stalin would give him the same guarantee he had given Sokolnikov. For some time Stalin refused to see him – but finally, it is said, he visited the Lubyanka and had a long talk with Radek in the presence of Yezhov. Radek then became the closest collaborator of the interrogation, and helped replan the scenario of the plot.[47] Muralov, who had held out so long, now gave in – reportedly

---

*In December, the Constitution of the R.S.F.S.R. provided a rather weaker echo of the same campaign.

under Radek's influence – and on the following day he too was confessing. Norkin started confessing about the same time. By January hundreds of pages of evidence from all the defendants were on the files.

On the anniversary of the founding of the Secret Police, 20 December 1936, Stalin gave a small banquet for the heads of the N.K.V.D. Yezhov, Frinovsky, Pauker and others were present. Afterwards, an account of what happened circulated among the N.K.V.D. When everyone had drunk a good deal, Pauker, supported by two other officers acting the parts of warders, played for Stalin the part of Zinoviev being dragged to execution. He hung by their arms, moaning and mouthing, then fell on his knees and, holding one of the warders by the boots, cried out 'Please, for God's sake, Comrade, call up Yosif Vissarionovich!'

Stalin roared with laughter, and Pauker gave a repeat performance. By this time, Stalin was almost helpless with laughing, and when Pauker brought in a new angle by raising his hands and crying 'Hear, Israel, our God is the only God!', Stalin choked with mirth and had to signal Pauker to stop the performance.[48]

In fact Stalin had good reason to be pleased with his Secret Policemen, who had their second production almost ready to go on. He now ordered pursuit of the line on which he had been blocked in the autumn. Bukharin and Rykov were to be implicated.

On 16 January 1937, Bukharin's name appeared for the last time as editor of *Izvestia*. It was at about this point that Radek had been induced after some resistance to implicate Bukharin, and it became possible for the plan against the Rightists to get moving again. On the very first day of the trial, 23 January, the whole Bukharin–Rykov–Tomsky group was incriminated. This time Stalin was fully prepared to face the resistance of his own 'moderates' squarely.

The intervention against Postyshev in the Nikolayenko case was made formal by a decision of the All-Union Central Committee, dated 13 January 1937 (and unpublished at the time), attacking 'unsatisfactory leadership' in the Kiev Party and faults in the Ukrainian Central Committee as a whole.[49]

Postyshev expressed his resentment. As a result, Kaganovich

was immediately sent to Kiev to straighten out the situation. In
his capacity as Secretary of the Central Committee he urgently
convoked a plenum of the Kiev Provincial Party Committee.[50] On
16 January 1937 he had Postyshev replaced as First Secretary of
the Kiev Provincial Committee, while leaving him his more important post. The official reason given was that Postyshev's duties
as Second Secretary of the Ukrainian Party were too demanding
to allow him to hold the Kiev post as well. This was plainly false:
indeed, when Khrushchev was appointed in 1938 to be First
Secretary of the Ukrainian Party, he held the Kiev post as well
without any difficulty arising.

So far this was no more than one of Stalin's typical first steps
against a victim. Meanwhile, the preparations for the Pyatakov
case was complete.

THE PYATAKOV TRIAL

On 23 January 1937 another gruesome little pageant assembled
among the florid columns of the October Hall. It was a bitterly
cold day and the hall was dark and gloomy. Just after midday,
Ulrikh and Matulevich, with Divisional Military Jurist Rychkov
in Nikitchenko's old place, took their seats at the judges' bench.
Vyshinsky sat at his old table on the left. The N.K.V.D. soldiers
were in their winter uniforms, with long coats and muffled hel-
mets.

The men who filed into dock were of a different sort from those
of the previous August. Then, genuine rivals had been crushed.
The new accused had presented no such obvious challenge. But
they were quite impressive figures. Pyatakov had never been a
member of the Politburo, but as we have seen he had long been
one of the most prominent, able and respected figures in the
Party. Sokolnikov, former candidate member of the Politburo,
was a most serious and respected politician. Serebryakov, former
Secretary of the Central Committee, was also no negligible figure.
And Radek was at least a widely known public person.

The new trial did not have the immediate and obvious aims of
the first. The motives remaining are plain enough. First, revenge.
Most of the leading ex-Trotskyites were now destroyed. And
revenge carried with it, of course, Stalin's idea of precautionary or

preventive measures. A clean sweep, even if there was no more compelling reason for action by normal standards, fitted Stalin's firm belief in 'Stone dead hath no fellow' and 'Better safe than sorry'.

Moreover, Stalin had been temporarily baulked of a more important prey – Bukharin and the Rightists. The trial was thus not the one he had intended, but a pale substitute. At the same time, it kept the pot boiling. It provided continuity. And it could be, and was, used to implicate the Right once again. A minor mystery, given this motive of Stalin's, is why Uglanov was not brought into it. He had been named as subject to investigation in the announcement of 21 August. He was not among those rehabilitated in September, and yet he was not tried. It would have been greatly to Stalin's advantage to have put up so prominent a Rightist in January 1937, as a bridge to Bukharin and Co. And even though Yagoda is alleged to have protected him, there was time, on ordinary reckoning, between Yagoda's fall and the January 1937 Trial for Yezhov to prepare him. One can only presume that, as we have said, he refused to talk.

The new batch of accused were designated simply 'the Anti-Soviet Trotskyite Centre'. No other group or faction was represented – unlike the case at the 1936 Trial of the 'Trotskyite–Zinovievite Terrorist Centre' or the later 'Bloc of Rights and Trotskyites'. The first trial had anyhow been, as we saw, unimpressive on the Trotskyite side. Radek was now put up to say:

If you take the composition of the old centre you will find that the Trotskyites did not have a single one of the old political leaders on it. There were Smirnov, who was more of an organizer than a political leader; Mrachkovsky, a soldier and a fighting man; and Ter-Vaganian, a propagandist.[51]

Since there were no genuine Trotskyites to hand, as there were genuine Zinovievites and genuine Rightists, the distinguished *ex-*Trotskyites had to serve.

In other ways, the new accused presented a different impression from their predecessors. Then there had been a seven-man 'Centre', plus various hangers-on. This time the Centre consisted of only four people, Pyatakov, Radek, Serebryakov and Sokolnikov. Radek and Sokolnikov were not accused of crimes as serious as those of the other two. Pyatakov and Serebryakov were charged with organizing three main sobatage groups (among dozens they had allegedly set up): the railway-wrecking organization headed by Livshits; the 'West Siberian Anti-Soviet Trotskyite Centre' at Novosibirsk, consisting of Muralov, Boguslavsky and Drobnis, having under them a variety of industrial wreckers in the area; and the three wreckers in the chemical industry, coming directly under Pyatakov. The specializations were not complete; for example, the railway wrecker Knyazev was also a Japanese spy, while the coal wreckers of Siberia were also the organizers of the attempted assassination of all visiting Politburo members.

As we have seen, these second-rank conspirators had more impressive backgrounds than their equivalents in the Zinoviev Trial. Between them, in fact, they formed a large and genuine group of Old Bolsheviks who had been Trotsky's closest followers in the struggles following Lenin's death.

The indictment differed greatly from that of August 1936. Then, it had simply been a matter of terrorism. It had been remarked by Vyshinsky and in evidence that the accused had no policy except the seizure of power from Stalin. But such a policy was by no means unpopular,[52] and soon after the executions the press had started to announce that Zinoviev did have a political programme after all – one involving the restoration of capitalism, which he had naturally tried to conceal.[53] Stalin was to remark:

> At the Trial in 1936, if you will remember, Kamenev and Zinoviev categorically denied that they had any kind of political platform. They had full opportunity to unfold their political platform at the Trial. Nevertheless, they did not do so, declaring that they had no political platform whatsoever. There can be no doubt that they both lied in denying that they had a platform.[54]

This theme was strongly put in the new indictment. The accused intended to renounce industrialization and collectivization, and they relied for support in particular on the German and Japanese Governments. They proposed to make territorial concessions to Germany, to allow German capital into the country, and in case of war with Germany to carry out wrecking in industry and at the Front. This had all been arranged at a meeting between Trotsky and Hess.

Trotsky had also at least implied the desirability of defeat in war, having allegedly written to Radek: 'It must be admitted that the question of power will become a practical issue for the bloc only as a result of the defeat of the U.S.S.R. in war. For this the bloc must make energetic preparations . . .'[55]

Espionage contact had been established with the Germans and Japanese. And, as in the Zinoviev Trial, a number of terrorist groups had been organized, 'in Moscow, Leningrad, Kiev, Rostov, Sochi, Novosibirsk and other towns'. An attempt had actually been made on Molotov's life by involving him in a car crash at Prokopyevsk in 1934. Nor had their practical activity been limited to the preparation of terrorist acts. In addition they had been responsible for many industrial accidents and deficiencies.

Other activities likely to prove more unpopular than assassination had been thrown in for good measure. For example, Knyazev was quoted as having confessed that 'the Japanese intelligence service strongly stressed the necessity of using bacteriological means in time of war with the object of contaminating troop trains, canteens and army sanitary centres with highly virulent bacilli . . .'[56]*

Though such accusations transferred unpleasant responsibilities to the accused, they had the disadvantage of appearing less plausible than those of 1936. Although the Zinoviev Trial was full of evident falsehoods, it could at least be argued that there *might* have been a genuine case, tarted up by the N.K.V.D. It was at least not incredible that the oppositionists might have shot Kirov, and even less so that they might have wished to shoot Stalin. The new accusations were highly unbelievable on any view. Sabotage, by Pyatakov and his subordinates, was most implausible. Moreover, it was virtually incompatible with the charges of terrorism. As we have said, a plot designed to break the Government by terrorist acts could scarcely divert its energies, and risk exposure, by a vast network of people blowing up mines and causing railway

*An early adumbration of the line to be used by the Chinese in Korea in the fifties.

accidents, simply to weaken the economy and sow distrust of the Government.

In the economic field, if not in the political, there is nevertheless some sort of rationale in Stalin's choice of victims. For there were genuine failures which required scapegoats. Men like Livshits were shot, it might be argued, like Admiral Byng* – *pour encourager les autres*. Even this peculiar style of common sense has its limits. To shoot the best economic organizers in order to encourage the second-best to be more effective than they had been is doubtful policy. It is true that Russia finally gained a fairly competent cadre of administrators capable of working under the threat of liquidation. But there are no doubt managers who do not give their best in such circumstances, and of whose services the country was deprived.

The sabotage theme was not, of course, new. It was in the old Shakhty Trial tradition – and indeed it was expressly stated in evidence that the old saboteurs had linked up with the new. The Shakhty/Metro-Vic Trial technique was also revived. An immense amount of confusing technical evidence was given. As a result, the trial of the present seventeen took seven days as against the five days which had been sufficient for the Zinoviev sixteen.

The accused were this time presented in a more logical order. First, the four leaders; then the seven West Siberian terrorists and saboteurs; then the three railwaymen; and lastly the three from the chemical industry.

First was *Pyatakov*. His appearance was still intellectual and dignified, but he had visibly aged and was thin and pale.

He made certain limitations in his evidence. Admitting the responsibility for forming terrorist and sabotage groups, and for planning acts of terror and 'diversion' to be carried out in the future, he at no time confessed to complicity in any particular act of violence, and specifically denied being in direct touch with all the plotters. After considerable revelations about the political

* One difference between Byng's situation and that of the Russian industrialists two hundred years later is that on his tomb in Southill, Bedfordshire, it was possible at once for his family to erect a monument, with the famous inscription beginning: 'To the Perpetual Disgrace of Public Justice . . .'

contacts of the alleged plot, he went on to confess to the organization of sabotage. But his sabotage acts were always of the following type:

In the Ukraine the work was carried on mainly in the coke industry by Loginov and a group of persons connected with him. Their work, in the main, consisted of starting coke ovens which were not really ready for operations, and of holding up the construction of very valuable and very important parts of the coke and chemical industry. They operated coke ovens without utilizing those very valuable by-products which are obtained in coking and thereby huge funds were rendered valueless.[57]

. . . Maryasin carried on the wrecking work along the following lines. First of all he sank money in piling up unnecessary materials, equipment and so on. I think that by the beginning of 1936 about fifty million roubles were frozen in the form of materials . . .

The wrecking activities in the last period assumed new forms. Despite the fact that, after a delay of two or three years, the plant began to enter on its operation stage, Maryasin created intolerable conditions, fomented intrigues, and in a word did everything to obstruct operation.[58]

. . . An absolutely faulty plan of development was drawn up for the war-chemical industry . . . a plan providing for a smaller output capacity and, consequently, for a larger outlay of capital than was required.[59]

Despite the fact that our country abounds in salt and raw materials for soda, and that the process of manufacturing soda is very well known, there is a shortage of soda in the country. The construction of new soda plants was delayed.[60]

That is, the overt acts he directly admitted were ones of negligence and bad planning by subordinates – which may well have been genuine.

He bluntly denied certain incriminations:

Vyshinsky: Accused Pyatakov, do you agree with what Shestov said?
Pyatakov: Shestov perhaps talked with somebody, but not with me when he says that somebody with pencil in hand calculated the cost of the ore. There was no such conversation with me.[61]

And again:

Vyshinsky: Do you now recall the conversation with Rataichak about espionage?
Pyatakov: No, I deny it.
Vyshinsky: And with Loginov?

Pyatakov: I also deny it.
Vyshinsky: And that members of your organization were connected with foreign intelligence services?
Pyatakov: As to the fact that there were such connections, I do not deny; but that I knew about the establishment . . .[62]

Whether the line he took was on his own initiative, as Smirnov's had been, or whether he was permitted to evade the more extreme responsibilities as part of the encouragement to him (and to Ordzhonikidze) to think that his offences would be held to be non-capital, is unclear.

Even as to his relations with Trotsky, he made certain vague reservations, as if to cast doubt on them. For example:

Vyshinsky: The conversation you had with Trotsky in December 1935 and the line he gave, did you accept it as a directive or simply as something said in a conversation but not binding for you?
Pyatakov: Of course as a directive.
Vyshinsky: Hence, we can take it that you subscribed to it?
Pyatakov: We can take it that I carried it out.
Vyshinsky: And carried it out.
Pyatakov: Not 'and carried it out,' but 'carried it out'.
Vyshinsky: There is no difference in that whatever.
Pyatakov: There is a difference for me.
Vyshinsky: What is it?
Pyatakov: As far as action is concerned, particularly criminally liable action, there is no difference whatever.[63]

The meeting with Trotsky here referred to was the central poin of the whole conspiracy. Trotsky had then laid down the entire programme of the plotters – seven pages in the official *Report of Court Proceedings.*[64] The difficulty was that Trotsky was in Norway, and Pyatakov never got nearer to him than Berlin where, in December 1935, he was conducting Soviet Government business. His absence for any length of time would be noticed, so his evidence was that by arrangement with an agent of Trotsky's he met in the Berlin Zoo, he arranged to fly to Norway. On the morning of 12 December he took off from the Tempelhof with a forged German passport, 'landed at the airdrome in Oslo' at 3 p.m., drove to Trotsky's home, and there conducted the conspiratorial business (in which Trotsky revealed for the first time that he had met the Nazi leader Hess and made arrangements for cooperation in war and peace).

This story was immediately proved false. Once again Stalin, at whose personal insistence this direct involvement of Trotsky had been inserted into the script,[65] was to find the disadvantages of a foreign venue for a fabrication. On 25 January the Norwegian paper *Aftenposten* published the information that no civil aircraft had landed at Oslo's Kjeller Airfield during the entire month of December 1935. On 29 January the Norwegian Social Democratic *Arbeiderbladet*, after further investigation, established that no aircraft had used the field at all between September 1935 and May 1936.

Trotsky now published a demand that Pyatakov be asked the full details of his alleged flight, including the name on his passport, by which entry could have been further checked. He went on to challenge Stalin to seek his extradition in a Norwegian court, where the facts could be judicially established.

No effective cover story could be found to offset this glaring falsification. In leading Party circles the truth soon circulated, as Raskolnikov, for example, makes clear (see p. 612).

Vyshinsky's counter, an extremely weak one, was made at the end of the trial, on 27 January:

Vyshinsky: I have an application to the Court. I interested myself in this matter and asked the People's Commissariat of Foreign Affairs to make an inquiry, for I wanted to verify Pyatakov's evidence from this side too. I have received an official communication which I ask to have put in the records.
(*Reads.*)
'The Consular Department of the People's Commissariat of Foreign Affairs hereby informs the Prosecutor of the U.S.S.R. that according to information received by the Embassy of the U.S.S.R. in Norway the Kjeller Airdrome near Oslo receives all the year round, in accordance with international regulations, airplanes of other countries, and that the arrival and departure of airplanes is possible also in winter months.'
(*To Pyatakov*): It was in December?
Pyatakov: Exactly.[66]

Thus, another agency of the Soviet Government 'certified' not the fact, but merely the technical possibility, of Pyatakov's flight. It might well be thought that this débâcle alone would have discredited the whole trial in foreign eyes. Anyone who may have hoped so soon found that Stalin's ideas about political gullibility were even better founded than had first appeared.

Radek, who had been partly responsible for the script of the trial, made a brilliant showing over the morning of 24 January. While the other accused spoke flatly and drearily, he put real feeling into his evidence. He developed the post-1927 history of Trotskyism, and the complex links between those now accused and the Zinoviev group. He then listed a number of fresh terrorist bands, implicated Bukharin, spoke of the 'Bonapartist' regime Trotsky intended which would in fact be under Fascist control, and added that Trotsky was already prepared to sacrifice the Ukraine and the Far East to the aggressors.

He aptly explained the belated Trotskyite call for Party democracy: 'People begin to argue about democracy only when they disagree on questions of principle. When they agree they do not feel the need for broad democracy, that goes without saying.'[67]

In spite of his agreement to cooperate, he made several points against the indictment, in an oblique fashion. When he complained, 'For nothing at all, just for the sake of Trotsky's beautiful eyes – the country was to return to capitalism',[68] he was in effect saying that the charge of a gratuitous wish to restore capitalism for no other motive than to put Trotsky in power was an extraordinary idea, especially as regards 'such men as Yakov Livshits or Serebryakov, with decades of revolutionary work behind them',[69] whose 'moral fibre' must now be 'utterly broken' if they 'could descend to wrecking' and 'act on the instructions of the class enemy'.

On the whole, Radek was a most cooperative and convincing defendant. Even so, when he had completed the main body of his evidence, Vyshinsky started to bully him, eliciting several sharp retorts, such as 'You are a profound reader of human hearts, but I must nevertheless comment on my thoughts in my own words.'[70] Or again:

Vyshinsky: You accepted this? And you held this conversation?
Radek: You have learned it from me, that means that I did hold it.[71]

Finally, Vyshinsky reminded him that he had not only failed to report the conspiracy, but had refused to confess for three months, and said 'Does not that cast doubt on what you said about your vacillations and misgivings?'

Radek became irritated and snapped out the weak point in the whole case:

Yes, if you ignore the fact that you learned about the program and about Trotsky's instructions only from me, of course, it does cast doubt on what I have said.[72]

In the course of Radek's evidence he had been made to remark that in 1935 'Vitaly [*sic*] Putna came to see me with some request from Tukhachevsky.'[73]

Thus Corps Commander Putna was once again implicated. More striking still was the mention of Tukhachevsky's name, even in an innocent context. Moscow was shaken by what appeared to be, conceivably, the first hint of trouble for the Marshal.

During the evening session Radek was recalled and exculpated Tukhachevsky in a long exchange with Vyshinsky (see p. 291). The threat had nevertheless been made, and understood.

The same day *Sokolnikov* was called. He had little to add, apart from identifying a few more terrorist groups. He had, it appeared, little direct connexion with terror or sabotage, and unlike the case with Pyatakov, Vyshinsky did not put questions implying the opposite. His main contribution of substance was to make the point about the older generation of saboteurs:

Sokolnikov: . . . It was pointed out that former wrecking organizations among the specialists should be found.
Vyshinsky: Among the former wreckers of the period of the Industrial Party and the Shakhty Trial. Well then, what was your line?
Sokolnikov: Trotsky's line, which permitted the wrecking groups of the bloc to establish contact with these groups.[74]

Serebryakov, who followed, exposed a number of railway chiefs and explained that the system of railway organization prior to Kaganovich's appointment in 1935 had amounted to intentional

sabotage. Otherwise he only contributed accounts of a few more terrorist groups to the already large pool.

On 25 and 26 January came the questioning of the 'Siberians'. The evidence was mainly concerned on the one hand with the establishment of the links between these men and Pyatakov and the Moscow Centre; and on the other with the detail of the ways in which they had contrived accidents and explosions.

Drobnis started with the usual examples of faulty planning in industry:

Needless to say, this retarded the speed and progress of construction work. It must be said that this was done rather cleverly. For example, there were plans for the main, basic buildings of the Combined Fertilizer Works, but for things like the gas mains, the steam supply pipes and so forth, which might appear of secondary importance but were really of very great importance for starting the plant on schedule, plans were not prepared in time, and of course this constant fussing in dealings with the organizations responsible for the designs led to the plan arriving much too late . . .[75]

. . . The Kemerovo district power station was put into such a state that, if it were deemed necessary for wrecking purposes, and when the order was given, the mine could be flooded. In addition, coal was supplied that was technically unsuitable for the power station, and this led to explosions. This was done quite deliberately.[76]

He went on to the case of the Tsentralnaya Mine. He ended, bus only after considerable bullying from Vyshinsky, with the confession that the plotters had hoped for as much loss of life as possible from the explosions. Though he had been in jail at the time of the disaster, he accepted responsibility.

Shestov, the N.K.V.D. agent, confirmed Sokolnikov on the old saboteurs. He gave a useful warning to engineers throughout the country:

. . . Although Ovsyannikov was not a member of our organization he was the sort of manager who left everything to the engineers and did not do anything himself, and he could quickly be converted into a Trotskyite.[77]

His own excavation system in Prokopyevsk had resulted in no fewer than sixty underground fires by the end of 1935.[78]

Shestov explained that it was Trotskyites rather than Government policy which was rendering the worker's life intolerable:

Instructions were issued to worry the life out of the workers. Before a worker reached his place of work, he must be made to heap two hundred curses on the heads of the pit management. Impossible conditions of work were created. Normal work was rendered impossible, not only for Stakhanov methods but even for ordinary methods.[79]

Norkin and Stroilov gave similar evidence of sabotage. *Norkin* had 'planned to put the State District Power Station out of action by means of explosions. In February 1936 there were three explosions.'[80] He had also been responsible for a faulty investment programme.[81] When asked the motives of his confession, he contrived to hint at the truth:

Vyshinsky: And why did you afterwards decide to give way?
Norkin: Because there is a limit to everything.
Vyshinsky: Perhaps pressure was brought to bear upon you?
Norkin: I was questioned, exposed, there were confrontations.
Vyshinsky: You were confronted with evidence, facts?
Norkin: There were confrontations.[82]

Stroilov's evidence is chiefly interesting for what is presumably Stalin's view of Trotsky's writings:

I said that I had read Trotsky's book *Mein Leben.* He asked me whether I liked it I said from the literary point of view he, as a journalist, wrote well, but because of the infinite number of 'I's' in it, I did not like it.[83]

At the end of his testimony, Vyshinsky, who had not bothered to check the Oslo airfield situation, went through a long rigmarole to establish the reality of a minor contact of Stroilov's from Berlin:

Vyshinsky: I request the court to have attached to the records a statement by the Savoy Hotel: 'Foreign tourist H. V. Berg, born 1874, German subject, merchant by profession, Hotel Savoy, Room 223 (it is identical with the telephone number), December 1–15, 1930, arrived from Berlin.
'In the room occupied by Berg there was a telephone No. 8–50, ext. 223. Director of the hotel. Seal and reference number.'[84]

Immediately afterwards he was doing the same thing about an address in Berlin Stroilov had visited:

Vyshinsky: I request the Court to have attached to the record this Berlin address and telephone number taken from this official publication [hands to the Court a big book in a red binding]. On page 206, against No. 8563 there is Wüster, Armstrasse, and the address of this Wüster, which is mentioned also in Stroilov's notebook.[85]

The Court acceded to both these requests, so that the *Telephone Address Directory of the German Reich*, 7th edition, vol. ii, now forms part of the dossier which, somewhere in the purlieus of the Soviet State Archives, has been gathering dust for a generation.

Like Drobnis, *Muralov* had been in jail at the time of the Tsentralnaya explosion. But he refused to accept responsibility.

The President: Did you know that at the Kemerovo coal mines the Trotskyites had gassed the pits and created absolutely intolerable conditions of work?
Muralov: Drobnis was at the Chemical Works – these are under one trust, and the mines are under another trust.
The President: I understand. I am speaking about the Kemerovo mine.
Muralov: I did not know that there they had adopted the course of gassing the Tsentralnaya Pit, and Drobnis did not report this to me. This occurred when I was already in prison.
The President: One of the passages in your testimony contains this sentence: 'At the Kemerovo mine the Trotskyites gassed pits and created intolerable conditions for the workers.'
Muralov: I learned about that while I was in prison, as being a result of all the undermining Trotskyite work.[86]

His main concern, in any case, was assassination. One of the weaknesses in the whole legend came to light:

Vyshinsky: But was it not said that terrorism in general produces no result if only one is killed and the others remain, and therefore it is necessary to act at one stroke?
Muralov: Both I and Pyatakov felt that it was no use working by Socialist-Revolutionary, guerrilla methods. We must organize it so as to cause panic at one stroke. We regarded causing panic and consternation in the leading ranks of the Party as one of the means by which we would come into power.[87]

But while admitting to the preparation of attempts on Eikhe and Molotov, he warmly repudiated the accusation that Ordzhonikidze was another intended victim:

Muralov: ... About 1932 and Shestov's reference to the attempt on the life of Ordzhonikidze, I categorically declare that this belongs to the realms of Shestov's phantasy. I never gave such instructions.
Vyshinsky: He is mixing things up?
Muralov: I do not know whether he is mixing things up or whether he is simply letting his phantasy run away with him.[88]

Vyshinsky was so annoyed that he referred to this in his closing speech:

Muralov, who will under no circumstances agree to having the preparation of an attempt on the life of Comrade Ordzhonikidze attributed to him ... admits that he did indeed organize a terrorist act against Comrade Molotov.

And it certainly is anomalous. We can hardly see it as other than a demonstration of loyalty to, and hope of help from, Ordzhonikidze.

As to the attempt on Molotov, this is interesting as the only piece of action the terrorists had accomplished since the Kirov murder. The presumable truth of the matter was given in 1961:

Here is still another example of Molotov's extreme cynicism. On a trip to the city of Prokopyevsk in 1934, the car in which he was riding went off the road, its right wheels landing in a ditch. None of the passengers was injured in any way. This episode subsequently provided grounds for a story about an 'attempt' on Molotov's life, and a group of completely innocent people was sentenced for it. Who knew better than Molotov that in reality there had been no such attempt? But he had not a word to say in defence of these innocent people.[89]

As explained by Muralov, the plan was for the driver to sacrifice himself by plunging Molotov to destruction:

Muralov: The car was to turn into a ditch while at full speed. Under such circumstances, the car by its own momentum would overturn and get smashed, while the people ...
Vyshinsky: Was the attempt made to overturn the car in the ditch?
Muralov: The attempt was made, but then the chauffeur funked and the car did not fall into the ditch ...

Shestov: . . . One spot – for those who know Prokopyevsk – was near Pit No. 5 on the way to the Mine Management Office, and the second spot was between the workers' settlement and Pit No. 3. There is a gully there, not a ditch, as Muralov said, a gully, about 15 metres deep.

Vyshinsky: A 'ditch' 15 metres deep! Who chose this spot?

Muralov: Permit me to say something about Shestov's explanation. I will not argue with Shestov about whether it was a ditch or a gully . . .

Vyshinsky: Have you yourself been at the spot where this ditch is?

Muralov: No, I have never been there.

Vyshinsky: So you have not seen it?

Muralov: No, but there are many gullies in Prokopyevsk, gully upon gully, hill after hill.

Vyshinsky: If you have not seen the place you cannot argue about it.

Muralov: I will not argue about it.[90]

Muralov's disturbing reference to the alleged ravine as a 'ditch' was presumably based on definite knowledge. Vyshinsky commented in his closing speech, 'But the fact remains a fact. An attempt on the life of Comrade Molotov was made. That the car overturned on the brink of the 15-metre "ditch", as Muralov here modestly called it, is a fact.'[91]

It is curious, moreover, that the only terrorist plot (apart from the Kirov murder) which actually reached the stage of any action was not committed by one of the trained and devoted Trotskyites, but by the locally recruited petty adventurer 'Arnold, alias Ivanov, alias Vasilyev, alias Rask, alias Kulpenen . . .' as Vyshinsky put it.[92] Although Trotsky had 'insisted . . . particularly strongly' on committing a number of terrorist acts 'more or less simultaneously', only the one against Molotov had come to anything. It is true (even officially) that Molotov was only rather shaken. But still, none of the proposed victims of Prigozhin or Golubenko, or the other professional assassins, was even shaken.

And now the court found the difficulty of mixing fact with fiction. Since there really had been an accident, which it was decided to inflate into an assassination attempt, the assassin was not a picked N.K.V.D. *agent provocateur* but the chauffeur actually involved. This proved to be a mistake. Instead of an Olberg or a Berman-Yurin, chosen and groomed for the occasion, the court was faced with a man who was wholly unsuited to the part chance had called on him to play.

At the evening session of 26 January Vyshinsky came to the examination of *Arnold*, the driver who had allegedly, under orders from the Siberian conspirators, made the attempt. The whole exchange was a ludicrous interlude. Vyshinsky for once seemed to lose control of the situation.[93]

Arnold said that he had lost his nerve and only produced a slight accident. But it was perfectly clear that no conspirator could ever have expected a man of his type to sacrifice himself, as the plan allegedly intended. In fact, his final remark completely contradicted the idea that he would be dead after the accident, since he explained his motives in becoming a Trotskyite as being based on their promise that when they came to power 'I would not be among the last people then'.

In the exchange (which goes on for thirty pages in the transcript) Vyshinsky no longer faced a more or less intellectual collaborator, but a small-time *lumpenproletarian* crook and adventurer. It took five or ten minutes to straighten out Arnold's real name from his various aliases, and even then this was not properly settled and caused further trouble later on.

Owing to the loose family life prevailing in the slums of Petrograd, he had already accumulated 'three surnames by the age of seven', Vyshinsky remarked. He had wandered to Finland, and then to Germany and Holland, while still in his early teens, with yet another surname, and then, during the war, to Norway and England. On his return, he was conscripted, but deserted and was then jailed for six months. . . . There are pages of this sort of interrogation, and now Vyshinsky again became entangled in the names, and also in a complicated muddle about the various regiments Arnold had joined and deserted from in the First World War and the ranks that he had held as compared with those he had gained by simply sewing a stripe on. What he said, moreover, contradicted the story he had given during the investigation. The President had to call him to order, but still little progress was made. . . . He had managed to steal some railway passes and got to Vladivostok and, finally, under yet another name, to New York, where he joined the American Army, although he could not then speak English. In America he was jailed for five or six months – though here Vyshinsky got bogged down in a further exchange about how many times he had been jailed (apparently twice). There was also confusion about whether he had or had not joined the American Army twice or never. He claimed he had got to France with the American Army, and a visit to South America also comes up. He had also enrolled as a Freemason in America, and at the same time as a member of the Communist Party of the United States. Twenty-three pages of evidence contain this extraordinary farrago, in which the only incriminating point established is the Freemasonry, which Arnold had concealed from the Party. He seems finally to have got himself shipped to Russia with a group of American specialists being sent to Kemerovo, and there joined the Russian Communist Party. In West Siberia he had been an office manager, then in charge of water transport, then in a commercial department, and then in charge of a 'telephone system', in big enterprises in Kemerovo and Kuznetsk. In 1932 he finally got in touch with the Trotskyites, being recruited by Shestov. Arnold had already been dismissed from some job for anti-Soviet remarks, and Shestov had something more on him, having discovered two of his names – though to establish this latter point Vyshinsky again became involved in a long argument about how many there were in all. The only relevant evidence is contained in about a page and a half.

This indicated that Shestov and Cherepukhin, the local Party secretary, had ordered him to have an accident with Ordzhonikidze, Eikhe and Rukhimovich in the car. But he lost his nerve.

When Molotov came, the plan was the same. But the 'ditch' had now become not a 'gully' but a 'bank':

Arnold: . . . On this curve there is not a gully, as Shestov called it, but what we call an embankment, the edge of the road, about eight or ten metres deep, a drop of nearly ninety degrees. When I came to the station, Molotov, Kurganov, Secretary of the District Committee of the Party, and Gryadinsky, Chairman of the Territory Executive Committee, got into the car. . .

However, he again funked it, and only turned just off the road when another lorry, evidently hired by the conspirators, drove at him. No one was hurt.

He was reprimanded for negligent driving, got a job in Tashkent, returned to Novosibirsk, became assistant manager in a supply department, and finally manager of a garage. And that was all.

After Arnold came Assistant People's Commissar of Railways *Livshits*, and the other railway plotters. This section of the trial was evidently Kaganovich's private preserve. In their final speeches both Livshits and Knyazev were to speak of the forfeit of Kaganovich's trust as a particularly heinous side of their offences. Livshits remarked:

Citizen Judges! The charge advanced against me by the State Prosecutor is still further aggravated by the fact that I was raised by the Party from the ranks to a high position in state administration – to that of Assistant People's Commissar of Railways. I enjoyed the confidence of the Party, I enjoyed the confidence of Stalin's comrade-in-arms, Kaganovich.[94]

while Knyazev mourned:

. . . I always experienced a dreadful feeling of pain when Lazar Moiseyevich [Kaganovich] said to me 'I know you as a railway worker who knows the railways both from the theoretical and from the practical side. But why do I not feel in you that wide range of activity which I have a right to demand of you?'[95]

Livshits, as a senior figure, was also involved in various assassination schemes, but the main evidence of the railway accused was of wrecking trains and espionage for Japan. The extent of the 'hostile' ring in the railways bears all the marks of Kaganovich's root-and-branch style. All the accused named whole lists of wreckers, pervading entire railway systems. Vyshinsky was particularly concerned to pin the killing of innocent citizens on the saboteurs:

Vyshinsky: You do not remember if these twenty-nine Red Army men were badly mutilated?
Knyazev: About fifteen were badly mutilated.
Vyshinsky: But what sort of serious injuries were there?
Knyazev: They had arms broken, heads pierced . . .
Vyshinsky: Heads pierced, arms broken, ribs broken, legs broken?
Knyazev: Yes, that is so.
Vyshinsky: This happened by the grace of you and your accomplices?[96]

But the extent of the criminal ring was equally well developed, as can be seen from the list of those involved in a single act of sabotage.

Vyshinsky: . . . But why was such a violation of railway service regulations possible? Was it not because the administration of the station was in league with the Trotskyites?
Knyazev: Quite right.
Vyshinsky: Name these persons.
Knyazev: Markevich, the station master, Rykov, the acting station master, Vaganov, assistant station master, Rodionov, assistant station master, Kolesnikov, head switchman.
Vyshinsky: Five.
Knyazev: Switchman Bezgin.
Vyshinsky: Six.
Kynazev: And then there was also the permanent way manager of that section, Brodovikov.
Vyshinsky: Yes, and the chief of the railroad, himself.[97]

On his single line, the South Urals Railway, Knyazev now implicated a long series of accomplices, in a way which adumbrates the extraordinary scope of the purge among railwaymen throughout Russia's lines. Leading figures at his own headquarters were supplemented by the permanent-way managers of the various sections; the traffic managers; the traffic inspectors; the heads of traction departments; locomotive foremen; depot engineers; and station-masters, assistant station-masters, drivers, switchmen. He named thirty-three men in all – as the 'cadres of my Trotskyite organization on the South Urals Railway'.[98]
Knyazev went on to say:

From thirteen to fifteen train wrecks were organized directly by us. I remember in 1934 there were altogether about 1,500 train wrecks and accidents.
Powerful locomotives of the F.D. type were introduced in the Kurgan depot. Taking advantage of the fact that not much was known about them in this depot, the management deliberately slackened the supervison of current repairs, frequently compelled the engine-drivers to leave before repairs were completed. Almost all the water gauges were reduced to a ruinous condition. As a result of this neglect, a boiler burst in January 1936 on the Rosa–Vargashi stretch . . .

Vyshinsky: . . . The train wreck on 7 February 1936, on the Yedinover–Berdyaush section, was carried out on your instructions?
Knyazev: Yes. . . . Railwaymen have a notion that if a rail splits no one on the road is to blame.
Vyshinsky: That is to say, they attribute it to objective causes?
Knyazev: They did not find the culprits.[99]

Last of all came the chemical criminals. The familiar charges recurred in a slightly different context. *Rataichak* made a slight attempt to defend himself:

Rataichak: . . . No, but I had to do that, Citizen Prosecutor, because if we had not taken this measure of precaution there was a danger that the lives of hundreds of workers might have been lost. That is why I myself directed the clearance work on the spot.
Vyshinsky: You directed it in such a way that 17 workers were killed and 15 wounded. Is that so?
Rataichak: (Remains silent.)
Vyshinsky: You directed the clearance operations in such a way that 17 workers were killed and 15 injured.
Rataichak: That is true, but it was the only thing to do.[100]

The prosecution ended with the reports of various Commissions of Expert Witnesses, who blamed all the explosions and pit fires on the accused. But Stroilov commented shrewdly that the excavating system the wreckers were accused of bringing in for their own purposes had in fact been in use for some time previously.

On 28 January at 4 p.m., Vyshinsky started on his speech for the prosecution:

This is the abyss of degradation!
This is the limit, the last boundary of moral and political decay!
This is the diabolical infinitude of crime![101]

These were, he exclaimed, the sentiments with which every honest man had condemned the Zinovievites. And now the cry should be raised again. For 'the conversion of the Trotskyite groups into groups of diversionists and murderers operating as the instruments of foreign secret services and of General Staffs of aggressors merely crowns the struggle Trotskyism has been waging against the working class and the Party, against Lenin and Leninism, for decades'.[102]

This was 'not a political party. It is a gang of criminals, merely the agency of foreign intelligence services.'[103] In fact they were worse than the Whites; 'they sank lower than the worst Denikinites or Kolchakites. The worst Denikinites or Kolchakites were superior to these traitors. The Denikinites, Kolchakites, Milyukovites, did not sink as low as these Trotskyite Judases ...'[104]

Rataichak was cited as a typical conspirator. Vyshinsky remarked, in a rather unbalanced fashion, 'Whether he is a German or a Polish spy is not clear, but that he is a spy there cannot be any doubt; and as is appropriate to his profession, a liar, a swindler and a rascal.'[105]

Such analyses, which may be translated as defining anti-Stalinism as criminal Fascism, naturally fitted in with Stalin's own predictions, now reinforced by Stalin's own court:

... Comrade Stalin's forecast has fully come true. Trotskyism has indeed become the central rallying point of all the forces hostile to socialism, the gang of mere bandits, spies and murderers who placed themselves entirely at the disposal of foreign secret services, became finally and irrevocably transformed into lackeys of capitalism, into restorers of capitalism in our country.[106]

More interesting than the direct assaults in Vyshinsky's speech were the preparations for further action. He said pointedly:

I would like to remind you of how, in the case of the united Trotskyite–Zinoviev centre, say, certain of the accused vowed, right here, in this very dock, during their last pleas, some begging, others not begging for clemency, that they had spoken the whole truth, that they had said everything, that in their hearts no opposition whatever remained against the working class, against our people, against our country. And later, when the revolting skein of monstrous crimes committed by these people became more and more unravelled, we found that at every step these people had lied and deceived when they already had one foot in the grave.

... I think that all these circumstances enable me to say that if there is any shortcoming in the present trial, it is not that the accused have said what they have done, but that, after all, the accused have not really told us all they have done, all the crimes they have committed against the Soviet State.[107]

The further charges to be made against Bukharin the following year were implicit in a particularly sinister passage:

Vyshinsky: . . . It was Pyatakov and Co. who in 1918, in a period of extreme danger for the land of Soviets, carried on negotiations with the Socialist-Revolutionaries with a view to bringing about a counter-revolutionary *coup d'état* and arresting Lenin so that Pyatakov might occupy the post of head of government, of chairman of the Council of People's Commissars. It was through the arrest of Lenin, through a *coup d'état*, that these political adventurers wanted to lay for themselves the road to power.[108]

Finally, he quoted Sokolnikov, on the essential unity of all the oppositions, based on the Ryutin programme,

As for the lines of the program, as far back as 1932 the Trotskyites, the Zinovievites and the Rights all agreed in the main on a program which was characterized as the program of the Rights. This was the so-called Ryutin platform; to a large extent, as far back as 1932, it expressed the program policy common to all three groups.[109]

Further personnel for new trials had already been adumbrated. In addition to Bukharin and Rykov, Rakovsky was implicated (by Drobnis).[110] Mdivani in Georgia was now incriminated by name.[111]

The present case had, Vyshinsky pointed out, been proved with a rigour not demanded in bourgeois courts:

With the assistance of the experts, we verified the evidence of the accused, and although we know that according to the laws of certain European countries the confession of an accused person is regarded as sufficient proof of guilt and the court does not consider itself obliged to call corroborating evidence, we, however, in order to observe strict impartiality, notwithstanding the confessions of the criminals themselves, verified their statements once again from the technical side and obtained a categorical reply concerning the explosion of 11 November, the fires in the Prokopyevsk mine, and the fires and explosions at the Kemerovo plant. Malicious intent was established without any possibility of doubt.[112]

Certain of the objections to the Zinoviev Trial were dealt with. For example, on the absence of documentary proof Vyshinsky now remarked:

The accused committed the deeds attributed to them. . . . But what proof have we in our arsenal from the point of view of judicial procedure? . . . The question can be put this way: a conspiracy, you say, but where are the documents? . . . I am bold enough to assert, in keeping with the fundamental requirements of the science of criminal procedure, that in cases of conspiracy such demands cannot be put.[113]

(On this point one of the defence lawyers, inadequately briefed, was to refer approvingly to 'documents available in the case'.)[114]

The popular rage line was heavily played:

They blow up mines, they burn down workshops, they wreck trains, they mutilate and kill hundreds of our best people, sons of our country. Eight hundred workers in the Gorlovka Nitrate Fertilizer Works, through *Pravda*, communicated the names of the best Stakhanovites in those works who died by the treacherous hand of the diversionists. Here is the list of these victims: Lunev – Stakhanovite, born 1902. Yudin – a talented engineer, born 1913. Kurkin – a member of the Young Communist League, Stakhanovite, 23 years of age. Strelnikova – girl shock brigade worker, born 1913. Mosiets – shock brigade worker, also born 1913. These were killed, over a dozen were injured. Maximenko, a Stakhanovite who fulfilled his norm 125 to 150 per cent, was killed. Nemikhin – one of the best shock brigade workers – sacrificed his ten days' leave to go down the Tsentralnaya Pit, and there somebody waited for him and killed him. Shot-firer Yurev – one of the men who took part in the fighting against the White Chinese – was killed. Lanin, an old miner, a participant in the Civil War, was killed. And so on and so forth.[115]

As a result, Vyshinsky felt justified in shouting, as he perorated:

I do not stand here alone! The victims may be in their graves, but I feel that they are standing here beside me, pointing at the dock, at you, accused, with their mutilated arms, which have mouldered in the graves to which you sent them!

I am not the only accuser! I am joined in my accusation by the whole of our people! I accuse these heinous criminals who deserve only one punishment – death by shooting![116]

Unlike the Zinoviev Trial, some of the junior accused this time had defence counsel. These took a different view of their duties from those in bourgeois courts. Braude started by saying, in a *locus classicus* for Stalinist defence lawyers:

Comrade Judges, I will not conceal from you the exceptionally difficult, the unprecedentedly difficult position in which the Defence finds itself in this case. First of all, Comrade Judges, the Counsel for Defence is a son of his country. He, too, is a citizen of the great Soviet Union, and the great indignation, anger and horror which is now felt by the whole population of our country, old and young, the feeling which the Prosecutor so strikingly expressed in his speech, cannot but be shared by Counsel . . .

In this case, Comrade Judges, there is no dispute about the facts. Comrade Prosecutor was quite right when he said that from all points of view, from the point of view of documents available in the case, from the point of view of the examination of the witnesses who were summoned here, and cross-examination of the accused, all this has deprived us of all possibility of disputing the evidence. All the facts have been proved, and in this sphere the Defence does not intend to enter into any controversy with the Procurator. Nor can there be any controversy with the Procurator concerning the appraisal of the political and moral aspects of the case. Here, too, the case is so clear, the political appraisal made here by the Procurator is so clear, that the Defence cannot but wholly and entirely associate itself with that part of his speech.[117]

When the 'defence' had finished, the last pleas followed. Pyatakov ended his, with downcast eyes,

In a few hours you will pass your sentence. And here I stand before you in filth, crushed by my own crimes, bereft of everything through my own fault, a man who has lost his Party, who has no friends, who has lost his family, who has lost his very self.[118]

Radek's most useful contribution was to make the point that there were still 'semi-Trotskyites, quarter-Trotskyites, one-eighth-Trotskyites, people who helped us, not knowing of the terrorist organization but sympathizing with us, people who from liberalism, from a Fronde against the Party, gave us this help . . .' This was in fact a charter for disposing of any critics of the Purge, even if 'seven-eighths-Stalinist'.

Yet, while both abject and cogent in his presentation of the charges against Trotsky and the accused, he managed to make a few two-edged remarks. He continued to dissociate himself and his co-defendants from the direct German connexion:

But when I read about Olberg and asked others whether they had known of the existence of Olberg, and none of them had heard about him, it became clear to me that in addition to the cadres who had passed through his school, Trotsky was organizing agents who had passed through the school of German Fascism.[119]

And finally he repeated the fact that it was only on his word, and Pyatakov's, that the entire case was erected:

What proofs are there in support of this fact? In support of this fact there is the evidence of two people – the testimony of myself, who received the directives and the letters from Trotsky (which, unfortunately, I burned), and the testimony of Pyatakov, who spoke to Trotsky. All the testimony of the other accused rests on our testimony. If you are dealing with mere criminals and spies, on what can you base your conviction that what we have said is the truth, the firm truth?[120]

The others took the more usual line. Drobnis, Muralov, Boguslavsky, referred to their splendid records and proletarian origins. Sokolnikov spoke at length and Serebryakov very briefly. All the politicals, though to very different degrees, attacked Trotsky in person. Arnold pleaded 'weak, low political development', as well he might.

At 3 a.m. on 30 January the verdict was pronounced. Death to all except Sokolnikov and Radek (as not 'directly participating in the organization and execution' of the various crimes) and Arnold, who got ten years each, and Stroilov, who got eight. A story circulating in N.K.V.D. circles has it that Stalin was asked for Radek's life to be spared by Lion Feuchtwanger, as the price for his agreeing to write his book (*Moscow 1937*) justifying the trials, which Stalin was particularly anxious to have written to counter the effect of André Gide's *Retour de L'URSS*.[121] The sentence on Arnold, supposed actually to have carried out a terrorist act, contrasts extraordinarily with those on the previous failed assassins like Fritz David. It has been suggested that Stalin had been so entertained by his evidence that, when he drafted the sentences, he indulged the caprice of showing special clemency.

When Radek heard the verdict his face showed relief. He turned to his fellow-accused with a shrug and a guilty smile, as though unable to explain his luck.*[122] All reports agree that he was sent to a labour camp in the Arctic, where he was, as was often the fate of politicals, murdered by a criminal prisoner.[124] This was in 1939. Sokolnikov also died, presumably in camp, in 1939.[125]

The relations of several prisoners are identified in camps or jail. Radek's daughter got eight years.[126] Drobnis's wife was seen in 1936 in the Krasnoyarsk isolator. She had become almost completely deaf as the result of treatment in the Lubyanka.[127] Galina Serebryakova, who spent nearly twenty years in Siberia from this time, had been married to two leading victims, Serebryakov and Sokolnikov. Through all this, she retained her Party-mindedness, and after her rehabilitation spoke up warmly at writers' meetings in 1962–3 against the liberalizing trends. During the early months of 1963, when heavy pressure was being put on the 'liberal' writers, Khrushchev was able to point to her as an example, comparing her with Ilya Ehrenburg, who during Stalin's lifetime had praised him warmly and lived comfortably, but was now departing from Party principles.[128]

There had been a progressive increase in the incredibility of the trials. At first (1936) the Party was only asked to accept the idea that Zinoviev and Kamenev, together with some genuine Trotsky-ites, had plotted to murder the leadership and had in fact been responsible for Kirov's death. Although the execution of Zinoviev and the others aroused a great revulsion, there were other factors. First of all, though it seems unlikely that any member of the Central Committee could have believed the charges literally, or taken the confessions at face value (and there were certainly rumours circulating about the true role of the N.K.V.D. in the Kirov killing), still the Zinoviev opposition had really fought Stalin by all the means at its disposal, in a political fight in which almost all the present Committee had been on Stalin's side. They had compromised themselves by lying their way back into the Party, as was quite evident. And it was at least possible that the assassination of Kirov was 'objectively' Zinoviev's responsibility.

*There were rumours put about that Radek was serving his sentence in comfort under little more than house arrest in a villa in the Urals.[123] It may be that he was briefly held in such conditions, but if so this was presumably only to impress the defendants at the third trial.

As to the more obvious falsehoods of the trial itself, the Party was quite used to falsehood for Party reasons, and, if it came to that, to fake trials designed to impress the public. Stalin was, it might have been felt, getting rid of irreconcilable enemies.

None of this applied to Pyatakov and his fellow-defendants. And, at the same time, the case produced all the anomalies and oddities of the previous one, in fact in an exaggerated form.

As with the Zinoviev group, it was alleged that Pyatakov and his fellow-defendants had organized a vast underground of assassins. Radek referred, perhaps ironically, in his evidence to 'scores of wandering terrorist groups waiting for the chance to assassinate some leader of the Party'.[129] At least fourteen separate groups or individuals are named, who had the task of assassinating Stalin (several of them), Kaganovich, Molotov, Voroshilov, Ordzhonikidze, Kossior, Postyshev, Eikhe, Yezhov and Beria. Again, in spite of the protection and complicity of high officials everywhere, they had been unable to carry out any overt act, successfully or unsuccessfully, with the sole exception of the attempt to murder Molotov, and even this did not sound very professional. Indeed, the sentencing of Arnold to only ten years' imprisonment was virtually an admission that he was not a political enthusiast. Why, when the conspiracy brimmed with fanatical Trotskyites, they should have entrusted this suicide operation to such a figure was not explained.

And the plotters were not even able to assassinate Kaganovich, though several of the men closest to him in his governmental post, like Livshits, Serebryakov and Knyazev, were members of the conspiracy.

Vyshinsky had to deal with the fact that Zinoviev and his colleagues who had supposedly made full confessions had (as it now appeared) concealed much of the story. He said flatly, as we saw, that they 'lied and deceived when they already had one foot in the grave'.[130] But in that case, while their confessions of fact might have been limited to what they could not deny, their abject expressions of guilt must have been insincere: that is, everything they said in their final speeches was retrospectively cancelled. People who believed in the trials, however, had no difficulty in reconciling, or rather ignoring, these contradictory versions.

A minor anomaly is, as we have seen, that the accused now admitted that they had plotted with Zinoviev and Kamenev to kill Molotov as well as the other leaders. Zinoviev and Kamenev had not confessed to this crime, since they had not been required to do so.

Once again, important plotters were mentioned and not produced. When the Old Bolshevik Byeloborodov, who had ordered the execution of the Royal Family, was implicated in a fashion which could not be cleared up properly, Vyshinsky remarked 'So now it will be necessary to ask Byeloborodov himself?'[131] But Byeloborodov was not produced, then or ever.* And the same applies, of course, to Smilga, Preobrazhensky, Uglanov and other important links, who were simply omitted without explanation.

In addition there were, of course, the factual mistakes, and particularly the Oslo visit. Yet in a version published in England under the sponsorship of the 'Anglo-Russian Parliamentary Committee', a preface by the Moscow correspondent of the *Daily Herald*, Mr R. T. Miller, could say 'They confessed because the State's collection of evidence forced them to. No other explanation fits the facts.' Mr Neil Maclean, Labour M.P. for Govan and Chairman of this committee, noted in a 'Foreword', 'Practically every foreign correspondent present at the Trial – with the exception of course of the Japanese and German – have expressed themselves as very much impressed by the weight of evidence presented by the Prosecution and the sincerity of the confessions of the accused.' This is an interesting (though untrue) smear on correspondents who thought otherwise. They were clearly in the same boat as the minority of committed Fascists, excluded from the company of all decent folk. (This is not the earliest, nor the only use of this polemical method.) Even when the trial was in progress, *Pravda* published a long article about how a British lawyer, Mr Dudley Collard, had described it (in the *Daily Herald*) as judicially unexceptionable.[133]

A couple of days earlier, on 27 January 1937, *Pravda* had printed a more suitable item: an idealized portrait of Yezhov

*There is a story of his being dragged down a prison corridor yelling 'I am Byeloborodov. Pass the word on to the Central Committee that I am being tortured!'[132]

with the information that he had been promoted to the new rank of General Commissar of State Security. In general, the press and 'public' had mounted the usual violent campaign. When the verdict was announced, a crowd of 200,000 assembled in the Red Square, in a temperature of − 27°C., to be harangued by Khrushchev and Shvernik, and to demonstrate spontaneously against the accused.[134] They carried banners demanding the immediate carrying-out of the death sentences − a demand readily acceded to by the authorities.

THE ORDZHONIKIDZE 'SUICIDE'

Once again the executions shocked the inner circles of the Party. This time Stalin had to face an immediate threat of firm opposition from a colleague who could not easily be dismissed − Sergo Ordzhonikidze. He had been double-crossed. Personally involved in the negotiations before the Pyatakov Case, he knew it to be faked and he had had Stalin's assurance that Pyatakov would not be executed. He saw in all this a fatal precedent. It became clear that he would now carry on the fight against the Purge by every means at his disposal.

One account describes his behaviour when he learned of the arrest of the head of one of the big trusts under his authority. He rang up Yezhov, calling him a 'filthy lickspittle', and demanded the documents in the case instantly. He then phoned Stalin on the direct circuit. By this time he was trembling and his eyes were bloodshot. He shouted 'Koba, why do you let the N.K.V.D. arrest my men without informing me?' After some reply from Stalin, he interrupted:

I demand that this authoritarianism cease! I am still a member of the Politburo! I am going to raise hell, Koba, if it's the last thing I do before I die![135]

As usual, Stalin was not caught unprepared. In fact, though we usually think of the dispute between the two men about Pyatakov as a matter of Stalin wanting to get rid of Pyatakov and being willing to put up with trouble from Ordzhonikidze in the process, it seems equally plausible that Stalin fully intended the destruction of Pyatakov as a blow against Ordzhonikidze too and that the destruction of Ordzhonikidze was not simply a by-product of the Pyatakov Case, but something planned from the start. (As we have suggested, it was perhaps as a political signal of some sort that at that trial Muralov, while freely admitting to kill Molotov and others, firmly denied any plans against Ordzhonikidze,[136] and was censured for it by Vyshinsky in his closing speech.) Ordzhonikidze's elder brother, Sergo-Papuli, was about this time 'shot after being tortured'.*[137] Stalin must therefore have been preparing to strike at his old colleague, but to have shown his hand only a short time before his final move.

Meanwhile in the Transcaucasus N.K.V.D. operatives were working 'to compel arrested people to give false testimonies against S. Ordzhonikidze'.† This would have been meaningless after Ordzhonikidze's death, and shows that Stalin was already preparing a dossier against his old friend.

It is also the case that most of Ordzhonikidze's associates fell before or after his death, and that this is a reasonable indication of Stalin's feelings. Among them was Gvakharia, Ordzhonikidze's nephew, the head of the great Makeyevka iron foundry.‡

The leaders of Soviet heavy industry followed: Gurevich (a leading figure in the metallurgical industries), Tochinsky and many others. The top directors and industrialists, the men who actually, under Pyatakov, created Stalin's one real achievement, disappeared.[143]

Ordzhonikidze himself was being increasingly harassed. Police officers 'arrived at Ordzhonikidze's flat with a search warrant. Humiliated and frantic with rage, Sergo spent the rest of the night trying to get through to Stalin on the telephone. As morning came he finally got through and heard the answer: "It is the sort of

* His close associate Mirzabekyan, shot with him, held a post in the Georgian government 'to 1937',[138] while we are told that Papuli's execution preceded Ordzhonikidze's death.[139]

† This charge was made at the Bagirov Trial in 1956.[140] Similarly, former N.K.V.D. officers tried in November 1955 were charged with 'collecting slanderous material' against him, and later of terrorist acts against members of his family and close friends in responsible posts.[141]

‡ Weissberg gives an interesting account of the brilliant and unorthodox methods by which he reorganized production.[142]

organ that is even liable to search my place. That is nothing extraordinary . . ."'[144]

On 17 February he had a conversation with Stalin lasting several hours. He made 'a last attempt to explain to Stalin, a friend of many years' standing, that dark forces were currently profiting from his pathological lifelong suspiciousness and that the Party was being deprived of its best cadres'.[145] So far, the 'cadres' the Party was being 'deprived of' were practically all oppositionists or ex-oppositionists, and Ordzhonikidze's formulation seems well suited to Pyatakov, and perhaps – in anticipation – Bukharin and Rykov. The talk of 'dark forces' is quite clearly an attack on Yezhov, and perhaps Kaganovich and others as well.

He worked in his People's Commissariat till 2 a.m. the next morning, the 18th. When he got home he had another equally fruitless conversation with Stalin on the telephone. At 5.30 in the afternoon he was dead.

His wife Zinaïda rang Stalin, who soon appeared. He 'didn't ask a single question, but merely expressed astonishment: "Heavens, what a tricky illness! The chap lay down to have a rest and the result was a fit and a heart attack."'[146]

The official medical report was as follows:

Comrade Ordzhonikidze suffered from sclerosis accompanied by serious sclerotic transformations of the cardiac muscle and cardiac vessels, and also from a chronic affection of the right kidney, the only one he possessed after the removal in 1929 of the left kidney owing to tuberculosis.

For two years Ordzhonikidze, from time to time, suffered from attacks of stenocardia (*angina pectoris*) and cardiac asthma. The last such attack, which was a very serious one, occurred at the beginning of November 1936.

On the morning of 18 February Ordzhonikidze made no complaint about his health, but at 17.30, while he was having his afternoon rest, he suddenly felt ill and a few minutes later died of paralysis of the heart.

G. Kaminsky, *People's Commissar for Health, U.S.S.R.*

I. Khodorovsky, *Head of the Kremlin Medical-Sanitary Administration*

L. Levin, *Consultant to the Kremlin Medical-Sanitary Administration*

S. Mets, *Duty Medical Officer of the Kremlin Clinic.*[147]

Of the four signatories, Kaminsky (who, we are told, was 'very unwilling'[148] to sign) was shot later in the year, Khodorovsky was referred to as a plotter in the Bukharin Trial, and Levin actually appeared as a defendant at that trial and was shot afterwards. What happened to the more obscure Mets is unknown.

Curiously enough, it was never alleged against the doctors, or anyone else, that Ordzhonikidze had been a victim of a murder plot by the opposition. It is true that at his funeral a few days later Khrushchev was to remark, 'It was they who struck a blow to thy noble heart. Pyatakov – the spy, the murderer, the enemy of the working people – is caught red-handed, caught and condemned, crushed like a reptile by the working class, but it was his counter-revolutionary work which hastened the death of our dear Sergo.'[149] And indeed, the authoritative article on him in the *Large Soviet Encyclopedia*, describing him as 'the favourite comrade-in-arms of the great Stalin' and saying that he 'died at his post as a warrior of the Lenin–Stalin Party', adds that 'the Trotskyite–Bukharinite degenerates of Fascism hated Ordzhonikidze with a bitter hatred. They wanted to kill Ordzhonikidze. In this the Fascist agents did not succeed. But the sabotage activity and monstrous treachery of the despicable Right-Trotskyite hirelings of Japanese–German Fascism greatly hastened the death of Ordzhonikidze.'[150]

But nevertheless, no one was ever charged with murdering him. This shows a curious restraint on Stalin's part (though of course he may have been saving the case for one of the post-Bukharin trials which never occurred, at least in public).

It is now no longer disputed that Stalin did in fact procure Ordzhonikidze's death. But the details are still debatable. And the way in which the original official version lost credence, first in the defector literature, and finally in Russia itself, is an interesting demonstration of the relative worth of the sources.

Soon after Ordzhonikidze's death, rumours began to come out of Russia. These varied as to detail, some saying that he had been forced to kill himself under threat of immediate arrest as a Trotskyite, others that he had actually been shot, or poisoned under the supervision of Poskrebyshev, Stalin's secretary.[151] For example, Kravchenko, in his book published a decade before Khrushchev's revelations at the XXth Party Congress, says that some believed he committed suicide, others that he was poisoned by Dr Levin.[152] But no one had any doubt that he died by violence, that his end was not 'natural'.

Khrushchev said in 1961 that he had believed what was said about Ordzhonikidze's heart attack, and only 'much later, after the war, I learned quite by chance that he had committed suicide'.[153] On the other hand we know from recent Soviet sources that the suicide story had circulated widely in the Party. Amirdzhanov, a 'worker of the Baku Soviet' – scarcely a very senior position – was 'repressed' in 1937 because when 'a certain section of the Party *aktiv*' had – already – learned of the suicide story, he had passed it on to 'an intimate circle of comrades'.[154] It was circulating in Kazan prison by April 1937.[155] Again, we are told that Nazaretyan, 'one of the first' to learn the truth about Ordzhonikidze's death, was arrested in June 1937 and had already learned it by then.[156] In the N.K.V.D., too, rumours circulated to the same effect.[157]

In the U.S.S.R. the natural death version remained official until in February 1956 Khrushchev remarked in his Secret Speech:

> Beria also cruelly treated the family of Comrade Ordzhonikidze. Why? Because Ordzhonikidze had tried to prevent Beria from realizing his shameful plans. Beria had cleared from his way all persons who could possibly interfere with him. Ordzhonikidze was always an opponent of Beria, which he told Stalin. Instead of examining this matter and taking appropriate steps, Stalin permitted the liquidation of Ordzhonikidze's brother and brought Ordzhonikidze himself to such a state that he was forced to shoot himself.

This account is clearly misleading. Khrushchev represents Ordzhonikidze's death as simply due to the failure of an attempt to hamper Beria, as a result of which Stalin turned against him. But at this time Beria was in the Caucasus, and though he was certainly influential he played little part in the great affairs of state going on at Politburo level in Moscow. The interest of the 1956 version is elsewhere, in the 'he was forced to shoot himself'.

Indeed, Khrushchev himself, when he raised the matter for the first time in a non-secret speech, omitted the Beria angle, which by 1961 was no longer a 'must'. He said:

Comrade Ordzhonikidze saw that he could no longer work with Stalin, although previously he had been one of his closest friends ... circumstances had become such that Ordzhonikidze could no longer work normally, and in order to avoid clashing with Stalin and sharing the responsibility for his abuse of power, he decided to take his life.[158]

This version has not since been amended or contradicted. It may be worth examining the other possibilities. There are, in effect, three stories (now that natural death has been eliminated): suicide out of despair – a voluntary act; straight murder; and suicide as the result of a threat of worse alternatives by Stalin. Khrushchev implies the first. But it seems reasonable to think that, at most, he is making the best of a forced suicide – just as, in the Kirov Case, he could not bring himself to accuse Stalin directly of murder.

A close friend of Ordzhonikidze's widow relates that she thought he had been killed by others, and had seen men running across the lawn away from the house at the time of his death.[159] A Caucasian Party official who was in Moscow at the time says that Stalin sent several secret policemen to Ordzhonikidze, offered him the alternative of arrest or suicide, and gave him a revolver. A doctor was waiting to certify heart failure.[160]

This account fits in with the fact that a dossier against Ordzhonikidze had been accumulated. It does not, of course, give any guarantee that the fatal shot was fired by Ordzhonikidze himself. (And though these accounts specifically speak of a shot, stories of poisoning are in a sense more plausible, in that a doctor would more easily certify, and a family more easily accept, a heart-failure verdict.)* In fact, there seems no real point in making him shoot himself, when the N.K.V.D. men could do that equally easily.

If it *was* suicide, it seems that the stories associating Poskrebyshev with the death are probable. Ordzhonikidze could scarcely have been expected to accept a political ultimatum or indeed to commit suicide at all, on a threat from a lesser N.K.V.D. officer; the presence of Stalin's personal representative is a reasonable

---

*When it was wished to get rid of Slutsky, Head of the Foreign Department of the N.K.V.D., on 17 February 1938, he was simply given cyanide in Frinovsky's office, and the death labelled a heart attack (see p. 588).

idea. Ordzhonikidze's own N.K V.D. guards must, of course, have been given suitable orders.

As to who else was implicated, it is interesting to note how often during the trials of 1953–6, notably of Beria, but also after his death of other police officials, the persecution of Ordzhonikidze is referred to. Among the vast selection of crimes which could have been urged against these men this insistence may be meaningful. It is worth remarking that the Bagirov Trial, of Beria's closest political associate (who was accused of persecuting Ordzhonikidze), took place more than two years after Beria's fall, but only a few weeks after Khrushchev had clashed at the XXth Congress with Kaganovich and others on the issue of repudiating Stalin. There is at least some sort of presumption that the raising of the Ordzhonikidze issue in this way may have had an immediate political aim. This would have been to compromise one or more of those closest to Stalin in 1937 and still living in 1956 – Poskrebyshev, Kaganovich, Malenkov, among others.

There was one obvious motive for at least pretending suicide. If the doctors, or any of them, had seen the body and been told it was suicide, it is of course understandable that they could have been induced to hush up the scandal in the interests of Party and State. Kaminsky, at least, was to prove a brave critic of the new Terror over the months that were left to him: it may perhaps have been his direct connexion with the Ordzhonikidze Case which brought him to his moral decision. Hushed up or not, and even taking it as suicide and not murder, at his political level (as candidate member of the Central Committee) he might have guessed what a suicide in those circumstances signified. But if it had *obviously* been murder, he might well have taken a stronger line.

The decisive argument against any but a forced suicide is different. If Ordzhonikidze had felt 'unable to share responsibility', if he 'did not want to play the scoundrel' as an accomplice in Stalin's plans, it is quite untrue that 'the only thing to do was to depart', as a recent Soviet account has it.[161] On the contrary, the Central Committee was about to meet. By 20 February the Ukrainian-based members of the Politburo (all three 'moderates') were already in Moscow,[162] and that body was probably in session. When the full plenum met on 23 February, a concerted attempt was made to block the Purge. The natural, in fact the 'only', thing for Ordzhonikidze to do was to throw himself into the struggle. Suicide at this moment was pointless. But from Stalin's point of view the opposite consideration prevailed. An opposition led by an angry Ordzhonikidze was likely to prove much more difficult to handle than one lacking his support. Suicide was pointless; but *murder* was logically indicated.

It is not uninteresting that Vyshinsky described the death of Zinoviev's secretary, Bogdan, who had allegedly been forced to commit suicide under the terms 'Kill yourself or else we will kill you', as 'really murder'.[163] In this sense, even accepting a forced suicide, we can in any case certainly speak of the murder of Ordzhonikidze.

On 19 February 1937,[164] the first photographs of Ordzhonikidze's corpse show, grouped around it, his wife and Stalin's own cabal – Stalin himself, Yezhov, Molotov, Zhdanov, Kaganovich, Mikoyan and Voroshilov. They all appear overcome with comradely sorrow.

A Central Committee announcement the same day spoke of him as 'an irreproachably pure and staunch Party man, a Bolshevik'.[165] And Ordzhonikidze continued to be honoured by Stalin, just as Kirov did. But there is one curious sign of the dictator's animus. Seven years later, in 1942, the main towns that had been named after Ordzhonikidze were quietly rechristened: Ordzhonikidzegrad (formerly Bezhitsa), Ordzhonikidze (formerly Yenakiyevo) and Sergo (formerly Kadiyevka) reverted to their earlier names, while Ordzhonikidze in the Caucasus, formerly Vladikavkaz, was given a new Ossetian name, Dzaudzhikau. Such action, in the Stalinist protocol, had hitherto invariably been a sign of disgrace (and was to be so in future under his successor as well, when the town of Molotov reverted to Perm, and so on). Yet no further public degradation was inflicted.

Five days after Ordzhonikidze's death the Central Committee assembled. In the last trial of strength which now took place, his presence was to be sorely missed among the elements attempting to halt the Purge.

THE FEBRUARY-MARCH PLENUM

Livshits's last words, as he was being led to execution, had been a cry of 'What for?' Or so a story went that now circulated in the upper levels of the Party. Army Commander Yakir, a full member of the Central Committee, commented privately when he heard it that the question was a good one as the men were quite clearly innocent.[166] This appears to have been the mood among the majority of the members of the Central Committee as the 'February–March plenum' opened, on 23 February.

The atmosphere was extremely tense. For the more moderate members of the Stalin leadership were about to make a strong, and last, attempt to wind up the Purge. And Stalin, on the other hand, was determined finally to overcome the hesitations and qualms which had for so long held him up and forced him to mark time. The struggle at the plenum is another of the cases in which long-standing rumour was, after decades of official silence, more or less confirmed by Khrushchev in 1956 and 1961.

The session was, of course, 'managed' by Stalin's men; the official *rapporteurs* were Yezhov, Zhdanov, Molotov and Stalin himself. Formally speaking, they dealt with different subjects – Yezhov with police affairs, Zhdanov with Party organization, Molotov with the economic side, while Stalin made the political report. But in practice all the reports centred on the Purge theme, from Yezhov's 'Lessons Emerging from the Harmful Activity, Diversion and Espionage of the Japanese–German–Trotskyite Agents',[167] through Zhdanov's condemnation of wrongful methods of expelling Party members and Molotov's 'report on wrecking and sabotage',[168] to Stalin's 'Deficiencies of Party Work and Methods for the Liquidation of the Trotskyites and other Two-faced People'.

In fact there was, in reality, only one item on the agenda – the expulsion and arrest of Bukharin and Rykov.

An account of the plenum was in circulation in the Vorkuta camps in 1940,[169] originating from several high officials including A. Butsenko, former Secretary of the Ukrainian Central Executive Committee, who had received a twenty-five-year sentence in connexion with the 'Ukrainian national fascist organization' and would have heard of these events from a number of sources. From this, from later Soviet evidence confirming and supplementing it, from the exiguous material published at the time, and from certain other sources, a coherent view can now be obtained of the desperate manoeuvring in that secret session.

A number of members of the Central Committee had agreed to oppose the attempts to bring Bukharin to trial, making it a test case of the exaggeration of the N.K.V.D.'s powers. Postyshev was to launch the debate.

During the weeks since January the indirect attacks on his position had continued. On 1 February his close supporter Karpov was denounced as 'an enemy of the Party, a loathsome Trotskyite'.[170] Over the following weeks, about sixty expulsions of his old nominees from the Kiev Party were announced. These lesser figures were more easily removable. They had no Old Bolshevik past, and even if their record as Stalinists was a sound one, it was not so widely known throughout the Party as to make charges against them sound unbelievable. In attacking men like Karpov, Stalin was undermining Postyshev without having the assault made directly. But at the same time, establishing the 'Trotskyism' of the second- and third-rank Stalinists in the entourages of men he wished to remove, Stalin was setting up precedents which, as resistance weakened, gave him a freer and freer hand to deal with more important men with perfect records.

On 8 February came attacks on faults that had been found in the Kiev, Azov–Black Sea, and Kursk provinces.[171] On the following day, 'lordly and immodest' actions that had come to light in the Party leaderships in Kiev and Rostov provinces were described.[172] The concentration on Kiev was obvious enough.*

These attacks had not so far cowed Postyshev, and he held himself ready to put the opposition's viewpoint. There was no intention of removing Stalin, but only of curbing him and getting him to abandon Yezhov and the Purge. There were precedents in

---

*Though we may note that the Secretary of the Azov–Black Sea Committee, Malinov, and the head of his Party Organs Department were to be denounced as Trotskyite conspirators.[173]

Russian history, but they were not encouraging ones. The *boyar*, Prince Michael Repnin, had called on Ivan the Terrible to rid himself of his Secret Police:

> 'To our misfortune, you have surrounded your throne with the *oprichnina* . . .
> Perish the *oprichnina*!' he said, making the Sign of the Cross;
> 'May he live for ever, our orthodox Tsar!
> May he rule over men as he ruled them of old!
> May he spurn, as treason, the voice of shameless flattery! . . .'

The declaration of loyalty to the ruler and hostility to his Secret Police was unsuccessful and Repnin was killed, a lesson to all who undertake such half-measures.

Stalin had learned of the plan in advance. Speaking first, he anticipated and refuted the arguments to be brought against him, and made an appeal for unity and responsibility in the Communist leadership.

Postyshev then went to the platform. In his 'dry, hoarse and unpleasant voice', he began to read his text. After a careful preamble, he spoke of the excesses of the Purge:

> I have philosophized that the severe years of the struggle have passed; Party members who lost their backbone broke down or joined the camp of the enemy, healthy elements fought for the Party. Those were the years of industrialization and collectivization. I never thought it possible that after this severe era had passed Karpov and people like him would find themselves in the camp of the enemy. And now, according to the testimony, it appears that Karpov was recruited in 1934 by the Trotskyites. I personally do not believe that in 1934 an honest Party member who had trod the long road of unrelenting fight against enemies, for the Party and for socialism, would now be in the camp of the enemies. I do not believe it . . . I cannot imagine how it would be possible to travel with the Party during the difficult years and then, in 1934, join the Trotskyites. It is an odd thing . . .[174]

He was about to come to grips with the charges against Rykov and Bukharin, when Stalin, who was listening without apparent emotion, uttered a loud interjection, which made it clear to everyone that he was aware of what was going on.

This was perhaps the occasion on which Stalin turned to Postyshev and said 'What are you, actually?', to which Postyshev replied 'I am a Bolshevik, Comrade Stalin, a Bolshevik'.[175] This reply, in any case, was at first represented in the Party as showing lack of respect for Stalin, and later 'it was considered a harmful act and consequently resulted in Postyshev's annihilation and in his being branded without reason as an enemy of the people'[176] – doubtless an exaggerated and compressed account.

Whatever Stalin said, Postyshev (according to the Vorkuta version) faltered, departed from the text of his speech, and while explaining the doubts that he and his associates had felt, said that after listening to Stalin's analysis he withdrew them and hoped that everyone else would do the same.

Most of the speakers who followed did do the same, but Rudzutak, Chubar, Eikhe and some of the military commanders are said not to have withdrawn. They argued that their doubts were not signs of treason or weakness but of their concern for the Soviet State. Chubar is said to have been particularly cogent. Kaminsky, the People's Commissar for Health, though only a candidate member of the Central Committee, is also reported as speaking with particular effect and firmness and presenting a full but calm indictment of Yezhov and his methods.[177]

But the solidarity of the attempt had been lost. The only chance lay in a firm front, rallying the sympathetic but timorous majority. As it was, the only real solidarity was that of the Stalinist *claque* – Zhdanov, Yezhov, Molotov, Voroshilov, Kaganovich, Mikoyan, Khrushchev and Shvernik in particular.

Stalin looked on with an indifferent air, smoking his pipe and taking notes. In the end he intervened in a mild tone, thanking everyone for their constructive criticism, but emphasizing the necessity of solidarity and firmness against the Trotskyite conspirators.

On 26 February Zhdanov made his organizational report, which was debated on 27 February. He took the opportunity to criticize sharply the situation in Kiev under Postyshev for 'incorrect leadership' and 'gross breaches of the Party constitution and the principles of democratic centralism' – the main point being that the Kiev and other organizations had been resorting to co-option instead of election, and that this was extremely undemocratic.[178]

Meanwhile the attack on Bukharin and Rykov was coming to its climax. They were, of course, present at the meeting as not-yet-expelled candidate members of the Committee. When their arrest was formally proposed, there was a stormy scene. Sokolnikov and Radek were brought in under guard, and testified against them.[179] But they faced them down and bitterly protested their innocence. 'They did not take the road of repentance.'[180] Every point raised against them they denied 'many times'.[181]

Bukharin is said to have made a strong and emotional speech, agreeing that a conspiracy existed but claiming that its leaders were Stalin and Yezhov, who were plotting to install an N.K.V.D. regime giving Stalin unlimited personal power.[182] He appealed in tears to the Committee to take the right decision. Stalin interrupted him, saying that he was behaving in a manner unbecoming to a revolutionary, and he could prove his innocence in a prison cell.[183]

The vote, taken under the eye of Stalin and Yezhov, with the N.K.V.D. guards waiting in the wings, was a mere formality. The two men were arrested on the spot and dragged off to the Lubyanka.

This was on 27 February. The plenum went on.

A resolution on Yezhov's report was accepted which repeated Stalin's formulation about the N.K.V.D.'s failure under Yagoda to act four years previously – that is, against Ryutin:

The Plenum of the Party Central Committee considers that all facts revealed during the investigation into the matter of an anti-Soviet Trotskyite centre and of its followers in the provinces show that People's Commissariat of Internal Affairs had fallen behind at least four years in the attempt to unmask these most inexorable enemies of the people . . .[184]

Stalin severely criticized Yagoda.[185] This must have been the occasion when Yagoda turned on the applauding members and snarled that six months earlier he could have arrested the lot of them.

In his economic report Molotov sneered at those who urged caution 'against conjuring up all sorts of conspiracies and sabotage and espionage centres', and called on the Party to annihilate enemies of the people 'hiding behind Party cards'. The present-day subversives and saboteurs were especially dangerous, he said, because they 'pretend to be Communists, ardent supporters of the Soviet regime'.[186]

On 3 March Stalin made his political report, and on the 5th a short 'final speech' closing the plenum. These two speeches were printed in full in the press on 29 March in a version believed to differ considerably, chiefly by omission, from what he had actually said. They were later in the year sponsored in England in one volume with the slightly compressed transcript of the Pyatakov Trial. Neil Maclean M.P., Chairman of the Anglo-Russian Parliamentary Committee, commented in a preface:

These speeches in that simple and clear style of which M. Stalin is such a master form an interesting background and commentary on the Trial . . .

They do indeed.

Stalin's report developed the theoretical justification for the Terror. Quoting the Central Committee letters of 18 January 1935 and 29 July 1936, he propounded his view (to be denounced in the Khrushchev period) that as socialism gets stronger, the class struggle gets sharper.

He pointed out that the fact of there only being a few counter-revolutionaries should not comfort the Party: 'Thousands of people are required to build a big railway bridge, but a few people are enough to blow it up. Tens and hundreds of such examples could be quoted . . .'

But his central theme was in effect a censure of leaders who had failed in their vigilance:

Some of our leading comrades, both in the centre and locally, not only failed to discern the real countenance of these wreckers, diversionists, spies, and murderers, but proved so unconcerned, complacent and naïve, that at times they themselves assisted in promoting the agents of the foreign States to one or other responsible post.[187]

'The espionage-diversionist work of the Trotskyite agents of the Japanese–German secret police,' he added, 'was a complete surprise to some of our comrades. . . . Our Party comrades have not noticed that Trotskyism has ceased to be a political tendency in the working class, that from the political tendency in the working class that it was seven or eight years ago, Trotskyism has become a frenzied and unprincipled band of wreckers, diversionists, spies and murderers, acting on instruction from intelligence service organs of foreign States.'[188]

He made the sinister suggestion, which was to prove a fair statement of his plans:

First of all it is necessary to suggest to our Party leaders, from cell secretaries to the secretaries of province and republic Party organizations, to select, within a certain period, two people in each case, two Party workers capable of being their real substitutes.[189]

His final speech touched only briefly on his older rivals, now crushed:

Two words about wreckers, diversionists, spies, etc. I think it is clear to everybody now that the present-day wreckers and diversionists, no matter what disguise they may adopt, either Trotskyite or Bukharinite, have long ceased to be a political trend in the labour movement, that they have become transformed into a gang of professional wreckers, diversionists, spies and assassins, without principles and without ideals. Of course, these gentlemen must be ruthlessly smashed and uprooted as the enemies of the working class, as betrayers of our country. This is clear and requires no further explanation.[190]

The bulk of the speech concentrated on a different matter – the censure, in effect, of his next batch of victims. His theme was incorrect conduct, and unjustified expulsions, by leading Communists still in high positions. Then, after remarking that:

We, the leaders, should not be conceited, and should understand that if we are members of the Central Committee or People's Commissars, this does not yet mean that we possess all the knowledge required to give correct leadership. The rank in itself gives neither knowledge nor experience. Still less so does the title.[191]

he went on to deal with the unfortunate case of Nikolayenko in Kiev:

Nikolayenko – is a rank and file member of the Party, she is an ordinary 'little person'. For a whole year she had signalled about a wrong situation in the Party organization in Kiev, exposing the family atmosphere, philistine approach to workers, gagging of self-criticism, high-handed action by the Trotskyite wreckers. She was shunned like a bothersome fly. At last, in order to get rid of her, they expelled her from the Party. Neither the Kiev organization nor the Central Committee of the Communist Party of the Ukraine helped her to obtain justice. It was only the intervention of the Central Committee of the Party which helped to disentangle that twisted knot. And what was revealed by an examination of the case? It was revealed that Nikolayenko was right, while the Kiev organization was wrong.[192]

and added, of the inhuman attitude to such expulsions by some Party bureaucrats, 'Only people who are essentially deeply anti-Party can have such an approach to members of the Party.'[193]

With these sinister words ringing in their ears, the defeated majority dispersed to their posts, where worse awaited them.

On 13 March *Pravda* gave prominence to a special article on 'The Struggle of Bukharin and Rykov against Lenin and the Party' which was specifically printed for the instruction of the younger generation who might not remember these earlier crimes. In it Tomsky too was accused of 'foul anti-Party activity', and all three were definitely denounced for criminal links with the Trotskyites. The author of the article was Peter Pospelov, still, as I write, a member of the Central Committee.

One of the first steps taken in the aftermath of victory came on 17 March, when the Ukrainian Central Committee relieved Postyshev of his post as Second Secretary.[194] He was demoted to be First Secretary in Kuibyshev province. There, though still officially retaining his rank as candidate member of the Politburo, he was to moulder, under constant criticism, for a year. The new post was supposed to be an opportunity to 'correct his errors', it was later to be said,[195] with the verdict that he had failed to measure up.

In Kiev, a resolution was passed saying that as a result of his leadership, and its 'un-Bolshevik style of work' which suppressed criticism and formed a solid clique, enemies of the Party had been able to penetrate the organization and sometimes to persecute honest Communists.[196]

In the following months the implications grew. At the Ukrainian

Congress in May, Kossior attacked Postyshev. In Kiev more than anywhere, he said, Trotskyites had been able to gain important posts.[197] Other speakers upbraided those in Kiev 'who had let in enemies'. Over several years of complacency the main thing had been a personality cult involving 'Greetings to Postyshev!', as the restored and rehabilitated Nikolayenko smugly remarked to the uneasy delegates.[198] He had been, in fact, 'intoxicated with success' because of 'the noise our press made round his name'.[199]

The defeat and demotion of Postyshev was only the beginning. Over the next few years the great majority (70 per cent) of the Central Committee which had just made a final and fumbling stand was to follow Bukharin and Rykov to the death cells.

For, politically, Stalin's battle had now been won. The way was at last completely open to the total annihilation of the old oppositionists. At the same time, by his actions against Postyshev, he had made the first moves to undermining and destroying that group of his own followers who had tried to block him.

But the main change was that the last attempt to preserve some sort of constitutional procedure had been defeated. In future he was not to observe any such limitations. Bukharin's and Rykov's were the last cases of Central Committee members whose expulsion and arrest was dealt with, in accordance with Party statutes, by the Committee itself.

In six months the position had changed radically. In the autumn of 1936, Stalin had had to argue and exert pressure to secure the arrest and trial even of potential rivals. Now, he could order the arrest of his closest colleagues without consulting anyone. He could strike when and where he liked, without appeal. The point at which his despotism became an absolute autocracy may be dated as the February–March plenum.

There were still steps to be taken to ensure the irrevocability of the victory. The demoralized and defeated majority of the Central Committee, convicted of the most capital of all crimes, ineffective disloyalty, had to be mopped up. The Purge had so far only affected a limited section of the Soviet people, among whom there remained much political indiscipline to be eradicated. And the Army remained – to all appearances wholly obedient, but tyrants have often been misled on this point, and Stalin was soon to insure himself against such a mistake.

But first, the instrument of terror needed retuning. The old N.K.V.D. of Yagoda's time was technically efficient, but in certain respects it lacked the true Stalinist spirit. In any case, its new master could not trust his predecessor's men.

In March, Yezhov ordered the departmental chiefs of the N.K.V.D. to proceed to various parts of the country on a massive inspection. Only Slutsky of the Foreign Department and – for the moment – Pauker were not so assigned. The others, leaving shortly afterwards, were arrested at the first stations out of Moscow in their various directions, and brought back to prison. Two days later the same trick was played on the deputy heads of the departments. At the same time, Yezhov changed the N.K.V.D. guards in all sensitive spots.[200] He had already barricaded himself in a separate wing of the N.K.V.D. building, surrounded by a formidable bodyguard and elaborate security precautions.[201]

On 18 March 1937[202] Yezhov addressed a meeting of senior officers of the N.K.V.D. in the Secret Police club-room at the Lubyanka. He denounced Yagoda as a former Tsarist police spy and a thief and an embezzler, and went on to speak of 'Yagoda's spies' in the N.K.V.D. He proceeded immediately to clean up the remaining Yagoda cadres. They were arrested in their offices by day or in their homes by night. Chertok, the bullying interrogator of Kamenev, threw himself from his twelfth-floor apartment. Other officers shot themselves, or committed suicide by jumping from their office windows.[203] Most went passively, Bulanov, arrested 'at the end of March', among them.[204] In all, 3,000 of Yagoda's N.K.V.D. officers are reported executed in 1937.[205] Of his departmental chiefs, Molchanov, Mironov and Shanin were to be denounced as Rightist conspirators,[206] organized as such in the O.G.P.U. in 1931–2, while Pauker (who disappeared in the summer) and Gay were transmuted to spies,[207] together with Pauker's deputy Volovich. (Pauker, a Jew, was spoken of as specifically a German spy.)[208]

On 3 April it was announced that Yagoda himself had been arrested for 'offences of a criminal nature in connexion with his

official duties'.[209] Next day an announcement was made of a new
People's Commissar and Assistant People's Commissar of Communications.[210] The transfer of the former Assistant People's
Commissar G. E. Prokofiev was also published. Though he was
still named as 'Comrade', he was arrested shortly afterwards as a
Rightist. The wives of both men were also arrested and were sent
to a camp.[211] Yagoda's dacha was taken over by Molotov.[212]

Yezhov now had his machine cleared and ready for action. At
the same time, the other main element in the Purge mechanism,
Vyshinsky's Prosecutor's apparatus, was being similarly reno-
vated. A number of the old Prosecutors had attempted to maintain a semblance of legality. For example, the Assistant Chief
Prosecutor of Water Transport had put in a memorandum on 26
June 1936 urging this. Similar protests were made by a number of
provincial Prosecutors – for example in Bryansk, where two were
arrested 'for spreading false and defamatory rumours'. Ninety per
cent of the provincial Prosecutors were removed, and many of
them were arrested. 'Vyshinsky carried out a mass purge in the
organs of the Prosecutor's office. With his sanction, many prominent workers in the Prosecutor's office who had tried in one way
or another to mitigate repressive measures and stop the lawless-
ness and arbitrariness were arrested and subsequently perished.'[213]
As late as the beginning of 1938 the ironically titled Stalinist law
journal *Socialist Legality*[214] called for further work in purging
'fascist agents' among the Prosecutors.

The authorities on Soviet law who had inculcated the 'formalist'
attitude to legality were held to responsibility. The Deputy
Commissar for Justice, the Soviet Union's leading legal theorist,
E. Pashukanis, was severely criticized in January 1937,[215] and in
April was linked by Vyshinsky with Bukharin as a wrecker 'who
has now been exposed'.[216] Another unsatisfactory Deputy Com-
missar for Justice, V. A. Degot, was arrested on 31 July 1937.
Sent to camp, he died in 1944.[217]

By early spring, all the machinery was in good order. The old
Communist police and prosecutors, ruthless as they had been,
had not proved sufficiently so for the new phase. Russians who
had thought that the country was already in the grip of terrorists
were now to see what terror really meant.

CHAPTER SEVEN

ASSAULT ON THE ARMY

Ils sauront bientôt que nos balles
Sont pour nos propres généraux.
THE INTERNATIONALE

ON 11 June 1937 it was announced that the flower of the Red Army Command had been charged with treason, and next day that they had been tried and executed. Unlike the victims of the political purges, there had been virtually no public build-up of feeling against the generals. For most people in Russia and outside, the news came as a complete and shocking surprise. No details were given of the 'treason'. The 'campaign' appearing in the papers on 12 June could hardly have the effect obtained on previous occasions by months or years of abuse. They did their best with meetings demanding the death penalty for the 'foul band of spies'; there had already been time for Demyan Bedny to compose a fifty-four-line poem including the names of the generals in the rhyme scheme; another poetaster, A. Bezimenski, provided similar verses; and in the pages around them, factory demonstrators, the Academy of Sciences, the polar explorers on Rudolph Island, and in fact representatives of the entire community, demanded the shooting of the traitors, which had, as it turned out, already taken place. On the 15th *Pravda* published Voroshilov's report to a meeting of members of the Government and the Military Soviet of the People's Commissariat of Defence on the crimes of the soldiers. They had 'admitted their treacherousness, wrecking and espionage'.

The men concerned were Marshal Tukhachevsky, Deputy People's Commissar of Defence; Army Commander Yakir, commanding the Kiev Military District; Army Commander Uborevich, commanding the Byelorussian Military District; Corps Commander Eideman, Head of the Civil Defence organization 'Osoaviakhim'; Army Commander Kork, Head of the Military Academy; Corps Commander Putna, Military Attaché

in London; Corps Commander Feldman, Head of the Red
Army Administration; and Corps Commander Primakov,
Deputy Commander of Leningrad Military District. In addition
Yan Gamarnik, Head of the Political Administration of the Red
Army and First Deputy Commissar of Defence, whose suicide
had been announced on 1 June, was implicated in the alleged
conspiracy. The original communiqué said that

> The above-named persons were accused of breach of military duty
> and oath of allegiance, treason to their country, treason against the
> peoples of the U.S.S.R. and treason against the workers' and peasants'
> Red Army.[1]

There was some discrepancy between these charges and those
given in Voroshilov's report, which associates the accused with
Trotsky and charges them with 'preparing the assassination of
leaders of the Party and Government', as well as with espionage.[2]
As we shall see, both the Trotskyite and the treason themes had
been prepared over many months; and the treason at least was
well 'documented'.

The accused were all leading members of the group around
Tukhachevsky which had pioneered military rethinking through
the thirties.* They had developed the ideas and to some degree
the organization of an efficient modern army.

The military leaders were still young men. They had been
commanding Armies while still in their twenties. Apart from
Kork, who was just fifty, those now seized were all in their forties.
Even now Tukhachevsky and Putna were forty-four, Yakir and
Uborevich only forty-one – the same age as Zhukov, who was to
play an important military and political role for many years to
come. Gamarnik, too, was only forty-three.

Tukhachevsky had by general recognition the finest military
brain in the Army, and the strongest powers of will and nerve. He
came of the minor aristocracy. During the First World War he
had served as a subaltern in the Semeonovsky Guards Regiment.
He had been taken prisoner by the Germans in 1915. After five

---

*Three prominent figures in that group did not die with them – Alksnis
of the Air Force, Muklevich of the Navy and Khalepsky of the armoured
forces – but their turn was to come soon .

attempts to escape, he was lodged in the security fortress of
Ingolstadt, the Colditz of the First World War (where his fellow
inmates included young Captain de Gaulle). In 1917 he got back
to Russia, where he joined the Bolsheviks.

Brilliant, quick of mind, with a streak of cruelty allied to an im-
petuousness which bordered on the rash, the young Red Army Commander cultivated a certain *hauteur* and an arrogance which was not
calculated to ease all his friendships.[3]

He was twenty-seven when, in 1920, he commanded the armies
attacking Poland, having several times saved the Communists on
the Eastern Front. He later commanded at Kronstadt and against
the Antonov rebellion in the Volga Basin.

The Kiev and Byelorussian Military Districts, under Yakir and
Uborevich respectively, were the two largest, containing between
them twenty-five of the ninety rifle divisions and twelve of the
twenty-six cavalry divisions.

Yakir, brisk and young in appearance and activity, was the son
of a small Jewish chemist in Kishinev. He had organized a
Bolshevik band in the Ukraine when only twenty-one, and risen
within three years to command the so-called 'Fastov army
groups' against the Poles. From 1926 he commanded the key
Ukrainian Military District, under its various successive names.
He was the only professional soldier who was a full member of
the Central Committee.*

Uborevich, a bespectacled military intellectual, had also
commanded an Army against the Poles in 1920, and had then
figured in the brilliant operations which finally led to the storming
of the Crimea at the end of 1920 and put an end to the Civil War.
He was a candidate member of the Central Committee, the only
Army one besides the four Marshals† and Gamarnik's Assistant
Head of the Political Administration, A. S. Bulin.

The others were almost equally distinguished. Kork and Eideman, too, had commanded Armies in the Civil and Polish Wars.
Eideman, a squareheaded, moustached, sergeant-major-looking
type, was in fact a Latvian writer. Putna, who had served with

*The other 'military' full members were Voroshilov and Gamarnik.
†Blyukher, Budenny, Tukhachevsky and Yegorov.

Tukhachevsky in the Semeonovsky Guards before the Revolution, had had lesser commands, but held major posts in the training side of the Army in the twenties. Feldman, of Jewish origin, was one of Tukhachevsky's closest associates.

The other main victim of Stalin's blow, Yan Gamarnik, Head of the Army Political Administration and First Deputy People's Commissar for War, was not in quite the same category. He had been engaged in controversies against the military leaders on matters of political-military organization. A typical Old Bolshevik, he had fought in very dangerous circumstances in the Ukraine in the Civil War, and had voted with the Sapronov faction at the time of its influence in the Republic.[4] But he had had no connexion with any oppositionists since the mid twenties. He had been appointed head of the Political Administration of the Red Army in 1929. With his long, rough beard and a resemblance to Dostoyevsky, he was thought of – in the Party context, it is true – as a sort of saint.

Far from their fine records being of any service to the generals, the contrary seems to apply. In 1937, one fifth of the officer corps were still veterans of the Civil War; this included almost all the High Command. But there were many grudges outstanding from those earlier times. During the battles for Tsaritsyn, a group had formed around Voroshilov and Stalin which continually disobeyed and stood out against the orders of Trotsky as Commissar for War. A long, bloody-minded intrigue, in which Voroshilov in particular behaved extremely badly, caused perhaps the worst ill-feeling to be found even among the freely quarrelling Bolshevik leadership.

Under this Tsaritsyn group had come a cavalry unit headed by Budenny, initially little better than bandits. He himself relates that Trotsky at the time spoke of them as 'a horde', under 'an Ataman ringleader. . . . Where he leads his gang, there they will go; for the Reds today, tomorrow for the Whites.'[5] One of Budenny's commanders actually shot a commissar for protesting against the sack of Rostov. As recruits came in, the 'horde' was later expanded, with Stalin's help, to be the First Cavalry Army. It had attracted efficient as well as erratic elements, and improved with organization. This Army's Military Council had consisted of Voroshilov, Shchadenko and Budenny.

The First Cavalry Army was involved in the fiercest controversy of all – the argument about responsibility for the Soviet defeat in the Battle of Warsaw in 1920. As Tukhachevsky had struck north of the Polish capital with the main bulk of the Soviet forces, Yegorov and Stalin with the Southern Front, including Budenny's men, had been attacking towards Lwow. Orders to divert Budenny northwards had been disregarded until too late, at best on technical excuses, at worst in a short-sighted attempt to secure local glory at the expense of the main effort. It is arguable that the Soviet forces were anyhow over-extended, but the bulk of Soviet military opinion followed Tukhachevsky in feeling that Stalin, Yegorov and Budenny had wantonly robbed the offensive of whatever chance it had. Lenin seems to have agreed, remarking 'Who on earth would want to get to Warsaw by going through Lwow?'[6] The whole matter was thrashed out in public in military lectures. There can be no doubt that it rankled bitterly with Stalin, and when he gained full control of the history books the whole episode was represented as a strategically sound drive on Lwow, sabotaged for motives of treason by Tukhachevsky and Trotsky.*

But at the time the controversy soon began to seem minor and academic. Compared with the true political virulences then prevailing, the Army gradually became a quiet area amid the storms of Soviet political life.

In the twenties, Communists in the armed forces were at first strongly and openly involved in the political arguments of the time. Antonov-Ovseenko, Head of the Army Political Administration, had been forthrightly Trotskyite. Lashevich, the Zinovievite Deputy Commissar for War, had actually held a more or less secret oppositionist meeting in a wood while still at his post.

But later, this sort of overt action ceased. For a time Army Communists still entered, though more discreetly than the civilians, into the controversies of the time. Yakir and Putna were among the officers signing some sort of confidential defence of the

* Stalin also put some of the blame for the Polish débâcle on Smilga.[7]

opposition in 1927.[8] Tukhachevsky had not been involved in this, or any similar, move. We may make a certain distinction between the professional soldiers who became Communists, like Tukhachevsky, Kork and Yegorov, and the Communists who had become professional soldiers, like Yakir, Blyukher and Alksnis. Even at this time the former played little part in politics – except when military matters were directly affected, as when Tukhachevsky and Uborevich opposed Trotsky's ideas of army organization.

But in any case, from the establishment of Stalin's primacy at the end of the twenties, the Army command had wholly withdrawn from the political struggle. In part, this was evidently due to the same ideas that had decided Pyatakov: the leadership question was settled. What remained was the professional problem of creating a sound military force. And, on the other hand, Stalin had been careful not to stir up trouble among the soldiery. Just as he had 'neutralized' the Ukraine by withdrawing Kaganovich in 1928, so he now left Tukhachevsky and his fellows a comparatively free hand. The Army's Communists had a high reputation in the Party. In the comparatively mild Party purge of 1929, some five per cent of military Communists were purged, compared with 11·7 per cent in the Party as a whole; in the 1933 purge, the figures were 4·3 per cent and 17 per cent respectively.

It is true that an occasional officer suffered. But this was usually a special case, like that of the military academic Snesarev, formerly a Tsarist general, lately rehabilitated.

In January 1930, on a charge of having participated in a counter-revolutionary monarchist officers' organization, he was arrested along with other military specialists

and at the age of sixty-five was deported to hard labour in the far north, where he died in 1937.[9]

But on the whole, the Army received more and more friendly attention, and less and less persecution. Its prestige began to be built up in a variety of ways. The principle of shared responsibility between the commander and the political commissar was abolished in March 1934, leaving the commander in full control with the commissar simply as his political adviser. The old military ranks up to, but not including, general, were restored on 22 September 1935. The same decree gave all except junior commanders the privilege of immunity from arrest by the civil organs without a special authorization from the People's Commissar of Defence. At the same time, the first five Marshals of the Soviet Union were named: Tukhachevsky, Blyukher and Yegorov of the genuine military, plus Stalin's nominees Voroshilov and Budenny.

Through 1936 and early 1937, however, a new factor arose. As we saw, a number of the military men were members of the Central Committee. Voroshilov and Budenny always supported Stalin. But Yakir and Gamarnik, as full members, and Tukhachevsky, Blyukher, Yegorov, Uborevich and Bulin, as candidate members, are all said[10] to have been, like the majority of civilian members, against the arrest of Bukharin.

At his trial in 1938 Bukharin was to speak vaguely of the 'military men' among his fellow plotters. When Vyshinsky asked 'Which military men?' he answered 'The Right conspirators'. Vyshinsky, accepting this, asked for the names in the particular context, and was given those of Tukhachevsky and Kork.[11] In his speaking of them as not simply members of the far-flung 'bloc' but as actual Rightists, we can perhaps find a clue to part of the reason for Stalin's resentment of the military. They had not been Rightists in the sense that Bukharin was. But it is more than likely that they had shown Rightism, in the sense that Rudzutak, Chubar and so on had done – that is, in exercising their votes or voices against Stalin at the plenums of the Central Committee during the final phase from September 1936 to February 1937. The military candidate members might perhaps have avoided giving their opinions about the fate of Bukharin, but the full members must have done so. Even abstention would certainly have been taken by Stalin as a sinister sign.

Not that we can so simply exhaust Stalin's motives. Former grudges and present nuisance-value certainly played a part. But there are more general, and more powerful, considerations.

Despotism enforced by a terrorist and terrorized bureaucracy may be in a general way extremely strong. But it presents certain points of vulnerability. There is a brittleness in the strength. Even the most rigorous precautions can never entirely rule out the possibility of assassination. There is no real evidence of any serious attempt on Stalin's life (unless, indeed, he died as the result of one in 1953: we have at present no final knowledge of the circumstances). There are a few vague reports of genuine plots, usually among young Communists, discovered before they came to fruition. And there are one or two individual incidents such as that reported during the Second World War of a soldier who shot at random at a car emerging from the Kremlin which chanced to contain Mikoyan.[12]

The other vulnerability was to a military *coup*. Even a few dozen determined men might conceivably have seized the Kremlin and the persons of the leadership. And in those circumstances the type of machine Stalin built can crack very easily. Even the farcical attempt by General Malet to overthrow Napoleon in 1812, by sheer bluff, had an almost incredible measure of preliminary success. The best chance of getting rid of Stalin would have been a *coup* by Tukhachevsky in alliance with the surviving oppositionists, just as the best chance of blocking Hitler in 1933 would have been a *coup* by Schleicher backed by the Social Democratic Party.

But just as the German Social Democrats were hobbled by their notions of constitutionality (and just as, later, most of Hitler's generals were hamstrung by their formal allegiance to Hitler as Head of State), the Soviet Marshals, like the civilian oppositionists, seem to have been mesmerized by the notion that the Stalin leadership, with all its faults, had inherited the Party legitimacy.

For there is no evidence that any conspiracy really existed. Isaac Deutscher has indeed written that 'all non-Stalinist versions concur in the following: the Generals did indeed plan a *coup d'état*'.[13] In reality, there is virtual unanimity that this was not the case. The leading defector information (including that deriving from N.K.V.D. officers in prison who discussed the matter with cell-mates who eventually came West),* and the present

* e.g. 'We ourselves believe that there was no such plot and this coincides with the interpretation put on events by the overwhelming majority of the Soviet intelligentsia and in particular the arrested officers themselves.'[14]

Soviet revelations, all agree on the non-existence of any plot. The Nazi secret archives contain no sort of evidence of anything of the kind. And the judgement of the most careful historians, such as Leonard Schapiro and John Erickson, is firmly of the opinion that there was no conspiracy. Admittedly, one cannot prove a negative, and we must not formally exclude the possibility of evidence one day turning up to show that some of the military were seriously considering action.* But it seems unlikely, to say the least. The curious thing is that the legend of a real conspiracy still persists, though the 'conspiracies' alleged at the three great political trials have either been rejected from the start or have long since been seen through.

The reason, paradoxically, seems to be that this is the one case in which Stalin did not produce his evidence. From Stalin's point of view, it was the best method. If a real military plot had suddenly been discovered, the immediate court-martial and execution of the conspirators was a natural-looking reaction. It had many precedents in other countries and, indeed, in Russia. Moreover, while the likelihood of the plots hitherto exposed in court was on the face of it dubious, the seizure of power by Tukhachevsky appeared a perfectly rational and possible move. In this case, public 'proofs' were not required. In a sense, this is itself a curious irony, as this is the only case in which Stalin did dispose of documentary evidence. It was, of course, faked, but it really was of German origin.

But Stalin had the wit not to publish these documents. They had not been devised solely for his benefit, and perhaps did not entirely suit his intention. On the other hand, if made public, it might, for all he knew, have been possible for experts to detect flaws, or even for the Germans to blow the gaff.

Thus the result of Stalin's sudden blow, and the absence of specific evidence, was that people found it easier to believe that a

---

*The same is true of vague reports that the idea of a *coup* occurred to some officers, in particular Feldman, but that none of the senior generals were involved. The other 'military conspiracy' mentioned at the Bukharin Trial – that of Peterson, Commander of the Kremlin Guard, who intended a palace *coup* – is only perfunctorily linked with Tukhachevsky;[15] but again, though not implausible, there is no evidence for it.

plot genuinely existed. As the Minister of War remarks in *Penguin Island* of the efforts of his Chief of Staff in providing reams of proofs against the accused Jewish officer, 'Proofs! Of course it is good to have proofs, but perhaps it is better to have none at all . . . the Pyrot affair, as I arranged it, left no room for criticism; there was no spot at which it could be touched. It defied assault. It was invulnerable because it was invisible. Now it gives an enormous handle for discussion.'

It was not so much that people believed the precise charges. Some of these, as later developed, were incredible – in particular that Yakir and Feldman, both Jews, had really worked for Nazi Germany. What was found tolerable was simply the central thesis that the generals were plotting to use their power against Stalin.

The essence of the plot, according to evidence in the Bukharin Trial,[16] was Tukhachevsky's 'favourite plan' – the seizure of the Kremlin and the killing of the leadership by a group of military men. Gamarnik had proposed also seizing the N.K.V.D. headquarters. He is represented as believing that 'some military under his direct command' would obey him. He considered he had sufficient Party and political prestige in the Army and that some of the commanders, 'especially the daredevils', would support him.[17]

A curious sidelight is that Gamarnik, with a choice of 'daredevil' officers allegedly at his disposal, and Yakir, the fighting general, are supposed to have instructed the Chief of the Department of Savings Banks of the Ministry of Finance, Ozeryansky, to prepare a terrorist act against Yezhov.[18] This is another of those little touches which might perhaps have fortified the scepticism of Mr Pritt.

Various versions were planted by the Russians. For example, the American Ambassador, Joseph Davies, says in his memoirs that he was told by Ambassador Troyanovsky on 7 October 1937, when he had queried the idea that Tukhachevsky would have become a German agent simply for money, that the Marshal had a mistress who was herself a German agent. This story was evidently planted elsewhere: Davies reports hearing it also from the French Ambassador on the authority of the Deuxième

Bureau, who are supposed to have got it from Prague. Walter Duranty recounts a similar story. There is no reason to believe it.

As we have said, the apparent suddenness of the blow at the Army, the great air of urgency, contributed to the plausibility of Stalin's story. And this theme was put about even in the outer circle of the N.K.V.D. A senior N.K.V.D. officer, as late as October 1937, was telling his subordinates in Spain 'That was a real conspiracy! That could be seen from the panic which spread there on the top: all the passes to the Kremlin were suddenly declared invalid; our [i.e. N.K.V.D.] troops were held in a state of alarm: as Frinovsky said, "the whole Soviet Government hung by a thread. . . ."'[19]

To another, Frinovsky remarked that the N.K.V.D. 'had uncovered a gigantic conspiracy – we have got them all!',[20] though this seems to have been said around 20 May, when the 'uncovery' by receipt of the forged dossier was accomplished, but three key arrests were yet to come.

This notion of a sudden, secret emergency was doubtless useful in providing a panic tension in military, Party and N.K.V.D. circles. But it was not in accord with the facts. The pressure against the Army, though little publicized, had on the contrary been gradual and cumulative.

It was eleven months since Stalin had in fact made the first moves against the High Command, which had now borne such fantastic fruit.

The first arrest in the series that was to lead up to the great blow at the generals had taken place on 5 July 1936, when the N.K.V.D. seized Divisional Commander Dmitri Shmidt, commanding a tank unit in the Kiev Military District, without informing or consulting his superior officer, Yakir. Yakir went to Moscow where Yezhov showed him 'material' implicating Shmidt.[21] This material presumably consisted of the confessions of Mrachkovsky, Dreitzer and Reingold which revealed Shmidt and his accomplice B. Kuzmichev (Chief of Staff of an Air Force unit) as having been under Mrachkovsky's instructions, through Dreitzer, to assassinate Voroshilov, in the interests of the Trotskyite element in the 'Bloc'.[22] In accordance with Stalin's style, Shmidt was a man against whom a particular individual grudge awaited settlement. Not only was he an ex-oppositionist, but he had given Stalin personal offence.

Shmidt, a Party member since 1915, was the son of a poor Jewish shoe-maker. He had become a sailor and then, through the Civil War, a brilliant cavalry commander in the Ukraine. During the period all sorts of rival factions were fighting right through the area: for example, Vassili Grossman recounts that Berdichev had changed hands fourteen times. It had been occupied 'by Petlyura, Denikin, the Bolsheviks, Galicians, Poles, Tutnik's and Maroussia's bands and "nobody's Ninth Regiment".'[23]

Amidst this chaos, Shmidt had risen to command first a regiment and then a brigade, had captured Kamenets-Podolsk, far to the west, surrounded by enemy forces, and had finally been ordered to prepare for the attempt, never in fact made, to break through Poland and Romania to help the Hungarian Soviet Republic in 1919. He had ridden into a camp of nationalist guerrillas with two aides and, after negotiations failed, engaged in a successful gunfight. In fact, he was a typical though not outstandingly gifted 'natural leader' of partisans – swashbuckling, simple, frightened of nothing, a true product of the Civil War. Later, in peace-time, he had shot, but failed to kill, a senior officer who had insulted his wife, the matter being hushed up.

During 1925–7 Shmidt had become associated with the opposition, though not in any significant way. Arriving in Moscow at the time of the 1927 Congress, when the expulsion of the Trotskyites was announced, he had met Stalin coming out of the Kremlin. Shmidt, in his black Caucasian cloak and silver-ornamented belt, with his fur cap cocked over his ear, had gone up to Stalin and, half-joking, half-serious, had started to curse him in the extravagant soldier fashion of the time. He ended by gesturing as though to draw his great curved sabre, and told Stalin that one day he would lop his ears off.[24]

Stalin said nothing, listening white and tight-lipped. The incident was taken as a bad joke, or at most an insult beneath political notice. Shmidt, after all, had accepted the Party decision which he objected to so strongly, and for nearly a decade he continued to serve. In fact the Trotskyites were allegedly to find him suitable conspiratorial material precisely because he was 'under no suspicion in the Party'.[25] As to his rudeness, after all, Stalin had defended 'rudeness' among comrades. And, indeed, that sort of thing from a rough soldier would not have been much regarded earlier on, or by any of the leaders but Stalin.

From the start it was clear that Shmidt's arrest was no isolated act. The 'cases' of Shmidt and Kuzmichev are among those named in the indictment of the Zinoviev Case as 'set aside for separate trial in view of the fact that investigation is still proceeding'. In court Mrachkovsky spoke of a 'terroristic group of people including Shmidt, Kuzmichev and some others whom I do not remember' which already implied a larger military organization. Reingold too mentioned them as forming only part of a 'Trotskyite group of military men', which had a number of other members whose names he did not know.

Kuzmichev, like Shmidt, was an old comrade of Yakir's. Another friend of his, Ivan Golubenko, Chairman of the Dniepropetrovsk Soviet, was also arrested in August 1936[26] as a Trotskyite, though later transmuted to a spy. Already a member of 'a counter-revolutionary Trotskyite–Zinovievite nationalist bloc'[27] in the summer of 1936, he was mentioned in January 1937 as a member of a terrorist group formed to assassinate both Stalin[28] and 'the leaders of the Communist Party and the Soviet Government of the Ukraine.'[29] He is said to have really been associated with Ordzhonikidze's attempts to halt the Terror.

These arrests, and particularly Shmidt's, caused considerable worry to military circles in the Ukraine. No one believed he was guilty. Though he had once voted for Trotsky, he had long since 'repented' of this. And throughout August there were further arrests. On 25 September came that of Divisional Commander Yu. Sablin. A woman N.K.V.D. officer, Nastya Ruban, who knew Yakir, went to him secretly and told him that she had seen the materials against Sablin and it was quite clear that he was not guilty. Three days later her death by heart attack was announced. It was soon learned that it had really been suicide.[30]

Meanwhile, in the Lubyanka, Shmidt was being interrogated 'in all degrees' by top-ranking N.K.V.D. operatives, including the Head of the Special Department, M. I. Gay, and the notorious

Z. M. Ushakov, on the charge of planning to kill Voroshilov. Documentary evidence was produced – a route card of Voroshilov's movements at the manoeuvres as issued to all commanders. For some time Shmidt denied all the accusations.[31]

While Shmidt and Kuzmichev had been implicated in the preliminary interrogations of the Zinoviev Trial prisoners and publicly named in the indictment, it was only in the course of the trial itself that, on 21 August 1936, a more senior figure, and one of the Tukhachevsky group proper, was unexpectedly brought in. Dreitzer, who had finished his evidence on the 19th, was recalled. And as the last evidence given in the whole trial, he implicated Putna. This officer was now alleged to have been in direct contact with Trotsky and Ivan Smirnov. Smirnov denied that Putna had anything to do with it. But Pickel, Reingold and Bakayev corroborated Dreitzer.[32] Putna, recalled from London, was under arrest by the beginning of September. His wife learned of the arrest in Warsaw on her way to join him.[33]

The next soldier who was to figure in the June 1937 Trial, Corps Commander Primakov, Deputy Commander of the Leningrad Military District, was under arrest no later than November 1936 (and probably earlier: he is now quoted as holding that post only until August).[34] His role in the whole affair is very obscure. But he had already been in N.K.V.D. hands in, apparently, 1934,[35] so was particularly vulnerable.

On the face of it it was no more extraordinary for Trotskyite plots to involve Communists in the Red Army than in any other field. It could not easily be complained of as an attack on the Army as such. On the other hand, according to Dreitzer, Trotsky's instructions had included as a particular duty 'to unfold work for organizing nuclei in the Army '[36] – a direct threat. During the autumn there were rumours that a show trial of 'Trotskyist' commanders in the Army was to be held, with Putna in the leading role. Tukhachevsky himself appeared to be under a cloud, if the lack of prominence given to him in the Army manoeuvres was any guide. Voroshilov made sinister comments on lack of vigilance to the Kiev commanders during his visit to their autumn exercises.[37]

The fall of Yagoda was interpreted as, in part, a victory for the

Army. German diplomatic reports of the time say that no more was to be heard of any Army trial, and that Tukhachevsky himself was fully 'reinstated'.[38]

As ever, this relaxation proved to be simply another manoeuvre of Stalin's. Shmidt and Putna were not released, and Yezhov was soon planning a more effective blow at the military. There is an unconfirmed report[39] that Putna was worked on from the start for evidence incriminating Tukhachevsky as a *British* spy. This would, indeed, be natural from Putna's London post. And in the trials, the accused were often charged with working for several foreign powers. But, anyhow, the charge was not developed in later propaganda, and may have been overtaken by the Nazi connexion.

As we have seen (p. 239), at the Pyatakov Trial Putna was again incriminated – though still for terrorism only, not treason. On 24 January 1937 Radek remarked, as if in passing, that Putna had come to him 'with some request from Tukhachevsky'. An extraordinary exchange between Vyshinsky and Radek on the following day ran like this:

Vyshinsky: Accused Radek, in your testimony you say: 'In 1935 . . . we resolved to call a conference, but before this, in January, when I arrived, Vitaly Putna came to me with a request from Tukhachevsky . . .' I want to know in what connexion you mention Tukhachevsky's name?

Radek: Tukhachevsky had been commissioned by the Government with some task for which he could not find the necessary material. I alone was in possession of this material. He rang me up and asked if I had this material. I had it, and he accordingly sent Putna, with whom he had to discharge this commission, to get this material from me. Of course, Tukhachevsky had no idea either of Putna's role or of my criminal role . . .

Vyshinsky: And Putna?

Radek: He was a member of the organization, and he did not come to talk about the organization, but I took advantage of his visit to have this talk.

Vyshinsky: So Putna came to you, having been sent by Tukhachevsky on official business having no bearing whatever on your affairs since he, Tukhachevsky, had no relations with them whatever?

Radek: Tukhachevsky never had any relations whatever with them.

Vyshinsky: He sent Putna on official business?

Radek: Yes.

Vyshinsky: And you took advantage of this in order to engage in your own particular affairs?

Radek: Yes.

Vyshinsky: Do I understand you correctly, that Putna had dealings with the members of your Trotskyite underground organization, and that your reference to Tukhachevsky was made in connexion with the fact that Putna came on official business on Tukhachevsky's orders?

Radek: I confirm that, and I say that I never had and could not have had any dealings with Tukhachevsky connected with counter-revolutionary activities, because I knew Tukhachevsky's attitude to the Party and the Government to be that of an absolutely devoted man.[40]

An experienced N.K.V.D. officer who read this at once remarked that Tukhachevsky was lost. Why, his wife asked, since Radek's evidence so emphatically exculpated him? Since when, was the reply, had Tukhachevsky needed a character reference from Radek?[41]

The whole clumsy interchange must have been a set-piece, doubtless dictated by Stalin himself, perhaps at Tukhachevsky's own insistence after the earlier mention of his name. Typically, it gave the Marshal full satisfaction in a superficial sense. He could hardly ask for a plainer assertion of his loyalty and innocence. But at the same time the idea had been launched. And when Vyshinsky in his final speech complained of the accused having confessed much, but not enough, of their criminal connexions, the foundations were laid for further development in his direction as in others.

When Shmidt finally broke down under severe interrogation, his confession was apparently circulated in the upper levels of the Party. Yakir determined to check the charges. He insisted on seeing Shmidt in jail. Shmidt had become very grey and thin, seemed apathetic, and spoke listlessly. Yakir described him as looking 'like a Martian', a being from another planet. But when Yakir asked him if his confessions were true, Shmidt repudiated them. Yakir was not allowed to question him on the details, but had Shmidt write a note to Voroshilov denying all the accusations. Yakir took this to Voroshilov and told him that the charges were clearly false.

Yakir went back to Kiev well pleased with this result, but his pleasure did not last long. For soon after, Voroshilov rang him up and said that on the very next day Shmidt had reaffirmed his confessions, and wished to inform Voroshilov and Yakir that his early evidence was true.[42] (Shmidt had given, or was shortly to give, evidence which was not to be circulated to Yakir and the other commanders – for this implicated Yakir himself. The Divisional Commander was required to confess that at Yakir's instigation he had planned to raise his tank unit in revolt.) *

After all this, Yakir could not have believed in the accusations. And he is also reported as having said that those shot in the Pyatakov Trial were innocent.[44] It seems more than probable from all this that Yakir, and presumably the other military men, did indeed oppose the Purge at the February–March plenum. At any rate his boldness in insisting on the interview with Shmidt shows him not lacking in the necessary courage.

On 3 March 1937, at the plenum itself, after the arrest of Rykov and Bukharin, Stalin spoke briefly about what harm 'a few spies in the Red Army' could do. And Molotov 'directly incited to the murder of the military cadres, accusing its participants of lack of desire to develop the struggle against "enemies of the people"'.[45]

The crucial political victory of the Purge had been won at the plenum. The organizational basis for extending it was also now becoming adequate. It was in April that the N.K.V.D., purged by Yezhov, became ready for further operations. It was 'soon after the plenum' that 'careerists and *provocateurs* in the organs of the N.K.V.D. fabricated a story "on the counter-revolutionary military fascist organization" in the armed forces'.[46]

Hitherto, Stalin's victims had almost all been former members of the oppositions. This was, of course, true even of Bukharin and Rykov. Now, for the first time, Stalin was to begin the massive offensive against his own supporters everywhere.

* Shmidt was being interrogated 'nine months before' the June Trial with a view to incriminating Yakir.[43]

With the oppositionists, even Bukharin and Rykov, the Party elite may to some degree have felt that this was a sort of very rough justice after all – and justice had been rough in the Soviet Union for a long time. Or they may have been influenced to some extent by the notion that at least a potential alternative leadership was being dealt with. But if undoubtedly loyal followers of Stalin, men who had taken no part in opposition movements, were now to be destroyed, then no one was safe. And no principle was involved. In such circumstances, it was quite reasonable for Stalin to have thought that the Army leadership, whose representatives had opposed even the Bukharin purge, or had only assented with obvious reluctance, might finally be driven into resistance. Stalin himself, in destroying the principle of political loyalty, would be undermining the restraints which had so far held them. Thus it is natural enough that he should have planned his blow at the Army leadership to coincide exactly with the period when he was turning on his own insufficiently subservient followers.

Meanwhile he proceeded gradually. On Yagoda's arrest on 3 April 1937 his post as Commissar of Communications was taken by Army Commander Khalepsky, Tukhachevsky's tank expert – an absurd as well as sinister transfer.

Corps Commander Gekker, Head of Red Army Foreign Liaison and thus a particularly sensitive figure in espionage charges, disappeared in April. During the same month, Corps Commander Garkavi, commanding the Urals Military District, was taken in. He was one of Yakir's closest associates: in fact, they were married to sisters. Again Yakir showed undesirable boldness, by going to see Voroshilov and eventually Stalin. Stalin soothed him, saying that serious charges against Garkavi had been made by those already under arrest, but that if he was innocent he would be released.[47]

On 28 April 1937 *Pravda* published a pointed call to the Red Army to master politics and to fight the internal, as well as the external, foe. This powerful, if oblique, blow was understood by the already shaken High Command.

At the May Day Parade, Tukhachevsky was the first to arrive

on the tribune reserved for the Army leaders. He walked alone, with his thumbs in his belt, to the reviewing stand. Yegorov then took position, but did not look at or salute his colleague. Gamarnik also joined the silent rank. A gloomy and icy atmosphere surrounded the soldiers. At the end of the Army parade Tukhachevsky did not wait for the civilian march-past, but walked out of the Red Square.⁴⁸

In April he had been nominated to attend the coronation of King George VI in London. On 3 May his documents were sent to the British Embassy, but on the 4th the British were told that for reasons of health Tukhachevsky would not now be able to come. Admiral Orlov took his place.

An officer who saw Tukhachevsky several times in May describes him as looking unusually gloomy after an interview with Voroshilov. A few days later he went to see Voroshilov again. Voroshilov was cold and formal, and simply announced to him his removal from his post as Deputy Commissar of Defence and transfer to the Volga Military District, a backwoods command with three infantry divisions and assorted troops.

Tukhachevsky commented to a friend, 'It is not so much a matter of Voroshilov as of Stalin.'⁴⁹

This posting, and others, were made official on 10–11 May, in a series of shifts among the higher officers which gave the clearest evidence yet of Stalin's animus. Gamarnik, as well as Tukhachevsky, was relieved of the position of Deputy Commissar of Defence. More deviously, Yakir was transferred from Kiev to Leningrad: unlike Tukhachevsky's posting, this was not an obvious demotion. Nor were either of the two officers ignominiously rushed to their posts, remaining in Moscow and Kiev respectively till near the end of the month.

At the same time a decree (dated 8 May)³⁰ restored the old system of 'dual command', with the powers of the political commissars being greatly increased *vis-à-vis* those of the fighting officers. The original powers of political commissars had been given them because the military specialists of the Civil War were mainly ex-Tsarist officers who were not regarded as trustworthy. The reimposition of the system upon a Communist officer corps was an extraordinary demonstration of lack of trust in the new cadres. On 9 May an 'instruction' was put out calling for greater vigilance.[51]

On 11 May came the first blow at the Far Eastern Army, with the arrest of Corps Commander Lapin, its Chief of Staff (who is reported committing suicide after torture in Khabarovsk jail).[52]

The same day saw the seizure of the biggest game yet – Army Commander Kork of the Frunze Military Academy. This meant that by mid May three of the destined victims of the Tukhachevsky operation were already under arrest, and the pressure was being increased upon Tukhachevsky and Yakir. But on the face of it, it looks as though the intention was to put the transfers through before the N.K.V.D. struck the final blow. If so, a change of plan came somewhere around the middle of May.

The 'dossier' of evidence that Tukhachevsky was a German spy came into possession of the Russians at about this time.[53] It had been forged in the 'Ostabteilung' of the German Sicherheitsdienst (S.D.). But the story is not as simple as that.

STALIN AND FASCISM

> I know how much the German people loves its Führer.
> I should therefore like to drink his health.
> STALIN, *24 August 1939*

Stalin's view of Fascism has some very peculiar features. It had, of course, long since been denounced as the worst form of bourgeois rule and 'analysed' as a form of control of the State by monopoly capitalists. But though 'Fascism' thus became a very evil word, the effects of this were considerably diluted by the method of calling the Social Democrats 'Fascists' too – 'Social Fascists'. In the resulting confusion, the German Communist Party had been ordered, against its will,[54] to direct its main force against not the Nazis but the Socialist-bourgeois coalition Governments, to the degree of the Prussian referendum of 1931 and the transport strike of 1932 in which Nazis and Communists actively cooperated against the moderates.

When such tactics resulted in the victory of Hitler,* the crushing of the German Communist Party was represented, according to the new Stalin style, as a victory. A new concept of Hitler as the 'icebreaker of revolution' – the last desperate stand of the bourgeoisie, whose failure would lead to the collapse of capitalism – came into vogue.

When it became apparent that Hitlerism was *not* going to collapse – a conclusion Stalin seems to have reached at the time of the Nazi Roehm Purge in June 1934 – he was not to be inhibited by doctrinal reasons from coming to an arrangement with the new dictator. The difficulty was rather that Hitler appeared to be quite intransigently anti-Communist. As he built up Germany's military and economic power, Stalin began a complex approach. Hitler's evident military threat could be blocked in two ways – by force or by agreement. If force was to be necessary, then a powerful anti-Fascist alliance needed to be built. If agreement were possible, it could best be achieved from strength. So from the mid-thirties Soviet foreign policy, and Comintern tactics, were directed to creating a system of Party and State alliances against German power.

In 1936, following this shift in foreign policy orientation, Foreign Commissar Litvinov, long an advocate of alliance with the West, received every sign of support. Leaving a discussion, Stalin put his arm around Litvinov's shoulder and said that now it appeared they could agree. Litvinov (or so he later told Ehrenburg) answered 'Not for long . . .'[56]

It has often been suggested that one of Stalin's motives for the Purge, and especially of the Army purge, was to give him the freedom of manoeuvre which finally produced the Nazi–Soviet Pact of 1939. The old pre-Nazi pro-German orientation had not been an ideological one, and alliance even with a very reactionary Germany against the 'have' powers was in principle long since accepted by the Army and most of the Party. Only when Nazism was seen as an overt threat to the Soviet Union did a change come, with the Popular Front campaigns of the Comintern, the

---

*Who himself remarked that he could always turn a Communist into a Nazi, but could not do the same with a Social Democrat.[55]

Franco-Soviet Pact, and so forth. But when it came it was warmly accepted. The Rightist mood in country and Party saw in these State and Party alliances the possibility of an 'opening to the Right', a reconciliation with democracy. Meanwhile, Tukhachevsky and the soldiery worked enthusiastically at a true modernization of the Army, to make it capable of facing not merely the Poles or Turks, but the high military potential of a mobilized Germany.

But for Stalin, the Fronts and Pacts were matters not of conviction but of calculation.

So long as any qualms were able to make themselves felt in the Communist International, Stalin's freedom of action to come to an arrangement with the Germans was limited. The ideological conceptions, the socialist sentiments, were directed firmly on to anti-Fascist lines. As far as the international field was concerned, the crushing of all independent, undisciplined motivations was necessary if Stalin was to make the best bargain. Prisoners were predicting the Nazi–Soviet Pact in 1938 on the basis of the categories being arrested – in particular the foreign Communists.[57]

When the Pact came in August 1939, the effects of years of hard organizational work and propaganda work in the Comintern became visible. All over the world, with negligible and temporary exceptions the Communist Parties accepted the switch and began to explain its necessity – sometimes in the later editions of papers which the same day had been urging a fight to the last against Nazism. Only individuals among the leaderships dropped out.

Even at the XVIIth Party Congress in 1934, Stalin had hinted of the alternative policy of agreement with Germany:

> Of course we are far from enthusiastic about the Fascist regime in Germany. But Fascism is beside the point, if only because Fascism in Italy, for example, has not kept the U.S.S.R. from establishing the best of relations with that country.[58]

A pessimistic estimate was presented to Stalin by the N.K.V.D. Foreign Department in August 1935 about the strength of elements in Germany favouring settlement with Russia. But the officer making the report noted that it made no impact on Stalin's feeling that accord could be achieved.[59]

For Litvinov was right. From 1936, and on the basis of the threat of his alternative anti-German policy, Stalin began to put out feelers to the Nazis, through his personal emissaries.

The representative of Stalin's personal secretariat, his old henchman David Kandelaki,* was sent as 'Commercial Attaché' to the Soviet Embassy in Berlin to make these delicate approaches. In December 1936 Kandelaki approached Dr Schacht at his own request to inquire about the possibility of enlarging Soviet–German trade. Schacht answered that a condition of this must be the ending of Soviet-sponsored Communist activity in Germany. Kandelaki went back to Moscow to consult Stalin and at about the turn of the year was given a written draft proposing the opening of negotiations either through ambassadors or, if the Germans so desired, in secret. The draft reminded the Germans that agreement had previously been suggested by the Russians.

On 29 January 1937 Kandelaki, with Friedrichson (a trusted N.K.V.D. man), again visited Schacht with a verbal proposal from Stalin and Molotov for the opening of direct negotiations. Schacht said that these suggestions should be passed to the German Foreign Ministry, and added once more that he felt that Communist agitation would have to be damped down. On 10 February Neurath saw Hitler about the proposals and wrote to Schacht on the 11th sensibly saying that there was no practical point in getting an agreement from the Russians to cease Communist propaganda. On the main issue, he said that as things were at the moment the Russian proposals were not worth proceeding with. If, however, Russia was 'to develop further along the lines of an absolute despotism supported by the Army', contact should certainly be made.

Meanwhile, the Pyatakov Trial had gone ahead, with its anti-Nazi implications. Even here, Stalin was able to have it both ways. General Köstring, the German Military Attaché who had been in effect implicated in the trial, was not declared *persona non grata*.

* He is supposed to have been arrested and to have died in camp.[60]

This decision seems to have been taken after considerable pressure from the Germans and is, to say the least, curious.

For the time being Stalin's approaches did not bear fruit. But the point had been made. The German leaders had had the advantages of an arrangement put before them.

Meanwhile, as Stalin's real approaches to Hitler went ahead, the non-existent contact between the Soviet High Command and the Nazis was made the subject of the decisive accusations of treason.

In the murky world of the secret organizations, some measure of contact had already been established between the N.K.V.D. and Reinhardt Heydrich's S.D.

After the suppression of the German Communist Party, operations against its underground remnant became simply a Secret Police matter. As with all sophisticated operations of this type, the Nazi secret agencies left some underground Communists untouched, with a view to retaining political contact.*

As early as December 1936, some sort of machinations to compromise the Soviet High Command were already afoot. In the first week of December, Slutsky, Head of the Foreign Department of the N.K.V.D., was seeking two agents capable of passing as German officers in this connexion. These were kept hanging about in Paris and finally told that the mission was postponed.[61]

Among the organizations penetrated by both the N.K.V.D. and German espionage was the 'Union of Tsarist Veterans' with its main body in Paris. On 22 September 1937 the N.K.V.D. was to carry out, as a special operation, the kidnapping and murder of General Miller, its leader. This seems to have been in an attempt to put General Skoblin, Miller's deputy, in command of the organization. Skoblin had long worked as a double agent with both the Soviet and German secret agencies, and there seems no doubt that he was one of the links by which information was

---

*Indeed, in the occupied countries during the war too, the Gestapo was in contact with the local Communist Parties, at least in the period before the German–Soviet War. In France, negotiations with the French C.P. had reached the stage of discussing permission to let *L'Humanité* appear. In occupied Norway Communist periodicals were briefly allowed. The position was similar in Belgium.

passed between the S.D. and the N.K.V.D. The first move in the whole dark business, which 'originated with Stalin',[62] appears to have been an N.K.V.D. story sent through Skoblin to Berlin to the effect that the Soviet High Command and Tukhachevsky in particular were engaged in a conspiracy with the German General Staff. Though this was understood in S.D. circles as an N.K.V.D. plant, Heydrich determined to use it, in the first place, against the German High Command with whom his organization was in intense rivalry.[63] For in Heydrich's motives, in this whole business, the compromising of the German Army ranked high. This side of it rather dropped into the background as the operation proceeded, and it does not anyhow particularly concern us.

The most probable account[64] (to which Gomulka, leader of the Polish Communist Party, has given his authority in a formal speech)[65] makes it out that towards the end of 1936, at a conversation with Hitler and Himmler, the pros and cons of 'betraying' Tukhachevsky and crippling the Red Army were discussed, and a decision taken. Several Soviet and other accounts[66] make it clear that the story of the German contacts with Tukhachevsky was originally 'leaked' by the Nazis through President Beneš of Czechoslovakia. Beneš had the information as early as the last months of 1936 (and confidentially passed it on to the French, whose confidence in the Franco-Soviet Pact was considerably weakened by it.)[67] He also, as several recent Soviet accounts agree, passed the reports to Stalin, in all good faith. Gomulka tells us that this false information had been planted some time before the documentary 'evidence' arrived, so that preliminary reports of the 'treason' were in Stalin's hands 'at the time of the February–March plenum'.[68]

The creation of the actual documentary evidence, however, was an artistic job and took time. In March–April 1937 Heydrich and Behrens (who later became Chief of the S.S. in Belgrade and was executed by the Tito Government in 1946) directed the forgery of a 'dossier' containing an exchange of letters over a period of a year between members of the German High Command and Tukhachevsky. Largely the work of the German engraver Franz Putzig, who had long been employed by the German secret agencies on false passports and so on, it consisted of thirty-two pages and had attached to it a photograph of Trotsky with German officials.[69] A recent Soviet book[70] quotes a number of Western and German accounts of the forgery of the dossier, and appears to accept that given by Colonel Naujocks, formerly one of Heydrich's men. This says that the German security service got genuine signatures of Tukhachevsky from the 1926 secret agreement between the two High Commands by which technical assistance to the Soviet Air Force was arranged. A letter was forged using this signature, and Tukhachevsky's style was imitated. The letter carried genuine German stamps, and the whole dossier consisted of it and fifteen other German documents. The German generals' signatures were obtained from bank cheques. Hitler and Himmler were shown the dossier in early May, and approved the operation. The S.D., after abandoning for security reasons an attempt to pass their creation through the Czechoslovak channel, got it directly to Yezhov, apparently through two captured N.K.V.D. agents and a third more indeterminate Soviet representative. It was in Stalin's hands by mid May.

Possession of this definite 'proof' of treason seems now to have produced a final decision on the conduct of the blow against the generals. The treason charge was to be the crux, and the Trotskyite and terrorist allegations, though persisted with, were to take second place. On 20 May Dmitri Shmidt, his appearance in person as the original link with Trotsky being no longer essential to the case, was shot in secret without further ado.[71] On the same day the emergency stories about a just-discovered plot began to be put about inside the N.K.V.D. And an official who left Russia on 22 May says that real panic was now gripping the officer corps.[72]

The same day saw the arrest of yet another of the leading figures in the alleged plot – Eideman. He was called out of a Moscow Party conference in the House of the Moscow Soviet, where he had been sitting on the presidium, and taken away by the N.K.V.D.[73] The original pretext was that he had signed a Party recommendation for Kork. Like Yakir, Eideman is represented as having become disillusioned with the Purges. After a Party meeting in the spring of 1937, he had remarked quietly to a friend, 'Last night they arrested another comrade here. It seems to me that he was an honest man. I don't understand . . .'[74]

The arrest of Feldman followed in a day or two. One officer describes a last conversation with Tukhachevsky. He was looking gloomy. When this was mentioned, he said that he had indeed had bad news. He had just learned of Feldman's arrest. 'What a monstrous provocation!' he commented.[75] Tukhachevsky knew, in fact, that he was cornered. As he drove to the station on his way to Kuibyshev his chauffeur suggested that he should write to Stalin to clear up the obvious misunderstandings. The Marshal replied that he had already written.[76]

On his arrival in Kuibyshev on 26 May, Tukhachevsky gave a short address in the evening to the District Military Conference. One who had known him well noted that in the two months since he had last seen him his hair had begun to turn grey.[77]

He did not turn up at the next session.[78]

For he had been asked to call in at the offices of the Provincial Committee of the Party on the way to his headquarters. After a while, Dybenko, whom he was relieving, came out pale-faced and told his wife that he had been arrested.[79]

On the evening of 28 May, news of the transfer of Tukhachevsky's case to the 'investigative organs' had reached the other generals, through some official though confidential channel.[80] So it is plain that the arrests after Tukhachevsky's were by no means bolts from the blue.

Army Commander Uborevich was the next to go. He was at a meeting in Minsk on 29 May when his A.D.C. passed him a note calling him urgently to Moscow. He excused himself and went to the station, where he was arrested as he entered his train. He told his wife and daughter, who were present, not to worry.[81]

Yakir was normally a cheerful man. A general who was present reports him as looking gloomy and *distrait* at a conference of the Kiev Military District, immediately after Tukhachevsky's arrest had become known to those present.[82] On 30 May Voroshilov telephoned Yakir and ordered him to come urgently to a meeting of the Military Revolutionary Soviet. Yakir offered to fly, but Voroshilov told him to take the train – a clear indication that the Defence Commissar knew the plans of the N.K.V.D. in detail.[83]

Yakir took the 1.15 p.m. train from Kiev the same day. At dawn on the 31st the train stopped at Bryansk, where N.K.V.D. men boarded it and arrested him. His A.D.C., Zakharchenko, was not taken, and Yakir was able to send a message to his wife and son that he was innocent.

Yakir asked to see the warrant for his arrest, and when this was shown him he asked to see in addition 'the decision of the Central Committee'. He was told that he could wait for that until he got to Moscow. He was bundled into a Black Maria, they drove to Moscow 'at a hundred kilometres an hour', and he was lodged in a solitary cell in the Lubyanka, where his chevrons and medals were ripped off.[84]

On 31 May the last of the 'conspirators' was dealt with. It was announced next day that 'former member of the Central Committee, Ya. B. Gamarnik, having entangled himself in connexion with anti-Soviet elements and evidently fearing that he would be arrested, has committed suicide'.[85] According to a senior Red Army officer under arrest, Gamarnik met his fate, not because he was himself to be implicated at that stage in the Tukhachevsky plot, but because he had been told that he would be a member of the court to try the generals; it is alternatively said that he was offered a reprieve if he would give evidence.[86] One recent Soviet account has it that he committed suicide 'on the eve of arrest'; another that he did it not to escape arrest but in protest against the purge.[87] The latest official account of his death is that at 5 p.m. on 31 May Bulin and another officer visited him at home, where he was ill, with the news of Yakir's arrest and his own removal from the Army Political Administration. After they left the room there were shots, and Gamarnik was found dead.[88] There have always been rumours that he did not kill himself, but was killed.[89] He was attacked as a Trotskyite, Fascist and spy on 6 June.[90]

Meanwhile, from his cell in the Lubyanka, Yakir had written at once to the Politburo demanding immediate release or a meeting with Stalin. He was, instead, subjected to nine days' harsh interrogation at which he was told that the 'whole Yakir nest' had been arrested.[91] The charges presented to him were 'so serious that in comparison the previous evidence for which Yezhov's interrogators had been working on Shmidt appeared to be amateurish concoctions'.[92] That is, the Nazi connexion was now being put forward, rather than mere Trotskyite terrorism.

Yakir sent a letter to Stalin assuring him of his complete innocence.

He wrote: '. . . My entire conscious life has been spent working self-lessly and honestly in full view of the Party and its leaders. . . . Every word I say is honest, and I shall die with words of love for you, the Party, and the country, with boundless faith in the victory of Com-munism.'

Stalin wrote on this letter: 'Scoundrel and prostitute.' Voroshilov added: 'A perfectly accurate description.' Molotov put his name to this and Kaganovich appended: 'For the traitor, scum and [next comes a scurrilous, obscene word] one punishment – the death sentence.'[93]

From 1 to 4 June the Military Revolutionary Soviet at the Commissariat of Defence, together with members of the Govern-ment, held an extraordinary session – the one to which Yakir had been invited, not knowing that the agenda consisted of a single item – the exposure of the counter-revolutionary military-fascist organization,[94] reported on by Stalin personally.

And now, after all the trouble and ingenuity which had been invested in it, he did not after all produce the 'dossier'. Instead, 'in his statement, and also in many interjections, he based himself on faked evidence from repressed military men'. He called for the execution of the accused, and also denounced a number of other officers including Army Commander A. I. Sedyakin, Head of Anti-Aircraft Command, and Divisional Commander D. A. Kuchinsky, Head of the General Staff Academy.[95]

The 'dossier' seems to have had its use in giving the limited Stalin–Yezhov circle a proper sense of outrage and urgency. And since we are told that Stalin used it 'to instruct the judges to pass a death sentence on Tukhachevsky',[96] it is possible that they, or some of them, were shown or told about the document. But it received no official use. Stalin seems to have decided that he could after all manage without it, and that the well-tried system of confession – even if not from *some* of the accused officers – could provide all the evidence needed. It would have been awkward even in a secret court if one of the officers could perhaps have exposed the fraud through some point which had escaped Yezhov's notice. And, good fakes though they doubtless were, they had not been planned with a full feeling for the nuances of Stalin's technique.*

It seems clear, in any case, that 'that quickfire court' found the accused guilty 'on the basis of the verbal statements of Stalin at the Military Soviet' without the 'dossier' being raised,[97] even to substantiate the charges of recruitment by Nazi intelligence which were laid.

In the indictment in the Bukharin Trial, it is asserted that that case was based on 'the materials not only of the present investigation, but also on the materials of the trials which have taken place in various parts of the U.S.S.R., and in particular the trial of the group of military conspirators, Tukhachevsky and others, who were convicted by a special session of the Supreme Court of the U.S.S.R. on 11 June 1937'.[98] Various allegations against the military were made in the Bukharin Trial, but they were all in the course of the evidence of various accused, and no 'materials' from the military trial itself were produced.

The membership of the court which is supposed to have tried the generals consisted, in addition to Ulrikh as Chairman, of Marshals Blyukher and Budenny, Army Commanders Shaposhnikov, Alksnis, Belov, Dybenko and Kashirin,† and Corps Commander Goryachev. Only the second and third survived the Purges.‡ Marshal Yegorov is reported as originally named as one of the judges, but his name did not appear in the final list.§[100]

But now, over the last days of the case, a thick obscurity descends, which has only very recently been relieved by occasional flashes of light. It has long been thought that no trial really took place. Well-informed and highly placed N.K.V.D. and Red Army

*A minor point is that, of the military men, they implicated Tukhachevsky only; and that they are said to have included Stalin's ambassador first in Berlin and then in Paris, Surits, who was (by a curious quirk) one of the very few ambassadors to survive the Purge.

†Shot 14 June 1938.[99]

‡Goryachev seems to have died a natural death.

§There are reports that one member of the 'court', Alksnis, was already himself under arrest. But he is mentioned in the press a number of times in July and later, and the story cannot be right.[101]

officer defectors have definitely taken this view,[102] and it has been on the whole accepted by the best Western experts.

On the other hand, a recent account published in the Soviet Union [103] says 'it was formally a court' and speaks of Yakir being harangued at it by Ulrikh to the effect that the German officer attached to him on his last visit to Berlin had recruited him for Hitler. Yakir is said to have denied it contemptuously.

Another equally circumstantial Soviet report says:

The court-martial was held behind closed doors. . . . Some witnesses' statements, which coincide, say that Tukhachevsky, speaking to one of the accused, who was talking about his connections with Trotsky, said 'Have you been dreaming about all this?'[104]

The implication certainly is that Tukhachevsky was brought before a court, and that, like Yakir, he did not confess, but that at least one of the others did. We are told elsewhere that 'Yakir, Tukhachevsky, Uborevich and others' denied the charges.[105] The death dates of Putna and Primakov are still given in all Soviet sources as 11 June or 12 June, which implies that they were, unlike Shmidt, still available to confess.

Every one of those named in the published verdict is now referred to as having appeared before 'a secret session of a Special Board of the Supreme Court'.[106] It is certainly quite possible that they appeared before Ulrikh only. Ilya Ehrenburg has indeed told us that Army Commander Belov once remarked in his presence that he had caught Uborevich's eye at the trial.[107] Either way, the military 'judges' clearly had no real say, and it is plausible that (as one account, based on a conversation with the Assistant Head of the N.K.V.D. Foreign Department, has it) their signatures were attached to the verdict after the executions at a conference with Yezhov.[108] It is at any rate clear even from the present account of Yakir's fate that the trial must have been perfunctory, for if he was interrogated for nine days before it, there was not much time left to go through even the Stalinist forms of trial then established.

Rumours of the manner of their end were many and various: that they were shot, not in the cellars, but in the courtyard of the N.K.V.D. building at 11 Dzerzhinsky Street, during the daytime, with N.K.V.D. trucks being revved up to cover the sound of the shots; that Marshal Blyukher, pale and shaken, was forced to take charge. The head of the N.K.V.D. firing-squad is said to have been Ivan Serov, then a young officer recently transferred from the Army into the N.K.V.D. as one of Yezhov's replacements for the old cadres, and later to serve as head of the K.G.B. (till 1958) and then, as late as 1964, as Head of Military Intelligence.

Khrushchev tells us that

> When Yakir was shot he exclaimed: 'Long live the Party, long live Stalin!' . . . When Stalin was told how Yakir had behaved before his death, he cursed Yakir.[109]

Khrushchev reports this 'Long live Stalin!' as if it were a simple case of political devotion. But the generals were not really naïve enough to believe that Stalin had no responsibility for their fate. Yakir was an old Communist, perfectly able to carry out political activity at the moment of death. And the programme of support for Stalin, combined with condemnation of the N.K.V.D., was already in existence. It was the line on which the maximum support for a programme opposed to the Purge could be mobilized. It seems plausible to think that Yakir may have been trying to show that those who had opposed the purge at the February–March plenum were not wishing the overthrow of the General Secretary – trying, in fact, to establish an anti-Yezhov 'platform'.

But, at least equally compelling, we know he had thought of his family; and it was clearly not in their interests for him to utter words of defiance or abuse. He had made a last appeal for them. The day before he was shot, he sent Voroshilov this letter:

> To K. Ye. Voroshilov. I ask you, in memory of my many years of honest service in the Red Army in the past, to give instructions that my family, helpless and quite innocent, shall be looked after and given assistance. I have addressed the same plea to N. I. Yezhov. Yakir, 9 June 1937.

On his copy Voroshilov minuted: 'In general I doubt the honesty of a dishonest person. K. Voroshilov. 10 June 1937.'[110]

Yakir's attempt to save his family was unsuccessful. His wife, his 'close companion for twenty years', was at once exiled to

Astrakhan with her son Peter, and their passports were confiscated. In the Volga town they met the families of Tukhachevsky, Uborevich, Gamarnik and others. The boy's grandfather had hidden the paper containing the charge against Yakir from the mother, and she only saw it when Uborevich's wife showed it to her.

The papers published a faked letter from Mrs Yakir repudiating her husband. She protested to the N.K.V.D., who rebuffed her, but later told her in a threatening manner that they were willing to receive a withdrawal, though not necessarily to publish it.[111]

At the beginning of September she was arrested. She was later liquidated, together with Yakir's brother, the wife of another brother and her son, and other relatives.[112] A woman cousin is reported as being sentenced to ten years' imprisonment in 1938.[113] Little 'Peti', now fourteen years old, was sent to a children's home. Two weeks later, at night, the N.K.V.D. took him, and he spent 'many years' in camps and prisons. He chanced to meet his father's A.D.C. in one of the Arctic camps and learned from him the full story of the arrest.[114] (In 1961, when Khrushchev was visiting Kazakhstan, Peter Yakir approached him. 'He asked me about his father. What could I tell him?'[115] At the time of Yakir's arrest and execution Khrushchev had spoken of him as 'riff-raff who wanted to let in the German Fascists'.[116])

Uborevich's wife was sent to Astrakhan on 10 June. She kept the charges against her husband from their little daughter, not yet in her teens: the girl learned of them from young Peter Yakir. On 5 September Mrs Uborevich was arrested by the N.K.V.D. She was able to give her daughter a few photographs, and they never met again. Nineteen years later, in 1956, the daughter learned that her mother had died in 1941.

The daughter was taken to a children's home, where she found other young girls – Veti Gamarnik, Svetlana Tukhachevsky and Slava Feldman. They were rounded up on 22 September and sent off, evidently to N.K.V.D. children's settlements.[117]

Tukhachevsky had a large family. It is said that one daughter, aged about twelve, hanged or attempted to hang herself, after being jeered at by her young friends.[118]

As for the others, 'on Stalin's direct instructions, the wife of the

Marshal, his sister Sofia Nikolayevna, and his brothers Alexander and Nikolai, were physically annihilated. Three of his sisters were sent to concentration camps, as well as a young daughter of the Marshal whom they interned when she reached the appropriate age.'[119] This was Svetlana, eleven years old at her father's death; given a five-year sentence when she was seventeen as 'socially dangerous', she is later reported in the Kotlas camp south of Vorkuta, together with Uborevich's daughter.[120] The Marshal's mother also perished:[121] she had refused to repudiate him. His wife is said to have first gone insane and to have been taken to the Urals in a strait-jacket.[122] Two former wives of Tukhachevsky's, together with Feldman's wife, are reported in a special 'Wives and Mistresses' section of Potmalag – a camp area strict as to discipline, but comparatively mild as to living conditions – in 1937, and to have later been transferred to the Segeta camp.[123] Another of the Marshal's sisters announced that she was seeking permission to change her name. (A daughter and three sisters survived to attend a memorial meeting in his honour at the Frunze Military Academy in Moscow in January 1963.)

Gamarnik's and Kork's wives were also shot.[124]

1937–1938

As the Red Army's best generals were dragged off to execution amid a vast campaign of public abuse, Stalin and Yezhov launched the N.K.V.D. on the officer corps as a whole. Corps Commanders Garkavi and Gekker were shot on 1 July.[125] Twenty younger generals from the Moscow headquarters alone were also executed.[126] Almost the whole command of the Kremlin Military School was arrested.[127] The Frunze Military Academy, which Kork had headed, was swept by arrests. The Head of its Political Department, Neronov, was arrested as a spy. For a time Shchadenko took over. Not a day passed without the arrest of a member of the staff. Almost all the instructors went to the jails.[128] Army Commander Vatsetis was giving a lecture. After an hour there was a short break, which ended with the announcement, 'Comrades! The lecture will not continue. Lecturer Vatsetis has been arrested as an enemy of the people.'[129] The students too were rounded up in droves. All who had references from Gamarnik, for example, were taken. So were those, and there were many of them, who had been sent to the Academy from units whose commanders had been arrested.[130]

In the provinces it was the same: in the Kiev Military District 600–700 officers of the 'Yakir nest' are said to have been arrested at this time.[131] A recent Soviet account tells us that

A new leadership arrived in the Kiev Military District. Shchadenko,* a member of the Military Council, from the very first started to take an attitude of suspicion towards the members of the staff. He kept watch, without bothering to conceal it, on the commanders and political officers of the units and was thereafter acting hand in hand with the Special Department. He was also extremely active in the campaign to compromise the commanding officer personnel, which was accompanied by the massive arrests of commander cadres and political cadres. The more people were arrested the more difficult it was to believe in the charges of treachery, sabotage and treason.[133]

A Soviet engineer officer was one of a number who had been working under Yakir (and Berzin) to prepare secret partisan bases, and to train partisans, in the Ukraine. In 1937 they were arrested and accused of 'lack of faith in the Socialist state' and 'preparation for enemy activity in the rear of the Soviet armies' – or 'training bandits and storing arms for them', as Voroshilov put it.[134] The bases were destroyed – to be much missed in 1941, when abortive attempts were made hastily to reconstruct them.

The commander of the 7th Cavalry Corps, Grigoriev, was called to the Kiev Military District Committee and accused of connexions with the enemy. He was allowed to go back to his post, where he was arrested the next day.[135] Here we have a picture of the N.K.V.D. not feeling any necessity to put a general officer under arrest immediately he must have realized his case was hopeless. They cannot, in fact, have had much real fear of desperate military action, as is sometimes suggested.

Even retired veterans became involved. In Kiev jail General Bougetsky, the Civil War hero whose wife had been crippled and his son blinded while in the hands of the Whites, and who himself had lost his right arm in battle, was interrogated in the inner

*Who had replaced M. P. Amelin, soon (8 September 1937) to be shot.[132]

prison at Kiev. On the heart of this dignified sexagenarian they pinned the Nazi swastika, and emptied a spittoon over his head. He was charged with an attempt to assassinate Voroshilov.[136]

In Minsk, Uborevich's 'judge' and successor as Commander of the Byelorussian Military District, Army Commander Belov, was almost immediately in trouble. A member of Uborevich's 'nest', Corps Commander Serdich (an officer of Yugoslav origin), was arrested on 15 July.[137] Imprudently enough, Belov intervened in his favour,[138] but he was shot on 28 July.[139] For the moment Belov was not proceeded against, and presided impotently over the further massacre of his subordinates.

PURGE OF THE POLITICAL COMMISSARS

At the beginning of August 1937, a conference of political workers in the Army was addressed by Stalin. He once more violently attacked enemies of the people.[140] Gamarnik's Political Administration suffered even more than the rest of the forces. At the top levels there was a clean sweep. Gamarnik's deputy, A. S. Bulin, had been dismissed by 28 May,[141] though he held the lesser post of Head of the Chief Administration of Cadres until the autumn, when he was arrested.[142] The other deputy, G. A. Osepyan, was also arrested, together with almost all the heads of the political administrations and most of the members of the soviets of the military districts.[143] Ippo, Head of the Military-Political Academy in Leningrad, who had been criticized in April, was dismissed on 1 June for political blunders[144] and later arrested. By rank, all seventeen of the Army Commissars went, with twenty-five of the twenty-eight Corps Commissars.[145]

This purge of politicals swept the units as well. In the two months following the June 1937 meeting of the Military Soviet, arrests in the 5th Mechanized Brigade of the Byelorussian Military District included the brigade commissar, the head of its political section, plus five out of the six battalion commissars, while the sixth was severely reprimanded.[146] A recent Soviet book speaks of 'thousands' of leading Party workers in the Army and Fleet being repressed.[147]

Mekhlis, one of the most sinister and unpleasant of all Stalin's agents, was confirmed as Head of the Political Administration of the Army in December 1937. He had lately worked as editor of *Pravda*, but in the Civil War had served as a political commissar at Army level. He had a special quirk – to cashier and arrest many political workers on the grounds of their connexion with the 'anti-Party Army Byelorussian–Tolmachevite Group'.[148] In fact, he was condemning the political commissars for this long-extinct deviation which had consisted of enthusiasm for *greater* political control in the Army! In any case, the grouping of senior political commissars who had criticized the Party leadership in the late twenties was, whatever its particular programme, far too independent-minded for the new regime. Mekhlis had insisted that any who attempted to defend them, such as the Head of the Political Administration of the Byelorussian Military District, I. I. Sychev, deserved the same fate as this 'band of spies'.[149]

At the beginning of 1938 the number of political workers in the armed forces was only one third of its official establishment. As the numbers still in position were 10,500, the implication is that at least 20,000 political workers had gone under.* By 1938, more than one third of all the Party political workers had had no political education at all.[150]

The number of Party members in the Army shrank by about a half.[151] At the XVIIth Congress Voroshilov had given 25·6 per cent of the Army as Party workers – the Army numbering in February 1935 approximately a million: the net deficit here was therefore some 125,000.

THE OFFICERS FADE AWAY

Everywhere – except as yet the Far East – the Purge began to strike at the whole command structure. The generals who had just been promoted to fill the vacant places now started to disappear.

At a meeting of the Military Soviet of the Caucasus Military District in November 1937, the new District Commander, N. V.

---

* 'At least', because that is not to allow for replacements who must have come in: the proportion who had gone through military political schools, compared with 1934, had gone down by half. So, of the 10,500, the assumption is that some 5,000 were fresh and raw.

Kuibyshev (brother of the dead Politburo member), criticized the purge of the Army as affecting the Army's battle-preparedness. He was shortly afterwards arrested.[152] And the same fate overtook the Military District commanders all over the Union. By the summer of 1938 all who had held these posts in June 1937 had disappeared. At the centre, a similar sweep took all eleven Deputy Commissars of Defence.

A recent Soviet account says that the Air Force and the tank and mechanized forces suffered most heavily.[153] Khalepsky of the Armoured Forces, Alksnis of the Air Force, and Khripin, Alksnis's deputy, had made an excellent impression on foreign military attachés in the autumn 1936 manoeuvres. Khalepsky, who had been relegated to the Communications Commissariat, was arrested in 1937 and shot in 1938.[154] Army Commander Alksnis was the youngest of the Tukhachevsky group, being barely forty. Backed by Corps Commander Todorsky, Head of the Air Force Academy, he had worked hard to save his juniors from persecution by N.K.V.D. Alksnis is given on the electoral lists as late as 13 November, and is now described as having 'commanded' the Air Force till 1938.[155] But it seems clear that by the last days of 1937 he was under arrest, together with Khripin (as was also Todorsky). According to one report, Alksnis was tortured and sentenced to penal servitude, but later shot.[156] Todorsky, arrested in the spring of 1938, was sentenced to fifteen years in May 1939. He survived and was released in 1953.[157]

The extraordinary deviousness of the N.K.V.D. is shown in Gorbatov's experiences. He learned he was in disfavour (for the second time) when, temporarily commanding the 6th Cavalry Corps, he went to the stores officer to draw his winter uniform, and found that orders had been received from the corps political officer, Fominykh, then in Moscow, not to give him one.[158] He went to Moscow and was arrested. His wife could not find out what had happened to him. No one would even tell her he had been arrested, until a girl whispered it to her in the corridor of the Red Army Officers' Hostel.

Gorbatov has given a brief account of his interrogation. At the Lubyanka he was at first treated fairly mildly, but bullying set in on the fifth day. He was in a cell with seven others, all of whom had confessed. He was then transferred to the Lefortovo prison where he shared a single one-man isolator with two others. Here he was tortured on the fourth interrogation, and there were five more torture sessions at two- to three-day intervals, from each of which he had to be carried back bleeding to the cell. There were then twenty days' rest, then five more bouts of torture. No confession could be wrested from Gorbatov, and on 8 May 1939 he was sentenced at a trial lasting four or five minutes to fifteen years' imprisonment plus five years' disfranchisement. The N.K.V.D. told his wife that as she was 'young and interesting' she could easily get married again.[159]

Another officer, a former revolutionary sailor in the Baltic Fleet, is reported as also having refused to confess and actually being acquitted, getting a civilian job on his release. He was, however, rearrested six months later.[160]

But 'many splendid comrades and political officers' confessed.

They were 'persuaded' – persuaded by quite definite techniques – that they were either German or British or some other kind of spies. . . . Even in cases when such people were told that the accusation of espionage had been withdrawn, they themselves insisted on their previous testimony, because they believed it was better to stand on their false testimony in order to put an end as quickly as possible to the torment and to die as quickly as possible.[161]

One divisional commander is reported as confessing that he had 'recruited' every officer in his division down to company commanders.[162] And there are many similar stories.

Rivalries between the N.K.V.D. and the Army were of course natural in various fields. (The possession by the Police of a large armed force was itself an irritant.) But in addition, the military intelligence network abroad operated to a certain extent independently of the Foreign Department of the N.K.V.D., and there was a struggle to win it. When Tukhachevsky was arrested the N.K.V.D. gained control. Almost all the military intelligence agents were recalled from abroad and shot.[163] S. P. Uritsky, Chief of Soviet Military Intelligence – the 'Fourth Bureau' – from 1935, was arrested on the night of 1 November 1937 and shot 'soon afterwards'.[164]

His predecessor as Head of the Fourth Bureau, from 1920 to 1935, J. K. Berzin, who had held a post in the short-lived Soviet Latvian Government of 1919, had been sent to the Far Eastern Army on handing over. From there he had gone to Spain, as virtual Commander-in-Chief of the Republican Armies under the name 'Grishin'. He had clashed with the N.K.V.D., and was shot on his return.[165]

The Commander of the International Brigade, 'General Kleber', a Soviet officer who was represented as a Canadian to suit international decorum, was seized and apparently executed in Spain itself.

Brigade Commander 'Gorev' (Skoblevsky), who had fought and won the Battle of Madrid for the Spanish Republic, was much fêted on his return to the U.S.S.R. But soon afterwards, about the end of 1937, 'the hero of Madrid was slandered' and shot.[166] He is said to have been arrested only two days after receiving the Order of Lenin.[167]

Other military victims among Soviet veterans of the Spanish War were to include the senior military adviser 'Grigorevich' – Shtern, later promoted Army Commander in the Far East; and the leading Soviet air ace in Spain 'Douglas' – later, as Lieutenant-General Smushkevich, Head of the Soviet Air Force; both were shot in 1941.[168] Marshal Malinovsky, until his recent death Minister of Defence, who was also in Spain, describes failing to obey two orders to return and finally getting a third threatening to list him as a 'non-returner', upon which he went back, at a time when, fortunately for him, the worst period of the Purge was over.[169] Soviet civilians in Spain also fared evilly. Antonov–Ovseenko, who had operated in the delicate position of Soviet Consul-General in Barcelona, likewise perished, as did Rosenberg, the Soviet Ambassador to the Republican Government. Rosenberg's crime seems to have been an attempt to arrange the exchange of prisoners with the Franco authorities. Stalin always regarded this sort of thing as suspicious, and was later to show resentment when the Yugoslav partisans entered into similar conversations with the German Command in the Balkans.[170]

PURGE IN THE NAVY

In the Navy the Purge was as sweeping as in the land forces. None of the eight men with the rank of Admiral ('Flagman') at the beginning of the purge remained at the end.[171] First to be arrested was the brains of the Navy, Admiral R. A. Muklevich. Muklevich, a comfortable, strong-looking man, was an Old Bolshevik with an extraordinary career behind him. Born in 1890, he had become a Party member at the age of sixteen, and in the difficult years, 1907–9, still in his teens, had been secretary of the Party's organization at Bialystok. He had been called up for the Imperial Navy in 1912 and been active in the Party's military work from then through the Revolution. During the Civil War he had served on the staff of various armies and fronts, become Deputy Director of the Army Academy in 1921, then served with military aviation from 1925, and finally taken over effective control of the fleet from 1926–7. As Director of Naval Construction, he had played a leading role in the modernization of the Soviet Navy. His clear view of the problems and unambitious efficiency made him a natural and welcome associate of Tukhachevsky's group.

He was arrested in May 1937.[172] He was not brought to public trial – indeed, there was no announcement made about the trial of any of the Naval leaders. He and the Naval Commander-in-Chief, Admiral Orlov, were, however, denounced as accomplices of Tukhachevsky at the XVIIIth Party Congress in 1939. The attack on them, unlike those made on the Army men, contained a specific criticism of their military policies. People's Commissar for Shipbuilding Tevosyan announced[173] that they had opposed the idea of a powerful surface fleet, and that their removal had made it possible to build 'a most mighty attacking force' – a chimera which diverted a large amount of Soviet effort into a hopeless and pointless attempt to match the major naval powers with a battle fleet.

This is doubtless the factual basis to be found, as so often, for one of the incidents in Arthur Koestler's *Darkness at Noon* – the execution of the Fleet Commander 'Bogrov' on account of a dispute about the nature of the future Soviet Navy. The precise issue, however, is rather different. Koestler has 'Bogrov' advocating large, long-range submarines as against Stalin's view that small, short-range craft were required, the political distinction being that the former implies a policy of aggression and world revolution, and the latter one of coastal defence and a general defensive policy. In reality, the Stalinist view was the more, rather than the less, aggressive ('Stalin had threatened to mete out heavy punishment to anyone objecting to heavy cruisers').[174] Muklevich's attitude, doubtless dictated by a realistic appraisal of the possibilities, given actual Soviet resources, was a short-range, defensive one. When war came, the Soviet Navy lost effective control of the vital seas, and Muklevich was proved right posthumously – the Soviet Admiralty reverting to his views, though not acknowledging them.

In any event, this argument cannot have been the main motive behind the Naval purge, whose origins were clearly the same as those of the purge in the Army and in the country as a whole. It was less a matter of settling technical disputes by executions than of using technical disputes as one excuse for executions. Muklevich confessed after a week's severe torture in the Lefortovo prison.[175] He was executed on 7 February 1938.[176]

Next to fall was the Commander of the Naval Forces Admiral Orlov, together with Admiral Sivkov, Commander of the Baltic Fleet, and Admiral Kozhanov, Commander of the Black Sea Fleet.* Orlov was arrested in November 1937, but he seems to have been dismissed as early as June, when Admiral Viktorov, Commander of the Pacific Fleet and himself shortly to fall, was acting as Head of the Navy.[178]

With the leaders, their subordinates fell in scores.

The Navy by its very nature gave contact, or the possibility of contact, with foreigners. Soviet warships paid courtesy visits. They cruised in international waters. During the Second World War these suspicious circumstances were to be much exacerbated, owing to collaboration with the Royal Navy at the Murmansk end of the Northern Convoy route. One of the chief figures in *One Day in the Life of Ivan Denisovich* is Buynovsky, 'The Captain', who has actually spent a whole month on a British cruiser as liaison officer. 'Then after the war some British admiral

* Shot, with Corps Commander Gittis, on 22 August 1938.[177]

who should've had more sense sent me a little souvenir with an inscription that said: "In gratitude". I was really shocked and I cursed like hell, so now I'm inside with all the others.'

The atmosphere had been established much earlier. Rear-Admiral Isakov, in his memoirs published in 1961,[179] tells a story of a flag officer of his acquaintance, Ozarovsky, who was wrecked in his small sailing-boat off the coast near Kronstadt. A Norwegian steamer came in sight and lowered a boat. Ozarovsky refused the offer of rescue, although his situation was desperate. Isakov describes Ozarovsky's feelings. He was bound to be saved. Though he himself could not have been seen from the shore, 'The foreign steamer entering a prohibited zone would be seen at once. A cutter would be sent to the scene.' And this in fact happened. Isakov visited him in hospital and asked why he had not let himself be brought to Leningrad by the Norwegians. Ozarovsky replied: 'I should have had to give an explanation: when and how this meeting with foreign agents had been arranged and for how much I had sold our operational plans while the ship was passing through the channel.' Isakov felt compelled to agree, and adds that even so Ozarovsky did not escape. He was arrested, interrogated and tortured for the very reasons he had advanced.

In fact, the occupational hazards of the Naval cadres were even higher than in the Army. They had one very minor advantage. Except in the case of the Pacific Fleet, naval officers were usually British 'spies', and, until 1939 at least, this carried slightly higher social status than attached to treason in favour of Germany, Japan and Poland.

A SECOND MILITARY MASSACRE

Orlov's case became associated with a new wave of military arrests launched in the early part of 1938, whose theme was made clear in a letter issued on Stalin's instructions calling for further purging of the armed forces, not only from enemies of the people, but also from 'the silent ones' who had failed to take an active part in the Purge.[180]

The replacements of the slaughtered commanders now went themselves to the Lubyanka. In the first days of January Belov was recalled to Moscow. The train journey, we are told, was gloomy, full of recollections of similar ones of the previous year. On arrival he was arrested: his intervention in favour of Serdich was now turned into a criminal matter.[181]

And now a second Marshal of the Soviet Union fell. Yegorov, a former Tsarist officer, was an older man than the members of the Tukhachevsky group, being fifty-five, a year younger than his former colleague in the Imperial Army, Shaposhnikov. He was one of Stalin's boon companions. Stalin is said to have offered Tukhachevsky's country villa to Yegorov after the execution, and Yegorov to have refused to take it.[182]

Yegorov had commanded the South-Western Front in the Polish Campaign, with Stalin as his political chief. He was the only important figure from Stalin's old military entourage to suffer.

The first blow in the military purge had taken out all the military members of the Central Committee except Voroshilov, Budenny, Blyukher and Yegorov. It seems possible that the offence Yegorov gave Stalin may have been at this political level, perhaps during the February–March plenum. He was removed from his post as Deputy People's Commissar of Defence at the end of February 1938.

According to one report, he was still in the Butyrka in the winter of 1939,[183] and his death date was given as 10 March 1941 in the *Small Soviet Encyclopedia* in 1959.* In any case, his removal from Tukhachevsky's old post set in motion a blow at the new High Command scarcely less stunning than that which had destroyed the old.

The same month, February 1938, saw the dismissal, and April the arrest on a civilian mission in the Urals, of Army Commander Dybenko,[184] who now commanded the Leningrad District. During the Civil War Dybenko had served with Voroshilov and Stalin, but that was no longer sure protection. The huge sailor had led the mutiny on the *Imperator Pavel I* in 1916, and had commanded the Baltic Fleet sailors in the Revolution. He had once been married to the fiery aristo-deviationist Alexandra

* But a later, equally official, publication, the *Soviet Historical Encyclopedia* (vol. v, 1961), gives 22 February 1939.

Kollontai. He had led the soldiers who suppressed the Constituent Assembly in 1918. But idealism had persisted for a time: he actually tried to resign from the Party when the death penalty was not, after all, abolished by the Soviet Government.[185] His closest friends at the Military Academy had been Uritsky, shot in 1937, and Fedko, who was brought on 2 February 1938 from Yakir's old post in the Ukraine to be Deputy Commissar for Defence for a short and insecure tenure.[186] They had all been sent from the Academy to take part in the assault on Kronstadt.[187]

Not only old associates of Stalin's like Dybenko were now to perish (together with his wife).[188] There were still grudges to be paid against former enemies. Among those in jail was, as we have seen, Army Commander Vatsetis, first Commander-in-Chief of the Red Army, whom Stalin and others had attempted to remove as a traitor in 1919, but whom Trotsky had successfully defended. He had meanwhile held important posts in the Army Inspectorate and in the Military Academy.[189]

A great slaughter of these and other military leaders took place on 27–29 July 1938: Admiral Orlov, Army Commanders Alksnis, Belov, Dubovoy (of the Kharkov Military District), Dybenko, Vatsetis, Velikanov[190] (of the Baikal Military District).* Others involved included Corps Commanders Gryaznov,† of the Central Asian Military District, and Kovtiukh‡ – the latter the legendary Civil War hero who appears under the name 'Kozhukh' in A. S. Serafimovich's novel *The Iron Flood*, which curiously enough continued to be sold without alteration after the purge of the hero. Admiral Viktorov and Corps Commander N. V. Kuibyshev went a day or two later, on 1 August.[194] A few more junior victims are known: A. A. Svechin, formerly a Tsarist major-general, and in the 30s a colleague of Vatsetis's at the Frunze Academy, was shot on 29 July; and K. A. Ozolin, Dubovoy's Commissar at the Kharkov Military District, on 1 August;[195] and

*And possibly Levandovsky whose date of death is given as 29 July 1937 in several reference books, but who seems to have been commanding after that date, and is mentioned elsewhere as dying in 1938.[191]

†Date of death 29 July 1938 in the *Soviet Historical Encyclopedia*, but elsewhere 21 August 1940.[192] Perhaps sentenced 1938, shot 1940.

‡'Died tortured in the Lefortovo.'[193]

no doubt there were others. This case was as broad an operation as that of June 1937; but it was kept entirely secret. It was also, presumably, connected with the execution of various major Party figures on the same days (see p. 606).

One last major blow, against the Far Eastern Army, remained to be struck. We shall deal with that in a later chapter, and afterwards consider the whole effect of this unprecedented destruction of the officer corps. But it will already be obvious that, if Stalin had destroyed a potential threat to his power, he had also inflicted enormous damage on Soviet defence.

CHAPTER EIGHT

THE PARTY CRUSHED

You have made of liberty a weapon for the executioner.
LERMONTOV

IN THE PROVINCES

APRIL 1937 saw the beginning of intra-Party elections, the occasion for a great campaign in the press against those elements interfering like Postyshev with Party democracy, who were found everywhere. Some failures in this respect were dealt with harshly in the set-piece article which launched the campaign, 'Internal Party Democracy and Bolshevik Discipline'.[1] The author was Boris Ponomarev, at present (1970) Secretary of the Central Committee of the Communist Party.

Among the first Central Committee members to be arrested were those from Leningrad. Outside Moscow, it was only in the northern capital, where Zhdanov ruled, and in Transcaucasia, under Beria, that local First Secretaries ready to purge without limit were already in control.

As a result of the Kirov murder,

The Leningrad Party organization suffered particularly large losses. . . . For a period of four years there was an uninterrupted wave of repressions in Leningrad against honest and completely innocent people. Promotion to a responsible post often amounted to a step toward the brink of a precipice. Many people were annihilated without a trial and investigation on the basis of false, hastily fabricated charges. Not only officials themselves, but also their families were subjected to repressions, even absolutely innocent children, whose lives were thus broken from the very beginning. . . . The repressions . . . were carried out either on Stalin's direct instructions or with his knowledge and approval.[2]

But in fact the first waves of terror had struck at non-Party people and the mass of minor functionaries. Zhdanov had pursued the Stalin method. He had weakened the old Kirov cadre from below, replacing many of its junior veterans at the district committee level. But he had not yet driven Kirov's leading supporters, a number of them members or candidate members of the Central Committee itself, from the higher posts they held in the city and the province. In particular there was Mikhail Chudov, Kirov's Second Secretary, who still held his position. A printer by trade, a Bolshevik since 1913, he had been imported into Leningrad from outside to reinforce Kirov in 1928. A full member of the Central Committee, he had been on the Presidium of the XVIIth Congress. In 1934 he had made Leningrad's funeral speech on Kirov in Red Square, and been on the Kirov Burial Commission. More than anyone, he represented the Kirov tradition in the city.

The old Party leaders at this level were to prove unacceptable to Stalin throughout the country. But the Leningrad men were particularly unsatisfactory. First, they had been closely associated with Kirov and his platform, both of which had been the special objects of Stalin's hostility. And secondly, they were the very men who, on that December afternoon over two years before, had rushed into the corridor when they heard the shot that killed Kirov, and must have noticed – indeed, we are now told, *did* notice – the absence of guards, and other suspicious signs.

To have removed them earlier would have given the very strong impression that Stalin was opposed to Kirov and perhaps that he wished all who knew anything about the Kirov affair out of the way. With the Stalinist victory in the February–March plenum, these inhibitions disappeared.

The Leningrad purge had already been violent even by Soviet standards. In the ensuing period, as it affected the entire political and industrial leadership, it was worse than almost anywhere else in the country – though this meant a matter of a nearly 100 per cent destruction, as compared with 80 or 90 per cent elsewhere.* We happen to have fuller information about it than about the lesser provincial massacres which succeeded it, and it shows the sort of operation which now involved Party and population alike.

*We are told by a Soviet historian that 90 per cent of the members of provincial and city committees and republican central committees were liquidated in 1937–8.[3]

Zhdanov reported back from the plenum on 20 March 1937, at a Party meeting notable for attacks on various district committees in the city. Zakovsky, now described as Commissar of State Security, First Rank, spoke of 'enemies still active' in the organization.[4]

Zakovsky was Zhdanov's right hand in the ensuing assault. His left – indeed his only trusted aide at an executive level – was the infamous A. S. Shcherbakov, who had served with him from 1924 to 1930 in the Nizhni-Novgorod (Gorki) province, becoming local chief of agitation and propaganda. Shcherbakov, a figure more personally disliked even than Zhdanov, was a plump man with glasses and Western-style hair, combed back. He had gone on from Gorki province to the Central Committee apparatus, and was then appointed, in 1934 – Secretary of the Union of Soviet Writers! After a year (1936–7) in Leningrad, he went on as a mobile purger to various reluctant provinces. During 1938 alone he was to serve in no less than four of these posts. Leaving Irkutsk completely crushed, he held two First Secretaryships in the Ukrainian provinces left empty by Khrushchev's purges, and then arrived in Moscow in the winter as the city's First Secretary. During the Second World War he was to take over political control of the Army and to become Secretary of the Central Committee and candidate member of the Politburo. He died in 1945, allegedly at the hands of doctor-poisoners. A typical Zhdanovite career.

This group soon set to work. In May 1937 Zhdanov assembled the executive workers of the provincial committee and announced: 'Two enemies – Chudov and Kodatsky – have been exposed in our ranks, in the Leningrad organization. They have been arrested in Moscow.' No one spoke: 'it was as if our tongues were frozen'. A woman Old Bolshevik, later to spend seventeen years in a labour camp, went up to Zhdanov, and said to him: 'Comrade Zhdanov, I don't know Chudov. He hasn't been in our Leningrad organization long. But I vouch for Kodatsky. He has been a Party member since 1913. I have known him for many years. He is an honest member of the Party. He fought all the oppositionists. This is incredible! It must be verified.' Zhdanov looked at her 'with his cruel eyes' and said: 'Lazurkina, stop this talk, otherwise it will end badly for you.'[5]

This conference of the Party organization 'uncovered and expelled from its ranks the Anti-Soviet Rightist-Trotskyite-double-dealers – the Japanese-German diversionists and spies'.[6] (Expulsion was the extreme measure of Party discipline proper. In these circumstances it almost invariably meant 'relaxation to the secular arm' of the N.K.V.D., followed by arrest.) And this was only the first step: of the sixty-five members of the new City Committee elected on 29 May, only two were re-elected on 4 June 1938 (while five others were transferred to posts outside the city).[7]

The long days of summer had set in in the northern capital, presenting a minor technical difficulty to Zakovsky's men. As the wave of arrests reached the top of the local Party, then swept downwards again, involving those promoted to Party positions in the past year or two, and then out beyond them to the already stricken masses of the population, operations could no longer be conducted under the decent cover of night. For Leningrad is easily the most northerly of the great cities of the world, on the same latitude as the Shetland Islands or northern Labrador. In winter daytime is extremely short, but in summer, as Pushkin says, one can read all night in one's room by the 'Transparent dusk and moonless glitter'. The rumbling and halting of police cars in the bright but deserted streets of the sub-arctic summer nights is said to have been particularly disturbing.

Nothing more is known of the fate of I. F. Kodatsky, Mayor of Leningrad and also a full member of the Central Committee, except that he was eventually shot, in 1939[8] (as was Leningrad's other full member of the Central Committee, P. A. Alexeyev, Chairman of the Leningrad Trade Unions). It is possible to trace Chudov's fate a little further.

A man called Rozenblum, a Party member since 1906, had been arrested in connexion with another case – that of the prominent Old Bolshevik Nikolai Komarov.

With the defeat of the Zinovievites in 1926, Komarov had taken over Zinoviev's own post as head of the Leningrad Soviet. In 1929 he became unsatisfactory to Stalin: without actually supporting Bukharin, he had shown no enthusiasm in the struggle against him. Bukharin had told Kamenev in July 1928 that the higher functionaries in Leningrad 'are mentally with us, but they are terrified when we speak of removing Stalin', so that they vacillated without being able to make up their minds. 'Stalin,' we are told elsewhere, 'had met with a set-back in attempting to win the Leningrad people over to his cause, Komarov and the others, the successors of Zinoviev.'[9] Komarov was removed and transferred to a post on the Council of National Economy in Moscow.* In 1934 he was no longer a full member of the Central Committee, but remained a candidate member.

Their transfer left Leningrad in the hands of men wholly loyal to the Party line. Yet the milieu at the beginning of the thirties was one in which genuine Stalinists, apart from Kirov himself and Chudov, were rare. Most are perhaps best thought of as Stalinists with a slight Rightist tinge, a position to which Kirov himself to some extent evolved.[10]

Komarov remained a link to them. He was to be named later as an important figure in 'the Leningrad group' of terrorists.[11] And through Rozenblum the Komarov Case was somehow linked with Chudov's. But this latter was designed as a far more important affair, a public trial with all the trimmings. Rozenblum, who had already been subjected to 'terrible torture',[12] was brought before Zakovsky,

who offered him freedom on condition that he make before the court a false confession fabricated in 1937 by the N.K.V.D. concerning 'sabotage, espionage and diversion in a terroristic centre in Leningrad'. With unbelievable cynicism Zakovsky told about the vile 'mechanism' for the crafty creation of fabricated 'anti-Soviet plots'.

'In order to illustrate it to me', stated Rozenblum, 'Zakovsky gave me several possible variants of the organization of this centre and of its branches. After he detailed the organization to me, Zakovsky told me that the N.K.V.D. would prepare the case of this centre, remarking that the trial would be public.'

'. . . You yourself', said Zakovsky, 'will not need to invent anything. The N.K.V.D. will prepare for you a ready outline for every branch of

*The only active Rightist in the Leningrad leadership, F. Ya. Ugarov, the then trade union chief, was also removed at that time.

the centre; you will have to study it carefully and to remember well all the questions and answers which the court might ask. This case will be ready in four or five months or perhaps half a year. During all this time you will be preparing yourself so that you will not compromise the investigation and yourself. Your future will depend on how the trial goes and on its results. If you begin to lie and to testify falsely, blame yourself. If you manage to endure it, you will save your head and we will feed and clothe you at the Government's cost until your death.'[13]

The trial, Zakovsky told Rozenblum, would involve Chudov, Chudov's wife Lyudmila Shaposhnikova,* and three other Secretaries of the City and Provincial Committees – Boris Pozern, Party member since 1903, A. I. Ugarov, and Pyotr Smorodin, all candidate members of the Party's Central Committee.

As so often, we may note that the ground had been well prepared. Already, in August 1936, it had been alleged that several members of the group associated with Nikolayev had 'enjoyed the confidence of a number of leading Party workers and officials of Soviet organizations in Leningrad'; it was this which had 'ensured them every possibility of pursuing their preparations for a terroristic act against Kirov without the least fear of being discovered'.[14]

There was a camp rumour[15] that the assassin Nikolayev had served under Chudov before the latter's transfer to Leningrad. Though the story, as it stands, cannot be reconciled with the facts of Chudov's career, it could possibly represent some genuine allegation of contact made against him by the authorities at the time of his arrest and trial.†

As to political complexion, it seems clear that the Leningraders were to be treated as 'Rightists'. There was some truth in this, and their end represented the final crushing of the Kirov line.

The Leningrad Centre Trial planned by Zakovsky never took place (in fact, announced trials of importance were held only in Moscow and Georgia). We do not know why. We might speculate

* Also a member of the Provincial Committee and Secretary of the Leningrad Trade Unions.
† Suitable terrorist groups from Leningrad, later than Nikolayev's, were also mentioned at the various trials: for example, one supposedly organized by the historian Prigozhin, operating as late as 1935.[16]

that the resistance of some of the Leningraders contributed to the downfall of Zakovsky, who was soon himself to be shot.

The fate of Zakovsky's list of victims presents some peculiar features. Chudov indeed was shot in 1937.[17] Smorodin's death is given variously as 1937[18] and 1941:[17] he succeeded Chudov as Second Secretary of the Provincial Committee in June, and was probably arrested in the late summer. But Pozern, who died in 1938,[19] 1939,[17] or 1940,[18, 20, 21] was still at large as late as May 1938, while A. I. Ugarov went on to promotion as First Secretary of the Moscow province, and only disappeared in the autumn of 1938. This certainly shows that, as Zakovsky said, variants must have existed, some of them implicating men with whom he was sitting daily in the Provincial Bureau.

The Leningrad purge is the provincial one of which we are best informed, and it is illuminating to look at its scope. Those arrested included all the seven Leningrad members and candidate members of the Central Committee.* Other victims were A. N. Petrovsky, who had headed the Executive Committee and was later a Secretary of the Provincial Committee, and I. S. Vayshlya, Secretary of the Leningrad Komsomol. In addition, most of the other members of the Bureau, and 'hundreds of the most active Party workers', including many secretaries of district committees in the city, perished. The purge also struck at the fighting service commands with Dybenko (G.O.C. Leningrad District and *ex officio* a member of the Provincial Bureau) and the Commander of the Baltic Fleet, A. K. Sivkov. At the same time the leading industrialists fell: the heads of all the great enterprises – 'Lenenergo', the Kirov Works, the 'Metallic' Factory – and many others.[22]

Of the 154 Leningrad delegates to the XVIIth Congress, only *two* were re-elected to the XVIIIth Congress – Andreyev and Shkiryatov, whose Leningrad affiliations were purely honorary. Of the sixty-five members even of the Leningrad Provincial Committee elected on 17 June 1937, only nine reappear a year later (four others had been transferred to positions outside the city).[23] As a survivor from among the lower officials in the

* Chudov, Kodatsky, Alexeyev, Smorodin, Pozern, Ugarov and P. I. Struppe, Chairman of the Provincial Executive Committee.

Committee's apparatus was later to comment, 'In 1937 I was to share the lot of many. I had an executive post in the Leningrad Province Party Committee and, of course, was also arrested.'[24]

As the old cadres were annihilated, Zhdanov promoted his own men. Some of these (like Voznesensky, who became chairman of the local Planning Commission and then deputy chairman of the town Soviet before transfer to the central Government and eventual membership of the Politburo; A. A. Kuznetsov, promoted through district secretaryships to Second Secretary of the Provincial Committee, and later to become Secretary of the Central Committee; and Popkov, later First Secretary of the Leningrad Committee), were shot in 1950 in a later 'Leningrad Case'. Others survived to, or almost to, this day, N. G. Ignatov, who had served in the old O.G.P.U., was secretary of a factory Party committee when Zhdanov took over in Leningrad. In 1937 he became First Secretary of a district committee in the city and a member of the City Committee. The following year he was sent to carry out the political side of the final operation against Postyshev, becoming Second and then First Secretary at Kuibyshev. After various ups and downs he was Vice-Premier of the U.S.S.R. when he died in 1966.

An even more interesting case is that of Alexei Kosygin, who 'played an active role'[25] in Party life as a member of the bureau of the city's Vyborg district (at a time when the main 'activity' was the denunciation and purge of the previous secretaries and bureaux), and in 1937 filled one of the economic gaps as director of the 'October' textile works. By July 1938 he headed the Transport-Industry Department of the Provincial Committee of the Party, and in October he was Chairman of the City Executive Committee, Kodatsky's old job. The following year he was transferred to a post in the Soviet Government, of which he has been a member ever since.

*

These Leningrad events were repeated in the Provincial Committees throughout the country, with the amendment that (except in Beria's Caucasian fief and under Khrushchev in Moscow) the local First Secretaries could not be trusted, as Zhdanov was, to conduct their own purges.

Kaganovich was sent to Ivanovo, the Kuban, Smolensk and elsewhere; Malenkov to Byelorussia, Armenia and so on; Shkiryatov to the North Caucasus. Everywhere they destroyed the old leaderships. So long as the Provincial Secretaries had to countersign orders for the arrest of prominent 'Trotskyites' (which Eikhe mentions as one of his prerogatives as First Secretary in West Siberia),[26] they were, at the earlier stages, able and willing to block action – or anyhow, to block the type of action now required by Stalin and Yezhov. In most cases Moscow itself had to destroy the local leaderships.*

And so, we are told, 'The investigative materials of that time show that in almost all territories, provinces and republics there supposedly existed "Rightist-Trotskyite, espionage-terror and diversionary-sabotage organizations and centres" and that the heads of such organizations as a rule – for no known reason – were First Secretaries of Provincial Party Committees or Republic Central Committees.'[27]

When Kaganovich went to Ivanovo, immediately on arrival he telegraphed Stalin: 'First acquaintance with the material shows that Provincial Secretary Yepanechnikov must be arrested at once. It is also necessary to arrest Mikhailov, head of the Provincial Committee's Propaganda Department.' Soon he was sending another telegram: 'Acquaintance with the situation shows that Right-Trotskyist sabotage has assumed wide scope here – in industry, agriculture, supply, trade, public health services, education and Party political work. The apparatus of provincial institutions and the Provincial Party Committee are deeply infected.'[28] His visit to the city became known as 'the black tornado'. 'He accused the entire Party organization, which had great revolutionary traditions, of supposedly standing aloof, of being off to the side of the high road. At a plenary session of the Provincial Committee he pinned the label "enemy of the people" on the majority of executive officials without any grounds.'[29]

*The other method used by the Secretariat was to intrude, under the reluctant First Secretaries, Second Secretaries from the purging faction (as N. G. Ignatov was sent to undermine Postyshev).

The expression now in use of this period is that Kaganovich or Malenkov went to So-and-so and 'routed' or 'crushed' (*razgromil*) the Provincial Committee. It is invariably one of these two, or Yezhov or Beria, who is held responsible. We have not yet heard from Soviet sources of the detail of the 'crushing' of the Ukrainian Central Committee, in which Khrushchev took part.* The role of Mikoyan in the destruction of the Armenian Party is hushed up and the whole action is attributed to Malenkov, as is the parallel *coup* in Byelorussia, where the acts of Yakovlev (now rehabilitated) are ignored.

A recent Soviet account,[31] in fictional form but evidently based on personal experience, describes the sort of scene which often occurred at the Provincial Committees. On 23 July 1937 a member arrives at a meeting of one of these. It has been called at a few hours' notice and no agenda notified. When he arrives the atmosphere is tense and silent. Everyone, as far as possible, sits in the back rows.

The first man to appear

was then very powerful, both a People's Commissar and a Secretary of the Central Committee, virtually one man with seven faces. The hall was quiet. The People's Commissar frowned and was evidently displeased at how he had been greeted, being used to a triumphal reception. Some bright lad came to his senses and started clapping. Other people joined in and things took their proper course.

After that the Bureau members of our Provincial Committee, headed by the First Secretary, appeared. They too were given a round of clapping, though a more feeble one . . .

The report on agitation and propaganda work in the countryside ought to have been delivered by the Propaganda Secretary, but it was Kostyukov, the head of the provincial agricultural land administration, who got up to speak. He was a great one for making speeches, especially when it came to plans, hectares and fertilizers, but this time you could see his lips moving but nothing was audible. Some bolder spirit in the hall shouted: 'Louder!'

Kostyukov raised his eyes from his notes and I felt ill – his eyes had the glassy look of a corpse . . .

* Though a post-Khrushchev publication lists in passing six Secretaries of his Moscow Committee, together with the Mayor, N. A. Filatov, as perishing in the purges.[30]

We heard him say:

> 'Two days ago Comrade Kazakov, Chairman of the Provincial Executive Committee, and I paid a visit to the Budenny Collective Farm . . .'

The People's Commissar put his hands on his hips and in a curious way, whether expressing astonishment or derision, asked the speaker: 'With whom? Who did you visit the collective farm with?'

'With Comrade Kazakov . . .'

It was only then that I noticed the absence of Kazakov from the Presidium. 'How's that?' I thought to myself. 'After all he is on the Bureau!'

The People's Commissar continued in the same incomprehensible tone: 'So that therefore, if I understand you correctly, you consider Kazakov a Comrade? Answer me!'

Kostyukov went white and started stuttering. . . . 'Of course . . . if that is the case. . . . Why shouldn't he be regarded . . . ?'

The People's Commissar looked at his wrist-watch, then glanced at the wings and some person there, not one of ours, immediately rushed over to him. The People's Commissar heard out this person's brief, momentary report and then declared . . . 'I don't understand how you can conduct yourself in this way. I simply refuse to understand . . .' He looked again at his wrist-watch and added, 'The enemy of the people, Kazakov, was arrested twenty minutes ago . . .'

. . . One of those sitting in the Presidium started applauding. The others backed him up, at first timidly, and then more energetically. A deep bass voice cried out: 'Hurrah for our glorious N.K.V.D.!'

And I, too, cried 'Hurrah!'

Kostyukov completely collapsed and, mumbling a few more words, left the rostrum to the sound of his own heels clicking on the floorboards. He was seen no more – he disappeared into the wings for good.

The People's Commissar again looked at his watch and in the same incomprehensible tone of voice addressed the Secretary for Propaganda: 'Perhaps you can do duty for the last inadequate speaker?'

The Secretary walked across to the rostrum, as white as a sheet, gave a little cough, and started off relatively confidently:

> '. . . As the previous speaker already stated, we must complete the harvesting in a shorter period. . . . At the same time, Comrade Kostyukov failed to point out that . . .'

At these last words the People's Commissar again put his hands to his hips and inquired sneeringly: 'Is Kostyukov your Comrade? Curious, very curious . . .' Again a glance at his watch and the pole-axing words:

'The accomplice of the enemy of the people Kazakov, his henchman Kostyukov, was arrested fifteen minutes ago . . .'

Within forty minutes the entire bureau of the Provincial Committee and the entire Presidium of the Provincial Executive Committee had been swept into oblivion.

At the end of June Kaganovich appeared before a specially summoned meeting of the Smolensk Provincial Committee and announced that the First Secretary Rumyantsev, who had held the area for Stalin since 1929, his Second Secretary Shulman, and a large group of the old leadership were 'traitors, spies of German and Japanese fascism and members of the Rightist-Trotskyite gang'.[32] They disappeared without trace. Rumyantsev was succeeded by D. Korotchenkov, under whose rule the province suffered the extremes of the Terror.*

In Smolensk, we chance to be able to trace the impact of the Purge at the local Party level. Belyi was a moderate-sized town and administrative area in the Smolensk province. The Provincial Committee, itself already in trouble following the February–March plenum, began to take it out on its subordinate bodies in March 1937. The Belyi First Secretary, Kovalev, was put up in a four-day ceremony, to be abused and denounced by his local subordinates. Various speakers attacked him for having lived with a Trotskyite in 1921, having behaved like a local dictator, having been a deserter from the Red Army, and so forth. There were more than 200 local Communists present, accounting for a large section of the local Party membership, and it is clear that a number of these had not yet grasped the tone of the new-style Party. Questions from the floor pointed out that everyone approved of Kovalev at the time and asked why they had not said anything earlier. But one of Kovalev's more sophisticated accusers

---

*Korotchenkov, who had previously been known and was later to be known again as Korotchenko, was at the time of his death in 1969 a member of the Central Committee, and Chairman of the Presidium of the Ukraine Supreme Soviet. He had been serving in 1937 as Party Secretary in Moscow under Khrushchev, and was later to accompany him to the Ukraine.

claimed that he had been silent because Kovalev had, for four years, forbidden him to speak!

The representative of the Provincial Committee, while arranging the removal of Kovalev, spoke more moderately than some of the rank-and-file delators, saying 'I do not have sufficient basis to call Kovalev a Trotskyite' but that the matter would be investigated.

When, in June, the Provincial Committee was itself unmasked, a hysteria of arrest and accusation seized Belyi. On 26–7 June a further meeting there saw violent denunciation of Kovalev and all the other members of the local leadership of his time. The whole of the Kovalev leadership fell, and on 18–19 September a plenum of the District Committee was held to destroy those who had succeeded him. The new local Secretary Karpovsky was accused of having been an agent of Rumyantsev's, of having once belonged to a bandit gang, of having relatives abroad, of maintaining connexions with a sister who had married a former merchant. Karpovsky defended himself, saying that he had not only not been a bandit but had himself killed several bandits. He had had a letter from an aunt in Romania but had never seen her since she left Russia in 1908. Both his sister and her former merchant husband were now employed in useful work. A friend who had fought with Karpovsky testified that the two of them had fought against bandits. But speaker after speaker attacked the Secretary in the most violent terms, and even this friend finally said weakly that he had just not been aware of Karpovsky's membership of a bandit gang. All Karpovsky's associates fell with him or shortly afterwards. By the end of the year a completely new team, all strangers to Belyi, was in charge. The Party membership, which had been 367 on 1 September 1934, had gone down to less than 200.[33]

Almost as striking as the calls for terror from above was this hysterical lynching mood of what now became a dominant section of the lowest Party organizations. For while the upper and middle levels of the Party were being wiped out, Moscow's envoys everywhere found denouncers, like Nikolayenko in Kiev, to give them 'evidence' against those they wished to destroy.

A recent Soviet article entitled 'The Dossier of a Provocateur'[34] describes how a Party member in Azerbaijan made his career during the purges by denouncing prominent Party colleagues to the N.K.V.D. Among those he denounced were three Secretaries of the Azerbaijan Central Committee, and the former Chairman of the local Council of People's Commissars. The 'provocateur', I. Ya. Myachin, was until recently a well-known and liked local Communist whom 'Communists for forty years had known simply as "Vanya"'. At one time he had held the post of Deputy People's Commissar for the Azerbaijan textile industry.

His belated undoing was the fact that he typed two copies of all his denunciations, sending one 'to the N.K.V.D., addressed to Bagirov's underlings', and another, which he signed, to the archives, where it was added to a file which lay on a shelf 'for a quarter of a century', until an archivist discovered it. It covered Myachin's activities for the period February to November 1937, and contained material 'compromising' fourteen Party, Soviet and economic leaders. A typical victim was accused of attempting 'to give instructions to counter-revolutionaries to keep their mouths shut' because once on a bus he advised against talking about sabotage. In justification of his activities Myachin said: 'We thought this was what we had to do. . . . Everybody was writing . . .' He was of course, by his standards, quite right.

And, by such means, the Purge struck everywhere. In the Urals, in the newest industrial area, a 'Ural Uprising Staff' was discovered, headed as was customary by the First Secretary – Kabakov, of the Sverdlovsk Provincial Committee, full member of the Central Committee. It was a 'bloc of Rights and Trotskyites' and also included Social Revolutionaries and Church leaders.[35]

In the Azov–Black Sea and Rostov provinces E. G. Evdokimov, the old N.K.V.D. chief, took over as provincial secretary. Even he is said to have complained to Moscow that the purge was going too far.[36] At all events he soon disappeared. As the arrests swept Rostov Provincial Committee, the young Party official Mikhail Suslov began his spectacular rise. He had been, in 1933–4, on a commission for purging the Party in a number of provinces. He was now appointed one of the Rostov provincial secretaries. (In 1939 he was to become First Secretary of the Stavropol Regional Committee, where in 1944 he became involved in the deportation of the Karachai people. Proving successful in this, he was made Chairman of the Bureau of the Central Committee for newly-occupied Lithuania, in 1944, and reimposed Soviet rule against a bitter partisan resistance. By 1947 he was secretary of the Central Committee, a post he has held continually ever since.)

There were some special cases. Yosif Vareikis, who had been very much in Stalin's confidence, and had served as First Secretary in Voronezh and Stalingrad, was now First Secretary of the Far Eastern Territory. He telephoned Stalin in September 1937 with a query about the reasons for the arrest of certain Communists.[37] In the conversation he put some question about the arrest of Tukhachevsky. He had served with him in the Civil War, when the two had at one time been seized by Social Revolutionary mutineers, whom they had eventually suppressed.

Stalin shouted 'That is not your business. Don't interfere in what doesn't concern you. The N.K.V.D. knows what it's doing.' He then went on to say 'Only an enemy would defend Tukhachevsky', and threw down the telephone. Vareikis was deeply shaken. He told his wife that he could hardly believe it was Stalin.

On 30 September he got a telegram summoning him to the capital on official business. On 9 October he was arrested a few stations out of Moscow. His wife was arrested four days later. He was mentioned as a plotter in the Bukharin Trial,[38] and was shot in 1939.[39] It seems very probable from the context that the conversation must have had something to do with the position of Marshal Blyukher, who commanded in the Far East, and that Stalin's lapse into open rage may have reflected a real anxiety about trouble from the Far Eastern Army.

IN THE REPUBLICS

In the Republics things went in the same way as in the provinces of Russia proper. In the Byelorussian Republic the 'verification' of Party cards ordered in 1935 and 1936 was used by Yezhov to expel, in connexion with an alleged anti-Soviet underground, 'more than half of the entire membership'.[40] The local officials opposed these actions, which amounted to the first phase in the destruction of the old Party and the rebuilding of another on its ruins. After the February–March plenum, on 17 March 1937, V. F. Sharangovich, as an emissary of the centre,* was sent to take over the Byelorussian First Secretaryship.

The resistance was widespread at the highest level in the Republic. M. M. Goloded, Chairman of its Council of People's Commissars, 'cast doubt upon the results of the verification' at a meeting of the local Central Committee.[41] This was made the occasion for the dispatch of Malenkov, in June 1937, to destroy the leadership.

Chervyakov, Chairman of the Byelorussian Supreme Soviet – i.e. 'Head of State' of this 'sovereign republic' – committed suicide. Goloded was charged with 'bourgeois nationalism',[42] arrested on the way to Moscow and shot.[43] Gikalo, Sharangovich's predecessor, and himself a notorious purger of others, went the same way.† Almost the entire leadership of the Republic, 'including the Central Committee secretaries ... the People's Commissars, and many leaders of local Party and Soviet bodies and representatives of the creative intelligentsia were expelled from the Party and many of them were arrested'.[44]

At a local Party Congress held in mid June, Sharangovich warmly celebrated the purge then in progress. His own fall came at a Byelorussian Central Committee plenum in August, when Ya. A. Yakovlev, sent from Moscow, denounced him in turn.[45] With him went a new batch of rulers, including Chervyakov's successor Natalevich. Throughout the summer and autumn the purge spread down to the local and mass level. Sharangovich's fate is typical of a significant phenomenon. The new generation of Stalinist careerists, who had adapted themselves completely to the new system, still found themselves arrested. This is particularly the case among the first and most energetic batch who

---

* He had served in Byelorussia until 1936.

† At the Bukharin Trial Goloded, Chervyakov, Gikalo, Zheborevsky (Byelorussia's Third Secretary), Benek (Commissar for Agriculture) and others were to be involved in a 'national fascist organization', whose main activities were espionage for Poland and the sabotage of agriculture.

had worked up to high positions. They were executed by younger but similar characters, who again often fell quickly. The shortness of their tenure has been explained as follows:

People of their type tended, in their unscrupulousness and zeal, to carry the Party line to absurd extremes, with the result that their actions had later to be explained away as deviations. People of this type were also inclined by nature to corruption and the exploitation of their positions for personal advantage. They thus roused the hatred and envy of their juniors. This further contributed to the shortness of their stay in office.[46]

Stalin's idea, announced at the February–March plenum, of having two stand-ins for every post, showed foresight, but did not go far enough. In many cases it was only the fourth or fifth nominee who was to keep the post through the ensuing years. Among those who began to rise in Byelorussia at this time was K. Mazurov (in 1970 Vice-Premier of the Soviet Union and member of the Politburo), who in 1938 held a position in the political departmcnt of the much purged Byelorussian railways.

Apart from politicians and engineers, the Byelorussian purge struck most heavily at the cultural leadership – and the Linguistic Institute and the Commissariat of Education in particular, where the principle of the separate Byelorussian nationality had been concentrated. Byelorussians, almost invariably, were *ex officio* Polish spies, owing to the geographical position of the Republic.[47]

The Byelorussian case is interesting in that it seems to show a slightly more stubborn opposition than that offered in the provincial committees, perhaps owing to some slight reliance on local feeling. This was to be far more noticeable in the Ukraine, where a large concentration of high officials made final subjugation a more difficult matter.

In Georgia (where in 1919 the Mensheviks had won 105 out of the 130 seats in the National Assembly)* there was by now no need of a purge at the top. The thin-faced, *pince-nez*'d Beria, the old O.G.P.U. operative Stalin had infiltrated into the Transcaucasian First Secretaryship in 1931, was in full control, and had

---

*The vote had been Menshevik 640,000, Bolshevik 24,000; the latter had won no seats at all.

already been purging enthusiastically. As early as 11 August 1936 he had even shot, in his own office, the Armenian First Secretary Khandzhian.[48]

So Georgia's intra-Party purge was violent but routine. No emissary of the Central Committee was required to enforce it. On the other hand the Republic was the scene of several publicly announced trials, though these were not actually *held* in public.

The most important came on 10–12 July 1937. Men as prominent – on the narrower stage of Georgian Bolshevism – as the leading victims of the Moscow Trials were brought to trial. It was evidently intended, originally, to make this too a show trial. For the men involved were all old enemies of Stalin's. Chief of them was Budu Mdivani, former Premier of Soviet Georgia, whose defence against Stalin Lenin had undertaken just before his death – whose case indeed had been Lenin's final reason for wishing to remove Stalin from the General Secretaryship. With him were the Old Bolshevik Okudzhava, father of the poet and balladist, and others.

Their trial is said to have been decided on at the February–March plenum.[49] But they had long since been incriminated. Mdivani had been denounced as long ago as 1929 for illegal Trotskyite activity,[50] but had become reconciled to the Party because, as he said, he felt too old to start another. At the Zinoviev Trial, though Mdivani's name was not mentioned, the 'Georgian deviationists' were, as we saw, specially noted as having had an attitude which 'as is well known was terroristic from 1928 onwards'. At the time of the Zinoviev Trial this was a record: no other group had then been charged with terrorist plans before the thirties. At the Pyatakov Trial Mdivani was accused of planning a terrorist act against Yezhov, and another against Beria.[51] And after his death, at the Bukharin Trial of 1938, he was described as a British agent.[52]

When attempts were made to get him to confess, he is said to have answered 'You are telling me that Stalin has promised to spare the lives of Old Bolsheviks! I have known Stalin for thirty years. Stalin won't rest until he has butchered all of us, beginning with the unweaned baby and ending with the blind-great-grandmother!'[53] He and Okudzhava 'fiercely denied their guilt'.[54] The Georgian Supreme Court sentenced them to death and they were shot.

Two parallel trials in the two Autonomous Republics within Georgia – Adzharia and Abkhazia – removed the equivalent veterans there on 29 September and 29 October respectively. In the former, the Old Bolshevik Nestor Lakoba, who had died on 28 December 1936 as a result (it is now said) of some intrigue of Beria's,[55] was posthumously accused of a plot on Stalin's life,[56] (and his son was shot).[57]

Meanwhile, a fresh assault on the new generation of second-line leaders was mounted. The dates of arrest of a number of Georgian and Transcaucasian Communists rehabilitated in 1964–5 are given as 1–3 September 1937. A general terror operation without the publicity of the oppositionist trials was starting. Over 1937–8, 4,238 promotions to senior Georgian Party, State and economic posts were made – that is, to leadership posts.[58] The *total* Party membership had been 34,000 at the XVIIth Congress, and the implication is that virtually the whole leading cadre was destroyed.

The Armenian Party had been under general attack since May. 'Suspicious people' were found to be in the Party apparatus.[59] During the summer, Ter-Gabrielian, who had been Chairman of the Council of People's Commissars in 1935, was interrogated for seven hours in the office of the head of the local N.K.V.D. about alleged embezzlement on the railways, and killed on the spot.

In September 1937 a plenum of the Armenian Central Committee was held in Erevan and the decisive blow was struck. The All-Union Central Committee was represented by Mikoyan, supported by Beria and Malenkov. Under the New Constitution, Armenia no longer formed part of the old 'Transcaucasian Socialist Federal Soviet Republic' ruled by Beria. It still came under his aegis in a general way, but in this case it was not thought to be an intrusion when Malenkov was sent 'on Stalin's direct instructions'[60] to carry out the operation. Malenkov stopped off at Tbilisi on his way to Erevan to concoct a story about the death of Khandzhian, whom Beria had shot, to their mutual satisfaction. The rest of the Armenian leadership were now to be blamed for the crime.[61]

Mikoyan led the attack on the local cadres. The First Secretary Amatouni is said to have put up a stout resistance and to have shouted back 'You lie!' He was, however, arrested, together with the Second Secretary, the Chairman of the Council of People's Commissars, and the head of the N.K.V.D., and was denounced as an enemy of the people on 23 September.[62] Almost the entire leadership of Armenia's Central Committee and Council of People's Commissars was illegally arrested. Malenkov personally interrogated the prisoners, 'using proscribed methods' in the process.

In this third week of September 1937 there was a wave of mass arrests throughout the Republic. Of the Bureau of sixteen members and candidate members elected in June 1935, none were left at the end of September 1937. Of those who formed the new Bureau in 1937, only two remained in 1940. Of the Central Committee of fifty-five elected in June 1937, only fifteen were re-elected just a year later in June 1938, and these included the non-local names of Stalin, Beria and Mikoyan. About thirty of those removed can be traced as having been expelled from the Party and probably arrested.

As in Georgia, the whole second level of the Party went too. 'Over 3,500 responsible Party, Soviet, economic, military and Komsomol officials were arrested . . . in a few months of 1937 alone. Many of them were shot without a trial and the requisite investigation.'[63] On the last day of the year, the execution of eight leading Armenian officials was announced, together with – ironically enough – the posthumous disgrace of Khandzhian.[64]

The launching of mass arrests in both Georgia and Armenia in September was not a coincidence. A general decision to destroy the old Parties in the national Republics seems to have been taken. By midsummer the entire Government of the Tatar Republic was under arrest.[65] September saw the sudden start of a press campaign conducted in more violent terms than ever, on a threat about which not much had been heard for some time – bourgeois nationalism. Such articles as 'The Rotten Position of the Daghestan Provincial Committee' became common. From about the 8th of the month, the Parties in the minority areas were subjected, under heavy headlines, to a continuous stream of abuse.

Uzbekistan, Kirghizia, Kazakhstan, Bashkiria, Karelia, everywhere large groups of traitors were found in the leaderships – in fact constituting the leaderships.*

The pattern that emerges in the Purge in the Republics and provinces is a striking one. It amounts to this: an operation planned in Moscow and carried into effect by missions from the centre almost everywhere destroyed the old Party, raising up instead from the rank and file a special selection of enthusiasts for a new organization of terrorists and denouncers. What requires the most emphasis is the sheer extent of the changes, the completeness of the liquidation of the hierarchy. At the centre, Stalin had already created his own cadres, and infiltrated them into high position. In the coming months the ravages were to be very great in Moscow too, but there was a continuity provided by a handful of men at the top and a group of Stalin's junior nominees in the instruments of power. In the provinces, the 'black tornado' really uprooted the old 'Party-line' Stalinists, the veterans who represented a continuity, however tenuous, with the old Party of the underground, of 1917 and of the Civil War. This amounted to a revolution as complete as, though more disguised than, any previous changes in Russia.

We may incidentally note a lesser point: whereas previously the Party Secretary had been the most powerful man in any area, it was now the N.K.V.D. chief who counted. Over the next year or two the new Party executives were to regain a good deal of their power. But for the moment, the police – themselves purged and purged again – were the direct agents of the centre and executors of its main missions.

DEVASTATED AREA: THE UKRAINE

And Kiev groaned with sorrow. The Armament of Igor

Stalin's victory over the Party was assured when he crushed the moderates at the February–March plenum. All that was left to do was to set the machinery of the purges in motion. There was to be one last flicker of resistance – in the Ukraine.

*The most prominent of these – the Uzbek – we will deal with in connexion with the Bukharin Trial (see pp. 516–20).

There is a certain shortage of recent official material on events in the Ukraine during 1937–8. While a good deal has been published in the past decade on other areas, it was published under the auspices of Khrushchev, with the result that it deals almost exclusively with areas with which he was not at the time associated – and very largely with those in which his various rivals carry most of the responsibility.

But we have other sources. And it can be seen that those in power in the Ukraine in the summer of 1937 continued, in spite of the removal of Postyshev, to show solidarity in opposing the extension of the Purge. This was action on a local scale, an attempt to defend a last outpost of comparative sanity. There was no longer any prospect of victory in the Union as a whole, and the struggle which now went on in Kiev might be compared to that of the garrison of an isolated fort which continues with a gallant but hopeless defence after its main armies have been defeated in the field.

In the Central Committee, in the great cities, the provincial capitals, the smaller Republics, those who had opposed the Purge were isolated figures impotently awaiting their fate. In the Ukraine alone, the old leadership, based on its local Central Committee, remained in control. The demotion of Postyshev had removed one hostile leader. And doubtless Stalin hoped to profit by whatever rivalries to the dismissed Second Secretary might be prevalent in the Ukrainian Politburo. But Kossior too was one of the doubters and so was Petrovsky. Postyshev's place was taken by his predecessor in the post, Khatayevich, a full member of the All-Union Central Committee, who had been on the Ukrainian Politburo since 1933. Though a considerable purge in the lower ranks took place under an order from the All-Union Central Committee in the weeks following the February–March plenum – nearly 20 per cent of Ukrainian Party members were expelled[66] – the old leadership was re-elected at the Ukrainian Party Congress in May–June. And when Stalin made an attempt to capture the position by a *coup de main*, the assault failed.

The Ukrainian Party had a special history. Lenin had underestimated Ukrainian national feeling. The 1917 vote in the

Ukraine for the Constituent Assembly was 77 per cent to the Social Revolutionary parties, 10 per cent to the Bolsheviks. The local Soviets were usually under anti-Bolshevik control. From 1917 to 1920 Ukrainian nationalist regimes of various types were in existence, and Bolshevik rule was imposed and re-imposed very largely from outside.

Unlike the situation in Russia proper, an important section of the Ukrainian Communist Party itself had originally come from the Left Social Revolutionaries. Their main body in the Ukraine had turned nationalist, under the name 'Borotbist'. This party was dissolved early in 1920 and its members entered the Communist Party.

Time and time again, Bolshevik leaders sent to the Ukraine with strong centralizing views modified them over the years. The attempt to rule solely as agents of a foreign power, through a handful of Quislings, was seen as in the long run non-viable. It was a problem of the type which repeated itself in Hungary after the Second World War.

Chubar, who was to be moderate on this issue, became Premier of the Ukraine in July 1923. But in 1925 Kaganovich was sent to Kiev as First Secretary. His ruthlessly centralizing policy was unpopular in the local Party, which otherwise had no quarrel with Stalin. Stalin himself writes of a demand from the Ukraine in 1926 that Kaganovich be replaced by Grinko and Chubar.[67] Stalin, involved in his great struggle at the centre, did not wish for a quarrel with the more moderate faction in the Ukraine simply on this local issue. When, in July 1928, Kaganovich was removed from the Republic, Stalin, as Bukharin put it, 'bought the Ukrainians by withdrawing Kaganovich from the Ukraine'.[68] He was replaced by Stanislav Kossior, a short, bald, bullet-headed Pole who backed Stalin unreservedly right up to the Yezhov period.

In the years of dispute with the Left and Right oppositions, Stalin's calculations proved correct. The Ukrainian Party gave no trouble. There seems to have been very little Trotskyism in it. And in fact, the national minorities in general disliked Trotsky more than Stalin. Even after experience of Stalin's rule, an

Ossetian Communist believed that while Trotsky's intended method of rule was in general identical with Stalin's, yet on the nationality question Trotsky was 'even more reactionary'.[69]

And the Ukrainian experience with the oppositionists had not been reassuring. Pyatakov, who had briefly ruled in Kiev in the Civil War, had put the view that the Ukraine must submit to Russia very bluntly: 'Can we declare that the form of existence of proletarian-peasant Ukraine can be determined solely and absolutely by the working masses of the Ukraine? Of course not!'[70]

In the early thirties the collectivization campaign had turned the Ukraine, more than anywhere else, into a battlefield between the Party and the population, and Party solidarity was the decisive criterion. Non-Communist nationalism remained powerful. The trial of forty-five leading cultural figures as a 'Union for the Liberation of the Ukraine' in March–April 1930, and the similar trials which followed it, were directed against a real resistance.

This extreme and rigorous purge erased the old Ukrainian intellectuals, and left the Old Bolshevik Skrypnik, in the Commissariat of Education, as the protector of only a residue of Ukrainian culture. This, however, he determined to defend.

There is no doubt that Skrypnik and his genuine feeling of resistance to Moscow represented a powerful trend among the rank and file of the Party. But the rest of the leadership were in a different position. Stalin's war on the peasants had truly placed them in a position in which, in Lenin's phrase, 'who-whom?' was the only immediate question. Whatever their hidden reservations and whatever they may have thought of the plans which had led to the crisis, they could no more be expected to indulge them than a general fighting a desperate battle can spend time arguing about the strategic errors of the High Command.

But still, they seem to have become shaken and exhausted by the loyal fulfilment of Stalin's collectivization orders.

On 24 January 1933 a resolution of the All-Union Central Committee attacked the Ukrainian Party:

The Party organs in the Ukraine have not succeeded in carrying out the Party charges entrusted to them in the areas of organization of grain storage and completion of the plan for grain collection.

Three of the seven Provincial Secretaries were censured and removed, together with three members of the local Politburo and Secretariat. And the major figure Postyshev, hitherto Secretary of the All-Union Central Committee, was sent to the Republic as Second Secretary, with plenary powers. Throughout 1933 non-Ukrainian Party workers of more unquestionable loyalty were transferred into the Republic from Russia. (It is estimated that there were some 5,000 of these.) [71]

On 8–11 June 1933 Skrypnik was strongly attacked. He refused to recant, and was violently rebuked by Postyshev for his attitude. Other attacks followed in the press, and on 7 July he committed suicide. His example may have been the Ukrainian writer Khvylovy, who had just done the same when accused of excessive Ukrainian feeling.

Skrypnik had been one of the three representatives of underground organizations who came to the conference of Bolshevik leaders in Paris in 1909. Next day *Pravda* described his suicide as 'an act of cowardice': Skrypnik, 'an unworthy member of the Central Committee', had fallen prey to bourgeois-nationalist mistakes. And, as Petrovsky said, 'It was not easy for us to ward off these nationalist attacks, since the chief aggressor was an Old Bolshevik, Skrypnik.' [72] However, Petrovsky added, Moscow had helped 'by sending well-known Party members to aid us'. And in particular he congratulated the new O.G.P.U. chief, Balitsky, who had accompanied Postyshev.

Skrypnik's supporters were disposed of by the unmasking of a 'Ukrainian Military Organization' consisting mainly of the post-1930 generation of academic leaders in the Institute of Linguistics, the State Publishing House, the School of Marxist Philosophy and the Shevchenko Institute of Literary Scholarship.

After Skrypnik's death there were no major attacks on the cadres of the Ukraine until Postyshev's fall in early 1937. When Chubar was called to Moscow to be All-Union Vice-Premier, he was replaced as Chairman of the Ukrainian Council of People's Commissars by Panas Lyubchenko, a former Borotbist, who shared his views – a slight and light-bearded figure with a sensitive, intellectual face, who had given satisfaction by his firmness in the collectivization struggle.

With Postyshev's ouster in March 1937, a purge swept the Party officials at the provincial and local level. Two thirds of the provincial and one third of the locality leaderships were changed.[73] This did not at first affect the remainder of the leadership, which, as we have said, was re-elected with all the correct formalities at the XIIIth Congress of the Communist Party of the Ukraine (May–June 1937), even though this Congress had to pass a resolution condemning errors in all ideological fields – the press, the Marx–Lenin Institute, the Institute of Red Professors and elsewhere – and make strong attacks on Postyshev and the old Kiev leadership.* Kossior, who had been comparatively mild at the time of Postyshev's demotion, now spoke of lack of vigilance at the top which had allowed Trotskyites to penetrate the Kiev Provincial Committee.[75] A day or two later, he denounced Postyshev by name for 'co-opting numerous enemies' into the provincial apparatus.[76] It was presumably the unfortunate Karpov who was meanwhile referred to by a Moscow Party periodical in a denunciation of 'a former secretary of the Central Committee' of the Ukraine, who had refused to believe accusations that one of his staff was a Trotskyite and had left him in a post in which, until his arrest, he had had access to secret documents.[77]

Signs began to accumulate of pressure being put on the Ukrainian leaders. When greetings were sent to Chkalov and his aircrew on 20 June 1937, those from Moscow were signed with the names of the leaders, but that from the Central Committee of the Communist Party of the Ukraine was anonymous, contrary to previous practice. On 15 July 'leading organs' in the Republic were attacked, in particular for the transfer of Postyshev's 'Trotskyites' from Kiev to other posts throughout the Republic. On 21 July the Ukrainian Radio came under heavy attack.[78] At the same time, the Ukrainian Komsomol was severely criticized and its secretary, Klinkov, denounced as an enemy of the people;[79] and the Central Committee of the

---

* At about this time, the Ukrainian N.K.V.D. chief, Balitsky, full member of the All-Union Central Committee, who had come to Kiev in Postyshev's entourage, was transferred and soon afterwards arrested. He was referred to by Khrushchev as a Fascist agent the following year.[74]

Ukrainian Party was criticized as such for 'tolerating the subversive work of the enemy among the youth'.[80] At some time in July the first member of the Ukrainian Politburo, Shelekhes, was arrested.[81]

In 'glorious, royal Kiev city', commanding the great plain from the cliffs of the Dnieper, everything appeared normal to the uninformed observer. In the tranquil Ukrainian summer, the concerts went on regularly in the cypress-walled outdoor auditorium. But even the musicians were under pressure, with all the other cultural agencies, and the Director of the Ukrainian State Opera, Yanovsky, was soon to be among those denounced as Fascists.

For though the Ukrainian leadership had accepted the Purge as far as resolutions were concerned, and though mass dismissals at the lower level, and unregulated arrests by the N.K.V.D., were rife, the local Politburo and Central Committee were still unbroken. Stalin decided that the time was ripe for crushing them.

Denunciations of treachery and corruption in the Ukraine were now being sent direct to the Kremlin, and the Ukrainian leaders protested that they were not even being given copies. This complaint was made the pretext for massive intervention. A Politburo commission consisting of Molotov, Khrushchev and Yezhov arrived in Kiev in August 1937 with a large force of 'special troops' of the N.K.V.D. At a session of the Ukrainian Central Committee, Molotov proposed the dismissal of Kossior, Petrovsky, Lyubchenko and others from their posts and from the Committee, and suggested the election of Khrushchev as Ukrainian First Secretary.

The Ukrainians refused to vote as instructed, in spite of Molotov ringing Moscow for Stalin's instructions. Finally, Molotov suggested that the Ukrainian Politburo should go to Moscow for a combined session with the U.S.S.R. Politburo.* This

---

*This account of an obscure episode is based on that given by A. Avtorkhanov.[82] There was later confirmation from the Yugoslav leadership that such a mission was sent, though this names only 'Molotov with two members of the Soviet Politburo' as going to Kiev to demand the expulsion of 'Kossior and two others'. It adds that this demand was rejected by the Ukrainian Politburo and Central Committee.[83]

manoeuvre could hardly be rejected without open breach of Party discipline. Rather than walk into the trap, on 30 August Lyubchenko shot himself and his wife. *Pravda*, announcing the suicide on 2 September, attributed it to his 'being entangled in anti-Soviet connexions'.

There are several slightly varying accounts of Lyubchenko's suicide, but they all agree that he and his wife died together. They had two children, a daughter at the university and a thirteen-year-old son. One account has the daughter dying with her parents.

Some members of the Ukrainian 'delegation' which went to Moscow seem to have been arrested at once, others returned to the Ukraine and disappeared *seriatim*. For if Stalin took a sweeping retaliation for the wholly abortive attempt of the All-Union Committee to block him in February and March, the temporarily successful resistance of the Ukrainians provoked even more complete revenge. Over the next year, the whole of the local Politburo, Orgburo and Secretariat were arrested, with the exception of Petrovsky (see p. 629). Of the 102 members and candidate members of the Ukrainian Central Committee, three survived. All the seventeen members of the Ukrainian Government were arrested. All the Provincial Secretaries in the Ukraine fell.

The Purge swept through every sort of establishment in the Republic. The State industrial enterprises, the municipal councils, the educational and scientific bodies – all lost their leaders by the hundred. The Ukrainian Union of Writers was practically annihilated.

Violent attacks on Ukrainian institutions started to appear. The Kiev and Kharkov radio stations were accused of having broadcast funeral marches after the announcement of the verdict in the first two trials, while Kiev had actually gone off the air while the verdict on the Generals was being transmitted. This was the result of 'an enemy organization' which the Ukrainian Central Committee had failed to understand.[84] The educational system was attacked as riddled with nationalists.[85] The museums were also full of spies concerned only to stress anti-Russian Ukrainianism.[86] The Republic had even failed to celebrate Peter the Great's victory at Poltava.[87]

Stalin's Ukrainian victims were slandered in a special way. The oppositionists in the three Great Trials were traitors, Trotskyites, spies and accomplices of the Fascists. But they were not shown as actually describing themselves as Fascists pure and simple. In the Ukraine on the other hand, it was no 'Bloc of Rights and Trotskyites' that was revealed but nothing less than a 'National Fascist Organization' headed by Lyubchenko, leader of the Soviet Government of the Republic, and including Grinko, People's Commissar of Finance in Moscow (another ex-Borotbist), Balitsky, Zatonsky, Yakir and a variety of leading figures in the Ukrainian Government and Central Committee, and such cultural lights as Yanovsky.

For the moment, however, Kossior was spared. He was sent back to Kiev having surrendered to strict instructions on destroying his followers. At a meeting of the Kiev Party organization from 15 to 16 September 1937, he delivered an attack on 'the band of bourgeois nationalists uncovered in the Ukraine'. Zatonsky, People's Commissar for Education, was 'severely blamed' and in reply 'could not say anything'.[88] Zatonsky, a moon-faced man with metal-rimmed glasses, a physics teacher, had, with Pyatakov, led the first Ukrainian Communist Government in 1918, which spent its brief existence in continuous fighting. He was refused entry to the October 1937 plenum of the Central Committee in Moscow; on 3 November he was called out of a university meeting in Kiev and arrested.[89]

Autumn also saw the arrest of Kossior's Third Secretary, N. N. (M. M.) Popov, of Vice-Premier Porayko, and others. K. V. Sukhomlin lasted at least till December, but was shortly afterwards arrested as a Japanese spy.[90] And Postyshev's successor Khatayevich was 'arrested and repressed' before the end of the year.[91]

The turnover was equally rapid at the local level. Kudryavtsev, who had replaced Postyshev in his lesser post as Secretary of the Kiev Provincial Committee of the Party, was removed at the end of 1937 to be denounced as an 'enemy of the people',[92] and his successor D. M. Evtushenko followed on 17 April 1938. They were later linked as the centres of a hostile leadership which had subverted most of the district secretaries of the province.[93]

352   *The Yezhov Years*

Lyubchenko was succeeded as Premier by a young Communist, M. I. Bondarenko. He too was arrested within two months,[94] and for a time there was no Premier at all. Instead, the names of unknown subordinates of Petrovsky appeared on decrees.

Then another Premier, Marchak, was appointed. He was demoted to Deputy Premier by February 1938,[95] and was soon afterwards under arrest.* He is said to have been drinking heavily with Balitsky's successor Leplevsky one night, and to have exchanged with him some remarks sceptical of Tukhachevsky's guilt. Next morning Marchak remembered this, and thought Leplevsky, as N.K.V.D. Commissar in Kiev, might have been acting as a *provocateur*. He rang Yezhov and denounced Leplevsky, who was arrested. Leplevsky in turn implicated Marchak, and they both confessed to conspiracy, terrorism and espionage.[96] Leplevsky's replacement, the third Ukraine N.K.V.D. Commissar to be appointed within a year, was Uspensky, himself to be executed within months.

The Purge was so complete and so quick that legal authority virtually disintegrated. There was no longer a genuine quorum of the Ukrainian Central Committee, nor a body capable of appointing a Government. People's Commissars, irregularly appointed, emerged for days or weeks and then themselves disappeared. The unprecedented sweep of the political leadership marked the effective destruction of the Ukrainian Party. The Republic became little more than an N.K.V.D. fief, where even the formalities of Party and Soviet activity were barely gone through.

Finally, in January 1938, a presumably spurious plenum of the Ukrainian Central Committee elected Khrushchev First Secretary.[97] Khrushchev brought with him from Moscow a new Second Secretary, Burmistenko, who had served in the Cheka for many years in the twenties and later worked closely with Stalin's personal secretariat. As Chairman of the Council of People's Commissars, he brought Demyan Korotchenko (Korotchenkov).†

* He had disappeared from local listings by 15 May.

† In 1939, in the *Stenographic Report of the XVIIIth Congress*, he is actually given with his Ukrainian spelling in the listing of the new Central Committee, and in his Russian spelling in the list of delegates to the Congress.

In May and June 1938 the entire Ukrainian Government was again replaced. Between February and June, all the twelve new Provincial Secretaries were again removed, together with most of their Second Secretaries.[98] At the XIVth. Congress of the Ukrainian Party in June 1938 the new Central Committee had, among its eighty-six members and candidates, only three survivors from the previous year – all non-political or honorary figures. The continuity of rule had for the first time been completely destroyed. Not one of the new Politburo, Orgburo or Secretariat had previously served.

The Politburo was a farcical rump with only six members: Khrushchev, Burmistenko and Korotchenko; the Commander of the Military District, Timoshenko; the latest N.K.V.D. chief of the Republic, Uspensky; and the ubiquitous Shcherbakov – in the Republic for a few months to purge a couple of provincial committees.

They reconstructed the Party from the ground up. In 1938, 1,600 Party members were raised to be secretaries of district and city committees in the Ukraine.[99] Among those who benefited was the young Leonid Brezhnev. He had been raised to Deputy Mayor of Dneprodzerzhinsk in May 1937. In 1938, under the Khrushchev regime, he was promoted to be head of a department of the Dneprodzerzhinsk Provincial Committee, and by the following year was a Secretary of that committee. He never looked back. Another beginning to do well was A. P. Kirilenko (now, 1970, a full member of the Politburo), who became a district Party Secretary in 1938, and a Secretary of the Zaporozhe Provincial Committee the following year.*

Stalin and Khrushchev had succeeded in destroying the old Party cadres in the Ukraine, and replacing them by men distinguished only by disciplined acquiescence in, or enthusiasm for, the new method of rule. This did not solve the problem of the Ukrainian people. Stalin was to tell Roosevelt at Yalta that 'his position in the Ukraine was difficult and insecure'.[100] And he later regretted that it was impracticable to deport the

---

*Few were so lucky. Between 1938 and the next Republican Party Congress in 1940 attrition remained high, if not so high. Of the 119 elected in 1940, seventy-three were new members.

entire nation, as he had done with the small Chechens and Kalmyks.[101]

AT THE CENTRE

While the punitive expeditions sent out by Stalin and Yezhov harried the provinces, Moscow remained the storm centre. Of the seventy-one full members of the Central Committee, about two thirds were normally stationed in the capital: all the full members of the Politburo except Kossior; the People's Commissars; the heads of Central Committee departments, of the Komsomol, of the trade unions; the Comintern's managers – all the concentration of power of a highly centralized machine.

Over this major sector of the Purge, Stalin and Yezhov themselves presided. They received valuable help from Molotov and Voroshilov when required, but on the whole Stalin kept an extremely tight personal grip on proceedings, working through Yezhov alone.

Over the period 1937–8, Yezhov sent in to Stalin 383 lists, containing thousands of names of figures important enough to require his personal approval for their execution.[102] As Yezhov was only in power for just over two years – and in fact his effective working period was rather less – this means that Stalin got such a list rather more often than every other day of 'persons whose cases were under the jurisdiction of the Military Collegium'. A Soviet historian tells us that the lists included 40,000 names.[103] We can envisage Stalin, on arrival at his office, as often as not finding in his In-tray a list of a hundred odd names for death, looking through, and approving them, as part of the ordinary routine of a Kremlin day.

The lists were in the following form:

Comrade Stalin.

I am sending for your approval four lists of people to be tried by the Military Collegium:

      List No. 1 (General)
      List No. 2 (Former military personnel)

List No. 3   (Former personnel of the N.K.V.D.)
List No. 4   (Wives of enemies of the people)*
I request sanction to convict all in the first degree.

                                                    Yezhov

The post-Stalin speaker who quotes this adds that 'first degree' conviction meant death by shooting. The lists were examined by Stalin and Molotov, and on each of them is the notation:

Approved – J. Stalin.
V. Molotov.[105]

Decisions to make an arrest, and even warrants, were often signed months before the arrest was carried out (see pp. 366–7). And, in the same way, leading figures were sometimes decorated with high Orders on the very day of their arrest.[106] The reason given by an N.K.V.D. officer is that the police only informed their immediate superior about the progress of their investigations and Yezhov informed only Stalin.[107]

As in the rest of the country, the new offensive started in May 1937.

Fitzroy Maclean, watching Stalin on the Red Square reviewing stand on 1 May, was already struck by the rest of the Politburo, who 'grinned nervously and moved uneasily from one foot to the other, forgetting the parade and the high office they held and everything else in their mingled joy and terror at being spoken to by him'. Stalin's own expression varied between 'benignity and bored inscrutability'.[108]

They might well feel alarm, for one of their members was absent. His colleagues had perhaps already 'discussed' his case, in the same way that Zhdanov's Leningrad Committee was to 'discuss' Chudov's. Yan Rudzutak, member of the Party since 1905, who had spent ten years in Tsarist prisons and exile, a former full member of the Politburo and now a candidate member, was not among his old comrades. His arrest had apparently just taken place.[109] He was seized at a supper party after the theatre. The N.K.V.D. arrested everyone present. Four women

---

* 'List 4' executions included the wives of Kossior, Eikhe, Chubar and Dybenko.[104]

among them are reported in the Butyrka, still in bedraggled evening dress, three months later.[110] His dacha was taken over by Zhdanov.[111]

Rudzutak was arrested as allegedly a Rightist, leader of a 'reserve centre' ready to take over if Bukharin's was exposed, because 'nobody had ever known of any difference between him and the Party'.[112] This is, in fact, an admission that Stalinists of long standing were now, for the first time, being arrested – especially (but not only) if they showed any signs of opposing the Purge. Rudzutak, in particular, had one very black mark against him, in his failure to recommend the death penalty for Ryutin when Head of the Control Commission in 1932. He had also, apparently, followed the same line at the February–March plenum.

Through May, another great heroic diversion, parallel to the exploits of the aviators of the previous year, was spread in the papers day after day. This was the landing, under the direction of O. Shmidt, of Papanin's group at the North Pole, a fine exploit. The officers of the airlift that took them in and set them up were welcomed by the Party leaders, decorated and followed round the usual celebrations. At the same time, the camp on the ice drifted south through the months, from time to time sending loyal greetings from – and receiving thanks at – the farthest flung outpost of the Party and State.

Through the spring and early summer the other great non-political news was a series of plays and ballets attended by the leaders of the Party and the announcement of long lists of awards to People's Artists in these fields.

Meanwhile, as a particularly fine summer lay on the great plain, the arrests went on. Former oppositionists continued to fall. Nikolai Krestinsky, former member of the Politburo and Secretary of the Central Committee, had been removed from the Foreign Commissariat to be Assistant People's Commissar of Justice of the R.S.F.S.R. in March.[113] On his transfer, he spoke approvingly of his removal to the Party cell, saying that even ex-oppositionists should not, in present circumstances, work in the Foreign Commissariat, where leading figures should have the absolute confidence of the leadership and a spotless past.[114]

At the end of May he was arrested. After a week-long interrogation,[115] he started to confess on about 5 June.[116] Bukharin, with whom he was to appear in court as a fellow-conspirator nine months later, had just begun his evidence.[117]

The way in which any sort of connexion with the arrested oppositionists was made a crime can be seen in the case of the veteran Lomov, Party member since 1903, who, representing the Moscow Bureau of the Bolshevik Party, had (after Trotsky) been Lenin's most enthusiastic supporter in the Central Committee in pressing for the seizure of power in November 1917.

In June 1937, an official of the U.S.S.R. State Planning Commission sent a letter to Stalin alleging that G. I. Lomov (Oppokov), a member of the Bureau of the U.S.S.R. Council of People's Commissars' Soviet Control Commission, had been on friendly terms with Rykov and Bukharin. Stalin wrote on this letter the instructions: 'To Comrade Molotov. What to do?' Molotov wrote: 'I'm for arresting this scum Lomov immediately, V. Molotov.'* A few days later Lomov was arrested, charged with membership in a Right Opportunist organization, and shot.[119]

Lomov (who seems to have been shot in 1938)[120] was to be mentioned at the Bukharin Trial as a fellow conspirator with Bukharin against Lenin.[121]

But even now opposition was not entirely crushed. In the last week of June, another plenum of the Central Committee was held – ostensibly to discuss vegetable production. It was the scene of mutual denunciations and disappearances on the spot. Nazaretyan (not, indeed, a member of the Central Committee, but of the lesser Central Revision Commission), whom Ordzhonikidze had saved in the early thirties, was arrested while actually on his way to the Kremlin to the plenum.[122] In a few months Stalin had progressed far in his ability to loose the secret police, without attention to political protocol, on to his opponents. His speech is said to have been in ruthless style, demanding, for example, less 'coddling' of prisoners.[123]

---

*Stalin seems to have gone through the formality of implicating Molotov in decisions to purge men working in the Government, as Lomov was. On the other hand, we are also told that Molotov countersigned the order to arrest Kabakov, a Party official pure and simple.[118]

In the meeting-hall, many faces were already missing – Bukharin's and Rykov's, Rudzutak's and Chudov's, Gamarnik's and Yakir's, Yagoda's and half a dozen others. But the spirit of resistance had not yet been entirely quelled. 'After the February plenum of the Central Committee a campaign was raised in the conspirators' circles against Yezhov . . . an attempt was made to discredit Yezhov and the work he was doing in the Party, to slander him.'[124] And even as late as this June plenum there was still at least one man brave enough to rise and speak against the Terror. This was the doomed Health Commissar Kaminsky, who again stuck to his point. Among other things he attacked Beria, denouncing him as a former agent of the Azerbaijan nationalist intelligence service.[125] Kaminsky, who had joined the Bolshevik Party as a medical student some years before the Revolution, was arrested the day he made his protest.[126]

In the midst of the swing into total terror, yet another diversion was provided by Russian airmen. In June, Chkalov and his crew flew their ANT–25 over the Pole to Falkland, Oregon, and in July Gromov flew another to San Jacinto, California, setting up a world distance record. The two flights, both fine achievements, were the occasion for a further great press campaign, pages and pages of newspapers being filled with greetings, meetings, lives of the airmen, photographs, and so on. When Chkalov finally crashed on 15 December 1938, Belyakin, Head of the Main Administration of the Aircraft Industry, Usachev, Director of the plant where the plane had been built, and Tomashevich, the designer, were shot for sabotage.[127]

The papers continued to carry general calls to vigilance, and accounts of various methods used by the enemy. *Pravda* drew attention to misprints in the local press which amounted to sabotage – for example, a reference to the *bedy* (sorrows) rather than the *pobedy* (victories) of Socialism. And local trials were frequently reported. But the great blow was that now being delivered against the leading cadres of the regime, which was to ravage the old Central Committee, and destroy the next level of the Party command in their thousands.

For it was now, starting in May 1937, that the flower of Stalin's long-nurtured administrative and political machine started to go.

After Rudzutak no member or candidate member of the Politburo was to be arrested during the year, and several officials only just junior to them hung on until a specially mounted top-level operation in November and December took them. But for the moment, there was a broad sweep of their subordinates, running as high as men like Antipov, Vice-Chairman of the Council of People's Commissars, Party member since 1902, several times arrested under Tsarism, and organizer of underground printing-plants, who had been among the half-dozen appearing with the Politburo on the May Day platform.* (Another who had been on that platform was the bald, Mongol-type Akulov. Stalin had tried to put him in control of the O.G.P.U., as his direct agent, in the early thirties. He had been Vyshinsky's predecessor as Prosecutor-General. He now held Yenukidze's old and prestigious post of Secretary of the Central Executive Committee. He was removed on 9 July and has not since been heard of.)

In the Central Committee apparatus, Malenkov's Department of Leading Party Organs was overseeing a thorough 'renewal'. Another figure who was to be named though not produced as one of the most important links in the Bukharin plot was Ya. A. Yakovlev, former People's Commissar for Agriculture, and now Head of the Agricultural Department of the Central Committee. He figured prominently in the press over June, and was the *rapporteur* on 28 June to the June plenum on its sole published item of discussion, vegetables. After that he fades out until his extraordinary transmogrification into a Rightist in March 1938 – an odd appellation for the man who had been a chief operator in the collectivization field.

Another head of a Central Committee Department now to disappear had at one time almost reached the summits of power – K. Ya. Bauman, head of the Central Committee's Scientific Department. He had been Secretary of the Central Committee and candidate member of the Politburo (as Uglanov's replacement) for a few months in 1929–30. An enthusiastic Stalinist, he had been the scapegoat for the first excesses of collectivization,

*His 'activity was cut short' in 1937[128] and he was named as a major conspirator, 'the leader of the parallel group of the Rights',[129] at the Bukharin Trial, without, however, appearing in dock.

but he had remained on the Central Committee. He was shot on 14 October 1937. With him went most of the staff of his department. The head of the parallel, but more important, Agitation and Propaganda Department, Stetsky, an old economist who had held the post since 1929, was also arrested about this time, and later shot.

Cynicism prevailed as well as terror. A senior Army officer in prison mentioned that he was once cheerfully greeted at a reception by Molotov's wife, with the words 'Ah, Sasha, whatever's this? Why haven't you been arrested yet?'[130] She had become head of the Cosmetics Trust (a post she was to hold for some years) through the elimination of her boss Chekalov, who was sent to the Vorkuta railway camps,[131] and she was to be a member of the 1939 Central Committee which replaced the men now disappearing. Her own arrest came in 1948.

An atmosphere of fear hung over the Party and Government offices. People's Commissars were arrested on their way to their jobs in the mornings. Every day another Central Committee member or Vice-Chairman of a People's Commissariat or one of their more important underlings was disappearing. In one sphere alone, for the moment, joy prevailed. Yezhov was awarded the Order of Lenin on 18 July, an occasion for photographs, leading articles and general celebrations. Vyshinsky received the same award on 21 July, though with less panache.

Orders were now also handed out to many leading police officials. On the completion of the Mdivani Case, the Georgian N.K.V.D. men received their reward. One notes among them the names of men who a year later were to replace the current operators in Moscow and elsewhere, and who were only to perish at the end of the Beria epoch, in 1953–5: Goglidze, Kobulov, Rapava and their like.[132] Other awards soon went to a group of Yezhov's men, including Ushakov (who was later to supervise the torture of Eikhe), Frinovsky and, as a junior, the long-surviving L. E. Vlodzimirsky, who was to serve Beria and be brought back by him in 1953 to be head of the Section for Investigating Specially Important Cases, and be shot in December of that year.

Yezhov himself was now to get the highest accolade, a town

named for him. On 22 July Kaganovich's protégé, the ex-O.G.P.U. man Bulganin, was appointed Chairman of the Council of People's Commissars of the Russian Republic. The fall of his predecessor, Sulimov, involved a change in the name of the town of Sulimov, capital of the Cherkess Autonomous Province, which was now suitably renamed Yezhovo-Cherkesk.

Bulganin's later colleague and rival Khrushchev was conducting his own purge in the local machine of the city and province to the satisfaction of the authorities. He had started in late March, as in Leningrad.[133] Now, at a meeting of the Moscow Provincial Committee on 23 August, he made a series of attacks on local leaders like Filatov, Chairman of the Provincial Executive Committee, which presaged his disappearance, with many others. Ukhanov, Khrushchev's Chairman of the Moscow Soviet up till recently, was now filling one of the ministerial vacancies as People's Commissar for Local Industry, and it was from there that he was seized – to die in 1939.[134] Like Antipov, Yakovlev, Stetsky and Sulimov, he was a full member of the Central Committee.

August saw one of the biggest tourist influxes ever to reach Russia. The visitors noted no public gloom. Once again a great Soviet flight was being celebrated – that of Levanevsky and his N-209 around the Union. The papers were full of celebrations, though they had time also, towards the end of the month, to announce the awards of Orders of Lenin to the hard-worked Military Jurists, including Ulrikh, Matulevich and Nikitchenko[135] (the two latter described as Vice-Presidents of the Military Collegium), and to Prosecutors like Roginsky.[136]

Meanwhile, the Commissars and Vice-Commissars of the economic Commissariats went the way of Ukhanov. Some, like Chernov, Commissar for Agriculture, removed on 30 October, Grinko, Commissar for Finance, and Ivanov, Commissar of the Timber Industry, were to appear in the next great trial. Others, like M. Rukhimovich, Commissar for the Defence Industry, who had been appearing with the highest leadership for a few months and lost his post in October 1937[137] (being replaced by Kaganovich's brother, M. M. Kaganovich), were not to be heard of again. Rukhimovich had supported Stalin against all the oppositionists; earlier he had been one of Stalin's and Voroshilov's closest accomplices in the intrigues against Trotsky in Tsaritsyn in the Civil War. He died in 1939.[138] In the same category comes Lyubimov, People's Commissar for Light Industry, who was removed, with both his Assistant Commissars, on 7 September.*[139]

By the end of the year few Commissars apart from Voroshilov and Kaganovich remained. In addition to those already named, the Commissars for Communications (Khalepsky), for Internal Trade (Veitser), for Heavy Industry (Mezhlauk), for Education (Bubnov), for Justice (Krylenko), for Sea and River Transport (Yanson) were arrested, together with successive heads of the National Bank and their subordinates.

For the moment we may consider one last case in more detail – that of the naturally sensitive Commissariat of Foreign Trade. Its head, Rosengolts, was removed on 15 June for 'other work'. Both his assistants, Eliava and Loganovsky, disappeared – Eliava to be shot during the year.[141]

Rosengolts, broad-shouldered, strong-minded and Jewish, was an excellent administrator. He had in the past few years accommodated himself to the new style of rule. He had been brought up in a revolutionary family. When only ten years old, 'My hand, the hand of a child, was used to hide illegal literature during the night and to recover it in the morning from a place where the hand of a grown-up could not reach.'[142] He joined the Bolshevik Party at fifteen or sixteen and was first arrested when sixteen years old. At the age of seventeen he was nominated as a delegate to the Party Congress. During the Revolution he had fought in Moscow, and in the Civil War had been prominent at various fronts. He had ruled the Donbas in a ruthless fashion. After a brief flirtation with the Trotsky opposition, he was appointed to the London Embassy. In 1928 he returned and had since worked in the Government, holding his present post since 1930.

Rosengolts was still referred to as 'Comrade' in the June decree releasing him from his post, and for some time no further move was made against him. This was in accordance with a

---

* Lyubimov seems to have been done away with almost at once. His death date is given as 1937 in a recent book.[140] But he was to be mentioned as a link to the Bukharinite 'Reserve Centre' at the March 1938 Trial.

common practice of Stalin's. Arrest was decided on, the dismissal occurred, and then for months the victim was left in some minor post, never knowing when the blow would fall. An American resident in Moscow in August 1937 describes a high official seen, day after day, waiting on a balcony opposite to be arrested. 'Waiting was killing him. He waited three more weeks while the G.P.U. watched and while his wife wasted away. Then the G.P.U. came.'[143] Some survivors have described this as psychologically more wearing and destructive even than the eventual imprisonment and interrogation, and they add that the state to which a man was reduced made the process of interrogation a fairly easy one for the N.K.V.D. In fact, some of its work had been done for it already without its officers having to move a finger, a useful saving of energy in a hard-worked organization.

Rosengolts was left to sweat it out for many weeks. He was still at large in August when he made several desperate attempts to get an interview with Stalin – later to be interpreted as an assassination attempt.[144] On his wife, 'a jolly, red-haired girl, very imperfectly educated and brought up in a religious household',[145] the weeks and months of anxiety must have been frightful. She did all she could think of.

When her husband was finally arrested, the routine N.K.V.D. search revealed, sewn into his hip pocket, a small piece of dry bread wrapped in a strip of cloth. Inside the bread was a piece of paper on which she had written out, as a charm against evil fortune, eight verses from the 68th and the 91st Psalms, ancient cries of the helpless against their oppressors:

LXVIII

1. Let God arise, and let his enemies be scattered: let them also that hate him, flee before him.
2. Like as the smoke vanisheth, so shalt thou drive them away: and like as wax melteth at the fire, so let the ungodly perish at the presence of God. . . .

XCI

1. Whoso dwelleth under the defence of the most High: shall abide under the shadow of the Almighty.

2. I will say unto the Lord, Thou art my hope, and my stronghold: my God, in him will I trust.

3. For he shall deliver thee from the snare of the hunter: and from the noisome pestilence.

4. He shall defend thee under his wings and thou shalt be safe under his feathers: his faithfulness and truth shall be thy shield and buckler.

5. Thou shalt not be afraid for any terror by night: nor for the arrow that flieth by day;

6. For the pestilence that walketh in darkness: nor for the sickness that destroyeth in the noon-day . . .[146]

CLOSING IN ON THE POLITBURO

As the tempo of the public side of the Purge eased somewhat in the autumn of 1937, Stalin began to prepare the next phase. A number of figures, including Bukharin and Rykov themselves, were under interrogation with a view to public trial. A number of unsatisfactory Stalinists like Rudzutak and Antipov, though they were still perhaps resisting, lay ready as a possible reserve for the Bukharin Case, or alternatively as the central figures of a later trial. But much remained to be done.

The rank and file of the February–March opposition had been crushed. But the senior figures involved were still in positions in the highest leadership. Until these, and any others who had shown restiveness or independence, could be eradicated, there was a flaw, a weak spot, in the structure of autocracy.

The problem presented by the Politburo Stalinists who had opposed the General Secretary at the February–March plenum was a new one. They were not, like Zinoviev and Bukharin, men long removed from the centres of power, nor even, like Pyatakov, men long relegated to second-rank positions in the Government and Party. It is true that they constituted a minority and that – except for Kossior and (previously) Postyshev's control of the Ukrainian machine – they had little grip on any true instruments of power. They nevertheless represented a higher potential of trouble than their predecessors. The one serious combination which, Stalin may have thought, remained was a combination of a group of 'moderate' leaders with the Army. Nor was the striking-down of the Army leaders in June 1937 entirely conclusive. Other commanders survived who could conceivably give trouble. In any case, Stalin proceeded with his usual combination of gradualness and ruthlessness.

But first, certain technical moves were called for. Since the decree of August 1936, people had been making a nuisance of themselves by complaining that their snap trials and executions were illegal. At any rate, on 14 September a decree was issued to introduce 'simplified trial procedures', in cases under Articles 58(vii), 58(viii) and 58(ix) of the Criminal Code. It forbade appeals and also petitions for clemency, the right to which had been restored in 1936 with the object of deceiving Zinoviev and Co. More interesting still, the new decree 'eliminated publicity in court trials'.[147] There are some obvious anomalies: in the first place, many trials must already have been held without any, or any effective, public attendance; second, the Bukharin Trial, with its vast publicity, was yet to come. Still, however we take the decree, it may perhaps reflect some sort of decision by Stalin to bring public trials to an end as soon as the one then in hand was over. It is sometimes argued that the partial failure of the Bukharin Trial itself led to the dropping of any further court proceedings. This decree shows that the decision may have been taken earlier. It is indeed true that the Bukharin Case seems to have been giving Yezhov a good deal of trouble. While Pyatakov and Radek were ready for open court in four months, nine months had already passed since Bukharin's and Rykov's arrest, and they were not to be adequately prepared for another three or four months yet. However, the plans for the Bukharin Trial were now, as we shall see, reaching the stage in which all possible ingredients had been established – assassination, medical murder, industrial and agricultural sabotage, espionage, bourgeois nationalism, and treason. Each trial so far had added crimes to the roster, but after this there would be no further lesson to rub in.

On 2 October came a law increasing the maximum term of imprisonment from ten to twenty-five years.[148] And a short plenum on 11–12 October celebrated the end of overt opposition by electing Yezhov a candidate member of the Politburo. This plenum also saw the fall of a prominent figure in circumstances even more high-handed than had previously been noted.

The People's Commissar for Education, Andrei Bubnov, was one of the most prominent of all Old Bolsheviks. He had been a delegate to the 1907 Congress, a candidate member of the Central Committee in 1912, and a member of the original Political Bureau set up to direct the Revolution in October 1917. With Pyatakov he had organized the Communist revolt in the Ukraine in August 1918. A Democratic Centralist in the early days, he had switched to Stalin's side as early as 1923, rigorously purging faction in the Army, and had served loyally ever since. At the October plenum he and his Ukrainian opposite number as Education Commissar, Zatonsky, went to the Central Committee building, but, on showing their Central Committee membership cards, were told by the N.K.V.D. officer on duty that they could not be admitted without further documents which had not been issued to them. Bubnov went back to his Ministry and worked late. At midnight his secretary came in trembling and told him that the radio had just announced his removal for inability to cope with his duties. Next day he handed over to the transient Tyurkin,[149] and was arrested in December.[150]

While Party trials and death sentences continued, they were now for a time rarer, and they were not given front-page treatment. The great propaganda campaign receded. The press began to fill with the preparations for elections to the Supreme Soviet. Every type of electoral article appropriate to a democracy began to appear – 'Women Voters, a Powerful Force', for example. And following them, the nominations of all the leaders in good odour, and page after page of enthusiastic meetings all around the Union, filled the papers day after day through October.

But Stalin was preparing for action against his unsatisfactory followers. A document (still in existence) was signed by Stalin, Molotov and Kaganovich in November, to sanction 'the arraignment ... before a court of the Military Collegium of a large number of comrades from the ranks of prominent Party, State and military workers'.[151] The 1961 speaker who gave this information went on to say:

Most of them were shot. Those innocently shot and posthumously rehabilitated include such prominent Party and State figures as Comrades Postyshev, Kossior, Eikhe, Rudzutak and Chubar; People's

Commissar of Justice Krylenko; Unshlikht, Secretary of the U.S.S.R. Central Executive Committee; People's Commissar of Education Bubnov, and others.

This strongly implies (though it does not actually assert) that these men were on the list referred to. Some, indeed, were already under arrest, but under the old procedure were presumably still being interrogated with the intention of any formal 'arraigning' being postponed until the confessions had been obtained.

The authorization by Stalin, Kaganovich and Molotov, presumably in the name of the Central Committee and the Council of Ministers, is a peculiar procedure. On the whole – except in the case of arrest of members of the Politburo itself – Stalin seems to have followed the forms of getting full Politburo permission for important arrests. At least, though this was perhaps not done during the critical period 1937–8, reports of later years give this pattern. *

What is more extraordinary is that some of the arrests now authorized were not carried out for weeks or months – that the accused remained in high posts for longish periods.

The procedure with regard to ordinary Party members seems to have been that just before an arrest, the N.K.V.D. would inform the local Party committee, or in the case of important members, the Central Committee, that a warrant had been issued. The member was then expelled from the Party in secret session and was not informed of the expulsion until arrested. Sometimes the period between these clandestine expulsions and the arrests was quite long. A case is reported of a District Party Secretary in the Ukraine who was secretly expelled by the Ukrainian Central Committee in March 1938 and not arrested until July, meanwhile carrying on as usual, and even expelling other members.[153] (Again, a foreign Communist arrested on 19 June 1938 was shown the order for her arrest dated 15 October 1937.)[154] Needless to say, the procedure was contrary to Party statutes.

Meanwhile, Postyshev still held his post in Kuibyshev and was

* An assistant Minister arrested in 1950 told his interrogator that Mikoyan would intercede for him and was shown the order for his arrest signed by the whole Politburo, including Mikoyan.[152]

still a candidate member of the Politburo. Kossior was still First Secretary of the Ukraine, and a full member of the Politburo; Chubar, Vice-Chairman of the Council of People's Commissars and full member of the Politburo; and the others in their relevant posts.

Who the 'prominent military workers' referred to were has not been made explicit, but these were now falling, or about to fall, in numbers, as we have seen. The 'others' must include the important figure of V. I. Mezhlauk, who now held the Commissariat of Heavy Industry, and had since the spring been appearing on platforms with the Politburo itself.[155] Mezhlauk, plumply square, balding, with glasses, was arrested in December 1937.[156]

Unshlikht, a Pole in the Dzerzhinsky tradition, had been a pro-Bolshevik member of the Polish Social Democratic Party since 1900. A member of the Petrograd Revolutionary Committee, he had served in the Civil War with Tukhachevsky, in the Sixteenth Army, and had been wounded. He had later been Vice-Chairman of the All-Russian Cheka. By the end of the year he too had been arrested.[157]

The lesser figure of Krylenko, who had impressed Bruce Lockhart in 1918 as an 'epileptic degenerate', is referred to in 1938 by a fellow-prisoner as 'notorious and universally despised'.[158]

We describe his disgraceful role at the Shakhty Trial in Appendix F. A recent Soviet article actually praises it:

In our courts the legal assessment is inevitably combined with the moral and political ones. Krylenko always gave that fact proper consideration. . . . Appearing in the Shakhty Trial, for example, this is how the orator stresses the special role of our Soviet court. 'Our court is an organ by means of which the directing vanguard of the proletariat, the working class as a whole, is building a new society. That is why its verdicts must be a definite instrument of political work, must be a definite instrument of educational, legal and political propaganda.'[159]

He had shown farcical dogmatism at a Congress of Chess Players in 1932:

We must finish once and for all with the neutrality of chess. We must condemn once and for all the formula 'chess for the sake of chess', like the formula 'art for art's sake'. We must organize shock-brigades of chess-players, and begin the immediate realization of a Five-Year Plan for chess.[160]

These qualities of doctrinaire fanaticism he took with him into the judicial side of Stalin's Purge. People's Commissar for Justice of the R.S.F.S.R. in 1931, in 1936 he took over the U.S.S.R. Commissariat for Justice.

On his arrest, he was treated in the Butyrka with special indignity, 'to take the conceit out of him'.[161] After a time he was taken to the Lefortovo, where all trace of him was lost. One of the charges seems to have been that he retarded the development of chess and cut it off from the social and political life of the nation.[162] He appears to have been shot in 1940.[163]

The doomed Politburo members remained free for the moment. Even Postyshev, in spite of demotion, was still not proceeded against. He is now said to have had a last conversation with Stalin, after he had been transferred to Kuibyshev, and to have frankly denounced the Purge, at least as it applied to loyal Party members.[164] However, in June, he had been given reasonable headlines for his speech to the Party conference in his new fief at Kuibyshev: it was a call, extreme even by the standards then prevailing, for the vigilant uprooting of Trotskyites.

Eikhe, a large, serious-looking man, smooth-moustached, with a reputation for ruthlessness, a Party member since 1905, was made People's Commissar for Agriculture in Chernov's place on 30 October.[165] In the West Siberian Territory, which had hitherto been his satrapy, Vyshinsky had alleged[166] an inadequate number of prosecutions for counter-revolutionary activity in 1937, a fact which may well be due to Eikhe's attitude or at least have figured in the later charges against him.

On 3 November 1937 a poster for the Republican elections, consisting of portraits of the Politburo, was put out. It contained all the full members, including Kossior and Chubar, but of the candidate members only Zhdanov and Yezhov were shown. Eikhe, Postyshev and Petrovsky were thus demonstratively snubbed. In fact, throughout this period, signs of degradation were visited on the candidate members of the Politburo who were later to fall. They were omitted from honorary Presidiums. Large numbers of lists of nominations for the December election of the Supreme Soviet starting in late October usually left them out (and often omitted Kossior too).* On the other hand, they were included in the conventional letter of important figures refusing multiple nomination on instructions of the Central Committee.[168] And all (Kossior, Postyshev, Eikhe, Chubar and Petrovsky) were returned in the elections which followed.

For the best part of two months, till the actual voting on 12 December and afterwards, these elections were given intense prominence and publicity. Every day, articles, photographs, lists of places where Politburo members would speak, the addresses of meetings to their candidates, and a vast apparatus of joyful expectancy reigned on paper. Mass resolutions were printed under such headings as 'With Joy We Vote for Nikolai Ivanovich Yezhov'; poems, such as one by Stalin's Kazakh hack bard Dzhambul, 'People's Commissar Yezhov', gave a view of the police chief which would have been thought excessively rosy if applied to a ruler like Good King Wenceslas.

Throughout December, articles and statements on the elections continued to appear. There were many reports from abroad of, for example, 'The Great Impression Made in England'. And so the days drew on. As the election publicity gradually petered out, there were other themes for the public – for example on the centenary of the Georgian poet Rustaveli – eked out with much Stakhanovite conferencing.

But the year was not to end without a demonstrative killing. Only five months had separated the Zinoviev and Pyatakov Trials. Since then eleven had passed, and the Bukharin case was still not ready. As an interim measure, a group of men who were not prepared to confess was tried *in camera* under the 14 September law.

On 20 December 1937 the papers ran page after page to celebrate the twentieth anniversary of the VCHEKA.-O.G.P.U.-N.K.V.D., with pictures of Dzerzhinsky and Yezhov. That body's vigilance had been demonstrated the previous day by the announcement of a purge in the bread distribution organizations. Workers' meetings sent applause, and poems about the

* Petrovsky and Eikhe, though not Postyshev, were included in one list.[167]

splendid role of the Secret Police appeared in profusion. *Pravda* carried a long article by Frinovsky, and also a long list of awards, including the Order of Lenin to Boris Berman. Among this feast of laudatory generalization, a short announcement, perhaps postponed for the occasion, drew attention to the more practical side of the work of Yezhov's men. It said that on 16 December Yenukidze, with Karakhan, Orakhelashvili and others, had been tried before the Military Collegium of the Supreme Court as spies, bourgeois nationalists and terrorists, had confessed and had been executed.[169]

Yenukidze is reported, in not very bad condition, being moved from Suzdal isolator to Moscow in the autumn of 1937.[170] In the Bukharin Trial he was to be made the central villain of terrorist activity, held responsible for the organization of the murder of Kirov, and said to have instructed Yagoda to tell Zaporozhets not to hinder the act.[171] He was also responsible for plotting the murder of Gorki.[172] It was rumoured less officially that in fact he not only refused to confess, but made statements implicating Stalin in the Kirov murder and other deaths.[173]

Orakhelashvili, who had been Secretary of the Georgian Central Committee, had for the past five years acted as Deputy Director of the Marx–Engels–Lenin Institute in Moscow. He is now said to have lost his life as a result of objecting to Beria's book on the Bolshevik movement in the Caucasus, which was heavily faked to give Stalin a major role. There is something of a mystery about Orakhelashvili's death. It was definitely stated that 'the sentence had been carried out'. But some recent reference books give his death date as 1940.[174] His wife Marya was also shot.[175]

On 21 December there was a grand ceremonial meeting for the N.K.V.D. in the Bolshoi Theatre in the presence of Kaganovich, Molotov, Voroshilov, Mikoyan and Khrushchev. The whole of the full membership of the Politburo, including Kossior and Chubar (who were not present), were elected to the honorary Presidium, but only Zhdanov and Yezhov among the candidate members, the remaining places being taken by Khrushchev and Bulganin. Mikoyan was the main speaker, lavishing praise on Yezhov as 'a talented faithful pupil of Stalin . . . beloved by the

Soviet people', and as having 'achieved the greatest victory in the history of the Party, a victory we will never forget'. He concluded, 'Learn the Stalinist style of work from Comrade Yezhov, as he learned it from Comrade Stalin!'[176]

In January came an important plenum of the Central Committee and the presentation of a new Government to the Supreme Soviet. The positions of Postyshev and Kossior were affected. Postyshev, still described as 'Comrade', was replaced as candidate member of the Politburo by Khrushchev.[177] (This was the last occasion on which a removal from the Politburo was officially announced. Henceforth names simply disappeared from lists and photographs.) *Pravda*'s leader of the same day denounced the heads of certain Party organizations, giving that of Kuibyshev as an example, for having around them 'sworn enemies of the people', while expelling honest elements. The Central Committee resolution menacingly noted that the N.K.V.D. had had to intervene to save slandered Party members expelled in the province.[178] Postyshev had also in fact received a confidential Party censure while in Kuibyshev for 'protecting enemies of the people'.[179] But he was not arrested immediately. He had a small flat in Moscow, where he was visited after this by his fighter-pilot son.[180] There he seems to have remained till his arrest in the spring.

Kossior, in Kiev among the crumbled remnants of his power, had had a bad year. His brother I. V. Kossior, also a member of the Central Committee, had died in apparent good odour on 3 July, though it has lately been revealed that this was, in reality, a suicide like Ordzhonikidze's.[181] Another brother, V. V. Kossior, an old oppositionist, had been given ten years' in 1934 and been implicated again in the Pyatakov Trial;[182] during the summer he had been one of a batch of oppositionists brought from Vorkuta to Moscow and shot. Kossior and Petrovsky went to Kiev on 26 January 1938 and were welcomed on the station by the supposititious Ukrainian Central Committee. On 27 January its 'plenum' released Kossior from his post.[183] The First Secretaryship of the Ukraine was transferred, as we have seen, to the coming man, Nikita Khrushchev.[184] But far from falling into immediate oblivion, Kossior was appointed instead Vice-Chairman of the

U.S.S.R. Council of People's Commissars and President of the Soviet Control Commission.

In fact, the new Government presented by Molotov to the Supreme Soviet on 19 January 1938 had as its three Vice-Premiers S. V. Kossior, Chubar and Mikoyan, while Eikhe was People's Commissar for Agriculture.[185]

The Vice-Chairmen of the Council of People's Commissars cannot indeed seriously have thought of themselves as holding powerful positions. Both Voroshilov and Kaganovich, in charge of important departments and invariably ranking senior to them in Party listings, were not at this time Vice-Premiers – an adequate demonstration of the post's comparatively decorative significance.

Even so, we have the extraordinary spectacle of Molotov taking the chair at a meeting of the Council of Ministers, the official order for the trial and arrest of several of whose members he had already signed. At meetings of himself and the Vice-Premiers, two out of the three supposedly contributing to policy discussions were actually no more than dead men talking, whose opinions were by now quite meaningless.

During the Khrushchev period it was customary to speak of the January 1938 plenum as marking a return to legality, it being thought suitable for such a turn of events to mark Khrushchev's promotion to the highest levels. Indeed, the Resolution of the plenum as ever speaks strongly against unjust expulsions from the Party, and this, with the attacks on Provincial Committees for the same error, which were to continue throughout the year, gave that impression to those who wished to receive it. But there was no sign of any real improvement. A Soviet account given in April 1964 managed to satisfy the demands both of Krushchev and of truth by saying 'The January 1938 plenum of the Central Committee of the All-Union Communist Party somewhat improved the situation. However, repressions did not cease.'[186]

It was Yezhov himself who made some of the most critical remarks about the wickedness of expelling members wrongly. Throughout the Terror the leadership had constantly spoken against unfair expulsions – with the aim, however, of destroying their subordinates. For example, as we have seen, in the 1937 attack on Postyshev, where the real motive was to remove an objection to the Terror, the official line was condemnation of inadequate Party democracy. In fact, this can be traced even in the Central Committee's letter of 24 June 1936, which spoke strongly against unprincipled expulsions.[187]

The January 1938 resolution criticizes a large number of local Party organizations in addition to that of Kuibyshev for such practices, blaming officials such as 'the former Secretary of the Kiev Provincial Committee of the Communist Party of the Ukraine, the enemy of the people Kudryavtsev', 'the exposed enemy of the people' Shatsky (head of the Leading Party Organs Administration of the Rostov Provincial Committee), and so on, and telling pathetic tales of honest Bolsheviks, and even their relatives by marriage, losing their jobs as a result of incorrect denunciation.

The persistence of this theme is remarkable. Clearly it was a great advantage to blame Postyshev and others for inhumanity rather than for belated humanity. In this way, the central leadership could, or might think it could, avoid some of the unpopularity arising from its own actions. But we might perhaps go further and see in this a sign that Stalin, right from the start, had determined to put the odium on his instruments and to destroy them when their task was completed. If so, he was to some degree successful. The 'Yezhovshchina' remained the popular name for the Reign of Terror, and with the disappearance of Yezhov himself some of the curse was taken off the surviving leadership.

To complete the changes brought about by the plenum, A. I. Ugarov, already under investigation in Zakovsky's 'Leningrad Case', was appointed on 11 February 1938 to succeed Khrushchev as First Secretary of the Moscow Provincial and City Committees of the Party, and for some months appeared on platforms with the leadership as one of the coming men. (He was to be replaced in October or November by Shcherbakov, and to disappear.)

The Party, as it had existed a year previously, had been broken. From District Secretaries to People's Commissars, the veterans of Stalin's first period of rule had fallen to Yezhov's assault. But further blows were being prepared for the terrified survivors.

CHAPTER NINE

A NATION IN TORMENT

*Of all the treasures a State can possess, the human lives
of its citizens are for us the most precious.*   STALIN

IT is very hard for the Western reader to envisage the sufferings of
the Soviet people as a whole during that time. And in considering
the Terror, it is precisely this moral and intellectual effort which
needs to be made. To demonstrate the facts is no more than
to provide the bare framework of evidence. It is not the province
of the investigator to do more. Yet it cannot but be that these
facts are offered for moral judgement. And however coolly we
consider them we should think in terms of Pasternak, breaking off
his *Sketch for an Autobiography* before the Terror with the words
'To continue it would be immeasurably difficult. . . . One would
have to talk in a manner which would grip the heart and make the
hair stand on end.'

Thus far we have dealt with the Purge as it struck the Party.
Information about this side of it, especially from Soviet sources,
is much richer than for the larger but less dramatic fate of the
ordinary Russian. Yet for every Party member who suffered – and
many of *them* were scarcely political in any real sense – eight or
ten ordinary citizens went to the cells.

The Party figures we have so far been covering were consciously
involved to a greater or lesser degree in a political struggle whose
rules they understood. They had themselves in many cases been
responsible for the imprisonment or death of peasants and others
by the million in the course of collectivization. Our pity for their
own sufferings should doubtless not be withheld, but it can at least
be qualified by a sense of their having a lesser claim to sympathy
than the ordinary people of the country. If Krylenko was to go to
the execution cellars, he had himself sent to their deaths, on false
charges, hundreds of others. If Trotsky was to be assassinated in
exile, he had himself ordered the shooting of thousands of the
rank and file, and gloried in it. Pushkin once described an earlier

generation of Russian revolutionaries as 'positively heartless men who care little for their own skins, and still less for those of others'. We may accept this about such people as Rosengolts. But it plainly does not apply to his wife. In her, we can already see the fate and the feelings of an ordinary non-Communist, caught up in the frightful tensions and agonies of the Great Purge.

The oppressive feeling that hung over everything is well illustrated in a comparison made by Dudorov, in *Doctor Zhivago*:

> It isn't only in comparison with your life as a convict, but compared to everything in the thirties, even to my favourable conditions at the university, in the midst of books and money and comfort; even to me there, the war came as a breath of fresh air, an omen of deliverance, a purifying storm. . . . And when the war broke out, its real horrors, its real dangers, its menace of real death, were a blessing compared with the inhuman power of the lie . . .

It is difficult for those of us who have lived in fairly stable societies to make the imaginative effort of realizing that the heads of a great State can be men who in the ordinary course of events would be thought of as criminals. It is almost equally hard to get the feel of life as it was for the Soviet citizen under the Great Terror. It is easy to speak of the constant fear of the 4 a.m. knock on the door, of the hunger, fatigue and hopelessness of the great labour camps. But to feel how this was worse than a particularly frightful war is not so simple.

Russia had undergone the Terror before. Lenin had spoken of it frankly as an instrument of policy. During the Civil War period executions simply of 'class enemies' were carried out on a large scale. But the circumstances were different in many ways. In those days it was, as it were, a hot Terror. Injustices and brutalities were perpetrated throughout the country; but they were seldom part of a big planned operation from above. They were, rather, fierce and uncontrolled blows at an enemy ready and able to strike back in kind. And they were openly described in their true colours. Those were indeed terrible days, when the Cheka squads were shooting class hostages in scores and hundreds. Those who went through them might have thought that nothing could be worse.

But Lenin's Terror was the product of the years of war and

violence, of the collapse of society and administration, the desperate acts of rulers precariously riding the flood, and fighting for control and survival.

Stalin, on the contrary, attained complete control of the country at a time when general conditions were calm. By the end of the twenties the country had, however reluctantly, accepted the existence and stability of the Soviet Government. And that Government had in turn made slight economic and other concessions which had led to comparative prosperity. It was in cold blood, quite deliberately and unprovokedly, that Stalin started a new cycle of suffering. First had come the Party's war on the peasantry. When this first Stalinist operation had done its worst, and things were settling down again in the mid thirties, the Great Terror was again launched cold-bloodedly at a helpless population. And the cold-bloodedness was compounded by the other distinguishing quality of the Stalin purge – the total falsehood of all the reasons given for it and accusations made during it.

There was another factor. In the First World War, as Robert Graves notes in *Goodbye to All That*, a soldier could stand the squalor and danger of the trenches only for a certain time. After that the wear and tear became too great. After the first month, under the tensions of trench life, an officer began to deteriorate a little. 'At six months, he was still more or less all right; but by nine or ten months . . . he became a drag on the other officers. After a year or fifteen months, he was often worse than useless.' Graves notes that over the age of about thirty-three, and particularly over forty, men had less resistance. Officers who had done two years or more often became dipsomaniacs. Men went about their tasks 'in an apathetic and doped condition, cheated into further endurance'. It had taken Graves himself, he says, some ten years to recover. He adds that none of this was due simply to physical conditions: in a good battalion, physical illness was rare.

What is so hard to convey about the feeling of Soviet citizens through 1936–8 is the similar long-drawn-out sweat of fear, night after night, that the moment of arrest might arrive before the next dawn. The comparison is reasonable even as to the casualty figures. The risk was a big enough one to be constantly present.

And again, while under other dictatorships arrests have been selective, falling on genuinely suspected enemies of the regime, in the Yezhov era, just as in the mud-holes of Verdun and Ypres, anyone at all could feel that he might be the next victim.

Fear by night, and a feverish effort by day to pretend enthusiasm for a system of lies, was the permanent condition of the Soviet citizen.

DENUNCIATION

For Stalin required not only submission but complicity. The moral crisis arose in a form well described by Pasternak. In 1937 (he later told Dr Nilsson),

> On one occasion they came to me . . . with something they wanted me to sign. It was to the effect that I approved of the Party's execution of the Generals. In a sense this was a proof of their confidence in me. They didn't go to those who were on the list for liquidation. My wife was pregnant. She cried and begged me to sign, but I couldn't. That day I examined the pros and cons of my own survival. I was convinced that I would be arrested – my turn had now come! I was prepared for it. I abhorred all this blood. I couldn't stand things any longer. But nothing happened. It was, I was told later, my colleagues who saved me indirectly. No one dared to report to the hierarchy that I hadn't signed.[1]

But few could match the moral grandeur of the great poet. Everyone was isolated. The individual, silently objecting, was faced with vast meetings calling for the death 'like dogs' of the opposition leaders, or approving the slaughter of the generals. How could he know if they were not genuine, or largely so? There was no sign of opposition or even neutrality; enthusiasm was the only visible phenomenon. Even the children and relatives of the arrested got up to denounce their parents.

The disintegration of family loyalty was a conscious Stalinist aim. When, in November 1938, Stalin destroyed the leadership of the Komsomol, headed by Kosarev, his complaint was that the organization was not devoting itself to vigilance activities, but sticking to its statutory obligation as a political training-ground for young Communists. Stalin's idea of a good young Communist demanded not this sort of political training, but the qualities of an enthusiastic young nark.

Many denunciations were made out of fear. If a Russian heard an incautious word, and failed to report it, it might be himself who would suffer. There are many accounts of Party members who were unable to think of any enemies of the people among their acquaintances being severely censured by their own branch secretaries as 'lacking in revolutionary vigilance'. There are many stories of conversations between old acquaintances which became too frank and ended with each of them denouncing the other. Any conversation that strayed even slightly from the orthodox could only be conducted between old and trusted friends, and with great circumspection. Ilya Ehrenburg's daughter had an old shaggy poodle which had learned the trick of closing the dining-room door as soon as the guests began to talk in a guarded way. As it was given a slice of sausage for its vigilance, it became expert at guessing the type of conversation.[2]

Not every responsible citizen did his duty as a delator. One director gave a lift to the mother of an enemy of the people, an old woman, and was told by his chauffeur: 'Comrade Director, I may be a son of a bitch who must report everything he sees and hears. Believe me or not, but I swear by my own mother that I will not report this time. My own mother is just a plain woman, not a fine lady like this one. But I love her and, anyhow, thank you, Victor Andreyevich, as one Russian to another.' And in fact this incident was never brought up against the director, though many less serious 'crimes' were to be alleged against him.[3]

Nevertheless, just as Nazism provided an institutionalized outlet for the sadist, so Stalinist totalitarianism on the whole automatically encouraged the mean and malicious. Even now, the Soviet press prints frequent stories of busybodies who report people to the police for imaginary offences, and still succeed in getting them deported. In Stalin's time this was routine. The carriers of personal or office feuds, the poison-pen letter-writers, who are a minor nuisance in any society, flourished and increased.

'I have seen,' says Ehrenburg, 'how in a progressive society people allegedly dedicated to moral ideas committed dishonourable acts for personal advantage, betrayed comrades and friends, how wives disavowed their husbands and resourceful sons heaped abuse upon hapless fathers.'[4] A recent Soviet story[5] tells, as reasonably typical, of a geological student who denounced another because he heard him, at a dance, telling his girl friend that his father had been executed – a fact that he had failed to disclose at the Institute. On the first student reporting it, his colleague disappeared, to serve fifteen years in a labour camp.

Individual denouncers operated on an extraordinary scale. In one district in Kiev sixty-nine persons were denounced by one man,[6] in another over a hundred.[7] In Odessa a single Communist denounced 230 people.[8] In Poltava a Party member denounced his entire organization.[9]

At the XVIIIth Party Congress, when the 'excesses' of the Purge period were being belatedly and peripherally criticized, one was now made to confess his methods, which had involved removing fifteen local Party Secretaries. Another well-known slanderer, in Kiev, applied for a free pass to a *kurort* on the grounds that he had worn out his strength in 'the struggle with the enemy', a remark which caused loud laughter in the Congress.[10]

Extraordinary results came from purely lunatic denunciations. Many poison-pen letters were mere malignant fantasy. There are odder cases yet, such as the Red Army deserter Sylakov who gave himself up in Kiev with a dramatic tale of an anti-Soviet plot in which he played the leading part. His original story was of planning an armed raid on a post office to provide funds for a terrorist organization, but of having decided instead to throw himself on the mercy of Soviet justice. This was not much use to the N.K.V.D. After Sylakov had been badly kicked and beaten, a quite different version was worked out, involving not himself and a few vague friends, but his military unit. The leader of the plot was now not Sylakov but his commanding officer. They had planned terroristic attacks on Government leaders. Almost the whole unit, from the C.O. to the drivers, were arrested, with many of their wives. Sylakov's two sisters, both working girls, his old and crippled mother and his father were all pulled in too. So was an uncle who had only met his nephew once, and who, having served as a corporal in the old Army, was transmuted into a 'Tsarist general'.

This absurd case proliferated fantastically till 'there was not a single cell in Kiev prison which did not contain someone involved in the Sylakov plot'.[11] When Yezhov, and his latest representative in Kiev, Uspensky, fell, late in 1938, Sylakov and his fellow-accused were reinterrogated with a view to getting them to withdraw their confessions.* Some of them, fearing a trick, refused, and had to be given tough treatment once again – to force them to withdraw false confessions involving them in crimes carrying the death penalty! Sylakov himself was finally sentenced to three years' imprisonment for desertion only.

But the N.K.V.D. did not, of course, leave denunciation on an amateur and voluntary basis. Everywhere it organized a special network – the *seksots*, recruited from among the general population.

Seksots were divided into two types: the voluntary – malicious degenerates out to injure their neighbours, together with 'idealists' who were convinced that they were working for the Cause; and the involuntary – who were drawn into it out of fear, or (very often) promises of the alleviation of the fate of an arrested member of the prospective *seksot*'s family. These last hoped that if they kept strictly to the truth and reported nothing disadvantageous about their friends, no harm would be done. But once started, they were trapped: the pressure became greater and greater. The *seksot* who failed to produce information was himself automatically suspect. As the population became more and more careful in its talk, more and more harmless acts and words had to be reported, misinterpreted, and finally invented, to slake the N.K.V.D.'s insatiable appetite for plots.[12]

One Ukrainian *seksot* is described as having become a genuine convert to Communism, though unable to join the Party owing to former White Army connexions, and therefore wishing to serve the cause in the one way which appeared to be open to him. At first he abused no confidences and reported impartially. 'He was only doing his duty, and doing one's duty is always pleasurable. When he had occasionally to overcome his own scruples or likes and dislikes in carrying it out, he felt a positive hero.'[13] But naturally, simple hints of feelings hostile to the Government were

*In fact, this may have been one of the excesses which brought the Yezhov system into disrepute.

not in themselves sufficient: for the N.K.V.D. of course knew that such could be found in a large section of the population. He put up a struggle, but was himself threatened as having concealed evidence. Gradually going to pieces, he started first to 'interpret' remarks, until gradually the distinction between truth and falsehood faded out in his mind. Even so, he failed to give satisfaction because he retained a sense of the plausible, and his inventions were too limited for his superiors, so he himself was arrested.

Every account of life in a Soviet office or institution, even before the Great Purge, is replete with intrigues. Such, doubtless, would be true of most other countries. But the resources available to a keen intriguer in Soviet conditions made it a far greater menace, since the normal method of getting on was to 'compromise' and have expelled from the Party, and as often as not arrested, either one's rival, or, if his position was for the time being too strong, one of his subordinates – through whom he could eventually be undermined. One rough estimate was that every fifth person in the average office was in one way or another an N.K.V.D. stool-pigeon.[14]

Weissberg speaks of the foundry industry, with which he had connexions through experiments to improve blast furnaces. Following Gvakharia, Ordzhonikidze's nephew and one of the geniuses of the industrialization drive, all the directors of the big foundries in the Ukraine were arrested:

A few months later their successors were arrested too. It was only the third or fourth batch who managed to keep their seats. In this way the direction of the foundry industry came into the hands of young and inexperienced men. They had not even the normal advantages of youth in their favour, for the choosing had been a very negative one. They were the men who had denounced others on innumerable occasions. They had bowed the knee whenever they had come up against higher authority. They were morally and intellectually crippled.[15]

Right through the Purge Stalin's blows were struck at every form of solidarity and comradeship outside of that provided by personal allegiance to himself. In general, the Terror destroyed personal confidence between private citizens everywhere. The heaviest impact of all was, of course, on the organizational and communal loyalties which still existed in the country after eighteen years of one-party rule. The most powerful and important organization drawing loyalty to itself and its ideas rather than to the General Secretary himself was the Party – or rather its pre-Stalinist membership. Then came the Army. Then the intellectual class, rightly seen as the potential bearer of heretical attitudes. These special allegiances attracted particularly violent attention. But in proceeding to attack the entire people on the same basis, Stalin was being perfectly logical. The atomization of society, the destruction of all trust and loyalty except to himself and his agents, could only be carried through by such methods.

In fact the stage was reached which the writer Isaac Babel summed up: 'Today a man only talks freely with his wife – at night, with the blankets pulled over his head.'[16] Only the very closest of friends could hint to each other of their disbelief of official views (and often not even then). The ordinary Russian had no means of discovering how far the official lies were accepted. He might be one of a scattered and helpless minority, and Stalin might have won his battle to destroy the idea of the truth in the Russian mind. Every man became in one sense what Donne says he is not, 'an island'.

Not that everyone blamed Stalin. His skill in remaining in the background deceived even minds like Pasternak and Meyerhold.[17] If men – albeit non-political – of this calibre could feel so, it is clear that the idea must have been widespread. The fear and hatred of the population was concentrated on Yezhov, who was thus unconsciously making himself ready to be the scapegoat, the eponym of the 'Yezhovshchina'.

MASS TERROR

As 'the number of arrests based on charges of counter-revolutionary crimes grew tenfold between 1936 and 1937',[18] the Purge extended itself outwards from the Party victims to include all their contacts, however slight. For example, in 1932 the Party Secretary in the Urals, Kabakov, had visited some workers' quarters and chanced to look in at an apartment where he found only the mother at home. She told him that her son had gone on a rest cure after being overworked, but had to do it at his own expense. Kabakov ordered the management of the trust employing the worker to pay the expenses. Five years later, when Kabakov was arrested (see p. 336), someone informed the N.K.V.D. that he had visited this worker and given him protection. He was himself at once pulled in, and accused of 'boot-licking' Kabakov.[19]

Thirteen accomplices had been found for Nikolayev, who had really acted alone. This became a general principle. 'Vigilance' was made the test of a good citizen or employee, as well as of a good Party member. The N.K.V.D. everywhere, and all public organizations and economic institutions, were under continual pressure to show their worth in uprooting the enemy. Every man arrested was pressed to denounce accomplices, and in any case all his acquaintances automatically became suspects.

In the show trials themselves, some of the confessions automatically implicated not just individuals, or groups of political associates, but wide circles completely outside the Party struggle. For example, in his evidence in the Bukharin Trial,[20] Zelensky pleaded guilty to the fact that 15 per cent of the staff of the Central Cooperative Union 'consisted of former Mensheviks, Socialist-Revolutionaries, anarchists, Trotskyites, etc. In certain regions the number of alien elements, former members of other parties, Kolchak officers and so on . . . was considerably higher.' These elements were, he said, assembled to 'act as a centre of attraction for all kinds of anti-Soviet elements'. The way this would snowball almost automatically, and throughout the country, is obvious.

Yet it was not only this process of association that gave the Purge its increasingly mass character. In the thirties, there were still hundreds of thousands who had been members of non-Bolshevik parties, the masses who had served in White armies, professional men who had been abroad, nationalist elements in the local intelligentsias, and so on. The increasingly virulent campaign for vigilance against the hidden enemy blanketed the whole country, not merely the Party, in a press and radio campaign. And while the destruction of hostile elements in the Party was going forward, it must have seemed natural to use the occasion to break all remaining elements suspected of not being reconciled to the regime.

For this sizeable part of the population was already listed in the files of the Special Department of the N.K.V.D., and its local branches, under various headings, such as:

AS   anti-Soviet element
Ts   active member of the Church
S   member of a religious sect
P   rebel – anyone who in the past was in
     any way involved in anti-Soviet uprisings
SI   anyone with contacts abroad.

Such categories were not in themselves legal grounds for prosecution, but they automatically made those listed natural suspects, and almost automatic victims when an N.K.V.D. branch was called upon to show its merits by mass arrests.

We have a more detailed division of these suspect categories in the lists of dangerous elements issued on the annexation of Lithuania by the U.S.S.R. in 1940.[21] Since even by January 1941, after half a year's occupation, there were admittedly only 2,500 Communists in the country,[22] few of the worst suspects – real Trotskyites – could be found. And no threat to Stalin's position as a whole could come from so small a territory. But in the selection of those whose elimination was required to turn the country into a more or less reliable fief, we can see some of the way of thinking which had been applied to Russia itself. The lists item all former officials of the State, Army and judiciary; all former members of non-Communist parties; all active members of student corporations; members of the National Guard; anyone who had fought against the Soviets (i.e. in 1918–20); refugees; representatives of foreign firms; employees and former employees of foreign legations, firms and companies; people in contact with foreign countries, including philatelists and Esperantists; all clergy; former noblemen, landlords, merchants, bankers, businessmen, owners of hotels and restaurants, shopkeepers; former Red Cross officials. It is estimated that this covered about 23 per cent of the population.[23]

In the Soviet Union many in these categories had already died

or emigrated. But many were left. And around each was a widen-
ing circle of colleagues and acquaintances who automatically
entered the field of suspicion by 'association with alien elements'.
Anyone in a job worked under a State official who might turn out
to be a Trotskyite. Anyone, anywhere, might find that he bought
his groceries from a former *kulak* or was neighbour to an Armenian bourgeois nationalist.

Thus by mid 1937 practically the entire population was potential Purge fodder. Few can have failed to wonder if their turn had
come. Pasternak, in the bitterly matter-of-fact passage with which
he ends the main body of *Doctor Zhivago*, gives the expectations
of the time:

> One day Lara went out and did not come back. She must have been
> arrested in the street, as so often happened in those days, and she died
> or vanished somewhere, forgotten as a nameless number on a list which
> later was mislaid, in one of the innumerable mixed or women's con-
> centration camps in the north.

Russians who had been abroad and come back towards the
autumn of 1937, like Ilya Ehrenburg, were deeply shocked by
the change. Even on his way through from Spain, when he rang
his daughter from Paris he could get nothing out of her except
conversation about the weather. In Moscow itself, he found
writer after writer and journalist after journalist had disappeared.
In the *Izvestia* office they had given up putting nameplates outside the doors of department heads: as the messenger girl explained, 'here today and gone tomorrow'. In the ministries and
the offices it was everywhere the same – empty seats, haggard
faces and an extreme unwillingness to talk.[24] An American
journalist living in a block of about 160 apartments in the summer
of 1937 notes that the Secret Police had made arrests in more than
half of them: 'and our house was no exception'.[25]

There were various methods of avoiding arrest. A well-known
scholar avoided the first wave of the Purge by pretending to be a
drunkard. Another, taking the same line a little further, got drunk
and created a disturbance in a public park, thus getting six months
for a minor criminal offence, and avoiding political trouble.[26]
By a curious irony, some genuine enemies of the regime – perhaps

more prescient than most – escaped by simply fading into the background. For example, Nicholas Stasiuk, who had actually been Minister of Supply in the anti-Communist Rada Government in the Ukraine in 1918, survived in Mariupol working as a park attendant until the German occupation during the Second World War, when he became a leading figure in the nationalist movement in the area.[27]

There was sometimes a period between disgrace and arrest which a lucky individual might make use of by leaving the main centres. S. G. Poplawski (who was to be installed by Stalin as Deputy Commander-in-Chief of the Polish Army after the war) was at the Frunze Academy in 1937. Expelled from the Party and the Academy, he at once left Moscow to avoid the next step. 'A year or a year and a half later' – that is, presumably after the fall of Yezhov – he reappeared and was then rehabilitated and readmitted to the course.[28]

In general, moving frequently was a certain protection, since it usually took 'at least six months or a year' before the local N.K.V.D. paid much attention or had accumulated enough evidence against a figure whom there was no exceptional reason to persecute. It also took a great deal of time before his personal documents from the N.K.V.D. of his previous place of residence were forwarded, 'particularly as all such documents were dispatched by special N.K.V.D. express messenger and not through the ordinary post'. Sometimes they never arrived at all.[29] Siberia, in particular, was a good place to go. Comparatively speaking, the local authorities were glad to have settlers, hardly distinguishing between people in forced exile and those freely arriving. The N.K.V.D. in a province in European Russia would have little interest in providing suspects for its Siberian opposite number, and though it could have a man under 'suspicion' brought back, this was troublesome and hardly worth going through except in important cases.

But such actions were open to few, and were often no more than temporary protection. The arrests came, eventually, in millions.

Vyshinsky's assistant, Roginsky, who got a fifteen-year sentence, continued to argue in camp that the regime was justified in isolating from the community large numbers of people who might cause trouble, and in continuing to exploit the labour to the maximum, regardless of any guilt or innocence, of those who were economically 'old and useless'.[30] More sophisticated N.K.V.D. and Party members would defend the Purges on subtler grounds. Even if mild jokes or criticisms of the Government was all that had taken place, this was a potential for future active opposition, and the N.K.V.D., by excising this group, was carrying out a justified preventive operation.

In the factories, public denunciation meetings of the established type spread to the workers as a whole. A recent Soviet novel describes such a works scene in 1937:

A short man in a lambskin cap angrily announced 'My foreman Sereda failed to issue me with cement. I thought at the time this was suspicious. Yesterday I learned that Sereda was concealing his relationship to one of Makhno's followers who married his cousin!'

'The fitter Tsvirkun when taking up employment concealed the fact that his old man was an elder of the church!' announced a second speaker.

A third speaker proceeded to expose his former comrade whose parents had been deprived of electoral rights for sabotage during the period of collectivization. . .[31]

The extension of the Purge throughout the country was not, as sometimes suggested, just the result of too much eagerness on the part of local N.K.V.D. officials who let things get out of control. On the contrary, it was insisted on from the centre. For example, on 29 November 1936 Vyshinsky was already ordering that within a month all 'criminal cases of major conflagrations, accidents and output of poor-quality products be reviewed and studied with the aim of exposing a counter-revolutionary and saboteur background in them'. In certain areas, where few prosecutions on charges of counter-revolutionary activity had been brought, severe censure was issued from the Public Prosecutor's Office in Moscow. In 1937 only eight cases in this category were brought to court through a large part of Siberia, and Moscow blamed this on 'a weak and inadequate struggle to stamp out the nests of saboteurs'.[32]

In general, occasional highly organized mass trials and much more frequent mass arrests marked the period. In May 1937 the

Far Eastern press announced fifty-five death sentences in such trials,[33] and in June another ninety-one, in July another eighty-three, and so on through the year. In Byelorussia from June onwards, hardly a week went by without wrecking and espionage being discovered in various industrial enterprises, the Academy of Sciences, the Polish theatre, the physical culture groups, the banks, the cement industry, the veterinary services, the bread supply organization, and the railways. (The local railway authorities were denounced on 8 October 1937 and charged with being not only Polish but also Japanese spies, in accordance with railway tradition.) In Central Asia it was the same: twenty-five executions were announced in Kazakhstan[34] and eighteen in Uzbekistan[35] in November. In January 1938 came twenty-six more in Kirghizia[36] and another 134 in Uzbekistan.[37]

On 28 July 1937 E. G. Evdokimov assembled the Party leadership of the North Caucasian area and gave instructions for a long-planned super-purge in the area. On 31 July, the local phase of this 'general operation' was launched in the Chechen-Ingush Republic in the North Caucasus: 5,000 prisoners were crammed into the N.K.V.D. prisons in Grozny, 5,000 in the main garage of the Grozny Oil Trust, and thousands of others into various requisitioned buildings. In the Republic as a whole about 14,000 were arrested, amounting to about 3 per cent of the population. Shkiryatov in person oversaw a further mass operation in October.[38]

The cold-blooded administrative organization of such mass arrest and deportation comes out very clearly in Serov's Order No. 001233 for the Baltic States:

Operations shall be begun at daybreak. Upon entering the home of the person to be deported, the senior member of the operative group shall assemble the entire family of the deportee into one room. . . . In view of the fact that a large number of deportees must be arrested and distributed in special camps and that their families must proceed to special settlements in distant regions, it is essential that the operations of removal of both the members of the deportee's family and its head shall be carried out simultaneously, without notifying them of the separation confronting them.

ARREST

Whether as part of such a special operation, or in the ordinary course of routine arrests, it was usual to take action in the small hours. Two or three N.K.V.D. men, sometimes brutal, sometimes formally correct, would knock and enter. A search was made which might be brief but could take hours, especially when books and documents had to be examined. The victim, and his wife if he had one, sat under guard meanwhile, till finally he was taken off. A quick-witted wife might in the long run save his life by getting him some warm clothes. By dawn he would usually have been through the formalities and be in his cell.

A general describes his arrest:

At two in the morning there was a knock at the door of my hotel room.
'Who's there?' I called.
A woman's voice answered: 'A telegram for you.'
'Obviously from my wife,' I thought as I opened the door.
Three uniformed men came into the room and one of them told me point-blank that I was under arrest.[39]

A poet writes of his, also at night:

'Go with you'
                         you ask, looking for your coat,
Your arm fumbles for the sleeve.
You feel overcome by a sudden weakness –
In such a moment you tire as in a lifetime . . .

It seems a ravine has opened under your feet,
And the ceiling seems to fall on you.
There is suddenly not enough air in the room –
You breathe
            with an effort.[40]

The New Constitution, indeed, had guarantees against unjustified arrest. Under its Article 127 no one might be 'arrested' except by order of a court or with the consent of the Prosecutor. This was anyhow not of much value in the absence of an independent judiciary: and the judicature of the U.S.S.R. was officially defined as 'a means of strengthening the Socialist regime, guarding the rights of citizens and repressing the enemies of the people and the Trotskyite–Bukharinist agents of foreign espionage organizations'.[41] But in any case, a distinction was made between 'arrest' and 'detention'. A man might be 'detained' without the sanction of the court or Prosecutor in 'all cases where public order and security is threatened'. Moreover, Article 45 of the Corrective Labour Codex reads: 'For reception into a place of deprivation of freedom it is obligatory to have a sentence or an order by organs legally empowered thereunto, *or an open warrant.*'

In fact a prosecutor's warrant seems generally to have been provided, though sometimes formalities were dispensed with. For example, a case is reported from the Ukraine in which the police arrested two chance visitors for whom they had no warrant together with the man they were after: each of the two accidentally arrested spent five months in jail before managing to get out.[42] Cases of mistaken identity, particularly with common names like Ivanov, are also occasionally noted. They were usually released after a few weeks or months, but cases are mentioned of their having confessed to espionage or other crimes before the mistake was discovered. Even then, they were sometimes released.[43]

Wives were not told where the arrested had been taken. The method of finding where they were was to go from prison to prison. In Moscow wives would go to the 'information centre' opposite the Lubyanka, at 24 Kuznetsky Most; then to the Sokolnika; then to the Taganka; then to the office of the Butyrka, in its small courtyard; then to the Lefortovo military prison; and back again. When the head of the queue of hundreds of women was reached, the official was asked to accept the 50 roubles a month to which as-yet unconvicted prisoners were entitled. Sometimes a prison, perhaps through bureaucratic incompetence, would not admit that they held the man in question until the second or third time round. One Moscow wife found a girl aged about ten in front of the queue with a dirty little wad of rouble notes. She was paying it in for her father and mother, both arrested.[44]

Anna Akhmatova's son, the young orientalist Lev Gumilev, was in jail in Leningrad. 'During the frightful years of the Yezhov terror,' the poetess says in the foreword to *Requiem*, 'I spent seventeen months in prison queues in Leningrad. One day someone "recognised" me. A woman with blue lips standing behind me, who had of course never heard my name, suddenly woke out of the benumbed condition in which we all found ourselves at that time and whispered into my ear (in those days everyone spoke in a whisper):

— Could you describe this?

And I said:

— I can.

Then something resembling a smile flickered over what once had been her face.'

Akhmatova speaks of her own mouth as one 'through which a hundred million people cry', and asks that if they ever put up a monument to her it should be at the prison gates in Leningrad where she stood for three hundred hours. In 1940 she was allowed to see her son, and afterwards wrote the poem which is no. 9 in *Requiem*, feeling that she was going mad.

Young Gumilev was again, or still, in jail in 1956, when Fadeyev made an appeal to the Prosecutor's Office, saying:

Certain eminent figures of the scientific and literary intelligentsia have doubts concerning the justice of his imprisonment. . . . In reviewing the case of L. N. Gumilev it is essential to bear in mind the fact that although he was only a child of nine when his father was no more, he, as the son of N. Gumilev and of A. Akhmatova, was at all times a convenient target for career-seeking and hostile elements who sought to make accusations against him.[45]

This makes it clear that he too was, like so many others, the victim of his relationships.

Women who actively tried to get their husbands released almost never succeeded. One typically describes being called to a local N.K.V.D. headquarters at midnight and simply being told, 'I order you to stop running about like a lunatic trying to get your husband released! I order you to stop bothering us! That's all! Get out!'[46]

After a husband had been sentenced, it was again difficult to trace him. One method was to write to the addresses of camps of whose existence a woman had heard from other wives. Sometimes, after receiving a long series of printed forms saying that he was not at such-and-such a camp, a husband could be found,[47] and, in certain types of sentence, parcels accepted.

For the wives, indeed, life was very bad. General Gorbatov remarks, 'I often thought of my wife. She was worse off than me. I was, after all, in the company of other outcasts, whereas she was among free people among whom there might be many who would shun her as the wife of an "enemy of the people".'[48] And all reports agree that the women lost their jobs, their rooms, their permits, had to sell possessions, live on occasional work or on the few relatives who might help them. Ignorant of their husbands' fate, they faced a worsening future.[49]

TO THE CELLS

The arrested man was first taken to a reception point in one of the prisons, signed in, and submitted to a strict physical search and an examination of his clothes seam by seam. Bootlaces and metal attachments, including buttons, were removed. These searches were made at intervals during imprisonment. At the same time thorough cell searches were carried out about once a fortnight.

In the cells, while there were variations around the country, the prisoner would find much the same routine – intense over-crowding, inadequate food, boredom and squalor, between bouts of interrogation. Life in the Tsarist prisons is universally described as very considerably preferable to those now developed. In particular, there had not been the overcrowding.

A prisoner who had been in Moscow's Butyrka Prison in 1933 says that while in that year there had already been seventy-two men in a twenty-four-man cell, there were no less than 140 in November 1937.[50] In a woman's cell supposed to hold twenty-five, 110 women were crowded. Planks covered the entire floor and the few beds, apart from a small part of the central gangway, a table and two large latrine buckets. It was impossible for the prisoners to lie on their backs, and when lying on their sides, if one wanted to turn over, it could only be done by negotiating with the prisoners on either side to do it all together.[51] The cell in which Pugachev had been held alone before his execution was now occupied by sixty-five people.[52]

Most of our descriptions of prisons are of those in Moscow, Leningrad or the Ukrainian capital. The impression given is scarcely a favourable one. But conditions seem to have been a good deal better there than those in the provincial jails. Several accounts remark on prisoners from Chelyabinsk or Sverdlovsk, on arrival in the packed cells of the Butyrka, exclaiming that the place seemed a holiday camp compared with their previous experiences.[53] Where the overflow was too great, as in some of the Siberian towns, vast pits were sometimes dug and roofed over and the prisoners simply herded in. By the autumn of 1937, a Kharkov prison built for about 800 held about 12,000.[54]

Overcrowding was treated differently in Moscow than in the provinces. In Moscow, space was gained by prisoners sleeping under the beds and on boards between the beds, By this means it was possible to accommodate up to three men to the square yard. In provincial prisons, beds and boards were taken out to make room for more inmates. In some, people slept in rows, lying on their sides. Other cells were even more crowded, half the occupants having to stand while the other half slept, packed, on the floors.[55]

Each cell elected its *starosta*, or cell-leader, who was responsible for keeping order, allocating sleeping places, and so forth. The new prisoner was put next to the reeking slop-bucket or *parasha*, getting better places as his seniority increased.

In the morning, a short time was given for ablution and excretion. For example, 110 women in one cell were allowed forty minutes with five lavatories and ten water taps.[56]

In prisons in the big cities, at least before they became too crowded, prisoners were taken to the baths every ten days. Sufficient soap was issued. Clothing was regularly disinfected. In most of the provincial prisons, however, conditions were already filthy.

During the 'Yezhovshchina' the usual daily ration was 500–600 grammes of black bread, 20 grammes of sugar, and thin cabbage soup twice a day. In some prisons there was also a tablespoonful of groats and hot water three times a day.

In the Butyrka, alternate days saw cabbage soup and fish soup, about a pound of black bread and a meal of lentils, barley or groats in the evening. This is described by a woman prisoner as being worse than what she was managing on in town after losing her husband and her son, but, even so, good in comparison with what she was to get in the camps.[57] These rations were usually delivered regularly and fully. Prison diet seems to have been calculated to be just enough to keep a more or less motionless prisoner alive.

It was unhealthy fare. But the general conditions were more unhealthy. Prisoners showed a peculiar greyish-blue tinge from long confinement without light and air.[58] The main diseases resulting were dysentery, scurvy, scabies, pneumonia and heart attacks. Gingivitis was universal.[59]

But the prison administration was held strictly responsible for the actual life of every prisoner. This was taken to such paradoxical lengths that 'in the same cell you would find prisoners suffering severely from the effects of interrogation about which nobody bothered, while every conceivable medicine for the prevention and cure of colds, coughs and headaches were regularly distributed.[60] And great precautions were taken against suicide.

Doctors reluctant to interfere with the course of the interrogation would sometimes treat prisoners whose ribs had been broken under a different diagnosis, but giving them the right treatment.[61] On the other hand, medical conduct in a provincial prison is quoted as being in a different spirit, the examination being conducted quite openly with a view to seeing how much the prisoner could stand. A certificate issued was quite frank about the beatings and was evidently entered in the official records without a qualm. This was in early 1938.[62]

The company, apart from a plague of stool-pigeons, was usually good, especially in Moscow, and innumerable cases are given of kindness and self-sacrifice – as when (a Hungarian Communist reports) a prisoner, back from even worse conditions, was allowed a bed to himself for a whole day by the 275 men crammed in a twenty-five-man cell, and was given extra sugar from their rations.[63] Lectures were given on a large variety of subjects, and much story-telling was also done. Herling mentions too that 'every cell contains at least one statistician, a scientific investigator of prison life, engrossed day and night in assembling a complicated jig-saw of stories, scraps of conversation overheard in corridors, old newspapers found in the latrine, administrative orders, movement of vehicles in the courtyards, and even the sound of advancing and receding footsteps in front of the gate'.[64]

All prisoners report cases of Party officials who remained loyal, and either held that Stalin and the Politburo knew nothing of what was happening, or, alternatively, that they themselves were not qualified to judge these decisions, and simply had the duty of obeying Party orders, including confession.

There were other types. In one of the cells of the Butyrka there were the sons of five moderately important officials. Four of them were the typical brutalized product of the new privileged youth of Stalinism. They had freely denounced their parents, and boasted of it, taking the view that there was no reason why they should harm their own prospects to look after relics of the past. Only the fifth, the son of General Gorbachov (the executed 'daredevil'),[65] was a decent youth.[66]

Smoking was permitted. All games were forbidden. Chess was, however, played illegally, with men made out of bread or other objects. In one of the women's cells in the Butyrka a fortune-telling game with matches was played. When a wardress saw people with matches she would count them, and if there were exactly the number required for the game (forty-one) the owner was punished.[67]

Books are only reported as available in two Moscow prisons, the Lubyanka and the Butyrka (and at the height of Yezhov's power these seem to have been stopped).* These libraries were good, containing the classics, translations, histories and scientific works – sounding much better than those of British prisons or, indeed, hospitals or Cunarders. The Butyrka's was particularly fine. The reason was that it had been used for political prisoners

---

*On Beria's appointment a certain relaxation took place. Games and books were again permitted.

in Tsarist times, and the big liberal publishing houses had always given free copies of their books to these jails.[68] That of the Lubyanka was largely of books confiscated from prisoners.

After Yezhov's appointment, new and harsher regulations came into force. All windows were blocked with shutters – still called 'Yezhov muzzles' – which left only a small piece of sky visible. (They had, indeed, been in use in the Lubyanka, and the equivalent Shpalerny prison in Leningrad, for some years.[69]) After the Bukharin Trial, as a 'reprisal', these panes were shut except for ten minutes a day. Bread became mouldy, clothes damp, walls green and 'joints aching as though some creature were gnawing them'.[70] The penalty for the slightest offence, such as the possession of a needle, was the punishment cells with only from one-half to two-thirds of the already small prison ration, deprivation of outer clothing, and being allowed to lie down only at night, and then on the stone floor.[71] Punishment cells had, logically enough, to be even worse than ordinary ones. A Soviet writer mentions three grades of them in Yaroslavl in 1937. In one there was light and the prisoner kept his or her clothes. The next was a mouldy hole in the wall, totally dark and cold, with vest only permitted and bread and water once a day. She was in it for five days for the offence (in any case not committed by her) of writing her name up in the washroom. From the remaining 'first' category, which she escaped, 'people came out only to die'.[72]

The trees and flowers which had grown in some prison yards were meanwhile cut down and asphalted over. Zabolotsky, in his poem 'The Ivanovs', had spoken of trees 'standing . . . behind railings, under lock and key'. He was himself to be deprived of the sight even of these.

At the same time, as far as possible, the more liberal warders were liquidated, and only the least popular guards were retained, after reindoctrination courses.[73]

Some prisoners, particularly those under interrogation in especially important cases, were kept in 'inner prisons'. So were certain men already serving sentences. The regime in these 'inner prisons' was quite different from the bullying squalor of the main buildings. Unlike the mass cells, with foetid air and prisoners pressed close together on bare boards, which nevertheless had a certain social life, of discussion and even occasional scientific and literary lectures from specialists, the inner prisons were 'living graves'.[74] The cells were clean, without overcrowding, each prisoner had his own bed, and even linen, and clothes were actually washed once a month. But no noise, not even loud speech, was permitted. The spy-hole in the cell door opened every few minutes. The prisoner had to be in bed from 11 p.m. to 6 a.m. During the day he could sit down but not lean on anything. There was nothing whatever to do – on inadequate diet. Isolation was complete: Weissberg, in isolator cells in the Ukraine and then in Moscow, only learned about the outbreak of war at the end of October 1939. There were only a few hundred prisoners in an inner prison at a time when thousands and tens of thousands might be in the outer one.

Such a prisoner had to undress and when sleeping to keep his arms outside the covers so that the hands could be seen. Weissberg says that this was because a prisoner had once plaited a length of string under the covering and hanged himself with it: in any case, it would have been the only opportunity for making any illegal object.*[75] If a warder saw a prisoner's hands hidden, he would come in and wake the prisoner each time he detected him.

In the 'inner prisons' proper communication by tapping was almost impossible, and was seldom replied to as being probably the work of a *provocateur*.[76] Elsewhere there was a certain amount of it.[77] The method is that described by Arthur Koestler in *Darkness at Noon* – the so-called 'Dekabrist' alphabet dating from the prisoners of the 1820s.†

In the isolation cells the psychological problem was intense. A former actor from the Bolshoi Theatre who had served five years gave the following 'lesson':

First, you must detach yourself from reality – stop thinking of your-

---

* Arthur Koestler says, in his *Spanish Testament*, which describes his experiences in the death cell at Seville, that it was recognized practice for prisoners to weaken themselves by continual masturbation, so that they would faint quickly under torture.

† The alphabet is arranged, in imagination, in a square of horizontal and vertical lines. To show a letter, you tap its co-ordinates in the horizontal, then the vertical.

self as a prisoner. Make believe that you are a tourist who temporarily finds himself in an unfamiliar environment. Don't admit to yourself that conditions here are very bad, because they may get even worse, and you should be prepared for that. Don't become too involved in the everyday life of the isolator. Try not to hear its sounds, especially at night, or to smell its smells. Try not to be aware of the guards, don't look at them, ignore the expression on their faces. Stop making-believe about the possibility of your being released soon from the isolator. Do not attempt to regain your freedom by means of a hunger strike, or by admitting your guilt, or by appealing for mercy to the authorities. Stop pining for the friends you have left behind in the free world.[78]

A special category of prison consisted of the half-dozen 'political isolators', notably those at Suzdal, Verkhne-Uralsk, Yaroslavl and Alexandrovsk. These dated from earlier days of the regime, when they had been thought of as a comparatively humane method of removing factious Communists and other left-wing 'politicals' from public life. Even in the early thirties, treatment in these prisons was comparatively humane. During the purge they sank to the normal level. A Soviet commentator says of the food in the Yaroslavl isolator in 1937 that it 'contained no vitamins whatever. For breakfast we got bread, hot water and two lumps of sugar, for dinner – soup and gruel cooked without any fat, and for supper – a kind of broth reeking of fish-oil.'[79] But they still preserved some special characteristics. They mostly held no more than four or five hundred prisoners. Typically at Verkhne-Uralsk, there were cells holding either 10–25 or 3–8 prisoners, with in addition a number of solitary cells. It was usual for important prisoners serving sentences, but not expendable – in that further trials were planned for them – to be held in these.

THE GREAT PRISONS

Of the five main prisons in Moscow, three – the Lubyanka, the Lefortovo and the Butyrka – were for 'politicals' only, though these were also held in the other places of detention with non-politicals. The Lefortovo was the great torture centre, though torture was also practised on a lesser scale in the Lubyanka and in the 'special section' of the Butyrka.

The *Lubyanka* was free of bugs, and the same is reported of some of the Kiev prisons, though bugs usually abounded. (In spite of the far cleaner and more sanitary conditions in the German concentration camps, as compared with the Soviet labour camps, the same does not seem to have been true of the prisons. The Berlin Central Prison on the Alexanderplatz is described as being more lice-ridden than those in Moscow.[80])

The corridors of the Lubyanka were clean, smelling of carbolic and disinfectant. It is the best-known of the N.K.V.D. prisons, since it lies within the headquarters of the Police Ministry, and has been the scene of the most famous imprisonments, interrogations and executions. But though its great wedge looming over Dzerzhinsky Square is only a few minutes' walk from the Bolshoi Theatre and the general tourist area, it is seldom pointed out to visitors even now.

It was originally the headquarters of an insurance company. The Cheka took over the old building, and over the years built over the entire block. The original building is pre-Revolutionary Gothic; the rest of the block was rebuilt in two bursts, one in 1930-functional, and the other in post-war wedding-cake style. The People's Commissariat consisted of the whole outer section. Inside is a courtyard, and within the courtyard is the nine-storey prison section. This was originally a hotel or boarding-house run by the insurance company, and though considerably adapted has not been rebuilt. As a result the rooms used as cells are less unpleasant than in the other prisons. The windows – though largely blocked by screens – are of good size.

The Lubyanka had about 110 cells, and these were fairly small ones. It seems improbable that more than a few hundred prisoners were held there at a time.

Prisoners who were unsatisfactory in the preliminary interrogations at the Lubyanka were often transferred to the *Lefortovo* – in particular the military. No clear account of the atrocities practised in the Lefortovo is available. We are told that prisoners who had been there and were transferred to the Butyrka regarded the beating-up in the latter prison as child's play compared with their previous sufferings.[81] The Lefortovo was built just before the First World War in a more or less star shape, with blocks radiating from a centre. It had the advantage that there were water-closets actually in the cells.

The *Butyrka*, started in the eighteenth century to house the captured rebels of the Pugachev insurrection, is by far the largest prison. It consists of a number of vast barrack-like blocks, centred on the old section, 'the Pugachev Tower', in which the great rebel had been held before his execution. In the Purge, it held about 30,000 prisoners.[82]

Gorbatov, who was tortured in the Lefortovo, says that the Butyrka was an immense improvement. Although there were seventy men in a twenty-five-man cell, they got half an hour's exercise a day instead of ten minutes every other day. It had large exercise yards, unlike the cramped squares of the Lefortovo.[83] Exercise was taken, walking in pairs, with hands behind backs and eyes to the ground. Any swinging of arms or raising of heads was immediately stopped.[84]

Women with new-born babies are reported in the Butyrka.[85] On the other hand, others were brought in who had had to leave children, and nursing babies, unattended at home. They had their breasts bandaged to stop the milk.[86]

The *Taganka*, and other prisons holding politicals and others, were like the Butyrka, but dirtier and less efficient.[87]

A special small prison some ten or twenty miles out of Moscow, the *Sukhanovka*, deserves mention. It had a particularly fearful reputation among prisoners, who knew it as 'the *dacha*'.[88] It was a single-floor building, out in the countryside, consisting of a set of isolators; and torture was the normal method of procedure. It is said to have been built specially for the Rudzutak–Postyshev intake. It was the one place where the regulations were observed so strictly that the warders literally never spoke at all to the prisoners. It had no library, or 'shop'.

In Leningrad there was a similar system. The *Shpalerny* prison, described as comparatively clean and orderly, fulfilled the role of the Lubyanka in Moscow with about 300 cells. The larger *Nizhegorodsky*, too, had a number of one-man cells for important prisoners. The *Kresti*, equivalent of the Butyrka, with about 30,000 prisoners,[89] was more squalid altogether, with sixteen men sharing what had been a one-man cell in Tsarist times.[90] A special *Transfer Prison* held those already sentenced to camps. (And outside, tourists were being shown as a horror of the past the cells of the old Peter Paul Fortress, where a handful of politicals had been held in considerably better circumstances before the Revolution.)

Whether in one of these, or in prisons of varying degrees of rigour, malnutrition and overcrowding, the arrested citizen awaited the authorities' next move. As a general thing, physical conditions were usually far worse in the provincial jails like Minsk, Gomel, Vyatka or Vologda, but regulations less tightly enforced; there was more offhand brutality, but also more chance of a comparatively sympathetic warder, who might even warn against informers.[91] As an experienced prisoner puts it, 'the dirtier the prison, the worse the food, the rougher and more undisciplined the guard, the less danger there was to life'.[92]

CRIMINAL TYPES

In his cell in this new community, the arrested man might be interrogated at once, or he might wait for some time. Meanwhile, he would discover in discussion with his cell-mates what his crime was likely to be. At the beginning of the Purge those arrested often thought that the other people in the prisons were actually guilty of something, and that only their own case was a mistake. By 1937 the outside public had come to realize that the accused were innocent, and people brought in took it for granted that their cell-mates were in the same boat as themselves. The chances of anyone there being actually guilty of anything whatever were very small. One sometimes hears the view still expressed in the West that the Great Purge, though unforgivably striking at many innocent men, at least destroyed, in passing, the genuine spy networks of hostile powers. Such is not the view of Gomulka, who remarks that the Terror 'only facilitated the work of the intelligence services of the imperialist states'.[93]

In fact, from the purely intelligence point of view, the Japanese, Polish and Latvian services at least seem to have gained all the information they required. And apart from direct operations, the mere fact of (for example) the defection owing to fear for his life of the Far East N.K.V.D. chief Lyushkov to the Japanese, in 1938, must have put them in possession of a veritable treasure-house of information – and this defection was a direct result of the Terror!

There is one important earlier case generally recognized as that of a genuine spy – Konar, who became Assistant People's Commissar of Agriculture until accidentally exposed. He was a Polish agent who had been given the papers of a dead Red Army soldier in 1920, and in ten years had thus risen high in the hierarchy, until exposed by someone who chanced to have seen the genuine Konar. As to minor agents, a number of books mention, as an extreme rarity, 'real' spies, or men who at least might possibly have been guilty.[94] There is one such, the 'Moldavian', in Solzhenitsyn's camp in *One Day in the Life of Ivan Denisovich*. In a Kiev prison in 1939 there was much pride and astonishment on all sides that one of the prisoners was a genuine Polish spy. Once he had admitted his own guilt he was badly beaten to get him to implicate Party officials in Kiev.[95]

Prisoners recognized, in most cases of arrest, that there was an 'objective characteristic' basic to the case. This might be social origins, past or present posts, relationship or friendship with someone, nationality or connexion with a foreign country, or activity in specific Soviet organizations. This probable 'real' cause of arrest was at once plain to cell-mates, though it was never mentioned by the interrogators.[96]

For although there were many categories, membership of which was liable to bring arrest – such as foreign connexions, high military rank, and so forth – these were not the crimes officially charged. Nor did they *automatically* lead to arrest. 'We can even quote cases of German Communists who were not arrested, although they were political refugees.'[97] Arrest depended on a variety of secondary factors.

One peasant in Kharkov jail accounted for his arrest by the fact that he had been arrested on a false charge four years previously, and released with apologies. This, he thought, must make the N.K.V.D. think that he had reason to dislike them. This was apparently not an unusual case. 'Hundreds of thousands of people were arrested during the Purge for no other reason than that at some time in the past the Soviet authorities had done them an injustice.[98]

To have had anything to do with foreigners was one almost certain road to arrest. People who had actually been abroad – for example, footballers like the three Starostin brothers, stars of the pre-war period* – were almost all in camps by the forties.[99] Professor Kalmanson, Assistant Director of the Moscow Zoo, had been educated abroad, so was assumed to be a 'spy' by his cell-mates. After his first interrogation he triumphantly told them that he was only a 'wrecker' – 16 per cent of his monkeys having died of TB (a lower figure, he pointed out, than the London Zoo's). But they were vindicated by his second interrogation, which reached 'the main question' – espionage for Germany.[100] Everyone connected with the organizations for contact with 'Friends of the Soviet Union' abroad was automatically suspect. These organizations sponsored pen-pal exchanges. One young science student is mentioned as being sentenced as a German spy because he had, on this basis, been writing to a Communist in Manchester, though his letters had consisted almost entirely of Soviet propaganda.[101]

All direct contact with foreign consulates was likely to prove fatal. Doctors who had treated German Consuls, a vet who had dealt with consular dogs, even more indirect connexions such as the vet's son, were arrested in the Ukraine, and another man, an old caretaker, always explained in prison that he was there as 'the brother of the woman who supplied the German Consul's milk'.[102] Another had copied and given to the Polish Consul the weather forecast pinned up in the public park.[103]

An opera singer who had danced longer than permitted with the Japanese Ambassador at an official ball is reported in camp. A cook had applied for a job advertised in *Vechernaya Moskva*, the evening paper. It turned out to be at the Japanese Embassy. She got the job but was arrested for espionage before she had had time to start it.[104] Another typical case is of two engineers and their families, arrested in the winter of 1937–38, because of a gift

*The field of sport was thoroughly purged. See H. W. Morton, *Soviet Sport*, New York, 1963, pp. 186–93.

parcel one of them had received from an uncle in Poland, consisting of two pairs of shoes, some crayons and a couple of dolls. The engineer who had not received the parcel, but was a friend of the one who had, got ten years.[105]

A Greek doctor was charged with espionage on the grounds that he had written to relatives in Salonika describing the characteristics of some fish being bred with a view to the extermination of malarial mosquitoes.[106] In December 1937, Greeks were arrested everywhere. Later, the Greek-inhabited area of Mariupol, on the Black Sea, was thoroughly purged in connexion with a special Greek nationalist plot which was to create a Greater Greek Republic over a large part of the Ukraine. Its 'Minister of Education' was in fact a Russian, but he had been Professor of Ancient Greek at Kharkov University and had spent a year in Athens. The 'Prime Minister' had been an adviser on minority questions to the Ukrainian Central Committee.[107]

Chinese were also arrested *en bloc*. One is reported as having been charged with taking a job as a tram-driver in Kharkov, with the aim of crashing it into any car on the tracks in front of him which carried members of the Soviet Government.[108] The national minorities in Russian towns were virtually eliminated. In September 1937 the Armenians in the Ukraine were rounded up. There were 600 of them in Kharkov.[109] The Latvians were arrested the same month. An alleged Latvian secret organization had worked for a Greater Latvia stretching over a large part of Russia, including Moscow.[110]

Members of the smaller national minorities were in as 'bourgeois nationalist' plotters. So were, in most cases, members of larger groups like the Ukrainians. One commented: 'I was bound in any event to be regarded as a Ukrainian bourgeois nationalist. True, I had never had anything to do with Ukrainian nationalism, and had never had any sympathy with it, but I had a typically Ukrainian surname, and I had had several sympathizers with Ukrainian nationalism among my acquaintances.'[111]

It is an interesting fact that there are almost no accusations through the Great Purge of allegiance to any genuinely reactionary idea. Those accused were almost always linked with the Mensheviks, the Armenian progressive nationalist 'Dashnaks', the Social Revolutionaries, or with Communist deviationist groups – practically never with Monarchists, Kadets, etc.

The Jewish Social-Democratic 'Bund' was a particularly fatal association; and many Jews qualified for accusation either as Bundists or as Zionists. A case is quoted of an elderly Jew who had worked as a defence lawyer in earlier trials in the Donets Basin, and conducted himself in a way that antagonized the N.K.V.D. – by asking them for documents which might be helpful to the defence and so forth. He had learned enough not to defend himself, and on his arrest signed everything that was put before him without reading it. He later found that he had installed himself as a leader of a 'Bund' group, in touch with other counter-revolutionary organizations, including one headed by the Provincial Party Secretary, Sarkissov (a candidate member of the Central Committee). On one occasion he was told that he was going to be 'confronted' by an important accomplice called Abramsohn, of whom he had never heard. When this man was brought in, the investigator said 'Stop looking at each other as if you'd never met before', so he immediately remarked, 'Hello, Abramsohn,' 'Hello, er . . . er . . .,' the other started, having to be prompted with his chief's name. They then both signed the records of their confessions about each other without looking at them.[112]

Genuine Bundists, on the other hand, are always reported as being the most refractory to interrogation, being better educated in Marxism than their interrogators, and toughened by a harder underground life in Tsarist times than that of the Bolsheviks.

All former Social Revolutionaries were arrested. In Kharkov jail, Weissberg tells[113] of a man who had joined the Bolsheviks in 1917, but who in 1905 had distributed among the Tsar's soldiers leaflets provided by the Social Revolutionaries. He had then been a young student and, far from being a member of the Social Revolutionary Party, did not even realize that there was any difference.

But everybody with unorthodox ideas of any sort was liable to end up in the camps. Jehovah's Witnesses were automatic victims. But there were also too-enthusiastic members of legal religions, such as the Baptist mentioned by Solzhenitsyn. Tolstoyans are widely reported, including an aged Tolstoyan woman whose twelve-year-old granddaughter had fought the N.K.V.D. officers to try and prevent her arrest.[114]

Priests had always had a difficult time under the Soviet regime. Now they became almost automatically suspect of capital crimes. Trials of priests were announced throughout the Union. One in Orel in the summer of 1937, involving a bishop, twelve priests and others, had as one of the accusations 'publishing prayers in Old Slavonic'.[115] Other accusations were less credible. Three bishops sentenced in February 1938 had 'agitated for the opening of previously closed churches', but their further crimes included sabotage.[116] The main Soviet authority of the time mentions that Buddhists were commonly agents of Japan, engaged in sabotaging bridges and farms.[117] It was also true that 'The activity of the counter-revolutionary Muslim priesthood in the U.S.S.R. is directed by the Japanese Secret Service'.[118] Many were accused of railway sabotage.[119] The authorities had also 'destroyed not a few nests of spies directed by "holy" Catholic priests', who had been responsible for the sabotage of factories, bridges and railways as well as espionage.[120]

If it were neither nationality, nor past, nor ideas, that brought a prisoner in, it might be relationship: the purge within the Party, the Government and the Army automatically spread in that way. Each of the accused had relations, and acquaintances who also had relations. We have already noted (p. 354) the four listings sent by Yezhov to Stalin of people to be shot, where List 4 is the simple 'Wives of Enemies of the People'.[121] We have seen the liquidation or imprisonment of the generals' relations. The military men had, it is true, been shot in comparative haste without public trial. Confessions in the longer-drawn-out affairs were in part obtained by promises not to kill the surviving dependants. Stalin's promises were sometimes kept. A woman prisoner met in labour camps twelve wives, two daughters, two sisters and a daughter-in-law of prominent purgees – including Yagoda's wife.[122] Eight years was the usual sentence.

Typical of purgees of the second rank was Salpeter, a commander of Stalin's bodyguard, a Lett, who was arrested, together with his wife. She refused to confess, but was finally confronted with her husband in a very bad state, who mumbled that she had said she would get rid of a picture of Stalin in their new flat (formerly Yagoda's). For this she too got eight years.[123]

The wives of the Soviet elite adjusted most slowly of all to their position in the cells. Their position was an especially difficult one. They had nothing to confess and were unable even to deny the charge, since that was simply of being 'wives of enemies of the people'.[124] In many cases they had not, as their husbands had, understood the dangerous possibilities before them. On arriving in the cells, they were priggish and intolerant of women who had been under arrest for a long time – believing that these earlier cases must have been guilty of some genuine offence.[125]

Even when not arrested, families suffered terribly. An attempted mass suicide is reported by a group of four thirteen- and fourteen-year-old children of executed N.K.V.D. officers, found badly wounded in the Prozorovsky Forest near Moscow.[126] The daughter of an Assistant Chief of Red Army Intelligence, Alexander Karin (who was arrested and shot, with his wife), was thirteen in the spring of 1937. The Karin apartment was taken by one of Yezhov's men. They turned her out into the street. She went to her father's best friend, Shpigelglas, Assistant Head of the Foreign Department of the N.K.V.D., who put her up for the night, but was virtually ordered next day by Yezhov's secretary to throw her out. Shpigelglas remembered she had relatives at Saratov and sent her off there. Two months later she came back: 'She was pale, thin, her eyes filled with bitterness. Nothing childish remained in her.' She had meanwhile been made to speak at a meeting of the Pioneers approving the execution of her father and mother and saying that they were spies.[127]

A Mrs Smirnov – though it is not clear of which of the three oppositionist Smirnovs she was the wife – is reported as left with a two-months-old baby, a six-year-old girl and a fourteen-year-old boy. The girl was fobbed off with stories about her father's travels, but the boy knew. As usual, after an interval, the mother was arrested, in spite of desperate appeals about the baby. She refused to denounce her husband, and got the usual eight years. What happened to the family is not known.[128]

When Weissberg was in the sick-bay in the Kharkov prison

there were a number of children there, including a boy nine years old.[129] When, early in 1939, the Soviet press started to report the arrest of various N.K.V.D. officers for extorting false confessions, one case at Leninsk-Kuznetsk in the Kemerovo province concerned children down to ten years old.[130] Four officers of the N.K.V.D. and the Prosecutor's Office received five to ten year sentences. In all, 160 children, mainly between twelve and fourteen, had been arrested and subjected to severe interrogation, and had confessed to espionage, terror, treason and links with the Gestapo.* Similar mass trials of children took place in various other cities.[131] There is indeed a report of a genuine children's organization which planned to avenge arrested parents by killing the N.K.V.D. officers they held responsible.[132]

In fact, in general, as a Soviet speaker has pointed out, 'not only the workers themselves were victims of repression, but also their families, down to the absolutely innocent children, whose lives were thus broken from the begining'.[133]

Another 'category' were automatic suspects – anyone connected with production, and in particular engineers. In their case no guesses were needed. They were saboteurs to a man. It did not matter if their record was generally good. Stalin himself had said, 'No wrecker will go on wrecking all the time, if he does not wish to be exposed very rapidly. On the contrary, the real wrecker will show success in his work from time to time, for this is the only means of staying on the job, of worming himself into confidence, and continuing his wrecking activity.'[134]

In the economy, the security mania of the N.K.V.D. seems to have been quite genuine. For, quite apart from the persecution of actual people, they imposed by about the end of 1935 a system through which guards and watchmen multiplied enormously in the factories, research institutes, and so forth throughout the country. This was in part supposed to be for the prevention of thieving, but also against the penetration of 'secrets', many of which were not secret by Soviet standards and almost none of which would have been regarded as secret in any ordinary com-

*These confessions were obtained with comparative ease. A ten-year-old broke down after a single night-long interrogation, and admitted to membership of a fascist organization from the age of seven.

munity. Moreover, there already existed in every Soviet institution a 'secret department', covering both political reliability of
personnel and the technical secrets; and into its safes anything
remotely confidential had to be put each night. It is now stated
that in 1939 there were, in a labour force of 78,811,000, no fewer
than 2,126,000 guards and watchmen – *not* counting N.K.V.D.
militia – and only 589,000 miners and 939,000 railwaymen.[135]

In this atmosphere, any failure, or any accident, in the economic sphere automatically became sabotage. In the absence of
genuine opposition acts any breakdown had to be made to serve,
just as Molotov's accident at Prokopyevsk had had to be inflated into an assassination attempt in the absence of any
genuine one. And already at the Pyatakov Trial, railway accidents
had been put to the account of the accused, with Vyshinsky
graphically recounting the sufferings of the murdered passengers.
In the Bukharin Trial, livestock deaths were attributed to the
conscious activities of the plotters. Sharangovich said in evidence, 'In 1932 we took measures to spread plague among pigs';
and later, speaking of horses, 'In 1936 we caused a wide outbreak
of anaemia.' Sharangovich also mentions a number of particular
plants – a cement works, a flax mill, a pipe foundry, a power
station – in Byelorussia (where he was First Secretary) as having
been sabotaged under his instructions. Failures in the grossly
over-extended first Five-Year Plan were very widespread indeed.
But even if the local First Secretary was usually responsible, in
every case subordinates were involved.

On the economic side, Soviet statistical and planning methods
led to an endless strain on skilled management. The planning
figures were always unrealistic. To admit failure meant instant
arrest, so the directors concealed it as best they could. This led
to a vicious circle with doubly erroneous figures in the ensuing
period. When the gap grew so large that it could not be concealed,
a scapegoat had to be found, and 'Then there is a crisis and the
Chief Director and a number of officials are sent to camps, but
those who take their place have to employ the same methods all
over again; the system as it stands leaves them no option.'[136]

The directors who organized the new works faced appalling
tasks. Lykhachev, of the Stalin Automobile Works in Moscow,

had to try and direct 25,000 men with crises about administration, raw material or simple negligence arising almost hourly. At the Gorki Works at Gorki, an even larger factory wore out the director Diakonov even before his arrest. The head of the automobile industry, Dybets, and his assistant were arrested in 1938. In the same year, in the metallurgical factory in Sverdlovsk, the Old Bolshevik director, Semion Magrilov, shot himself in his office, leaving a long letter attacking the Terror. All those suspected of having read it were arrested and disappeared.[137]

The railways were subjected to particularly Draconic laws. The Criminal Codex of the R.S.F.S.R. in its Article 59 covered 'crimes against the system of government', including various offences on the railways which 'lead, or might lead, to the breakdown of State transport plans' and of which some examples given are the accumulation of empty trucks and the dispatch of trains off schedule. The prescribed punishment was up to ten years or, if done with malicious intent, the death sentence.

Kaganovich also devised the so-called 'theory of counter-revolutionary limit-setting on output', with the help of which he organized the mass destruction of engineering and technical cadres. 'In a short period of time most of the directors of railroads and of the railroads' political departments and many executive officials of the central apparatus and lines were dismissed from their jobs and later arrested.'[138]

As to 'sabotage' itself, on the Russian railways at this time there was an accident of some sort about every five minutes. As we have seen in dealing with the Pyatakov Trial, this led to the slaughter of the railway cadres. Kaganovich had made a tour of the railways of the Far East early in 1936. Following this, the Military Collegium went on tour and handed down five death sentences and ten long jail terms in Krasnoyarsk and Tomsk in March, for wrecking for 'foreign intelligence services'. This was only a beginning.

In his speech at a meeting of railway activists on 10 March 1937, Kaganovich said: 'I cannot name a single road or a single system where there has not been Trotskyite–Japanese sabotage. Not only that, there is not a single branch of railway transport in which these saboteurs have not turned up . . .' Under Kaganovich arrests of railway officials were made by lists. His deputies, nearly all road chiefs and political-section chiefs, and other executive officials in transport were arrested without any grounds whatever.[139]

On 10 August 1937 Kaganovich wrote to the N.K.V.D. demanding the arrest of ten responsible officials in the People's Commissariat of Transport. The only grounds were that he thought their behaviour suspicious. They were arrested as spies and saboteurs and shot. He wrote in all thirty-two personal letters to Yezhov, demanding the arrest of eighty-three transport executives.[140]

The North Donets railway was the only line not involved in these sweeping arrests of early 1937. In August, the heads of the line were called to Moscow and instructed to find saboteurs. An estimate by the Director of Locomotive Service of the line is that about 1,700 out of the 45,000 employees were arrested within months. In mid-November he himself was called to the N.K.V.D. and asked how he proposed to end sabotage. As he was unable to think of any cases of sabotage – the line being an exceptionally efficient one – he was bitterly harangued and during the next wave of arrests was pulled in, on 2 December 1937, without a warrant or charge.

His wife and six-year-old son were thrown out of their house two days after his arrest, and he was subjected to severe interrogation, with beatings, together with a number of other prisoners, including several station-masters and the deputy head of the line.[141]

Special railwaymen's prisons were set up, in small towns like Poltava. Arrested railwaymen were kept in coaches in unused sidings. Special military courts travelled about the country dealing with them.[142] They were almost invariably Japanese spies. The reason for this was that the Soviet Union had in 1935 handed over the Chinese Eastern Railway to the Japanese. The Russian railwaymen who had operated it and who now returned to the Soviet Union were almost the only non-diplomatic Soviet personnel who had been living abroad, and on their return they were automatically high-grade suspects. (With their families, they are said to have numbered about 40,000.) And they had meanwhile worked on all the railway systems and recruited all their colleagues.

INTERROGATION

Whether soldier or intellectual, Ukrainian or engineer, the arrested man might thus deduce or learn from his acquaintances what the exact charge would be. And this was important. For when he went to interrogation it was N.K.V.D. practice not to tell him what he was in for, but to let him frame his own confession – unless he proved 'obstinate' after a few interrogations, when he might be enlightened.

Article 128 of the Code of Criminal Procedure of the R.S.F.S.R. laid down that the charge against a person under investigation must be presented not later than forty-eight hours after his arrest. This was not observed. In fact, it contradicted the basic N.K.V.D. method. In many cases charges were not presented until months, or years, afterwards; and in some cases not at all.

Sometimes there were special preliminaries. The Hungarian Communist writer, József Lengyel, describes being taken from the ordinary cell in which 275 men lived 'on, between, and under 25 iron bedsteads' to a much worse one for a fortnight's softening-up prior to interrogation. In this 'hermetically closed space' in the moist heat from human beings, and radiators, bread fresh in the morning was white with mould by midday. Some of his cell-mates had strokes and some went insane. Though he himself only got jaundice and open sores on arms and legs, his former cell-mates did not recognize him when he was returned to the ordinary prison.[143]

A woman teacher held in solitary confinement in darkness for forty days to confess her espionage motive in approaching the British Consulate for a visa also returned to her cell quite unrecognizable.[144] Worse was the 'kennel' at the Lubyanka, described by the critic Ivanov-Razumnik – a true Black Hole with sixty men packed in a heated basement cell about fifteen feet square, with no ventilation but the slit under the door, for a week or even more. Eczema, nausea and palpitations were universal.[145] This was a variation on the old 'steam room' technique used by the O.G.P.U. in the twenties. A Soviet writer describes also the 'standing cell', where, in darkness, a prisoner had room only to stand with his hands at his side, virtually immured. A Secretary of the Tatar Provincial Committee was held thus for two days and taken out unconscious.[146]

Interrogation took place mainly at night. In a mass cell, a warder would come and murmur the initial letter of a man's name, upon which those this fitted would give theirs until the right one answered. He would then be taken out.[147]

All accounts of experiences in the great prisons mention that when escorting prisoners along corridors to interrogation or for other purposes, the warders continually made a clicking sound with tongues or with their belt buckles, so that others on similar errands would know in advance. The purpose of this, evidently a definite regulation, was to stop anyone recognizing people outside their cells. If two were about to meet in the same corridor, one had his face to the wall while the other went by. In the Butyrka yard, which sometimes had to be crossed, were little sentry-box-style sheds, into which one or other of two passing prisoners could be shunted.

Eventually, down the stairs ringed with anti-suicide nets, the prisoner would arrive at the office of the interrogator where he might, for the moment, be fairly politely received. The routine questions started: 'Do you know where you are? . . . You are in the heart of Soviet Intelligence. . . . Why do you think you are here? . . .' A confession was now required. In the case of the ordinary prisoner preparation for public trial did not arise, and the confession was merely a horrible formality required under N.K.V.D. custom to justify a sentence which was usually ready for issue. That is, as far as the accused himself was concerned. For interrogation had one further important purpose – the implication of hitherto unnamed accomplices.

The interrogation technique almost invariably started, not with an accusation, but with the question: 'Will you tell me what hypothesis you have formed of the reason for your arrest?' This is said to have been based on a questionnaire used by the Holy Inquisition.[148]

The 'Yezhov method', as N.K.V.D. officers called it, threw the task of building the case against himself on the arrested man. If the accused simply gave an innocent account of everything he had done, tougher methods were used, but it still remained up to the victim to find the right line of confession. Prisoners, with the more or less obvious connivance of the authorities, became expert in helping the newly arrested to devise suitable and satisfactory confessions, thus saving everybody trouble, on both sides.[149]

There were various tricks of interrogation. The interrogator might be polite and speak rather in sorrow, and then change to abuse. The obscene cursing of the interrogated was routine. In some cases it had its effect. In others not: Weissberg recounts that he found it quite interesting.[150]

Many N.K.V.D. interrogators were often aware of the complete falsehood of all the charges, and some of them would even admit it. Most, however, even though not crediting the full details, 'professed to believe that they contained a grain of truth, and this sufficed to justify their actions in their own eyes'.[151] This applied particularly to the earlier generation of N.K.V.D. men. After they themselves were liquidated the newer intake were much simpler Stalinists, who often seem to have believed to a great extent in the accused's guilt.

The turnover of interrogators, as the N.K.V.D. itself was purged, was good for the morale of resisting prisoners. Two mention that 'Each of the present writers outlasted more than ten of his examining magistrates; one of them outlasted more than a dozen. In both instances this included the magistrate who had ordered the arrest.'[152] N.K.V.D. officers under arrest were usually interrogated more severely than others. They were more pessimistic about the outcome, and 'were extremely stubborn and reluctant to confess for they knew what lay ahead of them'.[153] They are reported as highly nervous, expecting to be taken out and executed at any moment.

We have already (in Chapter 5) dealt with the basic techniques of interrogation. In run-of-the-mill cases, the 'conveyor' remained at first the main system, punctuated by physical assault. A typical case is of the girl secretary of a factory director arrested as one of a Trotskyite sabotage ring. She was kept standing up for two days with short interruptions and then half-throttled by the examiner until she signed a confession which enabled the N.K.V.D. to arrest her chief and the thirty-odd other members of the factory's sabotage group.[154]

The conveyor would break down almost anyone in four to six days, and most people in two. Its single disadvantage was that it consumed time and energy. There came a point when the arrests outpaced the interrogative capacity of the N.K.V.D., and the simpler method of beating became routine. We can date this change precisely. It was on 17–18 August 1937. In Moscow, Kharkov and elsewhere, it suddenly came into force. At the Kholodnaya Gora Prison interrogation section a prisoner describes having to stuff his ears with bread to get any sleep that night on account of the shrieking of women being beaten.[155] In Kazan jail the first victim was the wife of the Premier of the Tatar A.S.S.R.[156] In the Butyrka that summer, one floor of a whole wing of one of the prison buildings was set aside for night interrogation. From 11 p.m. until 3 in the morning, the inmates of nearby women's cells were kept awake: 'over the screams of the tortured we could hear the shouts and curses of the torturers'. A woman would go half-mad thinking she recognized her husband's screams.[157]

The appearance of mere local initiative was preserved. The weapons were almost always boots, fists and table-legs. But Stalin and Yezhov no longer needed to heed any complaints from within the Party, and the rather half-hearted cover to a widely-known reality seems more a matter of preserving conventions than anything else. Stalin seems, in fact, to have issued official instructions on torture proper as early as the beginning of 1937, though it remained confidential even from Provincial Party Secretaries till he confirmed it, both retrospectively and prospectively, in the secret circular telegram to them on 20 January 1939 when, after the fall of Yezhov, one or two objectors had begun to make themselves heard[158] (see p.196).

Several victims note that the N.K.V.D. respected certain formalities. Of course their methods of interrogation were a clear breach of the law. But declarations signed by prisoners were very rarely suppressed. They had to be copied and filed in the dossier.[159] So when Beria took over, he found that some prosecutors were still attaching the complaints made by the accused about 'illegal methods of investigation' to the examination record. He took this up with Vyshinsky, who gave instructions that this was not to occur again, though in some cases the prisoners' statements could be preserved on file, not attached to the records of the case.[160]

Whichever interrogation method was applied to a given victim, the required confessions followed the same routines. As early as 1931 the foundations had been fully established. A surgeon had confessed his intention to poison the Dnieper River. A lawyer had confessed first to blowing up a bridge, then to planning terrorism, and finally to being a Japanese spy. An electrical engineer was to have commanded a battery of artillery to bombard the working-men's quarter of Dniepropetrovsk. Another accused confessed to having met ex-President Poincaré.[161]

There is a report of a former senior official in the Ukrainian timber industry who at the beginning of the thirties had made a confession in connexion with the Industrial Party Trial, that he had had too little timber felled in order to spare the woods for their former owners whose rights he aimed to restore. He had been sentenced to ten years but released after a year and – like many members of this particular conspiracy – restored to high position. On his re-arrest, he was required to confess that he had had too much timber felled in order to ruin the forests. Another forester had had to confess that he had special tracks cut in the forests to open the way for Polish or German tanks.[162]

One typical style of charge was that against Mrs Weissberg, arrested in April 1936. She was a ceramicist and it was alleged that she had surreptitiously inserted swastikas into the patterns of tea-cups she had designed, and also hidden two pistols under her bed with a view to killing Stalin.[163] A Jewish engineer was accused of designing a large scientific institute in the form of half a swastika, for reasons of Nazi ideology.[164] A woman potter had designed an ashtray which resembled, or could be made to re-semble, a Zionist Star of David. She was arrested and the stock destroyed.[165] Koestler mentions a German Communist doctor who was charged with injecting patients with VD, spreading rumours that VD was incurable, and being a German spy.[166] Professor Byelin, of Kiev University, was charged with espionage for mentioning in a textbook the depth of the Dnieper at various points. Another professor – a Jewish refugee from Germany – had given German agents details about the navigability of the Siberian River Ob. A third had forwarded to the Japanese reports about the political attitude of Jewish children.[167] One Kiev workman confessed to having tried to blow up a kilometre-long bridge over the Dnieper with a few kilograms of arsenic, but having had to abandon the attempt owing to rainy weather.[168] Speaking of a middle-aged washerwoman type, accused of consorting with foreigners in expensive restaurants and seducing Soviet diplomats to worm secrets out of them, a Soviet writer bitterly comments, 'this was July 1937, when no one cared any longer whether charges bore the slightest semblance of probability or not'.[169]

There is a recent Soviet account of an Old Bolshevik serving a fifteen-year sentence for 'terrorism', in that he had murdered himself. The N.K.V.D. maintained that he had stolen the dead man's papers and passed himself off in his place. When he had them call a witness who had known him since childhood, and identified him at once, they threw her out and sentenced him notwithstanding.[170]

When a big case was afoot, local interrogators sometimes tried to gain credit by finding accomplices for it, on their own initiative, among their prisoners. After the Tukhachevsky Case, a junior interrogator attempted to involve Weissberg in a connexion with the Reichswehr, to build up a new military conspiracy. His superior, on the other hand, meant to produce Weissberg as a witness in the Bukharin Trial, a role to which he was better suited since he had at least met Bukharin.[171]

There is an account of a case in the Ukraine in which fifty students were charged with forming an organization to assassinate Kossior, who had been named as one of the senior intended victims in the great Moscow Trials. A year's work on this case, which was a structure of great intricacy, had been performed by the interrogators. In 1938, however, it became known that Kossior himself had been arrested as a Trotskyite. Everyone thought that the students would be released. But a new interrogation immediately started and they were beaten up for having lied to the N.K.V.D. After a few days the stool-pigeons in the cells let them know what they were supposed to confess this time. It was to change their deposition, putting in the name of Kaganovich for Kossior. The N.K.V.D. could not face the trouble of constructing a completely new fabrication. Finally, everything was in order and the students were sent off to labour camps.[172]

The demand for denunciation of others was a difficult matter of conscience with many. One Armenian priest with a good memory confessed to recruiting all his fellow countrymen he had buried in the past three years. A newly-arrested prisoner would sometimes find a list of unused dead men made available by his cellmates.[173] The denunciation of people already arrested and sentenced was not regarded as discreditable.

But, of course, such tactics only seldom satisfied the examiners, and most people gave way enough to implicate outside contacts whose names were presented to them as already suspect by the very fact of acquaintance.

On the whole the N.K.V.D. officers showed a niggling, self-righteous and bureaucratic brutality, treating the prisoners like cattle about whom any question of sympathy simply did not arise. But there are many reports of odd exceptions, showing that even in these circumstances the Russian style of humanism sporadically persisted. Two ex-prisoners note that 'There were many officials of all grades, from simple warder to prison governor and even including examining magistrates, who again and again defied regulations and risked their own freedom by finding opportunities of making prisoners' lives easier by secretly giving them food or cigarettes, or even merely speaking a cheering and comforting word to them.'[174] (On the other hand József Lengyel recounts that though he remembers 'humane guards' and 'decent commandants', the investigators were without exception despicable.[175] This minor divergence certainly reflects the increasing brutalization of the N.K.V.D.: Koestler's 'Gletkin', even, is a figure of the Yagoda rather than of the Yezhov period.)

An N.K.V.D. sentry was returning a prisoner to his cell, after an interrogation in the Butyrka. They stopped at a tap for the prisoner to wash the blood off himself. As he did this he was shaken with sobs. The sentry said 'Don't take it too hard, Comrade! Life's hard on us all, one just has to bear it. Maybe he did beat you up for no good reason, but think nothing of it. Probably his black heart aches more than your white body. You can wash the blood off just like that, but what about him? Where's the water that can clean his black heart . . .?' The prisoner, an Army officer named Vasilev, returned to his cell much cheered, and spoke of the special humanity of the Russian people.[176]

A woman prisoner, a German Communist, reports a guard on the deportation train as saying to her, when she was in tears, 'Don't cry. It won't be as bad as all that. You'll live through it and get home again.' (She was later, when handed over to the Nazis, to note in the same way the occasional kind and thoughtful Gestapo man.[177])

In 1937 (though this is a somewhat different point) some of the old N.K.V.D. officers continued to show sympathy for obviously innocent and non-oppositionist Old Bolsheviks. A recent Soviet account by Antonina Levkovich, who was arrested as 'the wife of an enemy of the people' in 1937 following an appeal for her already arrested husband, quotes several instances of kindness. They often turned out badly for all concerned. After a month spent in bad conditions on the way from Moscow to Kirghizia, she and her companions found an N.K.V.D. officer who tried to save them from starvation. He was charged with 'intolerable pity for wives of enemies of the people' and had to shoot himself to avoid arrest.[178]

The Soviet press has lately (admittedly during a period of good-will towards the Police) published several such tales of N.K.V.D. men who in one way or another opposed the Purges. For example, a Kazakh officer called Sevikgali Dzhakupov, who after a career in the Cheka, including action in the extremely ruthless liquidation of the Basmachi – nationalist partisans – in Central Asia, was appointed in 1935 to a leading post in the Kazakh N.K.V.D., when 'the complicated international situation and a whole series of other reasons led to the start of the disastrous shooting of one's own people'. Dzhakupov's resistance centred on a friend of his, the Kazakh poet Saken Seifullin. He protested, even at open sessions, against the executions, and even after his own arrest in 1937 continued to defend his friend and others, writing to Stalin,

Yezhov and Vyshinsky. He was himself executed in January 1939.[179]

Such things are worth recording. But at the best of times they were most exceptional. The norm was callous brutality, or at best cloddish indifference to death and suffering. A Soviet writer remarks of the interrogators, 'They were all sadists of course. And only a handful found the courage to commit suicide. Pace by pace, as they followed one routine directive after another, they climbed down the steps from the human condition to that of beasts. . . . But all this happened only gradually.'[180] The few humane officers and guards did not anyhow survive Yezhov's purge of the N.K.V.D. His new intake of N.K.V.D. troopers were well-trained, well-fed, heartless young thugs. Any display of human sympathy, they had firmly implanted in them, was a concession to bourgeois feeling and a form of treachery in the class struggle. As the Purge broadened it also got worse.

'TRIAL'

With the interrogation completed, the cases were transferred to the judicial and quasi-judicial bodies for sentence. Since 1934 the competent court in political cases was the Military Collegium of the Supreme Court. This had a large staff and was able to mount many cases simultaneously. It took mere minutes even for leading officials (see p. 607) or generals (see p. 315). A lesser figure, Evgenia Ginzburg, describes her seven-minute trial before them in 1937. The Court returned in two minutes with a 'verdict' which she estimates must have taken twenty minutes to type.[181] Thus the Collegium got through tens of thousands of prisoners over the years of the Terror. But these thousands constituted a very small proportion of those condemned.

Those who came before a court were judged according to the Criminal Code, whose long Article 58 covered all forms of remotely political crime. This article was broad enough, or so it might have been thought, to encompass anyone the N.K.V.D. wished to 'repress'. And it had long been draconically interpreted. A Supreme Court ruling of 2 January 1928 had laid down that counter-revolutionary offences were committed 'when the person who committed them, although not directly pursuing a counter-revolutionary aim, wittingly entertained the possibility of this arising or should have foreseen the socially dangerous character of the consequences of his actions'.[182] The definition of terrorism was gradually extended to violent acts against a wide range of people. Not only all Party officials, but members of grain procurement commissions (in 1930), shock workers (in 1931), 'pioneers' (in 1934), were covered.[183]

A law of 7 August 1932 introduced the death penalty for a wide range of offences against State property, and the courts seem to have been invited to extend it still further in practical action.[184] Again, to take an example from the field of sabotage,[185] a law of August 1935 established as such the gleaning of wheat by peasant women, who had hitherto been able to save a certain amount in this way. Peasant women were commonly given ten years for this offence.[186]

Vyshinsky strengthened such tendencies by a simple interpretative method:

He proposed that the deliberate burning of State or public property be adjudicated, regardless of motive and intent, under Article 58, paragraph 9, of the Russian Republic Criminal Codex (Sabotage). Consequently, acts committed without counter-revolutionary intent (for instance, arson for reasons of personal enmity, revenge, etc.) had to be adjudicated under the articles on State crimes. Vyshinsky declared that there are no ordinary criminal offences, that these offences now become crimes of a political order. He recommended that ordinary criminal cases be reviewed for the purpose of imparting a political character to them.[187]

To take a specific crime:

Vyshinsky demanded that counter-revolutionary intent must mandatorily be sought in all criminal cases linked with shortcomings connected with the harvesting campaign. In his view, shortcomings in the harvesting campaign were in many cases caused by the activity of saboteurs, who had to be 'rendered harmless'. For example, during the harvesting campaign of 1937 it was revealed that a number of crops had become infested with ticks. This infection was ascribed to the activity of hostile counter-revolutionary elements, and in connection with this a great number of criminal cases were instituted. Many of the indictments linked with tick infection in grain crops were completely unfounded. Yet Vyshinsky demanded that the prosecutors insist on severe punishment in all criminal cases instituted in connection with crops infested with ticks.[188]

When it came to the actual trial,

He repeatedly maintained that in a criminal trial probability of guilt was perfectly adequate. Instructing prosecutors in the 'art of identifying saboteurs', Vyshinsky maintained that this is achieved not by comprehensive, full and objective evaluation of the evidence gathered in a criminal case but by so-called 'political flair'.[189]

And the legal processes were eased by his ruling that 'It is pointless to repeat without particular need what has already been established in the preliminary investigation.'[190]

As a result we get such extraordinary results as a woman who got ten years under Article 58, Section 10, for saying, after his arrest, that Tukhachevsky was handsome,[191] or an artist getting five years for adding to the slogan 'Life has become better, life has become more joyful: Stalin' the letter 'u', changing the meaning to 'Life has become better . . . for Stalin'.[192] Failure to inform, treated as complicity, was severely dealt with. In a minor case, only producing a six-year sentence even for the principal, the non-informer got three years under Article 58 (12).[193] Under the same Article a man was sentenced to three years for 'smiling in sympathy' while some drunken dockers at another table in Odessa were telling each other anti-Soviet anecdotes.[194] A Tatar woman, originally listed as a Trotskyite, was reallocated as a bourgeois nationalist by the N.K.V.D. official concerned, on the grounds that 'they'd exceeded the quota for Trotskyites, but were short on nationalists, even though they'd taken all the Tatar writers they could think of.'[195] A twenty-year-old mathematician, with no political interests, was sentenced simply because his mother, an old Social Revolutionary, was rounded up in 1937. He had actually been born in a Tsarist jail.[196]

But comparatively few cases were dealt with by a court. Article 8 of the Corrective Labour Codex states: 'Persons are directed to corrective labour who have been sentenced thereto by (*a*) sentence in a court of law; (*b*) decree of an administrative organ.' This latter was usually the N.K.V.D. 'Special Board', as set up by laws of 10 July and 5 November 1934. One prisoner who did six years in two camps and several prisons estimates that approximately 90 per cent of the 'political' prisoners had been sentenced by the Board.[197]

The Special Board consisted of the Deputy Head of the N.K.V.D., the Plenipotentiary of the N.K.V.D. for the R.S.F.S.R., the Head of the Main Administration of Militia and the Head of the Union Republic N.K.V.D. where the case had arisen. The Prosecutor-General of the U.S.S.R. or his deputy was also to participate.[198] It might pass, or rubber-stamp, hundreds of sentences a day.

The Special Board's sentences were originally limited to five years, but this was either abolished or ignored fairly soon. Terms of eight and ten years are mentioned.[199] But in any case, while a man who served out a term imposed by a court was often released, one sentenced by the Board was simply resentenced to a further period when his sentence expired. The formalities were completed in Moscow and the new sentence announced to the accused in camp by the local representative of the N.K.V.D. Special Department.

In the provinces, an entirely extra-legal body, the 'Troika', operated from about August 1937[200] – reviving in different form the emergency Tribunals of the Civil War. Its membership was the Party First Secretary, an N.K.V.D. representative and the Prosecutor. Unlike the Special Board, it had the power to inflict death sentences. It operated generally without even formal reference to articles of the Penal Code.

The Special Board was usually given 'cases for which the evidence was not sufficient for turning the defendant over to a court'.[201] The defendant had no right to defence, and cases were tried *in absentia*, which – as a Soviet law journal has lately remarked – 'created the preconditions for deliberately passing unjustified, harsh sentences'.[202]

And if the Criminal Code was interpreted with great elasticity by the courts, even that was found too restrictive for most cases before the Special Board. Article 58 was generally cited as a basis, but the accused were liable under the following heads:

K.R.T.D.	Counter-revolutionary Trotskyite Activity. Usual sentence five to ten years.
K.R.D.	Counter-revolutionary Activity. Usual sentence five years or over.
K.R.A.	Counter-revolutionary Agitation. Usual sentence five years or over.
Ch.S.I.R.	Member of the Family of a Traitor to the Fatherland. Usual sentence five to eight years.
P.Sh.	Suspicion of Espionage. Usual sentence eight years.

– the latter an offence perhaps unique in the world's legal history.

In addition, the following categories could be simply labelled by the Prosecutor and sent to camp without even the Special Board routine:

S.O.E.	Socially Dangerous Element. Usual sentence five years.
S.V.E.	Socially Harmful Element (that is, common criminals). Usual sentence five years.[203]

This power to inflict punishment where there was admittedly no crime was provided for in Article 22 of the 'Principles of Criminal Jurisdiction' given in the Basic Criminal Code, which reads as follows:

Punishment in the form of exile can be applied by a sentence of the State Prosecutor against persons recognized as being socially dangerous, without any criminal proceedings being taken against these persons on charges of committing a specific crime or of a specific offence and, also, even in those cases where these persons are acquitted by a court of the accusation of committing a specific crime.

In early 1937 sentences were still on the light side. A typical K.R.T.D. case is of an electrician arrested at that time, who had formerly known some Trotskyites and in whose room there was found, on his arrest, a copy of the first edition of *The History of the Civil War* (which, of course, gave many of the facts of Trotsky's role in the period covered). For this he got three years.[204] Another man, a former Trotskyite, was sentenced to a longer term because he had travelled from Moscow to Leningrad on 1 December 1934.[205] Another got three years for possession of a K.R.A. rhyme about Feuchtwanger and Gide.[206] A professor of astronomy got five years (K.R.A.) for objecting to his daughter marrying an N.K.V.D. man.[207] A typical P.Sh. case was of a professor who had been a prisoner of war in Austria in 1915 – his *sole* offence.[208] The decree of 14 September 1937[209] established what amounted to completely extra-judicial procedures for counter-revolutionary crimes, and sentences grew greater. Moreover those arrested in 1933 and 1935 were now retried, and the comparatively mild sentences of three or five years of those earlier days were 'translated . . . into the language of 1937'.[210]

After a Special Board 'trial' (in his absence), the accused eventually received the sentence, on some convenient occasion. One prisoner mentions simply being handed a grubby typewritten sheet in his cell by a woman trusty, an ex-prostitute, to the effect that the Special Board of the N.K.V.D. had condemned him to five years in camp.[211]

In spite of the vast amount of paperwork, loose ends proliferated. It is said that in the Butyrka a whole block was occupied by prisoners who could not be sent to camps because not only was there no warrant against them, but no papers of any sort existed in connexion with them. They had been condemned as groups and the judges had not been able to compile dossiers, while the labour camps would only accept prisoners with papers.[212]

For all the various forms of trial, death sentences are estimated at not over 10 per cent.[213] It was usually obvious when an execution was to take place. Several warders and an N.K.V.D. officer would appear at the cell door, which otherwise seldom happened. There was sometimes time to say goodbye and hand over any remaining property, such as clothes, to one's cell-mates.

A recent Soviet authority has remarked that 'Many were exterminated without trial or investigation'.[214] Vyshinsky himself favoured the extra-legal method. He several times said 'When it is a question of annihilating the enemy, we can do it just as well without a trial.'[215] There seem in fact to have been few executions without 'trial', apart from the liquidation of oppositionists already in camps, until 1937. The first blow seems to have been against foreigners resident in Russia, including naturalized Soviet citizens. With no important defenders in the Party and susceptible to the charge of contact with foreign espionage, they began to go to the execution cellars in large numbers late in 1936.

The cellars of the Lubyanka were really a sort of basement divided into a number of rooms off corridors. Later on, in ordinary routine, the condemned handed in their clothes in one of these rooms and changed into white underclothes only. They were then taken to the death cell and shot in the back of the neck with a TT eight-shot automatic. A doctor then signed the death certificate, the last document to be put in their files, and the tarpaulin on the floor was taken away to be cleaned by a woman specially employed for that purpose.[216]

And so it was elsewhere. In Gorki, for example, during the height of the Purge, one estimate is that from fifty to seventy executed corpses were taken out daily from the N.K.V.D. headquarters on Vorobievka Street. One prisoner was employed to whitewash the walls of the cells of executed prisoners immediately after they were taken over to the N.K.V.D. headquarters for execution. This was to cover the names that they had scratched on the walls.[217]

The main reason for believing that more were shot than condemned to death is that a common sentence was of imprisonment 'without the right to correspondence'. No one serving such a sentence is ever reported in the camps and prisons, and there is the evidence of the mass graves at Vinnitsa, containing men whose official condemnation had been such (see Appendix A).

So the Purge went on, striking further and further into every layer of the population until finally it reached the mass of the peasantry and the ordinary workers (often accessories in sabotage cases). 'Most peasants and unskilled workers escaped with a simple confession that, for purposes of counter-revolutionary agitation, they had alleged that there was a shortage of certain foods or of petrol or that shoes manufactured in Soviet fac-

428 The Yezhov Years

tories were of inferior quality, or something of the kind. This was sufficient for a sentence of from three to seven years' forced labour under Article 58.'[218]

Many accounts by former prisoners contain stories like the following: In September 1937 several hundred peasants were suddenly brought in to Kharkov prison. None of the officials in the prison knew what they had been arrested for, so they were beaten up to produce some sort of confession. But they did not know either. Finally, a case was put together:

> The charges against them were relatively light. Most of them were merely asked to confess that they had carried on counter-revolutionary agitation and sabotage. They had planned to poison wells and burn down barns, and they had put a spell on Stalin and agitated against the grain collections. All mere bagatelles. But about twenty of them were in more serious trouble. They were accused of a plot to steal horses, ride into the nearest town and proclaim an insurrection. The church bells were to ring out and at that sign the countryside was to rise. Nothing of all this had actually happened: the wells had not been poisoned, the cattle had not been harmed, the barns had not been burned down, the horses had not been stolen, the bells had not rung out, and the countryside had not risen. The whole thing was a complete invention.[219]

For the remainder of the Yezhov period they dominated the prison. They came in groups almost identically composed. First the chairman of the collective farm was arrested. He would give the names of his committee as accomplices, and they would name their foremen who would involve the ordinary peasants. Peasants usually confessed as soon as they found out what was required of them. The N.K.V.D. at this stage let them know what was needed informally through its own stool-pigeons. They went off to the camps in the far north in batches twice a week.[220]

Even out on the far Soviet periphery, a British observer, then in Lenkoran, Azerbaijan, saw lorry following lorry at intervals throughout the day, filled with Turkic peasants under N.K.V.D. escort. Ships, including the passenger boats taken off their ordinary routes for the purpose, were waiting to take them across the Caspian.[221]

Already in the summer of 1937 a Soviet writer notes 'the tremendous scale of the operation': 'All the agencies were inhumanly overworked. People were run off their feet; transport was insufficient; cells were crowded to bursting; courts sat twenty-four hours a day!'[222]

An N.K.V.D. officer arrested in November 1938 said that for six months it had become clear to the N.K.V.D. that the Purge could not go on in its present form.[223] The N.K.V.D. by now had files proving that almost every leading official everywhere was a spy. Many of them were never arrested. An example is Professor Bogomolets, at the time of his death President of the Ukrainian Academy of Science: at least ten statements from arrested scientists were on the record involving him as a Fascist spy.[224]

The snowball system had reached a stage where half the urban population were down on the N.K.V.D. lists. They could not all be arrested and there was no particular reason to take one rather than another. All the old 'categories' had been largely liquidated – former partisans, Old Bolsheviks, oppositionists, and so on. The new arrests in the N.K.V.D. itself were a sign that this was understood. The feeling also got around that a vast number of people had been arrested quite indiscriminately and now 'They don't even know what to do with them'.[225]

Not less than 5 per cent of the population had been arrested by the time of Yezhov's fall – that is, already at least one in twenty. One can virtually say that every other family in the country on average must have had one of its members in jail. The proportions were far higher among the educated classes.

In 1938, even from Stalin's point of view, the whole thing had become impossible. The first substantial question an interrogator asked was 'Who are your accomplices?' So from each arrest several other arrests more or less automatically followed. But if this had gone on for a few more months, and each new victim named only two or three accomplices, the next wave would have struck at 10 to 15 per cent of the population, and soon after that at 30 to 45 per cent. There are many theories of Stalin's motives throughout the whole horrible business, and the question of why he stopped the mass Terror at this stage has puzzled many commentators. But we can see that the extreme limits had been reached. To have gone on would have been impossible economically, politically – and even physically, in that interrogators, prisons and camps, already grotesquely overloaded, could not have managed it. And meanwhile, the work of the mass Purge had been done. Russia was crushed.

ON THE CULTURAL FRONT

The Russian intelligentsia had for over a century been the traditional repository of the ideas of resistance to despotism and above all to thought control. It was natural that the Purge struck at it with particular force. Not only did the Communists take seriously the whole principle of right and wrong ideas, and the necessity of crushing the latter, but they increasingly developed theories of form and method within the arts and sciences, so that someone otherwise an orthodox Party man in every way could yet hold opinions in biology or dramatic production which would lead directly to his fall.

In Soviet conditions, the academic world overlapped that of government to a larger degree than was then common elsewhere. The economists had been involved in the State Planning Commission, and had mostly been purged in the early thirties. But in other spheres too, such as foreign affairs and culture, there was a considerable overlap. We hear of a 'professor' in the Foreign Affairs Commissariat appealing to Molotov to intercede for his father, arrested through what he took to be a misunderstanding. Molotov minuted: 'To Yezhov: Can it be that this professor is still in the People's Commissariat of Foreign Affairs and not in the N.K.V.D. ?' Whereupon the writer of the letter was unlawfully arrested.[226]

During March, April and May 1937 articles appeared attacking deviation in history and economics, and among the 'cadres' of literature. A special article by Molotov sharpened the tone of the campaign.[227]

Historians were particularly vulnerable. The whole school of Party historians which had followed Pokrovsky were arrested. They were often labelled terrorists. In fact it is extraordinary how many of the leading terrorist bands were headed by historians. Sokolnikov mentions in the most natural way at his Trial that 'arrests had begun among the historians'.[228] Prigozhin, one of the leading terrorist executives of the group then before the court, was a historian. So were Karev, Zeidel, Anishev, Vanag, Zaks-Gladnev, Piontkovsky and Friedland, named at the 1936 and 1937 Trials as active terrorists. Friedland is mentioned by Radek as leading a terror group actually 'consisting of historians': this 'we, among ourselves, called the "historical or hysterical" group'.[229] Professors were a convenient class of suspect because they were in a position to recruit plausible terrorists in the person of students – also a much arrested class. It was said in evidence at the 1937 Trial, as a normal thing, that the terrorist organization in Siberia sought its cadres 'chiefly among the young people in the universities'.[230]

Friedland and the others were Party historians and automatically involved in controversy. But the non-Party academic world was also in a difficult position. While the man in the street could cease to talk a great deal, the professors were bound to go on giving lectures before public audiences which inevitably contained informers on the alert for anything which could possibly be interpreted as 'hostile'. (Colleagues, too, might be serving the police. A successful and erudite professor in Dniepropetrovsk, who had matters in his past which the N.K.V.D. used against him, is described as a most efficient *agent-provocateur*.)[231]

A professor of ancient history, Professor Konstantin Shteppa, first lost favour as a result of describing Joan of Arc as nervous and highly strung. Joan had been treated in a hostile fashion or ignored up to the mid thirties, but with the coming of the Popular Front in France she had been referred to as a heroine of a national resistance movement, so that the professor's remarks deviated from the Party line. After considerable trouble about this, he was again censured for a reference to the legend of Midas in an unfortunate context. Then, speaking of ancient and Christian demonology, he happened to remark that country people are always backward. Unfortunately, Trotsky, like many others, had expressed the same thought. Finally, in dealing with the Donatist movement in North Africa, at the time of the Roman Empire, he had shown that this was in part a national as well as a peasant rebellion, thus becoming a bourgeois nationalist. At this time, in 1937, his friends and colleagues were being arrested on a large scale.

I was naturally sorry for my friends, but I was not only sorry for
them. I was also afraid of them. After all, they could say things about
conversations we had had, in which we had not always expressed the
orthodox view. There had been nothing criminal in these conversations;
they had contained no attacks on the Soviet power. But the trivial
criticisms and grumbles and expressions of resentment and disappointment which occurred in every conversation forced every Soviet citizen
to feel guilty.[232]

Then came the suicide of Lyubchenko and his wife, N. Kru-
penik. Unfortunately, the wife had been a university lecturer, and
the whole staff of the Kiev University naturally became high-
grade suspects. A vast network of bourgeois nationalists in the
universities and cultural agencies came to light. Nevertheless, the
professor was not arrested until March 1938. After a severe
interrogation for fifty days, by a series of thirteen 'magistrates',
he was charged with complicity in an attempt to assassinate
Kossior. The fall of Kossior led to the withdrawal of this charge
in his and many other cases, and for it was substituted espionage
for Japan. This was based on the following facts: the professor
had for some time been head of the 'Byzantological' Committee
of the Ukrainian Academy of Sciences. The term then came to be
regarded as reactionary and was replaced by 'Near East'. This
connexion with the 'East' was regarded as adequate for at least
some suspicion of sympathy with, and espionage for, a country
a good deal farther east. It was shown that the professor had lectured on Alexander the Great and Hannibal to senior Red Army
officers. This had given him contact with the Army and therefore
the opportunity to carry out espionage. It was then proven that he
had actually met foreigners in the person of Professor Hrozný,
the great Czech specialist in Hittite history, who had 'recruited'
him through another Byzantologist who had lectured in the
Soviet Far East, thus getting very near Japan. Finally, an indirect contact was found with a professor in Odessa who had
actually met the Japanese Consul there. The reports passed
through this espionage link to Tokyo consisted of remarks about
the 'political morale' of the Army, and here a genuine fact was
established in that the accused had once told a colleague that

some senior officers had confused Napoleon III with Napoleon I, and Alexander the Great with Caesar.[233]

When things became easier, after Yezhov's fall, some of the surviving academics withdrew their confessions, the charges began to be toned down, and eventually, in the early autumn of 1939, the professor was released. He was lucky. Others were still going, from V. G. Sorin, of the Institute of Red Professors, repressed as an enemy of the people in 1939, who died in prison or camp in 1944,[234] down to non-Party lecturers.

At a Party meeting in a university, where a member was denounced with the approval of the chair, it sometimes happened that a supporter would rise and ask for proof of the charges against his colleague. The makers of such demands were invariably denounced for counter-revolutionary attitudes, always silenced, and often arrested. At a meeting of the Kiev Academy of Sciences, for example, someone denounced Professor Kopershinsky. Another Communist scientist, Kaminsky (not the Minister of Health), remarked 'Where class instinct speaks, proof is unnecessary.' He too was later arrested. The Secretary of the Academy was publicly accused in the local press for demanding proof about a similar denunciation.[235] He was one of the thirteen Secretaries of the Academy who succeeded each other between 1921 and 1938, all of whom were arrested. (Of the seven Principals of Kiev University in the same period, six were arrested and one died a natural death.)[236]

The Academy of Sciences covers a wide range of disciplines. But we should note that the purge was violent not only among Byzantologists and so on, whom a technologically-minded State can perhaps do without at a pinch, but also among scientists proper. The physicist Weissberg describes the situation at the Kharkov Physics Institute:

'Listen,' I said. 'Our Institute is one of the most important of its kind in Europe. In fact there is probably no other institute with so many different and well-equipped laboratories. The Soviet Government has spared no expense. Our leading scientists were partly trained abroad. They were constantly being sent to leading physicists all over the world at Government expense to supplement their knowledge and experience. Our Institute had eight departments each headed by a capable man. And what's the situation now? The head of the laboratory for crystallography, Obremov, is under arrest, and so is the head of the low-temperature laboratory, Shubnikov. The head of the second low-temperature laboratory, Ruhemann, has been deported. The head of the laboratory for atom-splitting, Leipunsky, is under arrest, and so are the head of the Röntgen department, Gorsky, the head of the department for theoretical physics, Landau, and the head of the experimental low-temperature station, myself. As far as I know, Slutski, the head of the ultra-short-wave department, is the only one still at work.

'Amongst those arrested is the founder of the Institute, Professor Obremov – its first director; Professor Leipunsky, member of the Academy of Sciences and later again director of the Institute; Professor Lev Davidovich Landau, the leading theoretical physicist in the Soviet Union.* Landau had already been forced out of the Institute by the G.P.U., and he went to Moscow to work with Professor Kapitza. I supervised the building of our low-temperature experimental station, but before it could be put into operation I was arrested. My successor was Komarov. He has also been arrested. Who is to carry on?

'... You need five years to train an engineer, and even then the Government had a very great deal of trouble before it could get suitable engineers for its new factories. But a capable physicist needs from ten to fifteen years' training.'[238]

Soviet publications of the sixties have confirmed such arrests. For example, Academician Berg writes:

Thereafter there came difficult times: 1937, the loss of one's close friends. Soon I too was arrested on a basis of a ridiculous and stupid denunciation. I spent precisely 900 days in prison. I was let out shortly before the war. During these years radio-technology suffered an enormous loss. Institutes and laboratories were closed down and people disappeared.[239]

Biology was, of course, a particularly sensitive field. With the rise of Lysenko in the early thirties, a fierce 'ideological' struggle commenced. Already in 1932 G. A. Levitsky and N. P. Avdoulov, cytologists, were arrested, but were later released. Other biologists were arrested about the same time.

* Landau, long one of Russia's foremost scientists, has described how he nearly died in prison as a 'German spy'. His colleague, Peter Kapitsa, with extraordinary bravery, finally persuaded Stalin of his value.[237]

In December 1936 the more prominent Professor I. J. Agol was arrested on charges of Trotskyism and executed. Professor S. G. Levit, head of the Medico-Genetic Institute, was expelled from the party on the grounds that his biological views were pro-Nazi. (The People's Commissar for Health, G. M. Kaminsky, was also criticized for defending him.)[240] Levit was arrested in about May 1937 and died in prison. A number of other prominent biologists, such as Levitsky, Karpechenko and Govorov, also perished, as did the celebrated N. M. Tulaikov, Director of the Cereals Institute, who was arrested in 1937 and died in 1938 in one of the White Sea labour camps.

In this field, as in the political, the lesser figures were arrested first and the net thus closed round their superiors. The biggest game was Academician N. I. Vavilov, the great geneticist, Lenin's favourite. He had given up his position as head of the Lenin All-Union Academy of Agricultural Sciences in 1935 to A. I. Muralov, until then Deputy Commissar for Agriculture. Muralov was arrested on 4 July 1937 and succeeded by Professor G. K. Meister. Meister was in turn arrested at the beginning of 1938, and Lysenko took the job after a squalid and deadly intrigue.

Vavilov himself was in trouble early in 1940 for some argument about the right agricultural policy to pursue in the parts annexed from Finland. An open quarrel with Lysenko followed. In August he was touring the Ukraine. While in Cernauti, he was suddenly recalled to Moscow, and arrested on 6 August. The files on his case (to which leading biologists were given access after the fall of Lysenko in 1964), contain a letter from Beria to Molotov as Politburo member in charge of Science, requesting permission for this arrest. Vavilov was under interrogation for eleven months and was questioned over a hundred times. He was tried on 9 July 1941 by the Military Collegium on charges of Rightist conspiracy, espionage for England and other matters. He was sentenced to death but his sentence was not carried out. (Beria, whose wife was a biologist, seems not to have approved the death sentence.)

The veteran biologist D. N. Pryanishnikov, together with Vavilov's brother the physicist, had interviews with Beria and Molotov to try to have him released, but without success. Pryanishnikov also seems to have intervened through Beria's wife to try to get better prison conditions for his old colleague, and he even had the extraordinary temerity to nominate him for a Stalin Prize in 1941.

Vavilov was now held in Saratov prison. He introduced himself to his cell-mates: 'You see before you, talking of the past, Academician Vavilov, but now, according to the opinion of the investigators, nothing but dung.' Held in the condemned cell, a windowless underground block, without any exercise, for nearly a year, he was almost saved by his election in 1942 as a Fellow of the Royal Society in London. But it was too late. Dystrophy had gone too far – he was a 'goner', and died on 26 January 1943. His wife and son had been evacuated from Leningrad to Saratov in 1942 and lived all this time within a few miles of the prison where he was dying. But they were informed that he was in Moscow and did not learn of his presence.[241]

The triumph of Lysenkoism was the most extraordinary of all the indications of the intellectual degeneracy of the Party mind which had followed on Stalin's replacement of the intellectual section of the apparatus by his own creatures like Mitin and Mekhlis in the early thirties. The villain of the piece from this point of view was the charlatan I. I. Prezent, who established the orthodoxy of the Lysenko line by a complex and superficially sophisticated manipulation of the Marxist phraseology. To do justice to Zhdanov, he at least was never wholly taken in by Lysenko, and the final destruction of Soviet biology was only accomplished in 1948, as part and parcel of his own political defeat and death. But meanwhile impressive verbalization, backed by vicious intrigue, secured Lysenko's position of supremacy even if not yet of monopoly.

Another field where a wholly erroneous doctrine was declared orthodox was linguistics. By the late twenties the teachings of N. Marr, who held that all language derives from the four sounds *rosh*, *sal*, *ber* and *yon*, became accepted as the Marxist line. It is a view otherwise universally dismissed. As a result old professors were first exiled, later had their books withdrawn, and in 1937–8 were usually arrested. A case has lately been mentioned of Professor E. D. Polivanov, a friend of Mayakovsky, arrested in 1937 and 'perished' in 1938, whose manuscripts of the thirties, all unpublished, are now being sought.[242] (Stalin abandoned Marrism in 1950, censuring its adherents for having bullied the anti-Marrites.)

But the heaviest toll of all seems to have been among the writers. They were threatened from two directions. A theory of correct aesthetic *method* was imposed upon them, and at the same time the *content* of their works was subject to intense scrutiny. It emerged a few years ago that of the 700 writers who met at the First Writers' Congress in 1934, only fifty survived to see the second in 1954.[243] Even allowing for deaths from old age (and the average age of delegates was 38·9[244] – in fact 71 per cent of them were under forty[245]), this is an astonishing figure.

It has lately been revealed that after the XXth Party Congress in 1956, it was confidentially admitted that 'there were more than 600 writers who were guilty of no crime, and whom the Union [of Writers] obediently left to their fate in the prisons and camps'. Alexander Solzhenitsyn, telling of this, adds that in reality 'the list is still longer . . .'[246] In all, from the 'cultural world', we are told by a Soviet historian that 'more that a thousand' perished.[247]

There were certain definite grudges to be paid off. Isaac Babel, Russia's finest short-story writer, had served in Budenny's Cavalry Army in the Civil War and the Polish Campaign, and in 1942 published his extraordinary collection of Civil War stories, *Konarmia*. Budenny had protested vigorously as each vignette forming the book came out. He regarded the ruthlessly clear-eyed stories as a slander, preferring the hack heroics of the ordinary correspondents. Gorki, recognizing Babel's very different talent, had protected him.

Babel wrote of the Revolution 'It's eaten with gunpowder and the very best blood is poured over it.' It was Babel who had at the Writers' Congress of 1934 spoken of the 'heroism of silence', a phrase and an activity to be condemned bitterly as a sign of alienation from the regime. Babel knew Yezhov's wife. Though he knew it was unwise, he sometimes went to see her to 'find a key to the puzzle'. He gathered that whatever Yezhov's role, it was not at the bottom of it.[248] He ceased to be published in 1937 and at the end of May 1938 was arrested in his *dacha* at the writers' settlement at Peredelkino. He died in prison or camp, in unknown circumstances, on 17 March 1941.[249]

Babel, in addition to offending a minor figure like Budenny, and bringing into disrepute the First Cavalry Army from which Stalin was now drawing an inadequate substitute for a High Command, is said to have made a rash joke about the General Secretary. But his offence was small compared to that of Boris Pilnyak, another, though lesser, talent to have arisen from the Revolution. His *The Naked Year*, about a provincial town in 1919, is the most extraordinary representation, in which the struggle for bare existence brings out the excess, the eccentricity, of the range of Russian character.

As early as the twenties he had become involved in one of the most obscure and doubtful crimes attributed to Stalin. In the spring of 1924 Frunze was appointed Deputy Commissar for War – and in practice took over control of the Army with little resistance from Trotsky before Trotsky's actual removal in 1925. He seems to have sympathized mainly with the Zinoviev–Kamenev group. In the later summer of 1925 he fell ill, and died on 31 October of that year. The rumour in Moscow was that he had been ordered by the Central Committee – that is in effect by Stalin – to undergo an operation which in fact killed him. If Frunze had died in 1936 or 1937 the existence of such a rumour would have been perfectly natural. The significant thing is that it circulated at so early a date – at a time, that is, when Stalin had not given any precedents.

Recent Soviet books on Frunze have been notably touchy on the point. A new biography[250] elaborates at some length about doctors who said that an operation was really necessary, and who tended him through his last illness. This is a book by one of those military historians who have elsewhere been so frankly hostile to Stalin's acts against the generals. Unless (as is of course quite possible) other interventions took place on its publication, one tends to think that exculpation from such a source shows that Stalin is really believed not guilty by some of those who would be anxious to know.

The most extraordinary thing is that the rumour was given

public circulation. On its basis Pilnyak, hitherto an almost entirely non-political writer (who had said that he knew nothing of politics and not being a Communist could not write like one), produced his *Tale of the Unextinguished Moon*, subtitled 'Murder of the Army Commander'. The hero, Gavrilov, is described as a well-known Red Army leader, who returns to Moscow on orders and reads in the papers that he has come back for an operation. He has had stomach ulcers, but is now fully recovered. He goes to see a man described as the most important of the 'three who lead' the Party, who orders him to have the operation. The doctors examine him, and report that an operation is necessary, but afterwards in private conversation say that it is not. The operation is performed and he dies of an overdose of chloroform. The story has a very sinister and gloomy tone. It was about to be printed in *Novy Mir*, but the issue was confiscated and the editors admitted in the following number that accepting it had been a mistake, and printed letters describing it as 'a malicious slander of our Party'. In the circumstances then prevailing there were many copies circulating, and the story was printed abroad in 1927, in Sofia.

It is clear, indeed, that no one with any political sense would have written a story like *The Tale of the Unextinguished Moon*, and it seems likely that Pilnyak was put up to it by some friend more deeply involved in the struggles of the time. But no more was said about the matter for the moment.

In 1929 Pilnyak was President of the All-Russian Union of Writers, a genuine association then resisting the manoeuvres of the Russian Association of Proletarian Writers (R.A.P.P.), founded in 1925, headed by Averbach, Yagoda's wife's nephew, and devoted to ideological and bureaucratic control of the writers. Mayakovsky's suicide in 1930 is now attributed, in part, to persecution by officials of R.A.P.P.[251] (In the face of opposition from all the best writers, and to a large degree from Maxim Gorki too, the R.A.P.P.ists failed in their task, and later lost favour and were themselves purged.)

Pilnyak's last effective work, *Mahogany*, served as a pretext for action against him. It was published in Germany as a preliminary to its coming out in Russia, then a common practice for copyright reasons. But it was then denounced as anti-Soviet and its publication abroad alleged to be a White Guard provocation. Pilnyak was now in great trouble and ready to submit to any ruling. Zamyatin, chairman of the Leningrad branch of the Writers' Union, was also under attack: his *We* (on which Orwell was to draw for *1984*) had been published abroad in much the same circumstances. He boldly demanded to be allowed to leave the country, refused to retract, and exposed the whole mechanism which literary persecution was already setting in motion, mild though its actions were compared with later developments. He said that the Moscow branch had passed its resolution 'without hearing any defence: first there was a condemnation and only then an investigation. I imagine that no court in the world has ever heard of such a procedure.' He added that he could not belong to an organization that behaved like this and resigned his membership of the Union. Finally, Maxim Gorki interceded for both Pilnyak and Zamyatin in *Izvestia*:[252]

... We have got into the stupid habit of raising people up into high positions only to cast them down into the mud and the dust. I need not quote examples of this absurd and cruel treatment of people, because such examples are known to everybody. I am reminded of the way in which petty thieves were lynched in 1917–18. These dramas were generally the work of *obyvateli* [obtuse philistines] and one is reminded of them every time one sees with what delight people throw themselves on to a man who has made a mistake, in order to take his place.

Pilnyak was 'allowed' to settle down to write pro-Soviet literature, while Zamyatin's boldness was rewarded by permission to leave the country. Zamyatin was one of the few trained Marxists among Soviet writers, and on this account he had rejected Bolshevism, which was welcomed in a vague and romantic fashion by futurists like Mayakovsky – at a time, indeed, when the futurists of Italy were showing a similar romanticism towards the other new and dynamic movement, Fascism.

Pilnyak settled down to write a conformist novel – *The Volga Flows into the Caspian Sea.* Yezhov personally oversaw the production, listing fifty-odd passages for amendment. Pilnyak became deeply depressed, and told Victor Serge 'There isn't a single thinking adult in this country who hasn't thought that he might get shot.'[253] (But he had the courage to intervene when Serge was arrested in 1933.) In May 1937 he was attacked flatly for 'counter-revolutionary writing',[254] and was arrested soon afterwards. He is supposed to have been shot as a Japanese spy, probably in 1938[255] or 1939 – he had actually visited Japan, so the report is a likely one.

Other prose writers of mark who perished include Pantaleimon Romanov, author of *Three Pairs of Silk Stockings*; Tarasov-Rodionov; Artyom Vesyoly; I. I. Kataev; S. Tretyakov, author of *Roar China*; Mikhail Koltsov, of *Pravda*, under suspicion as an agent of Lord Beaverbrook,[256] was arrested on 12 December 1938. Sentenced by Ulrikh on 1 February 1940 to ten years without the right of correspondence,[257] he seems to have died in 1942.[258] Others who were arrested but survived include Yuri Olesha and Ostap Vyshnia. Vyshnia, accused of planning to assassinate Postyshev and others, was released in 1943, and had to write deriding those abroad who had protested at his supposed liquidation.

Poetry in the U.S.S.R. was already a dangerous trade. Nikolai Gumilev, Anna Akhmatova's former husband, had been shot as a counter-revolutionary, on Agranov's orders, in August 1921, the month which also saw the death of Alexander Blok, long past his brief enthusiasm for the Red Guard, from anaemia due to malnutrition. Yesenin had committed suicide in 1925 and Mayakovsky in 1930.

And now many of the best surviving poets in Russia were destroyed.

The poet Vladimir Smirenski (Andrei Skorbny) had been given ten years as early as 1931, for participation in a group which had discussed politics almost entirely in relation to art.[259] We do not know the charges against most of the poets who now went to their deaths. It seems that they were seldom accused of poetic crimes as such, though a case is reported of a young poetess arrested for writing a 'hymn to freedom' which was construed as 'preparation for terrorism', and sentenced to eight years in the Karaganda camps.[260] The Ukrainian poets perished in their majority for 'nationalist' reasons: sixteen, starting with Vlyzko in 1934, are named as executed or dying in camps between then and 1942 –

almost all at Solovetsk, though a few were in Kolyma. There is no information about the charges against such men as Nikolai Klyuev, Yesenin's disciple, whose best poem, his 'Lament' for his friend and teacher, sighs 'If I could only touch peace'. He had already in the twenties spent three days in the Leningrad O.G.P.U.'s steam-room,[261] and been released. Again arrested in 1933, he was sent to Siberia. He is believed to have died there in about 1937.

The poet Pavel Vasiliev is said to have defended Bukharin as 'a man of the highest nobility and the conscience of peasant Russia' at the time of his denunciation at the Pyatakov Trial, and to have damned the writers then signing the routine attacks on him as 'pornographic scrawls on the margins of Russian literature'.[262] On 7 February 1937 he left his wife Elena to go over to a barber's shop for a shave, accompanied by his host's son.

Some minutes later the boy returned.
'Lena, they've arrested Pavel . . .'
. . . In all the prisons they answered alike, to the question: 'Is there a Vasiliev amongst those arrested?'
'No, Vasiliev, Pavel Nikolaevich, is not listed.'
Months went by. Some woman instructed her:
'Prepare a parcel. He'll be in the place where they accept it.'
It was true – the parcel was accepted in one of the prisons. Moreover they said that she could come again on 16 July.
On 16 July the person on duty said:
'He's been transferred to another place.'
And twenty years later, petitioning for her husband's posthumous rehabilitation, Elena Aleksandrovna discovered that it was precisely on 16 July that Pavel Vasiliev ceased to be.[263]

The leading Georgian poet Yashvili killed himself with a shotgun on 22 July 1937[264] as the result of the arrest of other Georgian literary figures, in particular his friend and equal the poet Titsian Tabidze.[265] In Boris Pasternak's *Letters to Georgian Friends*, we read of the Russian poet's brave and devoted attempts to help and console Tabidze's family for his disappearance, until his wife was finally informed of his execution (on 16 December 1937) when he was rehabilitated seventeen years later.

The Armenian poet, Gurgen Maari, who survived and returned to Erevan in 1954, has described his experiences.[266]

> I was arrested at night on 9 August 1936. I was not surprised. A month previously the First Secretary of the C.C. of the Armenian Communist Party, Agasi Khandzhyan, had tragically perished. The atmosphere in the House of Writers was very oppressive.

He was in solitary confinement for many months without even being allowed out for exercise. It was not until two years after his arrest that he was 'tried'.

> The Military Collegium of the Supreme Court of the Soviet Union is in session. I confess to terrorist acts, to the wish to separate Armenia from the Soviet Union and unite her to the imperialist camp. I intended to kill Beria . . .
> The Trial was a closed one, the trial lasted three minutes. . . . I was condemned to ten years' deprivation of liberty. Once again Sianos [a jailer, formerly in the same orphanage as Maari] accompanies me. This time to the cell for sentenced prisoners.
> 'How many did you get?' he asked in a whisper.
> 'Ten years.'
> 'Thank God. You've got off lightly.'
> 'Ten years,' I repeat.
> 'For the third night running, when they've taken people out, they've shot them,' he whispers . . .

The forty people in his cell included two architects, three writers, four engineers, and one People's Commissar; the rest were all Government employees and Party workers. The opinion of the pessimists was that their prison sentences of ten to twenty-five years were just for the sake of form and that they would be shot in any case. However, this did not happen.

> In the autumn of 1938 we were crammed into lorries one night and – covered with tarpaulin like forbidden goods – were taken to the station. It was empty at the station, there was not a living soul – only troops.

For six months the prisoners lived in the Vologda city jail. Then they were taken to Krasnoyarsk, where 'a large army of prisoners composed of representatives of many of the peoples of the Soviet

Union swarmed. Inhabitants of Central Asia stood out particularly in their bright national costumes.'

A medical examination determined who was to be sent on to Norilsk in the Arctic. It was then, for the second time in three years, that Maari managed to see himself in a mirror. He could hardly recognize himself. At the Siblag ('Siberian' Prison Camp) in Norilsk he made friends with Egert, once a famous film actor. He was marched with 200 others to another camp: most of the 200 died later. Maari himself was there until 1947. He briefly describes two different camp commandants: one hated 'intelligent swine' and sent them to do the heaviest work. The other, who liked books himself, eased his lot a good deal.

Released in 1947, Maari was not permitted to publish anything under his own name as his civic rights had not been restored, and in 1948 he was re-arrested. This time the cell was full of troops returning from German captivity. In 1948–9 he was incarcerated in nine prisons in nine different towns. He and his fellows were then classed as 'exiles for life'.

The Leningrad poet Nikolai Zabolotsky, who exalted a starling's song against 'the tambourines and kettledrums of history', was arrested on 19 March 1938 'on a faked political accusation'[267] and was long in labour camps. As the introduction to the latest Soviet edition of his works puts it, he spent the following years 'in the Far East, the Altai and Kazakhstan'. He was back in Moscow in May 1946, but he suffered from tuberculosis, caught in the camps, for the rest of his life.

The beautiful poetess Marina Tsvetaeva had gone abroad soon after the Revolution to join her husband, the literary critic Sergei Efron, who had fought in the White Army. She had written of the 'deadly days of October'. In the thirties her husband joined a Soviet-supported movement for the return of émigrés to Russia. He was one of the first to be allowed back by the Soviet authorities and he disappeared without trace soon after his arrival. Their daughter went from Paris to seek him and also disappeared. (He had been executed, while the girl was to spend sixteen years in prison camps.)[268] In 1939 Marina Tsvetaeva followed them. On 31 August 1941, worn out by long suffering, she committed suicide in the provincial town of Yelabug.[269]

Her scintillating poetry became widely known and circulated in manuscript. But in spite of its influence and popularity in literary circles, it was not to be published until 1957. Much of it has yet to be, in particular 'The White Flock', a cycle of romantic lyrics connected with the tragedy of the White Army:

> Where are the swans?
> The swans have left.
> Where are the ravens?
> The ravens have stayed.

Even the 1957 publication of a short selection of her most harmless verses is now called 'a gross political error'.[270]

Another talent of the first rank, Osip Mandelshtam, was a sick man, with a nervous complaint. In 1934 he was called in to the N.K.V.D. on an order signed by Yagoda himself, interrogated the whole night, and then sent to prison. He is said to have written an epigram on Stalin. Pasternak is reported to have pleaded for him with Bukharin, a sign of Pasternak's naïveté. (It seems to have been now that Stalin rang up Pasternak and asked if Mandelshtam was a good poet.) Other writers went to Yenukidze, still influential. At this time, when the Terror had not got into its stride, such interventions may have been helpful. In any case, the poet was sentenced merely to three years' exile at Cherdyn, a small town near Solikamsk, for 'conspiracy'. He attempted suicide, and his wife appealed to the Central Committee.

Mandelshtam was transferred to Voronezh, a tolerable provincial town. He was able to return to Moscow in May 1937, but could not get permission to remain. On 2 May 1938 he was again arrested, taken to the Butyrka and sentenced by the Special Board to five years' forced labour in the Far East. Near Vladivostok, in a transit camp for Magadan, he was robbed of his rations and viciously beaten up by a criminal group. Driven half-mad, he was finally thrown out of the hut and lived like an animal, begging occasional crusts outside the door. A doctor from Voronezh, working in the medical centre in the camp, saved his life for the time being, but he died on 27 December 1938, apparently in a psychiatric ward near by, to which the doctor had managed to transfer him.[271] He had written of his times:

But your spine has been smashed,
My beautiful, pitiful era,
And with an inane smile
You look back, cruel and weak,
Like a beast that has once been supple,
At the tracks of your own paws.

As with other citizens in all these arrests, the blind chance of 'objective characteristics' prevailed. In December 1937, so Ehrenburg tells us, his son-in-law Boris Lapin tried to account for various arrests of intellectuals:

Pilnyak has been to Japan; Tretyakov often met foreign writers; Pavel Vasilyev drank and talked too much; Bruno Jasienski was a Pole . . . Artyom Vesyoly had at one time been a member of the Pereval literary group; the wife of the painter Shukhayev was acquainted with the nephew of Gogoberidze . . .[272]

The fate of those who had conducted political manoeuvre and organization in the literary sphere depended directly on the course of politics proper. The leading R.A.P.P. writers, whose bureaucratic control of literature had been repudiated in 1932, had remained at liberty. But the main figure, Averbach, had come under the protection of his relation by marriage, Yagoda. Soon after Yagoda's arrest he was attacked as a Trotskyite, with other writers including Karev, who had been one of the Zinovievites disposed of without trial.[273] Kirshon came under fire soon afterwards and the whole group was charged with having had Yagoda's protection. The Polish poet Jasienski (see p. 585) was named with them, together with the critic Prince Dimitri Mirsky, who had returned to Russia from England a convinced Communist, and was now referred to as 'that filthy Wrangelist and White Guard officer'[274] (he is said to have died mad in a Siberian camp). On 15 May Kirshon's expulsion from the Party was announced:[275] by now they must all have been under arrest. Kirshon was also closely connected with politics, and it is interesting that he was shot in 1938 on a day of executions of politicians and soldiers (see p. 606). Their old colleague in R.A.P.P., Vladimir Ermilov, saved his skin as the principal witness against them.

For there were denouncers as well as victims, cowards and

bullies as well as brave men in the literary world, as elsewhere. When Pasternak was refusing to sign the authors' circular applauding the killing of the generals – only to escape because the organizers added his name anyway – Yakov Elsberg, the author of several books about Herzen, Shchedrin, etc., who had formerly been Kamenev's secretary, now embarked on a course of denunciation to remove the taint of this association. Another, N. V. Lesyuchevsky, is generally supposed in the Soviet Union to have denounced the poets Benedikt Livshits and Boris Kornilov, who were shot in 1937, the short-story writer Elena Tager, who spent many years in imprisonment, and Nikolai Zabolotsky.

During the 'Thaw' of 1962 the Moscow Writers' organization managed to secure the expulsion of Elsberg on a charge of informing in the thirties. The equally notorious case of Lesyuchevsky was raised, then shelved. But when the Moscow Writers' organization fell briefly into the hands of a liberal leadership at the end of that year they voted once more to reopen the case, again abortively.[276] Such men have lasted, indeed, while an honest Stalinist like Fadeyev, who tried to save some of his political enemies, committed suicide in 1956 on the exposure of his patron.

Besides mere police spies, there were men who had simply sold out to Stalin, like Alexei Tolstoy, who wrote that 'Dostoyevsky's Stavrogin was a typical potential Trotskyite', and made a career as a regime hack. There were others who just accepted the killing of their colleagues. Surkov remarked long after the rehabilitations, 'I have seen my friends, writers, disappear before my eyes, but at the time I believed it necessary, demanded by the Revolution.'[277]

The public arts suffered almost equally. The conductor E. Mikoladze was shot in 1937.[278] Many actors are reported in the camps – such as Shirin, sent to labour camp for saying 'Don't feed us Soviet straw; let's play the classics.'[279] Well-known actresses like O. Shcherbinskaya and Z. Smirnova followed them.[280] Actresses and ballerinas are frequently mentioned in the camp literature: a typical arrest was under Article 58, section 6, of a ballerina who attended a dinner arranged by foreign admirers.[281]

The celebrated Natalia Sats, creator of the Moscow Children's Theatre, had been Tukhachevsky's wife, and was arrested in 1937 and sent to Rybinsk camp. She is reported there at several dates in the forties, but survived, and was eventually released.

But the greatest victim in the theatre was Vsevolod Meyerhold. At the beginning of 1938 a short decree announced the 'liquidation' of the Meyerhold Theatre as 'alien to Soviet art'. It added that the question of Meyerhold's further work in the theatre was being 'studied'.[282]

On 15 June 1939 Meyerhold was invited to make a public self-criticism of himself at a meeting of producers presided over by Vyshinsky – himself, as the artist Yuri Annenkov remarks, a well-known producer of dramas of a certain type.[283] Meyerhold retracted, but also (in one account) counter-attacked with:

The pitiful and wretched thing that pretends to the title of the theatre of socialist realism has nothing in common with art. . . . People in the arts searched, erred, and frequently stumbled and turned aside, but they really created – sometimes badly and sometimes splendidly. Where once there were the best theatres in the world, now – by your leave – everything is gloomily well regulated, averagely arithmetical, stupefying, and murderous in its lack of talent. Is that your aim? If it is – oh! – you have done something monstrous! In hunting down formalism, you have eliminated art![284]

Meyerhold was arrested a few days later. He is now given as dying in Moscow – that is, presumably in prison or execution cellars rather than in camp – on 2 February 1940.[285] His wife, the actress Zinaida Raikh, who had formerly been married to Yesenin, was found dead in their flat after his arrest with, reportedly, her eyes cut out and seventeen knife wounds. Only documents were missing, and there was no police investigation.[286]

Meyerhold's theatre had predeceased him. The disappearance of anyone led also to the disappearance, or reassignment, of his artefacts. On the arrest of the sculptor Kratko, all his works disappeared from the galleries. When A. N. Tupolev the aircraft designer was arrested, the 'A.N.T.' types of plane were rechristened.* One prisoner reports a physicist who had with four collaborators completed a paper and lectured on it at the Academy

* Arrested in 1937, he confessed at once on Muklevich's advice, to avoid torture.[287] He and his wife (who had been sent to a labour camp) were later released.[288]

of Sciences. The paper appeared in the scientific journals under the name of the two collaborators who had not been arrested.[289] Unorthodox works simply vanished into the files of the N.K.V.D., where any that have not been destroyed still lie, with Gorky's last notebooks and Marina Tsvetaeva's last poems.

Nor have we dealt with the more general effect of actions such as those described in reducing what had been a lively culture to a terrified level of almost unrelieved conformism. We have only been able to give a few illustrations of the way in which the Purge hit the creative minds of Russia – half a dozen stories and a handful of names, including the greatest in the country. A Georgian paper recently asked rhetorically 'How many eminent writers, poets, artists, scholars and engineers perished in Georgia, repressed illegally, subjected to torture, exiled or shot?'[290] The same might be said of the U.S.S.R. as a whole. The few we have spoken of, and briefly, must stand for a holocaust of the things of the spirit.

CHAPTER TEN

IN THE LABOUR CAMPS

No one who has not sat in prison knows what the State
is like. TOLSTOY

THE fate of the prisoner who had the good fortune to escape being
taken down to the execution cellars was to be dispatched to a
Corrective Labour Camp.

The Corrective Labour Codex defines three types of camp:

1. Factory and agricultural colonies where 'people deprived of
   freedom' are 'trained and disciplined'. (Article 33.)
2. Camps for mass work which includes those in 'distant
   regions' for 'class-dangerous elements' requiring 'a more
   severe regime'. (Article 34.)
3. Punitive camps for the 'strict isolation' of those 'previously
   detained in other colonies and showing persistent insubor-
   dination'. (Article 35.)

The first category was mainly for very minor offences against
factory discipline, and for petty thieves. All sentenced under
Article 58 or by the Special Board went initially to Category 2.

The labour camp was one of the pillars of Stalin's whole
system. Concealment of its nature from the West was one of his
most extraordinary triumphs.

For the evidence on the camps was, by the late forties, overwhelming and detailed. Thousands of former inmates had
reached the West, and their wholly consistent stories were supported by a good deal of documentation – such as the many
labour-camp forms and letters reproduced in David J. Dallin's
and Boris I. Nicolaevsky's *Forced Labour in Soviet Russia* and
indeed by the Corrective Labour Codex of the R.S.F.S.R., produced with much effect by the British delegation to the United
Nations in 1949. Yet it was possible for Western intellectuals to
disbelieve this material, and to join in Soviet-sponsored campaigns condemning all who revealed it as slanderers.

And, indeed, there had long been an alternative Soviet story. There were, it is true, corrective labour establishments, of a highly beneficent type. Their operations could be seen in such works as Pogodin's play *The Aristocrats*, which showed how prisoners were reclaimed at labour on the White Sea Canal and elsewhere. Pogodin represents bandits, thieves and even 'wrecker' engineers being reformed by labour. A regenerated engineer, now working enthusiastically at a project, has his old mother visit him. The kindly camp chief puts his car at her disposal, and she is delighted at her son's healthy physical appearance. 'How beautifully you have re-educated me,' a thief remarks, while another sings: 'I am reborn, I want to live and sing.'

And much of the hostile evidence came from people who had been unjustly imprisoned in camps, and who had come to oppose the Stalin regime. They were, therefore, 'anti-Soviet', and pur-veyors of 'anti-Soviet propaganda'. By this system no evidence whatever of any facts unpalatable to Stalin could ever be admis-sible. As Bertrand Russell wrote of a labour camp book:

> The book ends with letters from eminent Communists saying that no such camps exist. Those who write these letters and those fellow-travellers who allow themselves to believe them share responsibility for the almost unbelievable horrors which are being inflicted upon millions of wretched men and women, slowly done to death by hard labour and starvation in the Arctic cold. Fellow-travellers who refuse to believe the evidence of books such as Mr Herling's are necessarily people devoid of humanity, for if they had any humanity they would not merely dis-miss the evidence, but would take some trouble to look into it.[1]

As Russell truly remarks, it was 'millions' who suffered. And here we have a point on which no official Soviet admissions have yet been made. While the publication of such books as *One Day in the Life of Ivan Denisovich*, and of various memoirs by former camp inmates, amounts to an acknowledgement that the long-disputed evidence produced in the West is accurate through and through, this applies to the nature of the camp system, not – or not explicitly – to its extent.

What many people of goodwill found hard to believe was less the existence of the system, in all its unpleasantness, than the numbers of prisoners alleged to be detained in them. When figures like 10 or 15 million, and more, were mentioned, it was an almost instinctive feeling that this did not accord with common sense, with normal experience. Nor, of course, did it. But then the reality of Stalin's activities was often disbelieved because they seemed to be unbelievable. His whole style consisted in doing what had previously been thought morally or physically inconceivable.

Even so, it is difficult not to reject the larger figures out of hand as 'obviously' exaggerated, and a very definite effort has to be made when we consider the evidence. This is multifarious, but inexact, and estimates have varied from about 5 million upwards. I am inclined (for reasons given in Appendix A) to accept a figure of about 8 million purgees in the camps in 1938. This cannot, in any case, be very far wrong.

A detailed list of camp groups covering thirty-five clusters was given as early as 1937[2] (a cluster usually included about two hundred camps of around 1,200 inmates each). In 1945, on the basis of reports from Poles allowed to leave under the Soviet–Polish treaty, a far more comprehensive account was given together with a map, showing thirty-eight administration clusters and groups (including eight under Dalstroy control).[3] In 1948, Dallin and Nicolaevsky, on the basis of careful research, were able to list and describe the operations of 125 camps or camp clusters, mentioning that a number of others had been reported but not wholly confirmed.[4]

Like the other mechanisms from which Stalin constructed the Purge, the labour camps were no new invention.

With a few exceptions, our major accounts of labour-camp life come from intellectuals who were sent to them from 1935 and 1936 on. For the victims of the Yezhov terror included a far higher proportion of urban, and of foreign, intellectuals than had the repressions of earlier years. As a result, we are inclined to think of the system as arising, or passing through an enormous quantitative or qualitative change, at the beginning of the Great Purge proper. There are, indeed, a few accounts by 'intellectuals' from the earlier period – for example, from Professor Tchernyavin – and these differ little from later ones. But on the whole those who suffered in the first half of the thirties were mainly peasantry, who were less inclined to write books about their experiences – even though an equivalent proportion of them ended up in Western Europe as a result of the captures and migrations of the war.

There is one important exception. When Victor Kravchenko sued *Les Lettres Françaises* in 1949 for having declared his book, *I Chose Freedom*, a fake, many otherwise unforthcoming refugees in the West sent in affidavits of experiences of theirs which confirmed his story, and a number of these were peasants who had been in camps from as early as 1930.

Their accounts[5] (and earlier ones) make it clear that the system already existed in much the same form, if with fewer inmates, at this earlier stage. Brutalities are described, indeed, which for a time became less common in the mid thirties. This probably signifies the automatic hostility of the N.K.V.D. cadres to those whom they were able to think of as a genuinely hostile class element – *kulaks*. At the same time, the tradition of the Russian *vlast*, of straightforward beating for the clods of peasants, as compared with a certain restraint towards the intelligentsia who might have influential friends and relations, still prevailed. Later on, of course, the latter class became, if anything, the target of yet greater extremes of brutality. But up to 1936 preferential treatment as political prisoners could still be claimed even by imprisoned Trotskyites, a category later to be marked out for specially vicious treatment.

Camps seem to have been in existence as early as mid 1918, but the decrees legalizing them were passed in September 1918[6] and April 1919.[7] The first true death camp seems to have been that at Kholmogori, near Archangel, in 1921. A list of sixty-five concentration camps administered in 1922 by the Main Administration of Forced Labour is given in the directory and address book *All Russia* of 1923.[8] This Administration was merged in October 1922 with the Corrective Labour Section of the Commissariat of Justice, and the whole brought under the N.K.V.D. as the Main Administration of Places of Detention.

The first great camps were in the Solovetsky Monasteries in the far north. Here, in Tsarist times, the monks of the oldest tradition of isolation from the world had withstood a siege from 1668 to 1676 defending their faith in the Old Belief against the reformism

454 The Yezhov Years

of the time. When the camps were set up, some of the old monks were retained for a time to teach the convicts how to operate the fisheries. They were later liquidated for sabotage.[9] At the Solovetsky camps health conditions were very bad. Epidemics reduced the population from 14,000 to 8,000 in 1929–30.[10] In general, these were bad times in all the camps springing up around the White Sea. The average lifetime in these between 1929 and 1934 'did not exceed one or two years'.[11] This was almost always due to corruption and inefficiency among the jailers. The remedy was a conventional one. 'The G.P.U. commission would come down from Moscow and shoot half the administration, after which convict life returned to its customary horror.'[12]

The statute on Corrective Labour Camps which governed the later period was adopted on 7 April 1930. The camps took their modern form at a time of vast expansion of the network.

Of the 10 million *kulaks* Stalin mentioned to Churchill as having been dealt with in the collectivization terror, a rough estimate is that about a third were sent to labour camps. In 1933–5 the peasant population of the camps is estimated at about $3\frac{1}{2}$ million – some 70 per cent of the then total.[13]

The most careful estimates of the camp population over the pre-Yezhov period run as follows:

In 1928, 30,000
In 1930, over 600,000.*
In 1931–2, a total of nearly 2 million in 'places of detention' can be estimated from figures given for the allotment per prisoner of newspapers.
In 1933–5, the estimates run mainly at the 5 million level.
In 1935–7, 6 million.[14]†

TO THE CAMPS

This established system awaited the new intake. After sentence the prisoners were crammed into Black Marias, of a type origin-

---

*Six main camp groups are known to have been in existence in 1930.

†The maximum numbers at forced labour (*katorga*) in Tsarist times was 32,000, in 1912, and the maximum total of all prisoners 183,949. (Vyshinsky, ed., *Prisons of Capitalist Countries*, Moscow, 1937, pp. 54, 61, 143.)

ally produced before the Revolution: they had then been designed
for seven persons, but by narrowing the cellular partitions to a
minimum now took twenty-eight.[15] Then, usually at night, they
were loaded into the railway wagons taking them to their destina-
tion, either cattle trucks which had carried twelve horses or forty-
eight men in the Tsarist wars and now held up to a hundred
prisoners,[16] or the specially-made 'Stolypin trucks', named after
the Tsarist Minister – though, as a recent Soviet writer says,
'Why were these appalling narrow penal wagons called Stolypin
trucks? They were of quite recent origin.'[17] These journeys to the
camps might last months. For example, one prisoner describes a
forty-seven-day railway journey from Leningrad to Vladivostok.[18]
Such trips are sometimes described as worse than the camps
themselves. The crowded goods trucks were practically unheated
in winter and unbearably hot in summer. Inadequate food and
drinking water and sanitary arrangements caused great suffering
and a high death rate. Lengyel complains of spending six weeks in
a ship's hold, on 'one of the widest rivers in the world', with only
seven fluid ounces of drinking water a day.[19]

The train guards, from the so-called 'convoy troops' of the
N.K.V.D., were particularly brutal and negligent. During transport to the camps the N.K.V.D.'s regulation mania was not even
formally observed when it came, for example, to rations. Sometimes there was nothing to drink the 'tea' ration from. Often the
ration gradually got smaller and smaller, and the guards started
failing to distribute it at all. Even the water to be provided was
often forgotten for a day or two.[20] A Soviet woman writer complains of the suffering caused by the provision of only one mug of
water a day for all purposes on the long run from Moscow to
Vladivostok.[21]

A Pole who collated the accounts of his fellow-countrymen
deported in 1939–40 remarks:

It seems almost impossible for any human being, when not experiencing any particular sensations of anger or vindictiveness and when
not in danger of thereby being deprived of it himself, persistently to refuse
to hand in a bucket of water to fifty or sixty human beings shut in under
such conditions. It is a fact that these men did refuse to do so, and could
keep up this attitude throughout journeys lasting four, five and six

weeks. There were whole days of twenty-four hours when not a drop of anything to drink passed into the cars. There were periods even of thirty-six hours.[22]

The writer adds that in examining 'many hundreds'[23] of accounts, he has noted one case of a guard passing in an extra bucket, and five others of the doors being opened for ten minutes or so to relieve the fetor of the cars. Of the doctors or medical orderlies attached to each train, he found a few cases of 'a little more than blank indifference' to particular children, and two records of decided kindness.[24] The brutalization Bukharin had noted in the Party had reached down and everywhere reinforced a more archaic brutality. These train journeys were highly debilitating. A Soviet writer, later rehabilitated, describes a party of men being marched from Vladivostok Transit Camp to the embarkation point for Magadan immediately after coming off the train, without food. After several had collapsed and died, the remainder refused to go on, whereupon the guards panicked, started kicking the corpses, and shot a number of others.[25]

There is an interesting post-war account in the *British Medical Journal** of a medical examination of twenty-four women, former inhabitants of East Prussia, who had just escaped to Western Germany after returning to the Eastern Zone from Russian labour camps. They had been packed about eighty to a truck, and they lived on bread and a spoonful of sugar a day. But the worst deprivation was the lack of water. It was estimated that about forty to fifty in one transport of 2,000 women died *en route*. In one of the camps described it was estimated that about half the women died in the first eight or nine months, mostly from intestinal diseases.

It was usual for political prisoners to be robbed almost at once of their most valued possessions, such as warm clothing and good footwear, either on the journey or immediately on arrival at camp. This was done quite openly under the eyes of the guards. The old criminal underworld of Tsarist Russia, which since the Time of Troubles had developed as an extraordinary milieu with

*23 April 1949. This was at a later time, but the conditions described are exactly parallel.

its own dialect and its own law, had been greatly reinforced, and its character much modified, by the tumults of the Civil War and the famine of the early twenties. Already then, the *bezprizorniye*, the homeless orphan children assembling in gangs and living by their wits, had become a problem. Collectivization and other social experiments disrupted millions more families and provided large reinforcements to these now maturing criminals.

The percentage of 'criminals' was around 10–15 per cent, but the majority of these were of the petty embezzler type, rather than *urkas* proper, who were seldom more than around 5 per cent of a camp total. In some camps, indeed, there were none or almost none – particularly the more severe camps like Solzhenitsyn's, where almost all prisoners were in under Article 58, as interpreted by the Special Board. In other camps their rule, which led to the slow murder of many politicals at night in the barracks when guards did not dare to interfere,* was the norm. By 1940 the N.K.V.D. were often more fully in control, permitting only, in mixed camps such as Kargopol, regular rape hunts. Even these were largely suppressed in 1941. But later a considerable relapse seems to have taken place. And in no case was there any serious interference with ordinary robbery and beating-up.

Soviet sources now confirm all this. General Gorbatov relates:

While we were in the Sea of Okhotsk misfortune befell me. Early in the morning, when I was lying half-awake as many of us did, two 'trusties' came up to me and dragged away my boots which I was using as a pillow. One of them hit me hard on the chest and then on the head and said with a leer: 'Look at him – sells me his boots days ago, pockets the cash, and then refuses to hand them over!'

Off they went with their loot, laughing for all they were worth and only stopping to beat me up again when, out of sheer despair, I followed them and asked for the boots back. The other 'trusties' watched, roaring with laughter. 'Let him have it!' 'Quit yelling – they're not your boots now.'

Only one of the political prisoners spoke up: 'Look, what are you up to? How can he manage in bare feet?' One of the thieves took off his pumps and threw them at me.[27]

* Karl Radek is reported by several sources[26] to have been beaten up and finally killed in these circumstances.

Similar things happened on several other occasions. Once, buying a tin of fish from a 'trusty', he had the money stolen, together with letters and photographs of his wife, by criminals who refused to return even the latter. (When he opened the tin it was full of sand.)[28]

He was surprised to see that the guards did nothing to discourage this sort of thing. At the Maldyak gold-field camp in the Magadan area where he served his sentence there were 400 politicals and fifty common criminals. The latter had all the privileges and in one way or another did the politicals out of much of their meagre food ration:

Work at the goldfield was pretty killing, particularly so considering the bad food we were given. The 'enemies of the people', as a rule, were detailed for the heaviest jobs, the lighter work being given to the 'trusties' or common criminals. As I have already said, it was they who were appointed foremen, cooks, orderlies and tent seniors. Naturally enough the small amounts of fat released for the pot chiefly found their way into the bellies of the 'trusties'. There were three types of rations: one for those who had not fulfilled their quota, another for those who had, and a third for those who had exceeded their quota. The latter automatically included the 'trusties'. They did little enough work, but the tally clerks were of their persuasion and so they swindled, putting to their own and their mates' credit the work that we had done. As a result the criminals fed well and the politicals went hungry.[29]

Outside the camps proper, that is in the transit camps and stations, the criminals continued to be almost completely out of control. One of their customs was to gamble with each other for the clothes of some strange political; the loser then had to pull them off the victim and hand them over to the winner. This game was also played for prisoners' lives. A Hungarian who was in Vorkuta in 1950–51 reports it played by fifteen-year-old juvenile criminals, the loser then knifing the chosen victim. These young delinquents, usually aged from fourteen to sixteen, were seldom seen in the usual camps, being held in special centres. They were far more terrifying than any other element in Soviet society: their egos were completely unsocialized. Killing meant nothing at all to them. They formed the hard core of the great 'hooligan' youth element which still persists in the Soviet Union and, politically speaking, may be thought to form the potential storm troops, on one side or another, in any future upsets in the country.

Gorbatov mentions a criminal with fingers missing who explained to him that he had 'lost' a political's clothes to another criminal, and before he could steal them to hand them over, the political had been transferred. So he was at once tried for negligence by his mates and sentenced to the loss of his fingers. The criminal 'prosecutor' demanded all five, but the 'court' finally settled for three. 'We also have our laws,' the victim commented.[30] In another case, one who, in a mass rape aboard the convict ship *Magadan* had taken a woman the leader of his band had marked down, had his eyes put out with a needle.[31] Another leader, also on a convict ship, had gambled his brigade's bread ration away at cards. He was tried and cut to pieces.[32]

In fact, the criminals (who had such names as 'The Louse', 'Hitler', 'The Knout') known at the time of the Purges as *urkas* and later as *blatniye*, in the fifties had come to call themselves 'Those with the Law' – that is, their own code.

One of its provisions (at this time, though it is said that it has since been modified) was refusal to work. Since the *urka* groups had sanctions just as effective as any disposed of by the camp administration, nothing could usually be done about this. One commandant is reported as giving the *urkas* jobs in the camp which existed only on paper. As Gorbatov describes above, the criminals in effect had arrangements with the authorities to ensure that the politicals worked on their behalf as well as on their own.

WOMEN IN CAMPS

Women criminals, who formed a high percentage of all women in the camps, were in the main tough and shameless – though one prisoner mentions a woman of the criminal class who never took her knickers off even in the washroom: it was said that the tattooing on her belly was so indecent that 'even she was a little embarrassed by it'.[33] The criminal women referred to themselves as 'little violets' and sneered at the politicals as 'little roses'. But they were somewhat restrained in their attitude to nuns.[34]

Women on the whole seem to have survived much better than

men. For this reason we have perhaps a disproportionate number of accounts of the camps from their hands. In fact, they seem to have numbered 'less than 10 per cent' of the total, and many of these were in the criminal group.[35] This was enough, all the same, to account for 'the innumerable mixed or women's concentration camps in the north', to which Pasternak refers in *Doctor Zhivago*.

In the mixed camps, non-criminal women were frequently mass-raped by *urkas*, or had to sell themselves for bread, or to get protection from camp officials. Those who did not were given the heaviest possible tasks until they gave in. A typical story from the Baltic–White Sea Canal camps is of a young woman who refused to give in to an official, who thereupon assigned her to a team of ordinary criminals who the same night blindfolded her, raped her and pulled out several gold teeth from her mouth. There was no one to whom she could complain, for the camp chief himself was known to have raped several prisoners.[36]

The guards were often brutal to them. A woman prisoner describes an attempt by a young girl to evade work by hiding under the floorboards. She was attacked by the guard dogs and dragged out so violently by the guards that she was literally scalped. Serving five years for stealing potatoes, she was one of the sixteen- or seventeen-year-old girls frequently reported in the camps.[37]

Decent prisoners did what they could for them. But the demoralization of their physical deterioration was intense. A man wrote of them 'I suppose there is no more horrifying sight for the normal man than a few hundred filthy, diseased-looking, shabby women. The deep-rooted romanticism of the male is outraged.'[38] And they felt this keenly. All accounts agree that even the debilitating work and diet did not damp down their sexual feelings, as it did in the case of men. Hysteria was common from this cause.

A French peasant woman, married and divorced from a Russian and unable to leave the country, got an eight-year sentence as the wife of a traitor in November 1937. She describes being marched twenty-five miles and then left standing in the freezing rain outside the barbed wire for two hours while the camp officers were being shown a film.[39]

In the labour camps there were seldom tractors or horses, and sleds of wood were pulled by the prisoners. If the team was made up of men, five were harnessed, if of women, seven.[40] A Polish journalist who served in the Pechora camps reports seeing several hundred women carrying heavy logs, and later rails for the railway.[41]

In 1937 a special camp, in the Potmalag complex, was set up which contained about 7,000 wives and sisters of enemies of the people. The camp was later broken up, some of the prisoners being sent to Karaganda, while 2,000 were held at Segeta on the Kirovsk railway. These wives are said to have been amnestied in 1945.[42]

SETTING UP CAMP

In general, the great expansion of the Yezhov period was marked by the setting-up of new camps. For example, in the Archangel area, the Kargopol 'camp', consisting of a number of smaller camps in a radius of about thirty-five miles, containing in 1940 about 30,000 prisoners, was founded in 1936 by 600 prisoners who were simply put out of the train in the middle of the forest and who built their own barracks and fences. The death rate had been very heavy. The Polish and German Communist prisoners had died first, followed by the national minorities from Asia.[43]

Pasternak, certainly drawing on the experiences of friends who had suffered, described in *Doctor Zhivago* the setting-up of a new camp:

We got off the train. – A snow desert. Forest in the distance. Guards with rifles muzzles pointing at us, wolf-dogs. At about the same time other groups were brought up. We were spread out and formed into a big polygon all over the field, facing outwards so that we shouldn't see each other. Then we were ordered down on our knees, and told to keep looking straight in front on pain of death. Then the roll-call, an endless, humiliating business going on for hours and hours, and all the time we were on our knees. Then we got up and the other groups were marched off in different directions, all except ours. We were told: 'Here you are. This is your camp.' – An open snow-field with a post in the middle and a notice on it saying: 'Gulag 92 Y.N.90' – that's all there was . . .

First we broke saplings with our bare hands in the frost to get wood to build our huts with. And in the end, believe it or not, we built our own camp. We put up our prison and our stockade and our punishment cells and our watch towers, all with our own hands. And then we began our job as lumber-jacks.[44]

In exactly the same way, a Pole describes being marched, in rags, to a spot on the frozen tundra where there was no more than a sign 'Camp Point No. 228'. The prisoners dug pits to live in and covered them with branches and earth. The food was simply raw rye flour, kneaded with water.[45]

Another prisoner of the 1939 period describes being marched to a temporary camp which would not hold, however squeezed, more than one fifth of the prisoners. The others were left out in the mud for several days. They began to light fires made of bits of parts of the barracks, and were charged and beaten up by the guards. Twice a day they had one third of a litre of soup, and once a day about half a kilo of bread.[46]

On entry into an established camp, prisoners were allotted their categories for work. This might be done by a quick examination of the prisoners' legs.[47] A certificate of 'first-class' health was required for the heaviest tasks. (A Soviet writer describes one being issued to a political four hours before her death from scurvy.[48]) Then they were marched to the barrack, where, typically, 'two hundred men slept in fifty bug-ridden bunks', on boards or mattresses 'full of heavy and hard-packed sawdust'.[49]

Crowding was intense. The former director of a Kemerovo works describes negotiating with the N.K.V.D. for 2,000 slave labourers.[50] The trouble was not the number, but how to accommodate them in the existing camps in the area. The officials concerned were shown around a camp which appeared to be packed solid, but the Commandant agreed with his superior that yet another layer of bunks could be put in.

There would be a stove, though not adequate to warm one of

the Arctic huts 'because the orderlies only brought in ten pounds of coal dust for each stove and you didn't get much warmth from that'.[51] In a corner would be the twenty-gallon latrine tank which prisoner orderlies carried off to empty daily – 'light work for people on the sick list!'[52]

The company, apart from the complement of *urkas* who in a non-penal camp would be lording it in the corridors, were of a varied lot of 'politicals'. There would be saboteurs – specialists and engineers. At first these mostly had technical jobs, but as the mass purges grew in scope, so many engineers and specialists flooded the camps that the chance of appointment to a technical position which had previously saved so many of them became proportionately rare.

An account of the Dzhezkazgan camp in a recent Moscow article mentions an ex-Ambassador to China, a soloist from the Bolshoi opera, an illiterate peasant, an Air Force general.[53] Common categories were soldiers, intellectuals, and especially Ukrainian and other nationalists on the one hand, and members of religious sects on the other. Solzhenitsyn points out that the Baptists were in the camps simply for praying. For this (at the time he writes of) 'They all got twenty-five years, because that's how it was now – twenty-five years for everybody.'[54] There are many reports of sectarians being beaten or sent to the isolator cells for refusal to work on Sundays.[55] A priest, beaten blind, was noted in 1937.[56]

For, as in all times of trouble and oppression, the millenarian sects flourished. In the great slave empires of the past similar voices had always spoken for the oppressed and hopeless. They sometimes preached that the horrors of the present were a special trial, and that from the Russian people, degraded and demoralized, a 'race of saints' would arise.[57] Even now, in Vorkuta, we are told that there is more religious organization (and sharper national feeling) among the minority groups still settled there after their camp experiences than in most other districts.[58]

Prisoners' rights were virtually limited to making written protests and complaints. The result: 'Either there was nothing or it was rejected.'[59] Such applications made a prisoner unpopular with the authorities.

In the penal camps proper, however, there was considerable freedom of speech:

> Somebody in the room was yelling: 'You think that old bastard in Moscow with the moustache is going to have mercy on *you*? He wouldn't give a damn about his own brother, never mind slobs like you!'
>
> The great thing about a penal camp was you had a hell of a lot of freedom. Back in Ust-Izhma if you said they couldn't get matches 'outside' they put you in the can and slapped on another ten years. But here you could yell your head off about anything you liked and the squealers didn't even bother to tell on you. The security fellows couldn't care less.
>
> The only trouble was you didn't have much time to talk about anything.[60]

Almost every account quotes cases of prisoners who remained devoted to 'the Party and the Government' and attributed their arrest to error.[61] These bored and annoyed the other prisoners considerably. In some cases, though not all, they turned informer. There were in any case a number of these by common N.K.V.D. practice. Informers who were recognized as such were always killed sooner or later. If the N.K.V.D. had been unable to extricate them in time, they made no complaint about their deaths. Herling gives an account of a revenge taken on a notorious former N.K.V.D. interrogator who was recognized in the camp, and when badly beaten up, but not killed, complained to the guards, who did nothing to save him so that he was finally killed a month later after endless persecution and attempts to appeal.

BEHIND THE WIRE

Reveille is usually reported as at 5 a.m. – a hammer pounding on a rail outside camp headquarters. Anyone caught a few minutes late getting up could be sentenced on the spot to a few days in the isolator. In the winter it would still be dark. Searchlights would be 'crisscrossing over the compound from the watchtowers at the far corners'.[62] Apart from the guards and the barbed wire, most camps also relied on dogs, their long chains fastened by a ring to a wire running from watchtower to watchtower. The noise of the ring screeching along the wire was a continual background.[63]

The prisoners' first thought, all day, was of food, and it was now that the breakfast, the best meal of the day, was served. (We will consider food, the centre of the entire norm system and the key to Stalin's plans for efficient slave labour, later.)

Then they were assembled and marched off to work, in gangs of twenty or thirty. The order would be given:

'Your attention, prisoners! You will keep strict column order on the line of march! You will not straggle or bunch up. You will not change places from one rank of five to another. You will not talk or look around to either side, and you will keep your arms behind you! A step to right or left will be considered an attempt at escape, and the escort will open fire *without* warning! First rank, forward march!'[64]

Apart from sleeping, the prisoners' time was their own only for ten minutes at breakfast, five minutes at the noon break, and another five minutes at supper.[65] They lost so much sleep that they fell asleep instantly if they found a warm spot, and on the Sundays they got off, which was not every Sunday, they slept as much as they could.[66]

The shoe situation varied. 'There'd been times when they'd gone around all winter without any felt boots at all, times when they hadn't even seen ordinary boots, but only shoes made of birch bark or shoes of the 'Chelyabinsk Tractor Factory model' (that is, made of strips of tires that left marks of the tread behind them).'[67]

Clothes were usually carefully patched and repaired: 'rags tied around with all their bits of string and their faces wrapped in rags from chin to eyes to protect them from the cold . . .'[68]

Ulcers are reported as common, through filthy clothes. These were cleaned and disinfected occasionally, and baths were also provided. Solzhenitsyn implies that in the penal camp he describes a bath was available about every two weeks.[69] But often there was 'no soap for either bathing or laundry'.[70]

To go sick for the odd day was possible with a minor complaint. But to be recognized as sick and put on sick diet was usually fatal. In any case, even a man feeling ill might not be allowed to go sick, as there was a quota: 'He was allowed to excuse only two men in the morning, and he'd already excused them.'[71] As a rule the infirmary took in only those who were plainly dying – 'and not all of them', a Soviet woman writer recalls.[72]

In one camp, still under construction, a sick inspection is described:

> The *naryadchik* and the *lekpom* (medical assistant), armed with clubs, enter the pit. The chief asks the first man he sees why he does not come out. 'I am sick,' is the answer. The *lekpom* feels his pulse and pronounces him all right. Then blows shower upon the man and he is kicked out into the open. 'Why don't you go to work?' the chief asks the next man. 'I am sick,' is the stubborn answer. The day before, this prisoner went to see the *lekpom* and gave him his last dirty louse-infected shirt. The *lekpom* feels his pulse and finds high fever. He is released from work. A third man replies that he has neither clothes nor shoes. 'Take the clothes and shoes of the sick one,' the chief rules sententiously. The sick one refuses, whereupon his things are taken off him by force.[73]

The veteran convicts in *One Day in the Life of Ivan Denisovich* have learned that it is necessary to march as slowly as possible to the morning job, otherwise they get too hot early, and 'won't last long'.[74] And in fact, those who survived the first months became fantastically skilled in the arts of survival. At the same time, customs useful to them became thoroughly established and traditional. For example, Solzhenitsyn describes the habit of the prisoners picking up odd scraps of wood on the building site and marching back with them.[75] This was illegal, but the guards did nothing about it until they reached camp again. They then ordered them to throw down the wood, as they too needed extra fuel and were unable to carry any in addition to their sub-machine-guns. But only a certain amount of the wood was now dropped. At the next check-point, the warders repeated the order. Again, only a certain amount of wood was dropped, and the prisoners reached the quarters with a proportion of their original gleanings. It was necessary, and in the interests of both guards and warders, that the prisoners should be able to get away with some wood, otherwise they would have had no incentive to bother to carry it in, and guards and warders would not have got their share. But no overt arrangement had ever been made. The agreement was wholly unspoken. We see, in such things, the development of the rules and traditions of a whole new social order, in microcosm.

A genuine caste feeling seems to have been arising, with the prisoner beginning to be regarded as actually an inferior being, just as in ancient times. The sentiment gradually spread that 'mere contact' with the prisoners was 'an insult to a free man'. 'It is considered inadmissible for a non-prisoner to eat the same food as a prisoner, to sleep under the same roof, or have any friendly relations with him.' Things reached the stage where the head of a camp admonished the man in charge of the disinfestation chamber for allowing a shirt belonging to a free mechanic employed in the power plant to be put in with the prisoners' clothes for delousing.[76]

Free citizens in Kolyma sometimes tried to help prisoners they came in contact with. In particular, we are told, 'doctors, engineers, geologists' would try to get their professional colleagues employed according to their capacities. A geologist now described as 'a hero of the north' lost his own life owing to an attempt to defend some of the Kolyma inmates. One of his interventions is described:

'These people might die!'
'What people?' the representative of the camp administration smiled, 'These are enemies of the people.'[77]

There are many accounts of camp officials, and even doctors, who came to regard the prisoners as their personal serfs. This selection of slaves was sometimes similar even in the details of its décor to the illustrations of books about Negro slavery, as when the chief of a Yertsevo camp section, Samsonov, honoured the medical examination with his presence, and with a smile of satisfaction felt the biceps, shoulders and backs of the new arrivals.[78] It has been maintained that the Soviet forced labour system might be considered as 'a stage on the way to a new social stratification which might have involved slavery' – that is, in the old-fashioned overt sense – though the trend was changed by later events.[79]

A Soviet critic has remarked that 'The whole system in the camps Ivan Denisovich passed through was calculated to choke and kill without mercy every feeling for justice and legality in man, demonstrating in general and in detail such impunity of despotism that any sort of noble or rebellious impulse was powerless before it. The camp administration did not allow the prisoners to forget for a single moment that they had no rights at all. . . .'[80]

In the forties, 'a prisoner had to take his cap off at a distance of five paces when he saw a warder, and keep it off till he was two paces past him'.[81] Solzhenitsyn tells of a muddled count, leading to recount after recount, and another time of an extra count when a missing prisoner has been found:

'What's all this about?' the chief escort screamed. 'D'you want to sit on your asses in the snow? That's where I'll put you if you like and that's where I'll keep you till morning!' And he sure would. He wouldn't think twice about it if he wanted. It'd happened plenty of times before and sometimes they had to go down on their knees with the guards pointing their guns at the ready.[82]

Reports of physical violence are common.[83] Refusal to work seems to have been punished variously: in the Far Eastern area by immediate shooting, elsewhere by stripping the offender and standing him in the snow until he submitted or by solitary confinement on 200 grammes of bread. For a second offence death was usual. And in camp, not only 'sabotage' but also 'anti-Soviet propaganda' was a capital crime.[84]

Occasional tightening of lax discipline in the camps led to the sudden infliction of penalties on a large scale. Appeals to the regulations were treated as repeated and wilful refusal to work. In 1937, 400 prisoners were executed in a batch in Karaganda on such charges.[85] A 'mutiny' is reported in a camp near Kemerovo near the end of 1938. It was in fact a strike against rotten food. Fourteen of the ringleaders, twelve men and two women, were shot in front of all the rest of the prisoners, then details from each hut helped to dig the graves.[86]

Apart from these executions for 'disciplinary' reasons, often announced openly in the camps with the purpose of intimidating the occupants further, there were many killings of a different kind. Orders would come from Moscow for the liquidation of a given number of ex-oppositionists, and the quota would then be fulfilled by a cursory reinterrogation – not on activity in the camps but on newly-discovered circumstances in connexion with the original offence, transforming it into a capital one. For mass operations of this kind, special commissions were on occasion sent down, and given special powers and premises where the doomed men were transferred for investigation and death. For example, one such centre was established in an abandoned brick factory in the Vorkuta area, where some 1,300 politicals are said to have been executed in the winter of 1937.[87]

In most of the main camp areas there seem also to have been established special and highly secret 'Central Isolation Prisons' covering a given group of camps. To one such, in Bamlag (the Baikal-Amur camp complex in Eastern Siberia), we are told that some 50,000 prisoners were 'transferred' for execution in the two years 1937–8. The victims were tied up with wire like logs, stacked in trucks and driven out to a selected area and shot.[88]

The Hungarian Communist writer Lengyel, himself a camp veteran, describes one of these special extermination camps in the Norilsk area, as what is evidently intended as authentic background, in his story 'The Yellow Poppies': the camp is wound up first by the execution of the remaining prisoners, and then by special N.K.V.D. squads who move in and execute all the staff and guards. Owing to the permafrost it is impossible to bury the bodies, and they are piled into veritable hills, and covered with truckloads of earth, the whole matter remaining unknown even in nearby camps, and even when the camp site itself is later re-occupied as a prison hospital.

But the routine punishment was the punitive 'isolators' built in each camp, and quite deadly. At Solzhenitsyn's,

> The fellows from 104 had built the place themselves and they knew how it looked – stone walls, a concrete floor, and no window. There was a stove, but that was only enough to melt the ice off the walls and make puddles on the floor. You slept on bare boards and your teeth chattered all night. You got six ounces of bread a day and they only gave you hot gruel every third day.

Ten days! If you had ten days in the cells here and sat them out to the end, it meant you'd be a wreck for the rest of your life. You got T.B. and you'd never be out of hospitals as long as you lived.

And the fellows who did fifteen days were dead and buried.[89]

Even among those who avoided the cells, all the deficiency diseases were rife. Solzhenitsyn's hero, who had lost teeth from scurvy in the Ust-Izhma camp in Pechora 'at a time when he thought he was on his last legs'[90] was lucky enough to recover. With scurvy, wounds opened and abscesses suppurated. Pellagra was equally common. Pneumonia, usually fatal, was a normal hazard. And the direct effects of undernourishment, 'swelling of the feet and face, and, in its final and lethal stage, swelling of the abdomen', were constantly to be seen.[91] In the farming camps, epidemics of brucellosis are reported.[92] In the northern camps gangrene, resulting in amputation, was frequent.[93] Tuberculosis was often the immediate cause of death. After about two years women prisoners tended to develop a continuous haemorrhage of the womb.[94]

It later became routine when a corpse was taken to the morgue 'to crack his skull with a big wooden mallet to make sure'.[95]

Escapes were occasionally made, but very seldom with any success. They were acts of desperation; but of course there was enough desperation to produce them. In the Pechora area the N.K.V.D. had a reward of 11 lb. of wheat to anyone turning in an escaped prisoner. In the early thirties, escaped prisoners in other regions were sometimes sheltered by the peasantry, but this was very seldom true among the terrorized *kolkhozniks* of the Purge period. There were, nevertheless, rare successes. Gypsies, in particular, sometimes reached encampments of their own race where complete solidarity saved them from discovery. And odd individuals, like the Spanish Communist general 'El Campesino', made completely successful escapes.

Recaptured prisoners were always brutally manhandled, and almost invariably shot.

For any escape on the march to the camps from the railheads the guards were charged with complicity and sentenced to two or three years which they continued to serve as guards but without pay. This made them extremely vigilant. In the camps too, 'If anybody got out it was hell on the guards and they kept on the go without food or sleep. It made 'em so mad they often didn't bring the fellow back alive.' [96]

One consequence of this vigilance was continual counting of prisoners:

> The lieutenant stood still and watched. He'd come outside to double-check the count. That was the routine when they left the camp.
> The men meant more to a guard than gold. If there was one man missing on the other side of the wire, he'd soon be taking his place . . .[97]
> They counted you twice on the way out – once with the gates still shut, so they knew if they could open them, and then a second time when you were going through the gates. And if they thought there was something wrong, they did a recount outside.[98]

This is one of several interesting parallels with Dostoyevsky's account of forced labour in the 1840s, in *The House of the Dead*:

> The prisoners are lined up, counted and called over at dawn, midday and nightfall, and sometimes more often during the day, depending on the suspicions of the guards and their ability to count. The guards often made mistakes, counted wrongly, went away and then came back again. Eventually the wretched guards would succeed in arriving at the right figure, and lock up the hut.

In a general comparison between this century and the last, we note that in Dostoyevsky's time prisoners have considerably more freedom of action inside the camp, and are not under such strict guard outside either, though Dostoyevsky mentions that his convicts are serving 'incomparably' the worst of the three types of hard labour. With the exception that in Dostoyevsky's camp the main sanction was frightful floggings, which sometimes resulted in death, rather that the 'isolators', the life of the convicts was on the whole preferable in his descriptions to those of Solzhenitsyn and the others. Each convict has his own box with a lock and key; prisoners keep domestic animals. They do not work on Sundays or feast days, or even on their own name days. Jews and Moslems have parallel privileges. The food is greatly superior, and prisoners on the sick list go into town and buy 'tobacco, tea, beef; on Christmas Day, sucking-pig, even goose'. They even have enough bread to spare for the horse of the water-carrier.

The convicts in *The House of the Dead* are all, indeed, really guilty of one or another offence – often murder, like the hero Goryanchikov – though there are about a dozen political prisoners out of thirty.

Dostoyevsky's type of camp was abolished in the 1850s. (He makes the point that he is 'describing the past'.) But even non-literary prisoners in Stalin's camps were able to make other comparisons – for example, one prisoner was a Polish Communist who had served two years in Wronki jail in Poland for political offences. In the Polish jail they had been locked in only at night, by day they were allowed in the garden; they were allowed any books from outside, unlimited correspondence and weekly baths; there were five of them in a large room.[99]

THE PENAL EMPIRE

In the vast empty spaces of the North and Far East, areas as big as fair-sized countries came under complete N.K.V.D. control. There were many camps scattered through the Urals, in the Archangel area, and more especially in and around Karaganda and on the new railway being built from Turkestan to Siberia. But in these, the N.K.V.D. administered only comparatively small enclaves. Even in Karaganda, where there were about 150,000 prisoners, they were in camps scattered among other settlements, mostly of deported 'free' labour.*

The two biggest true colonies of the N.K.V.D. empire were the great stretch of north-west Russia beyond Kotlas, comprising roughly what is shown on the map as the Komi Autonomous Soviet Socialist Republic, and the even vaster area of the Far East centred on the gold-fields of Kolyma. These regions had, before the N.K.V.D. took over, populations of a handful of

---

*These so-called 'free exiles' were men and women whose innocence was absolutely clear even to the examining judges. In some areas they were often little more than vagabonds, sleeping under bridges, begging their bread, and seeking work or even arrest to save themselves from starvation.[100]

Russians and a few thousand Arctic tribesmen. A decade later they held between them something between 1¼ and 2 million prisoners.

For both of these great areas we have accounts from both Soviet and émigré publications. *One Day in the Life of Ivan Denisovich* is set in the north-eastern camps. General Gorbatov's *Years Off My Life* covers his experiences in Kolyma. These and other Moscow-published works confirm and complement the large amount of material that has long been available in the West.

The Soviet Arctic is a world of its own. The feeling of having been thrown out from normal life was accentuated by the physical phenomena. In winter, there is the extreme, extravagant cold; the short days in which a swollen, livid sun raises itself for a few hours above the horizon – or, in the Arctic proper, simply lightens the sky somewhat without appearing; the soundlessly flickering ion-stream of the *aurora borealis*. In summer, the long days; the mosquitoes; the slushy swamp of the melted surface with its alien vegetation – bog-cotton and dwarf willow a few inches high; and below it, hard as rock, the permafrost. South of this true tundra is the even wilder forest belt, the taïga, where the great complex of timber camps lay.

Most of the northern camps were separated from the country as a whole by vast stretches of empty land, sparsely inhabited by tribal hunters, the Chukchi, Yakut, Nentsi – the last being the Samoyeds, cannibals, from whom Ivan the Terrible had recruited his fiercest guards. Most of these were happy to turn in prisoners for a bounty, having in any case a general hostility to Russians.

KOLYMA

The largest camp area was that which came under 'Dalstroy', the Far Eastern Construction Trust. The exact boundaries of Dalstroy's control have never been exactly determined, but it seems to have included all the territory beyond the Lena and north of the Aldan, at least as far east as the Gydan Range – a territory four times the size of France.

Its prison population was never quite as large as the Pechora region's, being usually around half a million. But the death rate was so high that more individual prisoners inhabited its camps at one time or another than any other region. Since it was supported by sea, and the number of ships, their capacity and their average of trips is known with reasonable accuracy, we can compute a probable *minimum* of 1 million deaths in 1937–41 alone.[101]

The main concentration of camps was in the Kolyma gold-fields, based on Magadan, with its port of Nagayevo.[102] Gold-mining started on a big scale in the early thirties. In 1935 a series of awards was announced in the gold-mining industry, with great publicity to all concerned. Most of those named were mentioned as working at Kolyma, under E. P. Berzin, the 'Director'. High among the awards of Orders, a different decree was inserted – commuting the sentences and restoring the civil rights of five engineers in the gold industry for their services.

Berzin is described as comparatively reasonable about prisoners' complaints.[103] He, his wife and his chief assistant, Filipov (who is said to have committed suicide in Magadan prison), were arrested, together with scores of others, in 1937, in Yezhov's purge of the N.K.V.D. There seems to have been some apprehension of resistance, and Berzin was promised awards and promotion, fêted by the N.K.V.D. 'delegation', and only arrested on the airfield.[104]

He was succeeded by Garanin, who launched on a campaign of, even by N.K.V.D. standards, maniac terror. Torture and execution, with the shooting in 1938 of an estimated 26,000 men in a special camp, Serpantinka, set up for the purpose, ended after a few months in his own recall and sentence of fifteen years or, according to other accounts, death. *His* successor Vyshnyevtsky also lasted a very short time, receiving fifteen years for a disastrous expedition intended to open up new areas.

The new man, Ivan Nikishov, described as 'icily, mercilessly cruel', lasted longer. He married an N.K.V.D. woman, Gridassova, who was put in charge of the women's camp at Magadan. They lived in a comfortable country house forty-five miles north-west of Magadan, in their own hunting preserve.[105]

The slave route to Kolyma had its own Middle Passage, the trip to Magadan from Vladivostok by boat, with thousands of prisoners battened down under hatches. The trip took eight or nine days, and was much feared. An alternative route was tried to Ambarchik on the Arctic Ocean, at the mouth of the Kolyma – a four-thousand-mile voyage through difficult seas, taking some two months. The first ship sent that way, the *Dzhurma*, was caught in the autumn ice, and when it arrived in Ambarchik the following year (1934), none of its 12,000 prisoners remained. This was at a time when the exploring ship *Chelyushkin* was caught in the ice and sank, and there was world-wide interest in the safety of its crew camped on the ice. American and other offers to try to rescue them by air were refused, and it has been suggested that the reason was that their camp was only a couple of hundred miles from the wintering place of the *Dzhurma*, which might have been stumbled on by foreign flyers.[106]

More usually, the shorter passage to Magadan, on the *Dzhurma*, the *Indigirka*, and other freighters,* was the prisoners' route. The ships were the scene of the worst of the *urkas'* acts. It was on the *Dzhurma* that General Gorbatov lost his boots (p. 457). By 1939, the guards were not entering the prisoners' hold, only waiting outside with raised guns when the prisoners were let out on deck in small groups to go to the latrine. As a result, the *urkas* had a freer hand than at any other time. There were always numbers of murders and rapes. In 1939, on the *Dzhurma*, the criminals managed to break through a wall and get at the provisions, after which they set the storeroom on fire. The fire was held in check, though it was still burning when the *Dzhurma* entered port. But there was no attempt to release the prisoners locked in the hold, and a great panic ensued when they realized that if it came to the point they would be abandoned.[108] A similar tale – perhaps a version of the same event – is told by a Soviet writer. The ship took fire. Male prisoners tried to break out and were battened down in the hold. 'When they went on rioting the crew hosed them down to keep them quiet. They then forgot about them. As the fire was still burning the water boiled and the wretched men died in it. For a long time afterwards the *Dzhurma* stank intolerably.'[109]

On another occasion several hundred young girls, sentenced for

* Lately referred to by a Soviet scientist as 'death-ships' of the Okhotsk Sea.[107]

unauthorized absence from arms factories and so on, were in a compartment of the hold on their own. Again the *urkas* managed to break through and raped many of them, killing a few male prisoners who tried to protect them. This time the combination of the rapes, the breakage and the murders resulted in the arrest of the commander of the ship's guard.[110]

On arrival at Nagayevo first 'the sick were carried ashore on stretchers and left on the beach in tidy rows. The dead were also neatly stacked so that they could be counted and the number of death certificates would tally.'[111]

The survivors found themselves in a strange land.

The Kolyma Basin alone is almost as big as the Ukraine. It is intensely cold: the temperature may go down to $-70°C$.[112] Outside work for prisoners was compulsory until it reached $-50°C$.[113] In spite of this, in 1938, fur was banned in the Dalstroy camps, and only wadding permitted; felt shoes were replaced by canvas. The rivers of the region are ice-bound eight to nine months of the year. A camp rhyme ran:

> Kolyma, wonderful planet,
> Twelve months winter, the rest summer.

For about two months in winter there is no sunrise at all. One calmly-written account of the Kolyma camps has as a natural chapter heading: 'Sickness, Self-mutilation, Suicide.'[114]

Not, of course, that these were limited to Kolyma. But in Kolyma the death rate was particularly high, and the despair rate too. Gorbatov, a strong man with great will-power who had even resisted interrogation successfully, tells us that he barely survived less than a year in the gold camps. The death rate among the miners is estimated in fact at about 30 per cent per annum,[115] though it varied to some extent with location, type of work, and personality of commandant. A Kolyma prisoner comments that it is rarely possible to live on the camp ration for more than two years. By the fourth year, at the very latest, the prisoner is incapable of work and by the fifth year he can no longer be alive.[116] In one of the Kolyma penal camps which had started a year with 3,000 inmates, 1,700 were dead by the end, and another 800 in hospital with dysentery.[117] In another – a regular camp – it is estimated that 2,000 out of 10,000 died in a year.[118] Of some 3,000 Poles, over a period of about fifteen months, about 60 per cent were counted dead.[119]

In a camp there recently described in the Soviet press,[120] inmates did a twelve-hour day. The food ration for 100 per cent norm was 800 grammes of bread per day. Non-fulfilment of norms, through whatever cause, automatically entailed a reduction of the bread ration to 500 grammes. This was just above starvation level: any further reduction to 300 grammes (as a punitive measure) meant certain death. Work at the surface gold sites was performed in accordance with a strict division of labour. Two men had to start a bonfire, and this had to be done without matches, by the ancient method of striking sparks with flints. Another man had to fetch water from the frozen river and melt it. Next, the deeply-frozen ground had to be softened, then excavated and the sand passed through sieves in search for gold.

Three youths of about seventeen appeared in this camp. They looked younger than their age, perhaps because they were so thin as to be almost emaciated. After the death of the father of one of them, his son had found a collection of Lenin's works, and in the last volume an envelope containing a copy of 'Lenin's Testament'. Not keeping it a secret, he and his closest associates were arrested on a charge of terrorism and counter-revolution, and sentenced to fifteen years' hard labour. So there they all were – three boys and two girls in Kolyma and others of the youthful group dispersed in other prison camps.

There were several women's camps in the Kolyma area. At Mylga they worked in the gypsum quarries.[121] Even worse was the women's disciplinary camp at Elgen. Evgenia Ginzburg (the mother of the writer Aksionov), who became a nurse just in time to save her life, and survived to be rehabilitated, gives an account of this camp which makes it clear that it was a killer. She describes the impossibility of the tree-felling norm, the trade in sex, the using up of the 'quota' of medical exemptions on the common criminals, and the sole methods of survival – 'threats, intrigue and graft'. Women prisoners who had become illegally pregnant in illicit camp intercourse were among those sent to Elgen. Several times a day they were allowed to try to feed their babies, but milk hardly came, owing to the rations and work, and after a few weeks usually ceased altogether, whereupon 'the baby would have to fight for its life' on patent foods. As a result, 'the turnover of "mothers", was very rapid'.[122]

Gorbatov and others note N.K.V.D. officers saving old mates in the services or the Party by giving them easy jobs. This old-boys' network was all very well for those with good connexions. A Soviet source gives the other side of the picture. A commandant discovered his former general among the doomed *dokhodyagi* – 'goners' – and gave him a post in the store. A little Jew called Dodya Shmuller, who had been a trouble to the authorities through constantly demanding his rights under the regulations, was then in the punitive isolator on 300 grammes of bread a day, and unlikely to survive. When he heard of the general being saved, he put in one last formal complaint, about his ration, but merely received a further spell in the isolator.[123]

Another disciplinary case is of a team accused of concealing gold which they had found. Their quarters were thoroughly searched but nothing was found. However, in order to 'teach the men a lesson', the whole team was sentenced to solitary confinement in a punitive section known as 'Stalin's Villa'. Only a few survived.[124]

For administration was even harsher than elsewhere, and more capricious too. One prisoner in Kolyma finished his sentence at the end of 1937 and was given a paper to sign stating that he had been notified of his liberation. However, he was not given any document to identify himself as a free citizen, and could not leave the camp without one. He continued to work as a convict with the ambiguous status of 'free prisoner'. He did not protest, as even so he was doing better than most people, who simply got a fresh sentence. At the end of 1939 he was finally given his certificate of liberation and allowed to choose a place of residence in European Russia apart from his own home area.[125]

By a circumstance unique in the history of the labour camp zones, Magadan was visited in 1944 by the Vice-President of the United States, Henry Wallace. With him, representing the Office of War Information, was Professor Owen Lattimore. They both

wrote accounts of what they saw, which differ in various respects
from the information we have from ex-prisoners.

Wallace found Magadan idyllic.[126] The horrible Nikishov, he
noted approvingly, 'gambolled about, enjoying the wonderful
air'. He noted Gridassova's maternal solicitude, and much
admired the needlework which she showed him. The true story of
the needlework[127] is that women prisoners capable of producing
this were able to sell it for extra rations to the N.K.V.D. aristocracy's wives to decorate their apartments. It was normally
produced, that is, after a ten- or twelve-hour working day in
conditions comparable with those adversely commented on by
Thomas Hood in *The Song of a Shirt*. (In a similar way, Solzhenitsyn mentions three 'artists'[128] in his camp, who gained
certain privileges 'as a reward for doing pictures free for the
higher-ups'.)

Lattimore[129] condemned the hardness of the Tsarist system in
Siberia. But this had now, fortunately, passed. The Soviet open-
ing-up of the north was 'orderly', being controlled by 'a remarkable concern, the Dalstroy (Far Northern Construction Company),
which can be roughly compared to a combination of the Hudson
Bay Company and the T.V.A.'.

He was equally impressed with 'Mr' Nikishov and his wife.
'Mr Nikishov, the head of Dalstroy, had just been decorated with
the Order of Hero of the Soviet Union for his extraordinary
achievement. Both he and his wife have a trained and sensitive
interest in art and music and a deep sense of civic responsibility.'

Lattimore approvingly quotes another member of his party on
a local ballet troupe which provided 'high-grade entertainment'
which, he adds, 'just naturally seems to go with gold and so does
high-powered executive ability'. Lattimore notes, too, that
unlike the old gold rushes with their 'sin, gin and brawling',
Dalstroy concentrated on greenhouses where tomatoes, cucum-
bers and even melons were grown to make sure that the hardy
miners got enough vitamins. The tomatoes that Lattimore was so
lyrical about were indeed grown in the area. A prisoner describes
some under the charge of a bullying but efficient woman doctor
at a prisoners' hospital in the northern region of Kolyma. Most

of the tomatoes went to officials and staff, but at least some reached the patients, which is remarked on as an extraordinary thing.[130]

Nikishov had indeed shown some of the executive ability Lattimore attributes to him. For the reception had been very well organized. All prisoners in the area were kept in their huts. Watch towers were demolished. Various other deceptions were undertaken. For example, Wallace was shown a farm, the best in the area: fake girl swineherds, who were in fact N.K.V.D. office staff, replaced the prisoners for the occasion. All the goods that could be scraped up in the neighbourhood were put in the shop windows, and so on.[131]

The party was actually taken to a gold-mine in the Kolyma Valley. Lattimore prints a photograph of a group of husky men bearing little resemblance to accounts of the prisoners from current Soviet or other sources. It is captioned 'They have to be strong to withstand winter's rigours'.[132] The comment is a sound one, but when it came to real prisoners it worked out the other way: since they were not expected to withstand the winter's rigours, it was unnecessary to keep them strong.

PECHORA

No camp area had quite the reputation of Kolyma for isolation, cold and death. But there were others which ran it close – in particular the vast prison region at the north-eastern corner of European Russia in the basin of the Pechora River. Even the name of this stream, though there is no river of Europe outside Russia larger than it, except only the Danube, is practically unknown in the West. Its basin is larger than the British Isles, or than New England, New York and New Jersey. Here, between Kotlas, the gateway to the area, and the Vorkuta coal-mine district, lay the largest single concentration of forced labour in Russia, holding more than a million prisoners.

In Vorkuta it is below zero Centigrade for two thirds of the year, and for more than a hundred days the *khanovey* or 'wind of winds' blows across the tundra. The climate killed those from the southern parts of Russia very quickly: few would be alive after a year or two.[133] As has been seen, much of our evidence comes from this region.

The head of the Pechora camps in 1936 was N.K.V.D. Major Moroz, who is variously described as particularly cruel and as sensible enough to try to give good rations and good conditions in exchange for good work. He himself had briefly been a convict between high N.K.V.D. appointments. And he later disappeared. His assistant Bogarov, a man of the most brutal and ferocious appearance, seems in fact to have been as humane as his post permitted, and to have been behind these improved conditions.

Moroz was succeeded by 'a confirmed sadist', Kashketin, of whom it was said that the only safety from him lay in his being ignorant of one's existence. After a few months of his rule, there were 2,000 convicts in the isolators of a single camp group, of whom only seventy-six survived. Kashketin's brutality availed him no more than Moroz's humanity: he too disappeared with all his subordinates at the end of the Yezhov period.

And so it was, on a smaller but still vast scale, throughout the N.K.V.D.'s realm, from the White Sea to Sakhalin, from the great complexes of Karaganda to the still virtually unrecorded 'death camps' of the Taymyr and Novaya Zemlya, from (as Solzhenitsyn puts it) the Pole of Cold at Oy-Myakoi to the copper-mines of Dzhezkazgan.

SLAVE ECONOMICS

The millions of slave-labourers at the disposal of GULAG played an important economic role, and indeed became accepted as a normal component of the Soviet economy.

An ad hoc Committee of the United Nations appointed under resolutions by U.N.E.S.C.O. and the I.L.O., and consisting of a prominent Indian lawyer, a former President of the Norwegian Supreme Court, and a former Peruvian Minister of Foreign Affairs, reported in 1953 in a sober document leaving no doubt of the 'considerable significance' of forced labour in the Soviet economy.

State-owned slaves were common in the ancient world. For example, the Laurion silver mines were operated by Athens on that basis. The Romans too had their *servi publici*. The head of the Department of War Engineering Armaments, R.S.F.S.R., wanting some hundreds of prisoners for urgent work during the war, was told by the N.K.V.D. official responsible that there was a shortage. 'Malenkov and Voznesensky need workers, Voroshilov is calling for road builders. . . . What are we to do? The fact is we haven't as yet fulfilled our plans for imprisonment. Demand is greater than supply.'[134]

We think of the lumber camps as typical. But the best estimate seems to be that (of the comparatively low camp population of early 1941) only about 400,000 were held at lumbering. The other main categories were:

Mining	1 million
Agriculture	200,000
Hired out to various State enterprises	1 million
Construction and maintenance of camps and manufacture of camp necessities	600,000
General construction	$3\frac{1}{2}$ million.[135]

Even in the great lumbering area of the north-west a high proportion of prisoners were building the Kotlas–Vorkuta railway. Many others were erecting (like Solzhenitsyn's hero) various industrial and mining buildings.

It has often been pointed out that slave labour is economically inefficient. Karl Marx had the same view:

The lowest possible wage which the slave earns appears to be a constant, independent of his work in contrast to the free workers. The slave obtains the means necessary to his subsistence in natural form, which is fixed both in kind and in quantity, whereas the remuneration of the free worker is not independent of his own work.[136]

Slavery owed part of its inefficiency to lack of incentives.

The same point is put by the Webbs, in a passage worth quoting at length as representing a certain way of looking at Soviet affairs common in the thirties. They are criticizing Professor Tchernyavin's first-hand account of the camps he served in:

It is to be regretted that this testimony – very naturally strongly biased – mixes up personal observation and experience of conditions that are, in all conscience, bad enough, with hearsay gossip unsupported by evidence, and with manifestly exaggerated statistical guesses incapable of verification. The account would have carried greater weight if it had been confined to the very serious conditions of which the author had personal knowledge. His naïve belief that this and other penal settlements are now maintained and continuously supplied with thousands of deported manual workers and technicians, deliberately for the purpose of making, out of this forced labour, a net pecuniary profit to add to the State revenue, will be incredible by anyone acquainted with the economic results of the chain-gang, or of prison labour, in any country in the world.[137]

It is quite true that the mass arrests remain basically a political phenomenon. The slave-labour motive can only have been secondary. The engineers and scientists, the doctors and lawyers, were not arrested simply to provide a corps of incompetent lumberjacks. As Weissberg says:

After twenty years of endless trouble and enormous expense the Soviet Government finally developed a working body of really capable physicists. And now what's happened? Shubnikov, one of the leading low-temperature physicists in the country, is to help dig a canal in the Arctic. So is our first director, Professor Obremov, also a leading Soviet physicist and an expert on crystallography. Can't you imagine what expensive navvies men like Shubnikov and Obremov are?[138]

But once arrested, the extraction of physical labour ensured at least some contribution to the economy, and (granted the initial irrationality of the whole Purge) there is nothing contrary to reason and common sense in Stalin's typical decision to integrate them into his economic machine. To this extent the Webbs are simply wrong as to Stalin's motives.

Moreover, Stalin was well aware of Marx's economic objection to slavery. And with his usual refusal to accept precedent, he sought to overcome it by the simple but untried method of *not* giving the slave a flat subsistence, but linking his rations to his output. In this way, it was thought, the lack of incentive Marx had pointed to was overcome.

It is quite true that the forced-labour projects were, anyhow, like much else in Stalin's economy, often totally misconceived even in their own terms. During the great wave of arrests in 1947, a Soviet account tells us, Stalin remarked at a meeting of the Council of Ministers that the 'Russian people had long dreamed of having a safe outlet on to the Arctic Ocean from the Ob River'. Simply on the basis of this remark decisions were taken to build a railway to Igarka. For more than four years, amid feet of snow, in temperatures down to $-55°$ C. in winter, and with swamps and mosquitoes in the summer, forced labourers toiled at this vast project, at more than eighty camp sites at intervals of fifteen kilometres along the 1,300-kilometre stretch. The estimated cost, if it had ever been completed, was from 4 to 6 million roubles per kilometre. In the end, 850 kilometres of rail, and 450 of telegraph poles only, had been constructed. After Stalin's death the line, the signals, the railway stations, the locomotives and all that had been erected were abandoned to rust in the snow.[139]

But this was an irrationality of the Soviet political and planning system itself. When it came to an ordinary operation, such as logging, it might seem that a method of providing very cheap labour had indeed been found.

Some prisoners made efforts on the spot to estimate the economic value of the camps. A friend of mine who was in a logging camp in the Vorkuta area worked for a time on the administrative side there (from 1950 to 1952) and says that the results were to a large degree faked or inflated, as in ordinary Soviet factories at that time. A great deal of the work which counted against norms was of a valueless nature, and though the prisoners themselves received the barest minimum of all necessities, the total cost of the camp, with guards, administration and so forth, was much in excess of the value of its output. Mr Antoni Ekart[140] reports much the same of the Vorkuta mines – which, however, would probably have been uneconomic even if run by free labour because of the distances involved and the total production effected. And a recent careful study[141] makes the suppposed savings due to forced labour over the whole economy at best marginal.

A Soviet account reinforces this view. The writer recalls a conversation in which one of the technicians on the job, himself a former prisoner, commented on the suggestion that the use of convict labour for constructional projects was relatively cheap:

It merely seems so. After all the prisoners have somehow to be fed, shod, clothed and guarded; special areas have to be constructed, provided with watch towers for the guards – yes, and for that matter the maintenance of the guards is a costly matter. Then also there is the physical training section and all the other 'sections' which in fact only exist on paper . . . in fact a sizeable establishment. Then there are those again who have to fetch the water for them, heat the baths and wash the floors. After all there are a lot of things that human beings need. There are also many duty officers and personnel, the hewers of wood and drawers of water, the countless carpenters, clerks and other 'scabs' as they are called in the camp! So that if one averages it out you must reckon one and a half ancillary persons for every one who actually works. The other main thing is that the guards cannot deploy the labour force as it ought to be: either one is not allowed to use the necessary machinery, or else the foremen, not to mention the convicts themselves, simply have no time to stop and think about how to organize the labour force because of the consequent parades, inspections and the rest of the to-ing and fro-ing.[142]

The maintenance of the guards, it may be remarked, was also a *military* debit. Throughout the war period the camps continued to be guarded by picked N.K.V.D. soldiers, in a proportion of about one guard to twenty inmates. The Soviet Government thus forfeited the use of certainly not less than 250,000 trained and healthy troops.

Even so, in certain circumstances, forced labour does seem to have paid: coal from Karaganda was sometimes noticeably cheaper than that from the Donets Basin.[143] Moreover, there are certain fields where free labour would be inordinately expensive, and where slave labour is probably economically preferable, for instance in the mines and strategic roads of north-east Siberia. In 1951, in the United States Congress, the immense labour cost of setting up an American air base in Greenland was disclosed. We can be sure that the equivalents in north Siberia were completed far more cheaply with slave labour than they could have been with even Soviet free labour. That is to say, while it is true that the forced-labour system was not limitlessly expandable, nevertheless it may have paid in certain fields.

In any case, to start examining the economics of the operation in an abstract way is clearly a mistake. A man killed by squeezing a year or two's effort out of him is of more use than a man kept in prison. The camps were *politically* efficient. They effectively isolated masses of potential troublemakers, and were a great disincentive to any sort of anti-Stalinist activity, or even talk. Assuming that the political purging was necessary, the camps were a useful end-product.

Like everything else in Stalin's epoch, the system operated by pressure from the top down. Every camp had its 'plan', and every camp chief worked under a system of penalties and rewards. There were some odd results. Camp chiefs are reported as having kept recaptured prisoners whom they should have returned to their original camps. Again, in the prison at Kotlas there was a group of prisoners consisting entirely of invalids and old people, whom none of the camps would accept, for obvious economic reasons. They remained there over a year, as the problem solved itself by their dying out.[144]

FOOD AND DEATH

In the camps, the commandants operated the norm system *vis-à-vis* the prisoners. As a general principle there were various 'cauldrons', or food allotments. The principle is simple enough. Precise figures varied considerably, but the following shows a typical proportion. In the Kolyma camps, for men doing twelve to sixteen hours' heavy physical labour a day, eight months of it in very low temperatures, the daily ration, of very poor bread, is given as follows by a former prisoner now in the West:

for more than 100 per cent of the norm	up to 930 grammes (32 oz.)
for 100 per cent	815 grammes (28½ oz.)
for 70–99 per cent	715 grammes (25 oz.)
for 50–69 per cent	500 grammes (17½ oz.)
disciplinary ration	300 grammes (10½ oz.)

plus 'soup', 3½ oz. of salt fish and just over 2 oz. of groats.[145]

A recent Soviet account of the same area gives:

for 100 per cent	800 grammes
non-fulfilment for whatever cause	500 grammes
punitive	300 grammes[146]

The first is given in ounces in the original, so the slight discrepancy has no significance. What seems to be the abolition of the intermediate stage may be due to the fact that the Russian was serving there later – from 1942 till at least 1950, as against the other's *circa* 1938 to 1946. A Polish account, of 1940–41, gives 500 grammes for 50 per cent norm and 300 for less.[147]

Another reported ration scheme, in one of the northern camps in the winter of 1941–2:

for the full norm	700 grammes of bread, plus soup and buckwheat
for those not attaining the norm	400 grammes of bread plus soup.[148]

Most Arctic arrangements were probably close to these two. The ration outside the Arctic proper was rather lower; typically:

over 100 per cent	750–1,000 grammes
100 per cent	600–650 grammes
50–100 per cent	400–475 grammes
penal (under 50 per cent)	300–400 grammes.[149]

These rations may be compared with those of a camp system more familiar to Western readers – that of one of the Japanese P.O.W. camps on the River Kwai (Tha Makham). There, prisoners got a daily ration norm of 700 grammes of rice, 600 of vegetables, 100 of meat, 20 of sugar, 20 of salt and 5 of oil for a total of 3,400 calories, but, as in Russia, very deficient in vitamins.[150] (Even today in the U.S.S.R. the camp norm is of 2,400 calories only, mainly based on 700 grammes of black bread.)

We can make certain other comparisons. In the Ukrainian cities in the famine period of the thirties, the bread ration was 800 grammes for industrial workers, 600 for manual workers, 400 for office employees. In the siege of Leningrad, in 1941–2, about one third to one half of the population remaining in the city died of hunger, mostly during the first winter. The rations in the worst period were:[151]

October 1941	The basic ration was down to 400 grammes of bread a day for workers and 200 grammes for dependants.

Late November 1941   250 grammes for workers,
                                 125 for dependants.
Late December 1941   Up to 350 grammes for workers
                                 and 200 for dependants.

At Leningrad there were small additional rations of meat and sugar; lumber workers got a supplementary ration above the norm; and a truly major difference is that in camps the prisoners never got their full ration, and that if there was a bad or inedible portion of the original bulk ration, that was the part that went to them. Solzhenitsyn describes what happens to the groat issue:

Shukhov had had thousands of these rations in prisons and camps, and though he'd never had a chance to weigh a single one of them on a scale . . . he and every other prisoner had known a long time that the people who cut up and issued your bread wouldn't last long if they gave you honest rations. Every ration was short. The only question was – by how much?[152]

The reason was obvious:

When they left in the morning, the cook got an issue of groats from the big kitchen in the camp. It worked out to about two ounces a head – about two pounds for each gang. That is, a little over twenty pounds for everybody working on the site. The cook didn't carry that stuff himself on the two-mile march from the camp. He had a trusty who carried it for him. He thought it was better to slip an extra portion of the stuff to a trusty at the expense of the prisoners' bellies rather than break his own back. Then there was water and firewood to carry and the stove to light. The cook didn't do that either. He had other prisoners and 'goners' to do it. And they got their cut too. It's easy to give away things that don't belong to you.

All the cook did was put groats and salt in the cauldron, and if there was any fat he split it between the cauldron and himself. (The good fat never got as far as the prisoners. Only the bad stuff went in the cauldron. . . .) Then his only job was to stir the mush when it was nearly ready. The sanitary inspector didn't even do that much. He just sat and watched. When the mush was ready, the cook gave him some right away and he could eat all he wanted. And so could the cook. Then one of the gang bosses – they took turns, a different one every day – came to taste it and see if it was good enough for the men to eat. He got a double portion too.

After all this, the whistle went off. Now the other gang bosses came and the cook handed them their bowls through a kind of hatch in the wall. The bowls had this watery mush in them. And you didn't ask how much of the ration they'd really put in it. You'd get hell if you opened your mouth.[153]

And so it was with everything: 'They stole all the way down the line – out here on the site, in the camp, and in the stores too.'[154]

The system was made more effective yet, in the lumber camps in particular, by turning it into a 'brigade', a gang, matter, with collective responsibility for inadequate work:

You might well ask why a prisoner worked so hard for ten years in a camp. Why didn't they say to hell with it and drag their feet all day long till the night, which was theirs?

But it wasn't so simple. . . . It was like this – either you all got something extra or you all starved. ('You're not pulling your weight, you swine, and I've got to go hungry because of you. So work, you bastard!')

So when a really tough job came along, like now, you couldn't sit on your hands. Like it or not, you had to get a move on. Either they made the place warm within two hours or they'd all be fucking well dead.[155]

The brigade leader, himself a prisoner, worked out with a foreman, 'the team surveyor', the amount of work done by his brigade. Other camp officials then estimated the production compared with the 'daily norm'. Their decisions were then sent to the food department for rationing according to the output.[156]

More depended on the work rates than on the work itself. A clever boss who knows his business really sweats over these work rates. That's where the ration comes from. If a job hasn't been done, make it look like it had. If the rates were low on a job, try to hike 'em up. You had to have brains for this and a lot of pull with the fellows who kept the work sheets. And they didn't do it for nothing.

But come to think of it, who were these rates for? For the people who ran the camps. They made thousands on the deal and got bonuses on top for the officers. Like old Volkovoy, with that whip of his. And all you got out of it was six ounces of bread in the evening. Your life depended on them.[157]

On one occasion this gang boss gets 'better rates'. This means that 'they'd have good bread rations for five days. Well, maybe four. The higher-ups always cheat on one day out of five.'[158]

As to the quality of the food, the convicts in Solzhenitsyn's book discuss the film *Battleship Potemkin*. The maggots on the meat which cause the mutiny are thought to be unrealistically large, and this is explained as necessary from the film point of view. Then comes the comment: 'If they brought that kind of meat to the camp, I can tell you, and put it in the cauldron instead of the rotten fish we get, I bet we'd . . .'[159]

He describes a meal:

The gruel didn't change from one day to the next. It depended on what vegetables they'd stored for the winter. The year before they'd only stocked up with salted carrots, so there was nothing but carrots in the gruel from September to June. And now it was cabbage. The camp was best fed in June, when they ran out of vegetables and started using groats instead. The worst time was July, when they put shredded nettles in the cauldron.

The fish was mostly bones. The flesh was boiled off except for bits on the tails and the heads. Not leaving a single scale or speck of flesh on the skeleton, Shukhov crunched and sucked the bones and spat them out on the table. He didn't leave anything – not even the gills or the tail. He ate the eyes too when they were still in place, but when they'd come off and were floating around in the bowl on their own he didn't eat them. The others laughed at him for this.

. . . The second course was a mush made out of *magara*. It was one solid lump, and Shukhov broke it off in pieces. When it was hot – never mind when it was cold – it had no taste and didn't fill you. It was nothing but grass that looked like millet. They'd gotten the bright idea of serving it instead of groats. It came from the Chinese, they said. They got ten ounces of it and that was that. It wasn't the real thing, but it passed for mush.[160]

The ration, and the whole estimate of norms, depended on all sorts of factors. First, the ideas of the officials in determining the piece-work. For some types of work it was on occasion set far above the possible, for example in building the Kotlas–Vorkuta railway. It was impossible to do more than about 30 per cent of the quota, so the ration, for this extremely hard work, was down to 400 grammes.[161] On the extension down to Khalmer-Yu, average expectation of life was about three months.[162]

Again, the goodness or badness of the year's harvest immediately affected rations. The bad harvest of 1936 produced an appalling level of mortality from starvation in the camps in 1937. Trouble was caused by the desire to eat anything at all. Rubbish boxes from the kitchens might be attacked by gangs. When these, in one camp, were thrown into the cesspool by the latrines, 'even there the gangs waded after them'.[163] When grass came up every blade might be put in a tin and boiled and eaten. Grass-eating was most common among intellectuals. Its long-term effects were deadly. Others tried to satisfy their appetites with boiling salt water, also ineffective.[164]

Even in Solzhenitsyn's penal camp, there are convicts who have served in worse places – a lumber camp where work went on till midnight if necessary to fill the quotas, and the basic ration was six ounces less.[165] In the area of the far north, to the east of the Urals, there seem to have been a number of camps of particularly rigorous regime, which are described as of 'complete isolation'. Only a few rumours about them have emerged, as no one seems in any circumstances to have been released. The death rate is said to have been very high. Norilsk was the centre of a group of camps more deadly than Kolyma. Novaya Zemlya also had an extremely bad reputation, with few, if any, returning.

Special punitive camps are often reported. After the introduction of a new and harsher regime of *katorga* in the early forties, those so sentenced were deprived of blankets and mattresses for the first three years and otherwise subjected to harder labour, longer hours and worse conditions.[166] Sometimes, as in the Dzhido camp, offending prisoners were put in chains for the remainder of their sentences.[167] For women the Stalinogorsk camp was particularly severe: inmates worked in iron- and coalmines. The second Alexeyevka camp, in the Kargopol group, a particularly bad one listed as a disciplinary camp but in fact full of foreign prisoners who had had no time to commit offences in other camps, had a large number of Polish Jews who had escaped from the Nazi persecution and died like flies. They hated the Soviet regime more bitterly and passionately than anyone in the camps.[168]

In one respect Solzhenitsyn was lucky. He was not in a lumber camp. Here rations were notoriously low and work extremely hard. Professor Swianiewicz, who was himself in a labour camp at one time, says that the former inmates are inclined to over-estimate the proportion of prisoners sent to such work, probably because they were 'under the constant fear of being sent to the forest. It was equivalent to a death sentence for a person not accustomed to heavy physical work to be assigned for a long period to a felling brigade.'[169] One former assistant to a doctor in a northern camp says that in two successive winters about 50 per cent of the workers in some forestry brigades died. Over all, about 30 per cent of the labour force was lost by death or total exhaustion per annum.[170] A Pole who was briefly in Alexeyevka describes the visible death as extraordinary. He saw two drop dead as they left the gates with other brigades. In his own brigade three died at the work site on his first day.[171] A very active man would sometimes remain healthy by producing 120 or 150 per cent of his quota for a year or eighteen months, and then one night would be found dead of heart failure in his bunk.[172]

Even comparatively mild lumber camps were great killers. Finnish prisoners who were experts in the matter held that the norms prevailing were impossible even for the best-fed workers. They could only be brought down even to the barely tolerable level by various forms of cheating (*tufta*), and bribery – using the same logs over again, by sawing off the stamped end, and so forth. Herling never came across a prisoner who had worked in the forest for more that two years. After a year they were usually incurable, and, following transfer as 'goners' to lighter work, retired to the mortuary.[173]

This was the last stage in the camps. When worn down, debilitated to the degree that no serious work could any longer be got out of them, prisoners were put on sub-starvation rations and allowed to hang around the camp doing odd jobs till they died. This category is recognized in recent Soviet as well as foreign books. Gorbatov, who describes the usual symptoms, confirms that to go sick was ordinarily fatal. For if you did, you had your ration cut and from that point there was no way out.[174] This corps commander was at one time able to sweep the camp office floors, and there found an occasional crust to keep him going. He was himself saved from death by a friendly doctor who got him transferred to an easier post. In general, throughout the period, all our sources emphasize that survival for any length of time was rare in most camps except among those qualifying for 'functions' – office jobs or other work enabling them to escape the main labour of the camp in question.

During bad periods 'the camps of the disabled and unfit . . . became the most populous, and the largest labour brigades were those of the woodcutters and the gravediggers'.[175] The dead were buried in pits, with small wooden tags attached with string to their legs.[176]

One estimate is that a batch of prisoners in the camps would, on the average, lose half its number in two to three years.[177] An N.K.V.D. functionary who worked on the Baltic–White Sea Canal group of camps gave evidence[178] that there were 250,000 prisoners in these camps at the beginning of the Purges, and the death rate was 700 a day, a figure also given elsewhere.[179] However, 1,500 new prisoners came in daily, so that the population continued to increase. A few survival times in the camps are known from Soviet sources. For example, we learn that Radek lasted two years, Rakovsky three years, Sokolnikov two years.[180]

The mortality rate in the camps in 1933 is estimated at about 10 per cent per annum, and in 1938 to be running at about 20 per cent.[181] The 1936 prisoners were almost all extinct by 1940. A woman who worked in a camp hospital notes that patients sentenced in 1937 and 1938 filled it in 1939 and 1940, but by 1941 there were few of them to be seen.[182]

One careful estimate makes the excess deaths due to forced-labour camps and forced settlements in the period 1927–38, 2·3 million;[183] and of course, the majority of those imprisoned in the 'Yezhovshchina' itself had yet to perish. Another thorough study gives a total of camp deaths in 1936–9 as 2·8 million, and in 1939–41 as 1·8 million.[184]

In any case, of those who went into the camps, only a small proportion ever came out again. For long, some of the best evidence we had came from German Communists withdrawn from the camps and handed over to the Nazis in 1939–40, from Poles released under the 1941 Treaty, and from others who, benefiting from exceptional circumstances, were in for equally short periods, In general, releases were very rare, and survival till the post-Stalin amnesties rarer still. The Soviet poet Olga Bergholtz (herself jailed for a time) remarks 'Why should I try to hide the fact that not many returned'.[181]

The length of sentence anyhow made little difference. (Those who were released were in any case all rearrested around 1947–8.) Upon the expiration of a sentence, it was usual for a prisoner to be called before a Special Department officer and given a few more years, though in some cases they were sent back to prisons in Moscow or elsewhere, reinterrogated, and sentenced for fresh crimes.

> Shukhov sort of liked the way they pointed at him – the lucky guy nearly through with his sentence. But he didn't really believe it. Take the fellows who should've been let out in the war. They were all kept in till forty-six – 'till further notice'. And then those with three years who'd gotten five more slapped on. They twisted the law any way they wanted. You finished a ten-year stretch and they gave you another one. Or if not, they still wouldn't let you go home.[186]

We do know of some people who lasted up to seventeen years and have since been rehabilitated – the Snegov referred to in Khrushchev's Secret Speech, for instance, or Lieutenant-General Todorsky. These seem to have served in the less severe camps. But most of the published Soviet evidence is from figures such as Gorbatov, who was among the rehabilitated officers of 1940 and would not otherwise have survived. (The routine of rehabilitation, in those few cases in which it applied, was slow. Gorbatov had, he later found out, been defended by Budenny, and on 20 March 1940 his sentence was rescinded and a review ordered. He did not get back from Magadan to the Butyrka prison until 25 December 1940. By 1 March 1941 he was in the Lubyanka, and on 5 March he was released.)

The other sort of Soviet witness is of the type of Solzhenitsyn, who says that though a man might possibly last ten years, any much longer period was out of the question – and this at a comparatively good period in camp history. Solzhenitsyn was in fact released after ten years in the post-Stalin rehabilitations. He had fortunately been sentenced later on in Stalin's life. A man sentenced in 1938 would have had to wait seventeen or eighteen years. Of those arrested in the period 1936–8, we can hardly allow 10 per cent to have survived: in fact, a Soviet historian tells us that 90 per cent of those who went to camp before the war perished, while Academician Sakharov notes that only 50,000 of the more than 600,000 party members sent to camp, rather than executed, survived.[187] A million would be an outside figure. Of the other 7 million odd, the number who died either by execution or in camps during the actual two-year Yezhov period may be taken as about 3 million.[188] The rest followed over a period of years, during which time their number was continually added to by the victims of later arrest.*

A contemporary Soviet poet has written:

> There – row on row, according to years,
> Kolyma, Magadan,
> Vorkuta and Narym
> Marched in invisible columns.
>
> The region of eternal frost
> Wrote men off into eternity,
> Moved them from the category of 'living'
> To that of 'dead' (little difference between them) –
>
> Behind that barbed wire,
> White and grizzled –
> With that Special Article of the law code
> Clipped to their case files.
>
> Who and what for and by those will –
> Figure it out, History.[189]

---

*The question of casualty figures in the Purge is dealt with more broadly in Appendix A.

CHAPTER ELEVEN

THE GREAT TRIAL

*Le dernier acte est sanglant, quelque belle que soit la
comédie en tout le reste.*   PASCAL

PREPARATIONS for the greatest trial of all were in less expert
hands than those which had produced the Zinoviev and Pyatakov
shows. The N.K.V.D. veterans had gone. Agranov had by now
followed Yagoda and his staff, being 'in 1937 expelled from the
Party for systematic breaches of socialist legality',[1] or so a current
Soviet footnote has it, as if asking us to believe that such practices were frowned on by the Party leadership of that year. He
died, presumed shot, in 1938.[2] His wife was also shot.[3]

Instead of Molchanov and Mironov, Agranov and Gay,
Yezhov's team for the new trial consisted basically of the
experienced Zakovsky, from Leningrad, Mikhail Frinovsky, who
under Yagoda had been Commander of the N.K.V.D's Frontier
Troops, and to some extent Matvei Berman,* who had headed
GULAG., the Labour Camp Administration, and Slutsky, of
the Foreign Department.[4] They were all to perish within the year,
but meanwhile they had after all contrived a show not grossly
inferior to its two predecessors. The plot was more complicated,
and more horrifying, and there were faults of detail which
attracted the censure of the stricter critics. But on the whole, it
was a fair success.

It might be thought that no public trial was now necessary.
The opposition, and the semi-independent voices among Stalin's
own supporters, had been crushed. The third trial was in this
sense little more than a victory parade. It brought together
publicly every type of opposition, terror, sabotage, treachery and
espionage, and turned them into branches of one single great
conspiracy. For the 1936 Trial, Molchanov had prepared for

* Berman was transferred from Deputy Commissar of the N.K.V.D. to be
People's Commissar of Communications in the Government appointed in
January 1938, being replaced by Zakovsky.

Stalin 'a special diagram . . . a system of many coloured lines on the diagram indicated when and through whom Trotsky had communicated with the leaders of the conspiracy in the U.S.S.R.'.[5] Such a diagram showing all the links in the Bukharin Case would be one of great complexity. The trial, which opened in the October Hall on 2 March 1938, had, indeed, taken over a year to prepare, but it was a production of far greater scope than the others.

For all the threads were now pulled together. The Rightists, Bukharin and Rykov, were linked to Trotsky; to the earlier Zinovievite and Trotskyite plotters; to Trotskyites, hitherto considered ex-Trotskyites, who had not yet been tried; to the usual dozens of terrorist action groups; to the espionage organizations of several powers. They had set up at least two 'reserve' centres; they had been involved in Yenukidze's plots; and they were closely concerned with that of Tukhachevsky. They had formed organizational connexions with underground nationalist conspirators in half a dozen of the non-Russian Soviet Republics. Their own 'Rightist' grouping had involved dozens of men thought to be loyal Stalinists, in high positions in the State. And, as a final touch, they had throughout had as a major accomplice Yagoda, with all his leading subordinates.

'In the dingy winter daylight and under the stale glare of the electric lamps',[6] a wide variety of prisoners sat in the dock. In the first trial Zinoviev and Kamenev, and to a lesser extent Smirnov, were the only well-known figures. The second, with Pyatakov, Radek and Sokolnikov, was less impressive still. And in each case the supporting cast consisted mainly of third-rate alleged terrorists and only slightly more interesting engineers.

This time three members of Lenin's Politburo stood in dock – Bukharin, Rykov and Krestinsky. With them were the legendary Rakovsky, leader of the Balkan and Ukrainian revolutionary movements, and the sinister figure of Yagoda, the Secret Police personified, looking right and left with a certain rat-like vitality. A group of the most senior officials of the Stalinist state who had for many years served it uncritically formed the bulk of the accused: Rosengolts, Ivanov, Chernov and Grinko – all People's Commissars until the previous year; Zelensky, Head of the

Cooperatives; Sharangovich, First Secretary in Byelorussia. For the first time two Asians, the Uzbek leaders Khodzhayev and Ikramov, denounced the previous year for bourgeois nationalism, took their places beside the European accused. These main political accused were supplemented by five minor figures – Bessonov, who had worked in the Soviet Trade Delegation in Berlin; Zubarev, an official of the Agriculture Commissariat; and the former secretaries of Yagoda, of Kuibyshev and of Maxim Gorki. Lastly, by a fearful innovation, there were three men far from public life, the Doctors Pletnev, Levin and Kazakov – the first two highly distinguished in their field and the oldest men in dock (sixty-six and sixty-eight respectively).

The indictment was a comprehensive one – of espionage, wrecking, undermining Soviet military power, provoking a military attack on the U.S.S.R., plotting the dismemberment of the U.S.S.R., and the overthrowing of the social system in favour of a return to capitalism. For these purposes the accused had assembled this vast conspiracy of Trotskyites, Zinovievites, Rightists, Mensheviks, Social Revolutionaries, and 'bourgeois-nationalists' from the whole Soviet periphery. They had been in close cooperation with the military plotters. A number of them had been spies of Germany, Britain, Japan and Poland since the early twenties. Several of them had been Tsarist agents in the revolutionary movement. Wrecking had been committed in industry, agriculture, trade and finance.

On the terror side, they had been responsible for the assassination of Kirov, which Yagoda had facilitated through Zaporozhets. But in addition they had caused the deaths of Kuibyshev and of Maxim Gorki, hitherto regarded as natural (and of the former O.G.P.U. chief Menzhinsky and of Gorki's son Peshkov into the bargain). This had been done by medical murder. Yagoda was also charged with an attempt to poison Yezhov. And a variety of the more usual fruitless plans to assassinate Stalin and other leaders were also alleged.

A brand-new charge, against Bukharin alone of those in dock, was of having plotted to seize power in 1918 and to murder Lenin and Stalin at the same time.

Once again Ulrikh presided, assisted by Matulevich and a new junior figure, Yevlev. And once again Vyshinsky conducted the prosecution. Only the three doctors had defence counsel, and they were represented by two of the same lawyers who had done their bit for the prosecution in the same roles in the Pyatakov Trial.

A CONFESSION WITHDRAWN

The first sensation of the trial came almost at once, when the accused were asked their pleas. These were all the usual 'guilty' until Krestinsky was reached.

Krestinsky, 'a pale, seedy, dim little figure, his steel-rimmed spectacles perched on his beaky nose',[7] replied firmly to Ulrikh:

I plead not guilty. I am not a Trotskyite. I was never a member of the bloc of Rights and Trotskyites, of whose existence I was not aware. Nor have I committed any of the crimes with which I personally am charged, in particular I plead not guilty to the charge of having had connections with German intelligence service.

The President: Do you corroborate the confession you made at the preliminary investigation?

Krestinsky: Yes, at the preliminary investigation I confessed, but I have never been a Trotskyite.

The President: I repeat the question, do you plead guilty?

Krestinsky: Before my arrest I was a member of the Communist Party of the Soviet Union (Bolsheviks) and I remain one now.

The President: Do you plead guilty to the charge of participating in espionage activities and of participating in terrorist activities?

Krestinsky: I have never been a Trotskyite. I have never belonged to the bloc of Rights and Trotskyites and have not committed a single crime.[8]

After the pleas the court recessed for twenty minutes. It has been suggested that this was to give time to put a little pressure on Krestinsky. Possibly: but the recess was only five minutes longer than that at the previous trials.

The court proceeded with the examination of Bessonov, who from his post as Counsellor in the Soviet Embassy in Berlin was the alleged contact man with Trotsky and Sedov. Bessonov, a grim, grey-faced man with the air of an automaton,[9] had been arrested on 28 February 1937, the day after Bukharin and Rykov. He had denied the main charges until 30 December 1937. But meanwhile, he had been tried on 13 August before the Military Collegium of the Supreme Court ('composed of almost the same people as in the present Trial')[10] which neither acquitted nor condemned him, but sent the case for further examination.

This can hardly mean other than that it had been decided to save him for a major trial: as a minor diplomat, and ex-Social Revolutionary, he was bound to be purged in any case. He must have appeared a suitable courier. The case is comparable with that of the Komsomols of 1935, saved up for the Zinoviev Trial.

When Bessonov now confessed that he had indeed been involved in Trotskyite plots with Krestinsky, Vyshinsky referred to Krestinsky's refusal to admit this. Bessonov smiled. Vyshinsky asked, 'Why are you smiling?' Bessonov replied: 'The reason why I am standing here is that Nikolai Nikolayevich Krestinsky named me as the liaison man with Trotsky. Besides him and Pyatakov nobody knew about this.'[11] Something of the mechanics of confessions implicating others, and of the whole tangled net of moral responsibility, comes through. In his final plea Bessonov was to remark that it was not until Krestinsky implicated him in October 1937 that his resistance to interrogation started to become hopeless.[12]

In general, after Bessonov had made a few points about his connexions with Sedov and Pyatakov, his examination was largely turned into an excuse for baiting Krestinsky. The latter admitted he had met Bessonov in the West, but denied any Trotskyite links:

Vyshinsky: And about Trotskyite affairs?
Krestinsky: We did not talk about them. I was not a Trotskyite.
Vyshinsky: You never talked about them.
Krestinsky: Never.
Vyshinsky: That means that Bessonov is not telling the truth, and that you are telling the truth. Do you always tell the truth?
Krestinsky: No.
Vyshinsky: Not always. Accused Krestinsky, you and I will have to examine serious matters and there is no need to get excited. Consequently, Bessonov is not telling the truth?

Krestinsky: No.
Vyshinsky: But you too do not always tell the truth. Is that not so?
Krestinsky: I did not always tell the truth during the investigation.
Vyshinsky: But at other times you always tell the truth?
Krestinsky: The truth.
Vyshinsky: Why this lack of respect for the investigation, why during the investigation did you tell untruths? Explain.
Krestinsky: (No reply.)[13]

A few minutes later Bessonov spoke of Krestinsky's formulations. Vyshinsky interrupted in an unpleasant tone, 'Briefly, because I think that Krestinsky will himself talk about these purposes later.' And, after Bessonov had made his point, Vyshinsky turned to Krestinsky and asked, 'Accused Krestinsky, do you recall such diplomatic conversations with Bessonov?' Krestinsky answered firmly, 'No, we never had such conversations.'[14]

Two minutes later it was:

Vyshinsky: You do not remember the details, but Bessonov does.
Krestinsky: There was not a word said about the Trotskyite stand.[15]

Finally, the question of Krestinsky's confession was faced directly:

Vyshinsky: But what about your admission?
Krestinsky: During the investigation I gave false testimony several times.
Vyshinsky: You said: 'I did not formally belong to the Trotskyite centre.' Is that true or not?
Krestinsky: I did not belong to it at all.
Vyshinsky: You say that formally you did not belong. What is true and what is not true here? Perhaps it is all true, or it is all untrue, or only half of it is true? What percentage, how many grams of it are true?
Krestinsky: I did not belong to the Trotskyite centre because I was not a Trotskyite.
Vyshinsky: You were not a Trotskyite?
Krestinsky: No.[16]

Krestinsky went on to point out that he had abandoned Trotsky in 1927:

Krestinsky: I date my rupture with Trotsky and Trotskyism from 27 November 1927, when, through Serebryakov, who had returned from

America and was in Moscow, I sent Trotsky a sharp letter containing sharp criticism. . . .

Vyshinsky: That letter is not in the records. We have another letter – your letter to Trotsky.

Krestinsky: The letter I am referring to is in the possession of the Court investigator, because it was taken from me during the search, and I request this letter to be attached to the records.

Vyshinsky: The records contain a letter dated 11 July 1927, taken from you during the search.

Krestinsky: But there is another letter of 27 November. . . .

Vyshinsky: There is no such letter.

Krestinsky: That cannot be. . . .[17]

This was to be significant.

Pressed continually in a long exchange, Krestinsky gave his motives for earlier confessions.

Krestinsky: At the preliminary investigation, before I was questioned by you, I had given false testimony.

Vyshinsky: . . . And then you stuck to it.

Krestinsky: . . . And then I stuck to it, because from personal experience I had arrived at the conviction that before the trial, if there was to be one, I would not succeed in refuting my testimony.[18]

Vyshinsky now called on Rosengolts, who confirmed Krestinsky's Trotskyism. Krestinsky, who had not been feeling well, slumped. Vyshinsky told him to listen. He replied that when he had taken a pill he would be all right, but asked not to be questioned for a few minutes.

Rosengolts, then Grinko, gave evidence of Krestinsky's guilt. Krestinsky, recovering, continued to deny it:

Vyshinsky: Here are three men on good terms with you who say what is not true?

Krestinsky: Yes.

After several more denials, Vyshinsky again asked him directly: 'When we interrogated you at the preliminary investigation, what did you say on this score?'

Krestinsky: In giving testimony I did not refute any of my previous testimony, which I deliberately confirmed.

Vyshinsky: You deliberately confirmed it. You were misleading the Prosecutor. Is that so, or not?

Krestinsky: No.

Vyshinsky: Why did you have to mislead me?

Krestinsky: I simply considered that if I were to say what I am saying today – that it was not in accordance with the facts – my declaration would not reach the leaders of the Party and the Government.[19]

This clear statement of the position was greeted with a 'shocked hush' from the audience.[20]

Questioning further about the preliminary examination, Vyshinsky asked 'If you were asked whether you had complaints, you should have answered that you had.' And Krestinsky replied 'I had in the sense that I did not speak voluntarily.'[21]

Vyshinsky then abandoned this line of questioning and turned to his official prey, Bessonov, who developed his connexions with Trotsky at length, adding that Trotsky had hinted at the physical extermination of Maxim Gorki. The session ended with a further exchange with, and denial from, Krestinsky.

After a two-hour adjournment, the evening started off with the evidence of Grinko, former People's Commissar for Finance. He had been a Borotbist, and in the early twenties had been dismissed from his post as Ukrainian Commissar for Education for excessive haste in carrying out Ukrainianization. In this capacity he now implicated Lyubchenko, and other lesser Ukrainians such as Porayko, Deputy Chairman of the Ukrainian Council of People's Commissars, as members of a 'national-fascist' organization. In his Moscow role, he brought in a number of other leading figures, such as Antipov, Rudzutak, Yakovlev and Vareikis, as Rightist plotters. He described how Yakir and Gamarnik had instructed the Head of the Department of Savings Banks to 'prepare a terrorist act' against Yezhov, and how other conspirators had arranged for an official of the Northern Sea Route to do the same by Stalin. His own main activity had been financial sabotage, which he had defined at the preliminary examination as follows:

The main object of undermining work in the People's Commissariat of Finance was the following: to weaken the Soviet rouble, to weaken the financial power of the U.S.S.R., to dislocate the economy and thus rouse among the population discontent with the financial policy of the Soviet power, discontent over taxes, discontent with the bad savings bank service, delays in paying wages, etc., which were to result in wide, organized discontent with the Soviet power and were to help the conspirators to recruit adherents and to develop insurrectionary activities.[22]

This sort of theme – the blaming of all the errors and malpractices of the Soviet economy on sabotage by the accused – was to run through the trial. For all spheres of life, there was someone in dock to answer for the discontent of the Soviet peoples.

Grinko, similarly, had been involved with Zelensky and others in trade hold-ups:

Grinko: ... Bolotin in the People's Commissariat of Internal Trade, carried on undermining activities, created a shortage of goods, goods difficulties in the country. ... Zelensky, on the instructions of the bloc of Rights and Trotskyites, sent huge quantities of goods to the districts where there was a poor harvest and small quantities of goods to the districts where there were good harvests, and this caused goods to remain on the shelves in some districts and a shortage of goods in others.[23]

But once again, Vyshinsky diverged to attack Krestinsky. Again he was rebuffed by a firm:

I deny that I talked with Fascists for Trotskyite purposes.

At this Rykov was called on. He too confirmed Krestinsky's guilt. Krestinsky once more asserted flatly that he knew nothing of any illegal activities, and the intervention of Ulrikh could get no more out of him.

But Rykov too proved unsatisfactory, though in a different way. In the period before his arrest, he had taken to heavy drinking, and reduced himself to a bad condition which the long strain of his imprisonment had, in its different way, done nothing to help. During cross-examination he sometimes seemed to have gone to pieces, punctuating his answers with inane giggles.[24] But he rallied. At first he was vague:

Grinko: From Rykov I learnt that Yagoda belonged to this organization, but I had no direct connections with Yagoda.
Vyshinsky: (to the court): Permit me to question Rykov. Accused Rykov, did you tell Grinko about this?

Rykov: I do not remember exactly, but I cannot exclude such a fact.
Vyshinsky: Hence, you told him about Yagoda's membership?
Rykov: Yes.[25]

Now, wrecking was raised:

Vyshinsky: Accused Rykov, do you corroborate this conversation with
Grinko about wrecking?
Rykov: I don't accept that. I deny it, not because I want to minimize
my guilt. I have done much worse things than this.[26]

But then he got into his stride on the line which both he and
(much more forcefully and consistently) Bukharin were to take
throughout. That is, they admitted forming an illegal organization, confessed to giving it a terrorist 'orientation', accepted full
responsibility in the abstract for all the acts allegedly committed,
but denied personal knowledge of or connexion with any
particular crime. They were thus able to point out that they were
freely confessing to capital crimes, so that their denials of the
particular acts could not be interpreted as attempts to evade the
penalty.

The last to be examined on 2 March was Chernov. Ex-Men-
shevik, and ex-theological student (like Bessonov – and Mikoyan
and Stalin), he had been in charge of grain collection in the
Ukraine in 1929–30, and had more recently been serving as All-
Union People's Commissar for Agriculture. He had been a ruthless executant of Stalin's will in the collectivization campaign, but
apparently not a convinced one. He is reported as having said,
during the 1930 slaughter of their livestock by the peasantry, that
at least 'for the first time in their sordid history, the Russian
peasants have eaten their fill of meat'.[27] He had started to confess
on the day of his arrest.[28]

He now confessed to qualms about collectivization, and admitted sharing them, at the time, with a wide range of Ukrainian
officials, including Zatonsky, But his main role in the dock was
to take the blame for agricultural failures. He had only been
removed from his post on 30 October 1937,[29] and could reasonably be blamed for much.

For example, there had been a good deal of livestock mortality.
Back in September 1937 a spread of infective anaemia among

Soviet horses had been countered by the arrest of the Head of
the Veterinary Administration of the People's Commissariat of
Agriculture, Nedachin, the Head of the Veterinary Services of
the Red Army,* Nikolsky, and a leading veterinary official in
the Agricultural Commissariat, Chernyak, whose forthcoming
trial was announced.[31] They had never again been heard of, but
Chernov was now able to accept the blame for similar epidemics,
spread through the agency of a different set of vets:

Chernov: ... I performed the following acts of diversion. In order to
cause heavy cattle mortality in Eastern Siberia, I instructed Ginsburg,
Chief of the Veterinary Department, who belonged to the organization
of the Rights, and through him the Chief of the Veterinary Supply
Department, who also belonged to the organization of the Rights, not
to supply anti-anthrax serum to Eastern Siberia. knowing that Eastern
Siberia was particularly liable to anthrax. The serum was not supplied
to Eastern Siberia. The preparations for this were made in 1935, and
when there was an outbreak of anthrax there in 1936 it turned out that
no serum was available, with the result that I cannot say how many
exactly, but at any rate over 25,000 horses perished.

Secondly, I instructed Ginsburg and Boyarshinov, Chief of the
Bacteriological Department, to artificially infect pigs with erysipelas in
the Leningrad Region and with plague in the Voronezh Region and the
Azov–Black Sea Territory ...

It is difficult to estimate the results, but at any rate it may be taken
for granted that several tens of thousands of pigs perished owing to
this diversive act.[32]

And a variety of other agricultural sabotage schemes, such as
wrong types of crop rotation, the provision of bad seed, and so
on, had contributed to 'lowering the harvest yield'.

In his Ukrainian period, he had also undertaken to incense the
middle peasants and Ukrainian national feeling generally, by
attributing the policies he had pursued to orders from Moscow.
He had contacted Mensheviks abroad, and become a German
spy. Rykov was his main connexion in the Rightist centre.

*The Senior Veterinary Surgeon of the Moscow Military District is re-
ported in the Butyrka about this time. He was charged with destroying
25,000 horses of the cavalry reserve by issuing poisoned vaccine, and sentenced to death.[30]

Recalled, the ex-Premier again admitted the plot but denied
approving the actions. 'All that he says is essentially and fundamentally true, but as to the part in which he said that I was in
favour of distortions [of the agricultural policy], it seems to me
he is wrong.'[33] On the overthrow of the Soviet power Rykov
added, 'I do not remember having such a conversation with
Chernov, but of course the possibility of such a conversation is not
precluded.'[34] Finally, he denied various meetings with Chernov
for wrecking purposes; and when Chernov said that to have
neglected to give such instructions would have marked him as a
very poor Rightist leader, he answered sardonically 'Perhaps I
should have done as he says. It was a mistake on my part.'[35] At
which Ulrikh abruptly closed the day's session.

The next day, 3 March, started with the ex-medical student
Ivanov, former People's Commissar for the Timber Industry. He
had, of course, sabotaged that industry, on instructions from
Rosengolts. Referring to the timber dumping which was a
notorious aspect of Soviet trade policy in the early thirties, he
said:

The most valuable timber was sold at reduced prices. This involved
a loss to the Soviet State of several million roubles in foreign currency.
Bukharin explained this measure as being an advance to the British
bourgeoisie in return for the support it had promised. Otherwise, he
said, we would not be taken seriously, and we would forfeit confidence.[36]

In the internal administration of lumbering, his main aim,
curiously enough, had been the disruption of culture:

Attention was chiefly devoted to hindering the technical re-equip-
ment of lumbering, preventing the fulfilment of the plans of capital
construction, especially in the cellulose and paper industry, in this way
placing the country on a short paper ration and aiming a blow at the
cultural revolution, interrupting the supply of exercise books and thus
rousing discontent among the masses.[37]

He confessed also to being involved in the 'Left Communist'
movement against Lenin, and to various attempts to organize
insurrectionary bands (partly on British orders) and terrorist
groups. In this connexion Bukharin was now questioned. He said
he had ordered the formation of illegal organizations, but not

insurrectionary bands. He had (though at a later date than that given by Ivanov) propounded an 'insurrectionary orientation' – the Ryutin Platform. He had given no actual instructions for insurrectionary preparations, but he accepted the responsibility, in that a 'practical worker' like Ivanov would doubtless go on to action on such a basis.[38]

When Vyshinky said to him, 'Hence, Ivanov's statements about connexions with the British Intelligence Service . . . ,' he interrupted, 'I was totally uninformed about the Intelligence Service.'[39]

The next questioning should, according to schedule, have been that of Krestinsky. But instead the minor agricultural specialist from Chernov's Commissariat, Zubarev, appeared. He gave a good deal of evidence about disrupting the food supply.

Vyshinsky: Tell us the nature of your wrecking activities.
Zubarev: . . . Causing confusion in seed cultivation, lowering the quality of the seeds, employing bad quality materials, bad sifting, careless storing, and the result of all this was not only a reduction in yield, but also a hostile mood of the peasantry, dissatisfaction with these so-called selected seeds. . . . My criminal activities consisted first of all in wrongly planning the sowing of vegetables. . . . Exactly the same kind of work was carried on in respect to retarding the development of fruit-tree nurseries.
In respect to State farms, the main wrecking activities were that up to the last moment no proper rotation of crops was established, and in a number of State farms there was no rotation of crops at all. All this naturally reduced the yields. A large number of State farms which possessed large herds of cattle were left without fodder owing to the wrong crop rotation, and as a result we had the dying-off of cattle and slow development of the livestock farming . . .[40]

and so on and so on. As well as with the Rights, he established connexions with Muralov from the 1937 Trial. He had also organized a terrorist group in the Agriculture Commissariat, choosing Molotov as the prospective victim. He had carried out agricultural spying for Germany.

Zubarev's main contribution, however, was his recruitment as a Tsarist agent in 1908 and later. For Vyshinsky now produced a surprise witness. This was a police inspector of pre-Revolutionary days, Vasilyev, who had allegedly recruited Zubarev. The production of this aged Tsarist gendarme was treated by the court and 'public' as a sort of comic turn. Even Vyshinsky was comparatively amiable to him, baiting him only with that puny malice which was the closest he could evidently get to good humour.[41]

With that, the morning session dragged to a close.

When the court reassembled at 6 p.m., Ulrikh announced to a tense court that the examination of Krestinsky would now take place. Vyshinsky interposed to say that he first wanted to put a few questions to Rakovsky.

He asked the old Bulgarian about the letter to Trotsky abandoning Trotskyism, which Krestinsky had referred to in the previous day's session. Rakovsky recalled it, and said it had been intended as a deception, and that Krestinsky had never broken with Trotskyism.

Vyshinsky then produced the letter, whose existence he would not acknowledge the previous day, and went on to argue that the letter itself, which spoke of the defeat of the opposition and the need to work in the Party, should be interpreted as a call to underhand subversion – a possible argument, indeed, but one scarcely compatible with an out-and-out deceptive surrender.

Finally he turned to Krestinsky. Did he accept this formulation?

Krestinsky, who was 'looking more than ever like a small bedraggled sparrow',[42] accepted it.

Vyshinsky asked if this meant that Krestinsky would now cease to deceive the court. The answer was a full confirmation of the evidence given at the preliminary inquiry. He admitted his guilt. On the first day, Krestinsky had occasionally been roused by Vyshinsky's taunts, but on the whole his tone is said to have been natural; it had now become flat and desperate.[43]

Vyshinsky pressed the point:

I have one question to ask Krestinsky: What, then, is the meaning of the statement you made yesterday, which cannot be regarded otherwise than as a piece of Trotskyite provocation in court?
Krestinsky: Yesterday, under the influence of a momentary keen feeling of false shame, evoked by the atmosphere of the dock and the painful

impression created by the public reading of the indictment, which was aggravated by my poor health, I could not bring myself to tell the truth, I could not bring myself to say that I was guilty. And instead of saying 'Yes, I am guilty,' I almost mechanically answered 'No, I am not guilty.'

Vyshinsky: Mechanically?

Krestinsky: In the face of world public opinion, I had not the strength to admit the truth that I had been conducting a Trotskyite struggle all along. I request the court to register my statement that I fully and completely admit that I am guilty of all the gravest charges brought against me personally, and that I admit my complete responsibility for the treason and treachery I have committed.[44]

And now, despite Ulrikh's earlier announcement that the examination of Krestinsky was due, Vyshinsky at once dropped him and turned to the examination of Rykov. All this has very much the air of the prosecution playing safe, and not willing to risk a further retraction at this stage.

We do not know what went on in the Lubyanka on the night of 2 March, but the consensus is that every form of pressure was put on Krestinsky to abandon his resistance. He seems to have been tortured. They dislocated his left shoulder, so that outwardly there was nothing to be seen. Bessonov is named as having told this version to the German engineer Hans Metzger in a prisoners' transfer train in 1939.[45] According to another variant, Krestinsky was also faced for hours with a battery of particularly bright lights, which damaged his already injured eyes, but only consented to confess on condition that the letter he had written to Trotsky should be put in the records.[46]

In any case, one can certainly imagine Stalin using his daughter against him, as he had used Ivan Smirnov's. And if Krestinsky had hoped to rouse the other defendants to defy the court, he had had to recognize defeat. Indeed, he may never have hoped or intended his retraction to go beyond the first day, making what demonstration he felt to be in his power.

An alternative account leaked through N.K.V.D. circles was that Krestinsky's retraction and reaffirmation were a put-up job. Stalin was wishing to show that the defendants did not all confess like automata and thought that this single and temporary lapse would add a touch of verisimilitude.[47]

The arguments against this notion are very powerful. Krestinsky's phrasing during the first day sounds, on the face of it, genuine, and some of the points he makes seem to be both valid and extremely embarrassing to the prosecution. Vyshinsky's attitude is sinister in a way which appears more compatible with a genuine threat to Krestinsky than the appeal to his reason and conscience which would be supposed to have produced the change in his evidence on the second day.

There is another and most suggestive piece of evidence from the trial itself. At the beginning, Vyshinsky announced the order in which he proposed to question the twenty-one prisoners. This was evidently a predetermined list, since it is repeated in the order in which they made their final pleas, except for one single transposition among the minor characters. But the actual order of questioning was different. The first day went according to schedule – Bessonov, Grinko, Chernov. But on the second Krestinsky should have had his examination-in-chief immediately after Ivanov. Instead, as we saw, the agricultural official Zubarev took the stand on the morning of 3 March, and in the afternoon Krestinsky was called upon not for a full examination, but only for a brief recantation. This, too, was preceded by the short and unscheduled interrogation of Rakovsky, undermining Krestinsky's point about the letter disavowing Trotskyism.

On the evening of 3 March, this was all that Krestinsky's examination amounted to. His full examination was postponed until the following afternoon, when the examinations of Rosengolts and Rakovsky were rescheduled, the former to precede and the latter to follow Krestinsky's. Rosengolts, as Krestinsky's alleged closest Trotskyite collaborator, established both Krestinsky's connexions with Trotsky and the joint plotting activity of himself, Krestinsky, and the Tukhachevsky group in the days after the Pyatakov Trial and Bukharin's arrest. Krestinsky confirmed and elaborated all this, and Rakovsky rubbed it in afterwards. All this seems to show an emergency procedure.

Nor is it difficult to see that the circumstances of his original interrogation were such as to make retraction possible. Krestinsky had been arrested at the end of May 1937. He confessed 'after the lapse of a week . . . at the end of the first interrogation'.[48] This strongly suggests that in his case the 'conveyor' was used in its most intensive form, and that he was not, therefore, broken in the long-drawn-out fashion described on pp. 199–202. It was just at that time that Bukharin was making his first confession, and it may be that it was momentarily intended to produce the next big trial at very short notice – and about as soon after the Pyatakov Trial as that had been after Zinoviev's.

If so, this perhaps came to nothing when Bukharin started to retract some of his confession (see p. 528), and the whole business of interrogating him had to begin over again. Meanwhile, with the spread of the Purge right through the Party, other useful additions to the case kept emerging, and it was nine months later that the trial took place.

However that may be, it is certainly the case that the N.K.V.D. seem to have had in their hands a leading prisoner who had not been brought into the right state for a trial by the most tried and successful procedure. The conveyor could produce confessions, but, as we have seen, the victim, once rested, recovered to the degree that he could retract them. He was not reduced to the degree of submission obtained by the longer method. Yet Krestinsky had confessed, and was being cooperative. There was no overt resistance to break.

Krestinsky's withdrawal of his confession was not unprecedented. During the Shakhty Trial one of the accused (Skorutto) had refused to confess, been kept out of the court for a day on the grounds of illness, and then come back and confessed, only to withdraw it again, and the following day to reaffirm it, under the appalling circumstances described in Appendix F. Again, in the Metro-Vic Trial, MacDonald withdrew, then reaffirmed, his original confession. It has never been thought that these withdrawals added anything to the credibility of the confession when finally produced.

Thus, on the whole, the argument that Stalin had planned the whole Krestinsky episode is a weak one. The N.K.V.D. defector source for it is good in general, but is less good for this period when his old colleagues and contacts in the higher ranks of the N.K.V.D. had already been removed. What seems more probable is that some such story was put round *within* the outer circles of the N.K.V.D., to account for the lapse.

Even if Stalin was not prepared for the particular lapse of Krestinsky, it may be that an emergency plan was in existence, which was rapidly put into play. In any case, Krestinsky's withdrawal, so dramatic and so cogent in its comments, barely affected the reception given to the trial by the foreign public. Stalin had won again.

AN EX-PREMIER

Rykov's examination-in-chief came almost as an anti-climax. It started off mildly, soon coming to the alleged complicity of Yagoda in Rightist activity back in 1929. And now Yagoda, in turn, was questioned and gave one of those half-hearted affirmatives which any objective observer might have interpreted as a negative: 'The fact is true, but not as Rykov puts it.'

Rykov went on to describe the supposed Rightist underground which arose after 1930. He then came to the Ryutin Platform – which, he said, he, Tomsky, Bukharin, Vasily Shmidt and Uglanov had been responsible for. Ryutin had merely fronted for them, and Yagoda's protection had saved the main culprits. The Platform 'recognized (as far as I remember, and I do remember, for I had a share in editing it) methods of violence in changing the leadership of the Party and of the country – terrorism and uprisings. It was formulated so broadly as to constitute an instruction that measures of violence should be applied in whatever forms might prove to be at our disposal.'[49] The Rightists were, he added, a large organization: 'it was not a question of a hundred or so people, but of numerous cadres', so that it was understandable that 'the name Ivanov has no place in my memory.'[50] A palpable irony about a People's Commissar and full member of the Central Committee.

When it came to *kulak* insurrections, Bukharin too was called on, and they both admitted vaguely a connexion with one in Siberia. Its location was put to Bukharin, who could not remember if the one given was right.

He too mentioned the Ryutin Platform: 'I have been questioned so many times about the Ryutin Platform . . .'

Rykov now admitted to forming a terrorist organization headed by his former secretary, Artemenko, which he had instructed 'to watch for passing Government automobiles', without result. He and Bukharin (again questioned) admitted forming another terrorist group, headed by a former Social Revolutionary, to assassinate Stalin and Kaganovich, but again without result. But both men were unsatisfactory as to details. Rykov said:

> The Centre did not adopt a decision in such-and-such a year to kill such-and-such a member of the Political Bureau or the Government. The Centre took means that would enable such a decision to be put into effect if one were adopted . . .

at which point he was understandably interrupted by Vyshinsky. Bukharin, asked on whose initiative Semyonov, the Social Revolutionary, had acted, said 'I do not remember. Perhaps it was mine. At all events, I do not deny it.'

Rykov involved the Rights with the supposed plan of 1935 to seize power, with Yenukidze, Yagoda, Peterson and others, which had also (he said) implicated Tukhachevsky and other generals. 'We did not,' he added, 'succeed in making a real attempt . . .' He went on to the connexions with Fascism, Menshevism, bourgeois nationalism and other groupings. But as to detail, he again said he could only suspect, not know, what Grinko represented; and when Grinko was now called on, Rykov said 'I do not remember' when asked if his evidence was correct.

There followed a further three-way exchange between Vyshinsky, Rykov and Bukharin on the dismemberment of the U.S.S.R. and defeatism. Bukharin said that he did not take a defeatist line 'but am responsible for this affair'. Rykov broke down and admitted the whole defeatist position on his own behalf and that of all the Rightists, but withdrew a suggestion he had made at the preliminary inquiry, that Bukharin was the man mainly responsible. At this Vyshinsky openly expressed his annoyance.

After further confession to treasonable actions in Byelorussia, Rykov again rejected the charge of organizing livestock wrecking. He again denied knowledge of Ivanov's connexions with the British. But he also, backed by Krestinsky and Rosengolts, confirmed the participation of Tukhachevsky in the bloc.

Rykov's testimony was not coherent, and took no perfectly clear line, but he had still contrived to make a number of substantial denials.

Next day, Sharangovich, the Byelorussian First Secretary, was first to be called. After the shifts and evasions of the previous evening, he made an excellent impression on observers sympathetic to the regime, with his frank and total admission of all charges. He had been a Polish spy since 1921, and had become a prominent member of the Byelorussian 'national-fascist' organization, whose other members included Goloded, Chervyakov, and most of the Party leaders in the Republic. Rykov and Bukharin were directly involved in their crimes, which had included the formation of three terrorist groups: two of these had been intended to attack Voroshilov during the 1936 manoeuvres.[51]

Sabotage, on a large scale, had been designed to cause discontent as well as disruption. He too had spread disease among animals:

I must also say that in 1932 we took measures to spread plague among pigs, which resulted in a high pig mortality; this was done by inoculating pigs against plague in a wrecking fashion.[52]
. . . Further, as regards rural economy, I should like to say something about our diversionist activities in horse-breeding. In 1936 we caused a wide outbreak of anaemia in Byelorussia. This was done intentionally, because in Byelorussia horses are extremely important for defence purposes. We endeavoured to undermine this powerful base in case it should be needed in connection with war . . .
As far as I can now recall, about 30,000 horses perished owing to this measure.[53]

More essentially, he took the blame for the early excesses of collectivization. These had been put through for anti-Party reasons:

At that period there were still about 100,000 individual peasants in Byelorussia. We gave it out that an individual peasant who failed to join the collective farm was an enemy of the Soviet power. This was done for provocative purposes; in accordance with our provocative stand, we applied to the individual peasants who resisted collectivization such taxation measures which caused discontent and an insurrectionary spirit among the individual peasants.[54]

But fortunately Moscow had known better:

... Later the Central Committee of the C.P.S.U. took measures to correct what we had done, and the situation changed. The spirit among the individual peasants, among those whom we had provoked, took a distinct turn for the better.

This interpretation of the events of 1929–30 is a striking one, and shows a continual preoccupation with the peasantry on Stalin's part.

In industry too, the 'national fascists' had operated on a large scale:

As to power development, here attention was mainly concentrated on the Byelorussian Regional Power Station, which feeds the industries of Vitebsk, Orsha and Moghilev. Fuel was supplied irregularly. Construction work was interfered with. Specifically, I can mention the Krichevsk Cement Works, the Orsha Flax Mills, the Moghilev Pipe Foundry...[55]

ASIAN NATIONALISTS

The Uzbek leader Khodzhayev followed Sharangovich. It will be convenient to take his case together with that of his colleague Ikramov, though the latter gave evidence the following day.

Hitherto 'bourgeois nationalism' had been represented by Sharangovich, and to a lesser extent Grinko. In the persons of the two Uzbeks it was put forward in a more forthright form. They were not mobile *apparatchiks* like the two just named. Their entire careers had been spent in Central Asia, where they had successfully fronted for the imposition of Moscow rule on long recalcitrant populations.

They represented, as others represented in their different spheres, a much larger set of Party and State officials – implicating the First Secretary and Chairman of the Council of People's Commissars in neighbouring Tadzhikistan, for example, as well as their own republic's deviationists.

Khodzhayev seems to have really resented in some degree the centralizing and denationalizing tendencies of Stalinism, but Ikramov had not. In fact they had led two opposed factions in the Uzbek Party, and they now attributed their alleged unity in struggling against the regime to pressure from the Rightist central group. Ikramov testified: 'Under the pressure of Bukharin and the direct guidance of Antipov, the two nationalist organizations co-ordinated their work.'[56]

Khodzhayev was by far the most prominent and effective Uzbek to have taken the Communist side right from the time of the Revolution, in the struggle against the old Emir of Bokhara. He had been a member of the Uzbek Central Committee Bureau since the first Congress of the Uzbek Party in 1925, and had long served as Chairman of the local Council of People's Commissars.

But he had not even been elected a delegate at the VIIth Congress of the Uzbek Communist Party ending on 17 June 1937. On 27 June, his removal from the Chairmanship of the Uzbek Council of People's Commissars and expulsion from the Uzbek Central Executive Committee was announced, together with an attack on his counter-revolutionary nationalist positions.[57] He was clearly under arrest by this time. His brother, also prominent in the local Party, committed suicide.[58]

In September, Andreyev was sent to Tashkent to supervise the extension of the purge in Uzbekistan. On 8 September Khodzhayev and seven others, including four members of the Bureau of the local Central Committee, were denounced as enemies of the people, and 'Comrade Ikramov', the First Secretary of the Republic, and the current local Bureau, censured for insufficient vigilance.[59] Two days later *Pravda* violently attacked Ikramov (this time without 'Comrade'), for defending a 'Trotskyite' Secretary of the Uzbekistan Central Committee.[60]

On 12 September, it was announced that Ikramov had been 'unmasked', expelled from the Party and his case handed over to the investigating authorities.[61] He does not seem to have been arrested yet. For 'before his arrest', made 'on Stalin's personal instructions',[62] he was shown evidence concerning him which had been given by others, and denied it completely in spite of the fact that Yezhov himself spoke to him four times.[63] This last presumably means that he had been brought to Moscow not yet technically under arrest – an odd, but not a unique, experience.

The Uzbek press now attacked him for weakness towards bourgeois nationalism, and specifically for supporting Khodzhayev.[64] It was presumably in support of Khodzhayev that Ikramov, as we are now told,[65] had protested in 1937 against the Purge, and thus incurred Stalin's displeasure. (As an otherwise loyal Stalinist, Ikramov was the first defendant in the public trials to be rehabilitated.)

His actual arrest was announced to the Party membership in Tashkent two weeks later, when the news was greeted 'with warm applause'.[66] He was confronted in jail with Bukharin,[67] who implicated him, but he only confessed on the 'sixth or seventh day' of the interrogation.[68]

Similar events, with similar timing, were sweeping Soviet Asia. In Kirghizia, the Chairman of the Council of People's Commissars was purged on 12 September,[69] and a call put out for ruthless measures against the local Central Committee.[70] In Tadzhikistan two Secretaries of the Central Committee and a number of others were denounced as nationalists or spies on 10 and 12 September.[71] (The Chairman of the Tadzhik Council of People's Commissars, Rakhimbayev, had also, it was announced, been guilty of keeping a harem of three wives.) And so, as we have seen (pp. 337–43), it had gone all round the Soviet periphery.

Under the cold lights of the October Hall, Khodzhayev now confessed that he had been anti-Soviet since 1920. He and Ikramov had been in contact with the Rights, through Antipov, and had been instructed to work with the British for the secession of Uzbekistan as 'a British protectorate'. They had done a good deal of industrial sabotage on much the same lines as Sharangovich's. 'Errors' of planning had been intentional:

The ramp for the delivery of coal was planned for a capacity of 75,000 kW., whereas the power house was built for 48,000 kW., and the planned capacity of the station is 70,000 kW. You see, therefore, that the elements of wrecking were present in the very planning of the station.[72]

Their agricultural policy had been disastrous, and this was also intentional, as it caused hostility to Moscow:

Khodzhayev: . . . This would have meant causing enormous discontent among the people, because we put it to them in this way: 'This is the Moscow plan, we are merely the servants of Moscow, we are carrying out Moscow's instructions. Don't you like it? Then complain to Moscow.' This is the task we set ourselves.
Vyshinsky: A provocative task?
Khodzhayev: A provocative task, set deliberately, and pursued for a number of years.
What did it lead to? It actually led to the destruction of the rotation of crops system, it led to diminution in the number of cattle, it led to a diminution in silk cultivation, because even here we pursued our wrecking activities, and in the long run it led to a diminution even of the cotton yield. And that is why for years Uzbekistan failed to fulfil its cotton plans. . . . If a peasant had ten hectares of land he had to sow eight or nine hectares with cotton. You will understand that if only one hectare is left for all the rest, the farm goes to ruin.[73]

But there was a more important economic aim – to develop an independent economy in Uzbekistan. This (in contradiction to the admissions made above) led to their planning the economy:

in such a way as to have less cotton, because it was an industrial crop which most of all bound Uzbekistan with the Union; secondly, we planned to develop agriculture in Uzbekistan so as to have more grain farming not only on the non-irrigated lands, but also on the irrigated lands, in order to be independent of Russian grain, and lastly, we planned the development of industry, road building, etc., in such a way as to be more economically independent than ever of Soviet Russia, of the Soviet Union, at the end of the First Five-Year Plan.

The economic side of 'bourgeois nationalism' was thus well shown, and Khodzhayev made it explicit:

I do not know whether the court is aware that the bourgeois nationalists, particularly in Central Asia, had a theory of organizing a self-contained economy, that is to say, of making the economy of the republic develop independently of the other parts of the Soviet Union, of making it possible for the republic to live without need for the rest of the Soviet Union in the event of possibilities arising for active, direct struggle.[74]

Ikramov gave similar evidence. Apart from contacts with Zelenksy, Antipov and A. P. Smirnov, Bukharin had stayed a few days with him in 1933. Bukharin, called on, admitted discussing with him the Ryutin Platform, and 'a vague allusion to terrorism', but denied any talk of wrecking.[75] At a further meeting, in 1935, the sinister point was raised that both Bukharin's and Ikramov's wives had been present, though the seditious conversation had taken place in their absence. Bukharin denied that on this occasion politics had been discussed at all. Here came a sharp exchange with Vyshinsky:

Vyshinsky: And you, the leader of an underground organization, met a member of your organization, one whom you enlisted, met him two years later, and did not try to verify whether he still adhered to your counter-revolutionary organization, you showed no interest in this, but began to discuss the weather in Uzbekistan. Is this how it was, or not?
Bukharin: No, this is not how it was. You are putting a question which contains in itself an ironical reply. As it happens, I figured I would meet Ikramov again, but by chance this meeting did not take place because he did not find me in.
Vyshinsky: You have an extraordinarily good memory for exactly those meetings which did not take place.
Bukharin: I do not remember the meetings which did not take place, because they are a phantom, but I do remember those which did materialize.[76]

Ikramov gave a long account of Antipov's vital role in organizing Central Asian subversion. Antipov had insisted on terrorism, and personally boasted that 'whoever the Rights had decided to kill would never reach Central Asia'.[77] And Ikramov, too, implicated the polygamist Rakhimbayev and his Tadzhik group.

TO RUIN THE ECONOMY

The examinations of Rosengolts and Krestinsky on the evening of 4 March were satisfactory to the prosecution. Rosengolts and

Krestinsky testified that they, with Rudzutak and Gamarnik, had constituted the main centre of the conspiracy after the arrest of Rykov and Bukharin in February 1937. They had then relied almost entirely on the projected Army *coup*.

Their connexions with German espionage, arranged through Trotsky, had dated back to 1922–3. Krestinsky admitted to the meeting with Trotsky in person which he had denied on 2 March. Trotsky had given full instructions for all types of treason, espionage, sabotage and terror.

The only slightly awkward moments were when Krestinsky said that he, Rosengolts and Gamarnik had 'discussed the necessity for a terrorist act' against Molotov, but had made no actual preparations for it (Vyshinsky commented sharply that this amounted to the same thing); and when Rykov, again called on briefly to confirm conversations with and about Tukhachevsky, denied them.[78]

Rykov, and Bukharin too, were incidentally all but exculpated of all the recent activity attributed to them by Krestinsky's remark that 'Trotsky said that we should not confine ourselves to Rykov, Bukharin and Tomsky, because although they were the recognized leaders of the Rights, they had already been compromised to a great extent and were under surveillance', so that Rudzutak, whom no one suspected, should be the connexion. But this 'surveillance', and the admission that it made Rykov and Bukharin unsuitable conspiratorial colleagues in effect disposes of the possibility of their guilt – and this is from 1933 on, covering the whole period of the Kirov and other alleged murders.

Rosengolts confessed to various embezzlements, including sabotage in the export of iron. This seems to refer to pig-iron exports, which in fact had been under a directive bearing Stalin's signature, with the deliveries superintended by Yezhov.[79]

Rakovsky was now questioned. He was the son of a landowner in the Southern Dobrudja, at first part of Bulgaria, but transferred to Romania a few years after his birth. He was prominent as a Bulgarian Socialist at the age of twenty, when he represented the party at the Congress of the Second International. He took a doctorate of medicine at Montpellier, and went back to the

Balkans, where he was arrested a number of times for involvement in the Romanian revolutionary movement. In 1916 he was
again arrested in Romania, and imprisoned at Jassy, where the
Russians freed him in May 1917. He went to Petrograd and in
1919 became a member of the Central Committee of the Russian
Communist Party and Chairman of the Council of People's
Commissars of the Ukraine. Becoming attached to Trotsky's
views, he lost his high posts and from 1924 to 1927 was Soviet
Chargé d'Affaires in London and then Ambassador in Paris. He
was recalled to Moscow in November 1927 and was expelled
from the Central Committee in the same month, for supporting
the Left opposition. He defended the opposition viewpoint at
the XVth Party Congress. In January 1928 he was expelled from
the Party and deported to Astrakhan, and later to Barnaul. It
had not been until February 1934, one of the very last, that he
had recanted and been readmitted to the Party. He had been
arrested about the end of 1936, and had been implicated in the
Pyatakov Trial.[80] Apart from the doctors, he was easily the oldest
of those in dock. And even among his veteran fellow-accused, his
record stood out as long and legendary.

The sixty-five-year-old revolutionary had refused to testify to
the N.K.V.D. for eight months,[81] one of the best records in the
trials. He now confessed that he had been a British spy since
1924. His disavowal of Trotskyism in February 1934 had been
designed to deceive the Party.[82]

On his rehabilitation he had been sent to Japan at the head of
a Red Cross delegation, and this was made the occasion for him
to incriminate the Soviet ambassadors in the Far East, Yurenev
and Bogomolov. He himself became a Japanese as well as a
British spy.

Vyshinsky got in one particularly unfair smear. Rakovsky's
father had been a landlord.

Vyshinsky: Hence I am not mistaken when I say that you were a landlord?
Rakovsky: You are not mistaken.
Vyshinsky: Well, now. It was important for me to establish whence you
received your income.

Rakovsky: But it is important for me to say what this income was spent for.

Vyshinsky: This is a different matter.[83]

Everyone among the old Bolsheviks knew that Rakovsky had spent everything he had on the revolutionary movement – financing the Romanian Socialist Party which he had founded, and its paper which he edited, and also subsidizing Russian and other revolutionaries. Now provoked enough to try to draw attention to these facts, he was instantly silenced.

When Rakovsky began to refer to the 'opposition', Vyshinsky interrupted briskly:

> In your explanations today you are generally permitting yourself to use quite a number of such expressions, as if you were forgetting that you are being tried here as a member of a counter-revolutionary bandit, espionage, diversionist organization of traitors. I consider it my duty to remind you of this in my interrogation of you and ask you to keep closer to the substance of the treasonable crimes which you have committed, to speak without philosophy and other such things which are entirely out of place here.[84]

Rakovsky finished by explaining that his surrender after eight months had been due to getting information, during the summer of 1937, about the Japanese attack on China and the extent of Nazi and Italian intervention in Spain.[85] This 'had a stunning effect on me. Rancour and ambition fell from me.' He decided that his 'duty was to help in this struggle with the aggressor, that I would go and expose myself fully and entirely, and I told the investigator that on the following day I would begin to give complete, exhaustive testimony'.

This sounds, in the context of interrogation and exhaustion, a credible exposition of the 'Rubashov' motive – more so, indeed, than the reluctant and partial confession of Bukharin, on whom 'Rubashov' was founded.

Rakovsky's evidence, adjourned over the night, had lasted till the morning of 5 March. The court then took Zelensky, a much less interesting figure. He had, however, a past in the highest Party ranks, as a former (1923–5) Secretary of the Central

Committee and Secretary of the Moscow Party organization, who had been removed for inadequate hostility to Zinoviev and Kamenev. He had merely been transferred to be Secretary of the Party's Central Asian Bureau from 1924 to 1931, and had never lost his place on the Central Committee. In his Asian capacity he had already been implicated as an agent of Trotsky by Ikramov and Khodzhayev. But his main role now was to explain how he had given rise to popular discontent: in the position he had held from 1931 to 1937, as Chairman of the Consumer Cooperatives – that is, virtually the entire official distribution network – he had had unexampled opportunities for doing this.

Starting with an account of his work as a Tsarist police agent in the Party from 1911, he admitted complicity in Kamenev's actions in 1924, and recruitment by A. P. Smirnov into the Rightist 'organization' in 1928–9. After Smirnov's exposure (i.e. in 1933), his contact became Antipov, under whose instructions the whole shop system was badly disrupted:

Zelensky: ... The Rights engineered interruptions in the supply of commodities of everyday use to the trading organizations. Thus, for instance, interruptions of this kind were engineered in the Kursk Region in the first quarter of 1936, in the sugar supply. Many shops were out of sugar for two or three weeks. Similar interruptions were engineered in the Leningrad Region in the *makhorka* supply; there were similar interruptions in the summer of 1936 in the bread trade in a number of rural districts of the Byelorussian S.S.R. situated near the frontier.

To give you some idea of the character of these interruptions, I will point out the following: out of 30,000 shops inspected by the co-operative trade sections of the Soviets and by trade inspectors, there was no salt in 3,700 shops in the first quarter of 1936. Out of 42,000 shops, 2,000 shops had no sugar on sale. In the third quarter of 1936, 1,600 shops out of 36,000 had no *makhorka*, so that these were not isolated cases, but rather widespread.[86]

And again:

Vyshinsky: Was there a case in 1936 when Moscow was left without eggs through your fault, through the fault not of you personally, but of one of the active participators in this conspiratorial bloc?
Zelensky: There was.

Vyshinsky: Do you remember when this made itself most acutely felt?
Zelensky: I cannot recall the month just now, but I can mention the following fact. In 1936 fifty carloads of eggs were allowed to spoil, from wrecking motives.[87]

He had also dislocated the accounts system:

Zelensky: It seems to me that the question of overcharging, short measure and short weight should be clear to everybody; it is very obvious. It consists in the following: when a man comes into a shop to make a purchase, he is overcharged, given short measure and short weight, that is, he is named a price higher than the one at which the goods should be sold, or is given shorter weight than he is entitled to, or is sold goods not of the proper quality.
Vyshinsky: Why is this done?
Zelensky: To arouse discontent among the population. . . . Prices are fixed by the trading organizations or by the salesmen in the shops very often at their own discretion, that is, without control. And so it is almost impossible to detect a man who overcharges the consumer. This matter assumed a serious and widespread character. To give some idea of the extent of this wrecking work, I may mention that of 135,000 shops that were inspected by the co-operative inspectorate, cases of overcharging and defrauding purchasers were established in 13,000 shops. The actual number was considerably larger.

Another important form of wrecking, also designed to arouse the discontent of the population, was the freezing of trade by dispatching goods to the wrong districts or at the wrong times. For example, there were cases when summer goods were sent in winter and vice versa, when winter goods arrived in the shops in summer.
Vyshinsky: That is, the public was offered felt boots in summer and summer shoes in winter?
Zelensky: Yes.[88]

All this was partly due to his staff:

Zelensky: . . . I had instructions, and I pursued the aim of contaminating the apparatus with alien, hostile, anti-Soviet and insurrectionary elements. How contaminated the apparatus of the Centrosoyuz was may be judged from the fact that when I was in charge of it about 15 per cent of the staff of the Centrosoyuz consisted of former Mensheviks, Socialist-Revolutionaries, anarchists, Trotskyites, etc. In certain regions the number of alien elements, former members of other parties, Kolchak officers, and so on, as, for example, in the Krasnoyarsk Territory, Irkutsk and West Siberia, was considerably higher.[89]

He then got into a curious altercation with Vyshinsky:

Vyshinsky: ... But how did matters stand with butter?

Zelensky: We don't sell butter in the rural districts.

Vyshinsky: I am not asking you what you sell. You were above all selling the main thing – your country. I am speaking about what measures were taken by your organization to disrupt trade and deprive the population of prime necessities. Apart from sugar and salt, do you know anything concerning butter?

Zelensky: I told you that the co-operatives do not sell butter in the rural districts ...

Vyshinsky: I am asking you: have you any knowledge of criminal operations with regard to supplying the population with butter, particularly cheap grades of butter, or not? Operations which were effected on the orders of your 'bloc of Rights and Trotskyites'; are they known to you or not?

Zelensky: Yes, they are.

Vyshinsky: In what did they consist?

Zelensky: They consisted in the following: in making butter, all the produce purchasing organizations used the international standards fixing quality of butter.

Vyshinsky: That is not the point.

Zelensky: That is the point.

Vyshinsky: No.

Zelensky: What do you mean? This was done ...

The President: Accused Zelensky, no cross-talk, and keep to the point ...

Vyshinsky: And was the butter which was issued for sale always of good quality, or did you try to spoil its quality too?

Zelensky: Yes.

Vyshinsky: Were there cases when members of your organization connected with the butter business threw glass into the butter?

Zelensky: There were cases when glass was found in butter.

Vyshinsky: Glass was not 'found', but thrown into the butter. You understand the difference: thrown into the butter. Were there such cases, or not?

Zelensky: There were cases when glass was thrown into the butter.

Vyshinsky: Were there cases when your accomplices, fellow participants in the criminal plot against the Soviet power and the Soviet people, threw nails into the butter?

Zelensky: There were.

Vyshinsky: For what purpose? to make it 'tastier'?

Zelensky: That is clear.
Vyshinsky: Well, that is organized wrecking and diversive activities. Do you admit that you are guilty of this?
Zelensky: I do . . .[90]

In addition to his vaguely unsatisfactory and undignified style of reply, Zelensky balked at a major question:

Vyshinsky: Did you take part in the wrecking, diversive, terrorist and espionage work of this bloc?
Zelensky: I did take part in wrecking and diversive work.
Vyshinsky: About espionage work you so far say nothing?
Zelensky: (No reply.)
Vyshinsky: Do you answer for all the criminal activities of the bloc?
Zelensky: I do.

– this last a weak ploy by Vyshinsky.

Zelensky did, however, admit contact with A. V. Alexander, the British Labour and Cooperative leader, with whom he had discussed the possibilities of a Rightist Government in Russia.

Ikramov's examination, which we have already covered, came next. When he had finished, first Bessonov was again questioned. He gave evidence of connexions with Social Revolutionary émigrés, with Trotsky, and with the Nazis.

BUKHARIN IN DOCK

And now, at last, the main subject of the trial was brought to questioning. Vyshinsky started his duel with Bukharin.

Bukharin had not been tortured.* Arrested on 27 February 1937, he had been confronted with Radek, who, however, had qualified his evidence against him, saying that Bukharin had objected to the degree of Trotsky's commitment to the Germans,[92] and refusing to confirm some of the more vicious charges.[93] After three months of interrogation, and threats to his young wife and child, Bukharin agreed, in a long talk with Yezhov and Voroshilov – as 'representative of the Politburo' – to confess to all the charges, including that of having planned to assassinate Lenin.

---

* Mikoyan insisted on this to Louis Fischer,[91] and it is also in accord with other accounts.

But when, two days later, his confession, amended and corrected by Stalin personally, had been given him to sign, he was so shocked that he withdrew his whole confession. The examination started all over again, with a double team of interrogators. He finally agreed to testify, but refused to say that he had planned Lenin's death.[94] One of the charges now brought against him, that of espionage, was not raised at all during his interrogation. It was doubtless felt that he was unlikely to agree to it, so it was sprung on him for the first time at the trial.[95]

He had evidently decided on his tactics after considering the earlier cases. His confession, like Rykov's, avoided admitting direct complicity in any of the worst overt acts, but accepted general responsibility. Anything less would have doubtless led to his omission from the trial and the execution of his wife. As it was, Vyshinsky threatened to stop his evidence.

Before Vyshinsky could speak, Bukharin asked the court to allow him to present his case 'freely' and to dwell on the ideological stand of the 'bloc'. Vyshinsky at once asked for the request to be denied, as limiting the legal rights of the prosecution. Bukharin then said that he confirmed his evidence at the preliminary inquiry. He then made his carefully phrased acceptance of guilt:

> I plead guilty to being one of the outstanding leaders of this 'bloc of Rights and Trotskyites'. Consequently, I plead guilty to what directly follows from this, the sum total of crimes committed by this counter-revolutionary organization, irrespective of whether or not I knew of, whether or not I took a direct part in, any particular act.[96]

He had, he admitted, planned the forcible overthrow of the Soviet power, and, 'with the help of a war which prognostically was in prospect', relied on the help of foreign States to which territorial concessions would be made.

Vyshinsky: And also by means of weakening the defensive power? *Bukharin:* You see, this question was not discussed, at least not in my presence.

As to wrecking, 'The orientation on wrecking was adopted.' But again, when a concrete question was put:

Vyshinsky: As you see from the trial, the circumstances were concrete enough. Did you and Khodzhayev discuss the fact that too little wrecking was being done, and being done badly?

Bukharin: About accelerating wrecking there was no talk.[97]

Bukharin then admitted that the bloc stood for the assassination of the leadership. Vyshinsky immediately asked whether the Kirov murder was committed on the instructions of the bloc.

Bukharin: I do not know.

Vyshinsky: I ask you, was this assassination committed with the knowledge and on the instructions of the 'bloc of Rights and Trotskyites'?

Bukharin: And I repeat that I do not know, Citizen Prosecutor.

Vyshinsky: You did not know about this specifically in relation to the assassination of S. M. Kirov?

Bukharin: Not specifically, but . . .

Vyshinsky: Permit me to question the accused Rykov.

The President: You may.

Vyshinsky: Accused Rykov, what do you know about the assassination of Sergei Mironovich Kirov?

Rykov: I know nothing about the participation of the Rights or the Right part of the bloc in the assassination of Kirov.

Vyshinsky: In general, were you aware of the preparations for terrorist acts, for the assassination of members of the Party and the Government?

Rykov: As one of the leaders of the Right part of this bloc, I took part in the organization of a number of terrorist groups and in preparations for terrorist acts. As I have said in my testimony, I do not know of a single decision of the Right centre, through which I was related with the 'bloc of Rights and Trotskyites', about the actual commission of assassinations . . .

Vyshinsky: About the actual commission. So. Do you know that one of the aims of the 'bloc of Rights and Trotskyites' was to organize and commit terrorist acts against leaders of the Party and the Government?

Rykov: I said more than that, I said that I personally organized terrorist groups. But you are asking me whether I knew of such aims through some third person.

Vyshinsky: I am asking whether the 'bloc of Rights and Trotskyites' had any relation to the assassination of Comrade Kirov.

Rykov: I have no information regarding the relation of the Right part to this assassination, and therefore I am convinced to this day that the assassination of Kirov was carried out by the Trotskyites without the knowledge of the Rights. Of course, I might not have known about it.[98]

Vyshinsky, baffled, then called on Yagoda, who said that both
Rykov and Bukharin were lying: Rykov had been present, with
Yenukidze, at the meeting which had discussed the question.
However, Yagoda now started to drop peculiar hints on his own:

Vyshinsky: After this, did you personally take any measures to effect
the assassination of Sergei Mironovich Kirov?
Yagoda: I personally?
Vyshinsky: Yes, as a member of the bloc.
Yagoda: I gave instructions . . .
Vyshinsky: To whom?
Yagoda: To Zaporozhets in Leningrad. That is not quite how it was . . .
Vyshinsky: And then you gave instructions not to place obstacles in
the way of the murder of Sergei Mironovich Kirov?
Yagoda: Yes, I did. . . . It was not like that.
Vyshinsky: In a somewhat different form?
Yagoda: It was not like that, but it is not important.[99]

Vyshinsky hastily dropped the matter and started to question
Bukharin about the allegation that he had intended to kill Lenin.
Bukharin admitted that there had been a plan in 1918 to arrest
Lenin, but when Vyshinsky asserted that this must mean to kill
him, he pointed out that Dzerzhinsky had actually been arrested
by Social Revolutionaries at the time, and not killed. Conceding
that Stalin and Sverdlov too were to have been arrested, he added
that 'under no circumstances' were the three to have been killed.
Vyshinsky postponed the question till witnesses were called.

Bukharin was then allowed to start to speak at length. Ulrikh
told him to stick to his 'criminal anti-Soviet activities', but after
ten or fifteen minutes he was still expounding a theory of the way
Rightism inevitably led to the restoration of capitalism. Ulrikh
interrupted to say he must not make his defence plea now.

Bukharin countered: 'This is not my defence, it is my self-
accusation. I have not said a single word in my defence . . .'[100]
Nor, strictly speaking, had he. And he now went on to admit that
his programme would have meant 'a lapse into bourgeois-
democratic freedom', which (Vyshinsky pointed out, and he
accepted) meant in effect 'outright rabid fascism'!

Vyshinsky turned to espionage:

Vyshinsky: Then why was it so easy for you to join a bloc which was engaged in espionage work?
Bukharin: Concerning espionage work I know absolutely nothing.
Vyshinsky: What do you mean, you don't know?
Bukharin: Just that.
Vyshinsky: And what was the bloc engaged in?
Bukharin: Two people testified here about espionage, Sharangovich and Ivanov, that is to say two *agents provocateurs*.[101]

Here Bukharin was cleverly turning the trial's tactics against its originators. Ivanov had, on his own evidence, been a Tsarist *agent provocateur* in the revolutionary movement – than which, for a Bolshevik audience, no lower form of life, no more untrustworthy character, could exist. His evidence was automatically worthless. But at the same time Bukharin was surely suggesting that he was still following the same trade, under different orders.

Vyshinsky now scored a point by turning to Rykov, who again admitted knowing that espionage was being conducted by the Byelorussian 'national fascists', and that 'in my opinion, Bukharin also knew'. Bukharin simply retorted that he had not known. His connexions with the Austrian police, which Vyshinsky raised, 'consisted of my imprisonment in an Austrian fortress'.

Vyshinsky: Accused Sharangovich, you were a Polish spy, although you have been in prison?
Sharangovich: Yes, although I have been in prison.
Bukharin: I have been in a Swedish prison, twice in a Russian prison, and in a German prison.[102]

Bukharin went on to elaborate the negotiations for and the structure of the alleged 'bloc', from his conversation with Kamenev in 1928 on, with special attention to the Ryutin Platform. Again Ulrikh intervened: 'So far you are still beating about the bush, you are saying nothing about your crimes.'

Bukharin spoke of the planned *coup* of 1935 by Yenukidze and Peterson – of which nothing had ever come. And, continuing his evidence at the next session, on the morning of 7 March, he developed this theme to include the Tukhachevsky group.

(Vyshinsky here objected to his use of the term 'palace *coup*'.) He admitted also sending insurrectionary organizers to the provinces, but denied all knowledge of their connexion with White Guard and German fascist circles. Again there was a long tussle as Vyshinsky tried to get him to admit and Rykov to confirm that he knew of this. But this time Rykov rallied and supported Bukharin's point.

Rykov went on to deny knowing that Karakhan was a spy. And on the whole issue of negotiation with Germany, Bukharin admitted that Trotsky had spoken of ceding the Ukraine, but that he himself 'did not consider Trotsky's instructions as binding on me'. On Karakhan's alleged negotiations:

Vyshinsky: Did you endorse these negotiations?
Bukharin: Or disavow? I did not disavow them; consequently I endorsed them.
Vyshinsky: I ask you, did you endorse them, or not?
Bukharin: I repeat, Citizen Prosecutor: since I did not disavow them, I consequently endorsed them.
Vyshinsky: Consequently, you endorsed them?
Bukharin: If I did not disavow them, consequently I endorsed them.
Vyshinsky: That's what I am asking you: that is to say, you endorsed them?
Bukharin: So then 'consequently' is the same as 'that is to say'.
Vyshinsky: What do you mean, 'that is to say'?
Bukharin: That is to say, I endorsed them.
Vyshinsky: But you say that you learnt of this *post factum*.
Bukharin: Yes, the one does not contradict the other in the slightest.[103]

Vyshinsky again started to hammer at the espionage theme, raising with Rykov the matter of the Byelorussians. And now, for half an hour, came one of the most striking exchanges in the whole of the public trials:

Vyshinsky: Isn't this an espionage connection?
Rykov: No.
Vyshinsky: What kind of connection is it?
Rykov: There was espionage connection there, too.
Vyshinsky: But was there an espionage connection maintained by a part of your organization with the Poles on your instructions?
Rykov: Of course.

Vyshinsky: Espionage?

Rykov: Of course.

Vyshinsky: Bukharin included?

Rykov: Of course.

Vyshinsky: Were you and Bukharin connected?

Rykov: Absolutely.

Vyshinsky: So you were spies?

Rykov: (No reply.)

Vyshinsky: And the organizers of espionage?

Rykov: I am in no way better than a spy.

Vyshinsky: You organized espionage, so you were spies.

Rykov: It may be said, yes.

Vyshinsky: It may be said, spies. I am asking, did you organize connections with the Polish intelligence service and the respective spy circles? Do you plead guilty to espionage?

Rykov: If it is a question of organization, then in this case, of course, I plead guilty.

Vyshinsky: Accused Bukharin, do you plead guilty to espionage?

Bukharin: I do not.

Vyshinsky: After what Rykov says, after what Sharangovich says?

Bukharin: I do not plead guilty.

Vyshinsky: When the organization of the Rights was set up in Byelorussia, you were at the head of it; do you admit that?

Bukharin: I have told you.

Vyshinsky: I am asking you, do you admit it or not?

Bukharin: I took no interest in Byelorussian affairs.

Vyshinsky: Did you take an interest in espionage affairs?

Bukharin: No.

Vyshinsky: And who did take an interest?

Bukharin: I received no information with regard to activities of this kind.

Vyshinsky: Accused Rykov, was Bukharin receiving any information with regard to activities of this kind?

Rykov: I never spoke to him about it.[104]

After going over the ground again, Vyshinsky only got Rykov back to his old line.

Rykov: I mean to say that we did not personally direct this development; however, it is not a question of direct leadership but of general leadership. We absolutely and definitely bear responsibility for this.

Vyshinsky: There is no point in making a pious face, accused Bukharin. Better admit what exists. And what exists is the following: you had a group of your accomplices, fellow-conspirators in Byelorussia, headed by Goloded, Chervyakov and Sharangovich. Is that right, Sharangovich?

Sharangovich: It is.

Vyshinsky: And on Bukharin's and Rykov's instructions, and under their leadership, you established connections with the Polish intelligence service and with the Polish General Staff? Is that right, Sharangovich?

Sharangovich: Absolutely right.

Vyshinsky: Under your leadership also with regard to the espionage connections. Is that right, Sharangovich?

Sharangovich: Absolutely right.

Vyshinsky: Consequently, who was the organizer of the espionage in which you engaged?

Sharangovich: Rykov, Bukharin.

Vyshinsky: Hence, they were spies.

Sharangovich: Quite right.

Vyshinsky: Just as . . .

Sharangovich: As I myself.

Vyshinsky: Be seated .

(To Rykov): Accused Rykov, did Goloded tell you in 1932 that all more or less important appointments of people to responsible posts in Byelorussia were first co-ordinated with the Polish intelligence service?

Rykov: Yes.

Vyshinsky: Did Bukharin know of this?

Rykov: I cannot say.

Vyshinsky: You do not know. You do not want to betray your pal?

Rykov: What I mean to say is that in those cases when I know that he is not telling the truth, I am exposing him, but in those cases when I do not know, I cannot and shall not do it.

Vyshinsky: I am asking you with regard to the fact that the Poles were giving their consent to the various appointments to official posts in Byelorussia. Was this known to your leading centre?

Rykov: I knew of it. As for Bukharin, I never spoke to him about it. I also knew that Chervyakov and Goloded maintained connections, not only with me, but with Bukharin and Tomsky as well. Whether they spoke of this to Bukharin I cannot say, because I was not present at those conversations.

Vyshinsky: Do you think that it would have been natural for Goloded to speak to Bukharin about this question? Or did they have to keep it a secret from Bukharin?

Rykov: I think that, naturally, he spoke to Bukharin, but what they talked about I do not know.

Vyshinsky: I shall ask you now by way of making a supposition: do you suppose that Bukharin knew of this?

Rykov: This circumstance ... I prefer to speak only of what I knew; and as to what I do not know – my position in the court room is not such as to allow me to advance suppositions.[105]

On his conversations with Bukharin, Rykov went on to say:

I do not recall any conversations dealing especially with this espionage work. I do not exclude the possibility that there were such conversations, but I do not remember.[106]

After a long exchange with Rykov about the meaning of some of his preliminary evidence, which Rykov pointed out was meant not as fact but as supposition, Vyshinsky turned to Bukharin, who immediately remarked:

I was not asked a single word about this during the preliminary investigation, and you, Citizen Prosecutor, did not question me for three months, not a single word.[107]

At this Vyshinsky lost his temper and shouted that Bukharin was not going to instruct him about how to conduct an investigation. He then turned on Rykov again, but got no further.

He concluded weakly: 'Permit me to consider it established that Rykov and Bukharin knew the substance of the treasonable connexion which included espionage. Is that correct, Rykov?'

Rykov: That is, espionage followed.

Bukharin: So it appears that I knew something from which something followed.[108]

Ulrikh turned the accused back to the theme of the proposed *coup d'état*. Following that, Bukharin denied having told Khodzhayev about an agreement with Germany, and after further argument about this Vyshinsky again lost his composure, and Bukharin was able to remark 'There is nothing for you to gesticulate about'. Ulrikh called him to order, and Vyshinsky launched on a harangue:

I will be compelled to cut the interrogation short because you are apparently following definite tactics and do not want to tell the truth, hiding behind a flood of words, pettifogging, making digressions into the sphere of politics, of philosophy, theory and so forth ...

Bukharin replied calmly, 'I am answering your questions', and went on to deny telling Khodzhayev about connexions with British spies. Vyshinsky had remarked, during his burst of rage, that 'According to all the material of the investigation you are obviously a spy of an intelligence service'. Bukharin now took him up on this point:

Bukharin: During the year I spent in prison I was not once asked about it.

Vyshinsky: We are asking you here in an open proletarian court, we are asking you here in this court before the whole world.

Bukharin: But you did not ask me this before.

Vyshinsky: I am asking you again, on the basis of the testimony which was here given against you: do you choose to admit before the Soviet Court by what intelligence service you were enlisted – the British, German or Japanese?

Bukharin: None.

Vyshinsky: I have no more questions to put to Bukharin.[109]

The court adjourned on that note. The Prosecutor had been defeated.

When the session resumed, Bukharin listed his contacts with émigré Mensheviks and Social Revolutionaries, and of the concessions to be made to Germany. He again went out of his way to deny espionage, and say that the military conspirators had spoken to Tomsky of 'opening the front' in case of war, but that he had disapproved:

Vyshinsky: And did you talk to Karakhan about opening the front?

Bukharin: Karakhan said that the Germans were demanding a military alliance with Germany.

Vyshinsky: And are the gates closed to an ally?

Bukharin: Karakhan gave me an answer to this question.

Vyshinsky: That the gates are closed to an ally?

Bukharin: No.

Vyshinsky: That means to open the gates?

Bukharin: Pardon me, there was no alliance yet.

Vyshinsky: But there were expectations, plans?

Bukharin: Well, just now the Soviet Union has an alliance with France, but that does not mean that it opens the Soviet frontiers.[110]

Vyshinsky now went on to the crime with which Bukharin alone of those on trial was charged – the plan to assassinate Lenin in 1918. The prosecution produced three prominent Left Communists of that period, Yakovleva, Mantsev and Ossinsky – the latter (originally Prince Obolensky) still a candidate member of the Central Committee elected in 1934.

At the time Varvara Yakovleva, a candidate member of the small 1917 Central Committee, had been the more prominent, and with Bukharin, Pyatakov and V. M. Smirnov had resigned when the decision to accept the Peace of Brest–Litovsk had been taken.

She now fully confirmed Vyshinsky's story. Bukharin had no difficulty in showing that the alleged illegal activities of early 1918 were not illegal at all, and that in fact the Leftists, with the Trotskyites then roughly aligned with them, held a majority and hoped to enforce their views through ordinary Party channels. *After* this majority had been lost, he admitted, conversations had taken place with a view to arresting Lenin and forming a new government. (Bukharin had indeed thought of arresting Lenin for twenty-four hours with a view to making it easier to change the Government, and had given the whole story as long ago as 1924.)[111]

There had also been conversations with the Left Social Revolutionaries, who had dropped out of the Soviet Government on the peace issue. What Bukharin denied was that there was any sort of plan to kill Lenin or complicity with the Social Revolutionaries.* He went on to point out that many who had been Left Communists at the time – including Kuibyshev and Menzhinsky – were not for that reason now regarded as enemies. He was ruled out of order. A series of points – including the fact

---

* Bukharin has been cleared of this charge. The 1959 edition of the *History of the Soviet Communist Party* simply said that 'the Left Social-Revolutionaries approached Bukharin with a proposal to remove Lenin from the post of Chairman of the Council and People's Commissars and set up a new government of Left Social-Revolutionaries and Left Communists'. The 1962 edition adds the following sentence: 'Bukharin did not accept the proposals of the Left Social-Revolutionaries, but the fact of their approach to him shows how the enemies attempted to use the fractional struggle of the Left Communists in their own interests.'

that he had been wounded by a bomb thrown by the Left Social Revolutionaries at a time when he was now charged with conspiring with them – were similarly ruled on.

Mantsev's evidence followed the same lines, and Ossinsky gave a rather more restricted account, omitting certain points against Bukharin. Bukharin denied the evidence about the assassination plan, and twice hinted strongly at the reason for the witnesses' attitude:

Vyshinsky: Consequently, you assert that Mantsev's testimony in this part and the testimony of witness Yakovleva are false?
Bukharin: Yes, I do.
Vyshinsky: How do you explain the fact that they are not telling the truth?
Bukharin: You had better ask them about it.[112]

And, later on,

Vyshinsky: You must somehow explain the fact that three of your former accomplices are speaking against you.
Bukharin: You see, I have neither sufficient material nor the psychological requisites to clear up this question.
Vyshinsky: You cannot explain.
Bukharin: Not that I cannot, I simply refuse to explain.[113]

Getting no further with this, Vyshinsky called two new witnesses – the old Social Revolutionaries Boris Kamkov and Vladimir Karelin. They were in 'neat blue suits', their faces 'grey and corpse-like'.[114] They had been in prison for years. An even more important Social Revolutionary, Maria Spiridonova, was implicated with her comrades.[115] But she seems to have refused to cooperate in the trial. An article by a Polish woman Communist who shared her cell in 1937 suggests that she was executed in the winter of that year as a result.[116]*

Kamkov, first to be called, had apparently been released during the twenties, but was back in prison no later than 1933.[117] Kamkov said that he understood from others that Bukharin had been informed of Social Revolutionary intentions, but he could not himself testify to this directly. He denied that there was any

*This article was strongly attacked by *Kommunist* for advocating 'humanist socialism'.

'joint decision' by the Left Social Revolutionaries and Left Communists. Vyshinsky again became flustered at the firm attitude of the old revolutionist, and when Bukharin tried to ask a question, he burst out with 'I request the accused Bukharin not to interfere in my interrogation. I am restraining myself enough, and I request my opponent to restrain himself . . .'[118] Kamkov again denied the point. Vyshinsky abandoned the witness without putting the point about Lenin's assassination.

Karelin was more amenable, and confirmed the plan to kill Lenin. He also brought in an entirely separate action – the genuine attempted assassination of Lenin on 30 August 1918 by the freelance *Right* Social Revolutionary Fanny Kaplan. This, he said, had been insisted on by Bukharin, and his insistence transmitted through the Left Social Revolutionaries. Ossinsky, called on to confirm this, said he had heard some vague gossip about Kaplan's shot being inspired by the anti-Government stand of the Lefts, but 'I can say nothing of Bukharin personally' in such a connexion.

Bukharin denied the whole thing.

Vyshinsky: Ossinsky spoke on the subject.
Bukharin: Ossinsky said that he could say nothing about me.[119]

Vyshinsky then tackled Bukharin directly, in an attempt to make him concede that the atmosphere in the Party was so heated in 1918 that assassination would have been rational. Bukharin denied this, and again denied the evidence.

Vyshinsky: But why do both former 'Left' Communists and 'Left' Social-Revolutionaries say so – everybody?
Bukharin: No, not everybody: of two 'Left' Socialist-Revolutionaries, only one said it.[120]

With a final 'categorical denial', Bukharin's examination was over.

In the indictment, the cases of Yakovleva, Mantsev, Ossinsky, Kamkov and Karelin are among those mentioned as being the subject of separate proceedings. The death dates of both Kamkov[121] and Karelin[122] are now given as 1938. Ossinsky, too, died in 1938, on 1 September.[123] We can presume that they were in fact executed for their alleged part in the plan to assassinate Lenin, Yakovleva, whose evidence had been the most satisfactory, survived until 1944.[124]

THE DOCTOR-POISONERS

On the morning of 8 March, the most horrible and obscure of all the crimes alleged against the bloc were reached. Over the next two days, the system of alleged 'medical murders' carried out directly under Yagoda's orders was the main subject of examination.

The plan to charge the opposition with these medical murders seems to have been adopted soon after Yezhov took over the N.K.V.D. Of the doctors concerned, as we shall see, Dr Pletnev was already embroiled in the N.K.V.D.'s plans by December 1936. Pletnev's hope 'as late as 5 March' (1937)[125] that the medical world would protect him presumably refers to the date of his arrest. Dr Levin was arrested some time between Ordzhonikidze's death in February and 12 June 1937.* Kryuchkov, Gorki's secretary, also involved, was denounced (with other writers associated with Yagoda) on 17 May.[126]

There were four of these alleged murders. First, in May 1934, Menzhinsky, Yagoda's predecessor as head of the O.G.P.U., had been killed by his favourite doctor, Kazakov, under instructions from Dr Levin. Then, in the same month, Gorki's son Maxim Peshkov had been killed by Levin and Professor Pletnev. Next came Kuibyshev, killed by Levin and Pletnev; and finally Gorki himself, killed by Levin and Pletnev.

The sixty-eight-year-old Dr Levin gave the first evidence. 'He, together with Yagoda, was the organiser'[127] of the medical killings. Levin's role is the most obscure in the whole story. For if it is unlikely that Yagoda could simply recruit outside doctors in unofficial practice to murder as he wished, the same does *not* apply to a man who had served in the Kremlin since 1920 'on the staff of the medical services of the N.K.V.D.'.[128] Levin had worked for Dzerzhinsky, Menzhinsky and Yagoda, which can certainly be taken as showing him not merely in the *medical*

* He is not listed among the Kremlin doctors in *Pravda* of that date.

confidence of the O.G.P.U.–N.K.V.D.: as he said himself, he enjoyed 'a definite recognition and confidence in me on the part of the head of' the O.G.P.U.[129] He also 'had a feeling that I would perish with Yagoda'.[130] In fact, he may be regarded as to some degree another of Yagoda's N.K.V.D. circle, all of whom were to go to the execution cellars.*

Levin remarks too that he has 'told the truth from the first day I entered prison'.[134] If that is taken at its face value, it is so different from the attitudes of other non-Party accused that it indicates a high state of discipline *vis-à-vis* the N.K.V.D. on the one hand and/or an indication that (again unlike most of the accused) his confessions were more or less factual.

Bukharin, in a brief cross-questioning of Dr Levin, asked if he had not been a counter-revolutionary saboteur in 1918 after the Bolshevik seizure of power, as if this were a generally known fact.[135] This question seems quite irrelevant – and indeed, if anything, damaging to the accused in general – but if we seek a special implication, it must be that Levin had been especially susceptible to becoming an O.G.P.U. agent as a result of his vulnerability to blackmail and threats about his past.

As we have seen (p. 262), there is a report that Levin was in some way involved in Ordzhonikidze's death – he was anyhow one of the signatories of the false death certificate, and is said to have been the only one actually present at the time. But if he was truly implicated in all these sinister actions, it is fair to say that the fact was not widely known. One Soviet diplomat took the view that he was simply a devoted medical man.[136]

Levin gave model evidence on the layout of the alleged crimes. As developed in his and the other testimony it amounted (1) to getting Kazakov, Menzhinsky's pet quack, to kill him by an overdose of his patent method, so that Yagoda could inherit the leadership of the O.G.P.U.; (2) killing Peshkov by having

---

* Apart from the other two doctors actually on trial, it may be noted that two more were implicated – Dr A. I. Vinogradov, of the medical service of the O G P U,[131] proceedings against whom had been 'terminated owing to his death',[132] and the political Khodorovsky, Head of the Kremlin Medical Administration till 1938, who had presumably not yet ripened (and whose death date is now given as 1940).[133]

Gorki's secretary Kryuchkov get him drunk and leave him passed out on a garden bench in the cold (though it was May), and loose Levin, Vinogradov and Pletnev on him when he caught a chill; and (3) arranging bonfires to affect Gorki's weak lungs,* and then taking him to see his granddaughters when they had colds, which he caught, thus also falling into the hands of Levin and Pletnev. Kuibyshev (4) had simply been given bad treatment for his heart, but had finally died for lack of medical attention which, in the circumstances, it might have been thought, he was lucky to avoid.

Levin explained how Yagoda had recruited him in a highly plausible way, which brought a sigh even from the trained audience:

Levin: He said: 'Have in mind that you cannot help obeying me, you cannot get away from me. Once I place confidence in you with regard to this thing, once confidence is placed in you with regard to this matter, you must appreciate it and you must carry this out. You cannot tell anybody about it. Nobody will believe you. They will believe not you, but me. Have no doubts about this but go ahead and do it. You think it over, how you could do it, whose services you could enlist for this. I will call you in a few days.' He reiterated that my refusal to carry this out would spell ruin for me and my family. I figured that I had no other way out, that I had to submit to him. Again, if you look at it retrospectively, if you look back at 1932 from today, when you consider how all-powerful Yagoda appeared to me, a non-Party person, then, of course, it was very difficult to evade his threats, his orders.[138]

Kazakov was called to corroborate Levin's story about Menzhinsky. Unlike Levin and Pletnev, Kazakov was not a doctor of reputation, though evidently honest in his eccentricities. He employed (as Bulanov was to remark) 'very intricate drugs that were not only unknown to medicine, but not very well known to Kazakov himself'.

Menzhinsky had sworn by Kazakov's 'lysates' method. In Dr

Levin: . . . Gorki loved fire, flames, and we made use of this. A bonfire would be lit up for him. Just when Gorki would feel the fatigue after his work all the chopped branches were gathered together, and a flame kindled. Gorki would stand near this bonfire, it was hot there, and all this had a harmful effect on his health.[137]

Levin's evidence, there is a sardonic description of 'much talk of a miraculous medicine' produced by a Professor Schwartzman, who had earlier made a good impression on Menzhinsky, ending in disappointment: 'Then there was another sensation, there was a lot of publicity about Ignaty Nikolaievich Kazakov and he (Menzhinsky) turned to Kazakov. . . . He was one of the small group of important people at that time who were under the impression that they were being helped by him a great deal.'[139] There had even been a special meeting of the Council of People's Commissars to discuss Kazakov's method.*

Kazakov confirmed Levin's evidence, and said he had been taken to see Yagoda personally, submitting out of fear on hearing the remark 'If you make any attempt to disobey me, I shall find quick means of exterminating you.'[140]

Yagoda was now called. He looked very different from his old self. His hair seemed whiter and his former jauntiness had gone.[141] But he still showed a certain bitter energy. His evidence was extraordinary, and must be significant – even though he was to withdraw it later in the day.

Vyshinsky: Accused Yagoda, did you instruct Levin to tell Kazakov that he would be asked to come and have a talk with you?
Yagoda: The first time I saw this man was here.
Vyshinsky: So you gave no such instructions to Levin?
Yagoda: I gave instructions to Levin to talk it over . . .
Vyshinsky: With whom?
Yagoda: With Kazakov, but I did not receive him personally.
Vyshinsky: I am not asking you whether you received him or not; I am asking you whether you instructed Levin to talk it over with Kazakov.
Yagoda: I gave no instructions to talk to Kazakov.
Vyshinsky: You just said here that you gave Levin such instructions.
Yagoda: I gave Levin instructions to bring about the death of Alexei Maximovich Gorki and Kuibyshev, and that's all.
Vyshinsky: And how about Menzhinsky?

*This is one of several examples of Soviet leaders' tendency to swallow ideas rejected by the specialists of the science concerned – as with Marrist linguistics and Lysenkoist biology. The latest medical example was early in the sixties, when a 'cancer cure' (the 'Kachugin method'), rejected by the medical profession, was given enthusiastic encouragement for several years by the Leningrad Party leadership.

Yagoda: I did not bring about the death of either Menzhinsky or Max Peshkov.[142]

Vyshinsky called Kryuchkov, who confirmed his role in killing Peshkov on Yagoda's orders. He then turned on Yagoda again and read from his evidence at the preliminary examination confessing to the Menzhinsky and Peshkov murders:

Vyshinsky: ... Did you depose this, accused Yagoda?
Yagoda: I said that I did, but it is not true.
Vyshinsky: Why did you make this deposition if it is not true?
Yagoda: I don't know why.
Vyshinsky: Be seated.
   'I summoned Kazakov and confirmed my orders. ... He did his work. Menzhinsky died.'
Did you depose this, accused Yagoda?
Yagoda: I did.
Vyshinsky: Hence, you met Kazakov?
Yagoda: No.
Vyshinsky: Why did you make a false deposition?
Yagoda: Permit me not to answer this question.
Vyshinsky: So you deny that you organized the murder of Menzhinsky?
Yagoda: I do.
Vyshinsky: Did you admit it in this deposition?
Yagoda: Yes.
Vyshinsky: When the Prosecutor of the Union interrogated you, what did you answer to this question about your part in the murder of Menzhinsky?
Yagoda: I confirmed it also then.
Vyshinsky: You confirmed it. Why did you confirm it?
Yagoda: Permit me not to answer this question.
Vyshinsky: Then answer my last question: Did you file any protest or complaint with regard to the preliminary investigation?
Yagoda: None.
Vyshinsky: Are you filing any now?
Yagoda: No.[143]

Taking up the Peshkov murder, Vyshinsky went on:

Vyshinsky: So everything that Kryuchkov says ...
Yagoda: It is all lies.
Vyshinsky: You gave him no such instructions regarding Maxim Peshkov?

Yagoda: I have stated, Citizen Prosecutor, that with regard to Maxim Peshkov I gave no instructions. I see no sense in his murder.
Vyshinsky: So Levin is lying?
Yagoda: He is lying.
Vyshinsky: Kazakov is lying?
Yagoda: Yes, lying.
Vyshinsky: Kryuchkov?
Yagoda: Is lying.
Vyshinsky: You gave Kryuchkov no instructions regarding the death of Maxim Peshkov? At the preliminary investigation you . . .
Yagoda: I lied.
Vyshinsky: And now?
Yagoda: I am telling the truth.
Vyshinsky: Why did you lie at the preliminary investigation?
Yagoda: I told you. Permit me not to reply to this question.[144]

This last was spoken 'with such concentrated venom and fury', an American observer notes, that the whole audience gasped with 'dismay and terror'. When Ulrikh intervened, Yagoda turned on him and said (in a phrase not included in the official report): 'You can drive me, but not too far. I'll say what I want to say . . . but . . . do not drive me too far.'[145] Again everyone was shaken. If Stalin was present in the hidden room above the Tribunal, where during this trial a trick of the light at one point made him clearly visible,[146] even he might for a moment have wondered whether his whole plan was not about to be wrecked.

Yagoda, more than any of the others, had reason to resent the trial. He, more than anyone, had performed irreplaceable services to Stalin. His arrest had so affected him that he could not sleep or eat, and Yezhov had feared for his sanity. Slutsky, the insinuating head of the N.K.V.D. Foreign Department, had been sent to talk to him. Yagoda complained about the ruin of the police organization he had built up over fifteen years, and one day remarked that God must after all exist: from Stalin he deserved only gratitude, but from God the fate which had actually overtaken him.[147]

But his present demoniac outburst was left in the air. Vyshinsky turned back to Levin. Levin now developed the Kuibyshev and Gorki murders, and Yagoda confirmed these. Towards the end of the morning, when Levin was going into the detail of Gorki's death, Yagoda suddenly said 'May I put a question to Levin?' Though such cross-examination by defendants had been usual practice in the previous days of the trial, Ulrikh hastily replied, 'After Levin finishes his testimony.' Yagoda, making it clear that his question was immediately relevant, insisted, 'This concerns Maxim Gorki's death!'

Ulrikh, evidently fearing the worst, cut him off, 'When the accused Levin finishes, then by all means.' He shortly ordered a thirty-minute adjournment. After this Vyshinsky said '... I think the accused Yagoda wanted to put questions to the accused Levin.'

The President: Accused Yagoda, you may put questions.
Yagoda: I ask Levin to answer in what year the Kremlin Medical Commission attached him, Levin, to me as my doctor, and to whom else he was attached.[148]

When this question had been answered, with no reference whatever to Gorki's death or to any of the other crimes, Yagoda said he had no more questions. It will be seen that what he had wanted to say before the adjournment cannot have been the same as what he actually asked after.

Levin was then questioned by his 'defending lawyer' Braude. Two points were made. First, Levin said of the 'directing organization' behind the murders, 'I knew nothing about it. I learnt about it only at the trial itself.' He then reiterated what was evidently, in one way or another, a powerful motive for obeying those capable of carrying out such measures: 'What frightened me most was his threat to destroy my family. And my family is a good, working, Soviet family.'[149]

The court had earlier announced an expert commission of five doctors. The morning session of 8 March concluded with the following exchange:

The President: Have the expert witnesses any questions to ask the accused Levin?
Shereshevsky and Vinogradov: * The expert witnesses have no questions to ask; everything is quite clear.[151]

---

*Professors Shereshevsky and (V. N.) Vinogradov were to survive Levin by many years. In 1952–3 they themselves were to go through the same

The evening session of 8 March saw the evidence-in-chief of Bulanov (Yagoda's personal assistant) and of Yagoda himself. Bulanov, a veteran N.K.V.D. officer – he had been in charge of the expulsion of Trotsky from the country in January 1929 – testified to the special version of the planned *coup* involving Yenukidze, Yagoda and the seizure of the Kremlin, and developed its links with the Tukhachevsky group, and with Karakhan's German negotiations. He went on to say that Yagoda had protected Uglanov and Ivan Smirnov in their interrogations and had ordered no search to be made when Zinoviev and Kamenev were arrested. He implicated all the old N.K.V.D. chiefs in the plot, and described how Yagoda had ordered Zaporozhets to 'facilitate' Kirov's assassination, and how Zaporozhets had released Nikolayev on his first attempt, and later killed Borisov. It must have seemed curious that Yagoda, arranging through Zaporozhets to let Nikolayev in to kill Kirov, had not thought to do something similar in Moscow by the agency of Pauker and Volovich, in charge of Stalin's personal security, and both now implicated as plotters.

A new crime was now developed – Yagoda's attempt to kill Yezhov after the latter had taken over the N.K.V.D. in September 1936. Bulanov and another officer, Savolainen (whose case was sent for separate trial), had sprayed a mercury solution six or seven times in Yezhov's office, and on the rugs and curtains, together with some other, unidentified poison.

Results can perhaps be obtained in this way. Mrs Clare Boothe

process. Vinogradov, who was seventy on 3 November 1952, was arrested a few days later, and proved to have been 'an old agent of British Intelligence'. He had, it was announced on 13 January 1953, been one of the murderers of Zhdanov (whose death certificate on 31 August 1948 he had signed). On Stalin's personal order, he was put in chains.[150] Shereshevsky's name was not announced as one of those arrested, but in the larger list of those released when the Doctors' Plot was repudiated by Beria on 4 April 1953, it turned out that he too had been implicated and arrested. This later batch of doctor-poisoners, who survived by the happy chance of Stalin himself dying in the meanwhile, had been treated with particular brutality. It was to them that Stalin's order 'Beat, beat and beat again' was applied by General of State Security M. D. Ryumin, head of the Section for Investigating Specially Important Cases and Assistant Minister of State Security (himself shot in July 1954).

Luce, when American Ambassadress in Rome, was reported to have suffered from poisoning due to the flaking of a toxic paint from the ceiling of her room. It may be that the poison in the office of the People's Commissar, if it existed at all, was of a similar nature. There was no suggestion of foul play in Mrs Luce's case, but the presumption in Yezhov's would be different.

Bulanov went on to describe the special poison laboratory Yagoda had had fixed up under his personal supervision. Yagoda was, Bulanov said, 'exceptionally' interested in poisons. This laboratory is generally believed to have really existed (Yagoda had been a pharmacist by profession before the Revolution). Given the characters and the motivations, this is one crime which might be genuine: Yezhov's health, it was alleged, was 'considerably impaired'.[152] But in Russia the whole story is almost universally regarded as the purest fantasy.

On the medical poisonings Bulanov remarked, plausibly enough, 'As far as I know, Yagoda drew Levin into, enlisted him in the affair, and in cases of poisoning generally, by taking advantage of some compromising material he had against him.'[153]

Bulanov asserted that Kazakov had indeed visited Yagoda, in spite of the latter's denials. Kazakov himself again confirmed this. Vyshinsky then put it once more to Yagoda:

Vyshinsky: After this testimony, which establishes your part in the poisoning, do you continue to deny it?
Yagoda: No, I confirm my part in it.

and then:

Vyshinsky: Accused Bulanov, and was the killing of Maxim Peshkov also Yagoda's work?
Bulanov: Of course.
Vyshinsky: Accused Yagoda, what do you say to that?
Yagoda: I admit my part in the illness of Peshkov. I request the court to hear this whole question *in camera*.[154]

Yagoda is described as having looked cornered and desperate during the earlier session, but he now appeared crushed, and gave his evidence in a toneless voice.

Vyshinsky next tried to implicate Rykov in Gorki's murder, on the grounds that Yenukidze had once allegedly said to him that an end should be put to Gorki's political activity. Rykov answered that doubtless Yenukidze meant murder by this, but that he himself had not so understood it at the time. He then himself put a question to Bulanov, who had spoken about 'Rykov's archives' being looked after by Yagoda: what were the contents? Bulanov said that he did not know, but Rykov had cleverly established that there was an alleged mass of documentary evidence which no one had produced in court.

Yagoda's own evidence-in-chief followed. His voice was now utterly weary and so faint that it could barely be heard. He stumbled through a written statement, 'reading it as though for the first time'.[155] He confirmed his long connexion with the Rightist plotters from 1928 on. In the early days he had supplied Rykov and Bukharin with tendentious material from the N.K.V.D. secret files, for use in their anti-Party struggle. It was due to his activities in the N.K.V.D. that the Rights, and the 'bloc of Rights and Trotskyites', had not been uncovered and liquidated until 1937-8. He had appointed conspirators to all the leading posts in the Secret Police – Molchanov (on Tomsky's express instructions), Prokofiev, Mironov, Shanin, Pauker, Gay, and others. He had joined in Yenukidze's plot to seize the Kremlin, and it was on Yenukidze's orders that he had arranged for Zaporozhets' collaboration in the Kirov assassination.

But when cross-examination started, he still showed a remnant of resistance. Bulanov's evidence about trying to kill Yezhov, he said, had been wrong in detail, and correct only in 'essence'.

Vyshinsky then taxed him with espionage. Yagoda replied, 'No, I do not admit being guilty of this activity.' He admitted shielding spies in the N.K.V.D.:

Vyshinsky: I consider that since you shielded this espionage activity, you helped them, assisted them.
Yagoda: No, I do not admit being guilty of that. Had I been a spy, I assure you that dozens of states would have been compelled to disband their intelligence services.[156]

This sensible remark did not deter the Soviet leaders from the practice of nominating the heads of their Secret Police as imperialist employees. Even at present the official story (originally put out in 1953) is that Beria was a long-service agent of British intelligence.

Rykov again raised the question of his 'archives'. Yagoda said 'I had no archives of Rykov's.' Bulanov then reaffirmed his evidence about these, and when Yagoda challenged him to mention any of their contents, he said he could not. Yagoda finally commented contemptuously, but tellingly, 'In any case, had the archives really existed, in comparison with the other crimes, the Rykov archives are a trifle.'

Later he refused to admit that he had protected Mensheviks:

Vyshinsky: But in any case you shielded this, even very insignificant role of the Mensheviks?
Yagoda: I shall not be able to give you an answer to this question.
Vyshinsky: Allow me to quote to Yagoda his testimony in Vol. II, p. 135: 'Question: You are shown a document from the materials of the People's Commissariat of Internal Affairs, containing a report on the Menshevik centre abroad and on its active work in the U.S.S.R.' Do you recall this fact?
Yagoda: Yes, I know, only I shall not be able to give you an answer to this here.[157]

When it came to the medical murders, he was still not entirely satisfactory. First he admitted his 'part in causing Max's [Peshkov's] sickness', but when Vyshinsky pressed him to plead 'guilty to causing, as you express it, Peshkov's sickness', he simply answered that he would give all his explanations *in camera.* Vyshinsky asked twice more, with the same result. Finally:

Vyshinsky: Do you plead guilty or do you not?
Yagoda: Permit me not to answer this question.[158]

The only distinction between what Yagoda had admitted and Vyshinsky's formulation was that the former spoke simply of 'his part in causing' and the latter of 'guilt for' Peshkov's death. Yagoda seems to be implying either that he had caused the fatal illness in an unintentional way, or, more likely, that he did not accept the major guilt. Whether either version is true is another matter.

Yagoda went on to admit killing Menzhinsky, and of reluctantly becoming involved in the murder of Gorki, at Yenukidze's insistence. When Vyshinsky went through his crimes at the end of the day, asking in turn whether Yagoda was guilty, in the cases of Kirov, Kuibyshev, Menzhinsky and Gorki, he did not refer to Peshkov – a minor victory for the accused.

Levin's defence counsel Braude then cross-examined:

Braude: Allow me to ask you, what methods did you employ to secure Levin's consent to commit these terrorist acts?
Yagoda: In any case not such as he described here.
Braude: You yourself went into detail about this at the preliminary investigation. Do you confirm this part of your testimony?
Yagoda: It is exaggerated, but that doesn't matter.[159]

Vyshinsky now attempted to involve Bukharin in the Gorki murder, Bukharin defended himself effectively. The 'evidence', even at its face value, was simply that Tomsky had once said to him in conversation that the Trotskyites were opposed to Gorki and had some idea of a 'hostile act' against him. A hostile act could be anything from a newspaper article up, and in any case such a conversation, as he pointed out, could not possibly prove that he, Bukharin, had murdered the writer.

Kryuchkov, Gorki's secretary, followed. He had left Peshkov lying in the snow in March or April, without result, and finally managed to leave him out to catch a chill in May: Levin and A. I. Vinogradov had managed to persuade other doctors and nurses to give the patient a fatal laxative. When Gorki in turn had been given a cold, Pletnev and Levin had insisted on overdoses of digitalis.

The most tragic of all the figures in the great trials was examined on the morning of 9 March. Professor Dmitry Pletnev, sixty-six-year-old heart specialist, had long enjoyed a reputation as Russia's leading doctor, the pride of the profession. Now, for the first time (if we except the petty crook Arnold), a figure from outside the whole machinery of state, the whole political controversy, stood for trial – and confessed. He, above all, represented the silent non-Party masses whose sufferings in the Purge were otherwise hidden from sight.

When Yezhov had decided that a confession from Levin alone would clearly not be impressive enough, he had turned his attention to Gorki's other main physician. But Pletnev had been before the Revolution a member of the liberal Constitutional Democratic (Kadet) Party. There was no question of appealing to him on the basis of Communist morality. But equally, he had avoided politics since the Revolution, and no political blackmail against him was possible.

Yezhov's solution was nasty even by Yezhov standards. The decision to go ahead with the story of medical murders must have been taken soon after he succeeded to Yagoda's post. An N.K.V.D. *provocateur*, a young woman usually employed to compromise foreigners, was sent as a patient to Pletnev. After a couple of consultations, she accused him of having assaulted her two years previously.[160] By December 1936 she was coming to his house, annoying his daughter and housekeeper, and he complained to the police.[161]

They affected to take up his complaint, but instead went into hers, and claimed to believe it. Pletnev appealed to his medical and personal connexions to help him. (He was treating Ordzhonikidze:[162] indeed, there is an N.K.V.D. report that he was in Ordzhonikidze's house at the time of the 'suicide'.)[163] As late as 5 March, the official account tells us, he was still expecting that such help would be forthcoming.[164]

But the contrary was true. On 8 June *Pravda*, by a very rare exception to its policy of not dealing with individual crimes, published under the sensational headline 'Professor – Rapist, Sadist', an account in three half-columns. Professor Pletnev had (it told) thrown himself upon the woman patient 'B' on 17 July 1934, and bitten her severely on the breast. This had done her a permanent injury which Pletnev, though no expert in breast disorders, had tried to cure. Not succeeding, and being pestered by the woman, he complained to the police, who took the matter up. On 17 January she had written him a letter, described by *Pravda* as 'a striking human document':

> Be accursed, criminal violator of my body! Be accursed, sadist, practising your foul perversions on my body! Let shame and disgrace fall on you, let terror and sorrow, weeping and anguish be yours as they

have been mine, ever since, criminal professor, you made me the victim
of your sexual corruption and criminal perversions. I curse you.

'B'

A short statement was added, signed by Vyshinsky, to the effect
that the Section for Investigating Important Cases had the matter
in hand.

On the day after the publication of this article, the papers were
full of accounts of meetings of a whole series of medical organizations vilifying him – the Moscow Association of Doctor–
Therapeutists, the Medical Union and others. The following day,
the equivalent organizations from other parts of the country sent
in their protests, from Kiev, Tula, Sverdlovsk and elsewhere,
denouncing the villainous doctor, the disgrace to Soviet medicine.
Among the doctors speaking to, and signing, violent resolutions
attacking Pletnev, one finds the names of Drs M. Vovsi, B. Kogan
and V. Zelenin, who were (like Drs Shereshevsky and V. N.
Vinogradov) to be tortured by the M.G.B. in 1952–3 in the later
Doctors' Plot.

Pletnev was sentenced, in a trial which took place on 17–18
July 1937, to two years' imprisonment. The press said that he had
confessed. And thus, crushed and dishonoured, denounced by his
colleagues, found guilty of a disgraceful offence, he found himself
in the cells of the Lubyanka 'where a still greater misfortune
awaited him'.[165]

Now, under Vyshinsky's questioning, he confessed his role in
the murders of Kuibyshev and Gorki. He spoke of the 'violent
threats [made by Yagoda] against me and against my family'.[166]

He mentioned a connexion with Dr Nikitin, Tolstoy's favourite physician, who had been one of a number of doctors exiled
some years earlier. But he said[167] that he did not believe Nikitin
to be politically-minded – an honourable rebuttal of what was
presumably a false charge against a distinguished colleague.

His defence lawyer Kommodov elicited his splendid medical
record. Then Vyshinsky re-examined on that, raising the assault
case. Pletnev made an attempt to reject the charge, but he was
borne down by Vyshinsky, now in one of his most arrogant and
bullying moods:

Vyshinsky: How many years did you say was your standing as a physician?
Pletnev: Forty.
Vyshinsky: You consider your standing as irreproachable?
Pletnev: Yes, I do.
Vyshinsky: Irreproachable?
Pletnev: Yes, I think so.
Vyshinsky: During these forty years you have never committed any crime in connection with your profession?
Pletnev: You are aware of one.
Vyshinsky: I am asking you because you state that your work for forty years was irreproachable.
Pletnev: Yes, but since I denied that time . . .
Vyshinsky: Do you think that the sentence in the case which is well known to you, the case of an outrage which you committed against a woman patient, is a blot on your reputation?
Pletnev: The sentence, yes . . .
Vyshinsky: Is that sentence a blot on your reputation or not?
Pletnev: It is.
Vyshinsky: So there were moments of disgrace during these forty years?
Pletnev: Yes.
Vyshinsky: Did you not plead guilty to anything?
Pletnev: I cannot say that I did not plead guilty to anything.
Vyshinsky: So you did plead guilty to something?
Pletnev: Yes.
Vyshinsky: Is this a blot on your reputation?
Pletnev: Yes.[168]

Kazakov, the remaining doctor, confirmed his part in Menzhinsky's death. But at the end of his evidence he defended his method and asserted that 'lysates' could after all not have harmed Menzhinsky.

Vyshinsky: For what purpose did you introduce these lysates? To kill Menzhinsky?
Kazakov: (No reply.)
Vyshinsky: Did you introduce the lysates for this end? Were you certain that they would assist your crimes?
Kazakov: You see, lysates have a dual effect.
Vyshinsky: You dare to assert that these lysates were harmless for Menzhinsky?
Kazakov: Yes. These three lysates were harmless.

Vyshinsky: And could you have fooled Yagoda?

Kazakov: (No reply.)

Vyshinsky: In view of the impossibility of getting a direct answer to this clear question, I request the court to adjourn the session and to make it possible for the Commission of Experts to answer the questions I have put to Kazakov.[169]

After a half-hour adjournment, the Commission of Experts supported Vyshinsky's view of the matter:

Such a combination of methods of treatment could not but lead to the exhaustion of the heart muscles of the patient V. R. Menzhinsky, and thereby to the acceleration of his death.

Moscow,   Expert Witnesses:
9 March 1938.[170]   Professor D. A. Burmin, Scientist of Merit
          Professor N. A. Shereshevsky, Scientist of Merit
          Professor V. N. Vinogradov
          Professor D. M. Rossisky
          V. D. Zipalov, Doctor of Medicine

Vyshinsky then read out admissions made by Kazakov at the preliminary investigation. Under these pressures, Kazakov finally confirmed his guilt in the matter. Vyshinsky was then finally able to say:

Inasmuch as we have a definite finding from the Commission of Experts, and Kazakov has repudiated his statement about the neutrality of these lysates, I think that the question can be considered closed.[171]

The last accused, Maximov-Dikovksy, was then examined. He admitted being placed in Kuibyshev's secretariat by Yenukidze, and explained how he had helped the medical killers to dispose of Kuibyshev.

Vyshinsky then produced a medical 'witness', Dr Belostotsky, who had been present in Gorki's last illness and now testified against Pletnev and Levin. The final report of the Expert Commission, confirming all the medical accusations and the attempt on Yezhov's health, was then presented.

It will be seen that the evidence in the case of these medical murders is confused and incomplete. We can be sure that those on trial were innocent of all the charges of treason, conspiracy, espionage and sabotage. We can be virtually certain, on the other hand, that Yagoda's responsibility for the murder of Kirov was correctly established – with the minor amendment that his instructions were received not from Yenukidze but from Stalin. But with the murky tale of the deaths of Menzhinsky, Peshkov, Kuibyshev and Gorki we are on different ground.

There are two problems: were they murdered? And if so, were they murdered by the doctors, or by one or any of them?

The first point to establish is that reliance on the binding force of the Hippocratic Oath will not take us far. Either the five doctors (Levin, Pletnev, Kazakov, A. I. Vinogradov and Khodorovsky) were guilty as charged; or the five doctors on the Expert Commission, and the witness Dr Belostotsky, were, in their capacity as doctors, accomplices in judicial murder.

A similar pattern was to be repeated in 1952–3. In the later Doctors' Plot, either the doctors, or some of them, procured the murder of Zhdanov (and in this atmosphere the fact of their rehabilitation by a political group not wishing the matter to go further by no means disproves this possibility), or Dr Timashuk – their denouncer – was actively willing to have her colleagues submitted to torture and death, and the new Commission of Medical Experts who certified that the doctors were guilty – and were afterwards censured for having done so – were accomplices in an action which would ordinarily have led to the liquidation of their colleagues. In neither case can the doctors be blamed as can the true instigators. On the contrary, the degradation of a humane profession under political terror makes the story even more revolting.

Drs A. I. Vinogradov and Khodorovsky, dead in unknown circumstances in the hands of the Secret Police, Professor Pletnev, dying disgraced and exhausted in some penal camp, and Drs Levin and Kazakov, shot to death in the cellars of the Lubyanka, most probably did not commit all or any of the crimes they were charged with. Even if one or other of them did so, it was clearly under extreme and intolerable pressures, backed by all the power of the State. In any case, they may seem to us to have been, in a way, martyrs – the unknown, confused and pathetic martyrdom suffered by ordinary people caught up more or less accidentally in manoeuvres of power by leaders to whom human life and standards of truth counted for nothing.

One thing is clear. If the medical murders took place as alleged, they took place on Stalin's orders. Levin, for example, working in the Kremlin and treating Stalin and his family, could have appealed to him personally as soon as Yagoda made his approaches – *unless* he knew that Stalin was behind it all. When it was alleged[172] that Levin would not take on the task merely on his, Yagoda's, orders, and had to be given direct instructions by Yenukidze, the depths of fatuousness were reached. Yenukidze was then a far less powerful and impressive figure than Yagoda. There was one single man in the U.S.S.R. more powerful than Yagoda, and giving him orders. The story (if true at all) is simply another example of the use of the code-word 'Yenukidze' to mean 'Stalin', as in Yagoda's similar account of the Kirov murder.

The argument that no murders in fact took place is a simple one. Stalin needed a few more assassinations to lay at the door of the oppositionists, and could only produce them by representing natural deaths as murders. This is a perfectly sound point as far as it goes. But it is an entirely negative one, and does not enable us to pronounce one way or the other, meaning no more than '*if* the deaths were natural, Stalin might have produced an identical story'.

The (equally general) argument on the other side is equally strong: that Kuibyshev and Gorki were obstacles to Stalin, and we all know what Stalin did to obstacles. Nor is it in the least out of character to suppose that he and Yagoda would have been prepared to use the method of medical murder, if available.

We must turn, rather, to the details. In the first place, there is Yagoda's evidence of the morning of 8 March, when he pleaded guilty to the murders of Kuibyshev and Gorki, and not guilty to those of Peshkov and Menzhinsky.

On the whole, Yagoda's initial evidence seems to have been true, or as true as was possible in the circumstances, on most other matters. His account of the Kirov murder seems quite authentic, except on the point of who instructed him to carry it out, and even that is hinted at in his remarks that 'it was not quite like that', when describing the relevant meetings: for this can best be taken as implying that someone's name has been left out or wrongly reported. Again, he pleaded not guilty to the charge of espionage, and there is no doubt that this was the truth. So when we come to his anomalous pleas on the four medical murders, there is at least some ground for paying attention to what he is saying.

On the Menzhinsky case we have the added detail of Kazakov's last-minute retraction of the whole essence of his evidence. This seems decisive. Menzhinsky was almost certainly not murdered by his doctors. (He may of course have been killed in some other fashion.)

On Peshkov, on the face of it the whole idea of his murder seems almost pointless. Yagoda justly remarked, 'I see no sense in his murder'. That Peshkova was Yagoda's mistress really adds little to his motive. He did not propose to marry her: he was married already and made no attempt to murder or divorce his wife over the following three years. Moreover, the murder method (reflected in the death of the loyal old sheep in *Animal Farm*) is a trifle unconvincing.

With Kuibyshev and Gorki on the other hand – that is, precisely the two killings Yagoda freely admitted to – we have cases in which Stalin had definite and pressing political motives for murder.

This does not prove that he killed them. In Kuibyshev's case all we can say is that he is now named as one of Stalin's three main opponents of the purge in the Politburo, and that Stalin procured the death of both the others (Kirov and Ordzhonikidze) by devious, though differing means – the latter by a faked heart attack. So Kuibyshev's 'heart attack' is not by any means to be accepted simply at face value. Moreover, his survival through 1935 might have constituted a severe obstacle to Stalin's plans, and he died at precisely the time Stalin was turning against the other main opponents of the killing of Zinoviev and Kamenev.

But as against that, we have no positive evidence of murder. We can, indeed, exculpate the doctors. In his case their alleged guilt is of gradually undermining his health and leaving him without medical supervision, to go to work as usual. As a murder method, it is perhaps implausibly oblique and uncertain. It seems probable that *if* Kuibyshev was murdered, it was not done by the doctors.

Gorki's death is the most interesting and important. For here we have a case where the survival of a sick man even for a few months might have gravely hampered Stalin's plans for the August 1936 Trial, whose postponement till after the holidays could have led to effective resistance in the Politburo and Central Committee. But how could Gorki be silenced, apart from the international scandal of arrest? As Vyshinsky put it, though with different intent, in his concluding speech:

How in our country, in the conditions that exist in the Soviet State, could it be made impossible for Gorki to display political activity except by taking his life?[173]

But again, it seems most unlikely that Pletnev was guilty. His general reputation speaks strongly against it. The methods by which the N.K.V.D. put pressure on him in 1936–7 powerfully imply that they were seeking to crush and compromise an innocent man. And, in this case at least, it seems unlikely that Levin could have given the sort of wrong treatment mentioned without Pletnev's knowledge and consent, so he too seems not responsible. Even such credulous observers as Walter Duranty strongly doubted the guilt of the doctors.

The probable alternative is perhaps that Gorki was indeed murdered, but not by Pletnev and Levin.

The Social Democratic journalist Brigitte Gerland, who was in one of the Vorkuta camps from 1948 to 1953, has described her acquaintance there with Dr Pletnev, then in his eighties, who was acting as camp doctor.[174] She says that his twenty-five-year sentence had been reduced to ten years, but that he had none the less not been released. Pletnev told her that Gorki had, physically speaking, made a good recovery from his heart condition, though he was in moral torment, wishing to leave Russia and return to Italy. His death took place in the crudest possible circumstances. A box of evidently poisoned sweetmeats had been given him, and he and two male nurses to whom he offered some all died quickly. An immediate autopsy showed that they had indeed been poisoned. The doctors kept silence (and a point to be made in favour of this account is that it would presumably be easier to persuade non-Party doctors – in the interests of the dead man, or of the country – to sign a fake death certificate than to make them commit murder).

Miss Gerland comments on the extraordinary crudity of this murder method, asking whether the N.K.V.D. did not have doctors capable of carrying out a subtler, 'medical' murder. She answers that the N.K.V.D. methods were indeed crude.

She adds that Pletnev died as late as the summer of 1953, just before her own release.

There is no way as yet of checking this story.* But as to its credibility, we can indeed note that Stalin's method of dealing with Ordzhonikidze did not take the reactions of the doctors signing his death certificate into account in any way, and cases of straightforward cyanide poisoning, with a heart attack certified, are noted within the N.K.V.D. – for example, that of Slutsky. And Yagoda was a poison man rather than a medical expert.

But of course, a story may be credible without being true. And we can do no more than give this account, adding that if true it tends to exculpate all the doctors, and hence casts a doubt on their having played a part in the other 'medical' murders. We may also note that recent Soviet articles on Kuibyshev, for example, do not state how he died.[175]

However, much more cogent testimony has appeared, in Gorki's case at least. In the summer of 1963 an old American acquaintance of Gorki visited his eighty-six-year-old widow, Ekaterina Peshkova, in Moscow. Of her son's death she said quite calmly that she had no doubt that it was natural. When the visitor remarked that people now said that Gorki's too had been natural, she became very agitated and exclaimed:

It's not quite so, but don't ask me to tell you about it! I won't be able to sleep a wink for three days and nights if I tell you.[176]

*Though we may note that Miss Gerland similarly obtained in camp what proved to be entirely accurate information about the then still secret 'Leningrad Affair'.

This seems reasonably conclusive. Meanwhile, Drs Pletnev and Levin have been referred to in favourable contexts.[177] The most probable assumption, then, is that Stalin did procure the murder of Gorki, through Yagoda, but not by means of the doctors. That is, he employed, if not the method reported by Miss Gerland, then something of that nature. That the Soviet authorities have not said anything of the Gorki case parallels their notable reluctance to give the full story even of the more political, and so perhaps less disgraceful, Kirov murder.

A final point arises. Mme Peshkova's evident conviction that Peshkov's death was natural and Gorki's not fits in with Yagoda's initial testimony in court. As with his evidence on the Kirov case, we seem to be driven to the ironic conclusion that, alone among the accused, the story told by the ex-Police Chief was essentially true! And if this is so, his confession to the Kuibyshev murder, alone among the other three, is best explicable as indicating that Kuibyshev, too, was really murdered. But this is a matter of deduction rather than evidence: we cannot at present at all exclude the possibility that in this one case the timely death of a man Stalin wanted out of the way was after all natural. Nor does it seem very probable that more will be forthcoming even when the Soviet archives are opened up. For it is rather unlikely that plans for this style of killing are committed to paper.

And there we must leave this murky and horrible episode.

When the doctors and their organizers and accomplices had been dealt with, the Expert Commission made its report, confirming their guilt, and for full measure establishing the damage to Yezhov's health, as evidenced in his urine. Apart from a short session *in camera* at which Yagoda (it was announced) 'fully admitted organizing the murder of Comrade M. A. Peshkov', the hearing was concluded. But before adjournment, Vyshinsky recalled Rosengolts for one petty smear.

He described the good-luck token found in Rosengolts's pocket (see p. 363), and asked the court's permission to read it. In a sneering tone, amid the titters of the audience, he read out eight verses of the Psalms – 'Let God arise, let his enemies be scattered . . .' – then asked Rosengolts 'How did this get into your pocket?'

Rosengolts: My wife put it in my pocket one day before I went to work. She said it was for good luck.

Vyshinsky continued on a humorous note, 'And you carried this "good luck" in your hip pocket for several months?'

Rosengolts: I did not even pay attention . . .
Vyshinsky: Nevertheless, you saw what your wife was doing?
Rosengolts: I was in a hurry.
Vyshinsky: But you were told that this was a family talisman for good luck?[178]

At this he winked at the crowd, who roared with laughter,[179] and the hearings were at an end.

THE LAST ACT

The court reassembled on 11 March for the final speeches and pleas. Vyshinsky's speech for the prosecution lasted all morning. He started with a violent harangue:

It is not for the first time that the Supreme Court of our country is examining a case involving the gravest crimes directed against the well-being of our country, against our Socialist fatherland, the fatherland of the working people of the whole world. But I will hardly be mistaken if I say that this is the first time that our court has had to examine a case like this, to examine a case of such crimes and such foul deeds as those that have passed at this trial before your eyes, before the eyes of the whole world, a case of such criminals as those you now see in the prisoners' dock.

With every day and hour that passed, as the court investigation on the present case proceeded, it brought to light even more of the horrors of the chain of shameful, unparalleled, monstrous crimes committed by the accused, the entire abominable chain of heinous deeds before which the base deeds of the most inveterate, vile, unbridled and despicable criminals fade and grow dim.[180]

He then came to the whole crux, from the point of view of Stalinist logic:

... The historical significance of this trial consists before all in the fact that at this trial it has been shown, proved and established with exceptional scrupulousness and exactitude that the Rights, Trotskyites, Mensheviks, Socialist-Revolutionaries, bourgeois nationalists, and so on and so forth, are nothing other than a gang of murderers, spies, diversionists and wreckers, without any principles or ideals ...

The Trotskyites and Bukharinites, that is to say, the 'bloc of Rights and Trotskyites', the leading lights of which are now in the prisoners' dock, is not a political party, a political tendency, but a band of felonious criminals, and not simply felonious criminals, but of criminals who have sold themselves to enemy intelligence services, criminals whom even ordinary felons treat as the basest, the lowest, the most contemptible, the most depraved of the depraved.[181]

Interrupting his argument with remarks about 'a foul-smelling heap of human garbage',[182] he traced the continuity of counter-revolution back to the Shakhty and Industrial Party Trials.

Attacking the entire past careers of Bukharin and the others, he rehearsed their current crimes. Of Zelensky, for example, he said:

I shall refer here to the most abominable practice of mixing glass and nails with foodstuffs, butter in particular, which hit at the most vital interests, the health and lives of our population. Glass and nails in butter! This is so monstrous a crime that, in my opinion, all other crimes of the kind pale before it.

He went on to explain:

In our country, rich in resources of all kinds, there could not have been and cannot be a situation in which a shortage of any product should exist ...

It is now clear why there are interruptions of supplies here and there, why, with our riches and abundance of products, there is a shortage first of one thing, then of another. It is these traitors who are responsible for it.[183]

A method of explaining economic failure which any Government might envy.

He attacked the line taken by Bukharin – 'that damnable cross of a fox and a swine' – and Rykov:

The former wanted to prove here that, actually speaking, he did not favour the defeat of the U.S.S.R., that he did not favour espionage, nor wrecking, nor diversive activities, because in general he was not supposed to have any connection with these practical matters, for he was the 'theoretician', a man who occupied himself with the problematics of universal questions.[184]

He was particularly incensed with the refusal of Bukharin and Rykov to accept responsibility for the Kirov murder:

Why did people who had organized espionage, who had organized insurrectionary movements and terrorist acts, and who, on their own admission, had received instructions from Trotsky on terrorism, suddenly, in 1934, stand aloof from the assassination of one of the greatest comrades-in-arms of Stalin, one of the most prominent leaders of the Party and the Government? . . .

Bukharin and Rykov have admitted that the assassination of leaders of the Party and the Government, of members of the Political Bureau, was part of their plans. . . . Why should we assume that, having entered into negotiations with Semyonov for the organization of the assassination of members of the Political Bureau, Bukharin deletes from this list of persons who are to be slain one of the most influential members of the Political Bureau who had distinguished himself by his irreconcilable fight against the Trotskyites, Zinovievites and Bukharinites? Where is the logic in such behaviour? There is no logic in it . . .

Finally Rykov admitted that in 1934 he instructed Artemenko to keep a watch on the automobiles of members of the Government. For what purpose? For terrorist purposes. Rykov was organizing the assassination of members of our Government, of members of the Political Bureau. Why should Rykov make an exception in the case of Sergei Mironovich Kirov, who nevertheless was assassinated on the decision of this accursed bloc? He made no such exception![185]

In the medical murders too he pointed out that Bukharin admitted everything but actual knowledge or responsibility. Dismissing 'an opinion current among criminologists that in order to establish complicity it is necessary to establish common agreement and an intent on the part of each of the criminals, of the accomplices, for each of the crimes',[186] he demanded the death penalty for all except Rakovsky and Bessonov.

He concluded that the others

must be shot like dirty dogs! Our people are demanding one thing: crush the accursed reptile! Time will pass. The graves of the hateful traitors will grow over with weeds and thistles. . . . Over the road cleared of the last scum and filth of the past, we, our people, with our beloved leader and teacher, the great Stalin, at our head will march as before onwards and onwards, towards Communism![187]

In the evening, the doctors' defence lawyers made their pleas, putting the blame on Yagoda.

Then came the last pleas of the accused. Bessonov remarked that he had loyally returned to Moscow from abroad even when under suspicion. Most of the others simply accused themselves, Bukharin and Rykov. Ivanov put in the remark, a sinister foreshadowing of future cases:

> The reason, I think, why Bukharin has not told the whole truth here is because throughout the whole period of the revolution he has fought the revolution and to this day has remained its enemy, and because he wants to preserve those remnants of the hostile forces which are still lurking in their dens.[188]

Krestinsky went into his splendid record in the Party, starting as an eighteen-year-old boy in 1901, his leadership in Bolshevik underground organizations, his many arrests, his work as Lenin's 'organizational assistant'. He made the telling point:

> I consider it necessary to stress the fact that I had absolutely no knowledge of the terrorist acts enumerated in the second section of the indictment, and that I learnt about them only when I was handed a copy of the indictment.[189]

and went on to explain his retraction as due in part to the fact that

> ... It seemed to me easier to die than to give the world the idea that I was even a remote accessory to the murder of Gorki, about which I actually knew nothing.[190]

Rykov, trembling and livid, made a sound defence. He admitted his general guilt, then added:

> ... But the State Prosecutor has charged me with something in which I had no direct part, and which I cannot admit. He has charged me with adopting a decision, or with giving directions for the murder of Kirov, Kuibyshev, Menzhinsky, Gorki and Peshkov. ...
> The evidence brought against me in this connection has been set forth here in detail; it is based upon the statements of Yagoda, who

refers to Yenukidze. Nothing more incriminating was brought against me at the trial . . .

The assassination of Kirov has formed the subject of two trials. Both the direct perpetrators and the organizers and leaders of this assassination have appeared in court. I do not recall that my name was mentioned then.[191]

He went on to rub in one extremely telling point. When it came to the alleged attempt on Lenin of twenty years previously, the prosecution had produced eyewitnesses, there were confrontations, and in fact direct evidence.

Why then, on the question of my participation in the assassination of five most important political figures, should a decision be taken on the basis of indirect evidence?

This, it seems to me, would be incorrect. At any rate, I deny any charge of my participation in these five assassinations.[192]

Until his arrest he had believed that Gorki had died a natural death. It was only at the trial itself that he had 'first learnt of such members of our counter-revolutionary organization as Ivanov'.[193]

He concluded with a formal plea of guilty – 'This responsibility of mine of course transcends all the discrepancies which still remain regarding certain facts and certain details' – and called on any surviving Rightists to 'disarm'.[194]

Rakovsky said: 'I confess to all my crimes. What would it matter for the substance of the case if I should attempt to establish here before you the fact that I learned of many of the crimes, and of the most appalling crimes of the "bloc of Rights and Trotskyites" here in court, and that it was here that I first met some of the participants?'[195] He went on to denounce Trotsky and Trotskyism, and to point out that his evidence had been entirely satisfactory to the prosecution.

Rosengolts rehearsed his revolutionary past, starting when, as a child of ten, he had hidden illegal literature. He ended his plea with a reference to his children.*

* It is a curious fact that Stalin was later (in his Report to the 1939 XVIIIth Congress) twice to name Rosengolts first among the 1938 conspirators – once in a general list of spies etc, running 'Trotsky, Zinoviev, Kamenev, Yakir, Tukhachevsky, Rosengolts, Bukharin', and then on the 1938 Trial alone,

Yagoda, too, 'in low fear-ridden tones',[196] dwelt on his underground work for the Party, from the age of fourteen, and of such later services as 'vast construction jobs – the canals' – that is, the forced-labour projects. He continued to oppose Vyshinsky on one point:

I am not a spy and have not been one. I think that in the definition of a spy or espionage we will not differ. But a fact is a fact. I had no direct connexions with abroad, there are no instances of my directly handing over any information. I am not jesting when I say that if I had been a spy dozens of countries could have closed down their intelligence services – there would have been no need for them to maintain such a mass of spies as have now been caught in the Soviet Union.[197]

The doctors and secretaries pleaded Yagoda's threats to them. Levin lapsed by referring to his great esteem for Gorki, and had to be called to order for 'blasphemy'. Pletnev mentioned his medical work, adding that the N.K.V.D. had given him facilities to write a monograph; he had known nothing of the 'bloc'. Bulanov criticized his fellow-accused:

I think, perhaps I am mistaken, that some of them showed signs of wanting to deceive the Party even now, although each of them invariably began by saying that he fully and entirely shares responsibility, pleads guilty and is answerable. But this was a matter of form, general declarations. In a number of cases they tried to deny their guilt by pleading ignorance of some point.[198]

Bukharin's speech, even more than Rykov's, was a brilliant development of the line he had taken throughout. He admitted leadership of the 'bloc of Rights and Trotskyites', and accepted political responsibility for all the crimes. For instance:

I admit that I am responsible both politically and legally for the defeatist orientation, for it did dominate in the 'bloc of Rights and Trotskyites', although I affirm that personally I did not hold this position . . .
I further consider myself responsible both politically and legally for wrecking activities, although I personally do not remember having

'Rosengolts, Rykov, Bukharin and others'. This seems to reflect some special animus on the part of the dictator, and fits in with the special jab at Rosengolts on the 'talisman', doubtless ordered from above.

given directions about wrecking activities. I did not talk about this. I once spoke positively on this subject to Grinko. Even in my testimony I mentioned that I had once told Radek that I considered this method of struggle as not very expedient. Yet Citizen the State Prosecutor makes me out to be a leader of the wrecking activities.[199]

As Bukharin destroyed the prosecution case against him, 'Vyshinsky, powerless to intervene, sat uneasily in his place, looking embarrassed and yawning ostentatiously'.[200]

While accepting group responsibility, Bukharin went on to deny that the group, as apart from the central 'bloc' of politicians existed:

Citizen the Prosecutor explained in the speech for the prosecution that the members of a gang of brigands might commit robberies in different places, but that they would nevertheless be responsible for each other. That is true, but in order to be a gang the members of the gang of brigands must know each other and be in more or less close contact with each other. Yet I first learnt the name of Sharangovich from the indictment, and I first saw him here in court. It was here that I first learnt about the existence of Maximov, I have never been acquainted with Pletnev, I have never been acquainted with Kazakov, I have never spoken about counter-revolutionary matters with Rosengolts, I have never spoken about it to Zelensky, I have never in my life spoken to Bulanov, and so on. Incidentally, even the Prosecutor did not ask me a single question about these people. . . . Consequently, the accused in this dock are not a group.[201]

The bloc had supposedly been formed in 1928, long before Hitler:

How then can it be asserted that the bloc was organized on the instructions of fascist intelligence services?

On espionage he took the same line:

Citizen the Prosecutor asserts that I was one of the major organizers of espionage, on a par with Rykov. What are the proofs? The testimony of Sharangovich, of whose existence I had not even heard until I read the indictment.[202]

The prosecution had proved that he had met Khodzhayev and discussed politics, and taken this as proof of espionage contact. There was no logic here.

He went on similarly to 'categorically deny my complicity in the assassination of Kirov, Menzhinsky, Kuibyshev, Gorki and Maxim Peshkov',[203] and in the 1918 case with Lenin:

> As to the plan of physical extermination, I categorically deny it, and here the logic to which Citizen the State Prosecutor referred, namely, that forcible arrest implied physical extermination, will not help in the least. The Constituent Assembly was arrested, but nobody suffered physically. We arrested the faction of the 'Left' Socialist-Revolutionaries, yet not a single man of them suffered physically. The 'Left' Socialist-Revolutionaries arrested Dzerzhinsky, yet he did not suffer physically.[204]

He then remarked tellingly, 'The confession of the accused is a medieval principle of jurisprudence.'[205]

Vyshinsky flushed at the words.

Thus Bukharin refuted the charges in detail. But he admitted them in general. He had been a counter-revolutionary conspirator in 'this stinking underground life'. He had 'degenerated' into an enemy of Socialism. He attacked Western commentators who had suggested that the confessions were not voluntary, and rejected the sympathy to be expected from Western Socialists. He was guilty of treason, the organization of *kulak* uprisings, the preparation of (unspecified) terrorist acts. He hoped that his execution would be 'the last severe lesson' to those who had wavered in their support of the U.S.S.R. and its leadership.[206]

At 9.25 p.m. on 12 March the court retired. It returned and pronounced verdict at 4 a.m. on 13 March. All the accused were found guilty on all charges. All were sentenced to death except for Pletnev, who got twenty-five years, Rakovsky, twenty years, and Bessonov, fifteen years.*

An old Bolshevik remarked that, apart from the use of relatives

---

*There is one slight oddity about the carrying-out of the sentences. We are told that Grinko perished on 15 March 1938.[207] That is, the usual immediate execution was not carried out, in his case at least, though Ikramov's death date is given as 13 March.[208] A rumour that Levin's sentence was commuted cannot be substantiated. It is based on the fact that a Dr Loevenstein, doing ten years as a 'Gorkyist', was met in the Yertsevo camp in 1940–41.[209] There were many 'Gorkyists', and the name is neither correct nor adequately disguised. (There was in fact a Kremlin doctor called Levinson.[210])

as hostages, he saw the 1938 confessions as based on total lack of political hope. In addition, in spite of everything, Stalin is said to have continued his promise not to execute the Bukharinites. They knew he had gone back on his word in most other cases, but 'a little hope goes a long way in such circumstances'.

Bukharin, nevertheless, must have known that his own attitude in court, fulfilling the minimum requirements only, would cost him his life. He had said in court that he was 'almost certain' he would be dead after the trial. He and Rykov, unlike Zinoviev and Kamenev, were ready for death. They are said to have died firmly defying their captors.[211]

In 1965 a 'last letter' of Bukharin's which had supposedly just been leaked to the West was published.[212] This was at a time when there was talk of an official rehabilitation of Bukharin and Rykov. And in fact they had at least been exculpated of spying and terrorism, though only at a fairly obscure conference of historians.[213] And Ikramov, Krestinsky, Zelensky, Khodzhayev, and Grinko have actually been rehabilitated, making nonsense of the charges against the rest. However, full rehabilitation of the two principals has not come.

(The 'last letter' appeals to future leaders of the Party, denounces the N.K.V.D. and its use of the 'pathological suspiciousness' of Stalin. This 'hellish machine' can transform any Party member into a 'terrorist' or 'spy'. He was not guilty, would cheerfully have died for Lenin, loved Kirov, and had done nothing against Stalin. He had had no connexion with Ryutin or Uglanov's illegal struggle. This 'letter' has yet to be authenticated. A careful student[214] who has examined the original has assured me that the Russian is far removed in literary style from the clear and scholarly writings of Bukharin, even allowing for the circumstances.)

The promises not to kill the wives seem to have been kept. Bukharin's widow was still alive recently. Yagoda's wife and sister are reported in camps, and Ivanov's wife too,[215] and the wives of Rakovsky and Ossinsky in the Butyrka.[216] Rykov's wife was also in the Butyrka, in 1937, anxious and ignorant of her husband's fate.[217] (Even Uglanov's wife is reported sent from Yaroslavl isolator to Vladivostok transit camp in the summer of

1939.[218]) During 1938 at least Rykov's daughter, Bukharin's father and Rosengolts's wife are said not even to have been arrested.[219]

During the whole period of the trial, from the announcement on 28 February that it would take place till the actual executions, the papers had, of course, been full of the demands of workers' meetings that no pity be shown to the 'foul band of murderers and spies'. Leaders and articles rubbed it in. A Conference on, Physiological Problems at the Academy of Sciences passed a resolution of thanks to the N.K.V.D. The folk 'poet' Dzhambul produced his regular verse contribution to *Pravda*, 'Annihilate'. The verdict of the court was received with many expressions of public joy.

Life, which had cast the Bukharin reactionaries aside, was represented mainly by the heroes of the Soviet Arctic expedition who had been landed at the Pole some months earlier, and were now in the news. First there was celebration of their rescue from the ice-floe and then, on 16 March, of their arrival back in Leningrad on the ice-breakers *Yermak* and *Murmanets*. Papanin and his gallant comrades were, as before, given the full treatment day after day, with receptions, decorations, public meetings and a vast press spread.

A further sign of the rejection by the forward-looking Soviet people of all the dark forces of the past was shown in the elections to Union Republic Supreme Soviets. As Stalin was to remark so tellingly in his Report to the XVIIIth Congress in 1939,[220] the executions of Tukhachevsky and Yakir were followed by the elections to the Supreme Soviet of the U.S.S.R., giving the Soviet power of 98·6 per cent of all taking part in the voting. At the beginning of 1938 'Rosengolts, Rykov, Bukharin and others' had been sentenced, and after this, elections to the Supreme Soviets of the Union Republics gave the Soviet power 99·4 per cent of all taking part in the voting.

As for the effects of the trial, once again neither the ineptitudes of the plot nor the partial denials of the accused made any difference. The extravagances included those long since established. Once more a vast network of assassins was discovered. At least eight groups were working on the destruction of Stalin,

Molotov, Kaganovich, Voroshilov and Yezhov. And, this time, they were shown to be not simply under the protection of high officials in the Party and Army, but actually to have been nourished and sponsored by the N.K.V.D. itself. Seldom can terrorists have had such advantages as those supposedly enjoyed by their plotters. Apart from half a dozen members of the Government, including the head of the Secret Police itself, they actually had on their side the N.K.V.D. officers Pauker and Volovich, responsible for guarding their prospective victims. But the results had been negligible. Assassinations had indeed been carried out, but only by doctors. By adding these in, the total successes of all the groups of assassins exposed at the three trials consisted of Kirov killed, Molotov perhaps slightly shaken in a car accident, Kuibyshev, Gorki and Menzhinsky 'poisoned' by their doctors, and Gorki's son given a chill and then doctored to death. It is an unimpressive result, and the conclusion – that the best way to assassinate anyone was to wait until he got ill – was not very encouraging to anyone desiring speedy action. A minor curiosity, again unnoticed by enthusiasts, is that the Indictment cites against the accused diversionary acts in the Far Eastern Territory, and in particular certain specified train wrecks, on the instructions of Japanese intelligence, and the Verdict finds them guilty of this, but no attempt at all is made to prove it in the evidence! The reason for this anomaly is not clear, though it might conceivably be that the relevant witness balked at the last moment.

Another oddity of the trial was again the implication of a whole series of important figures who were, however, not produced. As Grinko had remarked, the 'bloc' included 'a number of other people who are not now in the dock'.[221] Major roles in the conspiracy, as important as any of those appearing in court, were alleged to have been played by Yenukidze, Rudzu-tak[222] and Antipov,[223] while A. P. Smirnov, Karakhan, Uglanov, V. Shmidt and Yakovlev[224] had roles notably more important than the second level of those appearing in the dock.* Yenukidze

---

*Other members of the Central Committee implicated include Vareikis, Lyubimov, Lobov, Sulimov, Kabakov, Razumov, Rumyantsev and Komarov.

and Karakhan had indeed been shot without public trial. But why? And as to the others, why did they not appear? Such questions were scarcely asked.

On an even more essential point, Bukharin's calculation that his tactics would adequately expose the falsity of the charge against him seems to have been too subtle. It was, of course, plain that he denied all overt acts of terrorism and espionage. But who was affected by this? Serious independent observers in any case did not credit the charges, and would not have done so even if he *had* confessed to all of them – any more than they did in the case of Zinoviev. But, to the greater political audience for whom the trials were enacted, the impression received was simply that 'Bukharin had confessed'. For those who even noted that the confession had only been partial, the fact that he had admitted to organizing a terrorist conspiracy outweighed his rejection of actual terrorist acts. Indeed, this last even gave a certain colour to Vyshinsky's thesis that Bukharin, though driven to admit the essentials, was trying to wriggle out of particular crimes.

Stalin had once again won the battle of wits. For he understood, as the intellectual Bukharin did not, that political effects did not depend on simple logic; just as, in the twenties, his opponents 'won' the arguments at Congresses in the debating-point sense, without affecting his practical victory.

CHAPTER TWELVE

THE FOREIGN ELEMENT

The N.K.V.D. organs ... could extend the category of
'enemy of the people' to everyone who dared to utter a
word of criticism.   WLADISLAW GOMULKA

IN THE COMINTERN

THE Purge also operated abroad, and against foreigners in the
U.S.S.R. The most obviously purgeable of these latter were the
foreign Communists in the apparatus of the Comintern. It was
more particularly the Communist Parties which were illegal in
their own countries that bore the brunt. First of all, their leaderships were mainly ready to hand in Moscow. Then again, there
was no democratic opinion back in Germany, or Yugoslavia, or
Italy, or Poland, which could raise objections. There were no
victims, even in Moscow, among British or American Communists, who were thus not called upon to run the risks, either at
home or in Russia, which the rest of the Comintern Parties had
to face. Their protection derived from the nature of the regimes
they were working to overthrow.

Lenin, in creating the Comintern, skimmed off a lively section
of the European revolutionary Left, which might have otherwise
fertilized a broad and unified movement, and barred the way to
Fascism. They became instead a set of parties founded strictly
on the Bolshevik model, and constitutionally subordinated to the
Comintern – which always remained under effective Soviet control. After a while these parties' leaderships were selected and
their tactics dictated by Moscow – almost invariably with
disastrous results.

The last flicker of independence in the Comintern took place in
May 1927. In the presence of Stalin, Rykov, Bukharin, and
Manuilsky, the Executive Committee of the Comintern was asked
by Thälmann to condemn a document of Trotsky's on the Chinese
question. All present were prepared to do so, when the Italian
delegation – Togliatti and Silone – said that they had not seen the

document. It turned out that no one else had either. The Italians objected that though Trotsky was doubtless wrong, they could hardly be expected to subscribe to a formal condemnation of something they had not seen. It was explained to them that the Soviet Politburo thought it inexpedient to circulate it. The session was adjourned so that the old Bulgarian Communist Kolarov could go over the question with the recalcitrant Italians in private. He told them quite frankly that it was not a question of getting at the truth, but of the struggle for power. The Comintern must go along with the Soviet Politburo majority, and that was all there was to it. The Italians still persisted in their attitude, and Stalin typically withdrew the motion.[1] This appeal to independent judgement was, however, the last.

Silone left the Party. Togliatti must have decided that his choice was of submitting to Stalin and hoping to exert some influence, or going under; he chose the former course, and persisted in it, as an accomplice in many a far grosser breach of confidence, in later years.

Henceforward, the Comintern – after the removal, at that time peaceable, of various supporters of Trotsky and Bukharin – became merely another element in Stalin's political machine. As early as 1930 a member of the Yugoslav Politburo observed that apart from men of 'limited intelligence' like Pyatnitsky and Remmele, the Comintern leaders appeared to him to be 'men at one time remarkable, but now demoralized or exhausted'.[2]

The Comintern and its organs were by the nature of their work particularly liable to the charge of contact with foreign countries. The Communist Party of the Western Ukraine, which had been kept organizationally separate from the Communist Party of Poland, was already being purged as a nest of spies in the late twenties.[3] In 1936 a purge took place in the Communist Party of Latvia in which numbers of the Party's leadership then in Moscow were repressed 'for treachery and treason'. This amounted to 'in effect the dissolution' of the Party.[4] The Latvian Party had been little more than a branch of the C.P.S.U. – in earlier times even officially so – and on the other hand many Latvians, like Rudzutak, were prominent in Russia, and their origin was perhaps used against them. The Estonian Communist Party, too, was denounced as 'compromised'. So few Estonian Communists survived that on the Soviet annexation of their country in 1940 one of the highest posts went to a man of Estonian origin who had hitherto been an assistant station-master in the North Caucasus.[5] The entire Lithuanian Central Committee was also arrested, and charged with working for the Lithuanian government.[6] In any case, all this was a mere preliminary. In 1937 the storm broke over the main body of foreign Communists.

In the dingy corridors of the Hotel Lux the Comintern officials led a rather bohemian existence. Full of foreigners with nowhere else to go, the hotel became something like a frontier village raided nightly by bandits. Occasionally there was trouble. One Polish Communist shot down several N.K.V.D. men before he was overcome.[7]

On 28 April 1937 Heinz Neumann, former member of the German CP's Politburo, was arrested. After being one of the leading foreigners in the Canton Commune, with his friend Lominadze, he had been removed from the leadership of the German Communist Party early in the thirties, but had been working for the Party in Moscow since 1935.

Neumann's 'dark, petite, vivacious and gay'[8] wife describes his arrest. At one o'clock in the morning three uniformed G.P.U. officials and the manager of the Lux, Gurevich – himself certainly an agent – came in and roused Neumann. Forbidding the couple to speak in German, they made a long search, lasting till dawn, of his documents, taking a trunkful and sixty books of allegedly oppositionist content. When Neumann was finally taken out, he said to his wife 'Don't cry.'

'That's enough. Get a move on, now,' ordered the leader. At the door, Heinz turned and strode back, took me in his arms again and kissed me. 'Cry then,' he said. 'There's enough to cry about.'[9]

In December 1937 Neumann was removed from the Lubyanka, and he was evidently sentenced about then, since the order confiscating his goods was handed to his wife in January 1938.[10] He seems to have been transferred to the Butyrka in the summer of 1938 and still not to have signed any confession.[11] His wife had by then been sentenced to five years as a socially dangerous element.

Three other members of the German Politburo disappeared at about the same time – Hermann Remmele, Fritz Shulte and Hermann Schubert – the last arrested in July.[12] Schubert was denounced by an Austrian woman Communist for having mentioned Lenin's 1917 deal with the Germans in connexion with Trotsky's alleged relations with the Nazis. Togliatti then managed the attack on him.[13] Other prominent German victims included Hans Kippenberger, head of the Party's military apparatus, Leo Flieg, the organizational secretary of its Central Committee, Heinrich Susskind and Werner Hirsch, editors-in-chief of *Rote Fahne*, together with four of their assistant editors. (Hirsch seems to have been saved from a Nazi prison and allowed to go to the U.S.S.R. by the intervention of Goering's wife, who knew his family.)[14] Remmele is reported as going mad in camp, and always coming to blows with both guards and fellow-prisoners.[15]

The veteran Hugo Eberlein had been the only genuine delegate at the conference at which the Comintern was founded. The 'delegates' allegedly representing foreign countries were mostly just foreigners in the Soviet service: for example, Unshlikht represented Poland. Eberlein had instructions from Rosa Luxemburg to oppose the formation of the new International and did so firmly (though abstaining in the final vote).

His arrest was now reported in a Swiss paper and he gave a press conference denying it, only to be arrested next day. He is reported as being brutally interrogated while he was suffering from asthmatic attacks in the Lefortovo prison, and to have been sentenced to twenty-five years, dying in 1944.[16]

For lesser figures any excuse served, as with Soviet citizens. One German Communist was arrested for saying that the only Nazi with principles was Goebbels. This was construed as 'counter-revolutionary agitation'.[17] Another was accused of 'counter-revolutionary agitation against the Soviet State' on the grounds (in any case false) of having belonged to the opposition within the *German* Communist Party from 1931 to 1932.[18] A Soviet writer reports a German Communist in the Butyrka in 1937 with body scars from the Gestapo and crushed fingernails from the N.K.V.D.[19]

Several of the arrested were Jews. This did not save them from charges of fascist espionage, any more than it had Yakir. An interrogator is quoted as saying 'The Jewish refugees are Hitler's agents abroad'.[20] The German occupation of Czechoslovakia resulted in Czechs too being regarded as German agents. One Czech is reported as having had to confess that he became a German agent early in the First World War, at a time when neither Czechoslovakia nor the Soviet Union existed.[21]

Willi Münzenberg, the German Communist Party's propaganda genius, was summoned to Moscow to share the fate of Flieg, who had been arrested as he stepped off the train on arrival from Paris. (Flieg is evidently the leading German Communist who was brought in, in precisely these circumstances, to Ivanov-Razumnik's cell in the Butyrka, in his neat Western suit – horrified to learn from those present that he was, of course a Nazi spy.)[22] Münzenberg refused to go and was expelled from the Party in 1938. He was in France and was interned at the outbreak of war in the following year. When the refugee camps were opened by the French in view of the Nazi advance in 1940, Münzenberg struck for the Swiss border with another inmate. A few days later his body was found in a forest near Grenoble, hanging from a tree. His face was battered, and reports make it clear that suicide is unlikely.[23]

After the Nazi–Soviet Pact, in 1939, about 570 German Communists were assembled in the Moscow prisons.[24] A number of them were sentenced by the Russians, but the majority were told that they had been judged by a Special Commission of the N.K.V.D. and expelled as undesirable aliens. These German Communists, who included Jews and men especially wanted by the Nazis for armed resistance to them during the street fights of the early thirties, were hustled over the bridge to German-occupied Poland at Brest-Litovsk, while N.K.V.D. men checked the lists with Gestapo men. They included the widow of Erik Mühsam the poet, and the composer Hans David, a Jew eventually gassed by the Gestapo in the Maidanek concentration camp.* The actress Carola Neher, who was originally on the list, disappeared in Russia instead.[27]

The son of Ernst Torgler, the main German defendant at the Leipzig Trial, who had been Communist leader in the Reichstag, was then aged about thirteen. He appeared at protest meetings in the West and eventually went to Russia. There he got a long sentence as a German spy. He was reported at a camp in the Komi area in the far north, where he had the job of disposing of bodies. He had by this time become completely assimilated into the young criminal element. After the Nazi–Soviet Pact, he too was handed over to the Gestapo with the other German Communists.[28]

The Hungarian losses were also heavy. They included Béla Kun, leader of the 1919 Communist revolution in Hungary, himself. His conduct of the Terror in Budapest preceded even worse actions when, on fleeing to Moscow, he was put in charge of the newly conquered Crimea, and was censured and withdrawn by Lenin for his excessive cruelties. He then operated in the Comintern, and had been partly responsible for the Communist fiasco in Germany in 1921. He has been described as 'the incarnation of intellectual inadequacy, uncertainty of will, and authoritarian corruption'.[29]

A meeting of the Executive Committee of the Comintern in May 1937 saw his fall. Manuilsky made a speech violently denouncing him for insulting behaviour to Stalin and contacts with Romanian Secret Police since 1919. The other members of the E.C.C.I. looked on in silence.† Kun, who was quite unprepared for the attack, went white. He 'roared like a mortally wounded

---

*There were cases, the other way round, of people who had been in Nazi camps and came to Russia on release. A woman who had done three years in a Nazi concentration camp got eight years as a Trotskyite on arrival in Russia owing to acquaintance with a German Communist who had fallen under suspicion. Her husband had 'repudiated' her, but still contrived to send her occasional parcels.[25] Another case is quoted of a Viennese Jew, who had withstood nearly a year in Dachau, but committed suicide in a Soviet camp.[26]

†Among them were Wilhelm Pieck (later to precede Ulbricht in the leadership of East Germany), Kuusinen, Togliatti, Gottwald and Wang Ming.

lion: "This is a terrible provocation, a conspiracy to get me murdered. But I swear that I have not wanted to insult Comrade Stalin. I want to explain everything to Comrade Stalin himself." ' But everything had been set up in advance. As Kun, pale and shocked, left the room in a dead silence, two N.K.V.D. men escorted him out.[30] But he was not arrested immediately. A few days later Stalin telephoned and 'gaily asked Kun to receive a French reporter and refute a rumour of Kun's arrest'. This he did; the denial was published; and he was arrested a few days later – 30 or 31 May.[31] He had had several members of his own Politburo arrested earlier.[32]

Béla Kun was taken to the Lefortovo, where he was tortured. He is reported as having been kept standing on one foot for periods of from ten to twenty hours. When he returned to his cell after interrogation his legs were swollen and his face so black as to be unrecognizable.[33] He was in the same cell as Muklevich.[34] He was then held in the Butyrka until his execution for espionage.[35] This took place on the 30 November 1939. It seems clear that the formalities were complied with, for he is now described as having been 'sentenced on the basis of a faked indictment'.[36] Kun's frail wife Irina was arrested on 23 February 1938,[37] and got eight years, going first to Kolyma,[38] but survived and was eventually released. His son-in-law, the Hungarian poet Hidas, was also sent to a labour camp.[39]

Of the other leaders of the Hungarian Revolution of 1919, twelve more People's Commissars of the then Communist Government in Budapest were arrested. These included the Grand Old Man of Hungarian Communism Dezsö Bokányi, and Jozsef Pogány, known under the name of John Pepper as the Comintern's representative to the American Communist Party. Of the twelve, two survived imprisonment. Theorists like Lajos Magyar also perished.

Many Italian Communists died – such as Edmondo Peluso, who had been with Neumann in the Canton Commune. He got a letter out of prison begging friends for help, and saying that his strength was failing through torture, but that they should believe his innocence. Because this was suspected to be a police trap, there was no response. The few who were later released found that their stories of prison were not believed. Togliatti's brother-in-law Paoli Robotti was arrested in 1937. They broke his teeth and incurably injured his spine,[40] but he was eventually released and was later, in 1961, to say that he had kept silent about all this because it was not the business of Italian, but of Soviet, Communists to speak.[41]

Few had Robotti's luck. Most of the actual leadership were protected by Togliatti's docility in the face of Stalin's line. But about 200 Italian Communists perished. Evgenia Ginzburg mentions an Italian woman Communist screaming in the punishment cells of Yaroslavl on being beaten and hosed down with icy water.[42]

Gorkić, the General Secretary of the Yugoslav Communist Party, was arrested in Moscow in the summer of 1937. His Polish wife had already been seized as a British agent. Almost the whole of the Yugoslav Central Committee followed him, together with a large number of the remaining Yugoslav Communists: of these, more than a hundred 'found their death in Stalin's prisons and camps'.[43] They included such men as Vlada Copić, the Party's Organizational Secretary, newly back from command in the International Brigade in Spain. Tito came to Moscow at this time and lived on the fourth floor of the Lux. He later said that he never knew whether he would get out alive or awake in the night 'to hear the fatal knocking at my door'.[44] He noticed that there was a tendency in the Comintern to dissolve the entire Yugoslav Party – as was being done with the Polish and Korean parties. Finally, he was allowed to form a new Central Committee. As soon as he could, he transferred it to Yugoslavia and Western Europe, where it had some chance of survival.

The then First Secretary of the Finnish Communist Party, Avo Tuominen, gives a long list of Finnish leaders shot, and says that 'nearly all Finns then living in the Soviet Union were labelled "enemies of the people" '. These Finnish Communists were involved through a confession obtained from Otto Vilen, 'gained by Stalinist beating methods'.[45]

The tiny Romanian Party lost two of its most prominent

members, Marcel Pauker (not to be confused with the N.K.V.D. officer),* and Alexandru Dobrogeanu, who seems to have been shot in 1937. Pauker himself is said to have been accused of collusion with Zinoviev and shot without trial.[47] But in general it was the early connexion of the Romanians with Rakovsky which proved fatal. Little reference seems to have been made to this micro-purge until, at the trial in Bucharest in 1952 of the Polit-buro member Vasile Luca, an attack was made on 'the treason-able clique of Marcel Pauker'.† Bulgarian Communists were also much persecuted. Dimitrov's fellow defendants at the Leipzig Trial, Tanev and Popov, were jailed:[48] Popov survived and was rehabilitated in 1955. Chervenkov, later to be the Stalinist ruler of Bulgaria, hid out in Dimitrov's flat till interceded for. There were many other victims. One Bulgarian is mentioned in a Vologda camp being thrown into a hole in the ground without food for thirteen days, and dying.[49]

And so it was with all the émigré groups. But the heaviest casualties fell on the Poles. The Polish Communist Party was very much a special case in its relations with Moscow. It derived in the main from the Social Democratic Party of the Kingdom of Poland and Lithuania‡ – admitted on a basis of autonomy, to-gether with the Jewish Bund and the Lettish Social Democrats, into the IVth Congress of the Russian Social Democrats in 1906, when the Mensheviks and Bolsheviks were still technically united. A. S. Warski and Dzerzhinsky were then elected members of the joint Central Committee as its representatives.

The Poles on the whole backed the Bolsheviks, though with reservations. Their leader Rosa Luxemburg had written privately that the Bolsheviks' support would be valuable in spite of their 'Tartar-Mongolian savagery'. Although Lenin was soon involved

*Pauker is said to have been denounced by his wife, Anna Pauker.[46]

†The Luca Trial gives a curious example of nature imitating art – in this case, the career of Snowball in *Animal Farm*. Luca, who had hitherto featured as having played an heroic role in the Hungarian Revolution of 1919, was now exposed as having actually commanded a machine-gun unit on the other side.

‡This is not the place to go into the complex origins of Polish Commun-ism, in the two factions of the old Polish Social Democratic Party and the left wing of the Polish Socialist Party.

in organizing faction in the Polish Party, and in a series of polemics with Rosa Luxemburg and others, the quarrels were domestic in a sense which was not true of the relations with other foreign organizations. There was much coming and going between the Parties, then and later. When Poland became an independent State, Poles who had worked with the Bolsheviks and remained on Soviet soil became members of the Russian Communist Party pure and simple. We have only to think of names like Dzerzhinsky, Radek, Menzhinsky and Unshlikht (as with the parallel Lettish cases of Eikhe, Rudzutak, etc). A Pole could be transferred between the new Communist Party of Poland and the Russian Communist Party at will. Marchlewski, named head of the Polish 'Government' established behind the Red Army lines during the 1920 invasion of Poland, became, after the débâcle, a Soviet diplomat. As a natural corollary, the Polish Party, in so far as its organizations within Soviet territory were concerned, was involved in the Purge in much the same way as the Soviet Party proper – Warski was, after all, practically an 'Old Bolshevik' in almost the same sense as Rykov or Kamenev.

The Poles in Russia were to some degree comparable with the Irish in England; there were many of them, and they often played important roles in the life of the larger country. The Purge affected not only the Polish Party members, but the Polish population as a whole. The total Polish population is shown as 792,000 in the U.S.S.R. census of 1926. The 1939 census (not indeed reliable in certain respects) shows 626,000. Figures of their actual losses in the Purge are hard to come by. According to one Polish Communist, about 10,000 Poles from Moscow alone were shot at the time of the Bukharin Trial, with a total of 50,000 in the country as a whole.

Arrests of Polish Communists had taken place sporadically all through the thirties. Now the Party as a whole was caught up in an unprecedented campaign of almost literal annihilation, both organizationally and physically. The survivors in the whole of the Polish Communist movement and its following are said to have been about seventy or eighty in number. A Polish leader remarks, 'Almost all the leaders and active members of the K.P.P. then in the Soviet Union were arrested and sent to camps.'[50] It is certainly true that when a Polish Communist Government had to be formed in 1944, the leaders were scraped up from all over the place. The few who had the luck to remain in Polish jails, like Gomulka, had superimposed on them men like President Bierut, formerly (under the name Rutkowski) an N.K.V.D. interrogator, and as economic chief Minc, who had been a lecturer in an institute in Central Asia.

On 20–21 August 1937 Warski, Budzynski and others were shot.[51] Warski is said to have gone mad under interrogation and to have imagined that he was in the hands of the Gestapo. A number of Polish Communist leaders then in Poland were invited to Moscow for 'consultation'. They included Ring and Henrykowski, both members of the Polish Politburo. The latter saw what was going on, and for weeks never ventured out of his room at the Lux except on nocturnal shopping for supplies. All eventually disappeared.[52] From 1937 to 1939 all twelve members of the Central Committee present in Russia, and several hundred others, were executed. Among those who perished were all the Party's representatives on the Executive Committee and the Control Commission of the Comintern, including the veteran Walecki.

Before his arrest Walecki provided an example of the way old revolutionaries had become humiliated and degraded. Walecki, who had always given friendly greetings to Neumann's wife, met her in the Lux soon after Neumann's arrest. 'I smiled and nodded,' she remembers, 'but he looked away deliberately and there was an embarrassed, rather guilty expression on his face.'[53]

Usually Stalin, after purging a Party, could make use of the struggles over power and policy invariably prevalent to select a new leadership. But in this case 'both factions' in the Polish Communist Party in 1937 were accused of 'following the instructions of the Polish counter-revolutionary intelligence'.[54] It seems to have issued its last official statement on 8 June 1938 and to have been dissolved shortly afterwards. 'Agents of Polish fascism' had 'managed to gain positions of leadership' in it, according to the report of the Comintern delegate to the Soviet XVIIIth Party Congress, Manuilsky. (Manuilsky, making this report, referred also to police agents in the Hungarian and Yugoslav parties.)

The final batch of leaders, like Kostrzewa, were shot in 1939, when accounts were being settled with the whole Comintern apparatus. The Left-wing poets Stande and Wandurski and other literary men perished: the most important was Bruno Jasienski, who was arrested on 31 July 1937, sentenced to fifteen years on 17 September 1938, and died of typhus in the Vladivostok transit camp.[55] * His former wife, Cara, got ten years, as a spy.[56]

The total dissolution of the Polish Communist Party was an extraordinary measure. It reflected simply the physical destruction of its cadres. It probably suffered little more than the Ukrainian Party. But Stalin could not, indeed, simply dissolve the Ukrainian Party, since he needed someone to rule in Kiev. He did not, at the moment, have any immediate need of a group for ruling Poland and doubtless reflected that – as it turned out in practice – he could scrape one up from somewhere when and if required. The Polish Party, moreover, was one in which hostility to the forthcoming Nazi–Soviet Pact, with its partition of Poland, was likely to be strong.

The wives of the arrested foreigners suffered like those of the Russian victims. But they had no relations to turn to. They remained entirely at the mercy of official caprice. First, they were involved in a continual struggle with the manager of the Lux, who soon managed to transfer them from their rooms to a separate, older building on the other side of the courtyard, crowded in with other wives. From here too they were eventually evicted.

Their papers were not in order, and they had to queue up regularly every five days to renew them. It was impossible to get jobs. They could live only by selling their possessions and books.

It was common to try and keep the children from knowing what had happened to their fathers. Mrs Neumann quotes a conversation:

'Is your daddy arrested too?'

'No, my daddy's on holiday in the Caucasus.'

* Jasienski's fate illustrates the difficulty now met with in tracing even quite important figures. The Polish Communists have investigated the matter as closely as was in their power. But even now their two leading reference books give different dates for his death, while an official Soviet source gives yet a third. (Moreover, one Polish authority appears to be wrong on the date of arrest.) Fellow-inmates now in the West tend to confirm the Soviet dates.

And then the eleven-year-old daughter of one of the arrested comrades destroyed the child's illusion.

'Oh, he's in the Caucasus, is he? Why does your mother pay money into the prison, then? A fine Caucasus that is!'[57]

But sooner or later the wives were themselves arrested. On a single night in September 1937 all the Polish wives were taken. One that can be traced got eight years forced labour,[58] and this seems to have been the usual sentence.

The Soviet representatives in the Comintern machinery were also destroyed, being blamed for collusion in the penetration of the enemy into the constituent parties. The exception was Manuilsky himself, who acted as Stalin's agent throughout. Described as a third-rate mind, he was willing to be the Comintern equivalent of a Mekhlis or a Shkiryatov and thus survived.

In his report on Comintern matters to the XVIIIth Congress, after dealing with the Polish case, he significantly added: 'It was the failure of Comintern workers that they allowed themselves to be deceived ... and were late in taking measures against the contamination of the Communist Parties by enemy elements.'

This referred primarily to two other members of the Central Committee of the C.P.S.U. – Pyatnitsky and Knorin. Pyatnitsky was, apart from Manuilsky, the chief Soviet operator in the Comintern. He had served on its Executive Committee since 1923, and ran the key Organization Department.[59] He 'ended his life in prison'[60] on 30 October 1939.[61] He is said to have been executed in connexion with the Béla Kun case.

V. G. Knorin, another Soviet representative on the Comintern Executive Committee, controlled the German and other parties. A Latvian, he is described as an honest man, but a dogmatist.[62] He seems to have been denounced for permitting nationalist deviations as early as 1936. He was arrested in June 1937[63] as a Gestapo agent and is said to have been tortured particularly badly. He too was executed in 1939.[64]

Their subordinates fell with them. One of the 'lists' Stalin signed for execution consisted of 300 Comintern operatives.[65] The Head of the Foreign Communications Department, Mirov-Abramov, was arrested with all his staff in 1937. It is said that he was accused of espionage for no less than fifteen different countries.[66] Alikhanov, Head of the Cadre Department, was also arrested in the summer of 1937.[67] And, in general, a clean sweep was made of the organization, while at the top a handful of acquiescent figures like Kuusinen, Dimitrov and Togliatti remained.

KILLERS ABROAD

It was comparatively easy to deal with the foreigners in Moscow. The operation of the Purge in foreign countries called for more secret techniques.

In December 1936, Yezhov organized in the N.K.V.D. an 'Administration of Special Tasks'. Under it were the so-called 'mobile groups' charged with special assassinations outside Russia.[68]

There was one problem in particular which he faced. He could not so easily dispose of the old N.K.V.D. cadres operating abroad under the Foreign Department as he could those in the internal departments. They could refuse to come and be arrested. He coped with this by two methods. First of all, when he arrested the other heads of departments in the Lubyanka, he left Slutsky to carry on in the best of odours. The Foreign Department, it became known, was not to be submitted to the purge needed for its more corrupt confrères.

Numbers of operatives, impressed by this idea, returned to Russia, where they were mostly 'transferred' and executed. The fate of some of them became known. For example, in the summer of 1937 the N.K.V.D. Resident in France, Nikolai Smirnov, was recalled to Moscow and executed. At first Yezhov pretended that he had simply been transferred to an underground job in China. But the true story leaked out to the N.K.V.D. station in France because the wife of another officer had chanced to see the arrest of Smirnov, when she was about to call on him at the Hotel Moskva. Yezhov then put out the story that Smirnov had been a spy for France and Poland. The N.K.V.D. officers in France deduced that this was untrue from the simple fact that their cypher for communication with Moscow was not changed. If Smirnov had indeed been a French spy, it must then be assumed that he had betrayed the cypher. Similarly, the old network of informers he had built up continued to operate contrary to the laws of espionage.[69]

This sort of thing encouraged defection. Yezhov therefore strengthened his appeal for loyalty by another method. The mobile groups had as one of their first priorities the making of an example of any colleague who broke with Stalin.

Ignace Reiss, an N.K.V.D. Resident in Switzerland, broke with the regime in July 1937. His body was found on the road near Lausanne riddled with bullets. The Swiss police also found in the abandoned baggage of the friend of Reiss's who had betrayed him a box of poisoned chocolates, apparently intended for his children.[70]

Agabekov, former O.G.P.U. Resident in Turkey, had broken with the regime as early as 1929. He was murdered in Belgium in 1938.[71] Walter Krivitsky, whose book is a useful source for this period, had been N.K.V.D. Resident in Holland. On 10 February 1941 he was found shot in a hotel room in Washington.

When the situation among the spies abroad had been largely cleared up, it became possible finally to dispense with Slutsky. But in order to avoid troubling the agents still in the field, this was done tactfully. His death on 17 February 1938 was announced in a short friendly obituary next day.

In fact, he appears to have been poisoned by Frinovsky, by then Deputy Head of the N.K.V.D., in his office. Slutsky's deputy, Shpigelglas, was suddenly called in and told that Slutsky had had a heart attack. Slutsky lay in state in the main hall of the N.K.V.D. club, with a guard of honour. But many N.K.V.D. officers had some smattering of forensic medicine and at once noticed on his cheeks the spots indicating cyanide poisoning.[72]

IN SPAIN

Slutsky had recently given important service in Spain, which by now had become a major theatre of operation for the Purge – not only at the level of Yezhov's mobile groups, which roamed the country arresting and killing deviationists on the international scale like Camillo Bernini. For there were also larger political issues – the suppression of Spanish 'Trotskyism' and the gaining of effective control of the Spanish Government.

As early as December 1936, the Soviet press was speaking of the necessity for the elimination of P.O.U.M., the heretical Marxist Party of Catalonia,[73] equivalent of the British I.L.P. – that is to say, revolutionary Socialists opposed to Communist methods. It was not in any real sense 'Trotskyite' (and the few genuine Spanish Trotskyites did not belong to it). While its 29th Division was fighting against Franco on the Aragon front, the Russians were able to secure its suppression.

Jesús Hernández, one of the two Communists in the Spanish Republican Government, tells us how he was summoned by the Soviet Ambassador Rosenberg and introduced to Slutsky, then going under the pseudonym Marcos. Slutsky said that the suppression of P.O.U.M. was an urgent matter. Not only was it openly criticizing the Soviet Union, and in particular the Zinoviev and Pyatakov Trials, but it was attempting to bring Trotsky to Spain.

(There seems to be nothing in this latter allegation, but if the Russians believed it, Stalin might well have had qualms. In a civil war or revolution, it could have been argued, Trotsky's name was 'worth 40,000 bayonets'. In fact, such an idea was chimerical, and even to Spaniards not basically hostile to Trotsky the disadvantages of his presence must have outweighed the advantages.)

Rosenberg remarked that he had often told the Spanish Prime Minister Caballero that the liquidation of P.O.U.M. interested Stalin personally, but that Caballero would not listen to this. Slutsky made it clear that an alternative method was to be found – a provocation mounted by the N.K.V.D. which would allow the seizure of actual power in Barcelona by the Communists, and give them the excuse to get rid of Caballero if he attempted to undo the *fait accompli*.

The operation was prepared by Antonov-Ovseenko, then Soviet Consul-General in Barcelona, and Ernö Gerö, later to be overthrown in the leadership of the Hungarian Communist Party by the revolution of 1956, and at that time senior Comintern operative in Spain.

On the 3 May 1937, the subservient Spanish Communist whom they had intruded into the leadership of the Catalan police, Rodriguez Sala, seized the Barcelona telephone exchange from the anarcho-syndicalist C.N.T. trade unionists who had controlled it since the beginning of the war. The Left-wing organizations, including P.O.U.M., resisted, and after four days' fighting, which is said to have caused about a thousand deaths, they were put down by specially prepared police troops brought in from Valencia and elsewhere. On 15 May, the Communist Ministers in the Spanish Cabinet asked for the formal suppression of P.O.U.M. But even so Largo Caballero again refused.

Stalin's orders to get rid of Caballero and to put in Dr Negrin as Premier were now transmitted to the Spanish Politburo at a meeting with the Comintern representatives, including Togliatti and Gerö.[74]

Immediately after the formation of the Negrin Government, the new Director-General of Security, the Communist Colonel Ortega, told Hernández that Orlov, the N.K.V.D. chief for Spain, had had him sign a number of warrants for the arrest of P.O.U.M. leaders, without his superior, the Minister of the Interior, being informed. Orlov himself told Hernández that the leaders of P.O.U.M. would be 'exposed' as in collusion with a group of Franco spies already under arrest.

Hernández recounts that the majority of the Spanish Communist leadership, though acting loyally in accordance with the Comintern directives, was disgusted with the whole affair. The Secretary-General, José Díaz (who was later to jump or be pushed from his window in Moscow), spoke of 'this spiritual death' which had come over him. Togliatti and Dolores Ibarruri ('La Pasionaria' – a Communist who was never to be afflicted with qualms of conscience) had sent the Assault Guards' Commander in Catalonia an order to arrest the P.O.U.M. leadership.

On 16 June, Andrés Nin, Political Secretary of P.O.U.M., former Secretary of the Red Trade Union International in Moscow, who had held the portfolio of Justice in the Catalan autonomous Government, was arrested. He was taken to Alcalà, to a prison in Communist hands. There he was seized by a group of men including Orlov and Vittorio Vidali (an old Comintern agent later to be involved in the murder of Trotsky, and after the war to lead the anti-Titoite Communists in Trieste). He was removed to El Pardo and there submitted to a Soviet-style investigation. First he was interrogated for thirty hours in relays, without success, then tortured. 'At the end of a few days, his face was no more than a formless mass.'[75] However, no confession could be obtained from him and he seems either to have been killed or to have died under interrogation. El Campesino was told that he was buried on the spot.[76]

An interesting point about this particular crime is that most of those involved have been publicly named, and almost all of them – with the exception of Togliatti – are still alive. In fact, many of them (as Gorkin points out) were loyal adherents of the anti-Stalin line during its period of ascendancy.

The formation in France of a Committee for the Defence of P.O.U.M. and, even more, a strong but simple letter demanding merely a fair deal and treatment of the P.O.U.M. accused, signed by Gide, Mauriac, Duhamel, Roger Martin du Gard and others, seems to have had an effect in Spain and even on Negrin. In the case of the senior P.O.U.M. *leaders* still surviving, the Government was able to insist on no further 'disappearances', though the rank and file were shot freely. Julián Gorkin, representative of the P.O.U.M. on the Central Committee of the People's Militia, was one of those who survived.

Hernández takes the view that an important motive of Stalin's was to show that not only in Russia but also in a 'democratic' country governed by the Popular Front, Trotskyites had been proved traitors. Thus it was not simply the pursuing of the feud and the destruction of all Trotskyite bases, but also the obtaining of an ostensibly non-Soviet confirmation of the existence of a Trotskyite plot.

Meanwhile, the vulnerable units of the International Brigade were being combed for Trotskyites. For example, Walter Ulbricht was conducting among the German Brigaders the Spanish end of the purge which was sweeping the German Communists in Moscow. (The seconded Red Army commander 'Kleber', commanding the International Brigade, was removed in February 1937 and soon afterwards arrested.) The Soviet soldiers in Spain, who must have resented the N.K.V.D. actions, were often shot on return, as we have seen.

Ironically, as Stalin carried out his will as regards purges, and control over the political machinery in Spain, he had lost interest in the outcome of the actual war. Ehrenburg tells us that though the Soviet authorities expressed great indignation at Fascist and Nazi intervention in Spain, as soon as it became evident that the Republicans were fighting a losing battle this interest became a mere formality. Ehrenburg's own dispatches, sometimes sent with considerable risk, were cut, altered, or simply thrown into the waste-paper basket.[77]

Many Spaniards who managed to escape the final débâcle made their way to Moscow – 150 in a single boat.[78] Arriving there from May 1939 on, they found themselves facing a different danger.

This wave of political refugees of the Left had been preceded by others. After the defeat of the Socialist rising in Vienna in 1934, several hundred members of the Socialist defence organization 'Schutzbund' took refuge in Russia. They were welcomed as heroes, and marched past in a body in the Red Square to applause and congratulations. By mid 1937 they had been arrested and sent to camps 'almost without exception'.[79] Some of their dependants, with children to feed and no source of income (having been fired from their jobs), went in 1938 to the German Embassy, now controlled by the Nazis, in an attempt to get back to their homes. The Nazis put them up in the Embassy building and escorted them to the Soviet Registration Office for Foreigners to get permission to go back. Apparently, some succeeded.

The Austrians were, in the main, non-Communists. While, like them, the Spanish Republican rank and file was gradually deported to Central Asia and elsewhere, the leadership of the Spanish Communist Party became involved in the more political Purge that had long been sweeping the Comintern apparatus, and the foreign Parties based in Moscow. Soon General Gonzales ('El Campesino'), after a long wrangle with a Comintern commission, was digging in the Moscow Metro, preparatory to being sent to a northern labour camp; and the General Secretary of the Spanish Communist Party, Díaz, had died in dubious circumstances. They were known casualties among dozens lesser known.

THE TROTSKY MURDER

Abroad, one major piece of unfinished business remained. Rakovsky had remarked in his last plea that 'Even beyond the Mexican meridian Trotsky will not escape that complete, final, shameful ignominy which we all are undergoing here.' But this prediction had not yet been fulfilled in a literal sense.

Since his expulsion from the Soviet Union in 1929, Trotsky, from Turkey, Norway and finally Mexico, had loomed hugely in the Stalinist mythology as a diabolical figure, sunk in the morass of Nazi intelligence and finally responsible for the whole vast plot whose subordinate branches were continually being uprooted in Russia by a vigilant N.K.V.D. In reality, he was trying to organize a political movement on a world scale. Odd sects of the Communist movement joined his Fourth International. But in the U.S.S.R. itself his influence was practically nil. He was a figure off-stage in all the events we have recounted. His main participation in Soviet affairs was simply as a commentator and analyst from outside. In his *Bulletin of the Opposition*, he presented his ideas of the current situation in the country, and made recommendations for correct action by anti-Stalinist Communists.

For all his vigour and polemical skill, these are notable mainly for two things. First, a total lack of solicitude for the non-Communist victims of the regime: no sympathy whatever was expended, for example, on the dead of the collectivization famine. Secondly, an unbelievable ineptitude in political judgement. It is natural that there should hang about Trotsky the glamour of a Lost Cause. This is a normal historical sentimentalism, reminding one of Scottish feelings about Bonnie Prince Charlie, entertained by many who would admit when it came to it that there is a vast difference between their hero fleeing persecuted through the Western Isles and the certainly unpleasant results of an actual Jacobite restoration.

To attribute too much political virtue, or political intelligence, to Trotsky, as Malcolm Muggeridge has done, on account of his 'vivacious pen' or even to the combination of 'an independent mind ... courage, high spirits and unshakeable resolution', seems a similarly romantic view.[80] Muggeridge gives the impression of a 'rebel' against all tyranny. But this needs to be very severely qualified. During the period when Trotsky held power he was, whatever his personal magnetism, a ruthless imposer of the Party's will, who firmly crushed the democratic opposition within the Party, and fully supported the rules which in 1921 gave the ruling group total authority. And the crushing of the Kronstadt rebellion was as much his personal battle honour as the seizure of power had been. He was the leading figure among the doctrinaire 'Leftist' Old Bolsheviks who were finding it hard to stomach Lenin's concessions to the peasantry, and preferred a far more rigorous regime, even before Stalin came round to the same view. Trotsky might have carried out such policies less crudely than Stalin. But he would have used, as ever, as much violence as he thought necessary: and that would not have been a small amount.

But more destructive still to the image of the 'good old rebel' was his attitude to the Stalin regime. Even when in exile during the thirties, it was not by any means that of a forthright revolutionary out to destroy a tyranny. It was rather that of a 'loyal opposition'. In 1931 he published his key manifesto, 'The Problems of the Development of the U.S.S.R.'. This accepted the main lines of Stalin's programme, defined Stalinist Russia as 'a proletarian State', and simply quarrelled with Stalin about which 'phase' of evolution towards Socialism had been attained. Trotsky stood, in fact, not for the destruction of the Stalinist system but for its take-over and patching-up by an alternative group of leaders.

In the autumn of 1932 Trotsky wrote in a letter to his son: 'At present Miliukov, the Mensheviks and Thermidorians of all sorts . . . will willingly echo the cry "Remove Stalin". Yet, it may still happen within a few months that Stalin may have to defend himself against Thermidorian pressure, and that we may have temporarily to support him. . . . This being so, the slogan "Down with Stalin" is ambiguous and should not be raised as a war cry at this moment.'[81] In his *Bulletin* Trotsky wrote: 'If the bureaucratic equilibrium in the U.S.S.R. were to be upset at present, this would almost certainly benefit the forces of counter-revolution.'[82]

Trotsky was always arguing that a 'Thermidor' was being prepared, with the support of 'petit-bourgeois elements'. Obsessed with comparisons with the French Revolution, he continually spoke of Thermidor and Brumaire. The parallels between Stalin and either the Directory or Napoleon are interesting, but the differences are so great that for purposes of practical politics they are not worth taking into account. Stalin's regime – indeed Lenin's regime – had its own laws of development and potentialities. And when Stalin established his autocracy, it was comparable to other despotisms of the past, but hardly to those of eighteenth- and nineteenth-century France. Trotsky was attentive to the lessons of history, but they were not the lessons of Russian history. If instead of worrying about Barras and Bonaparte he had given some thought to Ivan the Terrible, it might have been more to the point.

Trotsky had objected to Lenin's machine right up to 1917, but having then accepted it, had never again denounced it in principle or seen that Stalinism, or something like it, was its natural product. The furthest he went was to say that it was 'rather tempting' to suggest that the Stalin system was 'already rooted in Bolshevik centralism, or, more sweepingly, in the underground hierarchy of professional revolutionaries'.[83]

Since Stalinist historiography is so extravagantly unreliable, there has been a tendency for historians to accept Trotsky's account of certain events. In particular, it has lately been shown that historians have depended too much on Trotsky's own account of Lenin's last period. His representation of Lenin wishing to 'form a bloc' with him alone, of a special mutual loyalty, political trust and personal friendship, is partisan eyewash. He was involved with the rest of the Politburo in resisting Lenin's attempts to influence public affairs from his sick-bed. In the ensuing intrigues he was by no means straightforward, but at once 'devious and faint-hearted', and his own account is 'pathetic in its half-truths and attempts to gloss over the facts'.[84] This is natural enough, and the only problem is why Trotsky's virtually unsupported word should have been so widely accepted. Partly, no doubt, because his books, written under the comparatively critical eye of the West, were not so wildly and unashamedly

falsified as their Stalinist competitors; partly because the Trotskyite tradition has trickled here and there into the mainstream of
independent historical writing. But Trotsky had never failed in
his duty to suppress or misrepresent facts in the interests of
politics. And his general reliability on the period in question
could have been considered in the light of his accusation that
Stalin poisoned Lenin. There is no evidence whatever that this is
true, and Trotsky himself only brought it up many years later –
in 1939. The only serious point in favour of it is not evidential at
all but simply a consideration of *cui bono* in so far as Lenin's death
saved Stalin from the loss of his main positions of power. But it is
more reasonable to see in Trotsky's accusation a lesser, mirror-
image, of Stalin's own habit of mind in making wild accusations
of treachery against political opponents.

When people say that Trotsky had an attractive personality,
they are speaking mainly of his public *persona*, his appearance
before great meetings, his writings, his dignity. But even so he
repelled many who felt him to be full of vanity, on the one hand,
and irresponsible on the other in the sense that he tended to make
a bright or 'brilliant' formulation and press it to the end regardless of danger.

Stalin's colourless, short-view remarks carried more conviction.
Their very drabness gave them a realism. In a period of comparatively down-to-earth problems, the great revolutionary (like the
great 'theoretician' Bukharin) did not feel at home. Whatever his
aberrations, Trotsky had a good deal in him of the European
Marxist tradition. As Russia lapsed into isolation, the Asian
element he had before the Revolution denounced in the Bolsheviks came to the fore. A Soviet diplomat told Ciliga that Russia
was after all Asiatic: 'The way of Gengis Khan and Stalin suits
it better than the European civilization of Leo Davidovich.'[85]

Trotsky's vanity, unlike Stalin's, was, practically speaking,
frivolous. There was something more histrionic about it. He had
shown himself no less ruthless than Stalin. Indeed, at the time of
the Civil War he had ordered executions on a greater scale than
Stalin or anyone else. Even in this, he showed some of the attributes of a *poseur* – the Great Revolutionary dramatically and in-
exorably carrying out the cruel will of history. If Trotsky had

come to power, this concern for his image would no doubt have made him rule in a less ruthless, or rather a less crudely ruthless, fashion than Stalin. The Russian people would perhaps have been able to say

> ... What his hard heart denies,
> His charitable vanity supplies.

Stalin's pragmatic approach gave the impression of a sounder man, and in a sense this was a true impression. He was always capable of retreat – from the calling-off of the disastrous collectivization wave in May 1930 to the ending of the Berlin Blockade in 1949. His skills in Soviet political methods make Trotsky look superficial, and the conclusion seems inevitable that he had far more to him than his rival. A mind may be intelligent, abilities may be brilliant; yet there are other qualities less apparent to the observer, without which such gifts have a certain slightness to them. Trotsky was a polished zircon; Stalin was a rough diamond.

Trotsky and his son Lev Sedov had been deprived of Soviet citizenship on 20 February 1932. They had not, as is sometimes said, been condemned to death by the courts. It had been announced as part of the verdicts in the Zinoviev and Pyatakov Cases that they would be liable to immediate arrest and trial 'in the event of their being discovered on the territory of the U.S.S.R.'.

Trotsky boldly challenged the Soviet Government to seek his extradition from Norway, which would have meant the examination of his evidence in the Norwegian courts. Instead, they put pressure on the Norwegian Government to expel Trotsky. Through the painter Diego Rivera he obtained asylum from President Cárdenas of Mexico, and on 9 January 1937 reached that country in a Norwegian tanker.

Like Lenin, who welcomed and protected Malinovsky and other Tsarist spies within the Bolshevik Party, even when they came under suspicion from the rest of his entourage, Trotsky proved gullible about his contacts. Lenin's defence had been the rather inadequate one that even while Malinovsky was betraying Bolsheviks he was also having to work hard and well to make new ones. Trotsky took the view that if he refused to meet any but his oldest and closest disciples, he would lose important opportunities to preach his doctrines and gain new followers.

The plot against Trotsky was tied in with the murky world of Soviet espionage in the United States, and some of it was only unravelled after the arrest of Jack Soble in 1957.

Soble had spied on Trotsky as early as 1931–2, with useful results. The next N.K.V.D. agent to penetrate Trotsky's political family was the extraordinary Mark Zborowski, of whom it has been said that he everywhere 'left behind a trail of duplicity and blood worthy of a Shakespearian villain', and who, after establishing himself in the United States as a respectable anthropologist at Columbia and Harvard, was finally exposed and convicted on charges of perjury in December 1958, getting a five- to seven-year term.[86]

Zborowski had managed to become Sedov's right-hand man, and had access to all the secrets of the Trotskyites. He was responsible for the robbery of the Trotsky archives in Paris in November 1936. Though he never committed any murders himself, remaining a finger-man, he seems to have played some role in the killing of Ignace Reiss.[87] He also nearly procured the death of Walter Krivitsky in 1937, and did succeed in having Trotsky's secretary Erwin Wolf murdered in Spain. The young German Rudolf Clement, secretary of Trotsky's 'Fourth International', seems also to have been conveyed into his murderer's hand by Zborowski, in 1938. A headless body found floating in the Seine in Paris was tentatively identified as Clement's: in any case, he has not been seen since. On 14 February 1938 Trotsky's son Lev Sedov died in suspicious circumstances in a Paris hospital.[88] Since Zborowski was the man who rushed him there, there is a very strong presumption that he informed the N.K.V.D. killer organization of the opportunity which now presented itself.

That Trotsky himself survived as late as 1940 is probably due to the breakdown of the N.K.V.D. Foreign Department as a result of Yezhov's and then Beria's purge of it and the difficulties produced by the defection of high officers like Lyushkov and Orlov.

Moreover, after some sort of attempt on Trotsky's life which seems to have been made in January 1938, very strict security measures were taken at the villa where he now settled at Coyoacán, outside Mexico City. Apart from Trotsky's own guards, considerable police protection was provided.

The planning of the attempts on Trotsky was now entrusted to a large staff, who made minute preparations. The Trotsky dossier in the N.K.V.D. registry at No. 2 Dzerzhinsky Street occupied three floors.[89]

We can certainly deduce a main motive of Stalin's as the simple physical destruction of all alternative leaderships. No further blackening of Trotsky's character was necessary or possible. In every sense except that of killing his great enemy, Stalin could only expect a political debit from the operation. It was the same concern as was to be shown in the execution of long lists of military and other men already serving in camps, at precisely the two defensive crises of the Second World War.

The organization of Trotsky's murder was assigned to Leonid Eitingon, a high N.K.V.D. officer, who was given virtually unlimited funds for the purpose. Eitingon had been sent to Spain to work under Orlov, taking the pseudonym Kotov, in 1936. He had already had considerable experience of terrorist activity abroad, and was now the leading figure in Yezhov's 'Special Tasks' organization. He continued with this career for many years. The agent Nikolai Khokhlov, sent to Germany to assassinate anti-Soviet émigré leaders, who defected to the West in April 1954, had worked under him. He seems finally to have been shot owing to his connexions with Beria.

Eitingon set off for Mexico, bringing with him Vittorio Codovilla (a founder of the Argentine Communist Party and a trusted Stalinist, who had been involved in the murder of Andrés Nin), and Vittorio Vidali, another of the most formidable of the killers from Spain.

The Mexican Communist Party, under its leader Hermán Laborde, had been a genuine political trend, and was lukewarm about such action against Trotsky. As part of the move against Trotsky, Laborde and his followers were purged and an intransigent group, including the painter Siqueiros, placed at the head of the Party.

Taking the name of Leonov, Eitingon organized his first attempt on Trotsky on a lavish scale. The central figure was Siqueiros.

On 23 May 1940 Siqueiros and two accomplices collected a number of sub-machine guns, police and Army uniforms, and some ladders and incendiary bombs, together with a rotary power saw. He dressed himself as a major in the Mexican Army and put on a disguise. At about 2 a.m. he assembled the twenty men he had chosen, and they drove in four cars to Trotsky's fortified villa. Some of the police had already been lured away; the others were trussed up at gunpoint. The telephone lines were cut and the sentry on duty, an American called Harte, was rushed and over-whelmed. The force broke into the patio and swept the bedrooms with tommy guns for several minutes. They then pulled out, leaving several incendiaries and a large dynamite bomb. The latter failed to explode. Trotsky was slightly wounded in the right leg; his ten-year-old grandson was also hit. His wife received some burns from the incendiaries. Otherwise, the attack was a failure.

The body of Harte was later found, shot, buried in the grounds of a villa rented by Siqueiros.

The Mexican Communist Party disowned the attack and dissociated itself from Siqueiros and Vidali. By 17 June the identity of the attackers had been established by the Mexican police.

Siqueiros was arrested in a hide-out in the provinces in September 1940, but although the facts were established, great political pressures were now brought to bear. At the same time, 'intellectuals and artists' urged the President to take into account the fact that 'artists and men of science are considered as the bulwark of culture and progress'.[90]

As a result, the court accepted Siqueiros's plea that the firing of three hundred bullets into the bedrooms had been for 'psychological purposes only', without any intention of killing or hurting anyone. Evidence that when Siqueiros heard of Trotsky's survival he had exclaimed 'All that work in vain!' was disregarded. The facts about Harte's death were found not to constitute a *prima facie* case of murder. The judge claimed that the accused did not form a 'criminal conspiracy', since a conspiracy could not be made for a single temporary job but must have 'stability and permanence'. They were even acquitted of impersonating police officers, on the grounds that though they had dressed up in uniforms, they had not actually attempted to usurp any police functions.

While Siqueiros was still out on bail, a convenient invitation to paint some murals in Chile, at the instance of the Chilean Communist poet Pablo Neruda, led to his decamping thither. So even the light sentence he might have got for the crime still attributed to him – of stealing the two automobiles outside the Trotsky house – was avoided.

On the failure of Siqueiros, Eitingon had put his second plan into operation. Four days after the first attempt, Ramón Mercader was introduced to Trotsky for the first time.

Mercader's mother, Caridad, a Spanish Communist, had become sexually entangled with Eitingon during the civil war in Spain, when she had herself worked in the liquidation squads. The N.K.V.D. made a practice of securing the passports of members of the International Brigade who had been killed. Mercader was given one which had originally belonged to a Yugoslav-Canadian volunteer killed in action early in the war. It had been reforged under the name of 'Jacson' – a curious example of the absurd slips which crop up in these otherwise highly skilled operations, though in fact this attracted no attention.

The plot now reached into the world of outwardly respectable New York Leftism, which at the time was seething with intra-Communist intrigue, and provided a ready recruiting ground for Yezhov's men. In fact, general supervision of the murder seems to have come under the permanent Resident of the N.K.V.D., the Soviet Consul-General in New York, Gaik Ovakimian, who was later exposed, in May 1941, and expelled from the country.

The details – some of which are even now a little obscure – do not concern us here. But it is at least interesting to note – in this as in the great espionage cases of the forties and fifties – how many people, of whom their non-Party acquaintances would have certainly denied any possibility of their joining in such activity, were, from factiousness, revolutionary romanticism, and even idealism, to become willing or half-willing accomplices in a vulgar murder.

These put Mercader in touch with Sylvia Ageloff, an American

Trotskyite who was a social worker. He seduced her and entered
into a relationship with her which passed for marriage. She was
entirely innocent of the planned crime. Through her, he was
admitted to the Trotsky household.

Over the next few months Mercader made five or six visits and,
as Sylvia Ageloff's husband, became reasonably established. On
20 August he arrived at Trotsky's villa, ostensibly to have an
article he had written criticized. He wore a raincoat. A long
dagger was sewn into the lining. A revolver was in his pocket.
But his actual weapon, a cut-down ice-axe, was in his raincoat
pocket. (An N.K.V.D. murder – of a Soviet ambassador – by a
strong assassin using an iron bar is reported by the Petrovs.)
Mercader was an experienced mountain-climber, and his choice
of the ice-axe as an assassination weapon was based on considerable experience of its use and power. Outside, his car was
parked facing the right way for a quick move, and round the
corner another car with his mother and an agent was waiting.
Eitingon in yet a third car was a block or so away.

Trotsky had two revolvers on his desk, and the switch to an
alarm system within reach. But as soon as he started to read
Mercader's article, the assassin took out his ice-axe and struck
him a 'tremendous blow' on the head.

Mercader had planned to leave quickly. But the blow was not
immediately lethal. Trotsky screamed 'very long, infinitely long',
as Mercader himself put it, 'a cry prolonged and agonized, half-
scream, half sob', according to one of the guards – who now
rushed in and seized the assassin.

Trotsky was operated on, and survived for more than a day
after that, dying on 21 August 1940. He was nearly sixty-two.

Mercader, coming to trial after Siqueiros, seems to have hoped
that he too might get a light sentence. Perhaps the judge would
hold that he had been teaching Trotsky how to climb the Alps.
But he was sentenced to twenty years' imprisonment, which he
served. Even after his identity had been established by finger-
prints he refused to admit who he was or why he had committed
the murder. The official Stalinist version was that he was a dis-
gruntled Trotskyite, and that the N.K.V.D. had nothing to do
with it.

Mercader's imprisonment was passed under conditions superior to those prevailing in Soviet prisons and camps. The Mexican revolution had effected genuine reform. A visitor notes:

His cell, spacious and sunny . . . with a little open-air patio in front, contained a neat bed and a table loaded with books and magazines.

He was also, under Mexican law, allowed women in his cell.

Eitingon and Señora Mercader left by the prepared escape route. She was received in Moscow by Beria, presented to Stalin, and decorated, for her son and herself.[91]

And indeed, the destruction of Stalin's last great opponent must have caused great satisfaction in the Kremlin. For once, it might have been noted, a prediction of Trotsky's had been literally fulfilled. He had written of Stalin, in 1936:

He seeks to strike, not at the ideas of his opponent, but at his skull.

CHAPTER THIRTEEN

CLIMAX

Each day too slew its thousands six or seven. BYRON

AFTER the Bukharin Trial, Stalin and Yezhov turned their attention to the remnant of opposition at the top.

This final wave of the Purge in the inner Party, directed against his own supporters, was well defined by a circular put out under Stalin's instructions, in April 1938, calling for a 'liquidation of the consequences of wrecking' in which the ' "silent" politically spineless people should also not be forgotten'.[1]

Various loose ends were tied up, such as the execution of minor figures who had perhaps been intended as victims in the Bukharin Trial, but had failed to give satisfaction – for example, the First Secretary in Kazakhstan, L. I. Mirzoyan, whom Stalin had attacked at the February–March plenum, and who had been arrested 'on Stalin's personal orders', was shot in May, denying the charges.[2]

There remained bigger game. Postyshev was arrested, probably in March or April. Eikhe, Kossior and Chubar, the doomed members of the Politburo, still featured, though not regularly, with the other members in formal listings, telegrams from the Soviet expedition at the North Pole, and so forth.

Eikhe and Kossior, appearing in good standing till the last week in April, went first. Eikhe was arrested on 29 April and Kossior (mentioned in an electoral list as late as 28 April) at about the same time[3] – in accordance with the N.K.V.D. custom of arresting people just before holidays, during which no attempt could be made to trace them.

Stalin was now wholly ignoring the formalities. We are told that there was no 'exchange of opinions or Political Bureau decisions' about the arrest of Kossior – nor in any 'other case of this type'.[4]

No announcement was made, then or ever, though his arrest must have become known immediately to those interested, for the Kiev Radio just ceased to announce itself as Radio Kossior, as it had done for some years.[5] The press had other matters to think of. For most of May and June, the new election campaign built up in newspapers, meetings, and any other feasible fashion, on the lines of the fanfares of the previous winter. (When the elections finally took place on 26 June, it was to the accompaniment of another exploit by 'Stalinist falcons' – a non-stop flight to Khabarovsk in the Far East by Kokkinaki.)

The absence of both men from the 1 May demonstrations was noted. Chubar was still there. He can be traced as receiving official greetings as late as 9 June. By 1 July, he is no longer listed.

Chubar is now said to have been concerned with shortcomings in industry, and to have had qualms about the new agricultural system. He had been closely associated with Ordzhonikidze, and was not pleased with the development of the cult of personality. In the period before his own removal, he had become 'deeply indignant' over the facts he had learned about illegal repressions. He did not believe that people he had known and worked with for years were really spies. His views on this became known to those in charge of the Purge. On his removal from membership of the Politburo and vice-chairmanship of the Council of People's Commissars, he was sent for the moment to work at Solikamsk in the Urals. But he remained there only 'a few months . . . soon he was arrested and shot'.[6]

Meanwhile Eikhe, in the new torture centre for top officials at Sukhanovka, was being interrogated by the notorious Z. M. Ushakov. Soon his ribs were broken, and he was confessing to being leader of a 'reserve net supposedly created by Bukharin in 1935'.

This was presumably what was mentioned as 'another reserve centre' at the Bukharin Trial, allegedly existing at the end of 1935 or the beginning of 1936, when Rykov was supposed to have urged Chernov to get in touch with it 'through Lyubimov'.[7] It was 'another' reserve centre because there was also reference to 'the parallel group of Rights' allegedly led by Antipov.

There is at least some slight logic in this representation of the latest victims as 'Rightists'. They had had no connexion whatever with the Trotsky or Zinoviev oppositions, and although they had

equally opposed the Bukharinites in 1929–33, they were advocates
of a lessening of the Terror and of reconciliation with Bukharin;
and some at least had opposed his arrest.

The plan for the next trial was, in any case, changed. Eikhe was
instructed to remove his name as reserve centre leader and substitute Mezhlauk's.[8] At the same time Rukhimovich also had his
name removed from the layout of this network.[9] His case, like
Eikhe's, seems to have been held over.

This left a number of ready victims for the first trial planned
wholly against Stalinists, leaving the more recently arrested
Politburo members and some others in reserve for future use.
Just what happened next we do not yet know. But it has lately
become apparent that a major case must have come to climax in
the last days of July 1938. We now know that on the 28th and
29th[10] of that month the following were shot:

Former Vice-Premier and Politburo member	Yan Rudzutak
Former Commissar for Heavy Industry	V. I. Mezhlauk
Former Secretary of the Central Executive Committee	I. S. Unshlikht
Former member of the Ukrainian Politburo	V. P. Zatonsky
Former Commander-in-Chief of the Navy	Admiral Orlov
Army Commanders (and – see p. 321 – a number of other leading officers)	Dybenko, Vatsetis, Velikanov, Belov, Dubovoy, Alksnis
A prominent playwright	V. Kirshon

Doubtless there are other characters among those whose precise death dates have not yet been given, who may also figure in
this group. But as it is, it plainly represents a mass execution of
the scale and significance of those already publicized. All we know
of the detail is that at a session of the Military Collegium of the
Supreme Court Rudzutak pleaded his innocence. He had made a
confession, but now retracted it and asked that:

the Party Central Committee be informed that there is in the N.K.V.D
an as yet not liquidated centre which is craftily manufacturing cases,
which forces innocent persons to confess; there is no opportunity to
prove one's non-participation in crimes to which the confessions of
various persons testify. The investigative methods are such that they
force people to lie and to slander entirely innocent persons in addition

to those who already stand accused. He asks the court that he be allowed to inform the Party Central Committee of all this in writing. He assures the court that he personally never had any evil designs in regard to the policy of our Party because he had always agreed with the Party policy pertaining to all spheres of economic and cultural activity.[11]

However, 'sentence was pronounced on him in twenty minutes and he was shot'.

We can trace a few relatives of the accused: Rudzutak's wife was sent to labour camp;[12] Unshlikht's sister, Stefanie Brun, got eight years;[13] Mezhlauk's first wife also got an eight-year sentence and died of dysentery in a transit camp in the Far East.[14]

This case marks a turning-point in the Purge. There were to be no more public trials of Party figures. But it is also interesting because it comes at the moment when Stalin was beginning to show distrust of Yezhov.

One Party organization had remained, not indeed exempt from purging, but only carrying out such purging as benefited its own leader – that of Georgia under Beria. It seems very out of character for Yezhov not to have attempted the destruction of the leading cadres in Tbilisi, and there are indeed reports that he was manoeuvring to do this in 1938.[15] It is said that Beria was to be arrested,[16] but successfully appealed, being supported by Molotov and others.[17]

Beria's appointment on 20 July 1938, just a week before the July massacre, to be Deputy Head of the N.K.V.D. can only be interpreted as the beginning of Yezhov's decline. It was a post that had previously been held by men like M. Berman and Agranov – that is, not one suitable for an important Party figure. In fact, Beria was quite clearly being prepared as a successor. He moved into the dacha just vacated by Chubar.[18]

There is a rumour that Yezhov and Kaganovich had clashed – not on any question of the desirability of the Great Purge, but on a more direct issue of power. Kaganovich himself supervised the purging of his personal ministries and other organs under his own control, but resented N.K.V.D. intrusion except for the technical purposes of arrest, shooting, etc. According to one account, Yezhov began to implicate Kaganovich himself, and had already forced Bondarenko, Head of the Kharkov Tractor Works, to make statements compromising him.[19]

On one view, the immediate reason why Stalin listened to the voices being raised against Yezhov is that he had failed to set up further public trials, in particular that of the Rightist 'Reserve Centre', plus a second Military Trial.[20]

It is quite conceivable that Yezhov had been charged with setting up a fourth great trial, and had failed in the assignment. If this were so, the coincidence of Beria's appointment and the immediately followed secret trial or trials would signify the winding-up of an unsatisfactory project by the new management.

But, on the other hand, Stalin had for some time been shooting prominent Central Committee members without such formality, and it is difficult to see what further benefit he could now gain from another public trial. Every possible lesson had been rubbed in in the Bukharin Trial. As far as a second Military Trial was concerned, the first had not taken place in public and the second could have been announced in precisely the same way. Indeed, the mere fact that the new batch of military conspirators was dispatched without public announcement seems to show that Stalin no longer felt the need for such.

Whatever plans Stalin may have had for the future, it was, anyhow, at this point that he abandoned public trials. None of the figures still under arrest was brought before public courts – though they all seem to have had confessions tortured out of them and to have been brought before these twenty-minute sessions of the Military Collegium.

It seems to have been more difficult to extract reliable and durable confessions from the new Stalinist prisoners. Rudzutak (and Eikhe after him) would not repeat before the secret courts which eventually tried them the confessions they had made under torture. This had been true of a number of those who had fallen in the earlier phase of the Purge, but there had been an adequate residuum of confessors. None of the new victims, on the other hand, had anything whatever to reproach themselves for from the point of view of having collaborated in any of the oppositions, and could hardly be asked to 'disarm'. This had been true only of one or two second-rank prisoners in the Bukharin Trial.

Some of the difficulty may have resided in the fact that this middle generation were still rather more than personal nominees or members of Stalin's extremist entourage. They were still men following their political convictions, attached to Stalin as a leader, but not committed to the idea of his leadership as a matter of ideological dogma. Unlike the men Stalin had assembled from the earlier generation, and against many of whom he was able to exert something like blackmail, the younger cadres were almost all secure in the consciousness of their general and political innocence (if not from our point of view, at least from their own).

As for Yezhov, for the time being he retained his power and position. One further bad omen was visited on him. On 21 August 1938 he was named People's Commissar of Water Transport, a post to be held in addition to the N.K.V.D.[21] (At the same time, Kaganovich was confirmed in control of heavy industry as well as railways, and made Vice-Chairman of the Council of People's Commissars.) But through the autumn the N.K.V.D. Commissar continued to appear with his old prominence; in fact, he was often named higher than his official standing in the Politburo – sometimes before Mikoyan, Andreyev and Zhdanov.

And he continued his policies. The Purge had grown in size, until finally it had reached such monstrous proportions that even Stalin seems to have seen that the time had come to ease off. This was a matter of major policy: the midsummer changes were perhaps no more than the first moves towards an alternative, based more on a particular failure than on the realization that a dead end was being reached in the entire Terror.

DIPLOMATS

Meanwhile, another rumoured trial failed to take place. After the Bukharin Trial it had been rumoured that a special trial of diplomats, centring on Antonov-Ovseenko, would be held.

Soviet diplomats had already suffered severely. For example, Tairov, Ambassador to Mongolia, had been shot in June 1937. Krestinsky and Sokolnikov had both served as Deputy People's Commissars for Foreign Affairs. Karakhan had been Ambassador in Berlin. Various lesser figures had been involved in the

trials, for example Chlenov,[22] of whom it was said in the Bukharin Trial indictment that his case would be subject to special proceedings. Others implicated in the Bukharin Trial were Yurenev, Ambassador to Tokyo, Bogomolov, Ambassador to China, and Sabanin, Director of the Legal Department of the People's Commissariat of Foreign Affairs.[23]

At that Commissariat, an N.K.V.D. officer, Vasily Korzhenko, was appointed Chief of Personnel[24] and he and his family moved into Krestinsky's Moscow house.[25] The treatment of Foreign Commissariat staff for comparatively minor offences has been interestingly described in a recent Soviet article.

V. N. Barkov was head of the Protocol Department:

On one occasion, on the instructions of Dekanozov, who was at that time a Deputy People's Commissar for Foreign Affairs and who, as it afterwards appeared, was one of the most active members of the Beria gang, Barkov had to meet a foreign correspondent. Under the regulations in force, on the day of his talk with the correspondent, Barkov had to see Dekanozov without fail, but Dekanozov was nowhere to be found. Obeying the orders he had received, Barkov saw the correspondent.

On the following day Dekanozov summoned him.

'Who gave you direct permission for the interview?'

'I could not find you anywhere.'

'You could not have tried very hard.'

The dressing-down went on for a long time. Barkov lost his temper and said:

'But on that day you could not be found!'

'Oh! It's like that is it?' said Dekanozov menacingly, and closed the interview.

On that day Barkov never returned home. His relations only saw him eighteen years later.[26]

The People's Commissar himself, Litvinov, beginning in 1937, and for the rest of his life, kept a revolver to hand, 'so that if the bell rang in the night, he would not have to live through the consequences'.[27]

Diplomats disappeared by the dozen. They had, indeed, had genuine contacts with foreigners, so that the presumption of their guilt was, by Yezhov's standards, overwhelming. They were recalled and shot: in his memoirs,[28] Ehrenburg says that few survived. He names nine that he knew personally whom Stalin liquidated.

But no trial took place. In particular, Antonov-Ovseenko simply went through a routine processing. He had been a Menshevik until 1917. He had led two local rebellions in 1905–6 and had been sentenced to death in 1906. He had been arrested several times for underground activity afterwards. (This record shows, incidentally, how mistaken is the notion that the Mensheviks were politically inactive because their views on party organization differed from Lenin's.) Joining the Bolsheviks in 1917, he had led the attack on the Winter Palace which overthrew the Provisional Government.

It was he who had burst into the Government room, announcing 'In the name of the Military Revolutionary Committee, I declare you arrested.' He commanded on the Ukrainian front in the Civil War and later became Head of the Political Administration of the Army.[29] Here he had supported Trotsky and was removed in favour of Bubnov. He remained a Trotskyite until 1928 when he submitted, like other oppositionists. He had since been employed in State and diplomatic posts, latterly in Spain.

Antonov-Ovseenko was held in a cell on the third floor of the Butyrka prison. He was ill and (as is often reported of the undernourished and over-interrogated) had swollen legs. But he bore himself boldly and entertained his cell-mates with stories of Lenin, the October Revolution and the Spanish War. One of them was Yuri Tomsky (son of the Mikhail Tomsky who had committed suicide in 1936), who has given an account of Antonov's last days.[30] At the interrogation Antonov refused to sign anything, though the protocols of the interrogation ran finally to 300 pages. One day when this was being gone through there happened to be a radio on in the investigator's office. The N.K.V.D. man called Antonov an 'enemy of the people'. The prisoner retorted '*You* are an enemy of the people. You are a regular Fascist.' The radio started to broadcast a mass meeting. 'Listen! Listen to how the people celebrate us. They trust us in everything, and you will be annihilated. There,' the N.K.V.D. official added, 'I have had a medal on your account.'

One day at the end of 1938[31] or the beginning of 1939[32] Antonov was called for execution. He took off his overcoat, shoes and jacket and distributed them to the other prisoners, and then remarked (young Tomsky tells us) 'I beg anyone who gets to freedom to tell the people that Antonov-Ovseenko was a Bolshevik and remained a Bolshevik till his last day.' The chief warders then led him away.

Antonov had himself served as State Prosecutor in the early thirties. He had to wait twenty-five years for his message to be published to the Russian people. All the same, he was lucky. Of the Mensheviks who died in camps after the 1931 Trial or the Social Revolutionaries like Spiridonova, there is no present prospect of our hearing the final messages. As yet, indeed, not even those of men like Kamenev have been given us.

Meanwhile, the other diplomats were being recalled for execution. The Soviet Minister in Bucharest, Ostrovsky, hesitated to return to Moscow, but went back when Voroshilov, with whom he had served in the Civil War, gave him a personal assurance of his safety. He was arrested on reaching the frontier.[33]

The veteran of the Baltic Fleet Mikhail Raskolnikov was Soviet Ambassador to Bulgaria. He refused to return to Russia when recalled in April 1939. He was nevertheless rehabilitated in Khrushchev's time (though later restored to the category of traitor). This must partly have been due to his particularly fine record in the Revolution and the Civil War, his total lack of involvement in any opposition, the fact that he proclaimed his loyalty to the last, and that he anyhow died within a few months (September 1939) of a nervous disorder. Even Ehrenburg in his memoirs mentions meeting him at the time when he was deciding to stay abroad and having sympathized with his position. Raskolnikov wrote an offensive letter to Stalin, which was published in the émigré *Novaya Rossiya* on 1 October 1939 after his death, and also a more moderate statement which appeared in another émigré journal, *Poslednie Novosti*, on 26 June 1939. In the latter, he says firmly to Stalin 'You yourself know that Pyatakov did not fly to Oslo' – showing that a good deal was known, and discussed, in Party circles.

KOMSOMOL

One major organization remained under its original Stalinist leadership – the Komsomol.

Kosarev had been sent by Stalin to purge the Leningrad Komsomol after the defeat of Zinoviev at the XIVth Party Congress in December 1925. In 1926, the opposition bloc had made a powerful attempt to secure the support of the young and of the students. Most of the 'Trotskyist' protest groups were composed of young intellectuals, who attacked Party control over the Komsomol. Half the Leningrad Komsomol Committee were expelled.

Kosarev had been boldly denounced by Kotolynov, then a leading Zinovievite in that body, for tactics of sheer bullying. He went on to practise these in Moscow, becoming a secretary of the Central Committee of the Komsomol in 1927 and its General Secretary in 1929.

Thenceforward, the organization had been a willing tool of the General Secretary, a sort of 'Stalinjugend'. Even this was not adequate, as Stalin held that 'The very first task of all Komsomol education work was the necessity to seek out and recognize the enemy, who had then to be removed forcibly, by methods of economic pressure, organizational-political isolation, and methods of physical destruction.'[34] In fact, he wanted the organization to become a youth auxiliary of the N.K.V.D.

On 21 July 1937 Kosarev was summoned by Stalin and Yezhov and harangued for an hour and a half about the inadequate role played by the youth organization in vigilance and denunciation.[35] He did his best to satisfy their demands. We have an account of action at the local level that autumn.

When the Smolensk Komsomol was cleaned up in October 1937, it was charged that 'Fascists, penetrating even into the Central Committee of the Komsomol, had now been exposed'. On 11 October 1937 the new local First Secretary Manayev reported that his predecessors 'the enemies of the people Kogan and Prikhodko' had 'undermined 700 *kolkhoz* Komsomol organizations'. The Pedagogical Institutes, the Technicum, the intermediate schools, had been 'filled' with hostile people, as were the Pioneer organizations. Local secretary after local secretary was listed as a criminal. Already, from a half to two thirds of the members of committees and secretaries of organizations had been replaced.

However, Manayev himself was criticized for giving money for medical treatment to enemies of the people under arrest and for 'criminal slowness' in uprooting enemies. The representative from Moscow said that the bad work of the provincial organization was possibly due to the fact that there were enemies in it yet to be unmasked.

The discussion consisted of a new torrent of denunciation. The Vyazma delegate, mentioning in passing that his district had lost five secretaries in the past few years, attacked the current holder of that office as 'completely corrupt' and 'a polygamist'. Though a number of hostile people had been expelled, so far they had only scratched the surface. As to teachers, another delegate claimed that out of 402 in his district, 180 were alien elements.[36]

As the denouncers came to the fore, Kosarev found that there were some more enthusiastic than himself.

A young woman called Mishakova from the Komsomol *apparat*, put up to it (it is now said) by Malenkov, made an attempt to compromise and destroy the leadership of Kosarev's appointees in the Komsomol organizations in the Chuvash Republic. Kosarev intervened directly, prevented the proposed purge, and removed her. Mishakova wrote to Stalin on 7 October 1938. Two or three days later she was invited to see Shkiryatov, whom Stalin had detailed to examine the case.

The whole incident, which had doubtless been arranged beforehand for that purpose, was used to complete the ruin of the last small power group which had gone through the Yezhov period unscathed. As late as 6 November, a speech of Kosarev's to a ceremonial Komsomol plenum was promptly reported in *Pravda*. But on 19–22 November a plenum of the Young Communist Central Committee was held. Stalin, Molotov and Malenkov attended. Stalin strongly defended Mishakova and turned the occasion into a violent attack on the Kosarev leadership. A few days later, the majority of that Central Committee were arrested. Beria in person came for Kosarev, the first time he had done such a thing.[37] This is almost certainly significant, as is the absence of

Yezhov's name from the entire investigation. For the Police Commissar was about to fall. According to one N.K.V.D. source, Kosarev was accused of plotting with him.[38]

By 1939 Mishakova was a secretary of the Komsomol, in which capacity she was able to tell this story, accompanied by references to the 'Kosarev gang', to the XVIIIth Congress, as a tribute to Stalin's sense of justice. By that time Kosarev, after torture at the hands of the N.K.V.D. interrogator Rodos, had been shot.

The purge of the Kosarev leadership, in its social aspect, has been interpreted as the removal of a genuine, if Stalinist, youth cadre in favour of a new conformity and anti-egalitarianism associated with the sons of the new bureaucracy.[39]

He was succeeded as Secretary-General of the Komsomol by Nikolai Mikhailov, then already over thirty and not previously associated with the organization. Mikhailov held the post until 1952, when he was promoted to be Secretary to the Central Committee of the Party and was succeeded by Alexander Shelepin. Mikhailov is still a member of the Central Committee of the Party and was until 1970 in charge of Soviet press affairs. Shelepin, Stalin's last selection to head the Komsomol, is of course one of the leading figures in the present regime.

A LAST BLOW AT THE ARMY

The Far Eastern Army had not been treated quite as the rest of the forces had. For strategic reasons it had been organized as something like an independent entity. It was the only great body of troops commanded by a Marshal – the tough, competent and practically experienced Blyukher.

Blyukher, though his name suggests a German origin, was in fact of pure Russian descent. His peasant grandfather had had the name given to him by some whim of his landlord during the days of serfdom.[40] Ironically enough, there was something of the German stance to him. Dark, grizzled, he had a square, bull-like face with a large close-clipped moustache in the *feldwebel* manner covering his large upper lip. He was now forty-eight.

He had been a worker in a wagon factory and served a thirty-two-month sentence for leading a strike while still twenty years old. He first came to prominence when, with V. V. Kuibyshev, he had established an isolated Bolshevik enclave amid a sea of White Armies, in the Samara area. In the distinguished Civil War career which followed he had been the first man awarded the new Order of the Red Banner. Later, under the pseudonym Galen, he had acted as chief military adviser to Chiang Kai-shek. He is said, back in the early thirties, to have opposed collectivization in the Far East on military grounds and, with Voroshilov's support, to have obtained a certain exemption there; and there was also talk of some connexion with Syrtsov.[41]

While Blyukher was still in Moscow in June 1937 in connexion with the Tukhachevsky 'Trial', the N.K.V.D. struck at his army. The new Chief of Staff, Sangursky, is said to have become involved (with the Party Secretary of the Far Eastern Territory, Kutev) in what Stalin felt to be some sort of political intrigue against the leadership.[42] He was now arrested and tortured. Another account[43] has him implicating literally hundreds of officers and in 1938 repudiating his confession and claiming that saboteurs in the N.K.V.D. were attempting to weaken the Army. Sangursky is reported as still alive in Irkutsk jail in 1939,[44] full of remorse for having, under torture, given away so many officers as fellow-conspirators. He was then facing a further charge – of conspiracy with Yezhov to wreck the Army!

With Sangursky went the Deputy Chief of Staff, the Chief of Combat Training and the Chief of Intelligence. In the autumn of 1937, Ingaunis, commanding the Far Eastern Air Force, was also in the Butyrka, having been severely tortured in the Lefortovo and confessing to espionage. The N.K.V.D. N.C.O. who tore off his insignia and Orders in the Lubyanka remarked, 'Well, they certainly handed out medals to all sorts of counter-revolutionary swine!'[45] The Head of the Army's Political Administration was arrested too. At the same time, most of the political leadership in the eastern provinces were seized.

Even so, as far as the Army is concerned, this phase only lasted about five weeks, and was not so intense or on such a mass scale as in the other military districts. It ended with Blyukher's return to his post.

For meanwhile an even more important consideration had arisen: on 30 June some patrol fighting had broken out between Soviet and Japanese troops on the Amur, and on 6 July the Japanese had seized Bolshoi Island in that stream. In spite of protests, the Russians made no attempt to dislodge them. There is no doubt that this was a probing action by Japanese military elements, who took the view that the local Soviet capacity to fight had been largely paralysed by the Purge.

Blyukher at once started to repair as far as possible the disorganization that had already set in. Tukhachevsky's execution, followed by the arrests in the Far Eastern Army, had left him deeply depressed.[46] But in the face of the military threat Stalin made no further move against him for the time being.

During the winter various arrests were carried out. Corps Commander Rokossovsky had been beaten senseless and dragged off to prison, together with a number of other officers of his unit. When Rokossovsky came before a 'court', its president said that it had the evidence of one of his fellow-conspirators, Adolf Kazimirovich Yushkevich, who had confessed that he and Rokossovsky had belonged to a counter-revolutionary centre, and had had certain instructions and tasks.

'Can the dead give evidence?' Rokossovsky asked, when he was allowed to comment.

'What do you mean, the dead?'

'Well, Adolf Kazimirovich Yushkevich was killed in 1920 at Perekop. I mentioned to the investigator that Yushkevich served in the Cavalry Group, but I accidentally forgot to mention his loss.'[47]

Rokossovsky was merely imprisoned, and was one of those lucky enough to be released when the pressure had died down.

Meanwhile, things were to get worse.

At the end of May 1938, when every other part of the Army, and of the country, had been dealt with, Mekhlis arrived in Khabarovsk with a group of new political commissars. At the same time the sinister Frinovsky steamed in, in a special train, with a large N.K.V.D. staff. The great purge of the Far Eastern Army, of which they had been cheated in 1937, was now at hand.

Mekhlis and Frinovsky first destroyed their own representatives. Mekhlis replaced the officers of the political administration – the 'Gamarnik–Bulin gang' were later said to have been particularly active in the Far East.[48] Frinovsky arrested and shot the sixteen leading N.K.V.D. officials of the area. He was balked of one major figure. The N.K.V.D. Commander of the Far Eastern Frontier Troops was G. Lyushkov, who had been Deputy Head of the Secret Political Department under Molchanov in the days of the Zinoviev Trial. One of the few still left over from the Yagoda regime, he had been so far spared because of his friendly relations with Yezhov. He now decided it was time to push his luck no further, and on 13 June he slipped across the Manchurian border with a vast amount of intelligence information for the Japanese.[49]

Having prepared the police and political striking forces, Stalin's emissaries turned on the Army proper. Blyukher's new staff and commanders were arrested wholesale. His Deputy Commander, his new Chief of Staff, his new Air Commander, Pumpur – who had served in Spain – and his leading Army Commander, Levandovsky, recently transferred from the Caucasus, all disappeared.* But now it was not only a matter of a few seniors. Forty per cent of the commanders up to regimental level, 70 per cent of divisional and corps staffs and over 80 per cent of the Front staff were seized, as N.K.V.D. lorries raided the officers' quarters night after night. By the end of June Blyukher was 'standing amidst the shambles of what had been his command'.[51]

Once again he was reprieved, and for the same reason as before. The Japanese had seen their chance. On 6 July 1938 they launched a probing attack with limited objectives on Lake Hassan.

Fortunately, there were still a few competent officers who had survived or been transferred to the area, in particular Corps Commander Shtern, who had recently been Chief Military Adviser in Spain and was now given command of one of the armies into which Blyukher's front had been reorganized. He was to

* Pumpur was released and promoted in June 1940. He seems to have been rearrested in the spring of 1941 and shot with Stern and the others in October of that year.[50]

have time to fight his battle and report on it to the next Party Congress and even to be elected to the new Central Committee before he too disappeared.

After five weeks of intermittent fighting, the Far Eastern troops first contained the Japanese and then pressed them back. By 11 August the battle was over. A week later, on 18 August, Blyukher was recalled to Moscow.[52]

The 'Stalin air route', pioneered with such panache at the time of the Zinoviev Trial, was being put to typical use by the General Secretary. A special pilot, Alexander Golovanov, later to rise to be Chief Marshal of the Soviet Air Force until his removal after Stalin's death in 1953, had been allotted by the N.K.V.D. for urgent travel by members of the Central Committee and Government. In 1935–6 he had served in the labour-camp administration in Siberia. Now he was provided with a special multi-engined aircraft, and in 1937–8 this was used to transport arrested officials from the Far East and elsewhere.[53] He had lately carried most of Blyukher's subordinates and their N.K.V.D. escorts back to Moscow.

Now the Marshal himself was taken aboard. He was not yet, however, under arrest. At the end of August he made a report to the Military Soviet of the People's Commissariat of Defence. 'Criticism was sharp and one-sided.' Voroshilov attacked him, while Stalin, who had always defended him previously, remained silent. Later Voroshilov told him that he was not to return to the Far East, but to remain at the disposal of the Military Revolutionary Soviet 'until a post suitable for a Marshal' could be found. Meanwhile he should go on leave to Sochi, the resort in the Caucasus.[54]

Blyukher telegraphed his wife to return, adding that his health was poor. He put some money aside for her, in case he was arrested. For the chances of this now seemed high. She and the family joined him soon afterwards, together with his brother, commander of an Air Force unit in the Far East. By this time he had learned of the arrest of Army Commander Fedko, Assistant Commissar of Defence, which seems in some way to have been associated with his own.

On 22 October, on Stalin's personal orders,[55] four men in black civilian suits entered the house and arrested all of them.* Blyukher was taken to the Lefortovo, where Beria personally conducted the first examination. He was then continuously interrogated by other N.K.V.D. officers working in shifts. The charge was of having been a Japanese spy since 1921, and of having planned to escape to Japan with the help of his brother (this second charge at least was not totally implausible: after all, Lyushkov had just done precisely that). The Marshal was now told that in addition to the rest of his family his first wife Galia had been arrested in Leningrad. Apart from using all these hostages, the N.K.V.D. also offered him an inducement: if he confessed he would get off with a ten-year sentence. However, he refused to sign the protocol.[57]

On 28 October 1938, medals were awarded to the heroes of the recent fighting in the Far East, including Shtern. The true victor was now undergoing severe torture by his N.K.V.D. interrogators. Within three weeks of his arrest, on 9 November, he was dead.

There is no evident reason for the N.K.V.D. to have practised or feigned on this occasion the haste with which the May–June purge of the Tukhachevsky group had been carried out. Unlike even that occasion – on which all official sources insist that there was a trial – we are told in a recent Soviet publication[58] that Blyukher was 'shot without court or sentence'. It has also been stated that 'uninterrupted interrogation broke down the health of this virile man'.[59] All this seems to point to his dying under interrogation. (Fedko, his presumed associate, was not to be executed until the following February.)

On the other hand, a pervasive labour-camp rumour held that Blyukher was killed by Yezhov personally.[60] (It is said, too, that Yezhov personally shot one of the Mezhlauk brothers during interrogation.)†[61] If this is so, it could all easily be represented to Stalin as showing that Yezhov had incompetently let things get

---

* Blyukher's son Vsevolod, who was sixteen when his father was arrested, was sent to an isolation camp for some years. In 1941 he was released, and when the war broke out was called up, concealing his name. He did well.[56]

† This was evidently the junior brother, I. I. Mezhlauk, who died 26 April 1938.[62]

out of hand: and it would perhaps contribute to the other wide-spread rumour that Yezhov finally went mad.

There is some rather sketchy evidence that information against Blyukher was being collected as early as the autumn of 1936. It is also said that Byeloborodov, who had been in jail for many months, had been interrogated to get evidence against the Marshal.[63] But this may only have been the routine collection of incriminating material which was being carried out in the case of every single leading figure, just in case.

There have always been rumours that Blyukher, or some of the officers round him, had seriously entertained the idea of a revolt. There is no reliable evidence of this, though Lyushkov gave information to the Japanese about 'opposition groupings' in Siberia. Much of this was seen, and transmitted back to Moscow, by the Soviet spy Richard Sorge. And whether it was factual or speculative, it seems from the timing that it may have been used against Blyukher.[64]

Blyukher had served with Postyshev on the Eastern Front in the Civil War, and also had connexions with Fedko and Kashirin. Fedko, appointed Commander of the Kiev Military District after Yakir's removal, had been replaced and brought to Moscow (as Assistant People's Commissar for War) in February 1938: that is, he was transferred with Kossior, and by the same method of kicking him upstairs to a high but powerless post. Fedko and Kossior (and Chubar) were executed – or at least sentenced – on the same day (26 February 1939).* We can very probably deduce a mixed military-political 'plot', which may have been linked with Blyukher.

The true reasons for proceeding against the Marshal seem to have been that he was an independent-minded soldier and (as a candidate member of the Central Committee) a politician, in a position of power and influence. His fall and death marks the end of the last tenuous hope of action against Stalin. By the beginning of November official listings of the military leadership ran: Voroshilov, Mekhlis, Shchadenko, Shaposhnikov, Budenny, Kulik, Timoshenko.[65] For the first time, the Purge operatives ranked before the surviving soldiery. A few weeks later the same

*The Ukrainians were also linked with Japan, through Sukhomlin.

order of listing contained an even more insulting and sympto-
matic insertion – that of Frinovsky, briefly become People's
Commissar for the Navy, immediately after Voroshilov.[66]

THE FALL OF YEZHOV

On 8 December 1938 it was announced that the rule, at once
pettifogging and bloodthirsty, of the horrible Yezhov had come to
an end. He had evidently lost effective control of the police by
mid-October, after which, as we have seen, the major investigations and interrogations were being conducted by Beria and
Shkiryatov. He was now replaced as People's Commissar for
Internal Affairs by Beria, retaining only his Commissariat of
Water Transport.

For a time Beria appeared together with Yezhov on the platforms and in the formal lists. Yezhov had by January dropped
back to his former 'correct' seniority in these lists, lowest of the
candidate members of the Politburo (Khrushchev being absent in
Kiev). He is last mentioned on the presidium for the anniversary
of Lenin's death, on 22 January.[67] By mid February he had disappeared. His fate is still obscure. There is a rumour that he was
produced at a secret party session in March, to be howled down –
but this may refer to an alleged attack on him (equally warm) by
Beria at a plenum in the autumn of 1938,[68] if it occurred at all.

But in any case, the 'bloodthirsty dwarf' thereafter slips into
the shadows with scarcely a trace. During the Stalin period, for
eighteen years, his name simply ceased to be mentioned. Rumours
abounded. He had been shot. He had gone mad and was under
restraint in an asylum.* There is a story that he was alive as late
as 1941, in one of the prisons near Moscow (reportedly the
Sukhanovka), in good health and granted privileges. There is
another that his body was found hanging on a tree in a prison
asylum with a sign round his neck, in a different hand, 'I am
filth'.[69] In the police, it was said that he was originally denounced
as a German spy.[70] But a good N.K.V.D. source maintains that

* The rumour of his madness seems to have been officially sponsored. To
some degree it 'explained' the excesses of the Purge in not too politically
damaging a fashion.

he was actually charged with being a British agent, which would indicate trial and execution *after* the signature of the Nazi-Soviet Pact.[71]

One positive piece of evidence that he was no longer well-regarded – if such were necessary – was the change of name when the town Yezhovo-Cherkessk dropped its prefix, confirming that he had not simply retired for reasons of health. Even after Stalin's death, some doubts remained. For example, though he is given in the index to Volume 50 of the *Large Soviet Encyclopedia*, published in 1957, it does not attach to his name the birth and death dates it provides not only for politicians in good standing and recently rehabilitated, but even for White Army generals. So we do not yet know in fact when Yezhov died. However, it seems clear that he was executed. In 1959 it was said[72] that 'Beria and Yezhov were duly punished for their criminal activity', and in 1962 he was referred to as having been 'repressed'[73] – a common euphemism. Finally, in 1966, a Soviet general described Stalin telling him in the summer of 1940, 'Yezhov was a scoundrel. In 1938 he killed many innocent people. We have executed him for this.'[74]

Beria soon made almost a clean sweep of the old N.K.V.D. The few who had survived from Yagoda's time, like Frinovsky and Zakovsky, who had prepared the Bukharin Trial, now followed their colleagues to execution. So did the Yezhov generation like Uspensky in the Ukraine, who also disappeared together with Redens, Nadezhda Alliluyeva's brother-in-law, and head of the Moscow N.K.V.D. The younger Kedrov's execution seems to have been earlier, though his father, with some friends, wrote letters to Stalin in February–April 1939[75] denouncing Beria – as a result of which they were shot, in spite of acquittal by the Military Collegium, on Beria's orders.[76]

By March 1939 Beria's men were everywhere in power: his own Georgian following held many of the major posts – in Moscow Merkulov and Kobulov, in Leningrad Goglidze, in the Maritime Province Gvishiani, in Byelorussia Tsanava.[77] These were what was later to be characterized as the 'Beria gang', until they all fell together in 1953.

The appointment of Beria is usually taken as a convenient date to mark the end of the Great Purge. Of Beria! – that is, of a man whose name, even in official Soviet circles, is now the very embodiment of terror and torture. And yet there is some sense in the convention.

Yezhov's removal was a simple piece of Stalinist expediency. The fact that most of his subordinates were executed under Beria was a simple matter of political mechanics. For apart from Yezhov himself and his personal nominees, the leading purgers, Stalin's own agents, did not suffer. Shkiryatov, who had acted as Yezhov's assistant, simply returned to Party work, and died, fully honoured as head of the Party Control Committee, a year after Stalin's own death, in 1954. Mekhlis and Vyshinsky also survived into the fifties. As for Malenkov, he flourished greatly in the years that followed, together with his rival Zhdanov.

In fact, throughout the Purge, Stalin had largely avoided public responsibility. And now, when the Terror had gone as far as it conceivably could, he could profitably sacrifice the man who had overtly carried out his secret orders, the man the Party and public then blamed most – and still, to some degree, do.

As we have said, by mid 1938 the N.K.V.D. itself, at the lower, operational level, had already wished to stop the progress of the Purge for obvious reasons. At the rate arrests were going, practically all the urban population would have been implicated within a few months. But they were caught in their own system. It was impossible for them not to arrest a man who had been denounced as an agent of Hitler. And an interrogator who did not demand the names of accomplices from each of his victims would soon himself come under denunciation for lack of vigilance or enthusiasm. By this time the idea had grown among prisoners that the more denunciations they made the better; 'Some even held the strange theory that the more people were jailed the sooner it would be realized that all this was nonsense and harmful to the Party.[78] ... My neighbour on the plank bed in the camp at Kolyma had once been head of the political department of a railway. He prided himself on having incriminated some 300 people. He said, as I had often heard in prison in Moscow, "The worse it is the better it is – like that, it will all be cleared up more quickly." '[79] In particular there was a keenness to involve as many loyal Stalinists as possible.

Weissberg[80] recounts the arrest in the spring of 1938 of the secretary of the Kharkov medical council. A man with an excellent memory, he knew the names of all the doctors in the city and denounced them all, pointing out that he was in an especially good position to have recruited them and that they were in any case largely from hostile social classes. He refused to name any of them as the leader of the plot, claiming that post for himself. The doctor told cell-mates that he had been inspired to take this course by reading about the case of a witch-burning in Germany at the time of the Inquisition when a young theologian charged with intelligence with the devil had at once pleaded guilty and named the members of the Inquisition as his accomplices. They were unable to torture him as he had confessed, and the case went up to the Archbishop who put an end to the business.

The climax of the mass Purge came in the first half of 1938, and the following months saw something of a diminution of pressure. Whether this was due solely to a simple loss of momentum at the lower operative level, or also to political pressures being put on Yezhov from above, is not clear. Stalin's discontent with Yezhov certainly begins in the early summer, when the plans to bring Beria in must have been laid. But he left Yezhov in office, and the veteran prisoner Ivanov-Razumnik speaks of a climax of brutality in September.[81]

It would perhaps be going too far to compare the situation too closely with one common in despotisms – like the Byzantine favourite who 'instead of being suffered to possess the reward of guilt was soon afterwards circumvented and destroyed by the more powerful villainy of the Minister himself, who retained sense and spirit enough to abhor the instrument of his own crimes'. Stalin had perhaps no strong liking for Yezhov, who never figures as one of his boon companions. But it would doubtless be Yezhov's narrow political comprehension, rather than any moral deficiency, that his superior might despise. The comparison is rather with the old autocratic tradition of disposing of the executioner who has killed one's rivals and thereby attracted to himself the main hatred of the survivors – a matter, in fact, of a common historical action which the wretched Yezhov had not the wit to foresee.

Even before Yezhov's fall was formalized, a significant case was reported from Omsk, where the Regional Prosecutor and his assistant were tried for abuse of authority, unjustified arrests, and the detaining of innocent people in prison, sometimes for as long as five months. They were sentenced to two years' imprisonment.[82]

This sentence seems only a partial triumph for justice. A few shootings of N.K.V.D. interrogators for extorting false confessions by violence are reported to symbolize the actual end of the Yezhov period. Captain Shiroky, of the Kiev N.K.V.D., was sentenced after having been made head of the Moldavian N.K.V.D. One prisoner mentions him as a 'not particularly harsh examining magistrate'.[83] Four others (according to other accounts) were charged with him.[84] There had, indeed, been occasional similar trials before, and speeches throughout the Purge period are full of condemnation of unjust persecutions. But this time the demonstration was clearly intentional. On the other hand, when certain Party officials became too free with their criticisms of police methods, Stalin pulled them up sharply with the circular telegram of 20 January 1939, explaining that torture was authorized (see p. 196).

At the same time certain cases which had become more of a nuisance than they were worth were dropped. For example, for the physicist Weissberg an agitation had been raised in the West to which even very Left-wing scientists had subscribed. Moreover, papers in his investigation had been inadequate, and muddled. It was now abandoned. (Weissberg explains how technical difficulties arose: when it was more or less accepted that the charges against him would be withdrawn, it was found that there were over twenty witnesses who had provided the evidence and it would be necessary to examine them all over again, and by this time they were of course scattered in camps throughout the country.)

The gross result of Beria's assumption of the N.K.V.D. was that a proportion of those in prison awaiting trial were released, making a good impression on the populace. Of those already in camp, apart from certain special rehabilitations like those of some military men in 1940, almost none were freed. An N.K.V.D. officer, himself under arrest, predicted this:

'Some of us will be released just to make it clear there has been a change; the remainder will go off to the camps to serve their sentences just the same.'
'What will be their criterion?'
'Chance. People are always trying to explain things by fixed laws. When you've looked behind the scenes as I have you know that blind chance rules a man's life in this country of ours.'[85]

But in the towns and villages of the Soviet Union, the pressure of haphazard mass arrests greatly eased. The country had been broken, and henceforward a limited number of arrests of men who had given some sort of cause for suspicion of disloyalty was sufficient to maintain the habit of submission and silence.

In general, Beria consolidated and institutionalized the system. From the 'Yezhovshchina' he developed, rather than an emergency operation against the people, a permanent method of rule.

STALIN AND BERIA CONSOLIDATE

The imprisoned Politburo members were not among those fortunate enough to benefit by the fall of Yezhov. While Ushakov and Nikolayev were at work on Eikhe, their colleague Rodos was submitting Kossior, Chubar and Kosarev to 'long tortures', receiving 'detailed instructions from Beria'.[86]

Rodos was to be described by Khrushchev[87] as 'a vile person with the brain of a bird and morally completely degenerate'. Summoned in 1956 before the Central Committee Presidium, he said 'I was told that Kossior and Chubar were enemies of the people and for this reason, I, as an investigative judge, had to make them confess that they were enemies. . . . I thought I was executing the orders of the Party.'[88] Khrushchev expressed great indignation at this answer, but all the same it is the only justification he gives for the activities of himself and his surviving colleagues during the same period.

One of Rodos's victims, Kosarev, was executed on 23 February.* Kossior followed him on 26 February.[89] Of the charges against Kossior, little is known except that he is supposed to have had communications 'with foreign counter-revolutionary organizations',[90] a phrase perhaps more applicable to émigré Ukrainian nationalists than to a foreign State. His two surviving brothers, Kazimir and Mikhail, perished too, as did his wife, put on 'List 4' and shot;[91] and the wife of one brother is reported attempting suicide on receiving a ten-year sentence.[92]

Apparently a public trial of Kossior and other high Ukrainian officials, together with scholars, scientists and technicians, had originally been designed, but this was now abandoned.[93] Nevertheless, as we have said, a joint trial seems to have taken place, of Kossior, Army Commander Fedko and Chubar.

It is logical to imagine Chubar and Kossior being tried together, as colleagues over a number of years in the Ukraine. But the obscurity of this phase is well illustrated by the fact that some recent Soviet works give the date of Chubar's death as 26 February 1939 and others as 12 August 1941. There are in fact two 'traditions', as historians of the Dark Ages would say, about the date of death in modern times of a Vice-Premier of a major country.† (Army Commander Fedko, too, is often given as dying on some unspecified date in 1943, as well as on 26 February 1939.)[97]

These two dates could be reconciled in some such way as the following – that Chubar was indeed sentenced with Kossior in February 1939, but not to death, or, if to death, was reprieved,

* If there is any truth in reports that Kosarev was seen in labour camps in the north later on, this may mean that the date given for his death is that of the sentence merely, and it was not carried out, or at least not immediately.

† To give a few examples: in the *Large Soviet Encyclopedia*, vol. 57, published in 1957, his death is given as 1939; in the *Small Soviet Encyclopedia*, vol. 10, published in 1960, it is 12 August 1941; in the *Ukrainian Soviet Encyclopedia*, vol. 16, published in 1964, it is 26 February 1939; in the notes to vol. 51 of Lenin's *Collected Works*, published in 1965, it is 1941. A biography of Chubar published in 1963[94] simply says that 'several months' after his dismissal in 1938 'he was arrested and shot', adding 'about a quarter of a century has passed since he died'. The commemorative articles in February 1966 for the seventy-fifth anniversary of his birth are also evasive. *Pravda* and *Pravda Ukrainy* say nothing. But a provincial paper[95] opts for the 1941 date. Chubar's wife was also executed.[96]

being finally dealt with during Stalin's panic after the first defeats, when many who had not been shot were liquidated – including, indeed, another ex-Vice-Premier, Antipov. And similarly with Fedko and the various parallel cases we have already noted. But we can hardly claim to have solved the point incontrovertibly.

There remained one Politburo figure who, though in bad odour, was not under arrest – Petrovsky. His position had now been extremely difficult for two years.

Among the Leningraders arrested in 1937 was his elder son Peter, who had edited the local *Leningradskaya Pravda*. Petrovsky, candidate member of the Politburo, Head of State of the Ukrainian Republic, was unable to get news of him. He met a 'stone wall of silence'. Friends, 'high officials in the Party and State', made several attempts to find out the facts. Finally they had to give up. The strictest instructions had been given to prevent anyone discovering what went on 'behind the walls of the Lubyanka'. Young Petrovsky never emerged alive.[98] Another son, Corps Commander L. G. Petrovsky, was expelled from the Party and Army, and though arrested was later released.[99]

Meanwhile, in July 1937, when various illegalities were being perpetrated in the Ukraine without the consent of the leadership, Petrovsky had written to Kalinin, his titular superior, complaining that the principles of Party democracy were being overborne.[100] This sounds as if it may have been his share of the reported complaint made to Moscow by the local leadership at the time, which was made the excuse for the Molotov Mission of August 1937.

He had, it is said, 'become critical of the personality cult'.[101] But on 4 February 1938 he was awarded the Order of Lenin for his sixtieth birthday. And he remained theoretically Chairman of the Ukrainian Supreme Soviet throughout the fall of all his colleagues. After a conversation with Stalin which he described as 'short and painful', he was removed, in June 1938, from his Ukrainian posts.[102] This was, it is now pointed out, done 'unconstitutionally'.[103]

He was posted to the Presidium of the All-Union Supreme Soviet, where he continued to sign decrees, in Kalinin's absence, as Deputy Chairman of that body, right up to late October 1938.[104] At the 7 November Parade he did not appear with the leadership, and was henceforth not to be named in the listings.

A political case was concocted against him in the usual way. During the Khrushchev era this was said to have been at Kaganovich's instigation, while 'only thanks to the support of N. S. Khrushchev, G. I. Petrovsky was able to escape physical repression'.[105] The caretaker of a villa near Kiev which had been used by the Ukrainian leaders made, after beatings, a confession incriminating Petrovsky. Petrovsky's secretary is also reported under arrest in the same circumstances.[106] A brother of Petrovsky is reported in the Butyrka in 1938.[107]

In March 1939, during the XVIIIth Congress, charges were made as a result of which he was not elected to the new Central Committee: he was accused of friendship with K. V. Sukhomlin, Ukrainian Politburo member since exposed as a Japanese spy; of failing to report his knowledge of S. V. Kossior's connexions with foreign counter-revolutionary organizations; and of having (presumably in the twenties) opposed Kaganovich's nomination as Ukrainian First Secretary.[108]

In fact, there is no doubt that a case against him, long prepared, was now to be launched. But (whatever the effect of Khrushchev's intervention) Stalin held his hand. Petrovsky was relieved of his membership of the Presidium of the Supreme Soviet (his last and titular appointment) on 31 May 1939 in a public fashion and with the title 'Comrade' – an indication that his name was not yet unsayable.

He had been unable to get any employment for some months, living on whatever his wife could earn. Finally, in June 1939, he was allowed to take up the post of Assistant Director of the Museum of the Revolution,* which he held till Stalin's death.[110] His name disappeared from reference books, and most foreigners imagined he had been executed. But it still continued to appear in one single list, that of the former Bolshevik members of the Tsarist Duma. It has been pointed out[111] that Stalin shot none of these: the others, all third-rate figures, survived to die natural

---

* There were vacancies there. The Director, Ya. S. Ganetsky, had been shot.[109]

deaths. Whether this is a special sentimentalism is, of course, unknown.

Petrovsky survived Stalin, only dying in 1958. In fact, he was the first figure to be restored to favour after Stalin's death. A decree on 28 April 1953[112] awarded him the Order of the Red Banner of Labour in connexion with his seventy-fifth birthday and 'his services to the Soviet State'. His real birthday had taken place on 4 February, at a time when Stalin was still alive, when nothing had been said of it. So the incident was quite plainly a conscious political demonstration, made during Beria's attack on the Stalin heritage.

During the Purge period Petrovsky had certainly suffered, if less than many. Yet it would perhaps not be inappropriate to recall that, when Commissar of Internal Affairs in 1918, he had ordered the unconditional shooting of all engaged in any sort of 'White Guard' activity.[113]

Meanwhile, the beginning of 1939 saw various governmental and Party shifts: for example, on 3 January Kosygin was made Minister of the Textile Industry. January and February saw heavy propaganda about economic discipline, the announcement of the theses of the new Five-Year Plan (1938–42) and the calling of the XVIIIth Party Congress for March.

Towards the end of February came an event which caused little stir. One last ex-oppositionist remained. Krupskaya had been able to do little during these years, though Stalin had allowed her to save one or two figures like I. D. Chigurin, arrested in 1937 – even though, his health ruined, and not fully rehabilitated, he had to live in poverty thereafter. Though still a member of the Central Committee, Krupskaya had only the minor job of Assistant People's Commissar for Education, and even there was 'deprived of the possibility of influencing decisions in education'.[114]

She died on 28 February, and Stalin himself carried the urn with her ashes at her funeral.

> Nadezhda Krupskaya will no more protect
> The innocent, the dying, those executed like rats[115]

even to the slight extent that she had done so. The very next day, the head of the Commissariat of Education's publishing house ordered his subordinates: 'Don't print another word about Krupskaya.' A part of her works was sent off to the 'special store' sections of libraries, part was buried in oblivion and not republished.[116]

THE XVIIITH CONGRESS

The XVIIIth Party Congress of 10–21 March 1939, which saw Petrovsky's fall, was the scene of the complete consolidation of all Stalin had striven for since that of 1934. The changes were extraordinary.

Of the 1,966 delegates to the previous Congress, 1,108 had been arrested for counter-revolutionary crimes.[117] Even of the residue lucky enough to survive, only fifty-nine now appeared as delegates. Of these, twenty-four were old Central Committee members, leaving *only thirty-five of the 1,827 rank-and-file delegates of five years previously – less than 2 per cent*! This is an indication of how literally we may take the thesis that Stalin created an entirely new Party in this period.

The list of the Central Committee membership now elected shows that fifty-five of the seventy-one who had been full members in 1934 had gone, and sixty of the sixty-eight candidate members. Of the 115 names no longer appearing, which included some natural and some possibly natural deaths, ninety-eight had been shot, as Khrushchev later stated in the 1956 Secret Speech. A later account by a Soviet historian maintains that this is an understatement, and that really 'about 110' of them were 'murdered'.[118] The discrepancy is possibly due to the inclusion or otherwise of suicides, assassinations and so on, and of those shot at a later date, such as Lozovsky.

In the new Committee one can note the groupings – no longer political factions as in the pre-Stalin period, but personal followings – which were to contend for Stalin's favour over the next fourteen years, and for power thereafter.

Zhdanov and his group are well represented with himself, Shcherbakov, Kosygin and A. A. Kuznetsov as full members, and Popkov and Rodionov as candidate members. The first two were to be the alleged victims of a later 'Doctors' Plot', and three out of the other four were to be shot in the 'Leningrad Case' of 1949–50.

Another group was associated with Malenkov: himself and V. M. Andrianov, in the Central Committee, Pervukhin, Ponomarenko, Pegov, Tevosyan and Malyshev as candidate members – together with Shatalin on the Revision Commission, his closest associate.

Beria was better represented still. With himself, Bagirov and V. N. Merkulov on the Central Committee and Gvishiani, Goglidze, Kobulov, Dekanozov, Arutinov, Bakradze, Charkviani as candidate members (plus Tsanava on the Revision Commission), we see his control in the Secret Police and in the political mechanism in the Caucasus. (There were two other N.K.V.D. representatives – Kruglov and Maslennikov as candidate members – a total of eight secret police on the Central Committee, by far the highest number yet. These last two were to survive Beria.)

Khrushchev too had his band – four full members of the Committee from his own selection in the Ukraine.

Stalin's own personal group were also of course fully represented, with Mekhlis, Shkiryatov, Poskrebyshev, Shchadenko and Vyshinsky.

In the Politburo the losses had been less great than at the lower level. But they were still remarkable. Kirov had been assassinated and Kuibyshev had died, or been poisoned. Ordzhonikidze had either been murdered, or forced into a suicide which was scarcely different from murder. Rudzutak had been shot eight months earlier, Kossior just before the Congress. Chubar (presumably) and Postyshev were in jail awaiting execution. Petrovsky had been removed, and was in Moscow, uncertain of his fate and begging for a menial post. Of the four who had been brought in between the Congresses, Khrushchev and Zhdanov were balanced by Eikhe and Yezhov, in prison awaiting execution. Of four of the fallen leaders it has now been specifically said that they were tortured (Rudzutak, Eikhe, Kossior and Chubar).

On 22 March 1939, four promotions were made in and to the

Politburo, of those who had served Stalin most satisfactorily during the recent period. Zhdanov and Khrushchev were raised to full membership, Beria became a candidate member, and so did Shvernik, who after Tomsky's removal in June 1929 had been appointed head of the unions. He had adequately transformed them into organizations for mobilizing and disciplining labour. Henceforth he was to serve continuously on the Politburo and its post-Stalin equivalent the Presidium, retiring in 1966, but keeping his Central Committee membership.

There is a notable difference in Stalin's treatment of the more senior generation of his supporters on the Politburo, and those promoted later. If we take the members of that body who supported him against the oppositions: of the eleven promoted to it up to July 1926, six survived right through the Purges, two were physically destroyed by informal means (Kirov and Ordzhonikidze), one died in doubtful circumstances (Kuibyshev), one, though removed from his posts, survived till after Stalin's own death (Petrovsky), and only one was 'tried' and shot (Rudzutak). But of the eight promoted from July 1926 until the end of 1937, only one (Zhdanov) survived. All the others were executed or presumed executed.

This distinction should perhaps be interpreted as follows: in the earlier period it was not a question of Stalin simply nominating rapidly promoted figures from the second rank of the Party. He was bound to rely on men who had reached high position to some extent on their reputations, and who in any case were widely enough known to the leading circles of the Party and had good enough Party records for their presence not to appear absurd on a body still containing distinguished and widely-known oppositionists.

They were men who, in however minor a way compared with the Trotskys and Bukharins, yet represented a continuity with Lenin's leading cadre. Some of them were eager supporters of the Great Terror, like Kaganovich. Others, like Molotov, may have had qualms but became enthusiastic accomplices, whether through fear or from other motives. More reluctant figures, like Kalinin, remained useful figureheads. In disposing of them, Stalin inclined to roundabout and concealed methods. But the Eikhes and

Postyshevs carried little more Party prestige than the other members of the Central Committee, and they were as readily expendable if they failed to satisfy.

The new leadership, Stalinist in every sense, made the Congress a triumphal celebration. At the same time, dissociating themselves from Yezhovism, the most notorious Purge operators deplored more strongly than ever the excesses of the Purge.

Shkiryatov quoted at length an incident of a man in Archangel wrongly removed from his job, arrested, and restored as a result of an appeal to the Central Committee. Zhdanov referred to a man who had written 142 denunciations, all false, and raised a number of cases in which individual Party members had been wrongly expelled, including such incidents as one in Tambov province where the expulsion and wrongful arrest of one man led to the expulsion from the Party of his wife, and seven other members, and from the Komsomol of twenty-eight Young Communists, while ten non-Party teachers lost their jobs.

Khrushchev's ally Serdyuk expressed horror at a denunciation of a large number of enemies of the people in the Party apparatus in Kiev in December 1938, which had turned out on investigation to be signed by a false name, and to be in the handwriting of the head of the Cultural Section of one of the district committees. Another case, also in Kiev, was of a woman teacher who in 1936–7 had denounced a large number of innocent people, and also obtained by blackmail and threats 5,000 roubles from various organizations and three free trips to a resort: Serdyuk explained to the disgusted delegates that her slanders had been written at the dictation of 'enemies of the people since unmasked', and that she herself had been sentenced to five years.

Stalin himself summed up: the Purge had been accompanied by 'grave mistakes', indeed 'more mistakes than might have been expected'. 'Undoubtedly,' he went on, 'we shall have no further need of resorting to the method of mass purges. Nevertheless, the Purge of 1933–6 was unavoidable and its results, on the whole, were beneficial.'[119]

The phrase '1933–6' might have struck the layman a little oddly. The fact is that the expulsions from the Party at that time had been constitutionally and publicly authorized, while the later

Purge had not ever been formalized, so could be taken as irrelevant.

Party executions, in fact, continued. The Congress itself was accompanied by that of Yakovlev, shot on 14 March. Over the next years Stalin and Beria wound up most of Yezhov's unfinished business.

In July 1939 the Prosecutor's sanction for Eikhe's arrest was at last obtained, to some extent legalizing the position. Eikhe was presented with the charges against him on 25 October 1939, and wrote to Stalin protesting his innocence – and blaming the frame-up in part on Trotskyites he now took credit for having persecuted in West Siberia. Ushakov and Nikolayev, he added, had 'utilized the knowledge that my broken ribs have not properly mended and have caused me great pain', as the result of which he had incriminated himself and others. He asked for an end to 'the vile provocation which wound itself like a snake round many persons, in large measure through my meanness and criminal slander'.[120] There is a story that, temporarily insane by torture in 1938, he had cried out that he confessed his 'guilt of belonging to a criminal organization which goes by the name of the Central Committee of the All-Union Communist Party (Bolsheviks)'.[121]

One of the charges against Eikhe is a trifle mysterious. He was accused of being responsible for certain 'resolutions of the Central Committee of the All-Union Communist Party (Bolsheviks) and of the Council of People's Commissars'. He pleaded that the resolutions in question 'were not made on my initiative and without my participation', and were 'in any case correct'. Those made without his 'participation' can only have been resolutions of the Council of People's Commissars, to which he did not belong until October 1937. The natural explanation would seem to be that the charge was a general one, made against a number of accused, some of whom *had* participated. As to the resolutions of the Central Committee, it seems plausible that as a charge brought against prominent political figures it may refer to decisions taken in the autumn of 1936, on the rehabilitation of Bukharin and Rykov. But doubtless other matters are also involved, and the point remains an obscure one.

Eikhe's letters to Stalin were ignored, though evidently kept on file. On 2 February 1940 he was finally brought before a court, where he withdrew his confessions and again attributed them to torture by the investigator. On 4 February he was shot. (His wife was also executed.)[122] It is interesting, in view of the previous association of political and military executions, that Admiral Dushenov, Commander of the Northern Fleet, former sailor on the *Aurora*, perished the same day.[123] In fact, there is some reason to suspect a major secret trial, or clearing up of an N.K.V.D. backlog, as in July 1938 and February 1939. For Meyerhold's death is given as 2 February 1940, while we learn that Mikhail Koltsov was also sentenced on 1 February.[124]

1939 had seen the executions of Rukhimovich, Ukhanov, Akulov, Sulimov and many others. Bubnov was shot on 12 January 1940. His daughter Valya was sent to labour camp.[125] Krylenko was now executed, and over the year others followed. On 10 December 1940 came Postyshev's turn. Stalin had decided that 'Postyshev . . . will be no more' and now came 'Postyshev's annihilation and branding without reason as an "enemy of the people" '. He was accused of 'diversion, conspiracy, and departure from Leninism'.[126] It will be remembered that Postyshev's Kiev Committee had been charged with Trotskyism. So, unlike the 'Bukharinism' alleged against Rudzutak and Eikhe, this may perhaps have figured in the indictment. Postyshev's eldest son, Valentin, was shot, and his other children sent to camps.[127]

The imprisoned officers went the same way as the politicals, Marshal Yegorov perhaps as late as 10 March 1941 (see p. 320).

The last leading figure of the Stalinist cadres to go was Antipov, who (like Chubar if our supposition is correct) was liquidated, in Stalin's elimination during the first German advance of the last remaining alternative leaders, on 24 August 1941. Stalin's victory on the political front had been complete. Now, in the disaster arising from his own miscalculation, no move to replace him was possible. Subjected to this very severe test, the Purge proved to have accomplished its object.

Epilogue

HERITAGE OF TERROR

None of the evils which totalitarianism ... claims to
remedy is worse than totalitarianism itself.

ALBERT CAMUS

'ZACHTO – why?' – the last words of Yakov Livshits, Old
Bolshevik and Deputy People's Commissar, as he awaited execution on 30 January 1937, got no answer. During the few remaining
months that old Party members were still at liberty and able,
occasionally at least, to talk of such things, his question was much
repeated. If experienced politicians felt baffled, the man in the
street was even more uncomprehending: 'I asked myself and
others, why, what for? No one could give me an answer.'[1] As for
victims, the first words on entering a cell were almost always, we
are told, a shaken 'But why, why?'[2] The prison and camp
literature tells of the same phrase, 'Why?', often found written
on cell walls, carved into the sides of prison wagons and on the
planks of the transit camps.[3] The old partisan Dubovoy* (whose
long white beard, of which he was very proud, the examining
magistrate had torn out) even developed in jail the theory that
the Purge was the result of an increase in the number of sun-
spots.[4]

The simplest form of true answer would of course be: 'to
destroy or disorganize all possible sources of opposition to
Stalin's progress to absolute rule'. But we can also see, in the
system he created after his victory, the specific form of despotism
for which he had sacrificed the nation and Party.

The victory was inevitably marked by a good deal of dislocation, and stability had not been achieved when the Soviet Union
was faced with international emergencies, starting with the
Finnish War of 1939–40, which became a desperate struggle for
mere existence in the four-year war with the Nazis from 1941 to
1945, and its aftermath of reconstruction. It was not until 1947–8

*Father of the Army Commander of that name.

that the Stalinist State became politically and institutionally stabilized.

But meanwhile two main objects had already been accomplished. A vast number of past or potential 'hostile' elements had been destroyed or sent to labour camps, and the rest of the population reduced to the most complete silence and obedience. And on the other hand, the Communist Party itself had been turned into something entirely new.

This political transformation is to some extent masked by the fact that the organizational forms remained the same. But in fact the discontinuity between the Party of 1934 and the Party of 1939 was radical. The people opposed to Stalin had already been almost entirely eliminated from the leading organs of the Party. Over the Purge period the Stalinists themselves, except for a small and peculiar personal following, were destroyed. The extent of the discontinuity is plain if we consider the delegates to the XVIIth and the XVIIIth Congresses. As we have seen, and it is worth repeating, *less than 2 per cent* of the rank-and-file delegates of 1934 held their position in 1939. The Communist Party of 1939 was as different from that of 1934 as Buchanan's Democratic Party was from Andrew Jackson's. If the latter case is more evident to historians, it is partly because, in the Communist case, emphasis on the continuous tradition, and thus concealment of the change, were of much greater political importance to the rulers.

The earlier leaders had wished to preserve all political rights for the limited leading membership of the old Party. Stalin, in destroying that Party, in a sense threw the positions of power open. He instituted the *carrière ouverte aux talents* in place of the old system. It is true that the 'talents' required were of a special type. But at least any man, whatever his origins and however recently he had joined the Party, could be sure of a good post if he exhibited adequate servility and ruthlessness. But at the same time, among the new cadres of Stalinism, Party theory in its old justificatory form was still to be a basis. As Hitler had remarked, 'Any violence which does not spring from a firm spiritual base, will be wavering and uncertain. It lacks the stability which can only rest in a fanatical outlook.'[5]

A close student of, and victim of, the Purge acutely analyses the thoughts of the truly orthodox among Stalin's operatives. Taking the case of a former N.K.V.D. officer known for his brutality, but gentle and even sentimental when himself a prisoner, he concludes:

What would a Prygov say if he were required to defend himself in a court of law? He would not, we believe, refer to superior orders, but to the teachings of Marxism and Leninism as he understood them. Prygov was as loyal and obedient as an S.S. man. But his faith was founded on a conviction that it fully accorded with the demands of reason and conscience. He was fully convinced that his was no blind faith, but was founded on science and logic. He was brutal because the general line required him to be brutal. The general line, so long as it accorded with the fundamental tenets of Marxism, was everything to him. Without the allegedly scientific foundation of the general line, which was the backbone of his faith, all the instructions of the Party authorities would have lost their significance for him. He was convinced of the logical and ethical correctness of his Marxist principles, and on this conviction his faith depended.[6]

For the Stalinist Party maintained, in theory, the old doctrine and the old loyalty. But the discipline which had hitherto been due, in theory at least, to a corporate collective leadership, now became the service of one man and his personal decisions. The loyalties and solidarities which had bound the membership now worked in one direction only – upwards; sideways, as regards the Party comrades among whom there had subsisted some degree of common trust, only mutual suspicion and 'vigilance' remained.

A new political system had been established. Not merely had the new men everywhere taken the place of the veteran cadres, but they had been given a long, severe and testing exercise in the methods and attitudes of the new style of rule. The experience of the Purge had hardened and tempered them, as the collectivization struggle, and before that the Civil War, had tempered their predecessors. The alloy, however, was a new one. Dostoyevsky remarks, in *The House of the Dead*, 'Tyranny is a habit; it grows upon us, and in the long run, turns into a disease. . . . The human being, member of society, is drowned for ever in the tyrant, and it is practically impossible for him to regain human dignity, repentance and regeneration.'

A Communist philosopher saw Stalin 'as the apex of a pyramid which widened gradually towards the base and was composed of many "little Stalins": they, seen from above, were the objects and, seen from below, the creators and guardians of the "cult of the personality". Without the regular and unchallenged functioning of this mechanism the "cult of the personality" would have remained a subjective dream, a pathological fact, and would not have attained the social effectiveness which it exercised for decades . . .'[7]

At the apex this led to an extravagant adulation of Stalin. A Congress delegate of 1939 remarked: '. . . At that moment I saw our beloved father, Stalin, and I lost consciousness. The "hurrahs" resounded for a long time, and it was probably this noise which brought me to myself . . .'[8] And this was reasonably typical. A whole literature was devoted to the *Vozhd*.

In the country as a whole a new public mood had been created. The experience had given the ruled as well as the rulers a new impress. The population had become habituated to silence and obedience, to fear and submission. In the years which remained of Stalin's rule after the Purges, the all-out mass terror was no longer necessary. The machine had been started up, and could now be kept rolling without extraordinary efforts. It is true, in a sense, that the comparative calm which may reign in an autocracy following the elimination of all opponents or potential opponents is no less a manifestation of terror than the original killings – is, in fact, merely a product and consolidation of them: '*Ubi solitudinem faciunt, pacem appellant.*'

In any case the security organs never cease to strike and strike brutally at all suspects. As late as 1940, Saratov jail was still holding ten men in cells for one or two.[9] Right through the period up to a million prisoners a year, replacing the losses by death, were dispatched to the camps, and the threat remained ever present in all minds; yet the intensity of 1936–8 was never reached again. In one vast operation Russia had been silenced and broken, and from then on more selective terror sufficed. This was partly because a good proportion of the new recruitment of forced labourers came from local and partial actions, starting with the Baltic and Eastern Poland, where the work of 1917–39 in Russia proper was compressed into a couple of years, in 1939–41.

Apart from the *c.* 440,000 Polish civilians sent to camp, in September 1939 the Russians took about 200,000 Polish prisoners of war. Most of the officers and several thousand soldiers were sent to camps at Starobelsk, Kozielsk and Ostachkov. In April 1940 there were about 15,000 of them there, including 8,700 officers. Only forty-eight were ever seen again: these had been removed from the camps and sent to Soviet prisons. The missing group included 800 doctors and a dozen university professors.

When, under the agreement between the Poles and Russians following the Soviet entry into the war, the former Polish prisoners were allowed to leave Russia and form their own army in the Middle East, the Polish representatives gave the Russians lists of names of soldiers who were known to have fallen into Russian hands and had not been released.

The Polish Ambassador Professor Kot raised the subject ten times with Molotov and Vyshinsky between October 1941 and July 1942, and always received the reply that all the prisoners had been released. When Kot met Stalin in November 1941, Stalin made a call to the N.K.V.D. on the subject. Whatever the answer was, Stalin then went on to the next point and would not discuss the matter further.

When General Sikorski saw Stalin on 3 December 1941, he was told that perhaps the missing men had got over the border into Manchuria. But Stalin promised to look into the question, saying that if any Poles had not been released, through local obstruction by N.K.V.D. officers, the latter would be disciplined.

In April 1943 the Germans announced the discovery of mass graves containing executed Poles in the Katyn Forest, near Smolensk. But within two days the Russians produced a clear-cut official story of Polish officers in camps in the Smolensk area who had been left behind and had fallen into German hands – a totally different account from those which had previously been given by Stalin and his subordinates.

Allied leaders, while not all actively accepting the Russian story, took the line that no trouble should now be caused in view of the overriding importance of unity against Hitler. The Western press, on the other hand, accepted the Russian version almost unanimously. The American military paper *Stars and Stripes* even published a caricature of a Polish officer, represented as falsely supposed to have been killed by the Russians.[10]

The Germans allowed access to the Katyn Forest to a large number of expert or interested parties – a European medical commission, containing experts from universities all over Europe including neutrals such as Dr Naville, Professor of Forensic Medicine at Geneva;* representatives of the Polish underground; senior Allied prisoners of war – who correctly refused to pronounce any opinion, but who reported confidentially to their Governments that the German story was quite clearly true.

Basically, the proof consisted of digging up previously untouched mass graves, examining the corpses, compacted under earth, finding on them Soviet newspapers and similar material going up to April 1940, and nothing later, and noting that they were mostly in thick clothing, as against the Russian story that the executions took place in the warmth of September 1941.

The bodies found at Katyn, 4,143 in number, represented only those who had been in the Kozielsk camp; 2,914 were identified, and 80 per cent of these were among the lists of missing the Polish authorities had assembled.

What happened to the Poles from the other two camps, numbering about 10,400 men, remains unknown. There are stories that a number of Polish prisoners were packed into old barges and scuttled in the White Sea. And there are also tales of a mass execution and burial resembling Katyn in the neighbourhood of Kharkov.[11]

The Nuremberg judges examined the Katyn Affair from 1 to 3 July 1946 in a derisory fashion, and did not mention Nazi responsibility for it in their verdict. No evidence of any sort has ever been forthcoming from German prisoners or captured material of Nazi responsibility for this particular crime.

* The only member to withdraw his evidence was the Bulgarian Dr Markov, who did so after some months in prison when arrested by the Russians on their entry into his country.

But it is now hardly necessary here to say more. It is nowhere believed any longer that the Germans were responsible, and the matter is simply not referred to in the Soviet or the Polish press – apart from one hint about 'the lack of news of those who were missing' in a Warsaw periodical.[12]

The significance, from the point of view of our theme, the Purges, is that we have here a clear-cut example of a mass execution carried out, without trial, and in complete secrecy, as a routine administrative measure – and in peacetime.

One further case, this time of two individuals, is equally illustrative. Henrik Ehrlich and Viktor Alter, the leaders of the Jewish 'Bund' Socialists in Poland, fell into Russian hands in September 1939 at the time of the Soviet–German invasion of Poland. They were both veterans of the Social Democratic movement in the old Russian Empire, and Ehrlich had been a member of the Executive of the Petrograd Soviet in 1917. They were taken to the Butyrka, charged with acting for the Polish Government in various infiltrations of saboteurs from 1919 to 1939. Ehrlich, who was on one occasion interrogated by Beria personally, insisted on writing all his answers. Alter replied simply to each question: 'It is absolutely false, and you know it well.'

After eighteen months, in July 1941, they were transferred to Saratov and condemned to death. They both refused to appeal, but after ten days their sentences were commuted to ten years' imprisonment. The amnesty granted to all Polish prisoners shortly afterwards resulted in their release in September and October respectively. They were asked to organize a Jewish anti-fascist committee, and it was clear that their connexions with old members of the Bund in the American trade unions – such as David Dubinsky – were much valued. Ehrlich became president and Alter secretary of this new organization, and the Soviet actor Mikhoels was named a member of its Presidium. Beria personally sponsored the organization, while telling them that on all international questions Stalin took the final decision.

On 4 December they went out of their hotel in Kuibyshev, and were never seen again. At first the pretence was kept up that what had happened to them was unknown. But after protests from Mr

Attlee and from the leading trade unionists in America and England, and also from important world figures like Albert Einstein and Reinholdt Niebuhr, Litvinov finally sent, in February 1943, a letter to the head of the American Federation of Labor, William Green, explaining that they had been arrested and executed for trying to persuade Soviet troops to cease contesting the advance of the German armies and to conclude an immediate peace with Nazi Germany. He added that they had been executed in December 1942 – but their colleague, Mr Lucjan Blit, who was with them in Kuibyshev until the moment of their arrest, believes that this is probably a mistake for December 1941.

Katyn and the Ehrlich–Alter Cases are representative of a host of similar actions, both having exceptionally come to the notice of the world public through special circumstances. Apart from continuous attrition in the old lands of Russia, particular operations provided a flow of victims. After the Poles and Balts in 1939–41, various other minorities were deported. In 1941, the Soviet Germans; in 1943–4, seven entire nations, mainly from the Caucasus, were arrested and deported *en bloc*.[13] German and Japanese prisoners of war filled the camps. In 1945–6 the Eastern territories were again ravaged, and with the end of the war those Russian soldiers who had fought for, or merely been captured by, the Germans were mostly sent to camps on their return.

THE PURGE AND THE WAR

Meanwhile, in 1941–5, the country had felt the effects of the measures taken by Stalin against his military leaders. A recent Soviet estimate, as yet unpublished in the U.S.S.R., gives figures slightly higher than those long accepted in the West. By its reckoning the purge accounted for:

> 3 of the 5 Marshals
> 14 of the 16 Army Commanders Class I and II
> 8 of the 8 Admirals ('Flagman') Class I and II
> 60 of the 67 Corps Commanders
> 136 of the 199 Divisional Commanders
> 221 of the 397 Brigade Commanders.[14]

All 11 of the Vice-Commissars of Defence went; and 75 out of 80 members of the Supreme Military Soviet. Nor was the effect confined to the upper echelons: about half the officer corps, some 35,000 in all, were shot or imprisoned.* As Khrushchev later said, the Purges started 'at Company and Battalion Commander level'.[15]

The Soviet novelist Konstantin Simonov, who associated much with military circles, gives an account of a conversation between two generals – 'Serpilin' and 'Ivan Alexeyevich' – in his *Soldiers Are Made, Not Born*.[16] Ivan Alexeyevich comments that the Purge was not merely a matter of individual generals.

'The whole thing goes deeper. In the autumn of 1940 when the Finnish war had already ended, the Inspector-General of the Infantry carried out an inspection of Regimental Commanders and in the course of my duties I saw the resulting data. The review was attended by 225 commanders of infantry regiments. How many of them do you think had at that time graduated from the Frunze Academy?'

'I cannot really guess,' said Serpilin, 'judging from the preceding events, presumably not very many.'

'What if I tell you that there was not a single one to have done so?'

'It just cannot be . . .'

'Don't believe it then, if you find that easier. Well, how many of the 225 do you think had gone through ordinary military college? 25 of them! and 200 of them had come from junior lieutenants' courses and regimental schools!'

As 'Ivan Alexeyevich' himself points out, 225 regiments constitute 75 divisions or half the strength of the peace-time Army, a reasonable sample. What Simonov is saying, in effect, is that the Army purge (plus the comparatively minor Finnish war of 1939–40) accounted for virtually every single Regimental Commander throughout the entire Soviet Army apart from those promoted to fill gaps higher up. Though fictional in form, this is given in such a way that it can certainly be taken as factual; and no rebuttal was made in the military press.

Similarly, in his labour camp, Gorbatov 'wondered how the

* Two figures are reported as having been discussed in recent confidential meetings of Soviet historians in the study of the period – a 'low' one of 33,000 and a 'high' one of 40,000.

officers newly appointed to high rank, with no battle experience, would deal with operations in a real war. Honest, brave men, devoted to their country they might be, but yesterday's battalion commander would be head of a division, yesterday's regimental commander of a corps; in charge of an army, or a whole front, there would be at best a former divisional commander or his deputy. How many futile losses and failures would there be? What would our country suffer just because of this?'[17]

As is now confirmed by Russian military writers, the Purge had indeed led to 'inexperienced commanders' being promoted. As early as 1937, 60 per cent of the commanding cadres in rifle units, 45 per cent in tank units and 25 per cent in air units are given as in this category.[18] Moreover, 'The cadre of leaders who had gained military experience in Spain and in the Far East was almost completely liquidated.'[19]

Nor could the atmosphere fail to affect the discipline of the Army:

The policy of large-scale repression against the military cadres led also to undermined military discipline, because for several years officers of all ranks and even soldiers in the Party and Komsomol cells were taught to 'unmask' their superiors as hidden enemies. It is natural that this caused a negative influence on the state of military discipline in the first war period.[20]

Mekhlis, in his report to the 1939 XVIIIth Congress, expressed horror and sorrow at 'incorrect expulsions' from the Party which had taken place in the Army in 1935, 1936 and 1937, on the basis of 'slander', instead of the correct method of 'documents and facts'.[21] And over the next few years a handful of generals were released – Rokossovsky and Gorbatov, for example. But still, as with the civilian purge (and the similar crocodile tears of Zhdanov), the arrests did not actually cease and cases continued to be processed. In 1940, Herling mentions a number of Soviet generals with whom he shared a cell. Most of them had been badly beaten, and showed the marks of ill-mended broken bones.

Even now, the Red Army had considerable striking power in the right hands. This was shown over the summer of 1939. After a very shaky start, a build-up of superior forces (itself a feat), luckily entrusted to the one superlative soldier of the old First Cavalry Army, Zhukov, threw back the Japanese invaders of Mongolia in model fashion at Khalkhin-Gol. But even as this was being done, the armoured tactics he had used, sponsored under Tukhachevsky (who with his group had by 1937 been beginning to create an 'elite army emerging from the mass'),[22] were being condemned and abandoned, and within months the tactical doctrine of the Red Army was back to old-fashioned 'mass', and the tanks were distributed in packets to lesser unit commands.

The post-Purge promotions placed men totally unsuited or untrained for high command in key positions. None of them showed any capacity for strategic thinking, and even the tactical dispositions on the frontier were proof of 'a dull or listless mind'.[23] The rigidity of the military-political machine meant that failure at the top produced certain dislocation. The 'mass' on which post-Tukhachevsky doctrine relied became too large and sluggish to be manipulated in such circumstances.

In the Finnish War of 1939–40 the 'initial incompetence of the Voroshilov–Mekhlis clique literally plunged the Red Army into disaster', says John Erickson.[24] He adds that apart from this high-level failure there was disastrous lack of the 'nerve' that Tukhachevsky had insisted on in junior commanders: independence of spirit had been destroyed by the Purges.

The German General Staff's secret rating of the Red Army at the end of 1939 spoke of it as a 'gigantic military instrument'. Though finding the 'principles of leadership good', it added 'the leadership itself is, however, too young and inexperienced'.[25] In 1940, German intelligence, warning against an underestimation of the Red Army, felt that nevertheless it would take four years before that Army was back to its 1937 level of efficiency.[26]

There were two positive ingredients in the gloomy post-Purge scene. First, Army Commander Shaposhnikov, the Tsarist colonel, had never lost Stalin's trust. Through the débâcle, he contrived to seek out and promote talent. As Chief of Staff his powers were limited, but he brought into the senior command posts a number of efficient officers, even though not enough to make up for those rising through the whims of Stalin, Mekhlis and Voroshilov.

Secondly, by great good luck, two of the old First Cavalry Army officers were good soldiers. After Voroshilov's Finnish effort, Timoshenko, who had picked up the pieces and was now (7 May 1940) a Marshal, was made Defence Commissar. At the same time Zhukov took the newly-revived rank of full General, and then various key commands, culminating in his appointment as Chief of Staff in January 1941.

The reforms which took place between 1940 and the German attack on Russia in 1941 were inadequate, but without them the Red Army would probably have been completely ruined in the first weeks of Hitler's assault. Timoshenko, in effect, attempted to restore the position as it had existed under Tukhachevsky. But three years of degeneration could not be recouped in a few months.

Moreover, with Timoshenko, the grotesque Kulik, also from Stalin's Tsaritsyn entourage of the Civil War, and described recently in the Soviet literature as a bullying incompetent,[27] was made Marshal, and put in charge of the artillery arm; and with Zhukov (and Meretskov, not long out of jail) another ineffective First Cavalry veteran, Tyulenev, became full general.

In fact, as a result of the 1940 promotions, four out of the five Marshals, two out of the three full generals and two of the new colonel-generals were from Stalin's Civil War group. Of the eight, two were to prove useful appointments. The others ranged from mediocre to disastrous. Stalin's concessions to military reality were not yet whole-hearted. We can be reasonably certain that but for the sharp jolt of the Finnish War Timoshenko would not have been allowed to carry out his partial programme of revitalization.

The task was tremendous – indeed, given the circumstances, impossible. But some improvement could be effected. The dual-command system was, after all, abandoned on 12 August 1940. In September Mekhlis was removed from the Political Administration of the Army. A partial reversion to Tukhachevsky's training methods set in. To create a new leadership and a new spirit could nevertheless not be done in the time remaining. Timoshenko was a vast improvement on Voroshilov, but the latter, and a large number of Stalinist *arrivistes*, remained in positions of power. And Stalin himself, with his long refusal to face the possibility of a German attack, was in final control.

When the German invasion was on the point of being launched, a leading commentator is doubtful 'whether any consistent plan for the defence of the Soviet Union existed, even at this late hour . . .'[28]

Stalin's attitude to the Nazi–Soviet Pact of 1939 is one of the most peculiar things about his entire career. The man who had never attached the slightest value to verbal assurances or paper promises does really seem to have thought, or hoped, that Hitler would not attack Russia. Even when overwhelming evidence was sent to him, by Soviet intelligence, by the British, by German deserters, that the Nazis were massing for attack, he gave strict orders that such reports should be treated as provocations. As far as can be seen, it was in the genuine hope of persuasion that he remarked to Schulenberg 'We must remain friends', and told Colonel Krebs 'We will remain friends with you in any event'.[29]

During the 1939–41 period attacks on the British were encouraged, but no mention even of the word Fascism was allowed. The Counsellor of the Soviet Embassy in Paris, Nikolai Ivanov, was actually sentenced to five years for 'anti-German views', and the sentence was confirmed – doubtless through bureaucratic inefficiency – in September 1941![30]

As an old Soviet diplomat remarked, the two years gained by the Nazi–Soviet Pact were almost completely wasted. He commented sourly, 'He suspected his own closest comrades, but he trusted Hitler.'[31]

It has been said that so much genuine enmity had been focused on Trotsky that Hitler, in comparison, seemed a shadowy figure, a bogeyman for use in frightening the Party rather than a real threat. There may be an element of truth in this, psychologically speaking. But Stalin's lack of contact with reality on the one point of the Nazi invasion had not been reflected in his attitude to Soviet–German relations during the earlier part of the Pact's duration. In 1939 and 1940 the Soviet Union had bargained hard, refused to make definite commitments, and though providing the Germans with various services appropriate to an ally such as the U-Boat 'Base North' near Murmansk, had conducted even the lowest-level negotiations with all the self-centred closeness and suspiciousness later shown in relations with the Anglo-American allies of a subsequent phase of the war period. The complete withdrawal from reality in the face of unpleasant facts is very much the aberration of 1941.

It seems likely that Stalin, realizing the incapacity of his army and his regime in the face of the Germans, hoped against hope at least for a further year or two's grace. Everything had gone his way for years. He could scarcely, it seems, conceive of his luck failing. Be that as it may, the result of his attitude was the despairing and absurd messages which poured in from the frontier on 22 June – 'We are being fired on. What shall we do?'

And yet the Soviet Army was larger in numbers, stronger in *matériel* and at least as well equipped technically as the German invaders. There was only one element in which the armies were not comparable: the German Command, staff and officer corps in general were of immensely superior quality. Though Hitler had removed a number of the higher officers, he had at least the sense to see that he could not fight a major war without a trained military cadre.

As the armies facing the Germans broke up under a task for which they had not been properly prepared or supported, Stalin reacted promptly. The Commander of the Western Front, Pavlov, his Chief of Staff, Klimovskikh, and his Signals and Artillery Commanders were shot. General Korobkov, commanding the battered Fourth Army, followed them. This did not save the three armies and four mechanized corps trapped between Minsk and Bialystok.

The Air Force, greatly superior in numbers to the Luftwaffe, was almost annihilated in the first days of the war. Only about one sixth of the Soviet fighter strength was in modern machines.[32] Soviet air superiority was nevertheless about 5:1 in the mere numbers of machines, so that this should not have been decisive.* But the other faults of Stalin's rule in the Air Force reinforced the errors of industrial and design policy. First, training had been

* More recently, Major-General P. Grigorenko has given the figures for modern machines alone as Soviet 2,700–2,800, against a German total of 3,000–3,500.

inadequate, and tactical methods were poor. Kesselring applied the term 'infanticide' to the Luftwaffe's destruction of Soviet bomber formations.

And all these long-established errors were compounded by Stalin's last and most fateful blunder, the failure to believe in the imminence of attack. Large parts of the Air Force were caught on the ground and destroyed in the first hours. Stalin's immediate answer to this destruction of planes on the ground was, typically, the execution of General Rychagov, the aviation commander of the North-Western Front. General Kopets, of the same arm, committed suicide for the same reason, having lost 600 aircraft while imposing negligible damage on the Luftwaffe.

The Russians also had a great superiority in the number of tanks and here design had not fallen behind.* The original Soviet tank defeats can be attributed almost entirely to bad tactical methods and worse staff work.[33]

In his biography of Stalin,[34] Isaac Deutscher mentions that imprisoned officers (like survivors of the purged opposition) were 'brought out of concentration camps and assigned to important national work'. This needs to be qualified.

A recent Soviet account[35] refers to as fact two lists of men 'still inside' who were liquidated in October 1941 and July 1942 respectively, at times when Stalin 'considered the situation to be desperate'. The lists included high Army officers. And in fact, the still surviving Shtern; Alksnis's successor as head of the Air Force, Loktionov; and Smushkevich – two Colonel-Generals and a Lieutenant-General (and all members of the new Central Committee) – were shot with a number of others on 28 October 1941 for 'treacherous activity'.[36]

Moreover, a Soviet Marshal makes it clear that while some of the officers brought out of camps and rehabilitated gave good service, in many cases the men concerned had been ruined: 'the moral, and often also the physical sufferings undergone in the prisons and camps had killed in them all the will, initiative and decisiveness necessary for a military man'. He gives the example of a general (a Civil War hero who had been eleven times wounded) who was arrested and sentenced in 1939 to twenty

* Grigorenko gives the tanks as: Soviet, 14,000–15,000; German, 3,712.

years' imprisonment without any charges being presented apart from the simple formula 'enemy of the people'. In a camp of 'severe regime' he became a bath-attendant and was given five years more for stealing a few underclothes. He was released in 1943 and made Chief of Staff of an Army, but his sufferings had broken his character.[37]

The 'Horse Marshals' commanded in 1941 – all three from the old First Cavalry Army. Timoshenko, in the centre, proved reasonably competent, though he too suffered heavy losses. On the southern and northern flanks, Budenny and Voroshilov were merely disastrous, especially the former. Stalin's other protégé, Marshal Kulik, came to grief in a clumsy operation before Leningrad. General Tyulenev became involved in the disasters in the Ukraine. All four were removed, but none was shot. As late as 1957 Tyulenev was defending Stalin's Lwow operations of 1920, the old wound in the side of the Soviet Army which had festered so long and so desperately.

With superior Russian resources, and vastly lengthened German communications, it was still only possible to avoid total defeat for two reasons. First was the continued existence of further reserves. Second, and more important, was the selection of better commanders. This could only be done in the course of the endless battles of the great retreat. The incompetents who had been put in to replace an adequate command in 1937–8 were weeded out by disaster. A new and efficient command was created by natural selection in the struggle itself. It was purchased, in fact, with the lives of hundreds of thousands of Russian soldiers, with hundreds of miles of Russian territory, and a great prolongation of the war.

Tukhachevsky's military doctrines were reinstated in the directives of the *Stavka* for the counter-offensive at Moscow in 1941. The turn had come. But, as a Soviet Army officer once remarked to the author, it was owing to the purges that the road to Berlin involved the long and painful detour via Stalingrad.

Far from the Great Purge eliminating a Soviet fifth column, it laid the foundation for one throughout the country in 1941–5. This was the first war fought by Russia in which a large force of its citizens joined the other side.

Among the more brilliant younger officers who had survived the Purge was General Vlasov. In the manoeuvres of 1940 his 99th Division had proved the best. A tall, powerful man with a stentorian voice and a fine flow of invective, he was, Ilya Ehrenburg tells us, popular with the troops and in favour with Stalin, who could not recognize a genuine potential 'traitor'.[38]

Vlasov, when captured, organized the Russian troops on the German side, in spite of great difficulties with the Nazi authorities. His programme shows that he was entirely out of sympathy with Nazism, and only concerned with a democratic Russia – he was comparable, in fact, to the Irish revolutionaries of 1916 who sought German support against Britain, or the Burmese and Indonesians of the last war who came to agreements (or tried to) with the Japanese against the West. As a Polish prisoner in Russia remarks more generally, of the expectations in the labour camps: 'I think with horror and shame of a Europe divided into two parts by the line of the Bug, on one side of which millions of Soviet slaves prayed for liberation by the armies of Hitler, and on the other millions of victims of German concentration camps awaited deliverance by the Red Army as their last hope'.[39]

Ehrenburg's implication that Stalin was effective at dealing with *imaginary* traitors is sound. In August 1941 he destroyed the last remnants of alternative political leadership. The two former Vice-Premiers, Chubar and Antipov, were apparently shot on the 12th and 24th respectively. It seems that such acts were widespread. A Pole mentions, in the Yertsevo camp, two generals, four lawyers, two journalists, four students, a high-ranking N.K.V.D. officer, two former camp administrators and five other assorted nobodies being selected and shot in June 1941.[40]

In fact, the outbreak of war was made the occasion for a general increase in police activity and power. Individual grudges were paid off and potential malcontents dealt with – as with the case of the widow of the Deputy People's Commissar of the N.K.V.D. in the Ukraine, Brunivoy, who had died under interrogation. She was arrested in 1937 and severely interrogated, with permanent injury to the kidneys and several broken ribs. She was released in 1939 and rehabilitated. She believed throughout that everything that happened was the result of hostile elements in the N.K.V.D., and wrote to Stalin and Vyshinsky to this effect. At the beginning of 1941 the N.K.V.D. officials in her case were tried and sentenced to short terms of imprisonment for the use of torture. She felt herself completely justified. Two days after the German invasion, on 24 June 1941, she disappeared once more.[41]

When the Russians withdrew before the German advance, attempts were made to evacuate N.K.V.D. prisoners. Not only was their labour needed, but they were of course expected to sympathize with liberators, even German ones. The retreat was so disorganized, especially in the Ukraine, that evacuation was often impossible. Killings on a mass scale took place. These are reported from Minsk, Smolensk, Kiev, Kharkov, Dniepropetrovsk, Zaporozhe and throughout the Baltic States. Near Nalchik, in the Caucasus, there was a molybdenum *kombinat* operated by the N.K.V.D. with convict labour. The prisoners were machine-gunned on the orders of the Kabardino-Balkar Republic's N.K.V.D. Commissar.[42] There is another report of a group of 29,000 prisoners accumulated in the Soviet retreat. When threatened with a further German advance and the abandonment of the camp at Olginskaya, the N.K.V.D. released all those serving less than five years and on 31 October 1941 shot the remainder.[43] *

And yet the war was also an occasion for relaxation of certain pressures. Religion, for example, was no longer persecuted. The public reversion to the old patriotism heartened at least the Russians. Above all, there was everywhere hope that once the war finished, things would become easier: the collective farm system would be abolished, the Terror would end.

Even apart from the sanguine mood of the people, the war brought a feeling of release, as Pasternak's characters remark:

You could volunteer for front-line service in a punitive battalion, and if you came out alive you were free. After that, attack after attack, mile after mile of electrified barbed wire, mines, mortars, month after month of artillery barrage. They called our company the death squad. It was practically wiped out. How and why I survived, I don't know.

---

*The custom persisted into peace-time. After the 8 December 1949 earthquake at Ashkhabad, the local camp was in ruins. Militia surrounded it and fired on all survivors. Out of 2,800, thirty-four came out.[44]

And yet – imagine – all that utter hell was nothing, it was bliss compared to the horrors of the concentration camp, and not because of the material conditions but for some other reason . . .

. . . It was not only felt by men in your position, in concentration camps, but by everyone without exception, at home and at the front, and they all took a deep breath and flung themselves into the furnace of this deadly, liberating struggle with real joy, with rapture.[45]

THE CONSOLIDATION OF STALINISM

But in proposing the toast at the victory banquet in the Kremlin in June 1945, Stalin spoke significantly of the 'ordinary' people as 'cogs in the wheels of the great State apparatus'.[46] His intention, completely fulfilled, was the restoration of the old machine.

In the same month it was made clear that the confession-trial system had been abandoned after 1938 because it was, in the then circumstances, no longer necessary, rather than because Stalin thought it unconvincing or useless. Sixteen leaders of the Polish underground Government and Army were placed on trial. The accused were headed by General Okulicki (who had taken over command of the Home Army following the surrender of General Bór Komorowski after the heroic Warsaw Rising) and Jankowski, the chief delegate in Poland of the Polish Government. (Okulicki, then underground, had been asked to contact the Soviet Command, with a guarantee of safe conduct, but was arrested when he presented himself.) They and thirteen of their fourteen co-defendants pleaded guilty to charges of anti-Soviet activity. This was the last of the great public trials to be held in Moscow. Its aim was to discredit the Polish Resistance and to bring pressure upon the Polish Government-in-exile to enter into a coalition with the Communist-sponsored Lublin Committee, then ruling Soviet-occupied Poland, on terms adequate to secure Communist predominance.

Though no more such trials were seen in Moscow, all over Eastern Europe the old method was employed, under direct Russian control, first (as in Russia) against non-Party elements such as the Agrarian leader Nikola Petkov in Bulgaria and Cardinal Mindszenty in Hungary, and later with Communist leaders like Lászlo Rajk in Hungary and Traicho Kostov in Bulgaria.

The system of public confession to entirely false charges came to an abrupt halt in December 1949 * when Kostov, Secretary of the Central Committee of the Bulgarian Communist Party, retracted his confession in open court and maintained this stand throughout the trial.

Kostov refused to change his mind in spite of the moral indignation of the court and the tearful appeals of his co-accused. Kostov was perhaps in a stronger position than most accused in earlier trials; he must long ago have become accustomed to the idea of death and torture in pursuit of his political aims. His conduct under 'Fascist' interrogation had been held up as an example to the Bulgarian Communist Party. He was still close to the period of his illegal life and had not – as perhaps Bukharin, etc., had – gone to seed after years of comfort. Moreover, he knew that the bulk of his party was silently behind him, and thus, perhaps, did not feel quite the isolation of the Russian oppositionists. In addition, he seems to have been particularly tough; in him typical Bulgarian mulishness and resilience were developed to a high degree.

In Russia itself there were almost no death sentences for three or four years after the war apart from those on a few leading Vlasovites. Genuine collaborators with the Germans had been

* The last show 'trial' of the Stalin period, that of Slansky and others in Prague in November 1952, was announced as public. But this time no Westerners were admitted.) The Slansky trial was conducted under Soviet supervision. At the political level Mikoyan was sent by Stalin in November 1951 to arrange for the next batch of arrests. At the Secret Police level, the scenario was supervised by M. T. Likhachev, Deputy Head of the Section for Investigating Specially Important Cases – himself to be shot with Abakumov in 1954 – and other M.G.B. officials.[47] (Both the basic idea of confession and the techniques devised by Yezhov for extracting them, were to receive significant employment in Asia in the 1950s. The Chinese accused the Americans of waging bacteriological warfare in Korea. The evidence they produced consisted of feathers, insects, clams, rats and other things riddled with germs and allegedly dropped from American planes. Such evidence was not, on the face of it, very convincing – though even this was accepted by one type of Westerner. To fortify their case, the Chinese resorted to confessions, extracted from American pilots.

rounded up by the tens of thousands, and merely sentenced to labour camps, where they were joined by the Soviet soldiers returned from internment in Germany. In 1946–7 a great wave of arrests struck at Jews, Army officers and others, and soon afterwards all those who had been released in the meanwhile were again arrested. This reversal of an act of 'rotten liberalism' was given official authorization by a decree of 1950, now said to have been adopted 'on the initiative of Beria and Abakumov'.[48]

The camps were at first more deadly than ever. Of those sentenced in 1945–6, few survived by 1953. The famine of 1947[49] was, of course, reflected in the camp rations with the usual results. By the beginning of the fifties, however, a reform and rationalization of the forced labour system led to a big drop in the death rate. Since almost no releases took place (one Kotlas commandant is quoted as saying that he had been eight years in his post and had released one prisoner),[50] the camp population mounted, by Stalin's death, to its probable maximum.

This general consolidation of the labour-camp system reflected a consolidation of the whole State and economy into the form Stalin had evidently been aiming at since his achievement of full power. In the new society, forced labour was evidently intended as permanent economic form.

What Stalin had established was essentially a command economy and a command society. This applied at every level. The collective farms, with their tractors, were producing less food than the ill-equipped *muzhik* of 1914. But they were now economically and politically under control. They could no longer hold the market to ransom.

And so it was the whole way up the scale. Everywhere, orders from the centre were not merely binding in principle but enforceable in practice. There was no significant area in which the important decisions could not be taken in the Kremlin.

The resemblances between this and 'Socialism', as Marx and others had envisaged it, were, formally speaking, not negligible. The capitalist no longer existed. The 'petit-bourgeois' individual peasant had gone. The State controlled the economy. For those who held that in a modern industrial society the absence of capitalists could only mean Socialism, this was enough. Defined more positively, Socialism had indeed always had one further characteristic – in effect its very keystone. The control of the State by the proletariat had been regarded as the essential. In Stalin's Russia, and for that matter in present-day Russia, there is no sign at all of any such thing. This point was got over by verbal means. All the phraseology of the Workers' State was employed, in every conceivable context.

One may wonder how far Stalin thought that he had produced the Socialism to securing which he had, as a young man, been converted. There was indeed no longer any 'ruling class'. Though Stalin created (and admitted he was creating) a large privileged stratum, it had no rights of ownership over the means of production. Every privilege was held, in the last analysis, at the whim of the ruler.

In this unitary system politics as such had disappeared, except in the form of intrigue at the highest level for Stalin's favour. In a sense this may sound paradoxical; there was more 'political' agitation and propaganda in the press and on the radio, in factory speeches and official literature, than anywhere in the world. But it was totally passive. It consisted solely of the handing-down of, and working-up of enthusiasms for, the decisions of the General Secretary. A new generation of industrial managers had risen, competent in the techniques of administration, in which the threat of the forced-labour camp spurred on the directors, just as a piece-work system drove the worker to his limits by the threat of hunger. The new industrialists – even those at the highest level like Tevosyan, Malyshev and Saburov – were little more than the unquestioning technicians of the new scheme of things.

The planning system, which had been quite chaotic in the thirties, now settled into a new rationality; increases in productivity – at least in the heavy industrial production which was Stalin's main interest – at last became regular. To say that the economy worked is not to give it any particular superiority over other systems. It too had its wastages and inefficiencies. Its planning was, in many fields, largely mythical. And the general unworkability of its distribution network was made up for by a large extra-legal market. But, all in all, the economy Stalin had created was at least an operating reality. Its built-in wastages were not great enough to prevent its one solid achievement – the continuing investment in industry of a high proportion of the national income. They were, however, great enough to hold the expansion bought at such sacrifice down to a level no greater than that of various capitalist countries.

Detailed comparisons were in any case impossible to make owing to the secrecy and distortion of the Soviet statistical system of the time. But what provided confidence to the Party elite, and gained the admiration of certain intellectuals abroad, was the more general fact that a booming industry had been created in a fairly backward country. It was hoped (and still is) that the method might be applicable in the really backward lands of the East.

But the old Russia was not all that backward. It had already been the fourth industrial power before the Revolution. In the reign of Nicholas II the railway network had doubled in length in ten years and there had been a great upsurge in the mining and metal industries. As Lenin said:

... The progress in the mining industry is more rapid in Russia than in Western Europe and even in North America. . . . In the last few years (1886–1896) the production of cast metal has tripled. . . . The development of capitalism in the younger countries is accelerated by the example and aid of the older.[51]

And the trend continued right up to 1914.

Since 1930 Stalin had greatly enlarged the industrial base. But he had done so by very wasteful methods – probably more wasteful economically, and in human suffering, than those of the original Industrial Revolution. He had not made the best use of his resources – solving the problem of rural over-population by removing precisely the most productive section of the peasantry, and wasting much of the original skilled engineering force by decimating it on false charges of sabotage. (It is true, indeed, that a high proportion of Russia's skill was killed or emigrated in the Revolution itself.) Even in 1929 it was reasonably clear, economically speaking, that milder measures could have produced equally good results, as they had in Meiji Japan, for example.

Kommunist, the main theoretical and political organ of the

Central Committee, has lately produced charges against Stalin's planning system. He personally interfered with the work of planning organizations; enforced arbitrary goals; and radically changed plans in a way that made whole sections of them meaningless. He thus inflicted lasting harm on the Soviet planning work and on the Soviet economy. Indeed (*Kommunist* goes on), it was Stalin who was responsible for lasting troubles in the Soviet economy which, to cover up his personal guilt, he used to ascribe to difficulties allegedly inherent in the rapid growth of the economy. In particular, 'arbitrary planning caused immense damage to agriculture which still suffers from the results of the cult of Stalin's personality'.[52]

I do not share the view that Stalin's method was the only, or the best, way available – even to a one-party regime – to attain the degree of increased industrialization actually realized. But in any case, the basic economic benefits obtained, or supposedly obtained, by the Stalin regime were already in hand before the Purge proper started. Economically, in fact, there is no doubt that the Purge was disadvantageous: it removed a high proportion of the most skilled industrial leaders, from Pyatakov down; and at the same time the camps were filled from an already overstretched labour pool. The rationale was that not of economics but of despotism. With all the incentives to attain, or at least claim, the opposite, economic advance admittedly slowed down in 1938–40.[53]

The lesson might seem to be that the use of terror in conditions, as in 1931–3, when it is to some degree economically effective is nevertheless not a good idea even economically. For it cannot simply be switched off. It builds up its own interests and institutions, its own cadres and habits of mind. Any good it may be (in this sense) at a particular moment is likely to be offset at a later stage when it is no longer applicable, but still applied.

But even if one were to accept the Stalin method as a whole, writing off later losses as the inevitable payment for earlier successes, other issues arise. Stalinism is one way of attaining industrialization, just as cannibalism is one way of attaining a high-protein diet. The desirability of the result hardly seems to balance the objections.

Meanwhile, Stalin pervaded every sphere. In philosophy, for example, he was celebrated as a profound critic of Hegel, as the first to elucidate certain pronouncements of Aristotle, as the only man to bring out the full significance of Kant's theories. On the tercentenary of Spinoza's birth, *Pravda* had put in several quotations from Stalin, having nothing to do with Spinoza or even philosophy.[54]

At a recent Moscow conference of experts a historian has complained that in those days 'it was impossible frankly to share one's thoughts and doubts even with one's comrades, for fear of placing them in a difficult position'.[55] Academician Evgeni M. Zhukov spoke of the 'psychological trauma' suffered by historians who were 'systematically imbued with the idea that theoretically sound works could only be written by a select *vozhd* and that profound thoughts and fresh deeds could proceed only from him.' Thus 'for almost twenty years – the period of the formation of the consciousness of a whole generation – independent creative thought by "ordinary mortals" in the sphere of theory was placed in doubt'.

A doctor, denouncing the effect on Soviet medicine, summed up:

The main harm caused to science by the cult of the personality lay in the proclamation of a single opinion . . . 'an inexhaustible fount of wisdom' as the supreme truth. . . . It is not accidental that in the course of discussions of concrete scientific problems, one concept or another was not verified by the experiments of its proposers but by references to scientific heritage, by mere quotation from the works of others.[56]

In the even more sensitive field of economics, independent thought was naturally treated with greater rigour. The Director of the Institute of Economics of the U.S.S.R. Academy of Sciences remarks:

Many Communists can still remember the havoc wreaked in the forties on the journal *Problems of Economics* for publishing an article by Professor Kubanin. In this article he expressed the completely correct thought that we were lagging behind America in labour productivity, in agriculture. The great scholar and major expert on the economics of agriculture paid for this correct thought with his life, while the journal was closed for its 'heresy'.[57]

The effect of the Stalinist attitude at the lower level is adumbrated by the First Secretary of the Georgian Communist Party, Mgeladze, who summoned workers from the Institute of Marxism-Leninism and the Institute of History of the Georgian Academy of Science and had them write a book on the history of the Party in Transcaucasia. When he was given the result, he announced 'I, as the author, like it. But be sure if there are any mistakes in it, you, dear friends, will all go to prison.'[58]

Again, Stalin happened to say in an aside that the Azerbaijanis were obviously descended from the Medes. Though there is no basis for such a notion, it became established doctrine among the historians. Linguists spent fifteen years trying to find Median words in Azeri. 'Eventually thirty-five dubious Median words were found, although the Median language itself is mythical.'[59]

These few examples – which omit, for instance, the major scandal of Lysenkoism in Soviet biology – must serve as a general impression of the effect of Stalin's new regime on the intellect.

In the less stormy atmosphere of the post-Yezhov years, moreover, more careful attention could be paid to thought-crime and face-crime. An authoritative instruction, typical of many, ran:

> One must not content oneself with merely paying attention to *what* is being said for that may well be in complete harmony with the Party programme. One must pay attention also to the *manner* – to the sincerity, for example, with which a school-mistress recites a poem the authorities regard as doubtful, or the pleasure revealed by a critic who goes into detail about a play he professes to condemn.[60]

The last years of Stalin's life saw a major though unpublicized series of purges. In 1949–50 came a new 'Leningrad Case'. Voznesensky, member of the Politburo, A. A. Kuznetsov, Secretary of the Central Committee, and other leaders were shot. About 3,000 senior Party members in Leningrad were arrested, and treated with particular brutality, many of them being shot; and there were similar purges elsewhere. In 1952–3, leading Jewish intellectuals perished by the hundred, and a wave of arrests culminated in the Doctors' Plot, with Stalin ordering the investigators, 'Beat, beat and beat again', as Khrushchev tells us.

Stalin's execution of the main Yiddish writers in the 'Crimean

Affair' of 1952 is among the most extraordinary of all State acts. As Manès Sperber has said, these were Communists who had submitted to all the imperatives of the regime and of Stalin. 'Like the others, they had betrayed their friends and their brothers every time that fidelity to the Party had demanded it; but they were to die because they remained incapable of betraying their language and their literature.' When Perets Markish, the poet, was shot he is said to have gone mad and to have been singing and laughing. David Bergelson, the Yiddish novelist, whose last book, *Killed, I Will Live*, was a quotation from the Psalms, picked another such for his last words: 'Earth, oh earth, do not cover my blood!'[61]

Not long before Stalin died, *Pravda*,[62] by an extraordinary exception, published an article by Mr Herbert Morrison, then British Foreign Secretary. It calmly but cogently set forth democratic objections to the Soviet system. An answer appeared at once, saying that Morrison was asking for freedom of speech for those it would be wrong to give it to – 'the criminals who . . . killed . . . Kirov'. It now turns out that it was precisely those people, and no others, who had freedom of speech.

The Stalinist version of the events of the purge was, of course, the only one permitted in Russia itself. Many people there knew at first hand that this version was false, but anyone susceptible of indoctrination by terror or by sheer pressure of propaganda fell in with the official line.

Abroad, things were different. The West was not forced to accept the Stalinist version. Freedom of judgement and freedom of information prevailed, then as now. This did not prevent an extraordinary degree of success for the official Communist view.

FOREIGN MISAPPREHENSIONS

If thou canst not realize the Ideal thou shalt at least
idealize the Real.   CALVERLEY

During the Purges, a young English Communist, John Cornford,
published a poem:

SERGEI MIRONOVICH KIROV

(Assassinated in Leningrad, December 1934)

Nothing is ever certain, nothing is ever safe,
To-day is overturning yesterday's settled good.
Everything dying keeps a hungry grip on life.
Nothing is ever born without screaming and blood.

Understand the weapon, understand the wound:
What shapeless past was hammered to action by his deeds,
Only in constant action was his constant certainty found.
He will throw a longer shadow as time recedes.[63]

Cornford, with a first-class record at Cambridge University,
went to Spain in 1936 and was killed near Córdoba, with the International Brigade, at the end of that year. There can hardly be a
better illustration of the way in which the generous impulse in
Western Communism could be befouled by Stalinism. The young
man who gave his life in the cause of a supposed revolutionary
humanism had been led by his allegiances to produce what is
little more than a versification of Stalin's theory that the class
struggle grows more bitter as the opponents of Communism
become weaker, using as its text a crime allegedly committed by
counter-revolutionaries, but actually by Stalin himself.

Time having, as Cornford suggests, receded, what has become
plain is that not even high intelligence and a sensitive spirit are of
any help once the facts of a situation are deduced from a political
theory, rather than vice versa.

Though Cornford's case is instructive, and not only as regards
his own time, he was not among those actively responsible for
propagating and compounding the falsehood; he was, rather, at
the receiving end. Between those in the West who accepted the
Stalinist version of events and those who originally issued that
version, there stood a number of journalists, ambassadors,

lawyers and students of Russia, whose direct and admitted duty it was to study the facts in detail and pronounce on them. Not every Western Communist, nor every Left-wing intellectual, could be expected to read with a critical eye the official reports of the Great Trials. Those who did, or who had actually attended them, and who from incompetence and blind (or cynical) partisanship transmitted a false analysis to the larger audience, may reasonably be thought somewhat blameworthy. A few examples of inadequate scepticism have already been noted.

Any recorder of these events must be tempted to compile a vast *sottisier* of misjudgements made by his compatriots and others in the West. It is scarcely a point that should be ignored, but it has been thought best to give no more than a few examples of the type of error which was made by many with high claims to clear judgement, moral enlightenment, and political knowledge. The contemporary effect on world opinion was an important aspect of the whole Purge operation. Stalin had himself considered it when he ordered the Zinoviev Trial:

> He is not impressed by the argument that public opinion in Western Europe must be taken into consideration. To all such arguments he replies contemptuously: 'Never mind, they'll swallow it.'[64]

The fact that so many did 'swallow' it was thus certainly a factor in making the whole Purge possible. The trials, in particular, would have carried little weight unless validated by some foreign, and so 'independent', commentators.

Foreign intervention had, as late as the mid thirties, been able to secure certain results, particularly in view of Stalin's post-1935 policy of alliances. For example, in June 1935, an International Congress of Writers for the Defence of Culture was held in Paris. It was intended as a large-scale Popular Front occasion. Magdalene Paz insisted on raising the case of Victor Serge, arrested in 1932. After an uproar, in which she was supported by Salvemini and Gide, she was allowed to speak. The Soviet delegation consisted of Pasternak, Nikolai Tikhonov, Ilya Ehrenburg, Mikhail Koltsov and the playwright Kirshon – the two latter themselves to perish shortly. Apart from Pasternak, these Soviet delegates resisted the debate strenuously and accused Serge of complicity in the Kirov murder, which had taken place two years after his arrest.[65] Afterwards, Gide went and conveyed the writers' displeasure to the Soviet Ambassador.

Serge was released at the end of the year. This is the last, and almost unique, occasion on which foreign opinion was able to influence Stalin. It would seem to show, however, that if articulate Western opinion had condemned the Zinoviev Trial with sufficient unanimity and force it is conceivable that Stalin might, in this Popular Front period, have acted at least slightly less ruthlessly. In fact, those who 'swallowed' the trials can hardly be acquitted of a certain degree of complicity in the continuation and exacerbation of the torture and execution of innocent men. The facts that were concealed from (or by) progressive opinion in the West were twofold: the existence and extent of the mass slaughter and the inconsistency and falsehood of the public trials.

From the start there were three basic objections to the evidence in the trials. First, the alleged plots were totally out of character with the accused leaders, who had always opposed individual assassination, and were now, moreover, charged also with having been enemy agents throughout their careers. Secondly, the allegations were often inherently absurd – like the charge against Zelensky that he had put nails into the masses' butter with a view to undermining Soviet health. Thirdly, some of the stories told in court were of events abroad, which could be checked: these contained demonstrable falsehoods – a meeting at a non-existent hotel in Copenhagen, a landing at a Norwegian airfield during a month when no landings had taken place.

In the West, the facts were readily available. Hundreds of articles and books were published in which all these points were clearly and flatly demonstrated. Trotsky, the one accused at liberty, exposed the frame-up with incisive skill. The distinguished Commission headed by Professor Dewey examined the whole evidence in the most judicious and meticulous fashion, and published its findings. It was not a question of political argument, properly speaking, but of facts. Yet, in spite of everything, these went unheard among large sections of well-informed people.

There was no reasonable excuse for believing the Stalinist story.
The excuses which can be advanced are irrational, though often
couched in the formulae of intensive rationalization.

The Communist Parties everywhere simply transmitted the
Soviet line. Communist intellectuals, some of them better
informed about Soviet conditions and more inclined to frame
their own answers, reacted variously. There were those who
simply repressed the difficult material. Mr Stephen Spender
quotes an English Communist friend, when asked what he
thought of the trials, as replying 'What trials? I have given up
thinking about such things long ago.'[66]

More representative was the attitude of Bertolt Brecht, who
remarked to Sydney Hook at the time of the first trials, 'The more
innocent they are, the more they deserve to die.'[67] Meanwhile, he
had written a play about Nazi Germany: a father and mother are
worried because friends of theirs are under investigation, and they
fear the block warden. The husband, a teacher, does not know if
they have anything against him at the school. 'I am ready to teach
whatever they want me to teach. But what do they want me to
teach? If only I were sure of that.' They worry about whether to
put Hitler's picture in a more prominent position, or whether that
will look like a confession of guilt.

Wife: But there's nothing against you, is there?
Husband: There's something against everybody. Everybody is suspected. It's enough if someone expresses any suspicion of you, to make
you a suspected person.

And later one remarks: 'Since when have they needed witnesses?'[68]

But the main theme of the play – taken as completely destroying
the moral basis of Nazism – is the father's and mother's fear that
their schoolboy son may have denounced them. This was at a time
when, as Brecht evidently knew, the same sort of thing was going
on in the Soviet Union. In fact, there was a widely praised and
celebrated Soviet example of sons denouncing their parents.
During collectivization Pavlik Morozov, leader of his village
group of young Communist 'Pioneers' who were acting as
auxiliaries in the attack on the peasantry, 'unmasked' his father –

who had previously been president of the village soviet but had 'fallen under the influence of *kulak* relations'. The father was shot, and on 3 September 1932 a group of peasants, including the boy's uncle, in turn killed the son, at the age of fourteen – thus, as it were, anticipating Stalin's age-limit for executions. The killers were themselves all executed, and young Morozov became, and has remained, a great hero of the Komsomol. The Palace of Culture of the Red Pioneers in Moscow was named after him.[69] The Soviet press lately celebrated the 'sacred and dear' Pavlik Morozov Museum in his own village: 'In this timbered house was held the court at which Pavlik unmasked his father who had sheltered the *kulaks*. Here are reliquaries dear to the heart of every inhabitant of Gerasimovka.'[70] (In 1965 a statue was set up to him in the village, as if to show that the principles he acted on are still considered admirable.)

In Brecht's own case it is noteworthy that a close connexion, his mistress, the actress Carola Neher (who had played the lead in the *Dreigroschenoper*), was arrested in Russia and never seen again.

As Herbert Luthy has argued, Brecht himself was not attracted to Communism as part of the 'Workers' Movement – which he had never known, but by a deep urge for a total authority, a total submission to a total power, the new Byzantine State Church – immutable, hierarchical, founded on the infallibility of the leader'.[71] His political and semi-political work invariably shows this pleasure at rolling in the muck for the sake of the idea. It seems to represent an extreme and degenerate version of Pyatakov's view of the Party.

It is perhaps natural that committed Communists should in principle have accepted and propagated untruths, in the old tradition of 'pious fraud'. But curiously enough, such a consideration seems partially to apply also to many elements of the non-Communist Left. Not in such a clear-cut manner, not so fraudulently nor so piously, they yet tended to temper criticism, to put the best complexion on, or ignore, refractory events.

There was, indeed, much resistance among the tougher-minded Left. Edmund Wilson, reading the charges against Zinoviev and Kamenev while still in Russia, saw at once that they were faked.

In the United States, the Commission headed by the eighty-year-old Professor Dewey had as its lawyer John F. Finerty, who had appeared for the defence in the Mooney and Sacco–Vanzetti trials. The Liberal *Manchester Guardian* was the strongest and most effective of British exposers of the trials. The orthodox Labour Party press did the same: that party also put out Frederick Adler's forthright and accurate pamphlet on the subject. And on the extreme Left some of the most effective exposure was done by Emrys Hughes in the Scottish *Forward*. In fact some Leftists (and not only Trotskyists and so on who had a direct partisan interest) were perfectly clear-headed about the matter, while some people opposed to the principles of Communism accepted the official versions.

But on the whole, in the atmosphere of the late thirties, Fascism was the enemy, and a partial logic repressed or rejected any criticism of its supposed main enemy, the U.S.S.R. The Western capitals thronged with 'the thousands of painters and writers and doctors and lawyers and debutantes chanting a diluted version of the Stalinist line'.[72]

Appeals in favour of the trials were made by various Western writers. Feuchtwanger, Barbusse – even the sensitive Gandhi-fan, Romain Rolland. In the United States, a manifesto attacking the Dewey Commission was signed by a number of authors, poets, professors and artists – Theodore Dreiser, Granville Hicks,* Corliss Lamont, Max Lerner and others.

Speaking of the attitude of many British intellectuals to the trials, Mr Julian Symons remarks on the 'monstrous incongruities that they willingly swallowed'. He adds: 'But they had not been deceived. In relation to the Soviet Union they had deceived themselves, and in the end one has to pay for such self-deceits.'[73]

In the non-Communist, Popular Front-style Left, there were signs of unease. Britain's leading journal of the intellectual Left, the *New Statesman*, found the first trial 'unconvincing', yet added: 'We do not deny . . . that the confessions may have contained a substance of truth.' On the 1937 Trial it said 'Few would now maintain that all or any of them were completely innocent.'

*Hicks later made the *amende honorable*.

On the 1938 Trial, which it claimed was 'undoubtedly very popular in the U.S.S.R.', it said that the confessions remained baffling, 'whether we regard them as true or false', but that it could be concluded that 'there has undoubtedly been much plotting in the U.S.S.R.' – curiously combining a sense of the incredibility of the charges with a willingness to believe them.

One of the achievements of Stalinism, was, in effect, that in spite of the fact that plenty of information was available contradicting the official picture, it was nevertheless possible to impose the latter upon journalists, sociologists and other visitors by methods which, on the face of it, seem crude and obvious, but which worked splendidly. Tourists visited Russia on a bigger scale in the Yezhov period than ever before. They saw nothing. The night-time arrests, the torture chambers of the Lefortovo and the crowded cells of the Butyrka, the millions of prisoners cold and hungry in the great camps of the north, were all hidden from them. The only dramatic scenes were the three great public trials. And these too were strictly controlled and did not depart much from a prepared script.

For if access to Russia was extensive, it was also imperfect. The Soviet Government at this time maintained its model prison at Bolshevo, which many foreign visitors were shown. The Webbs give it a laudatory account[74] and it had also attracted favourable comment from D. N. Pritt, Harold Laski, and many others. One friendly visitor had the opportunity of gaining a rather broader view – Mr Jerzy Gliksman, who, as a progressive member of the Warsaw City Council before the war, visited and reported enthusiastically on Bolshevo and the new humanitarian methods of criminology. A few years later he found himself in camps more representative of Soviet penal practice.[75]

Other prisoners report occasionally passing through the model blocks – known to prisoners as 'Intourist Prisons' – which were shown to foreign sociologists and journalists. Herling,[76] while in an ordinary cell in the Leningrad Transit Prison (which he describes as better than usual with only seventy prisoners in a cell for twenty), was taken by chance through a model wing – evidently that described by Lenka von Koerber in her enthusiastic book about the Soviet prison system, *Soviet Russia Fights Crime.*

On the other end of the judicial process, the trials themselves, we have already quoted one or two Western reports. Of others, that of the eminent British pro-Communist lawyer Mr D. N. Pritt, who attended the Zinoviev Trial, is especially interesting, since he says in his recent autobiography[77] that he had, and *still* has, 'a Socialist belief that a Socialist state would not try people unless there was a strong case against them'. He adds. 'What the Soviet views are now . . . I do not know.'

Every journalist Pritt spoke to thought the trial fair and, he remarks, 'certainly every foreign observer thought the same'. This is not so, of course, but the fact that even considerable partisanship could suggest it is presumably a sign that far too many did think so. One can certainly detect in some of the journalists, in particular, a certain professional vanity – that *they* could be duped was inconceivable. Then, once committed, a sort of blindness came over them.

Even a journalist like Walter Duranty, who spoke Russian, had been years in Russia, and knew some of the accused, could describe Ulrikh as 'a hard judge but a just one'; say 'No-one who heard Pyatakof or Muralof could doubt for a moment that what they said was true'; and conclude 'The future historian will probably accept the Stalinist version.'[78] He argues that Muralov and Pyatakov were so 'impervious to pressure' that their confessions could not have been false, and finds one of the strongest proofs of Pyatakov's guilt to be the fact that he was 'the brains of heavy industry' and that therefore Stalin would not have killed him unless his crimes were beyond pardon. As we have seen, this sort of common sense did not, in fact, apply.

Duranty's argument about Gamarnik's suicide is another example of the muddled thinking of the period: 'His suicide . . . proves that he had been engaged in some deal with the Germans.'[79] Of the other military conspirators, Duranty argues that 'they confessed' without long preparation, and this is an indication of the truth of the charges, while it also shows that confession was not necessarily the product of long interrogation. But of course the evidence that the Generals 'confessed', in any sense whatever, is simply that Stalin's press said they had done so! The trial (if there was a trial) was not public.

Not only Leftists and journalists wrote this sort of thing. The American Ambassador Joseph Davies reported to the Secretary of State that there was 'proof . . . beyond reasonable doubt to justify the verdict of guilty of treason'.[80]

During war-time lectures, Davies used to get a laugh, which he greatly appreciated, to his answer to questions about fifth-columnists in Russia: 'There aren't any, they shot them all.' Both parts of this piece of gallows wit are untrue. The men shot were not fifth-columnists. And fifth-columnists rose by the thousand, even in spite of the repulsive policies of the Germans. Most of them were, moreover, people who would never, under a moderately popular regime, have thought of going over to the enemy. Stalin's policies created a vast pool of potential treason which, had the Nazis not been foolish as well as foul, might well have decided the war.

This sort of reporting is more or less ephemeral. We should perhaps take more serious and studious treatments as still more reprehensible. Scholars and Russian experts were duped to the same degree as journalists and lawyers. When Beatrice and Sidney Webb examined Soviet matters, and put their conclusions into the vast tome *Soviet Communism: A New Civilization*, the Constitution much impressed them. So did the constitutions and the statutes of the Party, the trade unions, the consumer cooperatives, the collective farms. And, indeed, if these documents had ever been put into operation, they might have produced the society the Webbs thought they saw. It doubtless never occurred to the Webbs, brought up in Britain, that official documents do not necessarily bear much relation to fact. As it is, their book is to be regarded less as an account of a real country than as a successor to the works of Sir Thomas More, Campanella, Plato, Harrington and William Morris. It was unfortunate – and this of course applied not only to the Webbs – that the perfectly natural human activity of constructing Utopias should, through various misunderstandings, have been projected on to a real community with so little claim to it.

The Webbs assert flatly that Kirov's assassin 'was discovered to have secret connexions with conspiratorial circles of ever-widening range'. On the executions immediately following the assassination, they say that those shot did not seem to have been proven accomplices in the assassination 'or the conspiracies associated therewith', but that they were 'undoubtedly guilty of illegal entry and inexcusably bearing arms and bombs'.[81] 'Undoubtedly' seems a strong word, when the sole evidence was a brief announcement to that effect in the Soviet press.

They describe the Moscow trials as 'a tragic hangover from the violence of the revolution and the civil war'.[82] Of course, there is a sense in which all these events are connected: but the image does not seem appropriate as it stands. A hangover which suddenly reaches its climax sixteen years after the events supposed to have caused it requires some special explanation.

They comment, truly though not perhaps in the sense in which they meant it, that the trials produced some international revulsion against the Soviet Union and that therefore 'the Soviet Government must have had strong grounds for the action which has involved such unwelcome consequences'. Claiming to attempt 'a detached and philosophic interpretation' of the trials, they say that the whole manner of the confessions was convincing, and that 'careful perusal of the full reports of the proceedings' left them with the same impression, though they express a reservation about Trotsky.[83]

They explain the confessions as due to Russian prisoners 'behaving naturally and sensibly, as Englishmen would were they not virtually compelled by their highly artificial legal system to go through a routine which is useful to the accused only when there is some doubt as to the facts or as to the guilt or innocence of the conduct in question'.[84]

This curious view of the comparability of the Soviet and British legal systems was shared by Professor Harold Laski, who notes that 'Basically I did not observe much difference between the general character of a trial in Russia and in this country'. Vyshinsky, with whom he had a long discussion, he found 'a man whose passion was law reform. . . . He was doing what an ideal Minister of Justice would do if we had such a person in Great Britain – forcing his colleagues to consider what is meant by actual experience of the law in action.'[85] This was indeed published before Vyshinsky's great days. But trials had already taken place in Russia, and with Vyshinsky's active participation, which might have produced qualms.

Another serious student of Russia (and of agriculture in particular) was Sir John Maynard, from whom it had been possible to hide the Ukrainian famine. On the trials, he remarks:

> However much falsity of detail there may be, the Trials of the leading personages in 1936–38 were substantially justified by facts: and were probably the means of saving the U.S.S.R. from an attempted revolution which would have given to the Nazi Government an earlier opportunity.[86]

Sir Bernard Pares, a serious historian, and long-established expert on all things Russian, was equally duped. The later editions of Pares's *A History of Russia* cover the period to the end of the Second World War. Dealing with the Purges, he permits himself to say:

> Nearly all admitted having conspired against the life of Stalin and others, and on this point it is not necessary to doubt them. . . . Radek, who spoke with consummate lucidity, gave what is probably a true picture.[87]

On the Tukhachevsky case – of which, it may be remembered, no evidence whatever was presented – he merely points out that the Russian and German General Staffs had earlier been in contact and therefore 'It is by no means unlikely that there was a plot'. A generation earlier, the conscience of the civilized world could be aroused by the false condemnation to imprisonment of a single French captain for a crime which had actually been committed, though not by him. The Soviet equivalent of the Dreyfus Case involved the execution of thousands of officers, from Marshals and admirals down, on charges which were totally imaginary. It called forth instead, and not from Pares alone, comments like the above!

Of the trials in general Pares concludes: 'The plea that Stalin acted first to disrupt a potential fifth column . . . is by no means unwarranted.' Elsewhere[88] he remarks that 'the bulky verbatim reports were in any case impressive' – perhaps the most fatuous of all comments, and the fine fruit, as Walter Laqueur has said, 'of fifty years of study of Russian history, the Russian people, its country, its language'.

As an old authority on Russia, Pares had been opposed to the Soviet Government and revised his attitude in view of the Nazi threat. 'Towards the end of 1935,' his son comments,[89] 'my father set foot in Russia once more and any remaining doubts vanished at once. He had not left the Moscow railway station before his mind was flooded with the realization that the Bolsheviks were, after all, Russia.' This reliance on personal revelation and intuition, inadequately related to the real situation, is surely inappropriate and egocentric – a point worth making when we read similar accounts from more recently totalitarianized lands.

What happened in Russia under Stalin could not be understood or estimated in any commonsensical fashion, if by common sense we mean notions that sound reasonable and natural to the democratic Westerner. Many of the misunderstandings which appeared in Britain and America during the Great Trials were due to prejudice – not necessarily to prejudice in favour of the Soviet regime or of Stalin, but at least prejudice in regarding certain events and interpretations of them as inherently unlikely. The Great Trials were, and it should have been plain at the time, nothing but large-scale frame-ups. But it was extraordinarily difficult for many in the West to credit this: to believe that a State could really perpetrate on a vast scale such a cheap and third-rate system of falsehood. Bernard Shaw typically remarked 'I find it just as hard to believe that [Stalin] is a vulgar gangster as that Trotsky is an assassin.'[90] Presumably he would not have been surprised at some such events in quite highly organized societies like Imperial Rome or Renaissance Florence. But the Soviet State appeared to have a certain impersonality, and not obviously to lend itself to actions determined not so much by political ideas as by the overt personal plotting which had afflicted those earlier regimes.

There was another powerful factor. Both opponents of and sympathizers with the Russian Revolution thought of the Communists as a group of 'dedicated' (or 'fanatical') men whose faults or virtues were at any rate incompatible with common crime – something like the Jesuits of the Counter-Reformation. England has had little recent experience of revolutionary movements, and this idea persists. It is the type of general notion which the uninformed are likely to assume simply out of ignorance, and it has not lost its obscuring power to this day.

Men like Stalin, Kaganovich, Voroshilov, Molotov and Yagoda – indeed top operatives of the N.K.V.D. like Mironov and Molchanov – had been members of the underground Bolshevik Party in the time of its illegal struggle against Tsardom. Whatever their faults, they had thus established at least enough *bona fides* to exempt them from the suspicion that they did in fact behave as they are now known to have done. Even now, doubtless, there are those in the West who find it hard to swallow the notion of the top leaders of the Soviet Communist Party writing obscene and brutal comments on the appeals for mercy of the men they knew to be totally innocent. The mistake was in fact in the idea held in this country about revolutionary movements. In practice these are not joined only by Simon Pure idealists, but consist of a hodge-podge of members in which the idealist component is accompanied by all sorts of motivations – vanity, power-seeking and mere freakishness.

Perhaps the commonest reaction was to believe that the case against the accused in the trials was exaggerated, rather than false in every respect. This formula enabled those who subscribed to it to strike what they felt to be a decent commonsensical balance. In fact, it was simply a mediocre compromise between truth and falsehood, between right and wrong.

And the trials were at least directed against rivals of Stalin. The idea that Stalin had himself organized the murder of Kirov, on the face of it his closest ally and supporter – a murder in strictly criminal style – would have been rejected as absurd. When it was suggested by a few ex-oppositionists and defectors, who knew more about the circumstances than most people, it was hardly thought worth discussing.

Such attitudes showed a basic misunderstanding of the range of political possibility in a non-democratic culture. More particularly, they showed a failure to grasp Soviet circumstances and, above all, a misjudgement about Stalin personally. For Stalin's

political genius consisted precisely in this: that he recognized no
limitations, either moral or intellectual, in his methods of securing
power.

His calculation about the effect abroad was on the whole sound.
It is true that the frame-ups were clumsy fabrications. It is also
true that Stalin did not in fact silence everyone who knew anything about them. But he did not need to. The notion that things
would have been very different if the frame-ups had been seam-
lessly perfect and if everyone who had known the truth had
instantly been shot is a superficial one. Stalin had a clearer idea of
the state of the public mind both in Russia and in the West. It is
only too plain that he was right. Those who were prepared to
believe his story believed it regardless of its peripheral faults, and
rejected accounts put out by people who had had access to the
correct information.

Thus a State prepared flatly to deny its own malpractices, and
to prevent open access to the facts, could successfully persuade
many people abroad, even in spite of a large and growing body
of first-hand evidence from those who had actually experienced
the Terror. This is a lesson that has clearly been learned by similar
regimes in other parts of the world, and is still the basic principle
of much misinformation that appears in the West.

The trials were overt acts. The other acts of the Purge were
never announced. In particular, the size and nature of the labour-
camp system only became known in the West through defectors,
some of them former inmates. After the Poles in Russia were
released in 1941–2, thousands of accounts were available for
checking, and dozens of first-hand descriptions were readily
available in print. By 1948, as we have said, a very full analysis
of the system listing hundreds of camps, together with reproduc-
tions of camp documents, was published by David J. Dallin and
Boris I. Nicolaevsky.[91] The United Kingdom delegation to the
United Nations was able to circulate the Corrective Labour
Codex of the R.S.F.S.R.; free trade union bodies produced their
own analyses.

The evidence was as complete and as consistent as it could conceivably be. It was widely rejected. Jean-Paul Sartre even
defended the proposition that the evidence about the Soviet

forced labour-camp system should be ignored, even if true, on the grounds that otherwise the French proletariat might be thrown into despair. Why the labour-camp population should be sacrificed to the (rather smaller) membership of the C.G.T. is not clear; nor, indeed, has it ever been made plain why the views of the French proletariat, one of the few that has ever come largely under Communist influence, should prevail in world affairs any more than those of the anti-Communist British and American and German proletariats. Nor is it obvious at first sight why falsehood should demand the allegiance even of the intelligentsia. This sort of intellectual and ethical attitude might be treated as a passing aberration, a curiosity of history, and one might have thought that anyone holding it would have forfeited any public standing as a moral arbiter, at least in this sort of sphere. But this does not seem to be the case, and if only for that reason is worth referring to.

During the forties and fifties there were many attempts to silence or discredit the evidence of men who had been in the camps, or otherwise given information about the Purge. This was particularly the case in France. In 1950, the writer David Rousset, of the Commission Internationale Contre la Régime Concentrationnaire, sued the Communist weekly *Les Lettres Françaises* for libel. It had alleged that he had falsified a quotation from the Soviet penal code. As often in French political cases, themes much broader than the point supposedly at issue were developed. And, against a venomous defence by Communist lawyers, the facts of the forced labour system were publicly established. One of the witnesses was Dr Alexander Weissberg. An Austrian, a Jew, and (up to the time of his period in a Soviet prison) a Communist, he was continually subjected to abuse by the defence counsel in the style, 'It turns my stomach to see a German testifying before a French court'. The campaign to smear the witness did not work well in this instance, as he was able to produce an appeal which had been sent at the time of his imprisonment to the Soviet authorities testifying to his character and to his loyal service to the Soviet Union and signed by a number of leading physicists, including the Communist Joliot-Curie.

The most useful and interesting *I Chose Freedom* by Victor Kravchenko was similarly smeared in one of the most thorough and vicious campaigns of the time. Older readers will probably still recall the title with a vague feeling of unease, or hostility, induced by these methods.* Kravchenko too became involved in a court case in France, and in this instance the Russians sent witnesses to oppose him, while the French Communist Party mobilized a powerful legal and extra-legal team.

The French Communist literary weekly *Les Lettres Françaises* had published an article supposedly by an American journalist called Sim Thomas, who had allegedly alleged that a friend of his in the O.S.S. had admitted that Kravchenko's book was faked by that organization. Thomas was never produced and it is reasonably clear that he never existed. The trial proved a disaster to the Communists, although the French literary men concerned invariably countered facts supported by an impressive array of eyewitnesses by emotional appeals about the Battle of Stalingrad. They also put forward, to refute men who had actually been in labour camps, and otherwise suffered, witnesses such as the Dean of Canterbury and Mr Konni Zilliacus, who found themselves able to assert that full, or at least admirable, liberty prevailed in the Soviet Union. The Soviet Government also sent a number of witnesses, but these proved unused to hostile cross-questioning, and were on the whole disastrous.

For example, the Soviet witness Vassilenko, who had been an official in the Ukraine during the Purges, answered questions about the period:

Izard: What became of the following members of the Politburo who were in office before the purges in the Ukraine: Kossior?
Vassilenko: I don't know him.
Izard: Zatonsky?
Vassilenko: I don't recall that name.

* The obituary of Victor Kravchenko in *The Times* of 26 January 1966 is an extraordinary example of the carrying forward into the present of sentiments common in the forties. Ignoring the question of the truth of his book (long since established) and the falsehood of the libels against him (established even at the time by the court), it represented it all as a reprehensible 'Cold War' action.

Izard: They were the members of the Government of the Ukraine when you were working there. Balitsky?
Vassilenko: I don't recall that name.
Izard: Petrovsky?
Vassilenko: He's working in Moscow.
Izard: He wasn't purged?
Vassilenko: No.
Izard: Khatayevich?
Vassilenko: I don't know where he is.
Izard: Naturally! Lyubchenko?
Vassilenko: I don't recall that name.
Izard: Disappeared! Sukhomlin?
Vassilenko: I don't recall that name.
Izard: Yakir?
Vassilenko: I don't know.[92]

It will be seen that Vassilenko, under pressure, seems to have forgotten that the deaths in disgrace of both Yakir and Lyubchenko had been publicly announced. He was then asked what had happened to the four secretaries of his own local provincial party, and 'did not know'. Though himself a leading industrialist in the area, when asked about fifteen of the main managers and engineers, he denied knowing anything about what had happened to ten of them (two had died natural deaths). Unfortunately, when pressed about the missing ten, he snarled back, 'Why do you make yourself the defender of people like them?',[93] a remark not compatible with ignorance of their fate. This public illustration of the official Soviet mind at work is of interest far beyond the particular context of the trial.

Kravchenko won his case, and won it flatly and clearly, as the non-Communist press of the West agreed. Much credit went to his lawyer, the Resistance hero and former Socialist deputy, Maître Izard, who had himself been a prisoner of the Gestapo. But in the main the result depended on the chance that Kravchenko himself was of quick intelligence, capable of coping with skilled French lawyers. And even with his victory, as the details began to be forgotten, the mud was again picked up, was flung, and stuck. I am not aware that Messrs Zilliacus and Johnson, let alone the French, ever made the *amende honorable*. And as for Paris intellectuals without any knowledge of Russia, they had a sound safety mechanism: 'All they had to know was that Kravchenko was opposed to the Soviet system. This proved he was wrong.'[94]

Even when the existence of camps was admitted, they were described as of a most humane and reformatory nature. Mr Pat Sloan, the British Communist chiefly concerned with cultural liaison with the U.S.S.R., wrote:

Compared with the significance of that term in Britain, Soviet imprisonment stands out as an almost enjoyable experience. For the essence of Soviet imprisonment is isolation from the rest of the community, together with other persons similarly isolated, with the possibility to do useful work at the place of isolation, to earn a wage for this work, and to participate in running the isolation settlement or 'prison' in the same way as the children participate in running their school, or the workers their factory.[95]

and again:

The Soviet labour camp provides a freedom for its inmates not usual in our own prisons in this country.[96]

In 1966 he was prepared to comment on the above:

Among most writers on the U.S.S.R. in the 1930s, I have least to be ashamed of, or to wish to withdraw.[97]

The editor-in-chief of the Communist *Les Lettres Françaises*, M. Pierre Daix, wrote: 'The camps of re-education of the Soviet Union are the achievement of the complete suppression of the exploitation of men by men; the decisive sign of the effort by victorious Socialism to achieve the liberation of men from this exploitation in liberating also the oppressors, slaves of their own oppression.' By a considerable irony, when *One Day in the Life of Ivan Denisovich* came out in a French edition, sponsored by the Friends of the Soviet Union, they selected Daix to write the preface!

Active falsification by partisans and – worse – theoretical justification of falsehood by philosophers, were not the only causes of delusion. In addition, a general vague goodwill towards the Soviet Union, even in the thirties, led to a tendency to palliate or ignore the facts.

Dr Margolin remarks that 'an entire generation of Zionists has died in Soviet prisons, camps and in exile'; and he comments that the Zionists of the outside world were never able to help them, not only because of the difficulties, but because 'We did not care. I do not remember seeing a single article about them in the pre-war papers. Not the least effort was made to mobilize public opinion and alleviate their fate.'[98]

If this is true of the intelligent, inquisitive and internationally-minded Zionist movement, with an especial interest in a special group of prisoners, it applies much more to those in the West whose interest in the matter was, or might have been, the common bonds of humanity.

Whatever the Zionists felt, we should note that one great Jewish tradition remained clear and forthright in its attitude. The old 'Bund', the Jewish Social-Democratic organization which had played a most important part in the old Left, though crushed in Russia, had continued to work in the Baltic States and Poland. And in the United States, some of the most effective militants in the New York Jewish Left had sprung from Bund circles. A great example is David Dubinsky, who all through the period combined a firm radicalism with regard to the employers and an equally firm resistance to the Terror in Russia, and even during the war rebuffed pressures from 'liberals' and from the State Department which tried to dissuade him from protest against the executions of Ehrlich and Alter.

The effects of the Stalin era took a long time to sink in in the West. Indeed, they were rejected by many until admitted by the dictator's *diadochi*. A curious resistance prevailed in which evidence which would have been thought adequate about any other regime was rejected – a phenomenon ludicrously illustrated by (again) Jean-Paul Sartre in his introduction to Henri Alleg's book about torture in Algeria. Sartre says that we now know of the existence of torture in Communist countries as well, because of Khrushchev's admission and the evidence given at the trial of the Hungarian Police Minister Farkas. That is to say, evidence of the Alleg type, mere first-hand accounts, were to be admitted in the French, but excluded in the Russian case.

Khrushchev's revelations in February 1956 did not affect some

Soviet sympathizers in the West except to the degree that they feared they might prove disturbing to those whose faith was less firmly founded.

After the publication of Khrushchev's Secret Speech, Professor Joliot-Curie asked Ehrenburg to be cautious when speaking about it, especially to his children; Khrushchev's revelations were disturbing to many Communists; he personally knew of many errors and mistakes, even of crimes committed,* but he understood also that drastic changes of the whole structure of the State would cause troubles and personal hardships. These troubles could happen in any country, and they would not perturb him personally. They might, however, have a quite different effect on those who knew less. So he wished that Ehrenburg, when speaking about the Soviet Union, would choose positive rather than negative events.[100]

Such is the perhaps rational attitude of a Communist. It is charitable to imagine that the great physicist had not really faced the facts of what he still thought of as unavoidable hardships. In any event his case, and the various others we have dipped into, constitute a mere sketch and selection of an extraordinary *potpourri* of inhumanity and self-deception which a later generation might well take to heart.

THE HERITAGE

> In this country an avowed tyranny would be a mark of progress.   CUSTINE

When Stalin died on 5 March 1953, his successors appealed against 'panic and disarray'.[101] But their qualms were unnecessary. Though the single will of the creator of the new State had now gone, the machinery he had created remained in existence. And aspirations among the citizenry towards a different order of things had no possible means of expression and organization.

As much time has now passed since Stalin's death as the whole duration of Stalin's own regime after the end of the 'Yezhovsh-

* As Arthur Koestler points out,[99] Professor Joliot-Curie intervened in the case of certain physicists imprisoned in the Soviet Union, implying realization that charges were not always sound.

china'. We need not rehearse the history of the U.S.S.R. over that period. It will be enough to note that its politics have been dominated by the problem of Stalin – that the official line has tacked and veered between dramatic though partial denunciation of the old dictator (in, for example, 1956–61) and considerably more positive estimates (in, for example, 1957 and 1963), while at the present a policy of virtual rehabilitation is being pursued. During the interludes of severest criticism of the Stalinist past, the literature about the Purge period from which we have quoted was sporadically published.

'The cult of personality', a curiously inadequate description, is the invariable category in which the Stalinist past was criticized. This was, in effect, basically an allegation of vanity and flattery – not quite the essential which made the rule of Stalin so deplorable. It mattered much less to his victims that towns were named after him than that he was ruling by terror and falsehood. It is true that the expression implies autocracy, but it remains slightly off target.

It has proved compatible with allegations of extravagant tyranny, and equally with mere suggestions of the rather excessive application of necessary force – depending on the vagaries of recent politics. Above all, it has made it possible to claim that the Soviet State and the Party were essentially healthy throughout the period:

The successes that the working people of the Soviet Union were achieving under the leadership of the Communist Party . . . created an atmosphere in which individual errors and shortcomings seemed less significant against the background of tremendous success. . . . No personality cult could change the nature of the Socialist State, which is based on public ownership of the means of production, the alliance of the working class and the peasantry, and the friendship of peoples.[102]

But, as the Italian Communist leader, Palmiro Togliatti, commented:

First, all that was good was attributed to the superhuman, positive qualities of one man: now all that is evil is attributed to his equally exceptional and even astonishing faults. In the one case, as well as in the other, we are outside the criterion of judgement intrinsic in Marx-

686 *Epilogue*

ism. The true problems are evaded, which are why and how Soviet society could reach and did reach certain forms alien to the democratic way and to the legality that it had set for itself, even to the point of degeneration.[103]

Time and again the authorities have made it clear that, in the words of a 1963 Central Committee resolution, they 'oppose resolutely and implacably any attempt to undermine the foundations of Marxist-Leninist theory under the guise of the struggle against the personality cult, and all attempts to rehabilitate the anti-Marxist opinions and trends which were routed by the Party'.[104]

One of Stalin's principles – the theory that the intensity of the class conflict, and hence the necessity of terror, increases as the power of the defeated classes diminishes – has been denounced, though in its official form in the Party Programme adopted at the XXIInd Congress, this denunciation was hedged with reservations:

The general trend of class struggle within the socialist countries in conditions of successful socialist construction leads to the consolidation of the position of the socialist forces and weakens the resistance of the remnants of the hostile classes. But this development does follow a straight line. Changes in the domestic or external situation may cause the class struggle to intensify in specific periods. This calls for constant vigilance...[105]

The period also saw an evolution in the forms of the enforcement of State power. The Special Board of the M.V.D. was abolished in September 1953.[106] The 'Terror' Decree of 1 December 1934 was annulled on 19 April 1956.

In December 1958, a new Decree on State Crimes replaced the relevant articles of the Criminal Code dating from Stalin's time. Certain notorious excesses, such as Article 58 (i.c.), which openly inflicted penalties on the families of 'traitors' fleeing abroad, even if they were totally unimplicated, were dropped. On the other hand the Decree remained draconic and provided severe punishment for all forms of action, organization, or discussion hostile to the Government. Legal practice, too, received some degree of reform: Vyshinsky was denounced, together with his theory that confessions are the main element in a good case. But confessions were still used, and treated as valid – as in the Powers and the Penkovsky cases, in 1960 and 1963 respectively. And the more recent cases of Sinyavsky and Daniel and their successors show that nothing like equity has yet been attained.

The labour-camp system remains in being, and no information about it is officially available. The general impression is that measures had already been taken to cut the death rate and to make forced labour economically more rational in 1950 and 1951. After the death of Stalin, camp regulations seem to have been more equitably enforced, partly as the result of mass strikes in the northern camps. The release of a large number of prisoners took place under amnesties and through rehabilitations, though these seem to have ceased in about 1957.

The general picture is of some camps being virtually dissolved, some losing many of their inmates, and others remaining about the same. In many areas prisoners were released into free exile. After rebellions in the camps in 1953 (Norilsk and Vorkuta) and 1954 (Kingur),* prisoners seem to have been transferred further east. Reports at the end of 1956, when the operations to reduce the numbers of prisoners were virtually at an end, showed little change in the Kolyma–Magadan complex. Repatriated prisoners of war estimated that over a million then still remained in the Far Eastern camps. But it now seems that the more deadly complexes like Kolyma and Vorkuta have been largely wound up, and that only lesser groupings like Potmalag (where at least seventeen camps are known) continue.

In general, it is difficult to estimate how many prisoners remain in the camps (now humanely rechristened 'colonies'). Avram Tertz (Andrei Sinyavsky) remarks ironically of one camp, in *The Trial Begins*, that earlier 'The amnesty had virtually emptied the camp of its inmates. Only some ten thousand of us, dangerous criminals, were left.' P. I. Kudryavstsev, Assistant Prosecutor-General of the U.S.S.R., in an interview with Professor Harold Berman of the Harvard Law School in May 1957,[107] after the amnesties, said that two-thirds of the camps had then been

*The incident described in Constantine FitzGibbon's *When the Kissing Had to Stop*, where Latvian and Ukrainian women were crushed by tanks.

abolished, though he also spoke of new ones being built.* And, on the other hand, ex-prisoners reported that all the main complexes were still in operation.[108] In unofficial conversation, Russians are inclined to quote a figure of up to a million inmates, with the qualification that not more than about 10 per cent of these are political offenders – that is, still, more than the peace-time maximum in Nazi camps.

Discipline remains rigorous. Indeed, a decree of the Supreme Soviet of 5 May 1961 for the first time imposes the death penalty for certain 'acts of aggression against the administration', short of murder, in the camps.

However one looks at it, the penal and police systems have been reformed since Stalin's death. Equally, however one looks at it, they have not undergone essential change, have not become truly liberal.

The same ambiguity applies everywhere. It has deep political roots. Advantages accrue to the rulers if they can dissociate themselves as far as possible from the burden of the past, from the memory – enormously unpopular even in Party circles – both of the 'Yezhovshchina' and of Stalin's last few years, when no one at any level was safe.

Yet the present regime owes its legitimacy to its descent from Stalin, and is committed to the correctness of Stalin's 'general line' as against both the Left and the Right oppositions of the twenties and thirties, and hence to his correctness on basic policy matters. 'De-Stalinization', therefore, even in the Khrushchev period, was kept within bounds and confined to a special and partial denunciation. Stalin's body was removed from Lenin's tomb, but it still lies in a fairly honourable position under the Kremlin wall, among the bodies of important 'positive' figures of the second rank – and, perhaps significantly, next to that of Felix Dzerzhinsky, founder of the Secret Police.

---

*Berman took Kudryavstsev as apparently wanting 'to convey the impression' that there were only 800,000–900,000 inmates in camps in 1957. This seems to have been an under-estimate, since it was coupled with an estimate of 3 million for Stalin's last years, which is certainly very much too low.

Many of Stalin's personal group died in good odour after their patron's own death – Shkiryatov in 1954, Vyshinsky in 1955 (though his is rumoured as suicide). But Poskrebyshev is still alive and at liberty – writing his memoirs, or so it is said. Men like Kaganovich and Malenkov, though publicly accused by the Prosecutor-General of the U.S.S.R. of 'criminal violations of Socialist legality',[109] also remain at liberty. Most leading police officials of the old regime have been shot in one or other of the blows against particular factions which led to a series of trials in 1953–6. But others survive, such as Serov, who was Head of Army Intelligence until 1964. General Gorbatov speaks quite naturally of his torturer, Stolbunsky – 'I don't know where he is now' – and mentions meeting the despicable Commissar Fominykh, who had organized his removal, in a group of senior officers in 1962.

More basically, there has been no serious attempt to deal with the Terror as a whole. The great plot ostensibly headed by Trotsky, backed by the Nazis, involving politicians, generals engineers, doctors, and ordinary citizens by the thousand, has not been explicitly denounced as a fabrication. Statements have been made that demolish the authenticity of some of the main public accusations. Several of those named as conspirators in the 1938 Trial were rehabilitated a decade ago, making nonsense of the entire 'plot'. The main alleged crime of the 1937 accused – the 'attempt' on the life of Molotov – was openly described at the XXIInd Party Congress as a frameup. On the centrepiece of the whole Purge story (and the main crime of the 1936 accused in particular), the Kirov murder, we have seen that the official line was already rejected as unsatisfactory by Khrushchev in his Secret Speech of February 1956, and again, publicly, in his report to the 1961 Congress – each time with strong hints that Stalin was the real organizer of the assassination. So, although the full truth was being extracted with painful slowness, like some impacted wisdom tooth, enough had already been said to concede the total falsehood of the original Stalinist version.

The rehabilitations of the 1956–67 period have a parallel lack of logic. The military victims have been cleared. The executed

Stalinists – Rudzutak, Chubar, Postyshev, Eikhe, Kossior and the others – enjoy full honours. Yenukidze and Karakhan, of the December 1937 Trial, are now in good odour.

But no one has been cleared from the Zinoviev or Pyatakov Trials. And in the Bukharin Trial, a fantastic situation has persisted for years in which some of the accused are now fully rehabilitated, and others are not. Ikramov, Khodzhayev, Krestinsky, Zelensky and Grinko are now in favour. But to rehabilitate, for example, Krestinsky without rehabilitating Rosengolts is to rehabilitate Burke while leaving Hare accused.

Yugoslav sources said, in the autumn of 1962, that Bukharin would shortly be rehabilitated.[110] This did not take place, though at a meeting of an All-Union Conference on Measures to Improve the Training of Scientific-Pedagogical Cadres in the Historical Sciences,[111] Pospelov said: 'Students ask whether Bukharin and others were spies of foreign States. . . . I may state that it is sufficient to study the documents of the XXIInd Congress of the C.P.S.U. in order to say that neither Bukharin nor Rykov, of course, were spies or terrorists.' This little-publicized partial exculpation is important in principle. But Bukharin's and Rykov's names have not been restored to Party favour. And as I write, Zinoviev, Kamenev, Pyatakov, I. N. Smirnov, Sokolnikov, Rosengolts, to name some of the other leading figures at the public trials, still remain totally unrehabilitated. So do a good many men who did not even come to public trial: for example, Preobrazhensky, Smilga, Uglanov, Shlyapnikov, Medvedev, Sapronov, Sosnovsky.*

Rehabilitation, as well as being done in this illogical and partial fashion, has taken a variety of forms. The maximum has been the full-scale article with at least a remark at the end that the man named fell victim to slander as a result of the personality cult. The minimum has been simply the mention of the former purgee's name in a neutral or favourable context. There is, indeed, something even more minimal, if one can so express it, than the above.

---

*The present trend, moreover, is retrograde. Almost every time we have spoken of a 'recent' piece of Soviet evidence, we mean one no later than 1964–5.

It is now conventional in the 'biographical notes' on people who played a part in the earlier history of the Party and who are listed at the end of works dealing with that time, to give, in addition to those of birth and death, the date of entering the Party. In the case of all those in good odour, this is phrased 'Member of the Party from 1910', or whatever the date may be. In the case of those still unrehabilitated, this is invariably 'Got into the Party ["*Sostoyal v partii*"] 1910'. From this minor convention, it can be seen that, for example, Syrtsov is now, to this degree at least, restored to favour, while Preobrazhensky is not.

This curious, and typical, indirectness goes with a failure to come to grips with the past. It is easily explicable. After Stalin's death, the machine he created continued to rule the country, as it does to this day. The principle of one-party rule, the overriding competence of that party in all spheres of life, the preservation of its 'monolithic' nature – and rule over it by a small central body – all continued.

All the present leaders rose in the old machine during Stalin's time. The channels through which they rose remain as then established. And the principles of rule are, in general, those then brought to fruition.

The criticisms of the Great Terror which emerged during the Khrushchev interlude were general, and hedged with reservations. The rehabilitations which took place at that time were haphazard and inconsistent. At present they have virtually ceased. They may indeed be resumed at some later stage. But for the moment it is certainly true that the political advantages Khrushchev sought from his 'anti-Stalinism' have, as far as the present leadership is concerned, already been obtained with the expulsion from public life of a number of possible contenders for power.

After the fall of Khrushchev in October 1964, an end was put to speculative and risky initiatives in every field. This applies also to the matter of 'Stalinism'. The rehabilitation process virtually ceased, as did written discussions of the more sensitive areas of the Stalinist past. Stalin himself began to be treated at first with a rather cold respect and more recently with considerable favour, in spite of the protests of Party historians. The system of government he created, as amended and improved under Khrushchev, was consolidated.

The extent of the reaction since Khrushchev's time may be seen in the treatment of Raskolnikov. In his military *Memoirs* (published in 1964), the introduction states flatly 'The C.C. of the C.P.S.U. has completely rehabilitated him, and restored him posthumously to party membership and to Soviet citizenship.' Even as late as 1968 his Civil War record was favourably referred to;[112] but soon his photograph was removed from books, and various editors who had permitted favourable reference to him were reprimanded or dismissed. Finally an article in the authoritative party organ *Kommunist* spoke of him as 'a deserter to the side of the enemy and a slanderer of the party and the Soviet State'.[113]

The regime is, to a certain extent, in an illogical position. If its system is thoroughly accepted by the classes – now wholly non-capitalist – making up the population, then the compulsive elements might logically be relaxed; or, to put it in a more Western way, thirty years of indoctrination and terror might be expected to have produced a country in which opposition to the form of State would be negligible even if permitted. The beginnings of some such idea seem to have entered into the minds of one or two Party leaders around 1956 – if not Khrushchev's, then at least Shepilov's. A similar notion seems very temporarily to have affected the Chinese leaders in 1957; the Hundred Flowers Campaign is best explained as based on the idea that by now freedom could be allowed, since it would be used freely to support the regime. The immediate outbursts of heresy, in Russia as in China, showed that this was a miscalculation. And we still have the curious spectacle of a regime which claims almost unanimous support being extravagantly sensitive to the most minor criticisms – as was shown, for example, in the Sinyavsky–Daniel case. It is clear that the time has not yet come for a reconciliation with the people, for the re-creation of a Marxist democratic party as originally foreseen. For the moment, at least, the promise of better things after forty years in the wilderness shows little sign of fulfilment. The reason, basically, seems to be that the caravan is led by men skilled in the ways of the wilderness, and enjoying the powers they have gained and would certainly forfeit in a lusher land.

For Pyatakov's 'miracle' – the idea that by sheer political organization the Party could create industry and the proletariat which should in Marx's view have preceded the coming to power of socialism, and having done that, go back to the main line foreseen by Marx – has not worked out. The reason is plain. It had been a mistake to think that the Party would, after this un-Marxist detour, simply revert to a humanist democratic representation of the new proletariat. The 'temporary' alienation proved permanent. It was not the case that Stalinist methods could be used and then simply cast aside when specific economic and social aims had been achieved. Terror builds its own cadres, institutions and habits of mind. And the Party machine, whose loyalties for so long had been in practice simply to itself, whose interests had for so long been equally circumscribed, had become Djilas's 'New Class', no more capable of easily changing its ways than the old classes and bureaucracies of the past had been.

The Stalin era was a past so atrocious that its repudiation brought obvious dividends to any succeeding regime, but its successors also inherited a set of institutions and a ruling caste indoctrinated in certain habits and beliefs. It is difficult enough to induce the bureaucrats of the Party machine to accept changes that do *not* affect their right to rule. No approach to eroding that right has been made, and probably none could be made with any chance of success unless disintegration were to set in in the Soviet political scene. Yet, in an important sense, the essence of Stalinism is less the particular periods of terrorism or special views on industrial organization than the establishment of the political set-up. And that remains substantially unchanged.

It is common to equate 'de-Stalinization' with 'liberalization'. But even the Khrushchevite 'de-Stalinization' consisted of little more than the abandonment (or even the denunciation) of a specific set of excesses associated with the late dictator. It did not amount to any change of substance in the *system* of political rule in the U.S.S.R., or of the basic principles behind that system. Russia is still ridden by the Party machine, and the principle of *Partiinost* – the doctrine of the Party's right to ride and to decide

694   *Epilogue*

on all questions of speed and direction – remains untouched. What has taken place, in effect, is simply the denunciation and renunciation of excessive use of whip and spur.

There has recently been, indeed, a considerable effort to rehabilitate the N.K.V.D.: criticism is levelled at those who, basing themselves on the organization's role in the Purges, 'are not averse to putting practically all the officers of the Cheka under a cloud'.[114] Since Khrushchev's fall, a whole series of novels and plays has appeared featuring Secret Police heroes.*

There are complaints from present-day Soviet liberals that, for example, the former Georgian N.K.V.D. chief, Nadray, 'specialist in shooting wives and daughters', only received ten years after Beria's death and is now at liberty; that Colonel Monakhov, who shot several hundred foreign Communists in the Solovetsk camps at the beginning of the Finnish war, is living in a villa near Leningrad, an attempt to have him expelled from the Party having been prevented by Tolstikov, then First Secretary of the Leningrad province; that the leading interrogator of the Jewish doctors in 1952, A. G. Sugak, has a job as Assistant Director of a museum, and a villa near Moscow; and so on. Similarly with major delators: for example V. N. Astrov, who 'denounced hundreds of his colleagues', is reported as working in a publishing house and as having written, under pseudonyms, new slanders against his earlier victims.[115]

In the Party, the slight liberty of opposition of the early twenties, and even of the mid-twenties, has not been re-established. And the position as regards the country as a whole may be taken as roughly comparable to that at the beginning of the thirties. It might be added that there are no constitutional or other guarantees against repetition of something in the nature of the Stalin interlude, which started off from a similar civic level: any more than the rule of the comparatively liberal emperors in Roman times prevented reversions to tyranny when they had gone. Vespasian, who established sanity on the ruins of the Nero regime, was soon followed by Domitian.

*For example, Yuri German's *I Am Responsible* and *The New Year's Eve Party*, Kozhevnikov's *The Shield and the Sword*, Bylinov's *The Streets of Wrath* and Zalynsky's play *Pebbles in the Hand*.

Moreover, there has lately been a steady deterioration, even as to the view taken of Stalin. As early as the beginning of 1966 it was laid down that the phrase 'the period of the personality cult' – the mildest of all hostile descriptions of the Stalin period – was 'mistaken' and 'un-Marxist'.[116] A typical summary of the present position was made in a set-piece article in the Party's most authoritative organ, *Kommunist*, at the beginning of 1969, which said of Stalin's malpractices that 'these were mistakes in practical work which was essentially correct in fulfilling the scientifically based general line of the Party'.[117]

In September 1966, new articles were added to the Criminal Code, providing for the imprisonment of those given to uttering or writing material 'discrediting the Soviet State' or participating in 'group activities' involving 'disobedience in the face of the lawful demands of the authorities'[118] – laws clearly directed (as Soviet writers and scientists complained) against protests against such injustices as the Sinyavsky trial. They have since been applied in a number of notorious cases.

It was an Italian Communist Senator who remarked that the C.P.S.U. 'had not come to execution without a long process, which started neither in 1937 nor in 1934, but much earlier, when minorities were deprived of the right of expressing their views, and then were isolated and kept under suspicion and eventually expelled and imprisoned'.[119] On the other hand, the notion of permitting various views even within the Party was firmly rebuffed at the XXIInd Congress in 1961 and has not since been raised.

There are of course differences between the present period and the early thirties. It may be argued that the élan of the Party is dead and that only momentum, habit and institutions remain. If this view is taken, the present system might appear like the legitimist monarchies of the early nineteenth century – impressive, powerful, but dead at heart, and remaining only as an integument which eventually broke.

Moreover, the Stalin-style economy was viable only with strong political and police restraints, preventing the arising of consumer demand, and substituting threats for incentives. This worked fairly well in the old style steel- and coal-based production, but it is proving defective with a modern technical economy. The economic pressures for change are strong, and are so far being resisted in general, though certain adjustments have been made.

Several views are possible about the further evolution of the Soviet Union. But from the point of view of memories of the Terror, it has to be noted (as has been done by Pietro Nenni, the Italian Socialist leader) that there are no institutional or moral guarantees against a reversion to the habits of the thirties.

It would be putting it strongly to say with Milovan Djilas, 'Those who wish to live and to survive in a world different from the one Stalin created and which still exists and is as strong as ever, must fight for their lives.' Nevertheless, the present principle of rule in the Soviet Union – and indeed in all the other Communist States – remains that of the monolithic party created by Stalin after his political victory over the various oppositions. This does not, at any moment, necessarily, or even probably, lead to a Stalinist terror. But it is still susceptible – and *a fortiori* – to the criticism levelled by the Communist heroine and martyr Rosa Luxemburg against Lenin's regime.

Her argument against the suppression of hostile opinion, and the closed society, is not a moral one. It is simply that:

> Without general elections, without unrestricted freedom of press and assembly, without a free struggle of opinion, life dies out in every public institution, becomes a mere semblance of life, in which only the bureaucracy remains as the active element. ... Yes, we can go even further: such conditions must cause a brutalization of public life ...[120]

This was a sound prediction of development in Russia from the Revolution till the victory of Stalin. Until its recommendations are complied with, the Soviet Union can best be described as not fully cured, but still suffering from a milder and more chronic form of the affliction which reached its crisis in the Yezhov years. It is to be hoped that in one way or another a complete cure may soon be effected. One sign of it would be a frank confrontation with the past; so that Russians could freely and fully investigate the events of which some account has meanwhile been given in these pages.

Appendices

APPENDIX A

CASUALTY FIGURES

No exact numbers can yet be given of those who suffered in the Great Purge. In general Soviet citizens speak of 'millions of lives' broken, of 'millions of innocent people in camps and prisons'.[1] The estimates tentatively put forward in Chapter 10 are those which for various reasons have seemed reasonable to the author. We can indeed be sure that they are of the right order of magnitude, but the evidence will naturally lack precision until the N.K.V.D. archives are available for examination.

Nevertheless, there is much material which bears on the question. And without attempting to deduce from it a rigour which it will not at present support, we can list the main points which lead to the type of conclusion I have come to.

This can suitably be done under five main heads. First, the number arrested can be considered. Second, the number of these condemned to death, or at least executed. Third, the numbers in the labour camps. Fourth, the death rate in those camps. The figures for each of these depend to some degree on the others, but there is in every case a body of evidence directly bearing on the special point. Fifth and additionally, we can consider, looking back from the most recent Soviet census, the population deficit produced by the Purge. I have thought it best to give each train of evidence separately, and not make any explicit attempt to collate them. The extent to which they confirm each other, and the areas of uncertainty too, will be fairly apparent.

A. ARRESTS

1. We know from the Stalin–Molotov Secret Instruction of 8 May 1933[2] that there were at that time 800,000 persons in 'places of detention . . . *not* counting labour camps and colonies', that is, prisons. All accounts agree that crowding was much greater in 1937–8 than at any previous period: we can take 1,000,000 as a minimum, at any rate.

It fits with direct evidence from the cells. The Butyrka held about 30,000 prisoners.[3] If we conservatively allow another 20,000 for the other Moscow prisons, plus those of the towns of Moscow province, that would imply a total in the whole country of 950,000: Moscow province, with about 9 million inhabitants, had about one-nineteenth of the total population. Moscow is, indeed, not entirely typical. Its high concentration of Party members and Government officials were particularly liable to arrest; on the other hand, ordinary citizens are usually reported to have suffered less than the norm, and in general these factors are believed to balance out. (Leningrad, with a province population of about 6 million, reportedly had some 40,000 prisoners in 1940.)[4] A figure around a million might still be an underestimate of the number actually held in prisons proper at a given moment in 1937–8.

2. Another line of argument produces figures of the same order. In January 1927 the prison capacity was about 113,000; then overcrowded by about 1·7 to 1, the cells held about 198,000 prisoners. *If* we make the highly conservative assumption that there was no net increase in prison accommodation between 1927 and 1937, and apply the figures for overcrowding from Chapter Nine, where they run from about 4·5 to 1 up to 15 or 16 to 1, we get a figure of between half a million and a million and a half for the prison population proper.

3. An estimate which has found much support is that the average prisoner, over the whole two-year period, stayed in jail about three to four months.[5] This would give a total arrest figure for the two years of 6–8 million, if we accept an average jail population of only a million.

A complementary figure, given by an N.K.V.D. interrogator himself under arrest, is that there were 3,000 interrogators in Moscow alone.[6] *If* they concluded a case a week on the average – not a heavy demand – this would be at the level, for the whole country, of 6 million for the two years of 'political' prisoners only.

4. Dr Alexander Weissberg, the physicist, who was in the Kharkov prisons from March 1937 till February 1939, estimates that about 5·5 per cent of the population of the area feeding

these jails were arrested during this period.[7] Among other indications, a check was kept by following the numbers on the receipts given prisoners for their goods confiscated on arrest – money, braces, etc. But this was confirmed by other methods. (Avtorkhanov, a high official in the North Caucasus, estimates that about 4 per cent of the population of that region was arrested *in 1937 alone*, though he appears to grant that this is a higher figure than for the U.S.S.R. as a whole.)[8]

It has been objected to Dr Weissberg's figures that Kharkov too may not be representative. But Weissberg in fact compared the local figure with those made by prisoners who had done the same computation in other parts of the country,* and found that 5–5½ per cent was regularly reported. (Another prominent academic prisoner who conducted the same researches concluded that 5 per cent was a minimum figure for arrests.)[9]

Applied to the population total as given in the 1939 census,† this would mean about 8½ million arrests.

5. It can be estimated that during the most crowded period in the winter of 1937, over 4,000 men a week went from the Butyrka prison, mainly into camps, and were replaced.[14] For the whole of Moscow province one might postulate 7,000. If the *average* over the two years was of the lower order of *c.* 4,000, we get a total for the two years of 416,000; which applied to the whole country would give just under 8 million as the total number of arrests.

6. In 1934, at the XVIIth Party Congress, there were 2,817,000

*As another prisoner remarks: 'Every cell possesses at least one statistician.'[10]

† One of the difficulties is that we do not know what to make of the 1939 census. The census taken in January 1937 was suppressed, and publicly though vaguely denounced,[11] for 'gross breaches of the elementary bases of statistical science'. The Census Board is believed to have been shot. But what it was that proved unsatisfactory in their results is unknown. An N.K.V.D. rumour had it that the total population fell far below what was expected and required (a figure of 147 million instead of the 170 million reported in January 1939 was bruited).[12] On the other hand, the published total seems on the face of it compatible with the known and estimated population trends, and a quite different motive for the stifling of the 1937 figures – unsatisfactory social distribution – has been suggested.[13] Even so, in the circumstances, we can hardly repose unreserved confidence in any aspect of the 1939 census.

members and candidate members of the Party. Under the then regulations, candidates could not retain that intermediate position for more than three years. That is, by the XVIIIth Congress in 1939, they should all have been promoted – or expelled. The full membership in 1939 was 1,568,000, and of these *c.* 400,000 had not been in the Party at all in 1934. That is, there is a deficit of *c.* 1,640,000. About 300,000 had been expelled in 1934, when comparatively non-incriminating reasons were common. But the rest, including the 1935 expellees,* formed the first and hardest-hit target of the whole Purge. We can scarcely allow that a quarter of them escaped arrest. This would give a figure for party arrests of not far short of a million.

Another careful estimate[16] is that about 850,000 expulsions took place in the eighteen months January 1937–June 1938, which accords with the above estimate.

The figure most commonly found of the proportion of non-Party to Party arrests runs at 7–8 to 1. This would give some 8–9 million arrests.

7. Other estimates are of the same general type. A Yugoslav estimate is that there were about 7 million arrests in 1936–8.[17] An estimate by a responsible Party official is also 7 million arrests.[18] In fact all our chains of evidence (treated, in general, somewhat conservatively) lead, though without any real precision, to some such figure.

B. EXECUTIONS

1. Of the number of death sentences the impression of careful observers is that 'they did not exceed ten per cent of the whole'.[19] An analysis of reports on 471 random arrests in the period 1936–40 (relatives of 2,725 Soviet citizens later defecting to the West) included 52 known death sentences[20] – around 10–11 per cent. On the arrest figures we have, this would give *c.* 700,000 'legal' executions.

The Party official who estimates 7 million arrests suggests that the death sentences amounted to about 500,000.[21]

---

*A typical description of the reasons for expulsion being that they were '*kulaks*, White Guards, Trotskyites, Zinovievites, and all other filth'.[15]

2. We are told by a Soviet writer that in the Lefortovo, as early as August 1937, they were shooting seventy men a day.[22] The rate for the first five months of 1937 must have been a good deal lower; but, on the other hand, things were worse over the winter of 1937–8. If we take a total of 40,000 over the two years, we shall probably not be far wrong. This would give a figure of around 800,000 for the whole country if all the remaining prisons in it accounted for twenty times as many executions, which seems conservative even allowing for the special circumstances of the Lefortovo.* Then again, local N.K.V.D. branches in the provinces were ordered on occasion simply to execute a given number of 'enemies of the people' in their hands, that is, not prisoners held by GULAG in camps, but by the local authorities in prisons. For example, a former N.K.V.D. officer reports one telegram of which he was personally aware, and which is doubtless representative of others sent regularly throughout the Union, such is its air of routine formality: this was from Yezhov to the N.K.V.D. chief at Frunze, capital of Kirghizia:

You are charged with the task of exterminating 10,000 enemies of the people. Report results by signal.

The form of reply was:

In reply to yours of . . . , the following enemies of the people have been shot.

followed by a numbered list.[23] One order to the city N.K.V.D. of Sverdlovsk called for 15,000 executions. Another, to a small town near Novosibirsk, ordered 500, but the N.K.V.D. there could find only petty offenders available. In the end they had to shoot priests and their relatives, all who had spoken critically of conditions, amnestied former members of White Armies and so on – mostly people who would have ordinarily qualified for five-year sentences or less.[24] One example of this type of massacre has become known in physical detail. Mass graves were discovered in Vinnitsa, in the Ukraine,[25] in 1943 when the area was under German occupation, and were examined – like the Katyn graves – by an international commission of medical experts. The

*And see p. 427 for Gorki – provincial population *c.* 4m.

number of corpses, all killed by shots in the back of the neck, except for a few cases of braining with gun butts or clubs, was over 9,000. 1,670 corpses were examined. These shootings seem to have taken place in 1938. The identifications made by relatives give the latest arrests in June that year. The bodies were buried actually within the city limits in an orchard, a cemetery and a section of the municipal park. This implies a far greater likelihood of discovery than in the (presumably more natural and usual) selection of more isolated spots. The discovery was, in fact, made because various inhabitants had heard or seen suspicious actions. There is thus a presumption – as indeed can be deduced from Katyn – that other similar massacres remained undiscovered. (But we can also note in the selection of such sites that the N.K.V.D. in 1938 is shown as arrogantly sure of itself in its treatment of the population.)

The population of Vinnitsa before the war was about 70,000, and of the province about 1,000,000. *If* these 9,000 were the only executions in Vinnitsa, *if* they represented the entire province, and *if* the same proportion applied throughout the country, we get a figure of *c.* 1½ million executions. The same calculations applied to the (less solidly authenticated) Frunze and Sverdlovsk massacres mentioned above give a countrywide figure of over a million, from these one-shot operations alone.

3. Very significantly to estimates derived from known death sentences, there was also a sentence of forced labour 'without right of correspondence'. No ex-prisoner ever met anyone serving such a sentence. Moreover, when the mass grave at Vinnitsa was examined, a number of relatives identified corpses whose sentence had been notified to them as of (usually) ten years 'without right of correspondence'. We can conclude that this phrase was a method of concealing the execution rate. We have no means of estimating the numbers of deaths thus misrepresented. But the employment of this ruse was pointless unless it had substantial application, and one Moscow informant notes several out of his own limited acquaintance. An ex-N.K.V.D. officer says that it was quite a normal procedure.[26] Boris Efimov writes that his brother Mikhail Koltsov was sentenced to ten years 'without the right of correspondence'. When

he was rehabilitated in 1955 Efimov was told that he was dead. On his saying this could not be true, since Ulrikh had personally told him of this particular sentence, the official concerned shrugged and said, 'Ah, Ulrikh . . .'[27]

It is true that the date of Koltsov's death is now given as two years later than that of his trial. This seems to imply that this particular sentence, while in effect a death sentence, might mean one which was not, or not always, carried out immediately. Academician Sakharov, describing certain camps as 'prototypes of the fascist death camps' (in that they were places where 'thousands of prisoners were machine-gunned because of "overcrowding" or as a result of special orders'), tells us that these were 'camps without the right of correspondence'.[28] And this would certainly mean, for some of these sentences at least, a postponement of execution.

4. Mass executions were also ordered at this time in the camps. These were almost always carried out somewhat furtively. Prisoners would disappear to special centres, and thus not be reckoned by their mates among the camp death-rate estimates. Genuine old Trotskyists, of whom a few still survived even in 1938, were usually given a formal, if rapid, 'trial', but this was exceptional. An account from the central isolation prison of the Baikal-Amur railway group of camps, where executions were entirely clandestine and without sentence, estimates that in the two years 1937–38 some 50,000 people were executed here in this fashion.[29] (In addition to such operations, death sentences for sabotage and anti-Soviet propaganda were routine in camp.[30])

5. It will be seen that no exact estimate of total executions can be made, but that the number was most probably something around a million. One officer of the central N.K.V.D. estimates about two million 'liquidations' in 1936, 1937 and 1938.[31] An official Yugoslav statement estimated, as we have seen, that the total 'killed' in 1936, 1937 and 1938 was 3 million.[32] These seem high figures and perhaps include estimated camp deaths other than by shooting.

C. NUMBERS IN THE CAMPS

We are not able to give exact figures in this field any more than in the others. But there are methods of estimating which are sound in principle and cannot give answers that are far wrong, if carefully applied. Though arising independently, they tally with each other. And the results are in adequate accord with those deduced at the other end of the process – the rates of arrest.

1. First, we have a set of figures, authentic in themselves, but needing interpretation, for the forced labour resources expected by the N.K.V.D. to be available in 1941. These come in the secret 'State Plan for the Development of the National Economy of the U.S.S.R. in 1941'.[33] The version available is incomplete. From its list of the amount of production allotted one can make certain deductions on the amount of forced labour in lumbering, coal-mining and other spheres. But it omits gold-mining, agriculture and certain other branches, and, in particular, gives no figures for the out-contracting in construction work done by the N.K.V.D. for other Commissariats, one of its major spheres. Professor Swianiewicz, in a careful and conservative estimate based on this, arrives at a total of just under 7 million. It should be noted that late 1940 was a comparatively low period for camp population: Wiles, estimating 8 million for 1939, gives 6½ million for 1940.

2. The second method is also sound in theory – that based on prisoners' reports. Dr Julius Margolin, for example, was imprisoned in several camps of the Baltic–White Sea group from 1940 on. He found that the group contained a Division 28, that each division had at least 10 to 15 sites, and that these held a range from a few hundred to a few thousand prisoners. A rough deduction gives several hundred thousand prisoners for the whole. (The true total is believed to be about 300,000.) Obviously such individual estimates can give no more than a rough result. But when a considerable number of such reports are collated, plainly a very reasonable approximation can be attained. This was done, over the whole range of camps, by Dallin and Nicolaevsky in the mid forties, and their conclusion warrants considerable confidence. (Many of the survivors of the *c.* 440,000 Poles sent to labour camps in 1939–41, and allowed to leave the U.S.S.R. in

1942–3, gave useful indications.) Calculations so based give a figure, for the 1940–41 period, of 8–12 million.

3. There are various odd points in Soviet statistics published in the late thirties which have seemed to researchers to give indications of a possible labour-camp figure. For example, there is a discrepancy between the aggregate payroll for the whole economy and the total wage bill on the basis of official labour statistics, amounting to 18·5 per cent of the total payroll. Part of this is accounted for by the Army, but it has been estimated that 13·5 million involuntary workers remain after that has been done. These would include the large category of those doing 'forced labour' at the place of employ, then a common penalty though a short-term one.

Again, the author of the most authoritative study of the Soviet population (Lorimer) was puzzled by a residue of 6,790,000 unaccounted for in terms of employment, pensions, Army, etc., plus just under 1¼ million labelled 'social group not indicated'. Similarly, an analysis applying to the 1939 figures the proportion of population to labour force of the 1926 census – a point not given in that of 1939 – left a residue of 10 million.

Thus, those who take these approaches as genuinely significant can deduce from them figures of the right sort of magnitude. But the formal difficulties are great, and in none of these cases is it possible to say that the apparent anomaly is not accountable in some other way.

It is clear, again, that the 1939 census does *not* list the prisoners in the areas which actually contained them. Komi, for example, is given as having *c.* 319,000 population, half of them of the local nationality, and Magadan as a mere 173,000 (these figures are probably adequate to cover the free staff of the camp complexes, and their surroundings). Nor is it possible to establish whether or not the census contains the prisoners in any other way.

We must leave it that neither the census nor any other published Soviet statistics of the period have yet yielded any sound basis for an estimate; though it is worth noting that the expected population for 1937, as given in the preface, prepared in 1936, to *The Second Five Year Plan for the Development of the National*

Economy of the U.S.S.R. (English ed., New York, 1937), was 180,700,000, as compared with the census result of 170,467,000 two years later.

4. Other evidence is simply by report, but deserves consideration because it must often represent official leakage or at worst informed guesswork.[34] The general estimate in the camps themselves over 1938–41 was from 15 million upwards, and this was shared by many N.K.V.D. officers themselves under arrest. It was also the common rumour in official circles. GULAG officials arrested in 1938 gave about 10 million as their own estimate. There are a few lower estimates, such as that of an official who gave 6 million 'with a strong upward trend' in early 1941. A colonel connected with the inspectorate of camp guards from 1934 to 1941 said there were between 12 and 14 million just before the war. That these estimates run several million higher than those arrived at by other methods may be due to the inclusion of those charged under other articles of the Code than 58 – that is, 'common criminals' such as bandits, small peculators, breakers of labour discipline, etc. Most of these did not go through the processes described above but were held at detention centres attached to the police stations (Moscow had eleven prisons in addition to the five named in the Purge literature). There, their cases, involving simple and genuine facts, were processed in two or three days; and they went straight off to camp.*

5. No exact computation being possible, one can see that these figures, together with those for arrests and executions, are compatible with a highly conservative solution of the following type – not including 'criminals', as not specifically victims of the purge – for the end of 1938:

In jail or camp already January 1937	*c.* 5 million
Arrested January 1937–December 1938	*c.* 7 million
	c. 12 million

* After the war there was certainly an increase. N.K.V.D. functionaries imprisoned in 1948 spoke of 12 million. The commandant of a 'repatriation camp' feeding the labour camps spoke of the post-war total as 15–17 million. Solzhenitsyn notes that prisoners often exaggerated, giving higher numbers when 'the actual prison population was no more than 12 or 15 million.'[35]

of which executed	*c.*	1 million
died in camp 1937–38	*c.*	2 million
	c.	3 million
In captivity late 1938	*c.*	9 million
of which in prison	*c.*	1 million
in camps	*c.*	8 million

D. DEATH IN THE CAMPS

We are typically told that 'during the first year about one third of the prisoners die',[36] mainly of exhaustion. That is, those physically most unfitted to the extreme conditions of the camps went quickly. Taken as applying to the newly arrested of 1937–8, it would imply a loss of about 1 million of them each year, over the period immediately following admittance.

This 30 per cent death rate for the new intake is not of course the death rate for the camp population as a whole. A careful study of this has produced a rate in camps, in 1933, of about 10 per cent per annum. In 1938 it had risen to about 20 per cent.[37] This variation is compounded by another difficulty – that our information usually comes from particular areas, and there was much variation in conditions. Kolyma, as we have seen, had a death rate of up to 30 per cent. If we take its average population as 500,000, possibly an underestimate, this camp area alone probably accounted for over 2 million deaths up to 1950. Lumber work, and others in the far north – especially on the Vorkuta railway – were also dangerous employments. But in general, leaving aside a few very bad and a few notably moderate camps, the total impression is that the ration was always and everywhere insufficient to the work, and until 1950 always produced a death rate of a minimum of 10 per cent per annum.

An estimate in the broad scale, though still not a precise one, can be made in the case of the Polish prisoners of 1939–42. Of 1,060,000 Poles taken to labour camps, prisoner of war camps, or forced settlement, about 270,000 died. Of these, the great majority perished in the labour camps, which accounted for about 440,000 of the total detainees. Even allowing for the executions at Katyn and elsewhere, and starvation in a number of free settlements, it seems that not less than 40–50 per cent of the labour-camp inmates of Polish citizenship must have died during an average incarceration of around two to two and a half years.[38]

Release was very rare. Moreover, in the late forties, as is now admitted, those who had been released were all rearrested. Thus, the average prisoner had to go through bad years as well as fair, and except in a few favoured camps was most unlikely to survive. Of 3,000 Kursk 'collaborationists' sent to camp after the recapture of that city in 1943, only sixty were alive in 1951.[39]

After 1950 the death rate, at least in the main zones of northern Russia, became little higher (except for 'disciplinary' deaths) than the local civilian rate. The physical possibility of surviving a sentence existed, though the prospects at the time seemed poor, for, as the well-adjusted 'Ivan Denisovich' could say:

Maybe you could last ten years and still come out of it alive, but how the hell could you get through twenty-five?[40]

Fortunately, these later victims did not have to wait so long. But the average camp inmate arrested in the period before 1950 had usually been through killing years, as with the men from Kursk. The 1937–8 victims who did not go under in the first wave of deaths often survived right up to the war. But the bad years then ensuing killed the vast majority of them. They are only reported most exceptionally in the post-war evidence.

Taking the conservative figures of an *average* over the period 1936–50 inclusive of an 8 million population of the camps and a 10 per cent death rate per annum, we get a total casualty figure of 12 million dead. To this we must add a million for the executions of the period, certainly a low estimate. Then there are the casualties of the pre-Yezhov era of Stalin's rule, 1930–36: this includes as its main component the 7 million who perished in the collectivization famine itself and the deportations associated with it, and in camps before 1937; again, minimal estimates. Thus we get a figure of 20 million dead, which is almost certainly too low and might require an increase of 50 per cent or so, as the debit balance of the Stalin regime for twenty-three years.

THE SOVIET CENSUS OF JANUARY 1959

The total figure of 208,827,000 was some 20 million lower than Western observers had expected *after* making allowance for war losses – even though the first losses of the Purge, or such of them as may be registered in the 1939 Census, had also been taken into account. On the other hand war losses had probably been underestimated, and this remains to some degree an imponderable.

But the main point arises from a consideration of the figures for males and females in the different age groups:

Age (15 Jan. 1959)	Numbers (thousands)		Per cent	
	Male	Female	Male	Female
0– 9	23,608	22,755	50·9	49·1
10–19	16,066	15,742	50·5	49·5
20–24	10,056	10,287	49·4	50·6
25–29	8,917	9,273	49·0	51·0
30–34	8,611	10,388	45·3	54·7
35–39	4,528	7,062	39·1	60·9
40–44	3,998	6,410	38·4	61·6
45–49	4,706	7,558	38·4	61·6
50–54	4,010	6,437	38·4	61·6
55–59	2,906	5,793	33·4	66·6
60–69	4,099	7,637	34·9	65·1
70 and older	2,541	5,431	31·9	68·1
Age not given	4	4	—	—
Total	94,050	114,777	45·0	55·0

Many women died as a result of the war and the purges. But in both cases the great bulk of the victims was certainly male. From neither cause should there be much distinction in the figures for the sexes for the under-30 age groups in 1959. Nor is there. For the 30–34 block the proportion of 453 men to 547 women is a comparatively small difference, presumably indicating the losses of the young Army men in their late teens during the war. In the 35–39 group, which could have been expected to take the major war losses, we find figures of 391 men to 609 women. One would have thought that these men, in their early twenties in the war, would have had the highest losses.* But the proportion then gets worse still, and for the 40–44, 45–49 and 50–54 remains a set 384 to 616. Even more striking, the worst proportion of all comes for the 55–59 age group (334 to 666: in fact in this group alone there are almost exactly twice as many women as men). The figures for the 60–69 group (349 to 691) and for the 70 and over group (319 to 681) are also much worse than the soldiers' groups.† Now all authorities agree that the Purge struck in the main at people 'between thirty and fifty-five'[42]; 'generally, arrested people are all thirty or over. That's the dangerous age: you can remember things.'[43] There were few young or old, most of them being 'in the prime of life'.[44] Add twenty years for the 1959 position.

Precise deductions are not possible. Older men died as soldiers in the war. But on the other hand, the mass dispatch to labour camps of prisoners of war returned from Nazi hands in 1945 must have led to an extra, and non-military, death rate among the younger males. So must the guerrilla fighting in the Baltic States and the Western Ukraine which lasted for years after the war; and so must the deportations from the Caucasus and the general renewal of Purge activities in the post-war period. But in any case, the general effect of the figures is clear enough. The wastage of millions of males in the older age groups is too great to be masked, whatever saving assumptions we may make. We here have, frozen into the census figures, a striking indication of the magnitude of the losses inflicted in the Purge.

POSTSCRIPT (1970)

Since the above analysis was (apart from a section of para. B3.) published in 1968 further information has come from the Soviet Union, though not from official sources.

*This obvious point is backed by one of the few available age analyses of actual deaths in war. Losses in the German Army in World War I in proportion of age groups were distributed as follows: 15–19, 2·81 per cent; 20–24, 15·25 per cent; 25–29, 22·9 per cent; 30–34, 15·48 per cent; 35–39, 11·6 per cent; 40–44, 5·38 per cent; 45–49, 3·49 per cent.[41]

†It is true that losses in the First World War and the Civil War have some effect on this group, but in the census of 1926 there is none with a deficit of males of more than 10 per cent.

Academician Sakharov has told us that 'in 1936 to 1939 alone, more than 1·2 million party members, half the total membership, were arrested. Only 50,000 regained freedom. The others . . . were shot (600,000) or died in camps'.[45] It will be seen that Sakharov's figure for party arrests is rather higher than my estimate. His 600,000 party executions is, at the least, congruent with my rough figure of 1 million executions in all, tending if anything to imply that this was an underestimate. His statement that only 50,000 of the more than 600,000 who went to camp ever came out again is, again, in accord with my comment that 'we can hardly allow 10 per cent to have survived' (page 495). And another Soviet historian has also stated that '90 per cent of those arrested before the war and condemned to labour in the camps did not survive'.[46]

Sakharov tells us too that 'at least 10 to 15 million people perished . . . by torture or execution, in camps for exiled kulaks . . . and in camps "without the right to correspondence"'.[47] This, (omitting the deaths in the collectivization famine, which I have included), is close to the estimates I have given, especially as Sakharov is careful to say 'at least'. And it is at any rate interesting that Sakharov's figures are accepted by Roger Garaudy, at the time a member of the Politburo of the French Communist Party, in his book *Le Grand Tournant du Socialisme* (Paris, 1969); while Italian communist circles suggest that a figure of 8 million deaths from the great purge proper was given by Khrushchev to their delegation in Moscow in 1956.

LENIN ON HIS SUCCESSORS

(*Excerpts from his 'Testament'*)

24 *December* 1922: . . . I intend to examine here a number of considerations of a purely personal character.

I think that from this point of view the basic factor in the problem of stability are such members of the Central Committee as Stalin and Trotsky. In my view the relationship between them constitutes a good half of the danger of a split which could be avoided and the avoidance of which, in my opinion, should be served, among other things, by increasing the numbers of the Central Committee to fifty or one hundred persons.

Having become General Secretary, Comrade *Stalin* has acquired immense power in his hands, and I am not certain he will always know how to use this power with sufficient caution. On the other hand, Comrade *Trotsky*, as his struggle against the Central Committee over the question of the Commissariat of Railways has already shown, is distinguished not only by his remarkable abilities. Personally he is, no doubt, the most able person in the present Central Committee, but he also has excessive self-confidence and is overly attracted by the purely administrative aspect of affairs.

These two qualities of the two most prominent leaders of the present Central Committee might inadvertently lead to a split, and if our party does not take measures to prevent this, the split might arise unexpectedly.

I shall not go on to characterize the other members of the Central Committee according to their personal traits. I will only mention that the October episode of *Zinoviev* and *Kamenev* was not, of course, an accident, but that it should no more be held against them personally than his non-Bolshevism against Trotsky.

Of the younger members of the Central Committee I want to say a few words about *Bukharin* and *Pyatakov*. They are, in my opinion, the ablest forces (of the very youngest) and the following should be borne in mind regarding them: Bukharin is not only a most valuable and a most distinguished Party theoretician, he is also rightly regarded as the darling of the entire party, but it is only with the greatest reserve that his theoretical views can be classified as fully Marxist, for there is in him something scholastic (he has never studied and, I think, never fully understood dialectics).

25 December: Then as to *Pyatakov* – undoubtedly a man of exceptional will-power and abilities, but too attracted to administration and the administrative aspect of affairs to be relied upon in a serious political issue.

Of course, I make this and the other remarks only as regards the present, on the assumption that these two very able and loyal party workers will find occasion to increase their knowledge and correct their one-sidedness. Lenin 25 December 1922. Dictated to M. V.

Postscript: *Stalin* is too rude, and this fault, quite tolerable in our midst or in relations amongst communists, becomes intolerable for one who holds the office of General Secretary. Therefore I propose to the comrades that they consider a means of removing Stalin from the post and appointing to it another person who in all other respects differs from Stalin in one advantage alone, namely, that he is more patient, more loyal, more polite, and more considerate to comrades, less capricious, and so forth. This circumstance may seem to be an insignificant trifle. But I think that from the point of view of preventing a split and from the point of view of the relations between Stalin and Trotsky which I discussed above, this is not a trifle, or it is a trifle that may acquire decisive significance. Dictated to L. F. January 4 1923.

(Lenin, *Collected Works*, 4th Russian ed., vol. 36, pp. 544–6.)

POLITBURO MEMBERSHIP
1919–1938

	Candidate member	Full member	Fate
V. I. Lenin		1919	died 1924
L. B. Kamenev		1919	shot 1936
L. D. Trotsky		1919	assassinated 1940
J. V. Stalin		1919	died 1953
N. N. Krestinsky		1919	shot 1938
G. E. Zinoviev	1919	1921	shot 1936
N. I. Bukharin	1919	1924	shot 1938
V. M. Molotov	1921	1926	
M. I. Kalinin	1921	1926	died 1946
A. I. Rykov		1922	shot 1938
M. M. Tomsky		1922	suicide 1936
V. V. Kuibyshev	1922	1927	died (? naturally) 1934
G. Ya. Sokolnikov	1924		died in prison 1939
F. E. Dzerzhinsky	1924		died 1926
M. V. Frunze	1924		died 1925
K. E. Voroshilov		1926	died 1969
Ya. E. Rudzutak	1926	1926	shot 1938
G. I. Petrovsky	1926		died 1958
N. A. Uglanov	1926		shot or died in prison 1940
G. M. Ordzhonikidze	1926	1930	? suicide 1937
A. A. Andreyev	1926	1932	
S. M. Kirov	1926	1930	assassinated 1934
A. I. Mikoyan	1926	1935	
L. M. Kaganovich	1926	1930	
V. Ya. Chubar	1926	1935	shot ? 1941
S. V. Kossior	1927	1930	shot 1939
K. Ya. Bauman	1929		shot 1937
S. I. Syrtsov	1930		shot 1938
P. P. Postyshev	1934		shot 1940
A. A. Zhdanov	1935	1939	died (? naturally) 1948

	Candidate member	Full member	Fate
R. I. Eikhe	1935		shot 1940
N. I. Yezhov	1937		? shot *c.* 1939
N. S. Khrushchev	1938	1939	

THE 1934 CENTRAL COMMITTEE

FULL MEMBERS

Alekseyev, P. A.
Andreyev, A. A.*
Antipov, N. K.
Badaev, A. E.*
Balitsky, V. A.
Bauman, K. Ya.
Beria. L. P.*
Bubnov, A. S.
Chernov, M. A.
Chubar, V. Ya.
Chudov, M. S.
Chuvyrin, M. E.
Eikhe, R. I.
Gamarnik, Ya. B.
Ikramov, Akmal
Ivanov, V. I.
Kabakov, I. D.
Kaganovich, L. M.*
Kaganovich, M. M.*
Kalinin, M. I.*
Khatayevich, M. M.
Khrushchev, N. S.*
Kirov, S. M.
Knorin, V. G.
Kodatsky, I. F.
Kosarev, A. V.
Kossior, I. V.
Kossior, S. V.
Krinitsky, A. I.
Krupskaya, N. K.
Krzhizhanovsky, G. M.
Kuibyshev, V. V.
Lavrentiev, L. I.

Lebed, D. Z.
Litvinov, M. M.*
Lobov, S. S.
Lyubimov, I. E.
Manuilsky, D. Z.*
Mezhlauk, V. I.
Mikoyan, A. I.*
Mirzoyan, L. I.
Molotov, V. M.*
Nikolaeva, K. I.*
Nosov, I. P.
Ordzhonikidze, G. K.
Petrovsky, G. I.
Postyshev, P. P.
Pyatakov, Yu. L.
Pyatnitsky, I. A.
Razumov, M. O.
Rudzutak, Ya. E.
Rukhimovich, M. L.
Rumyantsev, I. P.
Ryndin, K. V.
Sheboldayev, B. P.
Shvernik, N. M.*
Stalin, J. V.*
Stetsky, A. I.
Sulimov, D. E.
Ukhanov, K. V.
Vareikis, I. M.
Voroshilov, K. E.*
Yagoda, G. G.
Yakir, I. E.
Yakovlev, Ya. A.
Yenukidze, A. S.

Yevdokimov, E. G.   Zhdanov, A. A.*
Yezhov, N. I.   Zhukov, I. P.
Zelensky, I. A.

* Re-elected to the Central Committee at the XVIIIth Congress, 1939.

CANDIDATE MEMBERS

(Here given in alphabetical order. The order given at the time, indicating seniority for filling gaps among the full membership, is shown by the numbering.)

23. Bagirov, M. A.*   27. Mikhailov, M. E.
44. Blagonravov, G. I.   9. Mikhailov, V. M.
13. Blyukher, V. K.   7. Musabekov, G. K.
58. Broydo, G. I.   33. Osinsky, V. V.
49. Budenny, S. M.*   4. Pakhomov, N. I.
59. Bukharin, N. I.   56. Pavlunovsky, I. P.
15. Bulganin, N. A.*   60. Polonsky, V. I.
17. Bulin, A. S.   35. Popov, N. N. (M. M.)
16. Bykin, Ya. B.   51. Poskrebyshev, A. N.*
50. Demchenko, N. N.   28. Pozern, B. P.
13. Deribas, T. D.   68. Pramnek, E. K.
29. Eliava, Sh. Z.   41. Ptukha, V. V.
53. Filatov, N. A.   45. Rosengolts, A. P.
39. Gikalo, N. F.   65. Rykov, A. I.
30. Goloded, N. M.   43. Sarkisov, S. A.
64. Grinko, G. F.   46. Sedelnikov, N. I.
 2. Gryadinsky, F. P.   18. Semenov, B. A.
 6. Isayev, U. D.   48. Serebrovsky, A. P.
21. Kalmanovich, M. I.   53. Shteingardt, A. M.
19. Kalygina, A. S.   1. Shubrikov, V. P.
 3. Kaminsky, G. I.   36. Shvarts, I. I.
55. Komarov, N. P.   8. Smorodin, P. I.
62. Kubyak, N. A.   57. Sokolnikov, G. Ya.
20. Kulkov, M. M.   34. Strievsky, K. K.
14. Kuritsyn, V. I.   10. Struppe, P. I.
22. Lepa, A. K.   67. Tomsky, M. P.
23. Lozovsky, S. A.*   11. Tovstukha, I. P.
66. Lyubchenko, P. P.   25. Tukhachevsky, M. N.
26. Makarov, I. G.†   61. Uborevich, I. P.
40. Mekhlis, L. Z.*   42. Ugarov, A. I.

12. Unshlikht, I. S.	5. Yeremin, I. G.
63. Veinberg, G. D.†	38. Yurkin, T. A.‡
37. Veger, E. I.	52. Zatonsky, V. P.
47. Yegorov, A. I.	32. Zavenyagin, A. P.§

* Re-elected full member († re-elected candidate member) at the XVIIIth Congress, 1939.

‡ Yurkin restored as candidate to Central Committee at XXth Party Congress, 1956.

§ Zavenyagin restored as candidate to Central Committee at XIXth Party Congress, 1952.

THE N.K.V.D. BACKGROUND

BY 1934 the political and psychological basis of the Great Purge was already in existence, and only one more prolonged effort of will on Stalin's part was needed to set it on its way. Its technical basis, the mechanisms of despotism, had long since been prepared.

Lenin (unlike Marx and Engels) had much admired the Jacobin terror, and as early as 1905 had envisaged a repetition of it in Russia.[1] (In accordance with this notion the police chief Dzerzhinsky was to be described by Bukharin, amongst others, as 'a real proletarian Jacobin'.)[2] From Lenin's views the theory arose that the Secret Police 'sprang from the very essence of the proletarian revolution', of which terror was 'the inevitable consequence'.[3]

Lenin did indeed remark in a speech just after the Revolution that the Bolsheviks would not use the French Revolutionary system of 'guillotining defenceless people'.[4] But Trotsky, though claiming that no executions were planned, soon hinted that it might not be possible to restrain 'popular fury'.[5]

The Secret Police, which under various names has persisted to this day, was founded on 20 December 1917 as the Cheka (Extraordinary Commission for Combating Counter-Revolution and Sabotage), and took over the old insurance company building, the Lubyanka, at which it is still established. Its origins were more or less illegal. An informal 'decision' of the Council of People's Commissars was later represented as an official decree. Even the statutes for the Cheka which were finally drawn up in November 1918 do not define its powers, and this had not been done when it was transformed into the G.P.U. in 1921.

The 'decision' of 20 December 1917 formulated the tasks of the Cheka as follows:

1. To investigate and liquidate all attempts or actions connected with counter-revolution or sabotage, no matter from whom they may come, throughout Russia.

2. The handing over for trial by Revolutionary Tribunal of all saboteurs and counter-revolutionaries, and the elaboration of measures to fight them.
3. The Commission carries out only a preliminary investigation in so far as this is necessary for preventive purposes.[6]

This document, published in 1924 and considered as the 'founding decree', is admitted in Soviet sources to be merely a rough outline. In practice, the Cheka was to be the punitive system of the dictatorship, answerable only to the top leaders themselves, and whatever actions it took were to be approved regardless of local opposition. In particular, it had no legal authority to carry out executions. Its first reported execution without trial took place on 24 February 1918. The Left Social Revolutionaries, who were still in the Government, tried to bring the matter up, but Lenin would not allow it to be put on the agenda.

As a Chekist official was to write:

Life had made it necessary to appropriate by revolutionary means the right to immediate execution. Comrade Dzerzhinsky had taken a step not foreseen by decree, not authorized by anyone. The Left Socialist Revolutionaries, heading the Commissariat of Justice, raised a cry, demanded that the question be brought up in the Council of People's Commissars. However, Vladimir Ilyich declined to include this question in the agenda of the *Sovnarkom*. He realized that Comrade Dzerzhinsky was right. One cannot go against life. In this way life itself legalized the right of the Cheka to immediate execution.[7]

As early as April 1918[8] the Cheka had set up its own three-man courts – the *troikas*, which were to become so notorious – to formalize these actions.

The assassination of Uritsky in September was made the excuse for increasing the Terror and for extending the power of the Cheka. First, 500 hostages were executed.[9] On 5 September 1918 came the famous decree 'On the Red Terror'.[10] Under it the Cheka was to be strengthened by sending a large number of Party members into it; concentration camps were to be set up; anyone in contact with counter-revolutionary organizations was to be shot; and the names and reasons for executions were to be published.

An 'instruction' of 17 September 1918 formally empowered the Cheka to sentence and execute without reference to the Revolutionary Tribunals.[11]

Dzerzhinsky was already excusing the shooting of innocents by the Cheka with the analogy that it was war, and in any war innocent members of the enemy were bound to be killed. The parallel is, of course, inexact. In battle there is no means of distinguishing between enemy soldiers, and it has never been suggested that wars were fought on any other basis. Arraignment before tribunals, on the other hand, is usually taken to be a matter of the establishment of facts and personal responsibilities.

Nor were Dzerzhinsky's views accepted by all Party members. Resistance came from a majority of the local Soviets whose opinions were canvassed in 1918.[12] A leading Old Bolshevik, the journalist Olminsky, wrote several critical pieces in *Pravda*, making it clear that a section of the Party opposed the extensive executions then being carried out and felt that the powers of the Cheka were greatly excessive. He also protested on one occasion against the scandalous and inhuman behaviour of a local Cheka which had stripped and flogged a number of peasants.[13] The Cheka's own organ had already printed letters from local Chekists demanding that torture be added to execution. (They protested against the release of Robert Bruce Lockhart, the British diplomat then under arrest on charges of conspiracy, urging that he should instead have been subjected to 'tortures, the very description of which would have filled counter-revolutionaries with cold terror'.)[14]

Prominent Chekists counter-attacked. One of them, Peters, complained that 'comrades occupied in journalism in offices and not actively fighting the enemies of the proletariat are attempting to limit the Cheka's activities'.[15]

Lenin backed them up. He attacked 'a narrow-minded intelligentsia' in the Party who 'sob and fuss' over mistakes made by the Cheka, adding 'when we are reproached with cruelty, we wonder how people can forget the most elementary Marxism'.[16] He did, however, reproach the Chekist Latsis for urging executions simply on a class basis, without any evidence of actual opposition to the regime. And though saying that they would soon be eliminated, he admitted that 'it is quite understandable that alien elements should attach themselves to the Cheka'.[17]

This early hint that unpleasant characters were getting into the Secret Police is supported by its own officials, who admitted, moreover, that the work corrupted even the better elements. One wrote:

Work in the Cheka, conducted in an atmosphere of physical coercion, attracts corrupt and outright criminal elements. . . . However honest a man is, however crystal-clear his heart, work in the Cheka, which is carried on with almost unlimited rights and under conditions greatly affecting the nervous system, begins to tell. Few escape the effect of the conditions under which they work.[18]

Another claimed that because they came into especially close contact with the 'dying bourgeois society', they were sometimes infected:[19] Dzerzhinsky himself remarked, 'Only saints or scoundrels can serve in the G.P.U., but now the saints are running away from me and I am left with the scoundrels.'[20]

It is ironic to find Bukharin, whose enthusiasm for the terror machine was always extravagant,[21] writing of its members as late as 1931, 'Do not let us forget how many of those who remain are nervous wrecks, and sometimes hopelessly ill. For their work was such torture, it demanded such gigantic concentration, it was such hellish work, that a truly iron character was required.'[22]

The police's powers continued to grow, and its practices to be inhumane, after the end of the Civil War. In March 1920 it was authorized to send people to forced labour camps for up to five years by administrative decision, if the investigation did not 'reveal sufficient evidence' for judicial proceedings.[23] Nor were the 'judicial proceedings' in any case laudable. The Cheka archives from Smolensk, for the period February–April 1921, give the minutes of many of them, including a summary of each case, and sentences. There is no reference to any laws on which the decisions are based, the accused are absent, and there is no record of any defence.[24]

The Kronstadt rebels of March 1921 wrote of the regime having 'brought the workers, instead of freedom, an ever present fear of being dragged into the torture chambers of the Cheka, which

exceeds by many times in its horrors the gendarmerie administration of the Tsarist regime'.[25] And this is the general impression
of the Cheka, which by now numbered 30,000 members.[26]

The Cheka was abolished by a decree of 6 February 1922 and
the G.P.U. (State Political Administration) established instead,
at this point forming part of the People's Commissariat for
Internal Affairs (N.K.V.D.); Dzerzhinsky was simultaneously
N.K.V.D. Commissar and Chairman of the G.P.U.

The G.P.U. was given legal functions which included 'the
fulfilment of special orders by the Presidium of the All-Russian
Central Executive Committee or the Council of People's Commissars for the protection of the revolutionary order'. It could
only keep people under arrest for two months without higher
permission, but in practice this amounted to almost unlimited
powers. In 1923 the G.P.U. was renamed the O.G.P.U., was
removed from the N.K.V.D. and became an independent ministry,
still headed by Dzerzhinsky.

Dzerzhinsky, who had been a strong political supporter of
Stalin, died in 1926 and was succeeded as head of the O.G.P.U.
by Menzhinsky, also of Polish noble origin. But already a much
more sinister figure was coming to the fore – Genrikh Yagoda.
He was a broad, sullen-looking, ruddy-faced man, with a small
moustache. Before the Revolution he had worked in a chemist's
shop in Nizhni-Novgorod (a background leading later to his
introduction of the serious study and use of poison into the
N.K.V.D.). He seems to have first been taken into the Cheka
during the Civil War, and soon to have come to Stalin's attention
in Tsaritsyn (the future Stalingrad). By the mid twenties, he was
effectively controlling much of the Secret Police administration –
since Dzerzhinsky had not only political responsibilities, but also
several other economic ministries to run.

During the intra-Party struggle of the late twenties, the role of
the O.G.P.U. leaders is variously interpreted. Though one
observer[27] speaks of many Trotskyites and few Rightists in the
police, there are signs that its leadership at least looked gloomily
at the prospect of further upheavals in the countryside. In
Kamenev's memorandum of his conversation with Bukharin on
11 July 1928 Bukharin is represented as saying 'Yagoda and

Trilisser [Head of the O.G.P.U. Foreign Administration] are with us. There have been 150 small rebellions.'[28] There is even a report that a delegation of the O.G.P.U., consisting of Menzhinsky, Yagoda and Trilisser, went to Stalin to warn him that the Secret Police could not guarantee quiet in the country, and were 'strongly rebuffed'.[29]

Bukharin's calculation that the O.G.P.U. supported him does not seem to have been sound. The Secret Police had certainly some cause for alarm in the peasant unrest which Stalin's policies were to develop into full-scale risings, but these tactical considerations do not seem to have led to any feeling in favour of a transfer of power to Bukharin and Rykov.

On the contrary, once engaged in the struggle, the police, like the Party as a whole, was thrown into Stalin's hands. There are a number of first-hand descriptions of peasant risings in this period, mainly in the Ukraine and the North Caucasus. One three-day battle in August 1930 in the Dniepropetrovsk province resulted in mass executions 'carried out near the ravines (*balkis*)', and thousands of sentences to labour camps.[30] Such actions committed the police to the repressive faction.

In fact, there seems to have been much fellow-feeling for Stalin, who treated the organization with tact and skill. Its members began to receive special privileges, as Stalinist social differentiation increased. Moreover, Stalin alone of the leaders had a thoroughgoing sympathy with the O.G.P.U. style. One prisoner describes a police official as telling her:

Comrade Stalin would have made an excellent Chekist. We Chekists sense it in him. He is one of us body and soul. We understand each other without words. We have a common language, a common method. Do you know what I mean? In the most difficult periods, Stalin has come to the Chekists for help, and each time the Chekists have helped him. Many of his friends and comrades-in-arms have betrayed Stalin, but never has he been betrayed by a Chekist! And Stalin appreciates this.[31]

The collectivization drive and the general revolutionary tension of the early thirties produced an enormous increase in both the activity and the size of the O.G.P.U. The number of prisoners pouring in from the countryside led in 1930 to the establishment of G U L A G, the Main Administration of Corrective Labour Camps which Yagoda headed.

The idea of arresting anybody who could possibly have done anything was also well established. For example, in 1930, when Britain still maintained a Consulate-General in Leningrad, an operation against its supposed sources of information was mounted by the O.G.P.U. They simply arrested anyone who had, or might have had, the slightest contact with the British – the captains of all ships plying between Leningrad and London, the chief harbour officials, and so on. About 200 people were given sentences of five years.[32] (In a sense, these light sentences were of course illogical, and amounted to admissions that those concerned were not spies.) And there are scores of other accounts from this earlier period of arrests as high-handed and baseless as those of the Great Purge proper.

On the defensive side, Stalin had made equally thorough preparations. Lenin's personal guard consisted of two men, later increased to four after the attempt on his life by Fanny Kaplan. Stalin's was several thousand strong, and the N.K.V.D. in addition kept other units at a state of readiness. The road to his country *dacha*, some twenty miles away, was guarded by over 3,000 agents, with cars, telephone connexions, etc. When Stalin was actually *en route*, the road was virtually under martial law.[33] Security arrangements in the Kremlin were extremely tight. Only two gates were in use – the Borovicheskye and the Spasskye. Documentary checks at these were immensely thorough and applied to everybody, including high officials of the N.K.V.D. At the buildings of the Council of Ministers and the Politburo, credentials and photographs were again checked, and there were other checks made at intervals along the corridors.

In 1931 Stalin briefly introduced one of his political entourage, A. I. Akulov, as Menzhinsky's senior deputy, but he withdrew him within the year, forming a satisfactory relationship with Yagoda instead. In 1933–4 he tuned up the police machine for further action. In March 1933 the O.G.P.U.'s right to order executions was given a legal, or at least an official, basis, by a fresh interpretation of earlier regulations.[34] 8 June 1934 saw the establishment of the hostage principle, under the extraordinary decree which we have quoted earlier. Though the overt application was only to the relatives of deserters, the principle was clear, and over the whole Terror pressure on relatives became the norm.

A month later, on 10 July, the O.G.P.U. was absorbed into a reorganized N.K.V.D. which now became the general police organization, with its Chief Administration of State Security in charge of the main body of Secret Police affairs proper.

Over the years the police had been growing into a highly-paid elite, 'rather like the officers' corps in old Prussia'.[35] They were among the most highly regarded of the new *priviligentsia* which was arising from Stalin's anti-egalitarian policies. New and more ostentatious uniforms came in. At the same time, N.K.V.D. officers were expected to learn the social graces. Many of them married smart and good-looking wives from the old educated classes, the type who gravitate to power and money in whatever form, and who, moreover, gained immunity from the otherwise unfortunate results of their social origins. N.K.V.D. children attended special schools. Junior posts often went to the sons of high officials. Many family connexions of the usual caste type sprang up.

Over the Purge period the N.K.V.D. maintained its status, but most of the earlier members were purged and replaced by others who shared the ruthlessness and pretensions of the older cadres, but were of an ever lower standard of education and intelligence. If the method of selection for party posts was, as Weissberg put it, 'negative', this was even more so the case with the police. A case is quoted of a Party Secretary in a small town who attracted attention by denouncing a sabotage organization concerned with releasing typhus lice in the city theatre, as a result of which he was recruited into the N.K.V.D. and became a prominent interrogator in the Donets Basin.[36]

A remarkable picture of an N.K.V.D. officer of the type who came forward in the Purge is given in a recent Soviet story.[37] 'Luminarski' is distinguished by an abnormal lack of any sort of feeling. He is an orphan, who has known no loyalties. The director of his orphanage was a cold-blooded, inhuman bully: Luminarski has no feeling for him any more than for anyone else, but discovers how to manage him by lies, presented as expressions of loyalty to the authorities. He learns to inform and denounce. Denunciations, he finds, are best based on facts, usually irrelevant, but combinable into impressive slander. The next move is to make the victims raise indignant denials, in which they can easily be caught in contradiction. He practises these methods right up the ladder. In the N.K.V.D. he rises by intrigue against his equally offensive but less talented colleagues. He learns to impress by always fulfilling and over-fulfilling his assignments. This means initiative in finding fresh victims, so that in an affair of a defective turbine, for example, it is necessary to implicate not merely the chief engineer, but various accomplices, thus inflating the importance of the case and gaining prestige with his superiors.

Such were the beneficiaries of the Purge, the men of the later Stalin period. But he already had to hand a force sufficiently lacking in ruth or truth, which we have seen in action in the earlier part of the period dealt with in these pages.

APPENDIX F

EARLIER SOVIET TRIALS

IF the Great Terror sprang from deep political roots and careful organizational preparation, it is also true that its most characteristic (or at least most striking) feature – the confession trial – was not a surprise innovation.

The only important political trials in the period after the Civil War were those of the Ukrainian and the Moscow Social Revolutionary 'centres' in 1921 and 1922, the latter, ironically enough, before a court presided over by Pyatakov. Apart from prejudicial campaigns, the use of *agents provocateurs* and so on, they were conducted comparatively fairly. And though Lenin pressed for death sentences, these were eventually dispensed with, under very strong pressure from European socialists. From then until 1928 there were no great public trials, and when the Shakhty Case broke, in that year, a new style was immediately apparent.

The Shakhty Case is supposed to have originated with the N.K.V.D. representative in the Caucasus, E. G. Evdokimov,* who reported a vast sabotage organization of veteran engineers in the city of Shakhty and its area. Evdokimov had been a common criminal, freed from jail by the Revolution, when he had joined the Party and distinguished himself in the Civil War. He became Stalin's special crony, was much decorated, and went with him on his vacations for several years running.[1]

It is said that when Menzhinsky received the report he pointed out that Evdokimov had produced no evidence at all. Evdokimov claimed that some private letters of the engineers were in code, but admitted that he had not decoded them. Menzhinsky then said that if a proper case was not presented within two weeks Evdokimov himself would be charged with sabotage – and, of course, the proposal to liquidate a number of skilled engineers without cause was indeed to sabotage the economy. Evdokimov, in the difficult situation into which he had got himself, went straight to Stalin. Stalin, though without the legal power to do so,

*Not to be confused with G. E. Evdokimov, the Zinovievite.

gave him *carte blanche* and he went back and had the engineers arrested. Menzhinsky, supported by Rykov and by Kuibyshev (naturally concerned as the Chairman of the Council of National Economy), objected strongly. Stalin silenced them by producing a telegram from Evdokimov hinting that attempts would be made in Moscow to hush the matter up. No decision was taken, but the case went ahead.[2]

Stalin's political motive was the discrediting of the Bukharinite line of peaceful cooperation with non-Party specialists, and 'proof' that the class struggle was getting sharper. He was to draw the specific lesson: 'We have internal enemies. We have external enemies. This, comrades, must not be forgotten for a single moment.'[3]

Dzerzhinsky had always stressed the value of confessions. Evdokimov and his subordinate Kursky set about extracting these. And eventually the case came to trial in public in Moscow. Vyshinsky was the presiding judge, and Krylenko prosecuted.

The trial opened in the huge Hall of Columns amid a press campaign of 'Death to the Wreckers!', the twelve-year-old son of one of the accused being among the demanders of the death penalty. Fifty Russian and three German technicians and engineers in the coal industry were charged with sabotage and espionage. Ten of the prisoners made full confessions, and six others partial ones. No other evidence was produced. A slight hitch was immediately evident. One of the prisoners, 'the accused Nekrasov', did not appear in the dock. He had, his counsel explained, gone mad. The written confessions were read out in court. They implicated all those present, including some who had not confessed.

Then Krylenko, 'narrowing his eyes and twisting his lips into a sneer', viciously attacked the engineers. One accused, Benbenko, tried to withdraw his confession. He had been in the hands of the G.P.U. for almost a year.

'I scarcely knew what I signed . . . I was driven to distraction by threats, so I signed . . . I tried to withdraw before the trial, but . . .'

Krylenko gazed at him and finally said quietly, 'Do you want to say that you were intimidated, threatened?'

Benbenko hesitated, and then said 'No'.[4]

Another of the accused, Skorutto, had denied his guilt from the beginning. One evening he was reported too ill to attend. Next morning he appeared, 'an ash-grey trembling figure', and said that the previous night he had confessed his guilt and the guilt of others. There was a woman's cry from the public benches, 'Kolya, darling, don't lie. Don't! You know you are innocent!' The prisoner burst into tears and collapsed into a chair. After a ten-minute recess he was brought back and said that though he had confessed he had withdrawn his confession earlier that morning. Krylenko went into the attack. Under intense badgering, Skorutto said that he had not slept for eight nights, and finally he had lied about his friends as they had lied about him. He had hoped that the court would be more lenient if he pleaded guilty. But he was not guilty. Next morning, Skorutto reaffirmed his confession and said that it had been his wife's outcry which had shaken his resolve to admit his guilt.[5]

And so the trial proceeded. Another of the accused failed to appear and it was announced that he had committed suicide.

Rabinovich, a man past seventy, 'all but worsted the terrifying and heretofore invincible prosecutor Krylenko in brain-to-brain combat'. When another witness spoke of his sabotage links, Rabinovich went up to him and glared him down, saying 'Why do you lie, eh? Who told you to lie?' Krylenko looked crestfallen.[6]

Another old man, Imineyetov, firmly maintained his innocence to the last. He boldly asserted that one day another Zola would write another *J'accuse* to restore their names.

An American present remarked that these flashes of illumination – the madness, the suicide, the withdrawals and reassertions of confession –

left us limp with the impact of horrors half-glimpsed. . . . How did men like Krylenko, who sneered and snarled while the world looked on, behave when there were no witnesses and no public records?[7]

Eleven death sentences were announced, of which six were commuted because of the prisoners' cooperation.

Although the public trial was not a complete success as a production, Evdokimov and his subordinates had constructed a pilot model which was to serve as a basis for the later trials. More important still, a technique had been found for Stalin. Once criminal charges were being investigated by the N.K.V.D., by methods no one in political circles was in a position to inquire into effectively, any attempts to oppose such action at once took on the air of defending criminals and attacking the State and its investigative organs. It was not an easy brief even for Politburo members to argue to. And later, when the oppositionists were in the hands of the N.K.V.D., Stalin had only to say that the investigation was not completed and might result in their acquittal, thus postponing the substantive argument, and then, after the confessions were in, say that the investigations had proved their guilt.

From 1930, a large number of secret trials, or executions without trial, took place in the spheres of economy and ideology. For example: in August 1930, the secret trial of a group of prominent bacteriologists charged with having organized a horse epidemic; September 1930, forty-eight leading officials of the food industry, headed by Professor Riazantsev, shot without trial for sabotaging food supplies (a method of coping with, or at least explaining, the food shortage which was to become conventional); February 1931, a number of distinguished historians, including Tarle, Platonov, Bukhrushin, Likachev, secretly sentenced to long prison terms (the survivors were released and restored to their university chairs within a few years); March 1933, thirty-five directors and other officials of State farms executed and forty others sent to prison without trial for belonging to a 'counter-revolutionary wrecking organization'; March 1933, thirty-five prominent officials of the People's Commissariat of Agriculture, headed by Vice-Commissar Konar, executed without trial [8] (in this case it seems likely that Konar actually was a genuine foreign spy). [9]

But the next true show trial was that of the so-called 'Industrial Party' headed by Professor Ramzin in November–December 1930. Ramzin had been a Bolshevik in 1905–7, and had worked for the regime during the twenties, but had then, it was alleged, fallen into bad company and become a wrecker. His 'party' was said to have had about 2,000 members, but only eight appeared in the dock. Most of the accused were high officials in Kuibyshev's State Planning Commission (Gosplan), the execution of forty-eight officials of which had already been announced. They had worked for Raymond Poincaré, President of France, for Lawrence of Arabia, for Sir Henry Deterding, the oil magnate, and others to undermine Soviet industry and prepare the ground for foreign attacks. Once again, there was a vast press campaign. Once again, the child of one of the accused demanded the death penalty for his father, Sitnin. There was no witness who was not himself a prisoner, and no documentary evidence of any sort was produced.

Among the 'witnesses' were the representatives of a so-called 'Labouring Peasants Party', consisting mainly of agricultural economists. They were accused of a separate, though complementary, plot to put the *kulaks* in power. They never came to separate public trial and their fate is not clear. They simply vanished. One of those involved, the engineer Palchinsky, is believed to have been killed during the preliminary investigation.[10]

Detailed confessions of contacts with the former big industrialist Ryabushinsky were made, with the dates and details of his sabotage instructions. It turned out that Ryabushinsky had been dead for years. The prosecution, which Krylenko was again conducting, then dug up a relative of his who had no money and had never been an industrialist and reassigned the dead man's role to this nonentity. The Minister of Finance in the new Government which the 'party' was supposedly planning was to have been Vishnegradsky, who had held that office in Tsarist times, but who had in fact also died some years previously.

It is reported that, though not in the form alleged, the Gosplan officials had really had pessimistic private conversations on the economic policy, and had 'envisaged the possibility of a socialist government in the event of a crash raising the question of a successor to Stalin'.[11]

Five of the accused were sentenced to death, but all sentences were commuted. A few years later Ramzin was released and restored to his posts.

In March 1931 came the 'Menshevik Trial'. With one exception, all the Mensheviks in dock had long since abandoned political activity and were valued economic and other specialists. A lone activist had been in contact with the Menshevik delegation in exile. His son was used to blackmail him. The G.P.U. built up this slight connexion into a visit by Raphael Abramovitch, one of the leaders of the Mensheviks in emigration, to Moscow.

Abramovitch was immediately shown by scores of witnesses in the West to have been attending the Congress of the Socialist International at a time when he was supposed to be in Moscow. (In fact, when he won a libel suit against newspapers in Berlin which had reported the trial, the attorney for the defence, a Communist member of the Reichstag, had to admit that the date was impossible.)

It is also significant that two genuine Mensheviks under arrest, who had actually entered the country illegally from abroad (Eva Broido and M. Braunstein), were not produced at the trial, even though Braunstein's name was mentioned.[12] The presumption has always been that they refused to cooperate. One of those actually on the list of accused, Bazarov, unaccountably failed to appear.

Promises were made to those on trial that if they confessed they would be secretly released and rewarded. The historian Sukhanov, whose *Memoirs* about the Revolution had been much praised by Lenin, is said, when the promises were not kept, to have revealed the whole affair to fellow-prisoners and finally to have gone on a series of long hunger strikes.[13] He cannot be traced after 1934 and presumably died or was executed about then. One of the accused ex-Mensheviks, M. P. Yakubovich, who got ten years, was rearrested and sentenced to another ten years in 1941; was released (two years after the end of his sentence) in 1953; and was rehabilitated, as to his second sentence only, in 1956. In 1967 in a statement to the Prosecutor-General he stated clearly that the Menshevik Case was entirely faked and revealed that Krylenko, with whom he had been associated in the revolutionary movement, had admitted as much to him at the time. In 1967 he saw Mikoyan, whom he had also known, and who told him he had never doubted his innocence. However, the official line is still that the Mensheviks were guilty as charged.[14]

The trial was made a convenient occasion to implicate the old democratic Bolshevik Ryazanov and to expel him from the Party by alleging illicit contacts between him and the Mensheviks.[15] Later released, he was to disappear in the Purges, dying in 1938.[16]

The trial was intended as a blow against the idea of a socialist coalition which had begun to be aired in certain Party circles. At the same time, it was a blow at moderate economic opinion. It was alleged that the defendants, several of whom had played an important part in preparing the Five-Year Plan, had tried to establish production targets far lower than the country's capability. In fact, the official Soviet figures prove that the accused planners had shown great prescience in forecasting the actual extent of fulfilment of the Plan. In almost every case they had actually tended to err slightly on the optimistic side. In steel, for example, they were accused of having criminally proposed the production in 1932 of 5·8 million tons. The Plan fixed the figure of 10·3 million; the defendants themselves confessed in court that 'much higher figures could and should have been fixed'. Actual production was 5·9 million tons. For pig-iron, they had envisaged a mere 7 million tons; the Plan demanded 17 million tons. Actual production in 1932 equalled 6·1 million tons.[17]

The Menshevik Trial was not all profit. For one thing, it completely alerted the Socialist leaders throughout Europe, who had good reason to examine it and who saw through its falsities.

The last of the great show trials held before the Purge proper has special interest for Westerners, since six of the eighteen accused were British. This was the famous Metro-Vickers Trial of April 1933. The theme was that the British engineers had organized a sabotage ring.

Ulrikh, the former N.K.V.D. man who had presided at various cases since the early twenties, was President of the Court, and Vyshinsky prosecuted. The team had been found which was to carry out all such operations in the future. Braude and Kommodov, defence lawyers in the later cases, fulfilled the same function here. Braude, as 'defence lawyer' of the British engineer Thornton, said 'We have against Thornton what is known as an almost complete chain of evidence, which places Thornton's defence in an extremely difficult position.' And yet, he complained, 'the accused Thornton insists on his categorical denials'. (Other defence lawyers, who assisted their clients, were not to appear again. One of them went to the length of pointing out that 'a foreigner cannot help taking an interest in his surroundings' and this did not necessarily constitute espionage.) Even the investigators were in some cases the same as in later trials. Sheinin, Investigator for Important Cases, helped work on MacDonald as he was later to do on I. N. Smirnov.[18] The case was to a certain extent a useful dress rehearsal from which directors and producers could draw a number of lessons, and learn to do better next time.

The particular technique of this trial was to produce a structure of immense complexity which was hard for the public to follow. This was particularly easy in a complicated matter like engineering breakdowns. In addition, every detail that could possibly be made to look bad was thrown at the Englishmen: for example, odd gifts or loans made by them to underpaid Russian engineers in a condition of near-starvation werc called 'bribes'. However, although all the office books and the private diaries and the expense accounts for eight to nine years were seized, very little could be squeezed out of them.

If the trial was on the whole not a success, it was mainly because the British engineers failed to cooperate. They had a number of advantages. First of all, they were not easily expendable during the investigation. That is, it would not have been easy to arrest them and then produce the one in six who was more or less satisfactory. (For of course, in the ordinary way, the organizers thought nothing of simply shooting without trial those leading 'conspirators' who did not come up to the mark.) Secondly, the authorities did not have the families of the accused Britons at their disposal. Thirdly, of course, the Britons could fall back on, feel behind them, the national solidarity which the Russian accused could nowhere find:

> Tonight before the foeman's frown
> He stands in Elgin's place
> Ambassador of Britain's crown
> And type of all her race.

Moreover, the British Government brought the heaviest possible economic and diplomatic pressure to bear.

Even so, most of them had made confessions at the preliminary investigations, and one, MacDonald, who seemed in a bad state, reaffirmed his at the end, after having withdrawn it during the trial. Vyshinsky had a long exchange with MacDonald, confronting him with his own original dossier, and showing him depositions written in his own handwriting, and took it very amiss when MacDonald replied that he only signed 'because it was not the open court'.

The main British accused, Thornton, said that his signed confessions were extracted 'under great pressure', adding 'I was interrogated for a very long time'. He had been interrogated every day but one since his arrest on 11 March until 1 April. The official records quoted in court show that Thornton was interrogated for 4¼ hours after his arrest and then, after an hour's break, for another eight hours.

He had finally made a confession, of the less concrete charges like espionage, though not of sabotage; and the prosecution and the court were particularly annoyed when he not so much withdrew it as treated it as a pointless formality he had had to go through before coming to court to plead not guilty.

Monkhouse said that he could understand how confessions were obtained, since he himself had been interrogated for eighteen hours when first arrested. Vyshinsky was able to show that this was an exaggeration: Monkhouse, without any means of measuring the time, had worked it out on the basis of the period between meals. In fact Monkhouse, who had been arrested at 3.15 a.m., was first interrogated for four hours; they then fed him in a two-hour break and he was then interrogated for seven hours. Vyshinsky made much of the outbursts produced in England by Monkhouse's remark that he had been interrogated for eighteen hours, and seemed to feel that by proving that it had been a shorter period he had undermined all accusations against the rectitude of the investigation. In fact, taking Monkhouse's firm assertion that the interrogation was continuous through the meal, it lasted thirteen hours.

Monkhouse defended himself firmly, and intervened at one stage to make the devastating point: 'After the showing which Sukhoruchkin made last night it is perfectly clear to me that this case is a frame-up against Metro-Vickers, based on the evidence of terrorized prisoners.'[19]

There were equally clear-cut retorts from other accused. For example:

Roginsky (for the prosecution): Did you hear the testimony of Zivert that you allowed sabotage in the work?
Gregory: Yes, but I do not attach any importance to that!

Another Briton, Cushny, spoke in his final plea of the Public Prosecutor's 'flimsy fabric' and repeated that 'there has not been a shred of real evidence brought against me'.

The sentences were comparatively light. The Russians received from eighteen months' to ten years' imprisonment. Thornton was sentenced to three years and MacDonald to two. Monkhouse, Cushny and Nordwall were expelled from the country and Gregory and one of the Russians were acquitted.

Thus, over the years before the Great Trials of the Purge itself, the system was developed and rehearsed. The technicians and producers of these affairs had learned a number of lessons. In the earlier trials the number of accused had been too high, and it had now been found that around eighteen was a suitable figure. The usefulness of a complicated story, in which the details were hard for the ordinary reader or observer to follow, leaving only a general effect, was established. And in Vyshinsky, a man had been found capable of mastering such a complexity, and imposing it upon the witnesses; he had also proved himself able to break up, and if necessary to interpret in a manner suitable to the plot, various unforeseen divagations, and he had been able to 'refute' a perfectly sound complaint by concentrating heavily and impressively on a discrepancy of detail.

There had indeed been faults in the trials, as presented. In the brief accounts I have given, these have stood out. But it must be remembered that, except in the case of the British engineers, they formed short passages in the evidence, coming amid days of interlocking and mutually confirmatory confessions. Even if some accused should plead not guilty, the evidence against them, from the other accused, remained. And though to the critical mind there were – as there were to be in the later trials too – inconsistencies and impossibilities which should have destroyed the credibility of each trial in turn, it was one of Stalin's most constant principles that most minds are not critical. A loyal Party member had no choice but to accept the official statements, and no objection was raised to the trials even by those who were later to suffer themselves. As to the Russian public as a whole, these cases at least provided scapegoats for economic failures which could otherwise only have been blamed on the regime – again, a principle to be carried right through the following period. The Soviet public, indeed, received censored versions in each case. But among the foreign journalists present, and still more the foreign observers at second hand, the trials were on the whole accepted or rejected according to the opinion held about the Soviet regime.*

*As Arthur Koestler remarks (of the *Brown Book of the Hitler Terror*, which he helped to prepare, and which later turned out to contain a number of erroneous guesses), 'that did not diminish the effect. In totalitarian propaganda the details do not matter.'[20]

ARTICLE 58 OF THE CRIMINAL CODE OF THE R.S.F.S.R.

(repealed December 1958)

SPECIAL SECTION: CHAPTER I

1. Counter-Revolutionary Crimes

Art. 58 (i). Any act designed to overthrow, undermine or weaken the authority of the workers' and peasants' Soviets and the workers' and peasants' government of the Union of Soviet Socialist Republics, of the Union and Autonomous Republics, elected by the Soviets on the basis of the Constitution of the U.S.S.R. and the Constitutions of the Union Republics or designed to undermine or weaken the external security of the U.S.S.R. and of the basic economic, political and national achievements of the proletarian revolution, is deemed to be a counter-revolutionary act.

In view of the international solidarity of the interests of all the toilers, such acts are also regarded as counter-revolutionary when they are directed against any other Workers' State, even though not forming part of the U.S.S.R.

Art. 58 (i.*a*). Treason against the homeland, i.e. acts committed by citizens of the U.S.S.R. to the detriment of the military strength of the U.S.S.R., its State independence, or the inviolability of its territory, such as: espionage, betrayal of a military or State secret, desertion to the enemy, flight abroad by land or air are punishable: by the supreme measure of criminal punishment – death by shooting and the confiscation of all property; in extenuating circumstances – by deprivation of liberty for a period of ten years and the confiscation of all property.

Art. 58 (i.*b*.) These same crimes, if committed by military personnel, are punishable by the supreme measure of criminal punishment – death by shooting and confiscation of all property.

Art. 58 (i.*c*). In the event of flight abroad by land or air of a member of the armed forces, the adult members of his family, if they in any way assisted the preparation or the commission of this act of treason, or even if they knew of it but failed to report it to the authorities, are to be punished: by deprivation of liberty for a period of from five to ten years and confiscation of all property.

The remaining adult members of the traitor's family, and those living with him or dependent on him at the time of the commission of the crime are liable to deprivation of their electoral rights and to exile to the remote areas of Siberia for a period of five years.

Art. 58 (i.*d*). Failure on the part of a member of the armed forces to report preparations for or the commission of an act of treason entails:

deprivation of liberty for ten years.

Failure on the part of other citizens (not members of the armed forces) to report is punished in accordance with Article 58 (xii).

Art. 58 (ii). Armed insurrection or incursion of armed bands into Soviet territory, with counter-revolutionary aims, the seizure of power at the centre or in the provinces with the same aims and, in particular, with the aim of forcibly separating from the U.S.S.R. or from a separate Union Republic any part of its territory or of violating treaties concluded between the U.S.S.R. and foreign States, entail:

the supreme measure of social defence – death by shooting, or declaration as an enemy of the labouring masses, and the confiscation of property and deprivation of citizenship of the Union Republic and thereby of the U.S.S.R., and banishment beyond the frontiers of the U.S.S.R. for ever; in extenuating circumstances a reduction of sentence is permitted to deprivation of liberty for a period of not less than three years and the confiscation of all or part of the property.

Art 58 (iii). Maintenance of relations for counter-revolutionary purposes with foreign States or with individual representatives of those States and also assistance, rendered by any means whatsoever, to a foreign State at war with the U.S.S.R. or engaged in fighting the U.S.S.R. by means of intervention or blockade entail:

> measures of social defence as indicated in Article 58 (ii) of the present Code.

Art. 58 (iv). The rendering of assistance, by any means whatsoever, to that section of the international bourgeoisie, which, not recognizing the equal rights of the communist system which is coming to replace the capitalist system, is endeavouring to overthrow it, and also to public groups and organizations, under the influence of or directly organized by that bourgeoisie in conducting activities hostile to the U.S.S.R. entails:

> deprivation of liberty for a period of not less than three years and confiscation of all or part of his property; to be increased in especially grave circumstances to the supreme measure of social defence – death by shooting, or declaration as an enemy of the toiling masses, coupled with deprivation of citizenship of the Union Republic and thereby of citizenship of the U.S.S.R., and banishment for ever beyond the frontiers of the U.S.S.R., and the confiscation of property.

Art. 58 (v). Influencing a foreign State or any public groups within that State, by maintaining relations with its representatives, use of false documents or by any other means to a declaration of war, to armed intervention in the affairs of the U.S.S.R., or to any other hostile acts, in particular: to blockade, to seize the State property of the U.S.S.R. or its Union Republics, to break off diplomatic relations, to break off agreements concluded with the U.S.S.R., etc. entails:

> measures of social defence enumerated in Article 58 (ii) of this Code.

Art. 58 (vi). Espionage, i.e. the transmission, theft or collection, with a view to transmission to foreign States, counter-revolutionary organizations or private persons, of information accounted by reason of its contents an especially guarded State secret is punishable by:

> deprivation of liberty for a period of not less than three years, with confiscation of all or part of property; in cases, when espionage has caused, or might have caused, especially grievous consequences to the interests of the U.S.S.R. the supreme measure of social defence – death by shooting, or the declaration to be an enemy of the labouring masses and the deprivation of citizenship of the Union Republic and thereby of the U.S.S.R. and banishment beyond the frontiers of the U.S.S.R. for ever, and confiscation of property.

The transmission, theft or collection with a view to transmission of economic information not constituting by virtue of its contents an especially guarded State secret but not intended for divulgence to the organizations or persons enumerated above, as the result of direct prohibition by law or by order of the heads of departments, establishments, or enterprises, either for recompense or gratis is punishable by:

> deprivation of liberty for a period not exceeding three years.

Art. 58 (vii). The undermining of State industry, transport, trade, monetary exchange or the credit system and also of the cooperative network, committed for counter-revolutionary purposes by means of making use to such ends of State establishments and enterprises, or by means of impeding their normal functioning, and also the utilization of State establishments and enterprises, or the impeding of their functioning in the interests of their former owners or of capitalist organizations interested in them is punishable by:

> the measures of social defence, indicated in Article 58 (ii) of the present Code.

Art. 58 (viii). The commission of terrorist acts, directed against representatives of the Soviet regime or members of revolutionary workers' and peasants' organizations, and participation in the commission of such acts, even by persons not belonging to a counter-revolutionary organization is punishable by:

the measures of social defence, indicated in Article 58 (ii) of the present Code.

Art. 58 (ix). The destruction or damage, for counter-revolutionary purposes, by explosives, arson or other means, of railways or other means of transportation, of the means of public communication, of water conduits, or public stores and other constructions or of State or public property, is punishable by:

the measures of social defence, indicated in Article 58 (ii) of the present Code.

Art. 58 (x). Propaganda or agitation containing an appeal to overthrow, undermine or weaken the Soviet regime, or to commit individual counter-revolutionary crimes (Articles 58 (ii) to 58 (ix) of the present Code), and also the distribution, the preparation, or the conservation of literature of this nature, entails:

deprivation of liberty for a period of not less than six months.

Similar actions undertaken under conditions of mass unrest or involving the exploitation of the religious or national prejudices of the masses, or under conditions of war, or in localities placed under martial law are punishable by:

measures of social defence, indicated in Article 58 (ii) of the present Code.

Art. 58 (xi). Any type of organizational activity, directed towards the preparation or the commission of crimes provided for in the present chapter, and also participation in an organization formed for the preparation or the commission of one of the crimes provided for in this chapter, is punishable by:

the measures of social defence, indicated in the relevant articles of the present chapter.

Art. 58 (xii). Failure to report reliable knowledge of preparations for, or commission of a counter-revolutionary crime entails:

deprivation of liberty for a period of not less than six months.

Art. 58 (xiii). Actions or active struggle directed against the working class and the revolutionary movement, if committed by those in a responsible or secret (agent's) post under the Tsarist regime, under counter-revolutionary Governments during the Civil War, are punishable by:

the measures of social defence indicated in Article 58 (ii) of the present Code.

Art. 58 (xiv). Counter-revolutionary sabotage, i.e. deliberate non-fulfilment by anyone of duties laid down or the wilfully careless execution of those duties with a view to weakening the authority of the Government, the functioning of the State apparatus, entails:

deprivation of liberty for a period of not less than one year, with confiscation of all or part of his property; to be increased in especially grave circumstances, to the supreme measure of social defence – death by shooting with confiscation of property.

(Juridical Publishing House, Moscow, 1949.)

Bibliographical Note
and
Select Bibliography

BIBLIOGRAPHICAL NOTE

IN a general way our sources are of two sorts: what we might call 'official' – that is, published in the Soviet Union; and 'unofficial' – from foreign victims, Soviet defectors and so on, published only in the West.

Generally speaking, it is now possible to treat these as complementary. For example, the accounts of labour camps by Alexander Solzhenitsyn, General Gorbatov and others, published in Moscow, confirm and supplement the numerous books and articles by ex-prisoners who over the past thirty years have made their way to the West.

It is a specially suitable moment to consolidate this various material into a single story. For since the fall of Khrushchev the flow of revelations about this period has virtually ceased. As the First Secretary of the Byelorussian Communist Party, Masherov, was able to tell his Congress in March 1966, there has been a great reduction in the number of cases 'where under the guise of criticism of the cult of personality the whole history of the Soviet Communist Party was being misinterpreted'.

1. *Contemporary official accounts* require little comment. They are, of course, false as to essentials, but they are still most informative. (It is untrue that Mdivani was a British spy, but it is true that he was executed.) Moreover the way in which official versions evolve is most significant – as with the variation and elaboration of the original simple story of the Kirov murder to the multifarious plot of 1938.

2. *Modern Official Accounts*: After Khrushchev's Secret Speech of February 1956, a great deal was published in the Soviet Union giving a true, or at any rate truer, version of trains of events, particular acts, and the fates of individuals. A certain imbalance is produced by the fact that this material concentrates almost entirely on the fate of Communist Party victims of the Purge – indeed, even oppositionist Communists have been virtually ignored. Nevertheless, there is an invaluable accumulation of

useful information on a wide variety of themes. The accounts are indeed scrappy and incomplete, and in some cases uncritically assembled on a basis more journalistic than scholarly. As the forthright A. V. Snegov insisted at a historians' conference,[1] in 1962 extraordinary distortions of Party history were still occurring 'in this seventh year after the XXth Party Congress'. And things have worsened since then.

The Secret Speech and Khrushchev's similar open speeches at the XXIInd Party Congress in October 1961 are a one-sided selection of vignettes of the purges. And since a large part of his motivation was plainly to blame his political opponents of the fifties – Beria, Molotov, Kaganovich, Malenkov and Voroshilov – these stories cannot just be taken at their face value – particularly the later ones, after these enemies had been silenced.

An example of his curious attitude – and indeed that of the Soviet leadership in general – is mentioned by Senator Reale, then a leading member of the Italian Communist Party, who describes how in 1954 the Italian Communist delegation heard from Khrushchev an account of how Beria was killed on the spot at a Presidium meeting in June 1953, and then had to sit and listen for some hours to an alleged tape recording of his December 1953 trial.

But although a certain amount of mythologizing is attached to the Khrushchev period, when he, or his subordinates, quote documents it seems most likely that these are entirely genuine. And in general a certain residual scepticism should not prevent us from accepting many at least of the stories made public in speeches and elsewhere. The same sort of consideration applies to the various books on formerly purged and now rehabilitated political and military figures which appeared in the Soviet Union in the past decade. As in all favourable biography, there is doubtless a certain tendency to present the subject in as favourable a light as possible. It is also true that where there are several such biographies – as in the cases of Tukhachevsky, Kirov, Yakir, Blyukher and others – there are a number of divergences on matters of detail, mostly (though not all) of a minor nature. But no doubt this usually means that the authors themselves faced difficulties in discovering the facts. It is clear that documents are in many cases inaccessible; and reliance must often be placed on the memories of surviving relatives and others.

The unsatisfactory nature of the documentation is strikingly shown in the divergence of Soviet sources over the dates of death, even of such prominent figures as Vlas Chubar, full member of the Politburo, or Marshal Yegorov, Chief of Staff. There are so many instances of two (and very occasionally instances of more than two) different dates for such deaths competing in the literature, that I am inclined to interpret it as follows: the earlier date may represent the imposition of the death sentence, which would be the last date to appear on the legal file on the accused, and would normally be carried out within days. If the sentence was thereupon commuted by administrative decision, the fact might not emerge on the documents available to a given researcher, but come out only in a different set of documents, or from the personal reports of surviving N.K.V.D. officers. But this is no more than logical speculation. And in some cases sheer muddle seems just as likely.

As Academician Maisky has remarked in a slightly different context, 'We know from the experience of the period of Stalin's cult of personality that not all documents are reliable';[2] he urged, too, that memoirs were likely to illuminate the motives of people's actions, even when the documents were more or less reliable. And, in fact, much of the Soviet information lately available has appeared in memoirs or biographical collections. These are of varying quality. Up to 1962, at least, only the Military Publishing House had set up a special editorial board and allowed memoir writers access to its archives.[3]

As we have said, the memoirs of Soviet citizens who themselves suffered in the purges are a most important source, particularly in confirming the prison and camp accounts given by non-Communists in the West. General Gorbatov, Marshal Rokossovsky, Grigory Shelest and others come to mind. One of the best descriptions of camp life is in *From Beginning to End* by József Lengyel. Lengyel, a Hungarian Communist of long standing, published this book in Budapest where it won the Kossuth Prize during a period of relaxation. In a different category is the novel *One Day in the Life of Ivan Denisovich*, which, though fictional in form, represents a true account of labour camp life. As a Soviet critic remarks, 'the author selected a relatively happy period in his hero's time at camp for the story. After all, it had happened that in the North, at Ust-Izhma, where Ivan Denisovich was first sent, there were no felt boots to wear all winter, there was nothing at all to eat, and Shukhov was "on the verge" of dying. And the discipline there was incomparably harsher . . . even in this comparatively easy period of his camp term, the author selects a day that is not merely ordinary but even lucky, "almost happy . . ."'⁴

Solzhenitsyn deals, indeed, with a later period in camp history than that of the purges; a time, moreover, when the death rate had been radically reduced. If I have quoted largely from his experience it is because it remains one of the most vivid, and at the same time is scarcely open to a charge of misrepresentation. Moreover, the changes in the system are unsubstantial, and may easily be seen from the other sources quoted, while the one day of Solzhenitsyn's hero represents the consolidated essence of the system in its state of perfection.

3. *There is also a certain amount of 'official' material of both periods, not intended for publication.* Among the most useful are the Smolensk Archives – the papers, up to 1938, of the Party headquarters at Smolensk which were captured in June 1941 by the Germans. Some 500 files were selected rather at random and sent back to Germany where they eventually fell into American hands. This 'Archive' contains a vivid documentation of the Purge – as it struck the Party rather than the population as a whole – in a province which from 1929 to 1937 covered the whole area between the Leningrad and Moscow provinces, Byelorussia and the Ukraine, with a population of 6½ million. Professor Merle Fainsod has splendidly digested it in his *Smolensk under Soviet Rule.*

We also have, though in incomplete form, the secret version of the State Plan for 1941, which is helpful in estimating the amount of forced labour controlled by the N.K.V.D. A certain amount of documentary evidence from the labour camps themselves has also been available in the West since the forties. The 'Secret

Speech', too, originally came to us through clandestine channels – and, indeed, it has never yet been published in the U.S.S.R., nor has the version published in the West been officially authenticated. More recently there have been leaks from the Soviet Union of similar, though lesser, documentary significance. For example, shorthand notes or summaries of the debates at certain confidential meetings of Soviet historians have reached the West.

4. *Accounts by victims* who later made their way to the West and published their experiences. These include very remarkable men and women, skilled in observation, vivid in description, and reliable as to their experiences. We are most lucky to have the memoirs of the leading Russian critic Ivanov-Razumnik; the Austrian physicist Alexander Weissberg; Margarete Buber-Neumann, widow of the German Communist Politburo member; the distinguished historian Professor Shteppa. It is fortunate that one of the leading students of the economics of forced labour, Professor Swianiewicz, should himself have been in camp (and, indeed, barely missed Katyn). Many of the less celebrated exprisoners are equally illuminating – for example, the Swiss-Belgian Communist Miss Eleanor Lipper, and the Russian defector Vladimir Petrov.

On the labour camps, we are in the fortunate position of having mutual confirmation, and in considerable detail, from Soviet and non-Soviet sources. Messrs Dallin and Nicolaevsky, as early as 1948, collated from defector sources a list of several hundred camps and camp groups. Some of the most distant and obscure of these, for example, have had this confirmation – for example, the gold camp Maldyak in the depths of Kolyma held General Gorbatov for a time. Again, camp conditions emerge identically from both types of source. Gorbatov's accounts of the treatment of politicals by the common criminal *urkas* might have come out of any of the defector stories. The bread-ration scheme in Kolyma is given almost identically by Eleanor Lipper in the West and by Grigory Shelest in his 'Kolyma Notes', published in the Soviet journal *Znamya*. And so on.

These distinguished and honest reporters were disbelieved. As Weissberg remarks in his book:

I know that I shall be fiercely assailed by those who have made it their business to defend the system of totalitarian lies. I know that like all others who have come forward in the past I shall be ruthlessly slandered. I cannot prevent that and there is no legal means of proving that what I say is true. The G.P.U. dismisses its victims without paper or documentary records. But History gives one weapon to truth which it denies to the lie. Lies have many versions, truth only one. Several hundred people left the Soviet Union when I did. Some of them will have lost their lives, or be in prison again, but others will probably have survived and be in freedom. I have no idea where they are now, but one day they too will come forward. What they say will agree with what I say, and that material agreement will confirm the truth of what I have said here.[5]

5. *The last and most controversial of our primary sources consists of the memoirs of defectors and others with access to political and police evidence.* Here we have to consider certain particular books.

In a totalitarian country, the question of evidence assumes a special form. No particular credence can be attached to official pronouncements, many of which, indeed, are extravagant false-hoods. The truth can thus only percolate in the form of hearsay.

Recent Soviet accounts make it clear that leaks even of highly secret information continued to take place even in 1937, when the unnatural nature of Ordzhonikidze's death became known to various quite minor Party officials – as it did, of course, to certain defectors who came West at that time. But of course not all hear-say and not all rumour is true. On political matters basically the best, though not infallible, source is rumour at a high political or police level. One of the most striking examples is the famous 'Letter of an Old Bolshevik'. This was originally published in the Menshevik *Sotsialisticheskii Vestnik*, then appearing in Paris, on 22 December 1936 and 17 January 1937, and was published as a pamphlet in New York later in 1937. Its (then anonymous) author was Mr Boris Nicolaevsky, not in fact an Old Bolshevik, but an Old Menshevik who had, however, worked as director of the Marx-Engels Institute for some time after the Revolution. He had, moreover, maintained his pre-Revolutionary links with a number of Bolsheviks. Rykov was his brother-in-law. And when Bukharin visited the West in March 1936, he had a number of conversations with him. Bukharin is the source of some of the general descriptions of Party feeling in the 'Letter'. But most of it, and in particular of course the passages dealing with the later part of 1936, come from other sources and in particular Charles Rappoport, the well-known Franco-Russian Communist and friend of Lenin. In the conditions then prevailing, which were easier than those of the later Stalinist period, the stories circulating at a reasonably high level of the old Party would percolate in this fashion – as indeed they did once again in the Khrushchev era. But the essay can nevertheless not be taken as more than this; nor should we fail to remember its second-hand nature. The 'Letter of an Old Bolshevik,' has lately been included in a selection of Mr Nicolaevsky's essays, *Power and the Soviet Elite* (New York, 1965). My references are to the latter edition.

Good rough criteria are whether an author is an authenticable figure, or a mere name on a book (like some writers who have had unexplained success in scholarly circles in the West); and whether the information checks against other – and particularly later – reports, and is itself consonant with the political and general atmosphere. Among the best and most accurate sources are some which, naturally enough from Stalin's point of view, were long made the subject of special campaigns of denigration and personal slander. For example, Mr Victor Kravchenko's *I Chose Freedom* was widely denounced as a Cold War fabrication (using the words 'Cold War' in a sense still sometimes attached to them, to mean, not international political actions, but the publication of facts or opinions unacceptable to the Soviet Government); the case was buttressed by allegations about his personal character. Kravchenko chances not to cover much of the area dealt with here, though his second book, *I Choose Justice*, an account of his lawsuit against *Les Lettres Françaises*, is useful as containing evidence from a number of ex-prisoners, much of which would doubtless not otherwise have been collected.

Another much smeared writer, Walter Krivitsky, is a useful, though a minor source. He has certain defects. First, his memory (or his capacity to check his memory against contemporary publication) is imperfect. As a result his narrative suffers the occasional 'chronological collapse' as John Erickson puts it.

That is, the information is normally of high integrity, but has become displaced. This can usually be allowed for. Secondly, his closeness to the best sources of information is not of the very highest. A point that is not often noted of Krivitsky, incidentally, is that he is remarkably careful not to give away any of the true State and military secrets of the regime, as against the particular acts of the ruling clique. Krivitsky defected on 5 December 1937, which gives the dividing line between his soundest and his more speculative information.

A more senior N.K.V.D. officer, Alexander Orlov, had served as deputy chief of the Economic Administration of the O.G.P.U. and had had close relations with a number of the leading Secret Police officials, and in particular Mironov, one of Yagoda's closest assistants in the preparation of the Zinoviev trial. His unfortunately named *The Secret History of Stalin's Crimes* seems to be most reliable – at least up to about the end of 1937, the time of the author's last visit to the Soviet Union. He defected on 13 July 1938. However, all his closest associates in the N.K.V.D. had long since been purged, and the few survivors of the old machine had for some time been both less likely to speak freely to him and less likely to get genuine information from the new N.K.V.D. leadership. Apart from this deterioration, reflected in an increasing lack of detail and certainty, Orlov stands up extremely well to our tests. (I have also been able to check, through an Eastern European Communist unfamiliar with Orlov's book, two striking, though minor, stories affecting acquaintances of my informant. And he has more recently been confirmed in a number of details by Soviet *samizdat* historians – for example on the suicides of leading police officials Pogrebinski [head of the Gorki Province N.K.V.D.] and Kozelski [head of the Secret Political Department of the Ukrainian N.K.V.D.].[6]) Another source which has stood up well to the emergence of later evidence is the Army officer and diplomat Alexander Barmine.

A number of defector reports do not have the same solidity. On the one hand their authors may not be authentically identifiable in their Soviet roles and may claim an improbable amount of personal contact with events; and on the other, it may be impossible to check the information they give – indeed, sections of it may be incompatible with or hard to relate to better sources; or it may merely be that, not being so closely involved in Soviet politics, the rumours they pass on are those of a less critical milieu. This applies to stories heard or misheard in prison or labour camp from others ostensibly more closely connected with the politics of the time. Much of this output is worthless, but there are books containing what seems to be a substratum of true material, or at least accurately reported rumour, which is in accord with known facts and gives possibly additional information. I have occasionally used such, with an 'it is said' when both the positive probability, and the negative lack of reason for falsification, have seemed to make it worth it.

The secondary sources are mostly the obvious ones. They include works in which masses of primary material have been collated, such as Dallin and Nicolaevsky's *Forced Labour in Soviet Russia*.

I have in general given the most accessible reference. In particular, where an English translation exists, I have normally quoted from it rather than from a Russian original.

SELECT BIBLIOGRAPHY

The two-hundred-odd volumes cited in the text are given in full at the first reference, and thereafter by the author's name only (unless more than one work by the same author is in question). The list below is of a smaller number of particularly useful, or comprehensive, books dealing with one aspect or another of the purges.

GENERAL

Armstrong, John A., *The Politics of Totalitarianism*, New York, 1961.

Balabanoff, Angelica, *Impressions of Lenin*, Ann Arbor, 1964.

Barmine, Alexander, *One Who Survived*, New York, 1945.

Carr, E. H., *Socialism in One Country*, 3 vols., London, 1958–64.

Ciliga, Anton, *The Russian Enigma*, London, 1940.

Daniels, Robert V., *The Conscience of the Revolution*, Oxford, 1960.

Deutscher, Isaac, *Stalin*, London, 1949.

——, *The Prophet Unarmed*, London, 1959.

Djilas, Milovan, *Conversations with Stalin*, London, 1962.

Ehrenburg, Ilya, *Men, Years and Life*, English ed., vol. iv, London, 1963; vol. v, 1964; vol. vi, 1966.

Fainsod, Merle, *Smolensk under Soviet Rule*, Cambridge, Mass., 1958; London, 1959.

Fischer, Louis, *Men and Politics*, London, 1941.

Jasny, Naum, *The Socialized Agriculture of the U.S.S.R.*, Stanford, 1949.

Krivitsky, Walter, *I Was Stalin's Agent*, London, 1940.

Lorimer, Frank, *The Population of the Soviet Union: History and Prospects*, League of Nations, Geneva, 1946.

Medvedev, Zhores A., *The Rise and Fall of T. D. Lysenko*, New York, 1969.

Orlov, Alexander, *The Secret History of Stalin's Crimes*, London, 1954.

Schapiro, Leonard, *The Communist Party of the Soviet Union*, London, 1960.

Serge, Victor, *From Lenin to Stalin*, London, 1937.

——, *Memoirs of a Revolutionary, 1901–1941*, London, 1963.

Souvarine, Boris, *Stalin*, London, 1939.

Trotsky, Leon, *My Life*, English ed., London, 1930.

760   *Select Bibliography*

Ulam, Adam, *The Bolsheviks*, New York, 1965.
Uralov, Alexander (A. Avtorkhanov), *The Reign of Stalin*, London, 1953.
Wolfe, Bertram D., *Three Who Made a Revolution*, Penguin ed., London, 1966.

Large Soviet Encyclopedia, 1st ed., 1926–47. (Bolshaya Sovetskaya Entsiklopediya)
——, 2nd ed., 1949–58.
——, 3rd ed., 1970–.
Small Soviet Encyclopedia, 3rd ed., 1958–60. (Malaya Sovetskaya Entsiklopediya)
Soviet Historical Encyclopedia, 1961–. (Sovetskaya Istoricheskaya Entsiklopediya)
Ukrainian Soviet Encyclopedia, 1959–65. (Ukrainska Radyanska Entsiklopediya)
Encyclopedic Dictionary, 1963–. (Entsiklopedicheskiy Slovar)
Short Literary Encyclopedia, 1963–. (Kratkaya Literaturnaya Entsiklopediya)
Ukrainian Soviet Encyclopedic Dictionary, 1966–. (Ukrainsky Radyanskiy Entsiklopedichniy Slovnik)
(References to these encyclopedias are to the article on the person in question unless otherwise stated.)

POLICE, TRIALS, PRISON, CAMPS, ETC.

Anon., *The Dark Side of the Moon*, with Preface by T. S. Eliot, London, 1946.
Beck, F., and Godin, W., *Russian Purge and the Extraction of Confession*, London, 1951.
Broué, Pierre, *Le Procès de Moscou*, Paris, 1964.
Brzezinski, Zbigniew, *The Permanent Purge*, Cambridge, Mass., 1956.
Buber (Neumann), Margarete, *Under Two Dictators*, London, 1949.
Dallin, D. J., and Nicolaevsky, B. I., *Forced Labour in the Soviet Union*, London, 1948.
Dewey Commission, Report of the, *Not guilty: The Case of Leon Trotsky*, London, 1937.
Ekart, Antoni, *Vanished Without Trace*, London, 1954.
Ginzburg, Evgenia S., *Into the Whirlwind*, English ed., London, 1967.
Gorbatov, General A. V., *Years off My Life*, English ed., London, 1964.
Herling, Gustav, *A World Apart*, New York, 1951.

Ivanov-Razumnik, R. V., *The Memoirs of Ivanov-Razumnik*, English ed., London, 1965.
Kravchenko, Victor, *I Chose Justice*, London, 1951.
Lengyel, Jozsef, *From Beginning to End*, English ed., London, 1966.
Lipper, Eleanor, *Eleven Years in Soviet Prison Camps*, London, 1951.
Maclean, Fitzroy, *Eastern Approaches*, London, 1941.
Medvedev, Roy, *Faut-il réhabiliter Staline?* Paris, 1969.
Petrov, V., *It Happens in Russia*, London, 1951.
Piontkovsky, A. A., Menshagin, V. D., *Course of Soviet Criminal Law*, Moscow, 1955.
Roeder, Bernhard, *Katorga: An Aspect of Modern Slavery*, London, 1958.
Sakharov, Andrei D., *Progress, Coexistence and Intellectual Freedom*, London, 1968.
Solzhenitsyn, Alexander, *One Day in the Life of Ivan Denisovich*, trans. Max Hayward and Ronald Hingley, New York, 1963.
Stypulkowski, Z., *Invitation to Moscow*, London, 1951.
Swianicwicz, S., *Forced Labour and Economic Development*, London, 1965.
Vyshinsky, Andrei, *The Judicial System of the U.S.S.R.*, Moscow, 1938.
Weissberg, Alexander, *Conspiracy of Silence*, London, 1952; U.S. title *The Accused*.
Wolin, Simon, and Slusser, Robert M., *The Soviet Secret Police*, New York, 1957.

TRANSCRIPTS, ETC.

The Menshevik Trial, Leningrad, n.d.
Wrecking Activities at Power Stations in the Soviet Union, English ed., Moscow, 1933.
Report of Court Proceedings: The Case of the Trotskyite-Zinovievite Terrorist Centre, English ed., Moscow, 1936. (Referred to as *Zinoviev Trial*.)
Report of the Court Proceedings in the Case of the Anti-Soviet Trotskyite Centre, English ed., Moscow, 1937. (Referred to as *Pyatakov Trial*.)
Report of the Court Proceedings in the Case of the Anti-Soviet 'Bloc of Rights and Trotskyites', English ed., Moscow, 1938. (Referred to as *Bukharin Trial*.)
Tucker, Robert C., and Cohen, Stephen F. (eds.), *The Great Purge Trial*, New York, 1965.
(This is a transcript of 689 pages of the 800 in the *Report of the Court Proceedings in the Case of the Anti-Soviet 'Bloc of Rights and Trotsky-*

ites', and contains in addition notes and a preface. It is more easily obtainable than the original, but after p. 199 its pagination is different. My references are to the original, but may be transferred as follows:

Original	Tucker and Cohen
pp. 1–199	identical
pp. 200–243	summarized pp. 200–201
pp. 244–512	pp. 202–470
pp. 513–51	summarized pp. 471–2
pp. 552–89	pp. 473–510
pp. 590–623	summarized pp. 511–12
pp. 624–800	pp. 513–689

The omissions are the examinations of Sharangovich, Khodzhayev, Levin, Pletnev, Kazakov and Maximov-Dikovsky, together with the medical witness Belostotsky and the answers of the Commission of Medical Experts.)

PARTY

Avtorkhanov, Abdurakhman, *Stalin and the Soviet Communist Party*, London, 1959.

Bega, F., and Aleksandrov, V., *Petrovsky*, Moscow, 1963.

The Communist Party of the Soviet Union in Resolutions, etc., 7th ed., Moscow, 1953–.

Drobzhiev, V., and Dumiova, N., *V. Ya. Chubar: A Biographical Sketch*, Moscow, 1963.

Dubinsky-Rukhadze, I., *Ordzhonikidze*, Moscow, 1963.

Essays on the History of the Communist Party of the Ukraine, 2nd ed., Kiev, 1964.

Essays on the History of Leningrad, vol. iv, Moscow-Leningrad, 1965.

Gruliow, Leo (ed.), *Current Soviet Politics, I*, New York, 1953. (XIXth Party Congress and period.)

——, *Current Soviet Policies, II*, New York, 1957. (XXth Party Congress.)

——, and Saikowski, Charlotte, *Current Soviet Policies, IV*, New York, 1962. (XXIInd Party Congress.)

Kostiuk, Hrihory, *Stalinist Rule in the Ukraine*, Munich, 1960.

Krasnikov, S., *Kirov*, Moscow, 1964.

Maryagin, G., *Postyshev*, Moscow, 1965.

Matossian, Mary, *The Impact of Soviet Policies in Armenia*, Leyden, 1962.

Nicolaevsky, Boris, I., *Power and the Soviet Elite*, New York, 1965.

Sinelnikov, S., *Sergei Mironovich Kirov: Life and Activity*, Moscow, 1964.

Stanislav Vinkentiyovich Kossior (in Ukrainian), Kiev, 1963.

Stenographic Report of the First Session of the Supreme Soviet, Moscow, 1938.

Stenographic Report of the VIIth Party Conference, Moscow, 1958.

Stenographic Report of the VIIIth Party Conference, Moscow, 1961.

Stenographic Report of the XIth Party Congress, Moscow, 1961.

Stenographic Report of the XVIIth Party Congress, Moscow, 1934.

Stenographic Report of the XVIIIth Party Congress, Moscow, 1939.

Stenographic Report of the All-Union Conference to Improve the Preparation of Scientific-Pedagogical Cadres in the Historical Sciences, Moscow, 1964.

Sullivant, Robert S., *Soviet Politics and the Ukraine, 1917–1957*, New York, 1962.

ARMY

Aleksandrov, P. N. *et al.*, *Komandarm Uborevich*, Moscow, 1964.

Bialer, Seweryn, *Stalin and His Generals*, New York, 1969.

Dubinsky, I. V., *Naperekor Vetram*, Moscow, 1964.

Dushenkin, V., *Ot Soldata do Marshala*, Moscow, 1961.

Erickson, John, *The Soviet High Command*, London, 1962.

Geroy Grazhdanskoy Voyny, Moscow, 1963.

Hoettl, Wilhelm, *The Secret Front*, London, 1954.

Kondryatsev, N., *Marshal Blyukher*, Moscow, 1965.

Koritsky, N. I., *et al.*, *Marshal Tukhachevsky*, Moscow, 1965.

Nikulin, Lev, *Marshal Tukhachevsky*, Moscow, 1964.

Petrov, Yu. P., *Partiynoe Stroitel'stvo v Sovetskoy Armii i Flote (1918–1961)*, Moscow, 1964.

Schellenberg, W., *The Schellenberg Memoirs*, London, 1956.

V. K. Blyukher, Moscow, 1963.

Wollenberg, E., *The Red Army*, London, 1938.

Yakir, P. I., and Geller, Ya. A., *Komandarm Yakir*, Moscow, 1963.

MISCELLANEOUS

On the Trotsky killing I have largely followed Isaac Don Levine's definitive *The Mind of an Assassin* (New York, 1959). I have not given references for the Katyn massacre, which falls outside the period of the purge proper: it may be followed in fuller detail in *The Crime of Katyn*, foreword by General W. Anders (London, 1965), Joseph Mackiewicz's *The Katyn Wood Murders* (London, 1951) and J. K. Zawodny's *Death in the Forest* (Notre Dame, 1962).

Other themes touched on in the Introduction and the Epilogue are more fully developed in the secondary sources there referred to.

PERIODICALS

SOVIET

Pravda, Izvestia, Krasnaya Zvezda, Kazakhstanskaya Pravda, Zarya Vostoka, Komsomolskaya Pravda, Bakinski Rabochy, Pravda Ukrainy, Pravda Vostoka, Rabochii, Sovietskaya Belorussia, Leningradskaya Pravda, Kommunist (Armenia), *Voprosy Istorii, Voprosy Istorii K.P.S.S., Voprosy Literatury, Voenno-Istoricheskiy Zhurnal, Bilshovik Ukrainy, Visti, Sovietskoye Gosudarstvo i Pravo, Znamya, Oktyabr, Novy Mir, Literaturnaya Gazeta, Neva, Belarus, Nauka i Religia, Vecherny Leningrad, Ogonek, Literaturnaya Rossiya, Molodoi Kommunist, Sovietskaya Sibir.*

OTHER

Na Rubezhe, Novy Zhurnal, Byulleten Oppozitsii, Bulletin d'Informations (Commission pour la vérité sur les crimes de Staline), *New Leader, Trybuna Ludu, Sotsialisticheskii Vestnik, Posev, Soviet Affairs* (St Antony's Papers), *Problems of Communism, Soviet Studies, Survey, Studies in Comparative Communism.*

Addendum

ADDENDUM

p. 73	Leonid Petrovsky's view is shared by other Soviet writers. (e.g. Yakir, pp. 93–4, 96; Medvedev, ch. V)
p. 80	We now have the detail that Borisov was killed with crowbars. (Medvedev, p. 159)
p. 81n	Indeed, on the informality and variety of Stalin's methods of liquidation we are now told, 'Some officials were murdered in their homes, in hotels, on hunting parties, in their offices, thrown out of windows, poisoned—and then were reported dead of heart attacks, accidents, or suicides.' (Medvedev, p. 367). Compare the fates of Khandzhian, Lakoba, Slutsky, Zinaida Raikh, etc.
p. 83	Two recent *samizdat* accounts of Nikolayev's interrogation, differing in details from this and from each other, agree that Nikolayev made it clear that he was aware of the N.K.V.D.'s involvement. (Yakir, p. 96; Medvedev, p. 159)
p. 90	I have not sufficiently stressed the fact that (apart from those of Nikolayev and two others) even the published confessions go no further than admitting membership of the Leningrad Centre while denying all responsibility for the murder. One of the judges, A. A. Batner, has since reported that in fact only Nikolayev confessed. (Yakir, p. 94)
p. 92	Stalin is reported as himself compiling the lists of members of the 'Moscow Centre' and the 'Leningrad Centre.' (Medvedev, p. 164)
p. 95	Fomin, it now appears, actually survived to the 1960s, giving no information to the Commission then investigating the Kirov case, and publishing uninformative memoirs in 1964. (Yakir, p. 93; Medvedev, p. 215)
p. 120	Further details on Kavtaradze, given in Medvedev, p. 311, show that this account, though accurate in substance, is much compressed.
p. 194	Torture was employed on the accused at the Menshevik Trial in 1931. (Medvedev, pp. 127, 133)
p. 195	For details of torture, see Medvedev, pp. 264 ff.
p. 197	The conveyor had been in use not later than 1928, when it was employed on the Shakhty victims. (Medvedev, p. 113)

p. 202   Both Bukharin and Krestinsky were directly threatened with the deaths of their wives and children, including the former's newborn baby. (Medvedev, p. 187)

p. 204   Drobnis, for one, was promised his life and seems to have believed it. (Medvedev, p. 188)

p. 206   Gaven, who had tuberculosis, was carried out on a stretcher to be shot. (Medvedev, p. 273)

p. 210   In the provinces, N.K.V.D. men are reported as forging the prisoners' signatures. (Medvedev, p. 303)

p. 254   We are now told that Sokolnikov was shot in 1941, after the outbreak of war. (Medvedev, p. 178)

p. 259   A false account of Papuli's interrogation was sent to Ordzhonikidze. (Medvedev, p. 193)

After the arrest of Ordzhonikidze's subordinates Stalin sent him excerpts from their interrogations which incriminated him, with the comment, 'Comrade Sergo, look what they're writing about you.' (Medvedev, p. 193)

p. 260   On Ordzhonikidze's death his secretary and his bodyguard were arrested. (Medvedev, p. 194)

p. 265   Two of Ordzhonikidze's brothers were arrested in May 1941. (Medvedev, pp. 194–6)

p. 270   On one account, the Plenum set up a commission chaired by Mikoyan to decide the fate of Bukharin and Rykov. (Medvedev, p. 174)

p. 306   The forgeries, it is now reported, were only attached to the documents of the case after the executions. (Medvedev, p. 301)

We are now told that Goryachev too in fact committed suicide. (Yakir, p. 95)

p. 307   The accused are named as tried in 'a room on the third floor' in a 'building on 25 October Street'— i.e. the Supreme Court (*Stepnoy Veter* by Robert Eideman, Moscow 1965, p. 20). Further details have since been given by Military Jurist A. A. Batner, who was secretary of the court. Frinovsky was court commandant, and Marshal Yegorov, though not a member of the court, was present. Blyukher said he felt ill and was allowed to leave: the verdict was brought to him at home to be signed. Two or three questions only were put, and by Ulrikh alone, to each accused. Shaposhnikov, in what was evidently an attempt to help the accused, asked Uborevich whether the alleged bad dispositions he had made in the Pinsk marshes were not really designed to trap the

Germans. Ulrikh silenced him and told Uborevich not to answer. Yakir insisted that Stalin could know nothing of the trial. Primakov retorted that, on the contrary, Stalin had obviously arranged it. The trial lasted four hours. Yegorov was in charge of the executions. (Yakir, pp. 94–5)

p. 308   For further details of the fate of the Yakir family (which was initially dealt with by Frinovsky in person), see *A Childhood in Prison* by Pyotr Yakir, London 1972.

p. 310   The wives of Tukhachevsky, Uborevich, Kork and Gamarnik were sentenced to 8 years, imprisonment but shot in October 1941. (Yakir, p. 34)
Also executed on 1 July 1937 was Corps Commander M. I. Vasilenko (*Large Soviet Encyclopedia*, 3rd edition). Garkavi, on the other hand, seems to have committed suicide. (Yakir, p. 30)

p. 316   Just as Rudolf Slansky was awarded the highest Czechoslovak order at a time when his 'accomplices' were giving decisive evidence against him. (*The Czechoslovak Political Trials 1950–1954*, Jiri Pelikan, London 1971, p. 104)

p. 320   Yegorov, whose case was discussed in the Politburo, is now said to have 'died in prison,' which could reconcile the two dates as those of sentence and death respectively. (Medvedev, pp. 325, 211)

p. 321   Army Commissar Ya. K. Berzin, the former effective C.-in-C. of the Spanish Republican Army, was also shot on 28 July 1938. (*Large Soviet Encyclopedia*, 3rd edition)

p. 336   In Gorki, for example, the entire City Committee was arrested. (*Essays on the History of the Gorki Organisation of the CPSU* [Gorki 1966] vol. III, p. 32)

p. 340   Khandzhian's death was represented as suicide and this was compounded by two forged farewell letters placed in his pockets. (Medvedev, p. 368)

p. 341   Lakoba, who seems to have been the scapegoat for a fake attempt on Stalin's life staged by Beria, is now said to have been poisoned by Beria. Lakoba's wife was tortured over a long period. A threat to shoot her fourteen-year-old son if she did not incriminate her dead husband was carried out. She finally died without signing. (Medvedev, pp. 299, 269)

p. 342   Malenkov's use of 'proscribed methods' is referred to in Shvernik's speech to the XXIInd Congress.

p. 354   The number on Yezhov's lists has more lately and more precisely been given as 44,000. (Medvedev, p. 294)

p. 356   And see G. A. Trukan: *Yan Rudzutak*, Moscow 1963.

p. 361   M. M. Kaganovich (a Jew) was to commit suicide some years later to avoid a charge of having been Hitler's choice for Vice-President of a Russian fascist government. He had also allegedly built aircraft factories close to the border so that the Germans could capture them. (Medvedev, p. 310)

p. 371   A most curious and significant point now appears in connection with the Yenukidze trial. One official source (*The Ukrainian Soviet Encyclopedic Dictionary*) now gives Yenukidze's death date as 30.X.1937, and Karakhan's as 20.IX.1937. This would mean that the December 'Trial' probably did not take place at all, and certainly not at the date stated. Whether they died under interrogation or were shot prematurely, the fact that they were no longer available would naturally account for the trial as announced not being held in public.

Eight members of Yenukidze's family also perished. (Medvedev, p. 341)

Orakhelashvili was reported tortured by having his eardrums pierced. (Medvedev, p. 264)

p. 372   Postyshev's wife had already been arrested. (Medvedev, p. 406)

p. 373   Kossior was censured for insufficient vigilance in January, on his recall to Moscow. (Medvedev, p. 192)

p. 408   A Soviet general tells us that eight years for wives and five for children was the norm. (Lt. Gen. A. I. Todorsky quoted in Medvedev, p. 342)

p. 409   A fourteen-year-old boy was charged with organising an anarchist group with a view to attacking the Red Army in the rear in case of war. A thirteen-year-old Kalmyk boy was sentenced for 'terrorist intentions' for shooting at a picture of Stalin with a catapult. (Yakir, pp. 34, 50)

p. 418   For other examples of extravagant accusations, see Medvedev, pp. 352 ff.

p. 424   An estimate of Special Board sentences in 1937 gives 80 per cent 8–10 years, 15 per cent 5 years, 5 per cent 3 years. (Yakir, p. 39)

p. 433   There was also, for example, a 'linguists plot' (Mandelstam, pp. 37, 47; Medvedev, pp. 137–8) and a trial of the staff of the Hermitage Museum. (Mandelstam, p. 364)

p. 438 Babel is reported to have resisted arrest, and to have seriously wounded an N.K.V.D. man. (Mandelstam, p. 5)

p. 445 A. A. Andreyev is reported as politically responsible for the sentence on Mandelstam, which was on KRA grounds. (Mandelstam, pp. 355, 373)

The poet's widow, Nadezhda Mandelstam, has since published the results of her own enquiries into the date and manner of his death (chapters 82 and 83, *Hope Against Hope*, London, 1971). She reports several rather different versions and is only able to conclude that he probably died between December 1938 and April 1939 in the Vtoraya Rechka transit camp near Vladivostok, perhaps during the typhus epidemic of that winter. She dismisses as improbable the story of the attack by criminals.

p. 448 A 'diversionary organisation of literary people' of which Babel and Meyerhold were supposed to be members was invented by the N.K.V.D. Meyerhold was also accused of having been a Tsarist police agent. He is reported as tortured with particular severity. (Medvedev, pp. 309, 316, 233)

A *samizdat* source now states flatly that Zinaida Raikh's murder was committed by the N.K.V.D. (Medvedev, p. 387)

p. 461 Akmolinsk Camp 26 also held 8000 women related to 'traitors,' including the wives of Krestinsky, Pilnyak and Sulimov. (Medvedev, pp. 341–2)

p. 473 Although it contains some material on the Northeastern camps, *One Day In the Life of Ivan Denisovich* is now known to be set at Ekibastuze in Kazakhstan.

p. 474 Garanin (who seems to have been technically assistant head under Pavlov) was shot in 1939. (Medvedev, pp. 281–2, 297)

p. 486 'Those who worked died of exhaustion, and those who didn't starved to death.' (Mandelstam, p. 378)

p. 500 Bessonov had a seventeen-day 'conveyor,' and was also badly beaten. (Medvedev, p. 187)

p. 510 A further report of Krestinsky's being tortured appears in Medvedev (p. 186).

p. 511 It is also significant that Soviet newspaper reports omitted much of Krestinsky's early evidence.

p. 538 A secret trial of surviving Social Revolutionaries,

774 *Addendum*

leading to the death of almost all concerned, is reported in 1937. But Maria Spiridonova is now reported not to have been actually shot till September-October 1941. (*Politichesky Dnevnik*, no. 67; *Kak Ya Iskal Shpiona Reyli* by P. I. Pimenov, *samizdat*, 1968, note 34)

p. 540   Yakovleva is nevertheless reported as eventually shot. (Medvedev, p. 181)

p. 569   Bessonov was shot in Orel in 1941. (Medvedev, p. 178)

p. 570   It is now reported that Bukharin's letter was genuine but was memorised by his wife, and put into writing only later. (Medvedev, p. 183)

p. 604   Kossior is reported as being brought before Stalin, Molotov, Kaganovich and Voroshilov, with Petrovsky (who tells the story) present. Kossior admitted he was a Polish spy, and Stalin told Petrovsky that he too should be shot, but would receive mercy instead. (Medvedev, p. 295)

p. 611   Antonov-Ovseenko's teenage daughter was also arrested. (Medvedev, p. 342)

p. 614   Even Shkiryatov was inclined to be milder to Kosarev than Stalin, who had to insist on greater rigour. (Medvedev, p. 293, quoting a speech of V. F. Pikina's, Nov. 21, 1963)

p. 622   On November 13, 1938, the Central Committee passed an unpublished resolution on 'regulating' the punitive organs: this naturally presaged Yezhov's fall. (Medvedev, p. 240)

p. 623   Yezhov seems to have been charged initially with trying to kill Stalin and seize power, and to have confessed. He is reported shot in 1940. (Medvedev, pp. 240–1)

p. 625   Sokolnikov is reported in prison as urging cell mates to denounce loyal Stalinists like Postyshev. (Medvedev, p. 341)

pp. 627–8   Kosarev's trial lasted fifteen minutes—remarked on as, at the time, on the long side. (Medvedev, p. 272)

p. 629   Peter Petrovsky was shot in 1942. (Medvedev, p. 246)

p. 630   Petrovsky's son-in-law S. A. Zager was also shot. (Medvedev, p. 200)

p. 631   At the June 1937 Plenum, Krupskaya is reported as speaking against the arrest of Pyatnitsky, evidently there decided upon. (Medvedev, p. 199)

p. 637   One of the charges against Postyshev was, ironically enough, of 'exterminating cadres' during his period in Kuibyshev, when he had sought to regain Stalin's favour by especially enthusiastic terror—including altering prison sentences to death on his own initiative. (Medvedev, p. 406)

p. 643   There are a number of accounts of the disposal of superfluous prisoners, especially the old and ill, by taking them out to sea and blowing up the barges. (e.g. Mandelstam, p. 383)

p. 646   Simonov's figures seem in fact to be taken from V. A. Anfilov *Nachalo Velikoi Otechestvennoi Voiny* (Moscow 1962) p. 28.

p. 647   We are told, too, that in the army medical service 900 doctors were shot and 1200 imprisoned. (Michel Garder, *A History of the Soviet Army*, English ed., London 1966, p. 103n)

p. 654   Other executions in the period of defeat are now reported as including those of survivors of the great trials, such as Sokolnikov and Bessonov; wives of executed generals; and members of other parties, like Maria Spiridonova (see Addendum, notes to pp. 254, 310, 538, 569)

p. 655   For executions in the retreat see also Yakir, p. 129; Medvedev, p. 249.

p. 658   Children of the victims of the Yezhovshchina too continued to be arrested in later years; e.g. Bubnov's and Lominadze's in 1944, Artem Vesyoli's, Shlyapnikov's and Smorodin's in 1949, etc. (Medvedev, p. 342)

p. 669   Brecht's poem on the death of his friend Tretyakov, written some years later, is cited as a sign of a more critical attitude. But even in that he wrote 'Among fifty who are condemned/One can be innocent,' a slight, but hardly a decisive improvement. Nor did he publish the poem or make any public protest.

p. 690   Other rehabilitations include V. I. Ivanov. (*Pravda Vostoka*, 20 July 1963)

p. 702   A similar estimate, of around a million party arrests, is given by Medvedev, p. 234.

p. 703   There were days when up to a thousand people were shot in Moscow alone. (Medvedev, p. 239)

p. 705   Two more recent reports by Soviet writers speak of the sentence to camp "without the right of correspondence" as in fact meaning execution. (Mandelstam, p. 259; Medvedev, p. 367)

p. 716–   See Addendum, notes to pp. 254, 623, above.
717

p. 728   In 1937 N.K.V.D. pay was approximately quad-
             rupled. (Medvedev, p. 392)

p. 735   Sukhanov was tried again in 1939 and shot on 29
             June 1940. (*Soviet Historical Encyclopedia*; Medve-
             dev, p. 137)

p. 751   On death dates it is even the case that in a single
             article the *Short Literary Encyclopedia* gives '1937
             or according to other information 1939' for the
             writer G. K. Nikoforov. My still rather inconclusive
             deductions can, however, now be improved on the
             basis of a comment by Nadezhda Mandelstam (*Hope
             Against Hope*, p. 389). She writes, "The dates on
             the certificate issued by the Registry Office also
             proved nothing. The dates put on such documents
             were often arbitrary: vast numbers of deaths, for
             instance, were post-dated to wartime. This was a
             statistical device to conceal the number of people
             who died in camps by blurring the difference be-
             tween them and the casualties of the war period.
             When the rehabilitations began in the days after
             Stalin's death, people were almost automatically put
             down as having died in 1941 or 1943."
             From a knowledgeable source, this certainly entitles
             us to reject, for example, the vague '1943' for
             Fedko (p. 628).

References to 'Medvedev' are from *Let History Judge* by Roy
Medvedev, English edition, London and New York, 1972; to
'Yakir,' from *A Childhood in Prison*, by Pyotr Yakir, English
edition, London, 1972; to 'Mandelstam,' from *Hope Against
Hope* by Nadezhda Mandelstam, English edition, London, 1971.

Notes

NOTES

INTRODUCTION

1. See Boris Souvarine, *Stalin*, London, 1939, p. 316.
2. See Isaac Deutscher, *Stalin*, London, 1949, p. 234.
3. See Souvarine, p. 302.
4. ibid., p. 303.
5. ibid., p. 317, quoting D. J. Dallin.
6. See Leonard Schapiro, *The Communist Party of the Soviet Union*, London, 1960, p. 215
7. Souvarine, p. 329.
8. Lenin, 'The Deception of the People' (speech of 19 May 1919).
9. *Kommunist*, no. 5, 1957, p. 21, quoted by Schapiro, p. 207.
10. See Louis Fischer, *The Life of Lenin*, London, 1965, p. 589.
11. Alexander Barmine, *One Who Survived*, New York, 1945, p. 94.
12. Sapronov's speech to the IXth Party Congress.
13. Victor Serge, *Memoirs of a Revolutionary, 1901–1941*, London, 1963, p. 190.
14. Anton Ciliga, *The Russian Enigma*, London, 1940, p. 86.
15. E. H. Carr, *Socialism in One Country*, vol. i, London, 1958, p. 151.
16. Barmine, pp. 93–4.
17. Milovan Djilas, *The New Class*, London, 1957, p. 50.
18. *Pravda*, 18 December 1923.
19. See Souvarine, p. 249.
20. ibid.
21. ibid.
22. See Robert V. Daniels, *The Conscience of the Revolution*, Oxford, 1960, p. 28.
23. *Report of the XIVth Party Congress*, Moscow, 1926.
24. Souvarine, p. 418.
25. *Pravda*, 17 October 1926.
26. Souvarine, pp. 489–90.
27. See Isaac Deutscher, *The Prophet Unarmed*, London, 1959, pp. 388–9.
28. ibid., p. 351.
29. Ciliga, p. 74.
30. Alexander Weissberg, *Conspiracy of Silence*, London, 1952, p. 501.
31. Victor Kravchenko, *I Chose Freedom*, London, 1947, p. 275.
32. Nikita Khrushchev, 'Confidential Report' to the XXth Party Congress (henceforward referred to as 'Secret Speech').

33. See Deutscher, *The Prophet Unarmed*, p. 548.
34. 'Letter of an Old Bolshevik', in Boris I. Nicolaevsky, *Power and the Soviet Élite*, New York, 1965, p. 48.
35. *Report of the Court Proceedings in the Case of the Anti-Soviet Trotskyite Centre*, English ed., Moscow, 1937, p. 482 (henceforward referred to as *Pyatakov Trial*).
36. Lenin, *Collected Works*, 3rd Russian ed., Moscow, 1935–7, vol. 29, p. 229.
37. See Souvarine, p. 246.
38. Deutscher, *The Prophet Unarmed*, p. 82.
39. Leon Trotsky, *My Life*, English ed., vol. ii, London, 1930, p. 207.
40. See Souvarine, p. 424.
41. D. J. Dallin and B. I. Nicolaevsky, *Forced Labour in the Soviet Union*, London, 1948, p. 116.
42. Speech of Rudzutak at the XVIth Party Congress.
43. Abdurakhman Avtorkhanov, *Stalin and the Soviet Communist Party*, London, 1959, p. 124.
44. *Report of the XVIth Party Congress*, Moscow, 1930.
45. *Voprosy Istorii*, May 1963.
46. *Pravda*, 1 December 1963.
47. ibid., 6 January 1930.
48. *Report of the Court Proceedings in the Case of the Anti-Soviet 'Bloc of Rights and Trotskyites'*, English ed., Moscow, 1938, p. 708 (henceforward referred to as *Bukharin Trial*).
49. e.g. Ciliga, p. 95.
50. *Leningradskaya Pravda*, 2 December 1962.
51. See Ciliga, p. 96.
52. G. A. Tokaev, *Betrayal of an Ideal*, London, 1954, pp. 167–8.
53. Deutscher, *Stalin*, p. 349.
54. *Izvestia*, 12 March 1933.
55. Fred. E. Beal, *Word from a Native*, London, 1937, pp. 254–5.
56. *Neva*, no. 12, 1962; and, for children, see Armstrong, *The Politics of Totalitarianism*, New York, 1961, p. 7, and Lorimer, pp. 142–3.
57. The evidence for the Ukrainian famine is exhaustively covered in an article in *Soviet Studies* of January 1964, by Dana G. Dalrymple.
58. Frank Lorimer, *The Population of the Soviet Union: History and Prospects*, League of Nations, Geneva, 1946.
59. Alexander Orlov, *The Secret History of Stalin's Crimes*, London, 1954, p. 42.
60. Souvarine, p. 670.
61. See Armstrong, *The Politics of Totalitarianism*, p. 7.
62. Merle Fainsod, *Smolensk under Soviet Rule*, Cambridge, Mass., 1958; chapter xii.
63. Ivan Stadnyuk in *Neva*, no. 12, 1962.

64. Winston S. Churchill, *The Second World War*, vol. iv, London, 1951, pp. 447–8.
65. S. Swianiewicz, *Forced Labour and Economic Development*, London, 1965, p. 98.
66. Naum Jasny, *The Socialized Agriculture of the U.S.S.R.*, Stanford, 1949, p. 458.
67. Kravchenko, *I Chose Freedom*, p. 130.
68. Barmine, pp. 199–200.
69. Raphael R. Abramovitch, *The Soviet Revolution*, London, 1962, pp. 346–7.
70. Nicolaevsky, p. 18.
71. ibid., pp. 18–19.

CHAPTER I: STALIN PREPARES

1. *IXth All-Union Congress of the Trade Unions of the U.S.S.R.*, Moscow, 1933, pp. 205, 253.
2. *Pravda*, 2 December 1930.
3. *The All-Union Communist Party (Bolsheviks) in Resolutions, etc.*, 5th ed., vol. ii, p. 668.
4. e.g. *Bukharin Trial*, p. 391.
5. e.g. Ciliga, Abramovitch, Nicolaevsky.
6. Ciliga, p. 279.
7. 'Letter of an Old Bolshevik' (Nicolaevsky, p. 29).
8. *Bukharin Trial*, p. 390.
9. 'Letter of an Old Bolshevik' (Nicolaevsky, p. 30).
10. Abramovitch, pp. 353, 355.
11. *Pravda*, 17 November 1964.
12. Ciliga, p. 279.
13. *The All-Union Communist Party (Bolsheviks) in Resolutions, etc*, 5th ed., vol. ii, p. 669.
14. *All-Union Conference on Measures to Improve the Training of Scientific-Pedagogic Cadres in the Historical Sciences* (18–21 December 1962), Moscow, 1964 (henceforward referred to as *Conference of Historians*, 1962), p. 291.
15. ibid.
16. Boris Nicolaevsky in *Sotsialisticheskii Vestnik*, June 1956.
17. *Bukharin Trial*, p. 644.
18. *Report of the XIth Party Congress*, Moscow, 1936, p. 806.
19. Ciliga, p. 278.
20. L. Shaumyan in *Pravda*, 7 February 1964.
21. *Bukharin Trial*, p. 381.
22. Karl Radek, *Portraits and Pamphlets*, London, 1935, p. 31.
23. Barmine, pp. 101–2.
24. *Byuletten Oppozitsii*, no. 34 (quoted by Deutscher, *Stalin*, p. 352).
25. *Report of the Court Proceedings: The Case of the Trotskyite–Zinovievite Terrorist Centre*, English ed., Moscow, 1936, p. 14 (henceforward

referred to as *Zinoviev Trial*).

26. Abramovitch, p. 343; see also Fainsod, p. 263.
27. *Pravda*, 25 May 1933.
28. In his Declaration of April 1930.
29. 'Letter of an Old Bolshevik' (Nicolaevsky, p. 56).
30. Radek, p. 31.
31. *Byuletten Oppozitsii*, no. 33.
32. See Ciliga, chaps. 5, 7.
33. Khrushchev, Secret Speech.
34. Stalin, Report to the XVIIth Party Congress.
35. *The XVIIth Party Congress*, Moscow, 1934.
36. See 'Letter of an Old Bolshevik', Barmine, etc.
37. L. Shaumyan in *Pravda*, 7 February 1964.
38. S. Sinelnikov, *Sergei Miron-ovich Kirov: Life and Activity*, Moscow, 1964, pp. 194-5.
39. *Kommunist*, no. 30, 1966.
40. Khrushchev, Secret Speech.
41. Tokaev, *Betrayal of an Ideal*, p. 166.
42. Nicolaevsky, p. 100.
43. Resolution of the XVIIth Party Congress, and Party Constitution of 1934.
44. N. Ruslanov in *Sotsialisticheskii Vestnik*, nos. 7-8, 1953.
45. Nicolaevsky, pp. 94-5.
46. *Large Soviet Encyclopedia*, 1st ed., Moscow 1926-47, *sub* Shkiryatov.
47. Speech to the 1st Soviet Writers' Congress, August 1934.
48. Orlov, pp. 24-5.
49. Sinelnikov, p. 196.
50. Orlov, pp. 26-7.

CHAPTER 2: THE KIROV MURDER

1. *Pravda*, 4 December 1934.
2. S. Krasnikov, *Kirov*, Moscow, 1964, p. 200; *S. M. Kirov v Leningrade*, Leningrad, 1966, p. 45.
3. *Essays on the History of Leningrad*, vol. iv, Moscow–Leningrad, 1965, p. 354.
4. For various rumoured details see also Tokaev, *Betrayal of an Ideal*, p. 242; Elizabeth Lermolo, *Face of a Victim*, London, 1956, p. 90 and *passim*; Orlov, p. 32.
5. L. P. Petrovsky, *Letter to the* *Central Committee*, 5 March 1969.
6. *Zinoviev Trial*, pp. 31, 32, 34.
7. Krasnikov, p. 200.
8. Orlov, p. 28.
9. ibid., pp. 259-60.
10. *Bukharin Trial*, p. 572.
11. ibid., p. 376.
12. Orlov., pp. 29-30.
13. Lermolo, p. 90.
14. Khrushchev, Secret Speech.
15. *S. M. Kirov v Leningrade*, p. 196.
16. Speech by Z. T. Serdyuk to

the XXIInd Party Congress
(*Pravda*, 31 October 1961).
17. Deutscher, *Stalin*, p. 355.
18. *S. M. Kirov v Leningrade*, p. 196.
19. Khrushchev, Secret Speech.
20. ibid.
21. Speech by A. N. Shelepin at the XXIInd Party Congress (*Pravda*, 27 October 1961).
22. *Essays on the History of Leningrad*, vol. iv, p. 355.
23. Orlov, p. 37.
24. Speech by N. S. Khrushchev to the XXIInd Party Congress.
25. *Bukharin Trial*, p. 558.
26. Svetlana Alliluyeva, *Twenty Letters to a Friend*, London, 1967, p. 150.
27. *Sovietskaya Byelorussia*, 13 January 1963; Svetlana Alliluyeva, *Only One Year*, London, 1969, p. 190.
28. Lermolo, p. 17.
29. 'Letter of an Old Bolshevik' (Nicolaevsky, p. 40).
30. *Pravda*, 21 December 1934.
31. 'Letter of an Old Bolshevik' (Nicolaevsky, p. 41).
32. e.g. Orlov.
33. Orlov, p. 35.
34. ibid., p. 34.
35. *Zinoviev Trial*, p. 136.
36. *Pravda*, 6 December 1934.
37. ibid., 18 December 1934.
38. Hrihory Kostiuk, *Stalinist Rule in the Ukraine*, Munich, 1960, pp. 98–100. See also article 'Vlyzko' in *Ukrainian Soviet Encyclopedic Dictionary*, vol. i, 1966.
39. *Pravda*, 10 June 1935.
40. Lermolo, pp. 264–5.
41. Fainsod, pp. 56–7.
42. Ciliga, p. 71.
43. Lermolo, p. 175.
44. *Vecherny Leningrad*, 30 December 1964.
45. *Proceedings of the VIIth Congress of the Komsomol*, p. 108.
46. *Pravda*, 27 December 1934.
47. ibid.
48. 'Letter of an Old Bolshevik' (Nicolaevsky, p. 51).
49. ibid.
50. ibid., pp. 51–2.
51. *Zinoviev Trial*, p. 74.
52. *Bukharin Trial*, pp. 556–7.
53. ibid., p. 557.
54. *Pravda*, 17 December 1934.
55. ibid., 22 December 1934.
56. ibid., 23 December 1934.
57. Lenin, *Collected Works*, vol. 49, Moscow, 1964; *Stenographic Report of the XIth Party Congress*, Moscow, 1961.
58. Lenin, *Collected Works*, vol. 53, Moscow, 1965; *Stenographic Report of the XIth Party Congress*.
59. Ciliga, p. 282.
60. *Byuletten Oppozitsii*, no. 52–3, p. 11.
61. Lermolo, p. 245.
62. Gustav Herling, *A World Apart*, New York, 1951, p. 123.
63. *Pravda*, 27 December 1934.
64. 'The Crime of the Zinoviev Opposition' p. 19, quoted by Pierre Broué in *Le Parti Bol-*

chévique, Paris, 1963, p. 351.
65. *Pravda*, 27 December 1934.
66. e.g. Lermolo, pp. 46–8.
67. ibid., pp. 45–6.
68. *Pravda*, 30 December 1934.
69. *Zinoviev Trial*, p. 145.
70. V. Petrov, *It Happens in Russia*, London, 1951, p. 31.
71. *Pravda*, 17 January 1935.
72. Deutscher, *Stalin*, p. 357.
73. *Zinoviev Trial*, p. 142.
74. ibid., p. 47.
75. ibid., pp. 147–8.
76. ibid., p. 143.
77. ibid., p. 145.
78. *Pravda*, 29 March 1937.

79. ibid., 24 January 1935.
80. *Bukharin Trial*, p. 480.
81. Orlov, pp. 23–4.
82. ibid., p. 22.
83. Victor Kravchenko, *I Chose Justice*, London, 1951, p. 260.
84. Orlov, pp. 21–2.
85. V. Petrov, p. 185.
86. Walter Krivitsky, *I Was Stalin's Agent*, London, 1940, p. 206.
87. V. Petrov, p. 185.
88. Khrushchev, Secret Speech.
89. V. Petrov, pp. 256–7.
90. Fainsod, p. 422.

CHAPTER 3: ARCHITECT OF TERROR

1. Weissberg, p. 507.
2. Arthur Koestler, *Darkness at Noon*, London, 1940, pp. 23–4.
3. Milovan Djilas, *Conversations with Stalin*, London, 1962, pp. 57–8.
4. Bukharin in conversation with Theodore and Lydia Dan in 1935 (Abramovitch, p. 416).
5. F. Beck and W. Godin, *Russian Purge and the Extraction of Confession*, London, 1951, p. 227.
6. Bernhard Roeder, *Katorga: An Aspect of Modern Slavery*, London, 1958, p. 196.
7. The problem is clearly and wittily unravelled in Bert-

ram D. Wolfe, *Three Who Made a Revolution*, Penguin ed., London, 1966.
8. Souvarine, p. 287.
9. ibid., p. 485.
10. Khrushchev, Secret Speech.
11. Tokaev, *Stalin Means War*, London, 1951, p. 115.
12. Ilya Ehrenburg in *Novy Mir*, no. 4, 1964.
13. Djilas, *Conversations with Stalin*, p. 172.
14. Iremashvili's *Memoirs* (quoted in Wolfe, p. 508).
15. Alliluyeva, *Twenty Letters to a Friend*, p. 117; Barmine, pp. 263–4; Orlov, pp. 316–18.
16. ibid., p. 122.
17. ibid., p. 116.

18. Orlov, pp. 314–25.
19. Alliluyeva, *Twenty Letters to a Friend*, p. 62.
20. Tokaev, *Stalin Means War*, p. 128.
21. ibid., p. 120; and see Alliluyeva, *Twenty Letters to a Friend*, chapter 19.
22. H. G. Wells, *The Outline of History*.
23. Barmine, p. 267; and see Alliluyeva, *Twenty Letters to a Friend*, pp. 54–5.
24. Souvarine, p. 244.
25. Khrushchev, Secret Speech.
26. Barmine, p. 305.
27. Trotsky, vol. ii, p. 225.
28. Deutscher, *Stalin*, p. 291.
29. *Nuovi Argomenti*, Special Issue for the XXIInd Party Congress, October 1961.
30. Djilas, *The New Class*, p. 128.
31. Deutscher, *Stalin*, chap. i.
32. Djilas, *The New Class*, p. 128.
33. Barmine, p. 161.
34. Djilas, *Conversations with Stalin*, p. 60.
35. Quoted in Daniels, p. 182.
36. Professor Tibor Szamuely.
37. *Novy Mir*, no. 5, 1962.
38. *Izvestia*, 6 February 1963.
39. *Mikhali Koltsov Kakim On Byl*, Moscow, 1965, p. 71.
40. B. Bazhanov, *Stalin der Rote Diktator*, p. 21.
41. Barmine, p. 257.
42. Konstantin Simonov in *Znamya*, May 1964.
43. Trotsky, vol. ii, p. 184.
44. Speech at the First Anniversary of Lenin's Death, 1925.
45. Djilas, *Conversations with Stalin*, p. 63.
46. Adolf Hitler, *Mein Kampf*, trans. James Murphy, London, 1939, p. 110.
47. Stalin, *Notes of a Delegate*, English ed., London, 1941, p. 13.
48. *Novy Mir*, no. 4, 1964.
49. *Pravda*, 1 July 1950 (official criticism of Academician Orbeli at a joint session of the Academy of Sciences and the Academy of Medical Sciences).
50. Souvarine, p. 267.
51. Khrushchev, Secret Speech.
52. Introduction to Nicolaevsky, p. xvii.
53. Alliluyeva, *Twenty Letters to a Friend*, p. 65.
54. *Novy Mir*, no. 4, 1964.
55. Humphrey Slater, *The Heretics*.
56. *Znamya*, May 1964.
57. Khrushchev, Speech to the XXIInd Party Congress (*Pravda*, 29 October 1961).
58. V. Petrov, pp. 122 ff.
59. e.g. *Large Soviet Encyclopedia*, 2nd ed., Moscow, 1949–58, *sub* Kavtaradze.
60. See Lavrentiy Beria, *Questions of the History of the Bolshevik Organisations in Transcaucasia*, Moscow, 1935; *Large Soviet Encyclopedia*, 2nd ed., vol. xxvi.
61. Barmine, p. 257.
62. In his conversation with Kamenev, July 1928.

CHAPTER 4: OLD BOLSHEVIKS CONFESS

1. e.g. Nicolaevsky, p. 66; Schapiro, p. 402; Tokaev, *Betrayal of an Ideal*, p. 248.
2. *Pravda*, 16 January 1935.
3. ibid., 23 January 1935.
4. *Bukharin Trial*, pp. 536–7.
5. ibid., p. 537.
6. ibid., p. 536.
7. 'Letter of an Old Bolshevik' (Nicolaevsky, p. 46).
8. Orlov, p. 216.
9. *Pravda*, 1 March 1935.
10. ibid., 9 March 1935.
11. Fainsod, p. 58.
12. ibid., p. 374.
13. ibid., p. 223.
14. ibid., pp. 223 ff.
15. ibid., pp. 56–7.
16. A. A. Piontkovsky and V. D. Menshagin, *Course of Soviet Criminal Law*, Moscow, 1955.
17. Alliluyeva, *Twenty Letters to a Friend*, p. 196.
18. *Izvestia*, 8 April 1935.
19. Orlov, p. 53.
20. e.g. Nicolaevsky, p. 224; Lermolo, pp. 206–7, 225–7.
21. *Byuletten Oppozitsii*, no. 47; Deutscher, *The Prophet Outcast*, p. 357; Frederick Adler, *The Witchcraft Trial in Moscow*, London, 1936, p. 26.
22. Ciliga, p. 283; and see Krivitsky, pp. 182–3.
23. *Bukharin Trial*, p. 419.
24. Lenin, *Collected Works*, vol. 53, Moscow, 1965.
25. *Bukharin Trial*, p. 396.
26. 'Letter of an Old Bolshevik' (Nicolaevsky, p. 56).
27. *Pravda*, 26 May 1935.
28. ibid., 19 May 1962.
29. *Znamya*, June 1964.
30. *Pravda*, 8 June 1935.
31. ibid., 16 and 19 June 1935.
32. Orlov, pp. 310–11.
33. Nicolaevsky, p. 224.
34. Orlov, p. 312.
35. Lermolo, pp. 121, 259–60.
36. *Pravda*, 28 June 1935.
37. *Zinoviev Trial*, p. 174.
38. Ciliga, p. 283.
39. *Pravda*, 8 February 1935.
40. Nicolaevsky, p. 22.
41. ibid., pp. 14–16.
42. 'Letter of an Old Bolshevik' (Nicolaevsky, p. 62).
43. Orlov, p. 73.
44. ibid., p. 89.
45. *Zinoviev Trial*, p. 24.
46. Orlov, p. 73.
47. See *Soviet Affairs*, no. 1 (St Antony's Papers), p. 13.
48. Orlov, p. 123.
49. ibid., pp. 338–51.
50. Andrei Vyshinsky, *The Judicial System of the U.S.S.R.* Moscow, 1936, p. 24.
51. Orlov, pp. 82–4.
52. ibid., p. 73.
53. ibid., p. 119.
54. *Zinoviev Trial*, p. 97.
55. 'Ivan Ivanov', in *Sotsialisticheskii Vestnik*, March 1951.
56. *Pyatakov Trial*, p. 40.
57. Orlov, pp. 110–11.
58. See Daniels, p. 170.
59. Orlov, p. 109.

60. *Zinoviev Trial*, p. 158.
61. Abramovitch, p. 414.
62. W. Krivitsky in *Sotsialisticheskii Vestnik*, no. 8, 1938.
63. *Zinoviev Trial*, pp. 13, 31.
64. ibid., p. 33.
65. Orlov, p. 86.
66. G. A. Tokaev, *Comrade X*, London, 1956, pp. 56–7.
67. Orlov, p. 130.
68. 'Ivan Ivanov', in *Sotsialisticheskii Vestnik*, March 1951.
69. Orlov, pp. 129–30.
70. ibid., pp. 124 ff.
71. 'Letter of an Old Bolshevik' (Nicolaevsky, p. 62).
72. *Bukharin Trial*, p. 510.
73. Orlov, p. 131.
74. Khrushchev, Secret Speech.
75. Krivitsky, p. 204.
76. *Pravda*, 24 March 1937; Fainsod, pp. 56–7.
77. ibid., p. 234.
78. Orlov and Krivitsky.
79. *Zinoviev Trial*, p. 159.
80. Orlov, p. 117.
81. 'Ivan Ivanov', in *Sotsialisticheskii Vestnik*, March 1951.
82. ibid.
83. *Bukharin Trial*, p. 556.
84. Orlov, p. 149.
85. 'Letter of an Old Bolshevik' (Nicolaevsky, p. 63).
86. ibid.
87. Orlov, p. 162.
88. ibid., chapter 13.
89. ibid., p. 174; and see V. and E. Petrov, p. 45.
90. ibid., pp. 167–8.
91. General A. V. Gorbatov, *Years off My Life*, English ed., London, 1964, pp. 117–18.
92. Khrushchev, Secret Speech.
93. Shelepin's speech to the XXIInd Party Congress.
94. *Pravda*, 3 April 1964.
95. *Nova Mysl*, no. 7, 10 July 1968.
96. Orlov, pp. 168–9.
97. *Zinoviev Trial*, p. 16.
98. ibid., p. 37.
99. ibid., p. 34.
100. ibid., p. 39.
101. Serge, *From Lenin to Stalin*, p. 82.
102. *Zinoviev Trial*, p. 151.
103. ibid., p. 51.
104. ibid., p. 61.
105. ibid.
106. ibid., p. 145.
107. ibid., pp. 63–4.
108. ibid., p. 66.
109. ibid., p. 54.
110. ibid., p. 68.
111. ibid., p. 70.
112. ibid., p. 81.
113. ibid., p. 72.
114. ibid., pp. 77–8.
115. ibid., pp. 84–5.
116. ibid., p. 81.
117. ibid., p. 154.
118. ibid., p. 153.
119. Isaac Don Levine, *The Mind of an Assassin*, New York, 1959, p. 26.
120. *Pravda*, 21 August 1936.
121. *Socialdemocraten*, 1 September 1936.
122. *Not Guilty* (Report of the Dewey Commission), New York, 1937, p. 85.
123. Orlov pp. 70–71.

124. *Zinoviev Trial*, p. 103.
125. ibid.
126. ibid., p. 105.
127. ibid., p. 147.
128. ibid., p. 116.
129. ibid., p. 119.
130. ibid., p. 120.
131. ibid., p. 128.
132. ibid., pp. 152–3.
133. ibid., p. 163.
134. Orlov, p. 174.
135. *Zinoviev Trial*, p. 166.
136. ibid.
137. Orlov, pp. 175–6.
138. *Zinoviev Trial*, p. 171.
139. ibid.
140. Victor Serge, *From Lenin to Stalin*, London, 1937, pp. 146–7.
141. ibid., p. 145.
142. Weissberg, p. 526.
143. Lenin, *Collected Works*, vol. 45, Moscow, 1963.
144. Peter Yakir, *Letter to the Editor of Kommunist*, 2 March 1969 (tr. *Survey*, nos. 70–71, 1969).

145. Margarete Buber (Neumann), *Under Two Dictators*, London, 1949, pp. 151 ff.
146. 'Letter of an Old Bolshevik' (Nicolaevsky, p. 63).
147. Enver Hoxha, speech of 24 May 1964 (Albanian Telegraph Agency, 27 May 1964).
148. Alliluyeva, *Only One Year*, p. 194.
149. *Zinoviev Trial*, p. 19.
150. Georgi Dimitrov, *Selected Articles*, English ed., London, 1951, pp. 22–3.
151. ibid., p. 203.
152. *Zinoviev Trial*, p. 55.
153. ibid., p. 20.
154. ibid., p. 31.
155. ibid., p. 33.
156. ibid., p. 59.
157. ibid., p. 67.
158. Orlov., p. 179.
159. Deutscher, *The Prophet Outcast*, pp. 416–18.
160. Dallin and Nicolaevsky, p. 39.

CHAPTER 5: THE PROBLEM OF CONFESSION

1. Beck and Godin, p. 38.
2. Avtorkhanov, p. 138.
3. Abramovitch, p. 416.
4. Nicolaevsky, p. 25.
5. Souvarine, pp. 362–3.
6. *Pravda*, 29 February 1928.
7. N. Valentinov (N. V. Volsky), quoted in Schapiro, p. 381.
8. ibid., unpublished MS. quoted in Abramovitch, p. 415.

9. ibid., quoted in Schapiro, p. 381.
10. Ciliga, p. 75.
11. ibid., p. 85.
12. Arthur Koestler, *Arrow in the Blue*, vol. 2, London, 1945, p. 155.
13. Ciliga, p. 255.
14. *Pravda*, 15 December 1923.
15. ibid., 18 January 1924.
16. Abramovitch, p. 288.

17. *Stenographic Report of the XIVth Party Congress*, Moscow, 1926.
18. See Souvarine, p. 459.
19. ibid., p. 440.
20. See Schapiro, pp. 294–5.
21. Angelica Balabanoff, *Impressions of Lenin*, Ann Arbor, 1964.
22. *Zinoviev Trial*, p. 133.
23. *Pravda*, 16 June 1933.
24. 'Letter of an Old Bolshevik' (Nicolaevsky, pp. 54–5).
25. Ginzburg, pp. 105–6.
26. Koestler, *Darkness at Noon*, p. 242.
27. Beck and Godin, p. 86.
28. ibid.
29. Koestler, *Arrow in the Blue*, vol. 2, p. 394.
30. A. Tairov before the French 'Commission Rogatoire' (quoted in Report of Dewey Commission, p. 370).
31. Koestler, *Darkness at Noon*, p. 183.
32. *Bukharin Trial*, pp. 777–8.
33. Orlov, pp. 117–18.
34. Serge, *From Lenin to Stalin*, p. 145.
35. Orlov, pp. 145–6.
36. ibid., p. 149.
37. Ciliga, p. 283.
38. *Pyatakov Trial*, p. 204.
39. Khrushchev, Concluding Remarks to the XXIInd Party Congress.
40. Khrushchev, Secret Speech.
41. Kravchenko, *I Chose Justice*, pp. 252–4.
42. ibid., p. 169.
43. ibid., p. 154.
44. Lermolo, p. 44.
45. Kravchenko, *I Chose Justice*, pp. 169–70.
46. Tokaev, *Betrayal of an Ideal*, pp. 264–6.
47. e.g. Neumann, p. 41; R. V. Ivanov-Razumnik, *Memoirs*, English ed., London, 1965, p. 222; Anon., *The Dark Side of the Moon*, London, 1946; Ginzburg, p. 97 etc.
48. Ivanov-Razumnik, p. 240.
49. ibid., p. 253.
50. ibid., p. 246; Ginzburg, pp. 118, 122; Kravchenko, *I Chose Justice*, pp. 274–5.
51. ibid., p. 238.
52. See notes by Boris Nicolaevsky to *The Crimes of the Stalin Era* (*New Leader* edition of Khrushchev's Secret Speech, New York, 1956).
53. Khrushchev, Secret Speech.
54. Gorbatov, p. 113.
55. Ivanov-Razumnik, pp. 248–9.
56. *Sovietskoye Gosudarstvo i Pravo*, no. 3, March 1965.
57. Weissberg, p. 236.
58. Antoni Ekart, *Vanished Without Trace*, London, 1954, p. 175.
59. Ginzburg, pp. 69–72.
60. *Bukharin Trial*, p. 252.
61. V. Dushenkin, *Ot Soldata do Marshala*, Moscow, 1964.
62. Beck and Godin, pp. 53–4.
63. Ivanov-Razumnik, pp. 244–6; and see Yakir, *Survey*, nos. 70–71, 1969.
64. Weissberg, pp. 163–4.

65. ibid., p. 297.
66. ibid., pp. 386–7.
67. Beck and Godin, p. 71.
68. El Campesino, *Listen, Comrades*, London, 1952, p. 132; and see Alexander Solzhenitsyn, *The First Circle*, London, 1968, p. 150.
69. Z. Stypulkowski, *Invitation to Moscow*, London, 1951, chapters xii-xiv.
70. Artur London, *L'Aveu*, Paris, 1969.
71. Evzen (Eugen) Loebl and Dusan Pokorny, *Die Revolution Rehabilitiert Ihre Kinder*, Vienna, 1968.
72. Ciliga, p. 154.
73. Orlov, p. 54.
74. Stypulkowski, p. 242.
75. Khrushchev, Concluding Remarks to the XXIInd Party Congress.
76. Arthur Koestler, Introduction to Weissberg, pp. xi–xii.
77. Kravchenko, *I Chose Freedom*, pp. 284–90.
78. Ivanov-Razumnik, p. 250.
79. *Nova Mysl*, no. 7, 10 July 1968.
80. Kostiuk, p. 119.
81. Weissberg, p. 415.
82. ibid., pp. 352–5.
83. *Novaya Zhizn*, 8 June 1918 (see J. E. Scott, 'The Cheka', *Soviet Affairs*, no. 1, p. 8).
84. *Sovietskoye Gosudarstvo i Pravo*, no. 3, March 1965.
85. Kravchenko, *I Chose Justice*, pp. 169–72.

CHAPTER 6: LAST STAND

1. 'Letter of an Old Bolshevik' (Nicolaevsky, p. 26).
2. *Pyatakov Case*, pp. 202, 214.
3. ibid., p. 561.
4. ibid., p. 167.
5. *Pravda*, 28 August 1936.
6. ibid., 1 September 1936.
7. 'Letter of an Old Bolshevik' (Nicolaevsky, p. 63).
8. *Pyatakov Trial*, p. 17.
9. Alexander Uralov (A. Avtorkhanov), *The Reign of Stalin*, London, 1959, p. 223.
10. e.g. Schapiro, p. 415.
11. *Bukharin Trial*, p. 125.
12. Khrushchev, Secret Speech.
13. 'Letter of an Old Bolshevik' (Nicolaevsky, p. 64).
14. Orlov, p. 143.
15. *Bukharin Trial*, p. 556.
16. Simon Wolin and Robert M. Slusser, *The Soviet Secret Police*, New York, 1957, p. 45.
17. *Bukharin Trial*, p. 553.
18. Tokaev, *Betrayal of an Ideal*, pp. 249–50.
19. 'Letter of an Old Bolshevik' (Nicolaevsky, p. 63).
20. Khrushchev, Secret Speech.
21. *Bukharin Trial*, p. 281.
22. Orlov, p. 180.
23. ibid., p. 206.
24. *Pyatakov Trial*, p. 134.
25. Orlov, p. 205.
26. Pierre Broué, *Le Procès de Moscou*, Paris, 1964, p. 276.
27. Weissberg, p. 56.

28. Orlov, p. 189.
29. ibid., pp. 187–9.
30. *Sovietskoye Gosudarstvo i Pravo*, no. 3, March 1965.
31. *Pyatakov Trial*, p. 287.
32. Orlov, p. 182.
33. Kravchenko, *I Chose Freedom*, p. 331.
34. Weissberg, p. 232.
35. Kravchenko, *I Chose Freedom*, pp. 329–30.
36. *Pyatakov Trial*, p. 257.
37. ibid., p. 537.
38. Orlov, p. 183.
39. *Pravda*, 30 May 1937.
40. *Essays on the History of the Communist Party of the Ukraine*, 2nd ed., Kiev, 1964, p. 466.
41. Stalin, speech to the February–March 1937 plenum, 5 March 1937.
42. *Pravda*, 29 May 1937.
43. G. Maryagin, *Postyshev*, Moscow, 1965, p. 291.
44. I. Dubinsky-Rukhadze, *Ordzhonikidze*, Moscow, 1963, p. 5.
45. *Bukharin Trial*, p. 126.
46. Orlov, p. 190.
47. ibid., p. 207.
48. ibid., p. 350.
49. Resolutions of the Congress of the Communist Party of the Ukraine (*Pravda*, 13 June 1937).
50. *Visti*, 1 June 1937.
51. *Pyatakov Trial*, p. 40.
52. Barmine, p. 295.
53. e.g. *Pravda*, 12 September 1936.
54. Stalin, speech to the February–March plenum of the Central Committee, 3 March 1937.
55. *Pyatakov Trial*, p. 7.
56. ibid., p. 14.
57. ibid., p. 43.
58. ibid., p. 48.
59. ibid., p. 49.
60. ibid.
61. ibid., p. 25.
62. ibid., p. 413.
63. ibid., p. 69.
64. ibid., pp. 58 ff.
65. Orlov, p. 191.
66. *Pyatakov Trial*, p. 443.
67. ibid., p. 85.
68. ibid., p. 125.
69. ibid.
70. ibid., p. 127.
71. ibid., p. 129.
72. ibid., p. 135.
73. ibid., p. 105.
74. ibid., p. 160.
75. ibid., p. 209.
76. ibid., p. 210.
77. ibid., p. 245.
78. ibid., p. 257.
79. ibid., p. 258.
80. ibid., p. 283.
81. ibid., p. 280.
82. ibid., p. 288.
83. ibid., p. 248.
84. ibid., p. 271.
85. ibid., p. 272.
86. ibid., p. 229.
87. ibid., p. 226.
88. ibid., p. 222.
89. N. M. Shvernik, speech at the XXIInd Party Congress (*Pravda*, 26 October 1961).
90. *Pyatakov Trial*, p. 222.
91. ibid., p. 511.

92. ibid., p. 475.
93. ibid., pp. 302–33.
94. ibid., pp. 566–7.
95. ibid., p. 569.
96. ibid., p. 367.
97. ibid., p. 368.
98. ibid., p. 365.
99. ibid., pp. 371–2, 378.
100. ibid., p. 412.
101. ibid., p. 463.
102. ibid., p. 466.
103. ibid., p. 480.
104. ibid., p. 494.
105. ibid., p. 474.
106. ibid., p. 468.
107. ibid., p. 514.
108. ibid., pp. 476–7.
109. ibid., p. 489.
110. ibid., p. 207.
111. ibid., p. 170.
112. ibid., p. 502.
113. ibid., p. 512.
114. ibid., p. 517.
115. ibid., p. 481.
116. ibid., p. 516.
117. ibid., p. 517.
118. ibid., p. 541.
119. ibid., p. 548.
120. ibid., p. 543.
121. Elisabeth K. Poretsky, *Our Own People*, London, 1969, p. 198.
122. Orlov, p. 212.
123. e.g. Walter Duranty, *The Kremlin and the People*, London, 1942, p. 73.
124. e.g. V. and E. Petrov, *Empire of Fear*, London, 1956, p. 69; Herling, p. 22.
125. *Stenographic Report of the XIth Party Congress*, Moscow, 1961.
126. Wolin and Slusser, p. 194.
127. Lermolo, pp. 134–5.
128. Khrushchev, speech of 8 March 1963.
129. *Pyatakov Trial*, p. 545.
130. ibid., p. 514.
131. ibid., p. 353.
132. Lermolo, p. 241.
133. *Pravda*, 29 January 1937.
134. ibid., 31 January 1937.
135. Kravchenko, *I Chose Freedom*, p. 239.
136. *Pyatakov Trial*, p. 510.
137. *Izvestia*, 22 November 1963.
138. *Kommunist* (Armenia), 26 June 1965.
139. Khrushchev, Report to the XXIInd Party Congress.
140. *Bakinski Rabochy*, 27 May 1956.
141. Robert Conquest, *Power and Policy in the U.S.S.R.*, London, 1961, pp. 449–53.
142. Weissberg, pp. 360–4.
143. Kravchenko, *I Chose Freedom*, p. 254.
144. *Izvestia*, 22 November 1963; and Dubinsky-Rukhadze, p. 6.
145. ibid.
146. ibid.
147. *Pravda*, 19 February, 1937.
148. Dubinsky-Rukhadze, p. 7.
149. *Pravda*, 22 February 1937.
150. *Large Soviet Encyclopedia*, 2nd ed., *sub* Ordzhonikidze.
151. *Na Rubezhe*, nos. 3–4, 1952.
152. Kravchenko, *I Chose Freedom*, p. 240.
153. Khrushchev, speech to the XXIInd Party Congress.

154. *Bakinski Rabochy*, 17 June 1962.
155. Ginzburg, p. 73.
156. *Pravda*, 17 November 1964.
157. e.g. Orlov, pp. 196–8.
158. Khrushchev, speech to the XXIInd Party Congress.
159. Private interview with author.
160. Avtorkhanov, p. 229.
161. *Izvestia*, 22 November 1963.
162. *Pravda*, 21 February 1937.
163. *Zinoviev Trial*, p. 162.
164. *Pravda*, 19 February 1937.
165. *Large Soviet Encyclopedia*, 2nd ed., vol. 31.
166. P. I. Yakir and Ya. A. Geller, *Komandarm Yakir*, Moscow, 1963, p. 211.
167. Khrushchev, Secret Speech.
168. Satyukov, speech to the XXIInd Party Congress.
169. Kostiuk, pp. 118–22, originally given in his paper *The Fall of Postyshev*, Research Program on the U.S.S.R. no. 6a, New York, 1954.
170. *Visti*, 1 February 1937.
171. *Pravda*, 8 February 1937.
172. ibid., 9 February 1937.
173. ibid., 5 June 1937.
174. Khrushchev, Secret Speech.
175. ibid.
176. ibid.
177. Oral information.
178. *Pravda*, 6 March 1937.
179. Litvinov's account, in Joseph E. Davies, *Mission to Moscow*, London, 1942, p. 172.
180. Khrushchev in *Pravda*, 17 March 1937.
181. Ikramov at the *Bukharin Trial*, p. 349.
182. Uralov, p. 118.
183. Krivitsky, p. 227.
184. Khrushchev, Secret Speech.
185. Krivitsky, p. 228.
186. Shvernik, speech to the XXIInd Party Congress (*Pravda*, 26 October 1961).
187. Quoted in *The Moscow Trial*, compiled by W. P. and Zelda K. Coates, London, 1937, p. 249.
188. ibid., p. 253.
189. ibid., p. 205.
190. Quoted by Vyshinsky (*Bukharin Trial*, p. 626).
191. Quoted in *The Moscow Trial*, pp. 275–6.
192. ibid., p. 277.
193. ibid., p. 279.
194. *Visti*, 17 March 1937.
195. *Pravda*, 19 January 1938 (Report of the January plenum of the Central Committee).
196. ibid., 23 March 1937.
197. ibid., 29 May 1937.
198. ibid., 30 May 1937.
199. *Visti*, 2 June 1937.
200. Orlov, p. 221.
201. ibid.
202. Krivitsky, p. 167.
203. Orlov, p. 222.
204. *Bukharin Trial*, p. 482.
205. Orlov, p. 225.
206. *Bukharin Trial*, p. 569
207. ibid., p. 571.
208. ibid., p. 556.
209. *Pravda*, 4 April 1937.
210. ibid., 5 April 1937.
211. Zbigniew Brzezinski, *The Permanent Purge*, Cam-

bridge, Mass., 1956, p. 229.

212. Alliluyeva, *Only One Year*, p. 388.

213. *Sovietskoye Gosudarstvo i Pravo*, no. 3, March 1965.

214. *Sotsialisticheskaya Zakonnost*, no. 1, 1938.

215. *Pravda*, 20 January 1937.

216. ibid., 9 April 1937.

217. *Voprosy Istorii K.P.S.S.*, no. 6, 1965

CHAPTER 7: ASSAULT ON THE ARMY

1. *Pravda*, 11 June 1937.
2. ibid., 15 June 1937.
3. John Erickson, *The Soviet High Command*, London, 1962, p. 58.
4. Robert S. Sullivant, *Soviet Politics and the Ukraine, 1917–1957*, New York, 1963, p. 342.
5. Quoted in Erickson, p. 51.
6. ibid., p. 99.
7. ibid.
8. Deutscher, *The Prophet Unarmed*, p. 350.
9. *Izvestia*, 24–30 January 1963; N. I. Koritsky *et al.*, *Marshal Tukhachevsky*, Moscow, 1965.
10. Uralov, p. 46; and see Kostiuk, p. 121.
11. *Bukharin Trial*, p. 188.
12. P. Deriabin and F. Gibney, *The Secret World*, London, 1960, pp. 110–11.
13. Deutscher, *Stalin*, p. 379.
14. Beck and Godin, p. 95.
15. *Bukharin Trial*, pp. 570, 177.
16. ibid., p. 253.
17. ibid., p. 256.
18. ibid., p. 71.
19. Orlov, p. 242.
20. Krivitsky, p. 7.

21. I. V. Dubinsky, *Naperekor Vetram*, Moscow, 1964, pp. 243 ff.
22. *Zinoviev Trial*, pp. 34, 41.
23. Vassili Grossman, *In the Town of Berdichev*.
24. Barmine, pp. 89–90.
25. *Zinoviev Trial*, p. 36.
26. Dubinsky, loc. cit.
27. *Pravda*, 23 August 1936.
28. *Pyatakov Trial*, p. 181.
29. ibid., p. 94.
30. Dubinsky, loc. cit.; *Voenno-Istoricheskiy Zhurnal*, no. 6, 1965.
31. ibid.
32. *Zinoviev Trial*, p. 116.
33. Barmine, p. 311.
34. *Geroy Grazhdanskoy Voyny*, Moscow, 1963, p. 218.
35. Erickson, pp. 376–7.
36. *Zinoviev Trial*, p. 22.
37. Dubinsky, loc. cit.
38. Erickson, p. 427.
39. Uralov, p. 48.
40. *Pyatakov Trial*, p. 146.
41. Krivitsky, p. 239.
42. Yakir and Geller, pp. 207 ff.
43. Dubinsky, loc. cit.
44. Yakir and Geller, p. 212.
45. Yu. P. Petrov, *Partiynoe Stroitel'stvo v Sovetskoy Ar-*

mii i Flote (1918–1961), Moscow, 1964, p. 299.

46. ibid.
47. Yakir and Geller, p. 212.
48. Krivitsky, pp. 250–51; Barmine, p. 7.
49. Koritsky, pp. 219 ff.
50. Yu. P. Petrov, p. 303.
51. Dubinsky, loc. cit.
52. *Voenno-Istoricheskiy Zhurnal*, no. 4, 1964; Alvin D. Coox in *Soviet Studies*, January 1968; Yakir, *Survey*, nos. 70–71, 1969.
53. W. Schellenberg, *The Schellenberg Memoirs*, London, 1956, p. 49.
54. See speech of O. Pyatnitsky at the XIIth plenum of the Executive Committee of the Comintern.
55. Hermann Rauschning, *Hitler Speaks*, New York, 1940, p. 134.
56. *Novy Mir*, no. 4, 1964.
57. Beck and Godin, p. 198.
58. *Stenographic Report of the XVIIth Party Congress*, Moscow, 1934.
59. Krivitsky, p. 31.
60. e.g. Geoffrey Bailey, *The Conspirators*, London, 1961, p. 147.
61. Krivitsky, p. 237.
62. Major V. Dapishev of the Soviet General Staff at a session of the Department for the History of the Great Patriotic War at the Institute of Marxism-Leninism, 18 February 1966, as quoted in *Posev*, 13 January 1967; see

also Ernst Genri (S. N. Rostovsky), as quoted in *Grani*, no. 63, 1967.
63. Erickson, pp. 433–4.
64. Wilhelm Hoettl, *The Secret Front*, London, 1954.
65. W. Gomulka, Report to the IXth Plenum of the Central Committee of the Polish Workers' Party (*Trybuna Ludu*, 23 November 1961).
66. e.g. Lev Nikulin, *Marshal Tukhachevsky*, Moscow, 1964; Khrushchev, speech to the XXIInd Party Congress; Winston Churchill, *The Second World War*, vol. i, London, 1948, p. 224.
67. Léon Blum, quoted by Erickson, p. 433.
68. *Trybuna Ludu*, 23 November 1961.
69. Private information from Mr John Erickson.
70. Nikulin, pp. 189–94.
71. *Ukrainian Soviet Encyclopedia*.
72. Krivitsky, p. 27.
73. D. V. Pankov, *Komkor Eideman*, Moscow, 1965, p. 103.
74. *Voprosy Istorii K.P.S.S.*, no. 12, 1964.
75. Koritsky, p. 134.
76. Nikulin, loc. cit.
77. Koritsky, pp. 128–9.
78. ibid.; *Voenno-Istoricheskiy-Zhurnal*, no. 10, 1965.
79. Nikulin, loc. cit.
80. Yakir and Geller, pp. 227 ff.
81. P. N. Aleksandrov *et al.*, *Komandarm Uborevich*, Moscow, 1964, pp. 230 ff.

82. Gorbatov, p. 103.
83. Yakir and Geller, loc. cit.
84. Dubinsky; Nikulin; Yakir and Geller.
85. *Pravda*, 1 June 1937.
86. Weissberg, p. 428; Krivitsky, p. 254.
87. Yu. P. Petrov, p. 299; *Krasnaya Zvezda*, 13 April 1962.
88. *Voenno-Istoricheskiy Zhurnal*, no. 5, 1964.
89. e.g. Krivitsky, p. 230.
90. *Krasnaya Zvezda*, 6 June 1937.
91. Yakir and Geller, pp. 230–2.
92. Dubinsky, chapter xiv.
93. A. N. Shelepin, speech to the XXIInd Party Congress.
94. Yu. P. Petrov, pp. 299–300.
95. ibid.
96. Nikulin, pp. 189–94.
97. Peter Yakir, at a session of the Department for the History of the Great Patriotic War at the Institute of Marxism-Leninism, 18 February 1966 (*Posev*, 13 January 1967).
98. *Bukharin Trial*, p. 5.
99. *Soviet Historical Encyclopedia*.
100. Serge, *From Lenin to Stalin*, p. 222.
101. Krivitsky, p. 255.
102. e.g. Orlov, Barmine.
103. Dubinsky, p. 267.
104. Lev Nikulin, in *Ogonëk*, no. 13, March 1963.
105. Dubinsky, p. 268.
106. *Geroy Grazhdanskoy Voyny*, p. 120.
107. Ilya Ehrenburg, *Men, Years and Life*, English ed., vol. iv, London, 1963, p. 147.
108. Orlov, p. 243.
109. Khrushchev, speech to the XXIInd Party Congress.
110. A. N. Shelepin, speech to the XXIInd Party Congress (*Pravda*, 27 October 1961).
111. Yakir and Geller, pp. 230–32.
112. *Kazakhstanskaya Pravda*, 15 October 1963.
113. Neumann, p. 56.
114. Yakir and Geller, p. 232.
115. Khrushchev, speech to the XXIInd Party Congress.
116. *Bilshovik Ukrainy*, no. 6, 1938.
117. Aleksandrov, pp. 265 ff.
118. Barmine, p. 8.
119. Lev Nikulin, in *Oktyabr*, 2–5, 1965.
120. Ekart, p. 244.
121. *Ogonyek*, no. 13, 1963.
122. Barmine, p. 8.
123. Wolin and Slusser, p. 194.
124. Yakir, *Survey*, nos. 70–71, 1969.
125. *Voenno-Istoricheskiy Zhurnal*, no. 5, 1966; *Soviet Historical Encyclopedia*.
126. Barmine, p. 8.
127. Tokaev, *Betrayal of an Ideal*, p. 244.
128. Marshal S. T. Biryuzov, *Sovietskii Soldat na Balkanakh*, Moscow, 1963, p. 141.
129. A. T. Stuchenko, *Zavidnaya Nasha Sudba*, Moscow, 1964, p. 63.
130. ibid., p. 64.
131. Barmine, pp. 6–8.

132. *Ukrainsky Istoricheskiy Zhurnal*, no. 6, 1963.
133. Gorbatov, p. 104.
134. I. T. Starinov, *Miny Zhdut Svoego Chasa*, Moscow, 1964, pp. 149–66.
135. Gorbatov, p. 104
136. Weissberg, pp. 422–3.
137. Stuchenko, op. cit.
138. *Byelarus*, no. 7, 1965.
139. Stuchenko, op. cit.; and see *Voenno-Istoricheskiy Zhurnal*, no. 8, 1966.
140. Yu. P. Petrov, pp. 299–300.
141. *Krasnaya Zvezda*, 2 June 1937.
142. L. Gaglov and I. Selishchev *Komissary*, Moscow, 1961.
143. Yu. P. Petrov, p. 302.
144. *Krasnaya Zvezda*, 1 June 1937.
145. Ernst Genri (S. N. Rostovsky): see *Grani*, no. 63, 1967.
146. Yu. P. Petrov, pp. 299–300.
147. ibid., p. 302.
148. ibid., pp. 301–2.
149. ibid., p. 302.
150. ibid., p. 304.
151. ibid., p. 312.
152. ibid., p. 303 n.
153. ibid., pp. 299–300.
154. Lenin, *Collected Works*, vol. 51, Moscow, 1965.
155. *Small Soviet Encyclopedia*.
156. Tokaev, *Betrayal of an Ideal*, p. 189.
157. A. Dyakov, in *Oktyabr*, no. 7, 1964.
158. Gorbatov, p. 107.
159. ibid., pp. 108 ff.
160. Beck and Godin, pp. 96–97.
161. Khrushchev, speech to the XXIInd Party Congress.
162. Beck and Godin, p. 48.
163. Weissberg, p. 27.
164. *Krasnaya Zvezda*, 2 March 1965.
165. *Komsomolskaya Pravda*, 13 November 1964.
166. Ilya Ehrenburg, in *Novy Mir*, no. 5, 1962.
167. Orlov, p. 241.
168. Ehrenburg, vol. iv, pp. 152, 146.
169. *Under the Flag of the Spanish Republic*, Moscow, 1965, p. 190.
170. Djilas, *Conversations with Stalin*, p. 13.
,171. Ernst Genri (S. N. Rostovsky): see *Grani*, no. 63, 1967.
172. Erickson, p. 475.
173. Tevosyan, speech to the XVIIIth Party Congress.
174. Admiral N. G. Kuznetsov, *Oktyabr*, no. 11, 1965.
175. Ivanov–Razumnik, p. 246.
176. *Voenno-Istoricheskiy Zhurnal*, no. 11, 1965.
177. *Soviet Historical Encyclopedia*.
178. ibid.; S. E. Zakharov, *et al.*, *Tikhookeansky Flot*, Moscow, 1966.
179. *Novy Mir*, no. 8, 1961, pp. 160–83.
180. Yu. P. Petrov, p. 301.
181. *Voenno-Istoricheskiy Zhurnal*, no. 6, 1963.
182. Orlov, p. 246.
183. Weissberg, p. 481.
184. *Pravda*, 17 February 1964.
185. Souvarine, p. 258.

186. *Geroy Grazhdanskoy Voyny*, p. 330.
187. Barmine, p. 95.
188. *Pravda*, 3 April 1964.
189. Erickson, pp. 66–7.
190. *Soviet Historical Encyclopedia*; *Ukrainian Soviet Encyclopedic Dictionary*; *Voennyy Vestnik*, no. 9, 1966; *Voenno-Istoricheskiy Zhurnal*, no. 9, 1966; *Large Soviet Encyclopedia*, 3rd ed., vol. i.
191. e.g. Koritsky; *Zarya Vostoka*, 21 March 1965; *Voenno-Istoricheskiy Zhurnal*, no. 4, 1965.
192. *Voenno-Istoricheskiy Zhurnal*, no. 2, 1963.
193. L. P. Petrovsky. *Letter to the Central Committee*.
194. *Soviet Historical Encyclopedia*.
195. ibid.

CHAPTER 8: THE PARTY CRUSHED

1. *Pravda*, 14 April 1937.
2. I. V. Spiridonov, speech to the XXIInd Party Congress.
3. Roy Medvedev, *Faut-il réhabiliter Staline?*, Paris, 1969, p. 42.
4. *Pravda*, 21 March 1937.
5. D. A. Lazurkina, speech to the XXIInd Party Congress.
6. *Pravda*, 30 May 1937.
7. ibid., 5 June 1938.
8. *Short Soviet Encyclopedia*, Addenda.
9. Ciliga, p. 48.
10. ibid., p. 160.
11. *Bukharin Trial*, p. 160.
12. Khrushchev, Secret Speech.
13. ibid.
14. *Zinoviev Trial*, p. 34.
15. Lermolo, p. 83.
16. *Pyatakov Trial*, pp. 95–7.
17. *Leningrad Encylopedia*, Leningrad, 1957.
18. *Encyclopedic Dictionary*.
19. Lenin, *Collected Works*, vol. 50, Moscow, 1965.
20. *Stenographic Report of the VIIth Party Congress*, Moscow, 1962.
21. *Ot Fevralya k Oktyabryu*, Moscow, 1957, notes.
22. *Essays on the History of Leningrad*, vol. iv, Moscow–Leningrad, 1964, p. 381.
23. Brzezinski, p. 226.
24. D. A. Lazurkina, speech to the XXIInd Party Congress.
25. *Large Soviet Encyclopedia*, 2nd ed., *sub* Kosygin.
26. Khrushchev, Secret Speech.
27. ibid.
28. Serdyuk, speech to the XXIInd Party Congress.
29. Yu. M. Vecherova, speech to the XXIInd Party Congress.
30. *Essays on the History of the Moscow Organization of the Party*, Moscow, 1966, p. 539.
31. A. N. Vasilev, 'Are There Any More Questions?', *Moskva*, June 1964.

32. Fainsod, p. 190.
33. ibid.
34. *Bakinski Rabochy*, 17 June 1962.
35. Khrushchev, Secret Speech.
36. Uralov, p. 147.
37. Radio Moscow, 18 September 1964.
38. *Bukharin Trial*, p. 76.
39. *Voprosy Istorii K.P.S.S.*, no. 11, 1963.
40. K. T. Mazurov, speech to the XXIInd Party Congress.
41. ibid.
42. *Rabochii* (Minsk), 8 June 1937.
43. *Izvestia*, 23 May 1964.
44. K. T. Mazurov, speech to the XXIInd Party Congress.
45. *Rabochii* (Minsk), 12 August 1937.
46. Beck and Godin, p. 92.
47. See Brzezhinski, pp. 180–84.
48. *Kommunist* (Armenia), 28 November 1963.
49. Nicolaevsky, note to *Crimes of the Stalin Era* (Khrushchev's Secret Speech, *New Leader* edition).
50. *Pravda*, 23 June 1929.
51. *Pyatakov Trial*, p. 74.
52. *Bukharin Trial*, p. 304.
53. Orlov, p. 249.
54. *Byuletten Oppozitsii*, nos. 56–7, 1937.
55. *Voprosy Istorii K.P.S.S.*, no. 5, 1963.
56. Souvarine, p. 638.
57. Yakir, *Survey*, nos. 70–71, 1964.
58. Dzhashi, speech to the XVIIIth Party Congress.
59. *Pravda*, 17 May 1937.
60. *Kommunist* (Armenia), 15 November 1961.
61. ibid.; Shelepin, speech to the XXIInd Party Congress.
62. Mary Matossian, *The Impact of Soviet Politics in Armenia*, Leyden, 1962.
63. *Kommunist* (Armenia), 15 November 1961.
64. *Zarya Vostoka*, 31 December 1937.
65. Ginzburg, p. 100.
66. Sullivant, p. 194.
67. *Stalin's Works* (Russian ed., 1946–51), vol. viii, pp. 149–50.
68. In his conversation with Kamenev in July 1928.
69. Tokaev, p. 57.
70. Pyatakov, speech to the VIIIth Party Congress (Sullivant, p. 32a).
71. Sullivant, p. 193.
72. G. Petrovsky, speech to the XVIIth Party Congress.
73. S. Kossior, speech to the XIIIth Congress of the Communist Party of the Ukraine, 27 May 1937.
74. Khrushchev, Speech of 5 June 1938 (*Bilshovik Ukrainy*, no. 6, 1938).
75. *Pravda*, 26 May 1937.
76. ibid., 29 May 1937.
77. *Partiinoe Stroitelstvo*, no. 15, 1937.
78. *Pravda*, 21 July 1937.
79. ibid., 22 July 1937.
80. ibid., 25 July 1937.
81. Sullivant, p. 222.
82. *Posev*, vol. vi, nos. 45, 50.

83. Vladimir Dedijer, *Tito Speaks*, London, 1953, p. 201.
84. *Pravda*, 18 September 1937.
85. ibid., 1 October and 29 December 1937.
86. ibid., 25 September 1937.
87. ibid., 4 October 1937.
88. ibid., 18 September 1937.
89. *Volodimir Petrovich Zatonsky* (in Ukrainian), Kiev, 1964, p. 132.
90. F. Bega and V. Aleksandrov, *Petrovsky*, Moscow, 1963.
91. *Voprosy Istorii K.P.S.S.*, no. 6, 1963.
92. *Pravda*, 19 January 1938.
93. Z. T. Serdyuk, speech to the XVIIIth Party Congress.
94. Brzezinski, p. 78.
95. *Pravda*, 22 February 1938.
96. Weissberg, pp. 461–2.
97. *Visti*, 28 January 1938.
98. Sullivant, p. 223.
99. Burmistenko, speech to the XVIIIth Party Congress.
100. Edward R. Stettinius, Jr., *Roosevelt and the Russians: The Yalta Conference*.
101. Khrushchev, Secret Speech.
102. ibid.
103. Roy Medvedev, p. 43.
104. *Pravda*, 3 April 1964.
105. Z. T. Serdyuk, speech to the XXIInd Party Congress (*Pravda*, 31 October 1961).
106. Ivanov–Razumnik, p. 307; Orlov, p. 241.
107. Weissberg, p. 168.
108. Fitzroy Maclean, *Eastern Approaches*, London, 1949, p. 28.
109. *Československy Časopis Historicky*, no. 4, 1964.
110. Ginzburg, p. 115.
111. Alliluyeva, *Only One Year*, p. 388.
112. *Bukharin Trial*, p. 277.
113. Louis Fischer, *Men and Politics*, London, 1941, p. 414.
114. Barmine, p. 307.
115. *Bukharin Trial*, p. 252.
116. ibid., p. 55.
117. ibid., p. 777.
118. A. N. Shelepin, speech to the XXIInd Party Congress (*Pravda*, 27 October 1961).
119. ibid.
120. *Stenographic Report of the XIth Party Congress*, Moscow, 1961.
121. *Bukharin Trial*, pp. 459–67.
122. *Pravda*, 17 November 1964.
123. Ginzburg, pp. 118, 139.
124. *Bukharin Trial*, p. 78.
125. Khrushchev, Secret Speech.
126. *Voprosy Istorii K.P.S.S.*, no. 11, 1965.
127. A. S. Yakovlev, *Tsel'Zhizni*, Moscow, 1966, p. 177.
128. *Izvestia*, 19 December 1964.
129. *Bukharin Trial*, p. 204.
130. Beck and Godin, p. 80.
131. Kravchenko, *I Chose Justice*, p. 235.
132. *Pravda*, 22 July 1937.
133. ibid., 17 March 1937.
134. *Large Soviet Encyclopedia*, 2nd ed., vol. li.
135. *Pravda*, 20 August 1937.
136. ibid., 29 August 1937.
137. ibid., 30 October 1937.
138. *History of the Civil War*, vol. i, Moscow, 1960.

139. *Pravda*, 8 September 1937.
140. *Ot Fevralya k Oktyabryu*, Moscow, 1957.
141. Lenin, *Collected Works*, vol. 50, Moscow, 1965.
142. *Bukharin Trial*, p. 764.
143. Louis Fischer, *Men and Politics*, p. 409.
144. *Bukharin Trial*, p. 796.
145. Barmine, p. 245.
146. *Bukharin Trial*, p. 623.
147. *Sovietskoye Gosudarstvo i Pravo*, no. 3, March 1965; see also Kravchenko, *I Chose Justice*, p. 157.
148. See *Bukharin Trial*, p. 696.
149. A. Binevich and Z. Serebryansky, *Andrei Bubnov*, Moscow, 1964, pp. 78–9.
150. *Voprosy Istorii K.P.S.S.*, no. 4, 1963.
151. A. N. Shelepin, speech to the XXIInd Party Congress (*Pravda*, 27 October 1961).
152. Personal information.
153. Beck and Godin, p. 97.
154. Neumann, p. 26.
155. e.g. *Pravda*, 2 May, 15 June, 29 October 1937, etc.
156. *Voprosy Istorii K.P.S.S.*, no. 2, 1963.
157. *Pravda*, 25 December 1964; *Voprosy Istorii K.P.S.S.*, no. 7, 1964.
158. Ivanov-Razumnik, p. 313.
159. *Sovietskaya Iustitsiya*, no. 10, 1965.
160. See Souvarine, p. 575.
161. Ivanov-Razumnik, p. 313.
162. See D. J. Richards, *Soviet Chess*, Oxford, 1965, p. 57.
163. *History of the Civil War*, Moscow, 1960.
164. G. Maryagin, *Postyshev*, Moscow, 1965, p. 247.
165. *Voprosy Istorii K.P.S.S.*, no. 7, 1965.
166. *Sovietskoye Gosudarstvo i Pravo*, no. 3, March 1965.
167. *Pravda*, 2 November 1937.
168. ibid., 7 November 1937.
169. ibid., 20 December 1937.
170. Lermolo, pp. 233–4.
171. *Bukharin Trial*, p. 22.
172. ibid., p. 23.
173. Lermolo, p. 275.
174. e.g. *Large Soviet Encyclopedia*, 2nd ed., vol. li; *The Party in the Period of Foreign Intervention and Civil War, 1918–1920*, Moscow, 1962. But the date is again given as 'December 1937' in the more recent *Soviet Historical Encyclopedia*, vol. 10, 1967.
175. *Pravda*, 10 June 1963.
176. ibid., 21 December 1937.
177. ibid., 19 January 1938.
178. *The Communist Party of the Soviet Union in Resolutions*, etc., 6th ed., vol. ii, 1953.
179. Maryagin, p. 298.
180. Radio Moscow, 8 February 1964.
181. Yakir, *Survey*, nos. 70–71, 1969.
182. *Pyatakov Trial*, p. 207.
183. *Stanislav Vinkentiyovich Kossior* (in Ukrainian), Kiev, 1963, p. 173.
184. *Pravda*, 28 January 1938.
185. *Stenographic Report of the*

First Session of the Supreme Soviet, *1938*.

186. Yu. P. Petrov, pp. 299–300.

187. *The Communist Party of the Soviet Union in Resolutions, etc.*, 7th ed., vol. ii, p. 851.

CHAPTER 9: A NATION IN TORMENT

1. *Daily Mail*, 24 October 1958.
2. Ilya Ehrenburg in *Novy Mir*, no. 5, 1962.
3. Kravchenko, *I Chose Freedom*, p. 211.
4. *Novy Mir*, no. 9, 1961.
5. *Moskva*, no. 4, 1965.
6. *Bilshovik Ukrainy*, no. 1, 1938, p. 53.
7. *Visti*, 23 May 1938.
8. ibid., 17 June 1938.
9. ibid., 14 February 1938.
10. *Stenographic Report of the XVIIIth Party Congress*, Moscow, 1939.
11. Beck and Godin, pp. 166–71.
12. ibid., p. 143.
13. ibid., pp. 174–9.
14. Kravchenko, *I Chose Freedom*, p. 448.
15. Weissberg, p. 364.
16. Ehrenburg, vol. iv, p. 195.
17. Ehrenburg in *Novy Mir*, no. 4, 1962.
18. Khrushchev, Secret Speech.
19. Brzezinski, p. 205.
20. *Bukharin Trial*, p. 335.
21. See e.g. *Lithuanian Bulletin*, New York, vols. iii–viii, 1945–50.
22. *Report of the Credentials Commission to the XIXth Party Congress*, *Pravda*, 9 October 1952.
23. Order 001233 (quoted in *Lithuanian Bulletin*); see also Order no. 0054 of Lithuanian N.K.V.D. Commissar Gusevitius, in *The Dark Side of the Moon*, pp. 50–51.
24. Ehrenburg, vol. iv, pp. 193 ff.
25. Fischer, *Men and Politics*, p. 409.
26. Beck and Godin, pp. 88–9.
27. John A. Armstrong, *Ukrainian Nationalism*, New York, 1963, p. 274.
28. Stuchenko, p. 65.
29. Beck and Godin, p. 88; and see Ginzburg, p. 25.
30. Ekart, p. 283.
31. Ivan Stadiuk, 'People are not Angels' (*Neva*, no. 12, 1962).
32. *Sovietskoye Gosudarstvo i Pravo*, no. 3, March 1965.
33. *Tikhookeanskaya Zvezda*, 9 May, 1937, etc.
34. *Sotsialistik Kazakhstan*, 23 November 1937.
35. *Kizil Uzbekistan*, 11 November 1937.
36. *Sovetskaya Kirghizia*, 11 January 1938.
37. *Kizil Uzbekistan*, 17 January 1938.
38. Uralov, pp. 140 ff.; Abdurakhman Avtorkhanov, *Narodoubistvo v S.S.S.R.*, Munich, 1952, *passim*.
39. Gorbatov, p. 108.
40. Harijs Heislers, 'The Un-

finished Story', *Zvaigzne* (Riga), no. 23, December 1956.
41. *Large Soviet Encyclopedia*, 2nd ed.
42. Kravchenko, *I Chose Justice*, p. 175.
43. Beck and Godin, p. 132.
44. Neumann, p. 10.
45. *Novy Mir*, no. 12, 1961.
46. Kravchenko, *I Chose Freedom*, p. 192.
47. ibid., pp. 192–4.
48. Gorbatov, p. 113.
49. See, e.g., Solzhenitsyn, *The First Circle*, pp. 155, 215–16.
50. Ivanov–Razumnik, p. 209.
51. e.g. Neumann, p. 32.
52. Eleanor Lipper, *Eleven Years in Soviet Prison Camps*, London, 1951, p. 57.
53. Ivanov–Razumnik, p. 349.
54. Weissberg, p. 89.
55. Beck and Godin, p. 66.
56. Neumann, p. 36.
57. ibid., p. 39.
58. ibid., p. 33.
59. Ivanov–Razumnik, p. 212.
60. Beck and Godin, p. 59.
61. ibid., p. 65.
62. Kravchenko, *I Chose Justice*, pp. 155–6.
63. József Lengyel, *From Beginning to End*, English ed., London, 1966, p. 15.
64. Herling, p. 9.
65. *Bukharin Trial*, p. 256.
66. Ivanov–Razumnik, p. 348.
67. Neumann, p. 38.
68. Weissberg, p. 469.
69. Ivanov–Razumnik, pp. 74, 116.
70. Ginzburg, chapter 41.
71. Beck and Godin, p. 62; and see Ivanov–Razumnik, p. 314.
72. Ginzburg, p. 185; and see Kravchenko, *I Chose Justice*, p. 253; Ivanov–Razumnik, p. 327.
73. e.g. Lermolo, pp. 163 ff.
74. Weissberg, p. 421.
75. ibid., p. 432.
76. Beck and Godin, p. 60.
77. See Ginzburg, pp. 60 ff.
78. Lermolo, pp. 191–2.
79. Ginzburg, p. 149.
80. Beck and Godin, p. 65.
81. e.g. Ivanov–Razumnik, p. 311.
82. Lipper, p. 7.
83. Gorbatov in *Novy Mir*, April 1964.
84. Neumann, p. 39.
85. ibid., p. 57.
86. Lipper, pp. 25–29; Ginzburg, p. 124.
87. Ivanov–Razumnik, pp. 342 ff.
88. Personal information; and see Solzhenitsyn, *The First Circle*, p. 150.
89. Herling, p. 9.
90. V. Petrov, *passim*.
91. Weissberg, p. 89.
92. Ginzburg, p. 83.
93. *Trybuna Ludu*, 23 November 1961.
94. e.g. Herling, p. 105.
95. Weissberg, pp. 447–51.
96. e.g. Beck and Godin, p. 45.
97. ibid., p. 87.
98. Weissberg, p. 285.
99. Ekart, p. 204.

100. Ivanov–Razumnik, pp. 305–6.
101. Beck and Godin, p. 118.
102. ibid., p. 119.
103. ibid., p. 46.
104. Neumann, p. 37.
105. Kravchenko, *I Chose Justice*, pp. 189–91.
106. Beck and Godin, p. 46.
107. ibid., pp. 122–3.
108. ibid., p. 110.
109. Weissberg, p. 326.
110. Beck and Godin, p. 114.
111. ibid., p. 154.
112. Kravchenko, *I Chose Justice*, pp. 161–2.
113. Weissberg, pp. 350–1.
114. Neumann, p. 133.
115. *Bezbozhnik* no. 7, 1937.
116. F. O. Oleshchuk, *Borba Tserkvi Protiv Naroda*, Moscow, 1939, pp. 85–6.
117. Oleshchuk, p. 65.
118. ibid., p. 87.
119. *Bolshevik*, no. 30, 1938.
120. Oleshchuk, p. 55.
121. Serdyuk, speech to the XXIInd Party Congress.
122. Brzezinski, p. 229.
123. Neumann, pp. 42–3.
124. Lermolo, p. 202.
125. ibid., chap. xviii; Neumann, pp. 40–41.
126. Orlov, pp. 226–7.
127. ibid., pp. 227–8.
128. Lipper, pp. 25–29.
129. Weissberg, pp. 407–8; and see Ivanov–Razumnik, p. 316.
130. Orlov, p. 251; *Sovetskaya Sibir*, 17 and 21–4 February 1939.
131. L. P. Petrovsky, *Letter to the Central Committee*, 5 March 1969.
132. Lipper, p. 72.
133. I. V. Spiridonov, speech to the XXIInd Party Congress.
134. Stalin, speech at the February–March plenum of the C.C., 3 March 1937.
135. *Itogi Vsesoyuznoi Perepisi Naselenie 1959 g*, vol. i, Moscow, 1962, pp. 161–4.
136. Ekart, p. 156.
137. Kravchenko, *I Chose Justice*, p. 288.
138. B. P. Beshchev, speech to the XXIInd Party Congress.
139. N. M. Shvernik, speech to the XXIInd Party Congress.
140. ibid.
141. Kravchenko, *I Chose Justice*, chap. 9.
142. Beck and Godin, p. 99.
143. Lengyel, p. 14.
144. Neumann, p. 49.
145. Ivanov–Razumnik, pp. 291–7.
146. Ginzburg, pp. 65–6.
147. e.g. Gorbatov, p. 111.
148. Ciliga, p. 141.
149. e.g. Beck and Godin, p. 47.
150. Weissberg, p. 238.
151. Beck and Godin, p. 57.
152. ibid., p. 145.
153. ibid., p. 147.
154. Neumann, pp. 63–4.
155. Weissberg, p. 281.
156. Ginzburg, p. 97.
157. ibid., p. 122.
158. Khrushchev, Secret Speech.
159. Weissberg, p. 241.

160. *Sovietskoye Gosudarstvo i Pravo*, no. 3, March 1965.
161. Kravchenko, *I Chose Justice*, pp. 177–9.
162. Beck and Godin, p. 101.
163. Arthur Koestler, Introduction to Weissberg, op. cit.
164. Beck and Godin, p. 102.
165. ibid.
166. Arthur Koestler *et al.*, *The God that Failed*, London, 1950, p. 77.
167. Beck and Godin, p. 46.
168. ibid.
169. Ginzburg, p. 122.
170. A. Dyakov in *Oktyabr*, no. 7, July 1964.
171. Weissberg, p. 231.
172. ibid., pp. 368–9.
173. Beck and Godin, p. 47.
174. ibid., p. 47.
175. Lengyel, pp. 92–3.
176. Ivanov–Razumnik, p. 248.
177. Neumann, p. 183.
178. *Izvestia*, 6 September 1964.
179. *Kazakhstanskaya Pravda*, 17 January 1965.
180. Ginzburg, p. 52.
181. ibid., pp. 130–31.
182. *Forty Years of Soviet Law*, Leningrad, 1957, p. 486.
183. Piontkovsky and Menshagin, p. 172.
184. *Forty Years of Soviet Law*, pp. 485–504.
185. Piontkovsky and Menshagin, p. 187.
186. Kravchenko, *I Chose Justice*, p. 91.
187. *Sovietskoye Gosudarstvo i Pravo*, no. 3, March 1965.
188. ibid.
189. ibid.
190. ibid.
191. Lipper, p. 48.
192. Wolin and Slusser, p. 186.
193. V. Petrov, p. 64.
194. Wolin and Slusser, p. 188.
195. Ginzburg, p. 105.
196. ibid., p. 88.
197. Wolin and Slusser, p. 182.
198. Kulski, *The Soviet Regime*, Syracuse, 1954, pp. 233–4.
199. Wolin and Slusser, *passim*.
200. Weissberg, p. 275.
201. *Sovietskoye Gosudarstvo Pravo*, no. 3, March 1965.
202. ibid.
203. See Wolin and Slusser, *passim*; Lipper, pp. 33–4.
204. Wolin and Slusser, p. 191.
205. Ivanov–Razumnik, p. 313.
206. ibid., p. 312.
207. V. and E. Petrov, p. 89.
208. Wolin and Slusser, p. 134.
209. *U.S.S.R. Laws 1937*, 61:266.
210. Ginzburg, p. 62.
211. Kravchenko, *I Chose Freedom*, p. 207.
212. Uralov, p. 147.
213. Beck and Godin, p. 72.
214. Spiridonov, speech to the XXIInd Party Congress.
215. *Sovietskoye Gosudarstvo i Pravo*, no. 3, March 1965.
216. V. and E. Petrov, p. 71.
217. Kravchenko, *I Chose Justice*, pp. 281–2.
218. Beck and Godin, p. 46.
219. Weissberg, p. 286.
220. ibid., pp. 288–9.
221. Maclean, *Eastern Approaches*, pp. 40–41.
222. Ginzburg, p. 109.

223. Weissberg, p. 414.
224. Beck and Godin, p. 49.
225. Weissberg, p. 414.
226. N. M. Shvernik, speech to the XXIInd Party Congress (*Pravda*, 26 October 1961).
227. *Pravda*, 21 April 1937.
228. *Pyatakov Trial*, p. 163.
229. ibid., p. 94.
230. ibid., p. 217.
231. Kravchenko, *I Chose Justice*, chap. ii.
232. Beck and Godin, p. 154.
233. ibid., pp. 149–65.
234. *Voprosy Istorii K.P.S.S.*, no. 1, 1965.
235. Beck and Godin, p. 29.
236. ibid., p. 37.
237. *Komsomolskaya Pravda*, 8 July 1965.
238. Weissberg, pp. 359–60.
239. *Nedelya* (*Izvestia* weekly supplement), 3–9 November 1963.
240. *New York Times*, 27 December 1936.
241. For the biologist Vavilov in particular see especially Zhores A. Medvedev, *The Rise and Fall of T. D. Lysenko*, New York, 1969. Much of this information was also given in a book published in the U.S.S.R., *Nikolai Vavilov*, by S. Reznik, which, however, has now been withdrawn (*Khronica*, no. 10).
242. *Pravda Vostoka*, 5 September 1964.
243. Ehrenburg in *Novy Mir*, no. 4, 1962.
244. *Protocols of the First Congress of Soviet Writers*, Moscow, 1937.
245. Speech of Mikhail Sholokhov at the IVth Congress of Soviet Writers, 1967.
246. Alexander Solzhenitsyn, Letter to the IVth Writers' Congress. *Survey*, no. 64, July 1967.
247. Roy Medvedev, p. 43.
248. Ehrenburg, vol. iv, p. 197.
249. *Short Literary Encyclopedia*.
250. F. N. Petrov, *M. V. Frunze*, Moscow, 1962.
251. *Small Soviet Encyclopedia*, vol. v, 1949.
252. See *Survey*, April–June 1961, p. 89.
253. Serge, *Memoirs of a Revolutionary*, p. 269.
254. *Pravda*, 17 May 1937.
255. Ivanov–Razumnik, pp. 220, 308; Ehrenburg, vol. iv, pp. 185–6.
256. Orlov, p. 196.
257. *Mikhail Koltsov Kakim On Byl*, p. 75.
258. *Large Soviet Encyclopedia*, 2nd ed., vol. li.
259. Wolin and Slusser, p. 187.
260. Neumann, p. 115.
261. Ivanov–Razumnik, p. 237.
262. *Na Rubezhe*, no. 3/4, 1952.
263. *Literaturnaya Rossiya*, 11 December, 1964.
264. Ehrenburg, vol. iv, p. 191.
265. *Large Soviet Encyclopedia*, 2nd ed., vol. li.
266. *Voprosy Literatury*, November 1964.

267. N. A. Zabolotsky, *Verse and Poems*, Moscow–Leningrad, 1965, p. 37.
268. Pavel Antokolsky in *Novy Mir*, no. 4, 1966.
269. Marina Tsvetaeva, *Selected Works*, Introduction by V. Orlov, Moscow–Leningrad, 1964.
270. Solzhenitsyn, quoted in *Survey*, no. 64, 1967.
271. See especially the biographical and critical commentary by Gleb Struve in *Osip Mandelshtam: Sobranie Sochineniy*, Washington, 1964.
272. Ehrenburg, vol. iv, p. 190.
273. *Literaturnaya Gazeta*, 20 April 1937.
274. ibid., 26 April 1937.
275. ibid., 15 May 1937.
276. Priscilla Johnson, *Khrushchev and the Arts*, Cambridge, Mass., 1965, pp. 13–14.
272. *Mladost* (Belgrade), 2 October 1957.
278. *Zarya Vostoka*, 28 June 1963.
279. Dallin and Nicolaevsky, p. 22.
280. Nikolai A. Gorchakov, *The Theater in Soviet Russia*, New York, 1957.
281. Ginzburg, p. 267.
282. *Pravda*, 8 January 1938.
283. Yuri (George) Annenkov, *Dnevnik Moikh Vstrech*, vol. ii, New York, 1966, p. 97.
284. Gorchakov, op. cit.
285. *Theatrical Encyclopaedia*.
286. Annenkov, p. 98; see also Dallin and Nicolaevsky, p. 123.
287. Ivanov–Razumnik, p. 246.
288. Brzezinski, p. 299.
289. Beck and Godin, p. 33.
290. *Zarya Vostoka*, 19 November 1961.

CHAPTER 10: IN THE LABOUR CAMPS

1. Herling, Introduction.
2. M. Z. Nikonov Smorodin, *Krasnaya Katorga*, Sofia, 1938.
3. Mora and Zwieznak, *La Justice Soviétique*, Rome, 1945.
4. D. J. Dallin and B. I. Nicolaevsky, *Forced Labour in Soviet Russia*, London, 1948.
5. Kravchenko, *I Chose Justice*, passim.
6. *Dekrety Sovetskoy Vlast*, vol. 3, Moscow, 1964, pp. 291–2.
7. See Slusser and Wolin, p. 42.
8. *All Russia*, Moscow, 1923, part 3, col. 55.
9. Kravchenko, *I Chose Justice*, p. 225.
10. Ciliga, p. 180.
11. ibid., p. 250.
12. ibid., p. 180.

13. Swianiewicz, p. 123.
14. Dallin and Nicolaevsky, p. 54.
15. Ekart, p. 71.
16. Lipper, p. 76.
17. Gurgen Maari in *Voprosy Literatury*, November 1964.
18. V. Petrov.
19. Lenygel, p. 15.
20. Neumann, pp. 62–3.
21. Ginzburg, pp. 212 ff.
22. *The Dark Side of the Moon*, p. 66.
23. ibid., p. 57.
24. ibid., p. 67.
25. Ginzburg, p. 263.
26. e.g. Herling, p. 22; V. and E. Petrov, pp. 68–9.
27. Gorbatov, pp. 125–6.
28. ibid., p. 133.
29. ibid., p. 129.
30. ibid., pp. 140–1.
31. Lipper, p. 95.
32. *The Dark Side of the Moon*, p. 158.
33. Neumann, p. 122.
34. Lipper, p. 149 etc.
35. Dallin and Nicolaevsky, p. 17.
36. Kravchenko, *I Chose Justice*, p. 258.
37. Andrée Sentaurens, *L'Air du Temps*, Paris, 1963.
38. Kravchenko, *I Chose Freedom*, p. 339.
39. Andrée Sentaurens, *passim*.
40. Kravchenko, *I Chose Justice*, p. 240.
41. Dallin and Nicolaevsky, p. 28.
42. Wolin and Slusser, p. 194.
43. Herling, pp. 21–2.
44. Pasternak, *Doctor Zhivago*, p. 452.
45. Dallin and Nicolaevsky, pp. 35–6.
46. ibid., pp. 34–5.
47. Neumann, p. 72.
48. Ginzburg, p. 254.
49. Alexander Solzhenitsyn, *One Day in the Life of Ivan Denisovich*, trans. Max Hayward and Ronald Hingley, New York, 1963, p. 7.
50. Kravchenko, *I Chose Freedom*, pp. 336–41.
51. Solzhenitsyn *One Day in the Life of Ivan Denisovich*, p. 136.
52. ibid., p. 3.
53. A. Dyakov in *Oktyabr*, no. 7, 1964.
54. Solzhenitsyn, *One Day in the Life of Ivan Denisovich*, p. 203.
55. Lipper, p. 144.
56. Ekart, p. 105.
57. Iulia de Beausobre (Lady Namier), *The Woman Who Could Not Die*, London, 1948.
58. *Nauki i Religiya*, November 1965.
59. Solzhenitsyn, *One Day in the Life of Ivan Denisovich*, p. 203.
60. ibid., p. 185.
61. e.g. Herling, p. 45.
62. Solzhenitsyn, *One Day in the Life of Ivan Denisovich*, p. 8.
63. e.g. Lengyel, p. 31.
64. Solzhenitsyn, *One Day in the Life of Ivan Denisovich*, pp. 43–4.

65. ibid., p. 28.
66. ibid., p. 198.
67. ibid., p. 12; and see Ekart, p. 57; Lipper, p. 138.
68. Solzhenitsyn, *One Day in the Life of Ivan Denisovich*, pp. 26–7.
69. ibid., pp. 23–4.
70. Dallin and Nicolaevsky, p. 12.
71. Solzhenitsyn, *One Day in the Life of Ivan Denisovich*, p. 22; see also V. Petrov, p. 185.
72. Ginzburg, p. 264.
73. Dallin and Nicolaevsky, p. 36.
74. Solzhenitsyn, *One Day in the Life of Ivan Denisovich*, p. 146.
75. ibid., pp. 150 ff.
76. Dallin and Nicolaevsky, p. 18.
77. *Literaturnaya Gazeta*, 4 April 1964.
78. Herling, p. 41.
79. Swianiewicz, pp. 21–2.
80. V. Lashkin in *Novy Mir*, no. 1, 1964.
81. Solzhenitsyn, *One Day in the Life of Ivan Denisovich*, p. 20.
82. ibid., p. 142.
83. e.g. ibid., pp. 36–7, 166–7.
84. e.g. Ginzburg, pp. 240, 279; Kravchenko, *I Chose Justice*, p. 237.
85. Neumann, p. 124.
86. Kravchenko, *I Chose Justice*, p. 341.
87. Abramovitch, pp. 418–20.
88. *Sotsialisticheskii Vestnik*, nos. 1–3, 1951.
89. Solzhenitsyn, *One Day in the Life of Ivan Denisovich*, pp. 193–4.
90. ibid., p. 14.
91. Dallin and Nicolaevsky, p. 13.
92. ibid., p. 24.
93. ibid., p. 37.
94. El Campesino, p. 162.
95. Solzhenitsyn, *The First Circle*, p. 175.
96. Solzhenitsyn, *One Day in the Life of Ivan Denisovich*, p. 137.
97. ibid., p. 41.
98. ibid., p. 128.
99. Ekart, p. 42.
100. Neumann, p. 111.
101. See Dallin and Nicolaevsky, p. 137.
102. For Kolyma, see especially Gorbatov; Lipper; Kravchenko, *I Chose Justice*, pp. 268–70; Slusser and Wolin, pp. 180–238; *The Dark Side of the Moon*, pp. 118–21, 155–64; Dallin and Nicolaevsky; Ginzburg, pp. 266–315; and 'Kolyma Notes' by G. Shelest, *Znamya*, no. 9, 1963.
103. Kravchenko, *I Chose Justice*, p. 269.
104. Dallin and Nicolaevsky, p. 130.
105. Lipper, *passim*.
106. Dallin and Nicolaevsky, pp. 128–9.
107. Andrei D. Sakharov, *Progress, Coexistence and Intellectual Freedom*, London, 1969, p. 53.

108. Lipper, p. 93.
109. Ginzburg, p. 270.
110. Lipper, p. 94.
111. Ginzburg, p. 272.
112. Lipper, p. 90.
113. ibid., p. 208.
114. ibid., chap. 9.
115. ibid., p. 108.
116. ibid., p. 197.
117. ibid., pp. 169–70.
118. *The Dark Side of the Moon*, p. 120.
119. ibid., p. 121.
120. G. Shelest, 'Kolyma Notes', *Znamya*, no. 9, 1963.
121. Lipper, pp. 125–33.
122. Ginzburg, chapter 55.
123. G. Shelest, loc. cit.
124. ibid.
125. Kravchenko, *I Chose Justice*, p. 270.
126. Henry A. Wallace, *Soviet Asia Mission*, New York, 1945.
127. Lipper, p. 113.
128. Solzhenitsyn, *One Day in the Life of Ivan Denisovich*, p. 33.
129. *National Geographic Magazine*, lxxxvi, December 1944.
130. Lipper, p. 253.
131. ibid., p. 268.
132. *National Geographic Magazine*, lxxxvi, December 1944.
133. Dallin and Nicolaevsky, p. 38.
134. Kravchenko, *I Chose Freedom*, pp. 405–6.
135. Swianiewicz, p. 39.
136. Karl Marx MS., published in *Bolshevik*, nos. 5–6, 1932.
137. Sidney and Beatrice Webb, *Soviet Communism: A New Civilization*, 2nd ed., London, 1937, p. 585.
138. Weissberg, p. 321.
139. Engineer Pobozhy in *Novy Mir*, August 1964.
140. Ekart, p. 259.
141. Swianiewicz, *passim*.
142. Pobozhy, loc. cit.
143. Naum Jasny, cited by Swianiewicz, pp. 193–4.
144. Kravchenko, *I Chose Justice*, p. 250.
145. Lipper, p. 198.
146. G. Shelest in *Znamya*, no. 9, 1963.
147. *The Dark Side of the Moon*, p. 161.
148. Dallin and Nicolaevsky, p. 10.
149. *The Dark Side of the Moon*, p. 97.
150. *Rights and Wrongs*, ed. Christopher Hill for Amnesty International, London, 1969.
151. L. Gouré, *The Siege of Leningrad*, Oxford, 1962. More detail is given in Dmitri V. Pavlov, *Leningrad and the Blockade*, English ed., Chicago, 1965.
152. Solzhenitsyn, *One Day in the Life of Ivan Denisovich*, p. 28.
153. ibid., pp. 84–5.
154. ibid., p. 86.
155. ibid., p. 69.
156. Dallin and Nicolaevsky, p. 7.
157. Solzhenitsyn, *One Day in the Life of Ivan Denisovich*, p. 71.
158. ibid., p. 99.
159. ibid., p. 140.
160. ibid., pp. 18–19.

161. Kravchenko, *I Chose Justice*, p. 235.
162. Ekart, p. 227.
163. Lengyel, p. 37.
164. ibid., pp. 37–8.
165. Solzhenitsyn, *One Day in the Life of Ivan Denisovich*, p. 81.
166. e.g. Lipper, pp. 168–9.
167. Dallin and Nicolaevsky, p. 72.
168. Herling, pp. 56–7.
169. Swianiewicz, p. 296.
170. ibid., p. 297.
171. ibid., p. 224.
172. Dallin and Nicolaevsky, p. 38.
173. Herling, p. 41.
174. Gorbatov, p. 130.
175. Lengyel, p. 15.
176. ibid., p. 17; see also Herling, p. 150.
177. Beck and Godin, p. 76.
178. *White Book*, p. 144.
179. Kravchenko, *I Chose Justice*, p. 259.
180. *Stenographic Report of the XIth Party Congress*, Moscow, 1961, Biographical Notes.
181. P. J. de la F. Wiles, quoted by Swianiewicz, p. 17.
182. Lipper, p. 232.
183. Wiles, in Swianiewicz, p. 17.
184. V. Kosyk, 'Concentration Camps in the U.S.S.R.' (in *Russian Oppresion in the Ukraine*, London, 1962).
185. 'That Year', *Novy Mir*, no. 8, 1956.
186. Solzhenitsyn, *One Day in the Life of Ivan Denisovich*, p. 78.
187. Roy Medvedev, p. 45; Sakharov, p. 55.
188. Yugoslav Politburo member Moša Pijade, speech of 1 August 1951 (V. Dedijer, p. 201).
189. Aleksander Tvardovsky, 'Tyorkin in the Other World', *Izvestia*, 18 August 1963.

CHAPTER 11: THE GREAT TRIAL

1. Lenin, *Collected Works*, vol. 53, Moscow, 1964, Biographical Notes.
2. ibid.
3. Yakir, *Survey*, no. 70–71, 1969.
4. Orlov, pp. 302, 264.
5. ibid., p. 119.
6. Maclean, *Eastern Approaches*, p. 93.
7. ibid., p. 86.
8. *Bukharin Trial*, p. 36.
9. Maclean, *Eastern Approaches*, p. 86.
10. *Bukharin Trial*, p. 716.
11. ibid., p. 49.
12. ibid., p. 716.
13. ibid., pp. 49–50.
14. ibid., p. 51.
15. ibid., p. 52.
16. ibid., p. 53.
17. ibid.
18. ibid., p. 54.
19. ibid., pp. 58–9.
20. Maclean, *Eastern Approaches*, p. 87.
21. *Bukharin Trial*, p. 59.
22. ibid., p. 18.

23. ibid., p. 81.
24. Maclean, *Eastern Approaches*, p. 98.
25. *Bukharin Trial*, p. 76.
26. ibid., p. 83.
27. Tokaev, *Stalin Means War*, p. 7.
28. *Bukharin Trial*, p. 724.
29. *Pravda*, 30 October 1937.
30. Ivanov–Razumnik, p. 310.
31. *Pravda*, 26 September 1937.
32. *Bukharin Trial*, p. 104.
33. ibid., p. 91.
34. ibid., pp. 96–7.
35. ibid., p. 109.
36. ibid., p. 123.
37. ibid., p. 124.
38. ibid., pp. 131–3.
39. ibid., p. 137.
40. ibid., pp. 143–4.
41. Maclean, *Eastern Approaches*, pp. 92–3.
42. ibid., p. 87.
43. Tokaev, *Comrade X*, p. 91.
44. *Bukharin Trial*, pp. 157–8.
45. Weissberg, p. 425.
46. e.g. in Robert Payne, *The Rise and Fall of Stalin*, London, 1966, p. 520.
47. Orlov, pp. 291–2.
48. *Bukharin Trial*, p. 252.
49. ibid., p. 163.
50. ibid., p. 164.
51. ibid., p. 210.
52. ibid., p. 206.
53. ibid., p. 207.
54. ibid.
55. ibid., p. 208.
56. ibid., p. 217.
57. *Pravda Vostoka*, 27 June 1937.
58. *Zarya Vostoka*, 10 July 1937.
59. *Pravda*, 8 September 1937.
60. ibid., 10 September 1937.
61. ibid., 12 September 1937.
62. ibid., 9 April 1964.
63. *Bukharin Trial*, p. 757.
64. *Pravda Vostoka*, 10, 11, 12 September 1937.
65. *Pravda*, 9 April 1964.
66. ibid., 27 September 1937.
67. *Bukharin Trial*, p. 348.
68. ibid., p. 757.
69. *Pravda*, 13 September 1937.
70. ibid., 20 September 1937.
71. ibid., 10, 12 September 1937.
72. *Bukharin Trial*, p. 234.
73. ibid., p. 225.
74. ibid., p. 223.
75. ibid., p. 348.
76. ibid., p. 351.
77. ibid., p. 361.
78. ibid., p. 250.
79. Barmine, pp. 228–9.
80. e.g. *Pyatakov Trial*, p. 207.
81. *Bukharin Trial*, p. 312.
82. ibid., p. 288.
83. ibid., p. 302.
84. ibid., p. 248.
85. ibid., p. 313.
86. ibid., p. 328.
87. ibid., p. 332.
88. ibid., p. 333.
89. ibid., p. 335.
90. ibid., p. 330.
91. Louis Fischer, *Russia Revisited*, London, 1957, p. 64.
92. *Bukharin Trial*, p. 430.
93. Orlov, p. 283.
94. ibid., pp. 284–5.
95. *Bukharin Trial*, p. 424.
96. ibid., p. 370.
97. ibid., p. 372.
98. ibid., p. 374.

99. ibid., p. 376.
100. ibid., p. 381.
101. ibid., p. 383.
102. ibid., p. 384.
103. ibid., p. 407.
104. ibid., p. 413.
105. ibid., p. 415.
106. ibid.
107. ibid., p. 417.
108. ibid., p. 419.
109. ibid., p. 424.
110. ibid., p. 437.
111. *Pravda*, 3 January 1924.
112. *Bukharin Trial*, p. 470.
113. ibid., p. 474.
114. Maclean, *Eastern Approaches*, p. 99.
115. *Bukharin Trial*, p. 492.
116. Jadwiga Sikierska in *Swiat* (Warsaw), 24 March 1957.
117. Ciliga, p. 292.
118. *Bukharin Trial*, p. 491.
119. ibid., p. 504.
120. ibid., pp. 508–9.
121. *Stenographic Report of the XIth Party Congress*, Moscow, 1961.
122. Lenin, *Collected Works*, vol. 50, Moscow, 1965.
123. *Soviet Historical Encyclopedia*, vol. 10, 1967.
124. *Pravda*, 12 September 1966; *Voprosy Istorii*, no. 6, 1967.
125. *Pravda*, 8 June 1937.
126. ibid., 17 May 1937.
127. *Bukharin Trial*, p. 590.
128. ibid., p. 544.
129. ibid., p. 516.
130. ibid., p. 546.
131. ibid., p. 518.
132. ibid., p. 35.
133. *Stenographic Report of the XIth Party Congress*, Moscow, 1961.
134. *Bukharin Trial*, p. 549.
135. ibid., p. 548.
136. Barmine, p. 207.
137. *Bukharin Trial*, p. 537.
138. ibid., p. 518.
139. ibid., p. 519.
140. ibid., p. 527.
141. Maclean, *Eastern Approaches*, p. 102.
142. *Bukharin Trial*, pp. 525–6.
143. ibid., p. 529.
144. ibid., p. 530.
145. Duranty, pp. 84–5.
146. Maclean, *Eastern Approaches*, pp. 119–20.
147. Orlov, p. 264.
148. *Bukharin Trial*, pp. 535, 539.
149. ibid., p. 546.
150. Khrushchev, Secret Speech.
151. *Bukharin Trial*, p. 551.
152. ibid., p. 511.
153. ibid., p. 562.
154. ibid., p. 564.
155. Maclean, *Eastern Approaches*, p. 105.
156. *Bukharin Trial*, p. 576.
157. ibid., pp. 578–9.
158. ibid., p. 573.
159. ibid., pp. 577–8.
160. Orlov, pp. 267–8.
161. *Pravda*, 8 June 1937.
162. Dubinsky–Rukhadze, p. 5.
163. See Armstrong, *The Politics of Totalitarianism*, p. 71.
164. *Pravda*, 8 June 1937.
165. Orlov, p. 268.
166. *Bukharin Trial*, p. 590.
167. ibid., p. 591.
168. ibid., pp. 596–7.

169. ibid., p. 608.
170. ibid., p. 609.
171. ibid., pp. 609–10.
172. ibid., p. 703.
173. ibid., p. 684.
174. *Sotsialisticheskii Vestnik*, no. 6 (671), June 1954.
175. e.g. *Pravda*, 6 June 1958.
176. Isaac Don Levine, *I Rediscover Russia*, New York, 1964, p. 175.
177. e.g. in Dubinsky–Rukhadze.
178. *Bukharin Trial*, pp. 622–3.
179. Maclean, *Eastern Approaches*, p. 107.
180. *Bukharin Trial*, p. 625.
181. ibid., p. 626.
182. ibid., p. 631.
183. ibid., p. 676.
184. ibid., p. 664.
185. ibid., p. 679.
186. ibid., p. 694.
187. ibid., p. 697.
188. ibid., p. 728.
189. ibid., p. 734.
190. ibid., p. 736.
191. ibid., pp. 737–8.
192. ibid., p. 738.
193. ibid., p. 739.
194. ibid., pp. 740–41.
195. ibid., p. 758.
196. V. and E. Petrov, p. 46.
197. *Bukharin Trial*, p. 786.
198. ibid., p. 782.
199. ibid., p. 769.
200. Maclean, *Eastern Approaches*, p. 110.
201. *Bukharin Trial*, p. 769.
202. ibid., p. 770
203. ibid., p. 771.
204. ibid., p. 774.
205. ibid., p. 778.
206. ibid., p. 779.
207. *Ukrainian Soviet Encyclopedia*, Addenda.
208. *Small Soviet Encyclopedia.*
209. Herling, Appendix.
210. *Pravda*, 13 June 1937.
211. Kravchenko, *I Chose Freedom*, p. 283.
212. *Politik*, 21 May 1965.
213. *Conference of Historians*, 1962, p. 298.
214. Mr George Katkov.
215. Brzezinski, p. 229; Lermolo, p. 207.
216. Lipper, p. 15.
217. Ginzburg, pp. 114–15.
218. ibid., p. 201.
219. Kravchenko, *I Chose Freedom*, p. 283.
220. *Stenographic Report of the XVIIIth Party Congress*, p. 26.
221. *Bukharin Trial*, p. 87.
222. e.g. ibid., pp. 80, 185–6, 235, etc.
223. e.g. ibid., pp. 182–3, 201, 293–4, 303, 314, 318–19, etc.
224. e.g. ibid., pp. 71, 80, etc.

CHAPTER 12: THE FOREIGN ELEMENT

1. Ignazio Silone in *The God That Failed*, pp. 109 ff.
2. Ciliga, p. 61.
3. *Conference of Historians*, 1962, p. 69; *Kommunist*, no. 10, 1963.

4. ibid., p. 286.
5. *Osteuropa*, no. viii, 1958, p. 33.
6. Arvo Tuominen, *Kremls Klockor*, Helsinki, 1958, p. 210. Quoted in *The Comintern – Historical Highlights*, ed. Milorad M. Drachkovitch and Branko Lazitch, New York, 1966.
7. Neumann, p. 8.
8. Koestler, *Arrow in the Blue*, vol. 2, p. 209.
9. Neumann, p. 5.
10. ibid., p. 23.
11. ibid., p. 168.
12. ibid., p. 143.
13. Herbert Wehner, *Erinnerungen*, Bonn, 1957, p. 160.
14. Poretsky, p. 181.
15. Neumann, p. 171.
16. Beck and Godin, p. 108; *Beiträge zur Geschichte der Arbeiterbewegung*, vol. 1, 1969.
17. Neumann, p. 55.
18. ibid., p. 53.
19. Ginzburg, p. 118.
20. Beck and Godin, p. 109.
21. ibid.
22. Ivanov–Razumnik, p. 307.
23. Koestler, *Arrow in the Blue*, vol. 2, p. 407; Ruth Fischer, *Stalin and German Communism*, London, 1948.
24. Herling, p. 62.
25. Lipper, p. 7.
26. Dallin and Nicolaevsky, p. 38.
27. Weissberg, pp. 487–9.
28. Beck and Godin, p. 76.
29. Serge, *Memoirs of a Revolutionary, 1901–1941*, p. 187.
30. Avro Tuominen (former Secretary-General of the Finnish Communist Party) in *Uusi Kavalehti*, no. 10/13, 1956.
31. Kun Béláné, *Kun Béla*, Budapest, 1966, pp. 489–90. (The date of his arrest is here given as the end of June, which conflicts with other accounts.)
32. Ciliga, p. 253.
33. Krivitsky, p. 217.
34. ibid., p. 219.
35. Ivanov–Razumnik, p. 315.
36. *Small Polish Encyclopedia*, Warsaw, 1958.
37. Kun Béláné, op. cit.
38. Lipper, p. 16.
39. Ivanov–Razumnik, p. 315.
40. Renato Mieli, *Togliatti 1937*, Milan, 1964; Guelfa Zaccaria, *200 Comuniste Italiani tra le vittime dello Stalinismo*, Milan, 1964.
41. Speech to the Central Committee of the Italian Communist Party, December 1961.
42. Ginzburg, pp. 169–70.
43. Tito, speech to the Central Committee of the Yugoslav Communist League, 19 April 1954 (*Borba*, 20 April 1949); speech to the IXth Party Congress, 11 March 1969.
44. Fitzroy Maclean, *Disputed Barricade*, London, 1957, pp. 103–4.

45. *Uusi Kavalehti*, 22 June 1956.
46. D. J. Dallin, *Soviet Espionage*, New Haven, 1956, p. 100.
47. Ivan Karaivanov, *Ljudi i Pigmeji*, Belgrade, 1953, p. 112.
48. Ivanov–Razumnik, p. 308.
49. Kravchenko, *I Chose Justice*, p. 279.
50. Jerzy Morawski, Secretary of the Polish C.C., speech of 27 March 1956.
51. *Polish Universal Encyclopedia* (P.W.N.).
52. Wehner, pp. 141–2.
53. Neumann, p. 6.
54. *Kommunist International*, nos. 1–3, 1938.
55. *Polish Universal Encyclopedia* (P.W.N.); *Ukrainian Soviet Encyclopedia*; *Polish Biographical Dictionary*, vol. xi, Warsaw, 1964–5 (see also Lipper, p. 40; Ginzburg, p. 248).
56. Lipper, p. 40.
57. Neumann, pp. 8–9.
58. ibid., p. 19.
59. *Survey*, no. 32, 1960.
60. *U Istokov Partii*, Moscow, 1963, notes.
61. Introduction to 1956 edition of Pyatnitsky's *Notes of a Bolshevik*.
62. *Survey*, no. 32, 1960.
63. *Voprosy Istorii K.P.S.S.*, no. 8, 1965.
64. *Ot Fevralya k Oktyabryu*, Moscow, 1957, Biographical Notes.
65. Roy Medvedev, p. 46.
66. Neumann, p. 34.
67. ibid., p. 6.
68. Orlov, p. 229.
69. ibid., pp. 230–31.
70. ibid., p. 232.
71. ibid., p. 233.
72. ibid., p. 238.
73. e.g. *Pravda*, 17 December 1936.
74. Jesús Hernández, *Yo Fui un Ministro de Stalin*, Mexico City, 1953.
75. Julián Gorkin, 'L'Assassinat d'Andres Nin', Commission pour la Vérité sur les Crimes de Staline, *Bullétin d'Informations*, no. 1, May 1962.
76. ibid.
77. *Novy Mir*, no. 5, 1962.
78. El Campesino, p. 35.
79. Beck and Godin, p. 108.
80. *Observer*, 10 October 1965.
81. See Deutscher, *The Prophet Outcast*, p. 175.
82. *Byulletten Oppozitsii*, no. 33.
83. See Wolfe, p. 520.
84. Adam B. Ulam, *The Bolsheviks*, New York, 1965, pp. 573–5.
85. Ciliga, p. 85.
86. Isaac Don Levine, *The Mind of an Assassin*, London, 1959, p. 27.
87. D. J. Dallin in *New Leader*, 19–26 March 1956.
88. Levine, p. 41; see also the *Bullétin d'Informations* of the Commission pour la Vérité sur les Crimes de Staline, no. 1, May 1962.

89. Levine, p. 50 (quoting V. and E. Petrov).
90. ibid., p. 188.

91. E. Castro Delgado, *J'ai perdu la foi à Moscou*, Paris, 1950.

CHAPTER 13: CLIMAX

1. Yu. P. Petrov, p. 301.
2. *Voprosy Istorii K.P.S.S.*, no. 1, 1965.
3. *Stanislav Vinkentiyovich Kossior*, p. 174.
4. Khrushchev, Secret Speech.
5. ibid.
6. V. Drobzhiev and N. Dumiova, *V. Ya. Chubar: A Biographical Sketch*, Moscow, 1963, pp. 65–71.
7. *Bukharin Trial*, p. 107.
8. Khrushchev, Secret Speech.
9. ibid.
10. See *Soviet Historical Encyclopedia*; *Small Soviet Encyclopedia*; *Short Literary Encyclopedia*; *Ukrainian Soviet Encyclopedia*; *Ukrainian Soviet Encyclopedic Dictionary*; etc.
11. Khrushchev, Secret Speech.
12. Brzezinski, p. 229.
13. Neumann, p. 55.
14. Lipper, p. 15.
15. e.g. Boris Nicolaevsky in the *New Leader*, 16 January 1956.
16. Nicolaevsky, p. 122.
17. Uralov, p. 80.
18. Alliluyeva, *Only One Year*, p. 388.
19. Weissberg, p. 399; see also Armstrong, *The Politics of Totalitarianism*, quoting the N.K.V.D. Lt. A. Zhigunov.
20. Avtorkhanov, p. 223.
21. *Pravda*, 21 August 1938.
22. *Bukharin Trial*, p. 426.
23. ibid., pp. 290–91.
24. Barmine, p. 8.
25. Nora Murray, *I Spied for Stalin*, London, 1950, Chapter 6.
26. *Molodoy Kommunist*, no. 1, January 1962.
27. Ehrenburg in *Novy Mir*, no. 4, 1964.
28. ibid.
29. *Soviet Historical Encyclopedia*.
30. *Novy Mir*, no. 11, 1964.
31. *Small Soviet Encyclopedia*.
32. *Soviet Historical Dictionary*.
33. Barmine, p. 21.
34. S. Pavlov, speech to the November 1962 plenum of the C.C., C.P.S.U.
35. *Izvestia*, 14 November 1963.
36 Fainsod, pp. 423–5.
37. Shkiryatov's and Poskrebyshev's speeches to the XVIIIth Party Congress; *Izvestia* and *Pravda*, 14 November 1963; *Aleksander Kosarev*, Moscow, 1963, pp. 111–12.
38. See Armstrong, *The Politics of Totalitarianism*, p. 75.
39. Dr S. Ploss in *Problems of Communism*, September–October 1958.

818 *Notes*

40. Admiral N. G. Kuznetsov in *Oktyabr*, no. 11, 1964.
41. See E. Wollenberg, *The Red Army*, London, 1938; Edgar O'Ballance, *The Red Army*, London, 1964, p. 121.
42. Bailey, p. 229.
43. *Na Rubezhe* (Paris), March 1952.
44. Bailey, p. 229.
45. Ivanov–Razumnik, p. 311.
46. Admiral N. G. Kuznetsov in *Oktyabr*, no. 11, 1964.
47. Marshal Rokossovsky in *Krasnaya Zvezda*, 13 December 1964.
48. Mekhlis, speech to the XVIIIth Party Congress.
49. On Lyushkov, see Alvin D. Coox in *Soviet Studies*, January 1968.
50. Yakir, *Survey*, nos. 70–71, 1969.
51. Erickson, p. 494; A. Svetlanin, *Dalnevostochni Zagovor*, Frankfurt, 1953, pp. 103 ff.
52. *V. K. Blyukher*, Moscow, 1963.
53. *Biographical Dictionary of the U.S.S.R.*
54. N. Kondryatsev, *Marshal Blyukher*, Moscow, 1965.
55. Tass, 22 February 1964.
56. K. A. Malamin, *The Regiments go West*, Moscow, 1964, pp. 97–8.
57. This account is based on those given by N. Kondryatsev (op. cit.) and V. Dushenkin (op. cit.).
58. *Voprosy Istorii K.P.S.S.*, no. 11, 1964.
59. Dushenkin, p. 223.
60. Personal information; and see Svetlanin, p. 127.
61. Ivanov–Razumnik, p. 307.
62. *Soviet Historical Encyclopedia*.
63. Lermolo, pp. 156, 241.
64. F. W. Deakin and G. R. Storry, *The Case of Richard Sorge*, London, 1966.
65. *Pravda*, 2 November 1938.
66. ibid., 16 December 1938.
67. ibid., 22 January 1961.
68. e.g. Tokaev, *Comrade X*, p. 119.
69. Swianiewicz, p. 133.
70. V. and E. Petrov, p. 77.
71. See Armstrong, *The Politics of Totalitarianism*.
72. *History of the Communist Party of the Soviet Union*, 1st. ed., Moscow, 1959, p. 484.
73. ibid., 2nd ed., Moscow, 1962. p. 505.
74. Yakovlev, p. 177.
75. *Leningradskaya Pravda*, 25 February 1964.
76. Khrushchev, Secret Speech.
77. See their sponsoring organizations at the XVIIIth Party Congress.
78. Gorbatov, p. 110.
79. ibid., p. 127.
80. Weissberg, pp. 311–12.
81. Ivanov–Razumnik, p. 323.
82. *Pravda*, 22 October 1938.
83. Beck and Godin, p. 146.
84. Weissberg, p. 12.
85. ibid., pp. 411–12.

86. Khrushchev, Secret Speech.
87. ibid.
88. ibid.
89. *Voprosy Istorii K.P.S.S.*, no. 11, 1964.
90. Bega and Aleksandrov, pp. 304–5.
91. *Stanislav Vinkentiyovich Kossior*, p. 174; *Pravda*, 3 April 1964.
92. Lipper, p. 16.
93. Beck and Godin, p. 181.
94. Drobzhiev and Dumiova, loc. cit.
95. *Sovetskaya Moldavia*, 22 February 1965.
96. *Pravda*, 3 April 1964.
97. See *Ukrainian Soviet Encyclopedia*; *Large Soviet Encyclopedia*, 2nd ed.; *Geroy Grazhdanskoy Voiny*; *Komandarm Yakir*; *Krasnaya Zvezda*, 6 June 1967; *Calendar of Significant and Memorable Dates*, Moscow, July 1967; *Voenno-Istoricheskiy Zhurnal*, no. 6, 1967; *Voennyy Vestnik*, no. 6, 1967.
98. Bega and Aleksandrov, p. 315.
99. *Izvestia*, 15 September 1966.; Petrovsky, *Letter to the Central Committee*.
100. *Voprosy Istorii K.P.S.S.*, no. 2, 1963.
101. *Ukrainian Soviet Encyclopedia*.
102. Bega and Aleksandrov, p. 304.
103. *U Istokov Partii*.
104. e.g. *Pravda*, 18, 25 October 1938.
105. *Voprosy Istorii K.P.S.S.*, no. 2, 1963.
106. Beck and Godin, p. 132.
107. Ivanov–Razumnik., p. 316.
108. Bega and Aleksandrov, pp. 304–5.
109. *Voprosy Istorii K.P.S.S.* no. 3, 1964.
110. Bega and Aleksandrov, pp. 305–6.
111. By Professor Tibor Szamuely.
112. *Pravda*, 6 May 1953.
113. *Izvestia*, 4 September 1918.
114. *Conference of Historians*, 1962, p. 260.
115. 'Meditations' by Jerzy Walenczyk (*Po Prostu*, 23 December 1956).
116. *Conference of Historians*, 1962, p. 260.
117. Khrushchev, Secret Speech.
118. Roy Medvedev, p. 42; Yakir, *Surrey* nos. 70–71, 1969.
119. J. Stalin, *Problems of Leninism*, Moscow, 1947. p. 625.
120. Khrushchev, Secret Speech.
121. Boris Nicolaevsky, Notes to *The Crimes of the Stalin Era*, New Leader edition of the Secret Speech.
122. *Pravda*, 3 April 1964.
123. *Soviet Historical Encyclopedia*; and see I. A. Kozlov, et al., *Severny Flot*, Moscow, 1966; *Voenno-Istoricheskiy Zhurnal*, no. 7, 1965.
124. *Mikhail Koltsov Kakim On Byl*, p. 75.
125. Brzezinski, p. 229.
126. Maryagin, p. 297.
127. Yakir, *Survey*, nos. 70–71, 1969.

EPILOGUE: HERITAGE OF TERROR

1. Ehrenburg, vol. iv., p. 196.
2. Ivanov–Razumnik, pp. 304–7.
3. Beck and Godin, pp. 182–3.
4. ibid., pp. 93, 203.
5. Hitler, p. 171.
6. Beck and Godin, p. 194.
7. Georg Lukács in *Nuovi Argomenti*, October 1962.
8. See Souvarine, p. 661.
9. Zhores A. Medvedev, p. 267.
10. Commission pour la Vérité sur les Crimes de Staline, *Bullétin d'Informations*, no. 3, January 1964.
11. ibid.
12. *Wspolczesnosc*, 16 February–1 March 1966.
13. See Conquest, *The Nation Killers*, London, 1970.
14. 'Ernst Genri' (S. N. Rostovsky), on the authority of Gen. Todorsky (*Grani*, no. 13, 1967, p. 194).
15. Khrushchev, Secret Speech.
16. *Znamya*, May 1964.
17. Gorbatov, p. 134.
18. Yu. P. Petrov, p. 304.
19. Khrushchev, Secret Speech.
20. ibid.
21. Mekhlis, speech to the XVIIIth Party Congress (*Stenographic Report*, p. 276).
22. Erickson, p. 583.
23. ibid.
24. ibid., p. 552.
25. See *Nazi Conspiracy and Aggression*, vol. vi, Washington, 1946, p. 981.
26. See Erickson, p. 566.
27. Yu. P. Petrov, p. 332.
28. Erickson, p. 583.
29. ibid., p. 578.
30. Ehrenburg, vol. iv, p. 256.
31. Ehrenburg in *Novy Mir*, no. 4, 1964.
32. Erickson, p. 583.
33. See ibid., chap. xvii.
34. Deutscher, *Stalin*, p. 486.
35. K. Simonov in *Znamya*, May 1964.
36. *Ukrainian Soviet Encyclopedia*; *Ukrainian Soviet Encyclopedic Dictionary*; Svetlanin; Ehrenburg, vol. iv.; Yakir, *Survey*, nos. 70–71, 1969.
37. Biryuzov, pp. 140–41.
38. *Novy Mir*, no. 1, 1965.
39. Herling, pp. 175–6.
40. ibid., pp. 221–4.
41. Beck and Godin, pp. 189–90.
42. Kravchenko, *I Chose Justice*, p. 405.
43. ibid., p. 282.
44. El Campesino, p. 198.
45. Pasternak, chapter xvi.
46. *Pravda*, 27 June 1945.
47. *Nova Mysl*, no. 7, 10 July 1968.
48. *Komsomolskaya Pravda*, 15 November 1964.
49. See Khrushchev's speech of 9 December 1963.
50. Personal information; see also Solzhenitsyn, *One Day in the Life of Ivan Denisovich*.
51. Lenin, *The Development of Capitalism in Russia* (1899).

52. *Kommunist,* no. 17, November 1962.
53. V. Frolov in *Voprosy Filosofii,* no. 3, 1967.
54. See Souvarine, pp. 578–9.
55. *Voprosy Istorii,* no. 1, 1964.
56. V. V. Parin in *Literaturnaya Gazeta,* 24 February 1962.
57. K. N. Plotnikov in *Conference of Historians 1962.*
58. D. G. Sturua, speech at the All-Union Conference on Ideological Work, 25–8 December 1961.
59. A. Sumbat-Zade, in *Conference of Historians 1962,* p. 338.
60. *Oktyabr,* no. 2, February 1949.
61. Commission pour la Vérité sur les Crimes de Staline, *Bullétin d'Informations,* no. 3, January 1964.
62. *Pravda,* 1 August 1951.
63. *John Cornford: A Memoir,* ed. Pat Sloan, London, 1938, p. 178.
64. 'Letter of an Old Bolshevik' (Nicolaevsky, p. 64); see also Krivitsky, p. 207.
65. Serge, *Memoirs of a Revolutionary, 1901–1941,* p. 318.
66. Julian Symons, *The Thirties,* London, 1960, p. 142.
67. *New Leader,* 10 October 1964.
68. Bertolt Brecht, *The Informer,* English translation, in *New Writing,* N.S., vol. II, London, 1939.
69. *Large Soviet Encyclopedia,* 2nd ed., vol. 28, Moscow, 1954.
70. *Komsomolskaya Pravda,* 2 September, 1962.
71. *Preuves,* March 1953.
72. Koestler, *Arrow in the Blue,* vol. 2, p. 208.
73. Symons, p. 143.
74. Sidney and Beatrice Webb, *Soviet Communism: A New Civilization,* 2nd ed., London, 1937, pp. 586–8.
75. Jerzy Gliksman, *Tell the West,* New York, 1948.
76. Herling, p. 11.
77. D. N. Pritt, *From Right to Left,* London, 1966, pp. 109–11.
78. Duranty, p. 37.
79. ibid., p. 55.
80. His dispatch of 7 March 1938; see also his *Mission to Moscow,* vol. i, London, 1942, p. 39.
81. S. and B. Webb, p. 1156.
82. ibid., p. 1145.
83. ibid., p. 1114.
84. ibid., p. 1153.
85. Harold J. Laski, *Law and Justice in Soviet Russia,* London, 1935, p. 21.
86. John Maynard, *The Russian Peasant and Other Studies,* London, 1942, p. 252.
87. Bernard Pares, *A History of Russia,* paperback ed., London, 1962, p. 584.
88. Bernard Pares, *Russia,* London, 1940, p. 33.
89. Introduction to Bernard Pares, *A History of Russia.*
90. Bernard Shaw, letter to the

Secretary of the British Committee for the Defence of Leon Trotsky, 21 July 1937 (quoted in Deutscher, *The Prophet Outcast*).

91. David J. Dallin and Boris I. Nicolaevsky, *Forced Labour in Soviet Russia*, London, 1948.
92. Kravchenko, *I Chose Justice*, pp. 134–5.
93. ibid.
94. *The God That Failed*, p. 256.
95. Pat Sloan, *Soviet Democracy*, London, 1937, p. 111.
96. Pat Sloan, *Russia Without Illusions*, Preface by B. Webb, London, 1938, p. 246.
97. *Spectator*, 3 June 1966.
98. Dallin and Nicolaevsky, p. 33.
99. *The God That Failed*, p. 79.
100. *Yunost*, no. 1, 1965.
101. Decision of a Joint Meeting of the Central Committee of the C.P.S.U., the Council of Ministers of the U.S.S.R., and the Presidium of the Supreme Soviet (*Pravda*, 7 March 1953).
102. Resolution of the C.C., C.P.S.U. (*Pravda*, 2 July 1956).
103. Palmiro Togliatti, 'Nine Questions on Stalinism', *Nuovi Argomenti*, 16 June 1956.
104. Tass, 1 February 1963.
105. *Programme of the C.P.S.U.*

(Moscow, 1961), Part I, Section 3.
106. *Sovietskoye Gosudarstvo i Pravo*, no. 1, 1956.
107. 'Soviet Law Reform', *Yale Law Journal*, vol. lvi, no. 8 (1957).
108. The evidence (up to that time) is discussed in 'An End to Concentration Camps?' by Paul Barton, *Problems of Communism*, March–April 1962.
109. *Pravda*, 26 December 1958.
110. *Politika*, 16 October 1962.
111. *Conference of Historians*, 1962, p. 298.
112. *History of the U.S.S.R.*, Book II, vol. 3, Moscow, 1968, pp. 103, 523.
113. *Kommunist*, no. 3, February 1969; and see Petrovsky, *Letter to the Central Committee*.
114. *Kazakhstanskaya Pravda*, 17 January 1965.
115. *Khronika*, no. 9.
116. *Pravda*, 30 January 1966.
117. *Kommunist*, no. 3, February 1969.
118. *Vedomosti Verkhovnogo Soveta R.S.F.S.R.*, no. 38 (416), 22 September 1966.
119. Senator Secchia, speech to the plenum of the C.C. of the Communist Party of Italy, November 1961.
120. Rosa Luxemburg, *The Russian Revolution*, English ed., Ann Arbor, 1961, p. 71.

APPENDIX A

1. e.g. Ginzburg, pp. 34, 193.
2. Fainsod, pp. 186–7.
3. Lipper, p. 7.
4. Herling, p. 8.
5. Weissberg, p. 89.
6. Ivanov–Razumnik, p. 149.
7. Weissberg, pp. 314, 319.
8. Uralov, p. 163.
9. Beck and Godin, pp. 66–7.
10. Herling, p. 9.
11. *Pravda*, 26 September 1937.
12. Beck and Godin, p. 68.
13. See Lorimer, p. 222.
14. Ivanov–Razumnik, pp. 209, 215.
15. *Sovietskaya Sibir*, 28 December 1935.
16. Brzezinski, p. 99.
17. Dedijer, p. 201.
18. Uralov, loc. cit.
19. Beck and Godin, pp. 71–2.
20. Brzezinski, p. 108.
21. Uralov, loc. cit.
22. Ginzburg, p. 136.
23. V. and E. Petrov, p. 73.
24. ibid., pp. 74–5.
25. Brzezinski, p. 108–9.
26. V. and E. Petrov, p. 71.
27. *Mikhail Koltsov Kakim On Byl*, p. 77.
28. Sakharov, p. 52.
29. Abramovitch, pp. 420, 421.
30. e.g. Ginzburg, pp. 279, 290; Kravchenko, *I Chose Justice*, p. 237.
31. V. and E. Petrov, p. 72.
32. Moša Pijade, speech of 6 August 1951 (Dedijer, p. 201).
33. See *Soviet Studies*, April 1952, for a description by J. Miller.
34. See *Le Livre Blanc*; Lipper; Kravchenko; Margolin; Herling; and especially Swianiewicz, and Dallin and Nicolaevsky.
35. Solzhenitsyn, *The First Circle*, p. 317.
36. Ekart, p. 11.
37. P. J. de la F. Wiles, quoted in Swianiewicz, p. 17.
38. Swianiewicz, pp. 41–2.
39. Information from Prof. Szamuely.
40. Solzhenitsyn *One Day in the Life of Ivan Denisovich*, p. 78.
41. Lorimer, p. 182.
42. Beck and Godin, p. 80.
43. Weissberg, p. 291.
44. Ivanov–Razumnik, p. 346.
45. Sakharov, p. 55.
46. Roy Medvedev, p. 45.
47. Sakharov, p. 52.

APPENDIX E

1. Lenin, *Collected Works*, 3rd ed., vol. viii, p. 64; and vol. vii, p. 270.
2. *F. Dzerzhinsky* (a collection of essays), Moscow, 1931, p. 141.
3. The historian Pokrovsky in *Pravda* 18 December 1927.

824   *Notes*

4. Lenin, *Collected Works*, vol. xxii, p. 50.
5. *Izvestia*, 6 December 1917.
6. 'The Cheka' by E. J. Scott, *Soviet Affairs*, no. 1, p. 6 (St Anthony's Papers, no. 1, 1956).
7. M. Latsis, in an article on Dzerzhinsky in *Proletarskaya Revolutsia*, no. 9 (56), 1926, quoted by Wolin and Slusser in *The Soviet Secret Police*, p. 33.
8. *Soviet Affairs*, no. 1, p. 10 (St Antony's Papers).
9. *Izvestia*, 3 September 1918.
10. *R.S.F.S.R. Laws*, 1918, 65–710.
11. *Soviet Affairs*, no. 1, p. 9 (St Antony's Papers).
12. ibid., p. 16.
13. *Pravda*, 19 December 1918.
14. *Yezhedelnik*, no. 3, 16 October 1918, quoted by Wolin and Slusser, p. 34.
15. *Pravda*, 26 October 1918.
16. ibid., 18 December 1918.
17. ibid.
18. Latsis, *The Extraordinary Commissions for Combating Counter-revolution*, Moscow, 1921 (quoted by Wolin and Slusser, p. 6).
19. Peters (quoted by E. J. Scott, *Soviet Affairs*, no. 1, p. 21).
20. See Deutscher, *The Prophet Unarmed*, p. 109.
21. See, e.g. his article on the tenth anniversary of the Cheka (*Pravda*, 18 December 1927).
22. *F. E. Dzerzhinsky*, pp. 334–45.
23. *R.S.F.S.R. Laws*, 1920, 22, 23: 115.
24. Wolin and Slusser, pp. 36–37.
25. *Izvestia* of the Temporary Revolutionary Committee of Sailors, Red Army Men and Workers of the Town of Kronstadt, 8 March 1921 (see E. J. Scott, *Soviet Affairs*, no. 1, p. 14).
26. Latsis, *The Extraordinary Commissions* (see E. J. Scott, *Soviet Affairs*, no. 1, p. 14).
27. Ciliga, p. 48.
28. Souvarine, p. 484.
29. Wolin and Slusser, p. 44.
30. Kravchenko, *I Chose Justice*, p. 99.
31. Lermolo, p. 36.
32. Ciliga, p. 177.
33. Orlov, pp. 339–40.
34. *Izvestia*, 12 March 1933.
35. Beck and Godin, p. 141.
36. Kravchenko, *I Chose Justice*, p. 149.
37. Aleksander Rozen, 'The Last Two Weeks', *Zvezda*, nos. 1 and 2, 1965.

APPENDIX F

1. Orlov, p. 28.
2. Avtorkhanov, p. 29.
3. Stalin, *Works*, English ed., vol. xi, Moscow, 1954.
4. Eugene Lyons, *Assignment in Utopia*, London, 1938, pp. 123–4.
5. ibid., pp. 124–6.
6. Louis Fischer in *The God That Failed*, pp. 211–12.
7. Lyons, p. 117.
8. G. P. Maximoff, *The Guillotine at Work*, Chicago, 1940, p. 304; Serge, *Memoirs of a Revolutionary*, p. 248; *Pravda*, 25 September 1930; K. F. Shteppa, *Russian Historians and the Soviet State*, New York, 1962, pp. 48–49; *Pravda*, 12 March 1933.
9. Cf. Orlov, p. 153.
10. Serge, *From Lenin to Stalin*, p. 151.
11. Souvarine, p. 530.
12. Abramovitch, p. 382–7.
13. Serge, *Memoirs of a Revolutionary*, p. 249.
14. *Khronika*, no. 10.
15. Schapiro, p. 394.
16. *Stenographic Report of the XIth Party Congress*, Moscow, 1961.
17. *The Menshevik Trial*, Leningrad, n.d., pp. 59, 62; *Itogi Vypolneniya Pervogo Piatiletnego Plana*, 1934, pp. 103–5. (See T. Szamuely, *Soviet Studies*, Jan. 1966, vol. xvii, no. 3.)
18. *Zinoviev Trial*, p. 45.
19. *Wrecking Activities at Power Stations in the Soviet Union*, Verbatim Report, English ed., Moscow, 1933, p. 423.
20. Koestler, *Arrow in the Blue*, vol. 2, p. 201.

BIBLIOGRAPHICAL NOTE

1. *Conference of Historians 1962*, pp. 268–75.
2. ibid., p. 148.
3. ibid.
4. V. Lakshin in *Novy Mir*, no. 1, 1964.
5. Weissberg, p. 14.
6. Yakir, *Survey*, nos. 70–71, 1969.

Index

INDEX

Doctor Zhivago (Pasternak), 386, 460–2
Doctors' Plot (1938), 194, 540–62; (1952–3), 116, 547n., 553, 556, 632, 663
Dostoievsky, Feodor, 471
Dreiser, Theodore, 670
Dreitzer, E. A., 155–7, 166, 287, 290
Drobnis, Y. N., 213, 223, 232, 240, 242, 251, 254
Dubinsky, David, 644, 683
Dubovoy, Army Commander I. N., 321, 606
Dubovoy, N., 638
Duranty, Walter, 672
Dushenov, Admiral, 637
Dybenko, Army Commander P. E., 121, 303, 306, 320–1, 329, 606
Dzerzhinsky, Felix, 23, 101, 209–10, 370, 530, 540, 569, 583, 688, 721–3, 725
Dzhakupov, Sevikgali, 420
Dzhambul, D., 571
Dzhezkazgan camp, 463
Dzhido camp, 491

Eberlein, Hugo, 577
Education, Commissariat for, 37
Efron, Sergei, 444
Ehrenburg, Ilya, 112–13, 116, 118, 255, 297, 307, 379, 386, 446, 592, 611–12, 654, 666, 684
Ehrlich, Henrik, 644–5
Eideman, Corps Commander R. P., 277, 279, 302
Eikhe, R. I., 126, 204, 243, 246, 256, 269, 331, 360, 369–70, 373, 604–6, 608, 633, 636–7, 690
Eisenberg, 198–9
Eisenstein, Sergei, 115
Eismont, V. V., 55–6
Eitingon, Leonid, 599–603
Ekart, Antoni, 484
Elgen camp, 477
Elsberg, Yakov, 447
Erickson, John, 648
Ermilov, Vladimir, 446
Estonian Communist Party, 575–6
Evdokimov, E. G., 75, 336–7, 389, 730–3
Evdokimov, G. E., 30–2, 87–8, 91–2, 141, 143, 154, 157, 161
Evtushenko, D. M., 351
executions, 426–7; number of, 702–5
extermination camps, 469–70

Fadeyev, Alexander, 68, 447
Fainsod, Professor Merle, 85
Far Eastern Air Force, 616
Far Eastern Army, 316, 322, 337, 615–22
Far Eastern Territory, 337, 572
Fascism, Stalin and, 296–310
February Revolution (1917), 30, 33, 175, 186

Fedko, Army Commander, 619–21, 628–9
Fedotov, 136
Feldman, Corps Commander, 278, 280, 285n., 286, 303, 309
Feuchtwanger, Leon, 116, 670
Filatov, N. A., 332n., 361
Finerty, John F., 670
Finnish Communist Party, 581
Finnish War (1939–40), 638, 646, 648–9
First Cavalry Army, 280–1, 438, 648, 653
FitzGibbon, Constantine, 687n.
Five-Year Plans, 43, 47–8, 64, 410, 631, 736
Flieg, Leo, 577–8
Fomin, 94
Fominykh, Commissar, 689
Foreign Affairs, People's Commissariat for, 609–10
Former Political Prisoners, Society of, 130–2
Fotieva, L. A., 120–1
Fourth Bureau (Military Intelligence), 315–16
French Communist Party, 680
Friedland, Ts., 431
Frinovsky, Mikhail, 219, 229, 263n., 287, 360, 371, 496, 588, 617–18, 622–3
Frunze, 703; Military Academy, 310
Frunze, M. V., 438

Gamarnik, Yan, 278–9, 283, 286, 295, 304, 309, 312, 503, 521, 672
Ganetsky, Ya. S., 630n.
Garkavi, Corps Commander, 294, 310
Gaven, Yuri, 206
Gay, M. I., 139, 149, 275, 289, 549
Gekker, Corps Commander, 294, 310
Georgia: Stalin's policy in, 20, 119–20; Lenin's intervention, 20; Bolshevism in, 100, 124, 340; intra-Party purge, 339–41; trials of Georgians, 204, 340–1
Gerland, Brigitte, 559–61
German Army, 648–55; and Red Army 'treason', 301–2
German Communist Party, 141, 296–7, 300; purging of, 575–9
German Social Democrats, 284
Germany: Stalin's policy towards, 296–310; Red Army espionage for, 286–7, 296–310, 521; and Second World War, 648–55
Gerö, Erno, 589–90
Gertik, A. M., 175
Gide, André, 666–7
Ginzburg, Evgenia, 421, 477, 581
Gliksman, Jerzy, 671
Gogliidze, S. A., 623, 633
Goloded, M. M., 338, 515, 534
Golovanov, Alexander, 619
Golubenko, Ivan, 289

844 *Index*

Rightist activity, 504–5, 513, 548–9;
trial, 530, 540–51; and medical killings,
540–51, 556–8, 561, 567
Yakir, Army Commander, 277–9, 281–3,
286–7, 289, 292–6, 303–9, 503, 571,
578, 621, 681
Yakir, Peti, 309
Yakovlev, Inspector, 503
Yakovlev, Professor, 159–60
Yakovlev, Ya. A., 332, 338, 359, 361, 572,
636
Yakovleva, Varvara, 537, 539–40
Yanovsky, 349, 351
Yaroslavl isolator, 397, 399, 570
Yashvili, Pavle D., 442
Yegorov, Marshal, 279n., 281–3, 295,
306, 320, 637
Yelabug, 444
Yenukidze, Abel, 73, 123–4, 371, 445,
497, 547, 549, 556–7, 690; removed
from posts, 130; denounced and out-
lawed, 130–3; alleged plan to seize
power, 514, 547, 549; and Gorki
murder, 548–9, 551
Yertsevo camp, 569n., 654
Yesenin, Sergei A., 441, 448
Yevlev, B. I., 499
Yezhov, Nikolai, 36–7, 128, 130–2, 164,
171, 203, 214–15, 226, 228–9, 231,
257–8, 260, 265, 286–7, 291, 307–8,
369–71, 381, 437, 440, 527, 552, 703;
in Purge Commission, 67; Great Purge
blamed on, 112, 374, 383; given key
posts, 127; and 'Trotskyite–Zinovievite
Centre' trial, 138, 140, 146–7, 153–4;
Commissar for Internal Affairs, 218;
alleged plots to kill, 256, 498, 547–9,
555, 561; and February–March plenum, 266, 269; purges N.K.V.D., 275–
6, 293; and Army purge, 287, 306, 310;
crushes Provincial and Republican
Committees, 332, 337, 340, 349; lists of
victims, 354–5, 407; resistance to, 358;
town named after, 361; and 'mobile
groups', 587–8; decline of power, 607–
9, 614–15; fall of, 620–7

Yezhovo-Cherkesk, 361, 623
Yiddish writers, 663–4
Yugoslav Communist Party, 581
Yurenev, K., 610
Yushkevich, A. K., 617

Zabolotsky, Nikolay, 397, 444, 447
Zakovsky, L. M., 137, 325–9, 496, 623
Zaks-Gladnev, 431
Zalutsky, P., 88–9
Zamyatin, Y. I., 145, 440
Zaporozhets, Ivan, 73, 75–7, 79–80, 83,
93–5, 275, 498, 530, 547, 549
Zatonsky, V. P., 351, 366, 505, 606,
680
Zborowski, Mark, 598
Zeidel, G. S., 431
Zelenin, Dr V., 553
Zelensky, Isaak, 384, 497, 504, 520, 523–
7, 563, 568, 570, 690
Zemlyachka, R. S., 121
Zhdanov, Andrei, 35, 66, 70, 126, 132,
218, 265, 371, 436, 547n., 624, 634–5,
647; replaces Kirov on Leningrad Com-
mittee, 88, 96, 323; alleged plot to kill,
151, 165; and February–March plenum, 266, 269; purges Leningrad,
323–5, 330; allegedly murdered, 547n.,
556
Zheliabov, A. I., 82
Zhukov, Academician Evgani M., 662
Zhukov, I. P., 278, 648–9
Zilliacus, Konni, 680
Zinoviev, Grigori E., 25, 33, 38–9, 54,
63–4, 69, 109, 123, 140, 178, 185, 191,
193, 214, 216, 229, 232–3, 326–7, 364,
497, 547, 613, 669, 714; character, 29;
alliance with Trotsky and Kamenev,
30–2; expelled from Party, 55, 187–8;
confesses error, 61, 186–8; and Kirov
murder, 73–4, 81–3, 86–92, 96, 255–7;
arrested, 87; trials, 141–4, 146–76, 206,
208, 217, 251–2, 340; execution, 169–
70, 255; Lenin's view of, 714
Zionism, 116, 683
Zubarev, P. T., 498, 508–9, 511